£1180

R M Hardy.

The Religious Orders in England

*

CANTERBURY FROM THE AIR

The Religious Orders in England

VOLUME I

BY

DOM DAVID KNOWLES

formerly Regius Professor of Modern History
in the University of Cambridge

CAMBRIDGE UNIVERSITY PRESS

CAMBRIDGE

LONDON · NEW YORK · MELBOURNE

Published by the Syndics of the Cambridge University Press
The Pitt Building, Trumpington Street, Cambridge CB2 1RP
Bentley House, 200 Euston Road, London NW1 2DB
32 East 57th Street, New York, NY 10022, USA
296 Beaconsfield Parade, Middle Park, Melbourne 3206, Australia

ISBN 0 521 05480 X hard covers
ISBN 0 521 29566 1 paperback

First published 1948
Reprinted 1950, 1956, 1960, 1962, 1974
First paperback edition 1979

First printed in Great Britain at the University Press, Cambridge
Reprinted in Great Britain by
REDWOOD BURN LIMITED
Trowbridge & Esher

CONTENTS

CANTERBURY FROM THE AIR   *Frontispiece*

The limits of the precinct can be clearly seen, together with the main
features of the monastic buildings, with the cloister, kitchen court,
Palace Court and Green Court. The high roof of the chapter-house,
added by Chillenden to Eastry's structure, is seen to the east of the
garth, with the infirmary range beyond. Eastry's memory is perpetuated by the central tower which, though dating from the fifteenth
century, takes its name, Bell Harry, from the great bell cast and hung
in the priorate of Henry of Eastry. (*Photo: by courtesy of the Friends of
Canterbury Cathedral*).

PREFACE   *page* ix

LIST OF ABBREVIATIONS   xv

Part One

The Old Orders, 1216–1340

Chap. I. The thirteenth century   3
Characteristics—the reforming bishops—the religious.

II. Reorganization among the Black Monks, 1216–1336   9
The early provincial chapters—domestic reforms—the monks
at Oxford.

III. The Augustinian chapters, 1216–1339   28
Organization of the chapters—the statutes of Helaugh Park.

IV. The exploitation of the land   32
Manor and demesne in the twelfth century—the resumption
of demesne—control of the estates—commercial farming—
administration of the manors: the wardens and the chequer—
improvement of the land—some great high farmers: Canterbury, Peterborough, Glastonbury.

V. Henry of Eastry   49

VI. The monastic administration   55
Centralization of finances—the treasury system—audit at
the chequer.

VII. The agrarian economy of the Cistercians   64
Sheep farming—credit transactions—corn for the market—
the Cistercian grange—finance and administration.

VIII. The system of visitation   78
Four kinds of visitor—the visitation procedure—interpretation of the documents.

IX. The first century of visitation: (I)   *page* 85
Introductory—the York registers—some troublesome cases
—the punishment of faults—financial mismanagement.

X. The first century of visitation: (II)   97
Worcester and Hereford—Wells and Exeter—Winchester
and London—the Cluniac houses—metropolitan visitations
—judgement on the system.

Part Two

The Friars, 1216—1340

Chap. XI. The Friars Minor   114
St Francis: his ideal and its originality—a new way of Christian life.

XII. The coming of the Minors   127
Thomas of Eccleston—the Minors in 1224—arrival in England
—the first friaries—early days in the province—the place of
the English friars in the order—examples of holy life—a share
in the controversies.

XIII. The order of Preachers   146
St Dominic: his life and genius—the Constitutions of the
Preachers: the two Distinctions—schools and chapters—
government by the most able—success of the legislation.

XIV. The Preachers in England   163
The first arrivals—the schools—confessors and diplomats.

XV. The evolution of the Franciscan ideal   171
The beginnings of an order—Haymo of Faversham—the
magistri, the *zelanti* and St Bonaventure.

XVI. The apostolic work of the Friars   180
Companions of the bishops—multiplication of privileges:
Nimis iniqua to *Ad fructus uberes*—the reactions and final
settlement—the working of *Super cathedram* in England—the
great controversies: William of St Amour to Jean de Pouilli—
the university question: Oxford and Cambridge—relations
between monks and friars.

XVII. Carmelites, Austin Hermits and lesser orders   194

XVIII. The early English Franciscan scholastics   205
Origins of the Oxford school: Grosseteste and Adam Marsh—
Thomas of York and his successors—Roger Bacon.

XIX. Doctrinal and moral controversies: Kilwardby and Pecham   217
The career of Kilwardby—rival theories of poverty—Augus-

tinians, Averroists and Thomists—the Question of Forms—
the condemnations of 1277—the career of Pecham—the condemnations of 1284–5.

XX. The Friars from the Council of Lyons to William of
Ockham (1272–1340)   *page* 233
The schools: Sutton and Trivet—Duns Scotus—William of
Ockham—John Baconthorpe—transition to modern thought
—the papal court: the Poverty of Christ—the case of Thomas
Waleys.

Part Three

The Monasteries and their World

Chap. XXI. The cathedral monasteries   254
The rights of the bishop—the convent and cathedral chapter
—the prior—the 'democratic' administration—Canterbury
and St Edmund Rich.

XXII. The monastic boroughs   263
Organization and administration—struggles and revolts, 1327
and 1381.

XXIII. The abbot   270
Powers of the abbot—his council—his household—abbots in
public life—exempt abbeys *vis-à-vis* Curia and Crown.

XXIV. The daily life of the monastery   280
The horarium—meat-eating—recreation—vacations—the
noviciate—lay brothers—the *peculium*—the monk's home—
personal sanctification.

XXV. Intellectual life—history, art and music   291
Matthew Paris, his life and work—monastic chronicles—Art:
the school of St Albans—psalters and apocalypses—the East
Anglian school—the writing of books—a Franciscan artist.
Music and the Chant: Gregorian chant and polyphony—the
Worcester school.

XXVI. Monastic England, 1216–1340   308
Survey of the black monks—the white monks and canons—
changes in the period.

Appendices   321

Bibliography   327

Index   341

PREFACE

In an earlier volume an attempt was made to write the history of the monastic order in England from the times of Dunstan to the Fourth Council of the Lateran. Between that Council and the Dissolution more than three centuries elapsed, but the story of the fortunes of the monks during that long space has never been told at length. The reasons for this neglect are not far to seek. During the earlier period monastic history abounds in notable events and striking personalities; new orders appear one after the other, and the older bodies undergo rapid changes; of all these vicissitudes we have vivid contemporary accounts, often written by the monks themselves, and the letters and biographies of the actors give depth and breadth, light and shade, to the picture. From the end of the twelfth century all this is changed. The monastic life and institutions, at least to a casual observer, appear to become static. There are no arresting developments, no revolutionary reforms, no leaders and saints of the stature of Dunstan, Lanfranc, Ailred and Hugh of Lincoln, and even a well-read student of the Middle Ages would be hard put to it to describe the changes that had taken place in the life of the monks between the age of Simon de Montfort and that of Thomas More.

Human institutions, however, are never wholly static, and it was a conviction that movement and change had taken place that led to the undertaking of a continuation of the earlier book through an age less familiar, and in a sense less grateful, to the monastic historian.

As the work went forward, at least three important developments in monastic life during the thirteenth century became apparent. The monasteries, at first under the impulse of the Lateran decrees, but later from a spontaneous effort from within, made considerable progress towards union for common action and for disciplinary and administrative reform; at the same time they entered upon new responsibilities as active landlords and commercial farmers on a large scale; and, lastly, they capitulated to the spirit of the age and took part in the intellectual life of the country by frequenting the universities. Whatever judgement may be made upon the wisdom or success of these new ventures, they are all evidence of a living energy and of a flexibility of movement and, so long as they were pursued with decision, they held the monasteries within the full stream of the country's life.

Yet while these new relations were being established in the intellectual and social spheres, the gradual evolution of European society was thrusting the monks slowly but without pause from the forefront of the national scene. In the eleventh and twelfth centuries they had been the very soul of the higher life of England; they were a principal influence in things of the mind; their most eminent representatives were known to all as leaders in Church and State; theirs was the country's literature, and they wrote its history. From the beginning of the thirteenth century and thence-forward ever more markedly their supremacy declined. The monasteries, though still a factor of importance in social and religious life, are no longer the most vital force. Abbots appear but rarely among the magnates and administrators of the new age; bishops and higher clergy trained in the schools set the tone and lead the reforms in the Church; the intellectual headship has passed to the friars and secular masters at the universities. The monasteries are no longer fountain-heads of the spiritual life of England, and the solidarity of the monastic world, so notable a feature in the age of Ordericus Vitalis and William of Malmesbury, has vanished entirely as a spontaneous sentiment despite all efforts made at the highest level to secure unity of action. Yet during all this period each monastery as a unit was consolidating its estates, multiplying its contacts with town and countryside, and adding to the extent and magnificence of its buildings.

Side by side with these developments, very great changes were taking place in the character of the sources from which our historical information is derived. For more than a century after the Conquest, while the history of the monasteries was an integral part of the history of England, many of the most distinguished historical writers and of the most important historical documents were of monastic provenance. Chronicles of individual houses abounded, and annalists, chroniclers and historians alike took the whole of monastic England within their purview, while many of them, from the most earnest to the most trivial—a William of Malmesbury, a Symeon of Durham, a Jocelin of Brakelond—answered at least by implication many of the questions we would most readily put to them. From the middle of the thirteenth century this is no longer so. The rare chronicles are purely domestic, there are no monastic historians of the national life, and only a very few writers—indeed, the compilers of the *Gesta Abbatum* of St Albans form a group almost unique—give us an intimate and sensitive account of the life of a great abbey. References to monastic affairs in secular chronicles are few, and collections of personal letters and biographies are entirely lacking.

As a compensation, official and administrative documents begin to multiply: decrees of chapters, records of visitations, financial accounts, bishops' registers, estate documents of all kinds, royal and papal letters, grants entered on the official rolls. But survival in many of these classes has been fragmentary and accidental, and tracts of time and space are without record, while the information supplied in such bulk is often without great historical significance, and is almost always valueless, if not positively misleading, until it has been submitted to a long process of synthesis and analysis at the hands of an expert. All who are conversant with monastic history are well aware, for example, that while the number of facts and figures recorded in the articles on the religious houses in the *Victoria County Histories* is very large, their significance for the general reader and often also for the historian is remarkably small. Similarly, the publication of a number of bishops' registers and monastic account-rolls in the nineteenth century was rendered almost valueless by well-intentioned abbreviation made on no scientific principle, and by the lack of intelligent comment of any kind.

The quality and incidence of the evidence available has necessarily affected the structure of the chapters that follow. For an earlier period it was not impossible to combine narrative with a treatment of particular points in such a way as to give some impression of ordered development in a body with many members. In later centuries this is not possible. The steady numerical increase in the houses and their population, the great reforms, the new beginnings, the connected sequence of events are all lacking. Consequently, the only possible course seemed to be that of selecting a number of important interests and pursuits, each of which might be treated in isolation from the others. The relation between these, and the assessment of their relative historical importance, must be left to the judgement of the reader, save for a few general conclusions: there is no common yardstick that may measure such varied activities as the organization of high farming, the illumination of manuscripts, the work of academic disputation, and the framing of disciplinary regulations; no scale that may balance the value of any or all of these against the evidence from visitation records or individual criticism, of decline, dissipation or torpor. Things so disparate cannot be set out as the factors of a single sum. All that the historian can attempt is to present as objectively as possible a whole mass of evidence of various kinds, in the hope that the reader may gain at least something of the impression given by a living organism with all its varied activities.

Two changes have been made in the plan of this book during the years —many of them very abnormal years—which have passed since it was undertaken. The original intention was to deal with the monastic bodies only, but it soon became clear that this would in effect make of the whole a narrower and perhaps less useful study than its predecessor. From the moment when the new orders of friars arrived in England they became a most important part of the regular religious life of the country, and any account which did not include them would be partial and incomplete. Their relations with the older bodies were many and complicated; their example attracted the monks out of their traditional orbit into that of the new universities; and, more important than all, the friars drew continually upon those very reserves of spiritual and intellectual power which might else have been available to the monks. In addition, it seemed of itself worth while to include between the covers of a single book the developments of the monastic life and those of the intellectual life of the schools, a subject all too unfamiliar to many English readers and, it may perhaps be said, to not a few of those who have written ably of the social and controversial activities of the friars. When once the decision had been taken to include the friars, the method adopted earlier with the Cistercians and Carthusians entailed the giving of some account of their origins, in order that the life of the early friars in England might be brought into some relation with the religious sentiment of Europe from which its inspiration was drawn.

This first change of design brought with it a second. The original intention had been to cover the whole period from the Fourth Lateran Council to the Dissolution in a single volume, but when the friars were added it became clear that the book would grow to an unwieldy size, and that its completion would be the work of many years. A limit was therefore set to the present volume, and a very elastic boundary, of no great significance in itself, was fixed in the middle decades of the fourteenth century. For both monks and friars alike the epoch which witnessed the end of the great constructive period of medieval speculation, and the social catastrophe of the Great Plague, was one of change; hitherto, they had been an accepted part of the life of church and country; henceforward, by slow degrees, they were to be put upon the defensive in more than one way. For the monks in particular, the Constitutions of Benedict XII in 1336 gave canonical recognition to much that had hitherto been controversial in matters of discipline, and made of the whole of England a single black monk province. That year, therefore, has been taken for them as a line of division. It is not, however, a very significant one, and where topics extend on either side, an arbitrary selection has been made of those to be included in the present volume. Thus the account of the academic activities of the monks at Oxford, where the first settlement was made only at the very end of the thirteenth century, has been postponed, as has also the treatment of their parish organization. Similarly, the history of the Carthusians and Premonstratensians, together with some aspects of Cistercian life, for which little information exists before c. 1350, has been reserved for future treatment. And in general, though no doubt there are omissions which no exigencies of planning can excuse, the absence of a topic from this volume does not necessarily imply that it has fallen entirely out of the reckoning.

My great debt to the numerous scholars and antiquaries who have investigated the history of the religious orders will be obvious from the footnotes, and Franciscan origins and scholastic philosophy have each a vast literature of which only a fraction can be cited in a general work. In a few cases, however, the debt has been so heavy that I may be allowed to express my obligation a little more fully.

All who have studied early Franciscan history or that of scholastic thought will speedily have realized how much is owing to those two great pioneers Heinrich Denifle and Franz Ehrle. The lapse of years serves only to throw into clearer relief their vast and accurate erudition, their tireless industry, and their pregnant genius; as with the peaks of a mountain group, a distant view serves only to enhance the impression of pre-eminence.

Two others were with us till yesterday, and I had hoped that both would read the expression of my gratitude. They were widely separated in years and achievement. Without the results of A. G. Little's patient work of more than half a century it would have been wholly impossible to write the history of the English Franciscans; in that province his name meets one at every turn, and he was always ready to answer at length any query. The other, R. A. L. Smith, died on the threshold of his career, but not before he had made one corner in the field of medieval studies, that of black monk finances and agrarian policy in the thirteenth century, peculiarly his own, and without his handful of papers and his enthusiastic companionship the chapters on those subjects could never have been written.

Finally, as I have written elsewhere, Mr W. A. Pantin's publication of all the available documents connected with the chapters of the black monks has made it possible, for the first time, to grasp the precise aims and assess the results of the endeavours made to unite and reorganize the scattered family of English black monk houses. His volumes are, in addition, a mine of information on details of monastic life, while the admirable historical notes and the copious lists and indices give order and lucidity to what might easily have become an impenetrable thicket.

Of those who have given me direct and personal help I must thank Miss Margaret Babington, who allowed me to use a Canterbury photograph as a frontispiece; Mr C. N. L. Brooke, who gave invaluable help in verifying references; Fr D. A. Callus, O.P., who read the chapters on the scholastics and added a number of precisions; Sir Sydney Cockerell, who read the pages on illumination and gave me access to many rare books during the war years; Dr G. R. Galbraith, who read the chapter on the Dominican organization; Mr W. A. Pantin, this time as a friendly critic, who read the whole book either in typescript or proof and suggested many additions and corrections; and Professor M. M. Postan, who read and suggested some alterations in the economic sections.

Finally, I may be permitted to acknowledge my indebtedness to all those who, in one way or another, have brought it about that the book should have been completed and this preface written at Peterhouse, the ancient and venerable foundation of Hugh of Balsham, bishop of Ely and monk and sometime subprior of the cathedral monastery of St Etheldreda.

DAVID KNOWLES

PETERHOUSE
April 21, 1947

A reprinting of this book has given the opportunity of making a few minor corrections and additions. Since the first publication in 1948 comparatively little work has been done on English monasticism, but Mr H. M. Colvin's account of the early Premonstratensians, Fr Hinnebusch's monograph on the English Dominicans, and Fr F. Roth's studies on the Austin Hermits have given precision in their particular fields. Meanwhile, the stream of literature on the history of scholasticism has continued to flow strongly, and has especially affected opinions on the chronology and doctrines of the English Dominicans, Robert Grosseteste, Roger Bacon, Duns Scotus and William of Ockham. For most of these, the section on the thirteenth century by Professor F. van Steenberghen in vol. 13 of the *Histoire de l'Eglise*, edited by MM. Fliche et Jarry (Paris, 1951), gives the new literature to date, and presents a picture which is sensibly different from those given by M. E. Gilson and Fr B. Geyer in their older works; at the moment of writing, a new survey by M. Gilson has just appeared. As it is the thought of Paris, rather than of Oxford, that has been chiefly reassessed, no great changes have been made in the text, but a passage on Ockham (p. 238) has been rewritten, the recent literature has been noted, and additional footnotes of some length will be found on pp. 216 and 227. For corrections and suggestions I am greatly indebted to reviews by Professor E. F. Jacob, Professor J. C. Russell, and Père H.-M. Vicaire, O.P.

DAVID KNOWLES

PETERHOUSE

December 8, 1955

LIST OF ABBREVIATIONS

AC	H. E. Salter, *Chapters of the Augustinian Canons*
AM	*Annales Monastici* (Rolls Series)
AFH	*Archivum Franciscanum Historicum*
ALKG	*Archiv für Litteratur- und Kirchengeschichte* (Denifle and Ehrle)
BGPM	*Beiträge zur Geschichte der Philosophie des Mittelalters*
BJRL	*Bulletin of the John Rylands Library*
BSFS	*British Society of Franciscan Studies*
CE	*Catholic Encyclopedia*
Chron. Abingd.	Chronicle of Abingdon
Chron. Evesh.	Chronicle of Evesham
Chron. Mels.	Chronicle of Meaux
CPL	Calendar of Papal Letters
CPR	Calendar of Patent Rolls
CS	Camden Series
C & YS	*Canterbury and York Society*
DHG	*Dictionnaire d'Histoire et de Géographie ecclésiastiques*
DNB	*Dictionary of National Biography*
DR	*Downside Review*
DS	*Dictionnaire de Spiritualité*
DTC	*Dictionnaire de Théologie Catholique*
Eccleston	Thomas of Eccleston, *De Adventu Fratrum Minorum* (ed. Little)
EcHR	*Economic History Review*
EHR	*English Historical Review*
FP	A. G. Little, *Franciscan Papers, Lists and Documents*
GASA	*Gesta Abbatum S. Albani*
Gerv. Cant.	Gervase of Canterbury
HBS	Henry Bradshaw Society
HMC	Historical Manuscripts Commission
JTS	*Journal of Theological Studies*
MC	W. A. Pantin, *Chapters of the Black Monks*
MGH, SS	*Monumenta Germaniae Historica. Scriptores*
MO	D. Knowles, *The Monastic Order in England*
MOPH	*Monumenta Ordinis Praedicatorum Historica*
MPAddit	Matthew Paris, *Additamenta*
MPChM	Matthew Paris, *Chronica Majora*
MPHA	Matthew Paris, *Historia Anglorum*
MSE	*Memorials of St Edmund's Abbey* (Rolls Series)
MU	H. Rashdall, *Medieval Universities* (ed. Powicke & Emden)
OHS	Oxford Historical Society

PBA	*Proceedings of the British Academy*
PhMA	E. Gilson, *La Philosophie au Moyen Age*
PL	Migne, *Patrologia Latina*
RB	*Revue Bénédictine*
RNP	*Revue néoscolastique de Philosophie*
RS	Rolls Series
SRS	Somerset Record Society
SS	Surtees Society
TRHS	*Transactions of the Royal Historical Society*
VCH	*Victoria County History*
ZfkT	*Zeitschrift für katholische Theologie*

Part One

THE OLD ORDERS, 1216–1340

CHAPTER I

THE THIRTEENTH CENTURY

I

The epoch of history which opens with the pontificate of Innocent III presents to the student of ecclesiastical institutions and of religious sentiment an appearance very different from that which had gone before. Even if we set aside the personal influence of the great pope himself in originating and determining the paths to be followed in European politics by his successors, and set aside also the circumstance that his reign coincided with the formal organization of university life in north-western Europe, two momentous and unpredictable events which occurred in the first decades of the thirteenth century gave a stamp to all that followed. The new orders of friars inaugurated a wholly original ideal and type of organization in the religious life, and the establishment at the Fourth Lateran Council of a code of disciplinary decrees gave a legal basis for a system of ecclesiastical administration different in method from all that had gone before. Necessary though it may be to trace the origins and causes of the new developments far back into the past, and to recognize the perseverance of much that was old, it yet remains true that the years between 1205 and 1215 are a watershed in religious history, and that no other decade has such significance for the spiritual and institutional life of the Church until the early years of the sixteenth century are reached.

This judgement, valid in a measure for all western Europe, is peculiarly true for England. Here, without a doubt, the Lateran Council marks a clear division in Church history. In the decades immediately preceding there had been in all degrees of life a growing spirit of independence, which in the reigns of Richard I and John threatened to become a spirit of antinomy. After the Lateran Council and the return of Stephen Langton to power, this gave place, at least among the higher clergy, to a spirit of order and reform, while the centralization of the Church as a whole, assisted by the attitude of the mendicant orders and by the direct action of a succession of distinguished popes, and stimulated by the close relations between England and Rome and by the prolonged residence, thrice within the space of fifty years, of an able and energetic papal legate in England, gave a permanent framework to the activities of individuals.

In consequence, bishops of the reign of Henry III and Edward I are of another type and have other interests from those of the contemporaries of Baldwin and Hubert Walter. In the twelfth century the most eminent bishops, with a few almost accidental exceptions, had been monks or regular canons—Anselm, Robert of Bethune, Theobald, Henry Murdac, Henry of Blois, Gilbert Foliot, Baldwin, Hugh of Lincoln—and of the others the most remarkable, such as Thomas Becket and Bartholomew of Exeter, had been in a sense individualists, holding a lone hand. In the thirteenth century, by contrast, from Stephen Langton onwards, there was a solid body (often a majority) of men formed in a single school, devoted to a single policy, and bound by common interests to each other and to Rome.[1] To these university-trained professional seculars the one interest was the administration of their dioceses according to the norm of councils and decretals, and in close dependence on Rome. It is true that there were always bishops of another type, royal officials or favourites of little spirituality, and men of family bent on a career, and that complaints are repeatedly made by contemporaries of widespread ignorance and vice, while modern students express disappointment at what they consider the failure of the English bishops to carry through the programme of reform inaugurated by Innocent III. Complaints of this kind, however, are a commonplace in every century, nor has any plan of reform been executed in all desirable completeness throughout the Church. Those who would judge aright the ebb and flow of the tide of spirituality must take a wide view of the hundred years that followed the death of St Bernard: they will then surely feel that the first half of the thirteenth century was, in the English Church at least, a time of life and growth, rather than one of stagnation and decay. It is not wholly accidental that the greatest ecclesiastic and the three canonized saints of the thirteenth century should all have been diocesan bishops with distinguished university careers behind them, and that more than half a dozen others from among the *magistri* bishops should have left behind them a name for sanctity sufficient to acquire for their tombs a reputation as places of pilgrimage and miraculous cure.[2] Nor should it be forgotten that it was these bishops who gave to England the Angel Choir at Lincoln, the west front at Wells, and the perfect symmetry of the one English cathedral to be completed in a generation, which reflects, perhaps more than any other building in Europe, the intellectual qualities of the age.

II

Along with the new type of scholar-bishop there came a new type of religious. The long reign of Henry III coincides almost exactly with the period of expansion and first fervour of the friars, which may be said to have opened with the council of the Lateran and closed with that of Lyons. Their work for the people and the neglected classes in town and country,

1 For an excellent study of the new episcopate *v. Bishops and Reform*, 1215–1272, by M. Gibbs and J. Lang; and for their activities, J. R. H. Moorman, *Church Life in England in the XIII Century*.

2 Besides the three canonized saints the following bishops of the reign of Henry III left an abiding reputation for holiness of life: Stephen Berksted (Chichester), Sewal de Bovill (York), Walter Button II (Bath and Wells), Walter Cantilupe (Worcester), Robert Grosseteste (Lincoln), Roger Niger (London), Richard Wendeue (Rochester), and Walter Suffield (Norwich).

though all but unrecorded by chroniclers, has received general and perhaps undiscriminating recognition from recent writers; the share that England took in moulding the destinies of the new orders, and in carrying to its highest pitch their intellectual achievement has been less understood, and must be examined more closely. Here it is only necessary to remark that Alexander of Hales, Adam Marsh, Haymo of Faversham and John Pecham among the Minors, Robert Kilwardby among the Preachers and Simon Stock among the Carmelites exerted an influence and won for themselves a reputation that extended throughout and beyond their orders, even though no adequate memorial may remain of their spiritual and intellectual greatness.

As regards the older orders, the thirteenth century, it must be acknowledged, has no striking changes to show. Here, also, the new leaven worked and, especially with the black monks and canons, produced a new organization with a considerable amount of legislation, but no new centre or scheme of fervent life developed, no saint arose, and a list of the twenty or thirty most eminent Englishmen of the age would not contain the name of a single monk or canon save Matthew Paris, who, for all his gifts, has few of the qualities of a ruler, or a reformer, or a divine. Yet although critics, and among them a papal legate in a solemn and public pronouncement, called attention to the need for reform among the black monks, and might have heard his words echoed a few years later by the highest authorities among the monks themselves, yet one familiar with the half-century that followed the death of King Stephen will probably feel that monastic life as a whole was more regular and amenable to authority in 1270 than it had been in 1190. Certainly, the decline so deplored by Gerald of Wales had been arrested, if not in part repaired, and his gloomy auguries for the immediate future of the order had proved false.

But while the monastic order showed a power of recuperation within itself, its early fertility had gone. The old orders made very few foundations after the reign of John. Though the rapid spread of the orders of friars was soon to show that there was as yet no dearth of religious vocations, the number of existing monasteries of the old model was so great that what may be called saturation point had been reached in the country at large. From 1216 onwards no plantation of any significance was made by the black monks save for the monastic colleges at Oxford, which drew their population from houses already existing. The white monks, likewise, had reached high-water mark, and no new plantations were made by any of the old established abbeys of England and Wales. King John's abbey of Beaulieu in the New Forest was an imported, not a spontaneous, growth; the monks came direct from France. It prospered, after slow beginnings, and during the reign of Henry III the monks for two royal foundations were drawn from it; the first group, to Netley, only a few miles across Southampton Water, founded by the king in 1239; the second to north Gloucestershire, where Richard, earl of Cornwall, established an abbey on the manor of Hayles, a hamlet to which a great theologian had already given European celebrity. To the newly built church, lying in rich meadows where the Cotswolds fall to the vale of Evesham and the eye travels across the wide champaign to Bredon and Malvern and the dark hills of Wales, the founder brought a relic of the Precious Blood that was soon to become a magnet to pilgrims. Here, on a Sunday in November, 1251, took place one of the most impressive public functions of the time. The ceremonies and entertainment were of such a splendour that even Matthew Paris, an eyewitness who was no stranger to such gatherings, feared to expatiate lest his recital should stagger belief.[1] King Henry and Queen Eleanor were there, together with the founder; twelve bishops, a vast concourse of magnates and prelates, three hundred knights and monks of various habits watched the ceremony and dined on a variety of dishes of meat and fish. Walter Cantilupe, the diocesan, was the consecrating prelate, but the eminent bishop of Lincoln celebrated at the high altar, and his twelve colleagues consecrated each a smaller altar in the church.

Yet the foundation of Hayles, little though it may have been realized at the time, was in a sense the end of a chapter. It was the furthest wash of the tide from Cîteaux. Only one more house of the white monks was to be founded, save for the academic Rewley, and that only after the lapse of a century. M. Stephen of Lexington and his seven associates, who in 1221 abandoned the schools of Oxford for the cloister of Quarr, were not alone in their conversion, but they were the last to hear the call of Cîteaux.[2] Nor is the story different for the canons. The rare plantations of the Austin canons in the thirteenth century were without exception small, and their names are known only to the antiquary; the white canons added only two houses to their list; the Gilbertines none at all. The nuns alone continued to multiply slowly, with several important new foundations.

The function at Hayles was only one of many such in an age that delighted in sumptuous religious pageants, and commanded the artistic skill capable of investing them with beauty of a high order. It was the full spring of Gothic architecture, the age of the greatest English sculpture, and the time when the painting of glass, metal work, mural decoration and the designing and embroidering of vestments had all reached a summit of harmonious excellence. The king himself was perhaps the most gifted connoisseur and the most lavish patron of religious art of the English medieval monarchs; his constructions and adornments at Westminster have no parallel in English monastic history; he was the patron of monk-artists and historians.

---

1 *Ann. Waverl. s.a. (Ann. Monast.* II, 343); *MPChM,* v, 262. The founder told Paris that the place had cost him 10,000 marks. Yet only twenty monks were on the foundation (*Monasticon,* v, 686). The scanty ruins of the abbey, lying deep in the fields away from habitation, have recently been cleared of grass and ivy.

2 *Ann. Dunstapl. s.a.* 1221. Had M. Stephen delayed his conversion for a few years, he would surely have become a friar. Isolated cases of transference of other religious to the Cistercians occur later (*v. Ann. Dunstapl. s.a.* 1231, 1240, 1249), but they are not typical.

Yet in more important matters the king, the bishops, the great nobles, the royal administration, and the monastic order were rapidly drawing apart, each to its own sphere. The solidarity of the educated ruling class was gone, and the relations between monarch and religious were now a personal matter. Less than thirty years after the foundation of Hayles came the statute *de Religiosis*, commonly called the Statute of Mortmain (1279), which, though by no means the rigid piece of anti-monastic legislation that it may at first sight appear, was a symptom of a new phase of social opinion in which the monks were no longer the animating or invigorating principle of the nation's higher life, but only one of many bodies of importance, each with rights against the others, whose private interests must be subordinated to the interests, as conceived by government, of the king and country as a whole.

III

The thirteenth century has been hailed as the 'greatest' or the 'most creative' epoch in the middle ages. Certainly, to those who see in Gothic art the supreme achievement of western Europe, that century must necessarily appear a nonpareil which gave birth to Notre Dame and La Sainte Chapelle in Paris, to the façades of Amiens and Rheims, to Westminster, Salisbury and Lincoln, and to the sculptures and glass of Chartres, Wells and York. Nor can there be a question as to the supreme position in the history of thought of the century which included the life-space of St Thomas, St Bonaventure, Albert the Great and Roger Bacon. If, in addition, we reflect that the opening years of the century saw St Francis giving new beauty to the Christian life and to his own exquisite motherland, that its first half coincided with the lifetime of St Louis and that the year of its close saw Dante, with half the Psalmist's span of years behind him, about to visit in spirit the realms beyond the grave, we shall perhaps have some sympathy with the judgements as to the preeminence of the thirteenth century, even if we cannot fully subscribe to them.

Yet the historian of religion may well think that the hundred years that passed between the pontificate of Leo IX and the death of St Bernard contained a more heroic and more significant age. Certainly, it was an age in which eminent men left in their letters and writings a more adequate and a more intimate picture of themselves than is given by their successors. As a general rule, the great ages of art and thought are also the great ages of literature and personal revelation. Pheidias and Praxiteles, and the Attic primitives before them, translate into stone the ideals and emotions that were embodied in words by Pericles and Aeschylus, by Sophocles and Plato; the Florence of Dante is also the Florence of Giotto; Michelangelo the poet is his own interpreter. With the greater part of the thirteenth century this is not so.[1] In speculative thought, indeed, the age was able to express itself in language of unrivalled precision and luminous clarity, and when we contemplate at Chartres, at Amiens, at Wells and at Sens the features of the men and women of that time in their strength and beauty and repose, their faces seem alight with an intelligence and a sympathy and a compelling nobility that call us across the centuries as does the letter of a friend long dead, but the individuals of the age, the men and women who walked and lived, are all but dumb; they do not, as do Anselm and Bernard and Héloïse and Ailred, show us their hearts; and the great doctors, who wrote so tirelessly in the schools, have not a word to spare for any personal affair. The age abounds in those who lay down principles or who dispute in law and philosophy, but the minds of the men of that time, more perhaps than at any other moment of history, found their employment and exercise in dealing with formal and abstract truth, rather than with the concrete realities of human life or with the emotions and appreciations of individuals. It is this silence of the men of the thirteenth century on all that concerns themselves and the beauties of their world that gives an added depth of wonder to those who hear, breaking the silence, the exquisite, rich and subtle tones of the clear and ranging voice of Dante.

1 St Francis of Assisi is, of course, a notable exception, and in a lesser degree Salimbene and other Franciscan chroniclers. Matthew Paris, though the broad traits of his character appear from his writings, tells us surprisingly little of himself and his *milieu*.

CHAPTER II

REORGANIZATION AMONG THE BLACK MONKS,
1215–1336

I

The period that opens with the Lateran Council was, as regards legislation affecting the life of the black monk abbeys, very different from that which had gone before. Hitherto, as readers of a previous volume will be aware, there had been, strictly speaking, no legislative authority at all either within or without the monastic body in England. The papacy, prior to the Council, had never attempted to put forward any comprehensive body of decrees; the bishops had no authority to do so; the very great activity of Lanfranc had been due entirely to his personal prestige and the circumstances of the time; and later enactments of provincial councils were directed solely against individual abuses and were, it must be said, never regarded very seriously by the monks. Among the black monks themselves, no legislative body of any kind existed; the houses were entirely autonomous, and all rested with the abbot or prior who could do little to affect the customary life of the house, as expressed in the uses which had crystallized around the Rule, when once an equilibrium had been reached after the Norman Conquest. Nor, it may be added, did any widespread sense of a need for further legislation exist.

With the thirteenth century all this was changed. Reform and the making of constitutions was in the air. In Rome, from the pontificate of Innocent III onwards, a series of energetic popes took a personal interest in the cause of monastic reform, and were encouraged and assisted in their endeavours by the position accorded to the Papacy by the new highly organized and highly centralized orders of friars. In England, the drift from autonomy to antinomy, the troubles of the times, and a few resounding scandals had awakened in many circles a desire for reorganization. Finally, the Lateran Council, by its decrees on general chapters and visitations, had created a legislative body for the black monks, together with officials charged with overseeing the execution of its enactments. It will be necessary in the present chapter to consider the nature, the extent, and the effect of all this new legislation upon the order.

In addition to the general chapters, three agencies, active at different times and places, worked for reorganization and reform: papal legates; visitors, both monastic and (in the case of non-exempt houses) episcopal; and, finally, individual abbots. The efforts of all these were in the main directed towards enforcing or introducing canonical and conciliar legislation on the same broad points, such as the abolition of private property, avoidance of indiscriminate exits from, or residence outside, the monastery, the regularization of the novitiate and the strict accountability of all officials, including superiors, for financial expenditure. These, being common to all throughout the century, need not receive detailed treatment here. Two matters, however, are significant enough to demand separate treatment: the one, the old question of meat-eating, was a chronic sore that successive generations attempted now to cauterize and now to mollify; the other, the reorganization of the horarium to admit theological studies, was of purely domestic origin and had consequences of some importance in the sequel.

The decree *In singulis regnis* of the Lateran Council of 1215 had enacted that the superiors of houses of black monks in each province should meet in chapter every three years, instructed at first by two Cistercian abbots, therein to take counsel and legislate for the 'reformation' of their order. This the abbots and priors in the province of Canterbury proceeded to do, though no doubt hindered by the disturbances of the times, and the first meeting was held at Oxford, probably in the autumn or winter of 1218–19, under the presidency of two distinguished abbots, William of St Albans and Hugh of Bury, assisted by the Cistercian abbots of Thame and Wardon.[1] The number and composition of the gathering is not known, nor is any account of their deliberations extant, but their decrees exist in the form in which they were to be applied by the visitors appointed by the chapter for each diocese. These decrees, grouped under twenty-five headings and suggested rather by recent conciliar discussion than by peculiar local needs, follow no recognizable order and are in no sense a comprehensive code. It is noteworthy that the abbots begin by setting their own house in order by a series of enactments limiting abbatial expenses and liberties and aimed at restoring the heads of houses to the full regular life. Apart from this, the most imperative decrees were directed against any sort of private possession by monks, including the practice of making to individuals a money allowance from which to purchase the necessaries of life, and against travelling on the part of monks.[2]

The neuralgic spot touched by the fathers of the chapter was, however, connected with none of these matters, but with dietary regulations. These will be discussed later; here it is only necessary to say that the first chapter, treading delicately on miry and unfamiliar ground, let it be known after long discussion that all their decrees, after a short period of probation, would be amenable to revision at a second chapter, or, rather, a second session of the first chapter, which was to be held at St Albans on 14 Sep-

---

1 *Chapters of the English Black Monks*, 1215–1540, ed. W. A. Pantin (*CS*, xlv), vol. I (1931). This most valuable collection of documents, carefully dated and annotated, contains much matter formerly unprinted; it is a model of exact scholarship and a mine of carefully digested information; the data it provides, essential for the understanding of monastic history in the period concerned, have not hitherto been fully used. The work will henceforth be quoted as *MC* by volume and page. The dates of the two first meetings of the chapter are uncertain; *v. MC*, I, 3–4.   2 *MC*, I, 8–13.

tember 1219. At this meeting protests were duly made on behalf of the weaker brethren to whom some of the earlier decrees had seemed heavy and unbearable.[1] What these points were is not specifically stated, but to judge by the new decrees, they concerned only the travelling of monks and the dietary regulations. Such changes as were made, however, did not take effect, owing to the death of one of the presidents, and as presumably the earlier version continued to be regarded as tentative by those who disliked its provisions, the black monks remained for all practical purposes temporarily unaffected by any legislation. Indeed, it might have seemed that the new system would fail altogether to function. The second (or third) chapter was called for 1222. We do not know the exact date, but the rendezvous was Bermondsey, where, however, something of a fiasco occurred owing to the non-appearance of one of the presidents, the abbot of Gloucester. As no constitutional machinery existed to meet such a situation, the chapter apparently considered itself unable to legislate;[2] it did, however, provide for the future by fixing a meeting for Northampton three years later, and by electing as presidents two abbots who might, if necessary, be represented by their priors. In the event, neither prelates nor priors put in an appearance, and only some fifteen heads of houses out of more than sixty who were liable to summons arrived, but those present, undaunted by these facts, not only proceeded to hold the chapter, but passed a number of constitutional ordinances governing visitations and various emergencies, and instructed the two *de facto* presidents, the abbots of Evesham and Abingdon, to promulgate the statutes of the Oxford chapter of 1218 as revised by that of St Albans. Henceforward it may be assumed that chapters were held at fairly regular intervals, though little record survives of their activities.

Meanwhile, their decrees were supplemented from another quarter. From 1234 onward the papal legate, Cardinal Otho, had held a series of visitations; in 1237, at a council held at St Paul's, he gave his approval to a recent reaffirmation of a decree against meat-eating,[3] and shortly after, in November 1238, he summoned the black monk abbots to meet him in St Martin's, London, where he presented them with a comprehensive set of statutes composed by Pope Gregory IX. These covered all aspects of the regular and administrative life, and the abbots are said to have received the presentation with joy, but the same authority tells us that three months later the legate put out a short and milder set of decrees.[4]

Such legislation as was forthcoming during the following ten years has only come down in fragments, and would seem to have been of no great importance; in 1249, however, the chapter passed the most comprehensive

---

1 *MC*, I, 17: 'Statuta primi capituli sui, que quibusdam infirmioribus videbantur onerosa et importabilia...cum moderatione declarata sunt.' Cf. *ibid.* 7–8.
2 *MC*, I, 18: 'Capitulum...non processit.'
3 Wilkins, *Concilia*, I, 653; *MPChM*, III, 432–3.
4 *MPChM*, III, 499, 516–17, 524.

set of decrees yet produced, reiterating and adding to those already in existence, and ordering that they, together with the Lateran decrees and the statutes of Gregory IX, should be publicly read at stated intervals. This is perhaps the first occasion on which we can see something like a formal body of 'constitutions' recognized as permanently binding all the houses.[1] Three years later Innocent IV transmitted the statutes of Gregory IX to all the bishops of England with a covering letter in which he commanded them to see to their observance.[2] This step produced the inevitable reactions, which we are fortunate enough to be able to trace in part. Although a chapter had met that spring at Osney before the news came through, a special meeting of all superiors was convoked for September at Oxford.[3] No account of its decisions has survived, but a letter has been preserved, dating from the following year, in which the abbot of Evesham sends to the abbot of St Albans a copy of a privilege granted by the pope to the non-exempt abbots of the province of Rouen, enabling them, in view of the alleged severity of Gregory's statutes, to dispense their subjects in all matters save where this is expressly forbidden by the Rule. The writer suggests that exempt abbots may be successful in obtaining a similar privilege, and Paris informs us that St Albans forthwith did so, though the comments on the statutes made by the community in chapter show that, with few exceptions, they were being observed by the house.[4]

Hitherto mention has been made only of the southern or Canterbury chapters. In the northern province of York similar, though independent, meetings were held, though as the province contained only half a dozen black monk houses, the most important of which were closely confederated, these deliberations could neither possess the significance nor arouse the opposition which have been noticed in the south. Indeed, it would appear to have been the practice of the northern chapters to publish, with slight changes, recent southern legislation; thus at their first meeting, at Northallerton in 1221, the northern abbots made their own in essentials the southern statutes of 1218–19.[5] Later chapters, however, such as that of 1273, passed decrees, commonplace indeed in content, which cannot be traced directly to any extant southern source.

II

What may be regarded as the peak of capitular legislative efficiency was attained in the eighth decade of the century. This, it would seem, was neither accidental nor due to an immediate crisis, but reflected the movement of contemporary sentiment. The generation of men now in high

1 *MC*, I, 34–45.
2 The decrees are in *MPChM*, VI (Additamenta), 235 *seqq.*
3 *MC*, I, 53; *Ann. Wint.* (*AM*, II, 94), *s.a.* 1253.
4 *MPChM*, VI, 290–3 (letter), 247 *seqq.* (comments of community).
5 *MC*, I, 232–5. For the resemblances between northern and southern statutes see table in *MC*, Appendix IV.

office had grown to manhood and received their intellectual formation in the new world. They had become acquainted on the one hand with the great legislative and constitutional achievements of the Preachers and the Minors, with the work of Humbert de Romanis, of Haymo, of Raymond of Pennafort and of Bonaventura, and on the other with the repeated endeavours of successive popes to reorganize the monastic life. Their minds had been aroused by the success of Albert the Great and Thomas Aquinas in producing a logical synthesis of the whole of Christian thought; they had followed the bitter controversies between seculars and mendicants as to the more perfect life, and those between Preachers and Minors, and among the Minors themselves, as to the meaning and scope of evangelical poverty and the literal observance of the Rule. They had felt the need of definition and uniformity in their own life, especially, perhaps, as they watched the reforming activities of Kilwardby and Pecham, and at a moment when their material prosperity was, on the whole, great, they had been singled out by the legate Ottoboni in a solemn council at London in 1268 as the part of the Church that was most relaxed, and had been the recipients of a new set of decrees.[1] Finally, the flood tide of the scholastic movement, which had already engulfed all the orders of friars, was now drawing many of the monks, or at least awaking in them a consciousness that their way of life no longer ran in the main paths of the age's progress.

Moreover, it is clear that a number of unusually alert and spiritually minded men were leaders of the body at the time. Roger of St Albans (1260–90), for example, was a man of virtue, with an expert knowledge of the recent publications and commentaries in canon law;[2] Richard of Ware, abbot of Westminster (1259–83), knew the Curia well, though at the same time he was a trusted royal servant in England, and was in his own monastic home the energetic ruler who drew up the long list of uses that bears his name,[3] though it was itself based upon the work of an eminent contemporary. At St Augustine's, Canterbury, the abbot, Nicholas de Spina (1273–83), was a distinguished man, alive to the needs of the time. His reputation had caused him to be chosen conservator of the Premonstratensians in England; within his house he made a number of changes to be mentioned later, and was probably the author of the elaborate customary which formed the basis of that of Abbot Ware; under his rule, so the chronicler says, St Augustine's attained a degree of prosperity, spiritual and temporal, never surpassed before or after.[4] At Glastonbury, John of Taunton (1274–90) was equally abreast of the times. His library shows that he was familiar with the works of Albert

---

1 Wilkins, *Concilia*, II, 15–19.

2 *GASA*, I, 400: 'Quem a primaevo juventutis flore vitae sanctitas et morum gravitas commendabat.' *Ibid.* 483. Among his books were: *Duo paria Decretalium, Summae Reymundi, Gaufridi et Bernardi super Decretales.*

3 Cf. Flete's *History of Westminster*, 113–14.

4 Thorne, 1925, 1935 *seqq.*

the Great and St Thomas, including the *Summa*, as well as with those of spiritual writers.[1]

The legate Ottoboni in 1268 had, after declaring the need for reform among the black monks, ended his decrees for the Church in England with a number of monastic regulations which were little more than a repetition of those already given by Gregory IX. Nine years later, at the chapter of 1277 over which the abbots of St Augustine's and Glastonbury presided, a long and complete set of constitutions was approved.[2] Besides their great length, these were distinguished by the care taken to survey the whole life and to arrange the decrees in divisions with an appropriate rubric. In a preface, the presidents declare their intention of restoring to the monastic order its primitive perfection by putting an end to the novel and diverse customs which had been introduced, to the destruction of both regularity and uniformity.[3] As a secondary end they declared their intention of making radical changes in the daily time table in the interests of intellectual work.

As regards reform, the principal, or at least the most controversial point was connected with diet, and will be considered later, as will the whole movement towards theological study which issued in the establishment of a house for the province at Oxford. Some other decrees of this chapter will also be considered on a later page. For the moment it is enough to remark that the statutes form a sane and practical, if somewhat severe, body of law, and though their general tone is one of restriction and reform they are clearly the work, not of an external legislator endeavouring to impose discipline upon a decadent or recalcitrant body, but of authority within the body itself, animated by a real desire for a fully regular life, and inspired with a serious hope of attaining the end desired.

Nevertheless, the decrees were in the sequel subjected to a sharp fire on both flanks: while their alleged severity elicited protests from one section of the monks, another group, conservative in sentiment, professed to see relaxation in the rearrangement of the liturgical life, and they received a tardy support from a quarter whence it could hardly have been expected when the matter was taken up by Archbishop Pecham and other members of the hierarchy.

Consequently, as in 1218–25, certain revisions were effected.[4] The first, a thoroughgoing piece of work in 1278, changed many details but left

1 *Adam de Domerham*, II, 574–5. Among his books were a Gospel annotated 'secundum glosam novam fratris Thomae...postillos super Mathaeum fr. Alberti Magni...librum de perfeccione spiritalis vitae, et primam, secundam, tertiam, quartam partem fr. Thomae; quaestiones de malo, de mortalibus criminibus disputatas a fr. Thoma.' He also had the 1a 2ae and 2a 2ae of the *Summa* and a work of Kilwardby.

2 *MC*, I, 64–92.

3 *MC*, I, 64: 'Statum monastici ordinis ad suam excellenciam primitivam...reducere... impellamur, advertentes quod s. patris nostri Benedicti regularibus observanciis intermissis... in singulis...monasteriis per diversarum consuetudinum novitates, que parere discordias dinoscuntur, predicte regule professores a se disiuncti appareant et diversi.'

4 *MC*, I, 95–100, 103–5.

essentials unaltered. The second, dating from the following year, was apparently still less significant. In any case, though a few concessions softened the severity of the 1277 decrees, the changes which simplified and shortened the liturgical services stood, though there is some evidence that they were only slowly and incompletely obeyed in conservative houses.

That the legislation of 1277–9 was the outcome of a widespread desire for regularity and uniformity in influential circles among the monks is shown by a number of satellite and contemporary documents. There is, for example, the interesting list of suggestions and petitions as well for 'mitigation' of the Rule as for a return to the old practices which were put before chapter with a view to their submission to the Holy See,[1] and the long series of regulations for the training of novices, also drawn up, it would appear, by authority of chapter.[2] When to these are added the customaries and individual ordinances of the time, some of which have been mentioned above, it will be seen that the later decades of the century were a time of great and healthy activity among the black monks in high place. The climax of capitular efficiency was perhaps reached in 1291 and the following years, when *diffinitores* were elected to draw up regulations for the new house at Oxford and for its financial support, but the whole series of documents from 1270 to *c.* 1300 shows that there existed a sense of solidarity and corporate responsibility in the southern province, together with a desire and an ability on the part of the chapter and its officials to propose the policy and direct the life of the whole body. The administrative activities of the presidents, the manifold legislation of chapter and the use of it as an agency for petition to Rome, the endeavour to establish uniform regulations for the training and education of novices, the coming into being of a common house of studies at Oxford, erected, maintained and governed through the chapter and its diffinitors—all this, no doubt largely inspired by the sight of the organization of the Preachers,[3] and perhaps also by the contemporary work of king and parliament, marks a very great development, not only from the days of Samson and Roger Norreys, but even from those of the first provincial chapters. The whole tone, indeed, of the documents of the time, were it not for their cumbrous phraseology, would go far to create in the mind of one familiar with later monastic history the illusion that he was reading of the monks of the early counter-Reformation, and it is not surprising that lawyers and antiquaries such as Clement Reyner and Augustine Baker, who guided the legislation

---

1 The petitions are in *MC*, I, 106–7, 114–19; the *tradicio generalis capituli* is *ibid.* 110–11. These may, however, be a response to a request of the chapter of 1298. Cf. *MC*, I, 139.

2 These were printed by Sir E. M. Thompson at the end of the *Customary of St Augustine's, Canterbury* (*HBS*, XXIII, 1902), I, 399–429.

3 The office and title of *diffinitor*, wholly foreign to the old monastic order, were perhaps directly derived from the Preachers. It is worth remarking that these decades witnessed the strongest efforts of the Augustinian chapters for regularity and uniformity, culminating in the Statutes of Helaugh Park (*v. infra*, p. 29).

of the revived English congregation at the dawn of the seventeenth century, having discovered later capitular decrees based upon these, should have used them when formulating their own constitutions.[1]

These characteristics were not long maintained. The disastrous events in social, political and ecclesiastical history of the fourteenth century may have had their share in destroying them, but already in the early decades of the century centrifugal forces were at work, and there is evidence that the ablest prelates were no longer interested in affairs of the order as a whole, or in securing uniformity of observance and discipline.[2] The corporate efficiency of the reign of Edward I was never surpassed, and not long maintained. Nevertheless, its existence, almost universally ignored, should be appreciated as marking an important and interesting moment in English monastic life which has hitherto escaped the notice of historians.

III

The above review will have shown that general chapter, through its ordinances and its officials, was a living force in the thirteenth century. How far the system of visitation was effective and how far cases of serious disorder continued to occur will be discussed elsewhere.[3] A few points, however, directly concerning the chapters may be mentioned here. It is natural to inquire whether the attendance was satisfactory throughout. Unfortunately, there are few complete lists of those present. We know, however, that at the chapter of 1225 only some fifteen out of the sixty-odd superiors of the province were present in person, and that the meeting of 1246 was prorogued owing to the paucity of numbers, as was likewise that of 1252, when a list, unfortunately fragmentary, records fourteen prelates who sent excuses and another nine who neither appeared nor gave reasons for their absence.[4] When this chapter reassembled in 1253 fifteen were present in person, twenty-three others were represented by proctors, and eleven others are recorded as absent without excuse.[5] This would seem to leave a few still unaccounted for, though it is not altogether clear how many of the small priories at this time considered themselves liable, or entitled, to a summons. At the great chapter of 1277 forty-five abbots are said to have been present,[6] while at the important meeting of 1290 some thirty were present in person and others by proctor.[7]

On the whole it seems clear that in the thirteenth century, especially in its latter half, the attendance, though never universal, was satisfactory,

---

1 Cf. *MC*, II, 185-6.

2 E.g. de Wenlok, abbot of Westminster, and Henry Eastry, prior of Christ Church; this last, however, a house which always held aloof from chapter.

3 *Infra*, p. 110.

4 *MC*, I, 21, 24, 47-8. *Ann. Theok.* (*AM*, I, 135, 150), *s.a.* 1246, 1252. Mr Pantin has tabulated the attendances in an appendix to his essay on the chapters in *TRHS*, ser. 4, x (1927).   5 *MC*, I, 51-2.

6 So an entry in a Reading chronicle printed in *MC*, I, 59.   7 *MC*, I, 129-30.

once granted the validity of vicarious attendance, especially as the greater houses were well represented. So far as the scanty evidence for the period goes, the regular absentees would seem to have been the heads of a few insignificant priories and the superiors of two or three large houses absent on principle. Of these latter the most constant and important was the prior of Christ Church, Canterbury; others, who had some traditional motives for refusal to co-operate, were the abbots of Battle, Faversham and Spalding.[1]

An analysis of the names of the presidents between 1215 and 1336 indicates that the office never became the perquisite of an individual or of a house.[2] In all, seventeen abbeys are known to have provided a president: most of these were, as was only right, the larger houses, and a closer examination shows that they were usually the most distinguished abbots of the day. Westminster heads the list with at least seven terms of office; Bury and St Albans have but two each; at the end of the period a series of badly attended chapters were for twenty years presided over by the abbots of Chertsey, Walden and Ramsey. An isolated reference in a chronicle suggests that one of the two presidents was by custom chosen from among the abbots of exempt houses,[3] and in fact, one at least of the names, so far as they are known, from 1218 to 1292 is always that of an exempt abbot.[4] Later, however, the rule, if rule it was, ceased to be honoured.

With the beginning of the fourteenth century, indeed, attendance was falling off badly, and the chapter showed signs of going the way followed so many centuries later by the League of Nations. In 1309 the presidents, who had prorogued a sparsely attended meeting, sent a circular letter, couched in the strongest terms, to defaulters, and the same letter was re-issued in 1315 and a similar one twice in 1319 after successive prorogations. In the last edition the two presidents, Walden and Chertsey, threatened to throw in their hand and report the whole matter to Rome unless notice were taken of the summons.[5] The machinery of chapter, however, did not cease to function either then or at any later date.

IV

Two matters with which the chapters were repeatedly concerned are of particular interest, and deserve separate examination. The first of these is the question of meat-eating and fasting.

As was seen in a previous volume, the exact observance of the Rule on

1 The position of Christ Church will be discussed elsewhere. For Spalding *v. MC*, I, 209 *seqq.*; for Faversham *ibid.* 138, and *Reg. Pecham*, III, 959.

2 *V.* the table of presidents in *MC*, I, Appendix v.

3 *GASA*, I, 392. Five exempt houses agree in 1253 to appoint as referee the 'abbas exemptus qui in ultimo Generali Capitulo praesideat' (*sic*).

4 In 1292 Abingdon and Ramsey were presidents. Our list of chapters is, however, incomplete.   5 *MC*, I, 164, 192, 194.

two important points, viz. the regime of a single meal from 14 September to Easter and the abstinence from all meat save in the infirmary had broken down very generally by the end of the twelfth century.[1] House differed from house in details and degrees, but roughly speaking it may be said that most houses kept the double meal until November, and thenceforward on all important feasts till Lent and during two or three weeks at Christmastide; as regards meat, complete abstinence save in the infirmary, which was undoubtedly universal in the early Anglo-Norman monasticism, had been breached by three practices: the eating of meat in the infirmary by those supposed to stand in need of a fortifying diet; the invitation by the superior to his private room of individuals at discretion; and, finally, certain fixed periods of 'recreation', during which sections of the community ate meat in a special room apart from the main body. It will readily be seen that the last, though a wholly 'irregular' proceeding, was an almost inevitable development from the two former, as thus only could discontent and charges of favouritism or malingering be avoided. It was, however, a frank abandonment of the Rule. At a few houses, however, complete abstinence appears still to have been practised as late as c. 1200.

The thirteenth century saw earnest attempts, from within and without, to stem the tide of relaxation, and for more than a century the struggle continued between the party of strictness, which gradually lost strength, and the larger, though less defined group of the lax, having between them the great body of those who desired a limited and authorized mitigation. The first chapter of 1218–19, while decreeing that all superfluities in diet were to be cut off, and ordering superiors to discuss ways and means of effecting this with a small committee of monks, nevertheless authorized two important relaxations: the second meal was to be continued till 1 November, and thenceforward allowed at Christmastide and all feasts 'in copes'; and monks of the cloister might when necessary eat meat with permission in a separate room, that is, one distinct from both refectory and infirmary.[2] In the revised version of these decrees, however, it was laid down that the Rule was to be followed absolutely as to fasting (i.e. the single meal from 14 September), but the clause on meat-eating was retained.[3] In view of the presidents' declaration that they were modifying various enactments that had seemed unbearably hard to some, this revision is a little difficult to understand; we know, however, from other sources that influential abbots, such as William of St Albans and Robert of Peterborough, were

1 *MO*, 460–2.
2 *MC*, I, 10–12. The 'fratres qui pondus diei et estum portant' recurring in these statutes are the 'monks of the cloister'. Officials would in the course of their duties and travels have opportunities for 'recreation'. On the subject of meat-eating the essay of Edmund Bishop in *DR*, XLV (1925), 184–238, should be consulted. Bishop's treatment is exhaustive, with the relevant passages printed, often from MSS. The present writer, however, does not find himself able to agree with all the findings, e.g. the interpretation of the *Quum ad monasterium*, for which *v. infra*, p. 19.
3 *GASA*, I, 294. 'Statuit abb. Willielmus ut Regula S. Benedicti inviolabilius observetur.'

against any relaxation and persuaded their communities to adopt the full regime of the Rule.[1]

A few years later orders were issued by Gregory IX for a special visitation of the religious houses of England. Among the visitors were a Cistercian and a Premonstratensian abbot, and among their injunctions was one forbidding flesh-meat anywhere outside the infirmary; other visitors, however, such as those at Westminster and Bury, allowed monks who were in need of a generous diet to join the sick in the infirmary;[2] while Grosseteste, visiting Peterborough a little later, caused resentment by putting a stop to regular 'recreations' and the eating of meat by monks in the guesthouse and elsewhere, and restricted it to those specially invited by the abbot to his room.[3] These various experiences would seem to show that even after the statutes of 1218–25 the widest variety of practice obtained.

This, indeed, is borne out by the events of the next few years. The chapter of 1237 met in the expectation of imminent action by the legate Otho; perhaps in order to forestall him they decreed that the Rule was to be observed literally, and all 'recreations' abolished; only the sick were to be allowed meat in the infirmary.[4] Later in the year the legate, at a Council held in London, included among its decrees one in which he recorded this decision of the chapter and gave it his solemn approval.[5] In the following year he promulgated the decrees of Gregory IX. These put an absolute ban upon flesh-meat, save for the sickly in the infirmary, but a decretal which accompanied the statutes was destined to have considerable influence in the sequel. This was the celebrated *Quum ad monasterium Sublacense*, originally issued as a letter by Innocent III in 1202.[6] In it, the pope forbade the eating of meat, not only in the refectory, but also with the abbot as a community act elsewhere, as had apparently been the custom at Subiaco on feast days. It was expressly stated that meat was to be eaten only in the infirmary, and that even the sick and weakly were never to eat meat privately, but only there. The abbot's right (which rested, indeed, on a passage of the Rule) to invite individuals to dine with him, that they might have a more generous diet, was safeguarded. Bearing in mind the circumstances and the aim of the original letter, it may be argued that the pope's intention was to bar flesh-meat, even from the abbot's table, when monks were present. In the sequel, however, the ambiguous phrases of a similar kind in which meat-eating was alluded to

1 *MC*, 1, 17: Swapham, *Coen. Burgensis Historia* (ed. Sparke, 1723), 111.
2 For this visitation *v.* Bishop, *art. cit.*; *MPChM*, 111, 239; *Ann. Theok.* (*AM*, 1, 89), s.a. 1232; *Ann. Dunstapl.* (*AM*, 111, 133), s.a. 1232; cf. R. Graham, *Visitation of Bury St Edmund's and Westminster in* 1234, in *EHR*, xxvii (Oct. 1912), 728–39.
3 Swapham, *Historia*, 110.
4 *MC*, 1, 24.
5 Wilkins, *Concilia*, 1, 653: 'Quod utique approbantes statuimus inviolabiliter observari.'
6 *MPChM*, 111, 507. Innocent's letter (Potthast 1734, *PL*, ccxiv, 1064) was embodied in canon law by Gregory IX in III tit. 35 (not 34 as in *RS* followed by Bishop), cap. 6.

in English documents allowed of a kindly interpretation being put upon the pope's words, and the decretal *Quum ad monasterium* was later undoubtedly used as giving sanction to a current practice which resembled the very one that Innocent III had intended to abolish by his letter.[1]

For the moment, however, it is not clear that the decretal received this lax interpretation, and a few years after Otho's departure Innocent IV, in reaffirming the Gregorian decrees, specifically condemned 'recreations'. Consequently, it was this strict standard that was reiterated by chapters during the next forty years.[2]

For how long, and in how many quarters this regime was held to cannot be said with any certainty, but in some houses a breach was made almost at once. Thus at Bury, as early as 1256 a bull was obtained from Alexander IV which allowed those in need of it to eat meat in the infirmary or with the abbot in his room,[3] and there is evidence that periodical recreations for the whole community in relays became more common during the century. The great code of 1277 allowed meat, apart from the infirmary, only in the abbot's room, but the revised version of 1278 permits monks of the cloister, together with the weakly and those recently bled, to take meat in a special room,[4] and this practice, which is noted as a regularized novelty at St Augustine's in 1275,[5] was widespread. Moreover, there are indications that most great houses had established a country-house in their neighbourhood to which the monks went in turn, and here it was customary to eat meat,[6] while the fact that one of the *dubia* to be put to Rome *c.* 1275 concerned the lawfulness of eating the flesh of bipeds suggests that this was not currently considered to be a breach of the Rule.[7] Finally, in 1300 very wide dispensing powers were given by chapter to superiors in the matter of meat.[8]

---

1 It is not easy to be sure of the correct interpretation of *Quum ad monasterium*. The 'operative clause' runs: 'quanquam ex indulgentia possit abbas interdum aliquos fratrum... advocare, ipsosque in camera sua melius et plenius exhibere.' This at first sight bears out the opinion of Bishop, who held that it allowed no meat at the abbot's table. But the language (as so often when meat is concerned) is confessedly ambiguous, and the following facts must be reckoned with: (*a*) the use of the letter from 1277 onwards by all the chapters as authority for eating meat, and (*b*) the permission of the practice in visitation by such a strict prelate as Grosseteste *c.* 1245. *V.* Swapham, *Hist. Burg.* 110.

2 *MPChM*, vi, Additamenta, 239: 'Nullus monachus in quocumque loco, sive in domo sit ordinis sive extra, carnes comedat. Illas autem carnium refectiones, quae sanis in quibusdam monasteriis certis temporibus consueverunt hactenus exhiberi, penitus inhibemus.' Cf. chapter of 1256 (*MC*, I, 56): 'Firmiter inhibemus, ne de cetero ab aliquibus nostri ordinis, cuiuscumque persone gracia vel favore carnes comedantur, exceptis omnino debilibus et egrotis.'

3 Alexander IV to Bury, 4 Aug. 1256, in B.M. MS. Harl. 1005, fol. 120a, quoted by E. Bishop, *art. cit.* 231–2.

4 (1277) *MC*, I, 78; (1278) *ibid.* 100.

5 *Customary of St Augustine's*, I, 39–40: 'Ad tempus, licet cum timore, etc.'

6 Thorne, 1937: 'Fratres qui secum (in cellis) per vices moraturi sunt ad recreationem.' Cf. *GASA*, II, 202 (Redburn).

7 *MC*, I, 116–7.

8 *Ann. Wig.* (*AM*, IV, 547), *s.a.* 1300: 'De esu carnium quilibet prelatus, sicut viderit expedire, potest cum suis subditis dispensare.'

Thus after a hundred years the position was very much what it had been in the reign of John: meat was still barred from the refectory, from which the community as a whole was never absent, but either by invitation from the superior or by rotation in periods of 'recreation', or by absence from the monastery for business or repose, meat was, in fact, eaten not infrequently and in some cases at regular intervals by all members of the community. In other words, though theoretically the situation had changed little between 1215 and 1300 there was by the latter year no serious possibility (as there had seemed to be at the time of Gregory IX and again perhaps c. 1270–80) that the strict and genuine observance of the Rule might again become the norm. It was not long before direct action from Rome gave formal and wide dispensing power to superiors and, shortly after, explicitly countenanced the eating of meat on three days a week. Despite this, however, it should be remarked that a few of the greatest houses long endeavoured to maintain the strict observance, which conservative opinion was still defending in the days of Wiclif.[1]

V

The second matter which repeatedly came up for consideration at the chapter is perhaps of wider interest. This was nothing less than the abandonment of some or all of the liturgical accretions and elaborations in the interests of theological study.

St Benedict, as has often been remarked, divided the monk's day into three equally important parts, devoted respectively to liturgical prayer, sacred reading and manual, or at least physical, work. When the custom of monks receiving a literary education and Holy Orders grew, when agricultural and domestic work passed entirely to serfs and servants, and when the liturgy and chant developed in Italy and Gaul, purely physical work disappeared and its place was taken, and often more than taken, by additions to the psalmody, intercessory prayers of various kinds, and elaborations in ceremonial and chant. As has been seen, the time left for other employments was, in the greater Anglo-Norman houses, very limited and divided, and of this, much was consumed by the younger monks in learning by heart the words and chant of the Office; consequently, it had been part of the programme of Cîteaux and other reforms to make the reintroduction of manual work possible by shearing away all, or almost all, the accretions of chant, ceremonial and vocal prayer. Among the black monks of England no changes had been made, but the employment of many in administration had led to wholesale exemptions and to the splitting of communities into the two classes of obedientiaries and monks of the cloister. This division, felt by some as invidious and by all as undesirable,

1 Cf. MS. Bodley 240 of c. 1377 discussed in MC, I, 22–3.

hastened the sentiment of the time which was moving away from the cult of an elaborate liturgical life. Meanwhile, the prodigious development and *éclat* of the university discipline, which had already swept three of the great orders of friars away from their primitive form of life, could not but fascinate many of the monks, while their lack of scholastic organization and the prospect presented to postulants of several years devoted purely to the rehearsal and execution of liturgical offices, deterred many young men of parts from entering the novitiate.[1] In addition, many of the superiors, aware that their order had lost the position of intellectual leadership held by it a century before, failed to realize that this was due primarily to profound changes in the cultural life and aims of Europe; they hoped, therefore, to be able to regain their position by restoring study to a position of honour.

Their programme had necessarily two parts: the provision of time and encouragement for study, and the establishment of a house at a university whither might be sent individuals or a quota from all the monasteries. The second point, which issued in the foundation of Gloucester College, may be dealt with later; here we are concerned with the changes in domestic life ordered by chapter.

The first indications of changing sentiment are perhaps to be seen in decisions such as that of abbot William of St Albans to reduce the elaborations of the Kyrie and shorten the extra psalmody.[2] A little later, general chapter, to secure unanimity of practice and avoid undue burdens, abolished the recitation of the psalms for benefactors on big feasts.[3] Six years later, the office of All Saints was done away with, and superiors were authorized to make still further reductions; the twofold reason is given, that thus the task of learning by heart what remains will be less exacting, and the monks will have more time to give to reading and other similar pursuits.[4] Fifteen years more, and the presidents are found writing to the abbot of Ramsey to enjoin observance of the decrees.[5]

The great change, however, came with the code of 1277. The moving spirits, the abbots of St Augustine's and Glastonbury, were, as has been seen, themselves students, and they enunciate their aims very clearly. While the length of the office causes fatigue and distaste, the studies which formerly flourished now languish; at the same time, those with intellectual interests are repelled from the monastic life by the prospect of having to

---

1 For the great quantity of matter to be learnt by heart by novices *v. Customary of St Augustine's*, I, 420–1. It included the whole Rule, Psalter, Common Offices of Saints, etc., even after reductions had been made; cf. *MC*, I, 74.

2 *GASA*, I, 295.

3 *MC*, I, 44 (1249): 'Ne supra vires, propter (psalmorum) multitudinem, que in quibusdam locis singularitate quadam fieri consuevit, monachi de cetero graventur, et ut eadem sit observantia apud omnes et idem ordo', etc.

4 *MC*, I, 55 (1255): 'Liceat prelatis racionabiliter in officiis divinis...resecare superflua, ut sic facilius a fratribus addiscantur cetera et sacris leccionibus,...inserviatur studiosius.'

5 *MC*, I, 58 (1271).

learn by heart most of the liturgical services.[1] First, therefore, many of the repetitions of chant in the Office and Mass are abolished; next, a clean sweep is made of almost all the accretions of psalmody and intercessory prayers, leaving only the Office of Our Lady, suffrages for those recently dead, and certain prayers in Lent. What remains is to be recited more slowly and devoutly, and all are to be present.[2] Less memory-work is henceforth to be demanded of novices, and those of unusual brilliance may be dispensed even from what remains.[3] The revised version of 1278 went still further, cutting out more repetitions, certain lessons, and the Athanasian Creed, which was now to be recited only on Sundays, not on all feast-days.[4]

As constructive measures, there are two rubrics in the statutes: *de occupacione* and *de studio*. The place of the manual work of the distant past is to be taken by study, and by writing, emending, illuminating and binding manuscripts.[5] As regards study, until the common house at Oxford is established, such monasteries as are able should make provision for a public lecturer in theology. These decrees, though unanimously approved by the chapter,[6] provoked a lively opposition. A chronicler at St Albans branded the omission of psalmody and prayers for benefactors as sloth and ingratitude, and pointed to the contemporary Statute of Mortmain as a just retribution; another affected to fear that the *Paternoster* would soon go the way of the *Quicumque vult*.[7] More substantial opposition was shown by a number of petitions to chapter for a maintenance of the *status quo* in psalmody and ceremonial, and by similar requests in the *dubia* to be submitted to Rome. There is, moreover, evidence that many houses disregarded the new legislation altogether.[8]

The conservatives received unexpected support from outside. At Worcester, the bishop, Godfrey Giffard, took exception to the changes, both in themselves and as having been introduced without his permission, and ordered a return to the old usage.[9] At about the same time, Archbishop Pecham took still more drastic action. It is impossible not to suspect that this distinguished Franciscan theologian and inveterate controversialist viewed the move of the monks towards the universities as a trespass upon

---

1 *MC*, 1, 64: 'Per prolixitatem officii preter regulam ampliati que fastidias generans devocionem extinguit pocius quam accendit, studium quod retroactis temporibus in nostra religione strenue floruit proth dolor emarcescat, etc.'

2 *MC*, 1, 69: 'Divinum officium de cetero fiat devocius quam hucusque.'

3 *MC*, 1, 74.

4 *MC*, 1, 98.

5 *MC*, 1, 74: 'Abbates...monachos...loco operis manualis...ceteris occupacionibus deputent, in studendo, libros scribendo, corrigendo, illuminando, ligando, etc.'

6 *MC*, 1, 65: 'De tocius capituli antedicti consensu expresso.'

7 *GASA*, 1, 464. For the persistence of this spirit *c*. 1377, v. *MC*, 1, 22.

8 *MC*, 1, 106–7. E.g. 'De xv salmis, petimus quod more solito cantentur, etc.', and cf. decrees of 1298, regarding houses that have made no change, in *MC*, 1, 138–9.

9 *MC*, 1, 93–4, quoting *Register of G. Giffard* (Worc. Hist. Soc. 1902), 96.

the preserves of the student orders;[1] his ostensible reason, however, is that the monks, in abolishing the prayers that have taken the place of manual work, are actuated by sloth and are abandoning their allotted task.[2] He persuaded the bishops in council to condemn the change and himself, in the visitations throughout the country which he made as metropolitan, included this condemnation in his articles and instructed his suffragans to observe it.[3] From his letters we learn, somewhat unexpectedly, that even the nunneries had followed the decrees of chapter in this matter.

Despite domestic resistance and the opposition of Pecham, who even went so far beyond his powers as to forbid the payment of the tax levied on all houses for the maintenance of the Oxford establishment, presidents and chapters held to their course, though how far the thorough reorientation implied by their decrees was effected throughout England cannot easily be decided. Had the vocal prayer been curtailed without a corresponding increase in work and study the critics would clearly have been justified, and there are indications that the new programme was fully desired and envisaged only at a few of the greater houses and among the more en-lightened superiors. It is easy to appreciate the reluctance which the mature members of undistinguished communities must have felt to change their whole time-table without the prospect of advantage for themselves or the bulk of their body, nor could 'study' ever become the occupation of a group of men of varied gifts and abilities cut off from any permanent intercourse with the schools and from the opportunities of preaching and apostolic work enjoyed by the friars. At the same time, the presidents and chapters of 1278–9 deserve the praise of having made a bold, reasoned and adequate attempt to rejuvenate the old monasticism by restoring discip-line and observance, by endeavouring to secure uniformity, by courage-ously abandoning what seemed outworn and by taking all possible steps to substitute other employment more in harmony with the fashions of the age. That their plans failed to effect as complete and immediate a revolution as they had hoped was due as much to the circumstances of the times and to failure in co-operation on the part of the monasteries as to any intrinsic fault in their programme. It cannot, however, be denied that their endeavour, if wholly successful, would not have been simply a re-storation of the monastic body to its pristine purity, but would have assimilated it very nearly to the student orders of friars, very much as

1 Cf. *Reg. Pecham, ep.* CXXVI (*RS*, I, 150), where he forbids the payment of the quotas levied by the chapter for the support of the Oxford house. For a fuller treatment of the episode v. D. Knowles, *Some Aspects of the career of Archbishop Pecham* in *EHR*, LVII (Jan. and April 1943).

2 For all this v. *Reg. Pecham epp.* LXX (Barking), CXXVI (Ely), CLXXXIX (Reading), CCXIII (Glastonbury), DCX (Godstow). The fullest statement is in his injunctions to Glastonbury (*Reg.* I, 259).

3 Cf. his letter to the bishop of Ely, 17 Nov. 1280 (*ep.* CXXVI, *Reg.* I, 150 *seqq.*): 'Licet dudum in congregationibus nostris Londin', de consensu omnium episcoporum ibidem praesentium, etc.'

more than one monastic congregation after the Reformation endeavoured to avoid the evils of the past and take its part in the contemporary renaissance of religious life by undertaking some of the active employments, and adopting a part of the organization of the new congregations of clerics that led the van of the counter-Reformation. In each case, success could only be bought at the price of the sacrifice of a part of the monastic heritage. And, we may think, the movement of reform in the thirteenth century had in it a fundamental flaw—a flaw that ran through so much of the official religious achievement of the time, even through the work of Gregory IX, of Innocent IV, of Grosseteste and of Haymo of Faversham: the substitution, that is, of a legal, calculated, logical programme, apparently capable of rapid and complete execution, for the ardour of a call to the ideal, based not upon law but upon love.

VI

Of all the decisions of the provincial chapter the most important in its consequences was that of establishing a common house of studies at Oxford. The spectacular development of scholastic theology at the universities of Paris and Oxford, and the suppression or absorption of many of the previously existing forms of education and intellectual pursuit by its exclusive and exacting discipline, made it seem to many contemporary observers that those who failed to associate with the life of the schools were standing apart from the stream of mental and spiritual life, to say nothing of their ineligibility for the positions of influence in the Church which were becoming more and more exclusively reserved to Masters. The orders of the friars had without exception identified themselves with the movement by the middle of the century. In 1245 the Cistercians, tacitly but none the less really breaking with their primitive aims, began not only to send monks to the universities, but to establish schools of theology in their own houses.[1]

It is perhaps typical of the conservative habits of thought of the black monks that they were among the last to be swept into the stream. In 1247, however, the chapter decreed that wherever conditions permitted, a daily lecture on theology or canon law was to be given to selected monks by a lecturer who might be either a religious or a secular.[2] The tentative wording of the decree is characteristic; it gave more than one loophole of escape to those who wished to make no move, and all indications show that its practical effect was small. Meanwhile, it had become clear that no serious theological studies were possible for a body which had no foothold at a university, and in consequence, the establishment of a common house of studies at Oxford was part of the programme of the presidents of 1277, while, since a fund of money was a *sine qua non* of any such establishment,

---

1 *ALKG*, I, 570; *MPChM*, v, 79.   2 *MC*, I, 27–8.

a tax was imposed on all houses *pro rata* for its purchase and maintenance.[1] This imposition, which was extended inadvisedly to several small and quasi-foreign priories, was resisted by two dependencies of Bec, Stoke-by-Clare and St Neot's, and the abbot of Bec enlisted the help of Archbishop Pecham.[2] Their protest was successful, but when Pecham went on to forbid the levying of the tax in any quarter he was clearly acting beyond his authority and met with no success. He relieved his feelings, we are told, by calling the monks boors, dunces and dullards.[3]

Meanwhile, the Oxford project had only partially materialized. Contributions were scanty, although a private benefactor of a west country family had in 1283 given a site in Oxford, where a small priory had been inaugurated in the common interest under the auspices of Gloucester Abbey.[4] This modest establishment, which adjoined the Carmelite house in Stockwell Street on the site of the present Worcester College, had been put into the shade by the development of the neighbouring Cistercian house of studies, Rewley Abbey, founded in 1281. The presidents of 1288, therefore, made an urgent appeal to the chapter, pointing to the achievement of the white monks, recalling their own large numbers, and calling upon them to show that the black monks were capable of finishing the tower which they had begun to build.[5] They put forward a scheme to constitute a priory, with a small permanent community, subject directly to the presidents, to which monks from all houses might be sent. This, it was stated, was what the whole chapter had asked for.[6]

Even so, the negotiations, and perhaps also the pecuniary contributions, hung fire, and although the chapter of 1291 elected four diffinitors to draw up constitutions for the new foundation which was to be directly

---

1 *MC*, I, 75: 'Et ut nostra religione refloreat studium, ad locum vel ad edificia idonea Oxonie providenda, ubi nostri ordinis fratres de diversis monasteriis causa studii transmittendi decenter habitare valeant et honeste, etc.' The fullest account of the early days of Gloucester College is by Prof. V. H. Galbraith, *New Documents about Gloucester College* in *Snappe's Formulary*, ed. H. E. Salter (*OHS*, LXXX, 1924), 336–86b, where a number of the sources are printed.   2 *New Docs*. 343, 355–6; *MC*, I, 119–20.

3 *MC*, I, 133: 'Consuevit nos in suis visitacionibus nominare musardos (= idlers, boors) brevitores (?), fatuos et bollardos (dunces).' The writer is no other then Walter de Wenlok of Westminster, writing to the abbot of Thorney, *c.* 1290–1. For Pecham's action *v.* pp. 23–4.

4 The reply to Giffard by Walter de Wenlok *c.* 1290 makes it clear that the house had never been a private venture: 'Remandavit se semper in proposito habuisse locum illum communitati ordinis et non abacie Glovernie assignare.' In view of this declaration Prof. Galbraith's description of 'the little priory...which had been founded in 1283 by Sir John Giffard of Brimpsfield as a cell of St Peter's, Gloucester', is perhaps somewhat misleading. The house was never a mere cell; it always had an academic character. Giffard, a west-country man, clearly wished from the start to help the black monks to realize their scheme, and in default of adequate funds for equipping a common house—a kind of establishment wholly foreign to their habits of thought—he made his gift and gave control to the abbey with which he was most familiar. Moreover, the transfer to Gloucester was not at first absolute, nor had release from Mortmain been obtained.

5 *MC*, I, 126–7. The writers, Walter de Wenlok of Westminster and John of Brockhampton of Evesham, after praising Rewley remark that the black monks, too, had had similar successes in the past 'quando, sicut ipsi (*sc*. Cistercienses), veritati regule adherebant'.

6 *MC*, I, 132 (Wenlok is writing): 'Hoc enim universitatis fuit peticio sicut nostis.'

subject to the common body, the house, to which numerous students were now resorting, remained under the control of Gloucester and ill-equipped with buildings.[1] At last, in 1298, when Giffard was on the point of reclaiming his property, the chapter decided to make a new start with a nucleus of four monks from Eynsham (chosen, no doubt, on account of its proximity), and entrusted all arrangements to a committee of four abbots.[2] Eynsham, for some reason that does not appear, failed to supply the group required; the original founder, Sir John Giffard, turned in consequence to the abbot of Malmesbury where he himself was living, and where he was shortly to die. In the subsequent arrangement Malmesbury became the owner of the priory, or, to speak more accurately, of the site and a part of the fabric; the abbot of Malmesbury had jurisdiction over the permanent community, while the right of passing novices for profession rested with the presidents.[3] The establishment, therefore, taken as a whole, was neither a priory nor a college; the abbot and community of Malmesbury were the ground landlords, who also owned a part of the buildings; the public rooms, such as refectory, chapel and the rest, were erected and maintained at the common cost of the province; the rooms or staircases occupied by the monks from the various houses were erected and maintained by the houses concerned. The whole was under the direct administration of a prior, but the presidents appointed the regent master.[4]

A chronic lack of funds would appear to have hindered building operations for a quarter of a century. At last, by a piece of good fortune, the Carmelites in 1320–1 moved across the road into some new property. The presidents, therefore, urged by the bishop of Norwich, and acting on their own authority without waiting for a decision of chapter, did a quick deal and secured the vacated quarters, thus becoming owners of property along Stockwell Street for the whole extent covered by the modern front of Worcester College.[5] With this event the external development of the establishment ceased until the fusion of the northern and southern provincial chapters, and the Benedictine constitutions of 1338, opened a new epoch at Oxford for the black monks.

1 *Ibid.*: 'Convenerunt de diversis monasteriis... multi habiles ad studendum invenientes amplam aream (= site), set pro numerosa multitudine domos paucas.' They had in consequence to lodge out.

2 *MC*, I, 136–8.   3 *New Docs.* 346–8.

4 Cf. the request of the presidents to Worcester, *c.* 1311–19, to send a monk to be regent, in *MC*, I, 174–5.

5 *V.* the letter of the presidents in *New Docs.* 379–80.

CHAPTER III

THE AUGUSTINIAN CHAPTERS

The history of the Augustinian general chapters between the Fourth Lateran Council and the Constitutions of Benedict XII is very similar to that of the black monks.[1] Although the organization and procedure had been established in all fullness by the decrees of the Council, Innocent III gave special attention to the English black canons. The abbot of Leicester was detained in Rome till the end of February 1216, in order to carry home with him a letter from the pope to his fellow-canons; in this, Innocent, doubtless after previous arrangements with the abbot, fixed the first chapter for 8 November of that year, and gave Leicester as the place of meeting; instead of the white monks of the Council's decree, two white canons, the abbots of Welbeck and Croxton, were appointed as assessors to the presidents.[2]

At this chapter the heads of houses from the two provinces of Canterbury and York met together, but after a few years, and in all probability soon after the chapter at Bedford in 1220,[3] the provinces were separated. In contrast, however, to the records of the black monks, the acts of the northern province have survived in greater bulk than those of the southern, and its decrees would seem to have been at least as important. While our knowledge of the northern activities is due to the accident which has preserved a single important manuscript,[4] it should, nevertheless, be noted that while the northern province contained but a fraction (twenty out of a hundred and eighty) of the total number of houses, the majority of these twenty were in fact members of the group of fervent and distinguished houses that had come into being under Thurstan and Henry Murdac, and had joined with the Yorkshire Cistercians in the cause of reform.

The black canons, though even less linked together than the black monks, proceeded to legislate rapidly, and at a chapter in 1220 a fairly full, though unsystematic, list of decrees was framed, including one or two of considerable importance which will be discussed elsewhere. In general, the points dealt with are similar to those which occur in the contemporary monastic chapters—the example of regular life to be given by superiors, silence in the monastery, the extirpation of private ownership—but such

---

1 The available material has been edited by Dr H. E. Salter, *Chapters of the Augustinian Canons* (*OHS*, LXXIV, 1920), henceforth referred to as *AC*.

2 *AC*, 1–2.

3 Not before 1223, in which year the prior of Dunstable appears as visitor in Yorkshire; cf. *Ann. Dunstapl.* (*AM*, III, 80), *s.a. V.* also Salter, introd. xi.

4 B.M. roll Cott. XIII, 3.

similarity of matter and even of phraseology as may be noticed reflects rather the contemporary sentiment common to all religious circles than a direct imitation of the monks.

After the first few chapters legislation in both provinces became, to judge by the surviving records, scanty and sporadic. The canons were never presented with a code of regulations from Rome, as were the monks on two occasions, and there never appeared in their midst a movement of thought, or a group of superiors, anxious to produce a programme of common action suited to the changing times such as the monastic chapter of 1277 endeavoured to implement. In 1265, however, shortly before the legislative activity of the black monks reached its height in the southern province, the canons of the north made a brave attempt to reduce their varieties of observance to a single norm. For this end they proposed no new legislation, but decreed that delegates elected by seven of the oldest and most influential houses should meet at Drax, having with them the customaries of their respective homes; from these they were by common consent to frame a single code which, duly approved by a subsequent chapter, was to be applied to all the houses as a binding norm.[1] This scheme, so reasonable and practical and, to all appearances, sc simple, was destined to end in frustration. The full sequence of events cannot be traced, but the meeting of the delegates, or at least their final meeting, was held not at Drax but at Helaugh Park, and the fact earned for their decrees the name of *statuta de Parco*. But though the chapter might desiderate uniformity, it was a jealous refusal to abandon domestic usages, rather than any hostility to pure observance, that nullified all the endeavours of the committee at the Park. In 1282 discontent with the novelty and alleged severity of some of the statutes led the chapter to propose a revision.[2] This was apparently not effected, and in the subsequent chapter at Gisburn the priors and proctors solemnly undertook to observe the statutes of the Park, while offering to consider at their next meeting any complaints from individual houses.[3] When the next chapter met in 1288 protests were heard from all sides that the new statutes traversed universally approved usage, and that the presidents had complicated the matter still further by imposing their observance under pain of canonical censure. Ultimately, a promise was once more given to consider all grievances at the following chapter; in the meantime, the censures were lifted.[4] Unfortunately, a lacuna in the records prevents us from learning what the upshot of the matter was.

Meanwhile, in 1325 the southern province produced a short and incoherent set of decrees which appears to have been regarded as a code of

1 *AC*, 36.
2 *AC*, 39: 'Que pluribus nostri ordinis monasteriis, ut aliquibus videtur, sunt onerosa et usitatis eorum consuetudinibus nimis dissona.'
3 *AC*, 41-2
4 *AC*, 43-4. The archbishop of York wrote to the presidents on behalf of the dissidents (*v. Guisborough Cartulary*, II, 364-5, SS).

observance.[1] Shortly afterwards, in 1340, the provinces were united by Benedict XII; for a time, north and south abounded each in its own sense, but in 1380 the statutes of the Park, still, after a hundred years, more honoured in the breach than the observance, were declared null, void and of no effect in favour of the Northampton decrees of 1325.[2] Three years later they were restored to force; the record of this is the last reference to them that has survived.[3] As no text is known to exist it is impossible to judge of their intrinsic merits, but their chequered history is a significant proof of the tenacity and success with which the Augustinian houses resisted all attempts to secure uniformity at the expense of individual usage. Unimportant as they may have been in a period of fervour, the manifold, if minute, differences in practice thus perpetuated were to be, in a time of decay, no small barrier to all external and general attempts at reform.

So far as can be seen, the chapters were usually held at an important centre, such as Oxford or London, and later, when the provinces were united, most often in a house near the boundaries of north and south such as Leicester, Northampton, or Newstead near Stamford. The assemblies were directed by two presidents, who also exercised an undefined authority in the intervals between chapters; indications, however, go to show that these officials had in practice less influence than the presidents of the black monks, perhaps by reason of the very large number of houses involved and the insignificance of even the more important as compared with the greater monasteries. Like the monks, the canons appointed diffinitors; but whereas among the monks these officials appeared late, were rarely elected and then only for specified tasks, the canons, whose capitular body was at least three times as numerous, came in time—perhaps, indeed, very early[4]—to give all legislative business into their hands, reserving for the chapter no more than a ratification. Here again the similarity to Dominican practice will be noted, but indeed no other procedure would in practice have been workable. A large body of men meeting together for the first time and for a few days only would have been quite unable to decide upon the topics and draw up the decrees of a body of legislation. Visitors, likewise, were elected by chapter: in the northern for the whole province, which had few houses outside the diocese of York; in the southern, two to each small group of dioceses;[5] of their activites, even less record survives than with the monks.

Like the monks, also, the canons had as regular visitor the Ordinary, and only two of their numerous houses enjoyed exemption. Many communities lay within the vast diocese of Lincoln and came in for much

---

1 *AC*, 10–15 (Northampton, 1325).

2 *AC*, 73.

3 *AC*, 76.

4 *V*. Salter, introd. xv. The first official mention of diffinitors is in 1325.

5 E.g. in 1228 the priors of Dunstable and Newenham were appointed visitors for Lincoln and Coventry dioceses; *v. Ann. Dunstapl.* (*AM*, III, 112), *s.a.*

attention at the hands of the energetic, reforming, Grosseteste. His activities are recorded by chroniclers over a wide number of years; in 1236, in particular, he deposed no less than seven Augustinian abbots and four priors in his diocese, and for the rest of the century the bishop's visitations attract far more attention among the annalists than do the domestic visitations from members of the chapter. Besides the bishop, the archbishop of Canterbury claimed and exercised the right from *c.* 1240 onwards, as he did over the houses of black monks.[1]

1 For detailed references, *v.* Cheney, *Episcopal Visitation*; Gibbs and Lang, *Bishops and Reform*, 150–4. *V.* also *infra* chaps. VIII–X.

CHAPTER IV

THE EXPLOITATION OF THE LAND

I

The student of English monastic institutions in the later centuries of the middle ages cannot afford to neglect the economic basis upon which the life of the monks rested. Whereas in an earlier period the black monks of the autonomous houses had taken little or no direct part in the exploitation of their estates, during the two centuries from *c.* 1200 onwards there was a very general tendency not indeed to work upon the land, as did the first Cistercians, but to direct and oversee the exploitation with interest and full responsibility. This direct intervention gave rise to a whole series of readjustments in the administrative and financial machinery of the monasteries, and determined the lines along which the lives of many of the ablest members of a community ran, giving to the outlook of the house and to the policy and occupations of its superior a character notably different from that of the preceding age. In other words, while in the old English and early Anglo-Norman monasticism the main care of the abbot and administrative officials had been to establish and secure the income, in money and kind, from their properties, in some such way as does a college bursar at the present day, and had only rarely undertaken the further task of directing the economic policy and supervising its execution, during the thirteenth and early fourteenth centuries a change is noticeable; activities previously exceptional now appear more normal, and the monks become high farmers. Superior and monks, indeed, now often filled the roles both of an enlightened great land-owner—a duke of Portland or Sutherland—and of his estate agent. To grasp the full significance of this change it will be necessary to consider briefly the economic development of great estates in England between the Conquest and the reign of Henry III.

A recent historian has remarked that monastic estates were in two respects at least better fitted for exploitation than the great majority of lay fiefs: they were more compact, and there was greater continuity of administration.[1] The first of these assertions is open to question: while it is true that certain houses, such as Battle and St Augustine's, Canterbury, were owners of a solid *bloc* of estates in the near neighbourhood of the abbey, others, such as Westminister and Christ Church, held large properties at great distances from the administrative centre. The second advantage, however, is incontrovertible. An undying community, controlling estates which never escheated and were never broken up, trans-

---

1 N. Denholm-Young, *Seignorial Administration in England,* 1.

ferred or subjected to reorganization at the death of an owner, was clearly in a strong position to develop the fief as a whole for commercial purposes. It was doubtless this continuity of administration which gave, first to the Cistercians and later to the black monks, a leading place among the pioneers of commercial sheep and dairy-farming, as well as among the first promoters of the corn trade of England.

II

The agrarian basis upon which the monasteries of England rested at the time of the Conquest was at once simple in outline and complex in its parts. Its simplicity was due to the elementary nature of the husbandry, to the similarity (which was, however, not uniformity) of the methods and conditions of cultivation in all districts, and to the absence of any considerable production for distant markets.[1] Speaking generally, there was in 1066 little export trade in grain, dairy produce, or live-stock, and there were very few towns in England whose needs created a market. The members of each village group cultivated grain and kept animals for their own livelihood and clothing and for that of the landowner and his dependents; only a small proportion of the produce, or the surplus of a good year, was marketed. The conditions of cultivation, though differing in details as between the open-field system of the Midlands, the tenements of East Anglia, the small-holdings of Kent and certain peculiarities of Yorkshire and Lincolnshire, were in their main lines similar all over the country east of Cornwall, Wales and Cumberland. Everywhere the village community was the social unit and the land was cultivated by co-operative methods of husbandry, with communal grazing and forage rights. Each group therefore grew the same crops and reared the same stock for its own needs— bread, beer, milk, cheese, pork, lard, eggs—using the same implements, employing the same methods and regulated by the same or similar customs. There was no broad division of the country into grain and root, dairy and stock- or sheep-farming districts as in recent centuries, and the nucleus of exploitation was the village or hamlet surrounded by its arable and meadows, not the single farmhouse among the fields. Though the term 'self-sufficient' cannot be applied to the English system of agriculture without reserves, least of all after c. 1150, it nevertheless has a meaning when used of the epoch of *Domesday*, and this relative self-sufficiency, added to the

1 A general survey of the agrarian life of western Europe before and after its feudalization will be found in the relevant chapters of the *Cambridge Economic History*, vol. 1. Normal English conditions, as obtaining especially in the Midlands and Wessex, can still best be studied in Vinogradoff's *The Growth of the Manor* and *English Society in the Eleventh Century*. Regional peculiarities are described in *Types of Manorial Structure in the Northern Danelaw*, by F. M. Stenton (*Oxford Studies in Social and Legal History*, II); *Northumbrian Institutions*, by J. E. A. Joliffe in *EHR*, XLI (1926); *The Bilsington Cartulary*, ed. with introd. by N. Neilson (*Proc. Brit. Academy*, 1928): this deals with Kent and Sussex weald and marsh customs; *The Social Structure of Medieval East Anglia*, by D. C. Douglas (*Oxford Studies in Social and Legal History*, IX, 1927).

communal, customary methods of cultivation, made the control of the agricultural unit a simple affair. A single bailiff, possessed of an adequate knowledge of the craft and supported by the authority of the lord above and by the routine set up by the reeve below, could keep the machinery in motion indefinitely without the necessity of taking any decisions save the practical ones called for by the vagaries of the climate and of human nature.

Yet though the working of the economic unit was simple, the pattern of its structure and of its relations with its neighbours was extremely complex. On the purely agricultural side, the intermingled strip-cultivation, the rotation of crop and fallow, the communal enjoyment of pasture, waste and wood, the co-operative methods of ploughing and harvesting, and the dues of land-service to the lord, gave to each cell of agricultural life something of the complexity of a piece of machinery. On the administrative side, the simplicity of pattern given by the villages scattered all over the land was confused by an independent design which was superimposed upon it, that of the manorial organization. The economic essentials of the manor—a lordship of undetermined size, containing demesne land, villein land and (most frequently) the holdings of free tenants, together with common and waste, the demesne being exploited in great part by the compulsory service of the villeins—all existed before the Conquest at least in embryo, but the individual estates were not gathered up into a higher unity and the name of manor and the feudal administration associated with it were imposed by the Normans as a standard pattern on a pre-existing variety of usage. As the Anglo-Norman manor was an administrative unit based on existing tenures, it did not always bear direct relation to the village, which was in fact often divided between two or more manors, while gifts, purchases and inheritance of parcels of land often created extremely complicated interrelationships between lords and tenants. With this, however, we are not directly concerned, save to note that from the Conquest onwards the manor and not the village was the economic and administrative unit of the estates of a monastery, at least south of the Trent and Wash.

The Old English estate, however limited its production for market, was always required to produce a considerable quantity of food and material for the lord who, save in the case of very small properties, was not a regular resident on the land, and who supported a greater or lesser number of dependents. Originally, it would appear that owners of a complex of estates had more than one place of residence, and these were so chosen as to reduce to a minimum the transport of foodstuffs over long distances; bishops' registers bear witness to the survival of this practice throughout the greater part of the middle ages. In the case of the monasteries, however, perambulation of this sort was always out of the question, and consequently the food-farm made an early appearance; the obligation, that is, upon an estate to render to the lord a fixed amount of provisions annually. Gradually, in the case of the larger monasteries, a scheme was elaborated to cover the whole year, each manor sending up a quota—

estimated as a week's or fortnight's farm—on a specified date once or more during the year. In this way the house was assured of a constant supply of wheat, barley, malt, hay, fodder, cheese, bacon, lard, honey, poultry, eggs, fish and the like. The cartage was performed as a labour service by the villeins and the whole kept the monastery and its dependents and guests in essential foodstuffs during the whole year.[1]

III

Since, as has been noted, the routine of a manor's husbandry needed no superior skill in planning and no subordination to, or co-ordination with, the requirements of any other estate, but only the steady control of authority, the monks before the middle of the twelfth century took little part in the direct exploitation of their lands. While food farms were as a rule levied on all the monastic manors, direct control of manorial agriculture and especially of the demesne farming through a bailiff accountable to the monks was only practised on estates adjoining the monastery.[2] Elsewhere the monks, anxious apparently to avoid the risks of fluctuating income and the responsibilities of direct supervision, often farmed out whole estates to 'farmers' who rented them for a fixed annual payment in kind and money. Sometimes, also, the monks let out the demesne, or portions of it, to tenants, thus relieving themselves in permanence of the onus of demesne farming. These leases ran for a period sometimes as short as a year, but often as long as two lives; this practice was widespread, and became more and more common during the twelfth century; sometimes, even, the 'men' of a manor took up the farm themselves, or the demesne might be parcelled out to small tenants.[3] These methods were, however, far from giving the maximum financial returns, and it was not uncommon for a more irregular, though more profitable, expedient to be adopted by sending out monks to farm a manor or group of manors; in such cases it would obviously be possible to demand a revenue up to the capacity of the land.[4] None of these methods, save perhaps the last, led directly to any grouping or co-operation among the manors, but the unity of administration of the manorial and higher courts, together with the inevitable solidarity created between the lands of a single lord and by constant communication with the centre of the honor, led to a certain amount of mutual assistance and co-operation, as is shown from the earliest records that survive.

1 For monastic food-farms, v. MO, 441–4, with references there given.
2 In the pre-manorial structure the reeve (*praepositus*) was the lord's agent and organizer on each estate, though the ambiguous Latin term was also used of superior officials; from the Norman period to the late fourteenth century the bailiff (*ballivus*) or sergeant (*serviens*) was the lord's agent and the reeve, elected by the villeins usually from among themselves, allotted the services and paid the hired labourers; in the late fourteenth century the two functions (of reeve and bailiff) were often merged and the terms are interchangeable (cf. H. S. Bennett, *The Reeve and the Manor in the Fourteenth Century* in *EHR*, XLI, 1926).
3 MO, 442, note 1.   4 MO, 443.

But while the tendency of the monasteries to farm out their super-fluous demesne increased in the twelfth century, aided by the growing devolution of the obedientiary system, economic forces were at work that set up a contrary current. Chief among these was the gradual but steady growth of population, with the consequent development of trade in corn, cheese and wool. These in turn were stimulated by the increase of commerce in general and the growth of towns, and resulted in the multiplication of markets and the appearance of dealers in corn and wool.[1] At the same time prices were steadily rising. In consequence, it became both possible and desirable to dispose of all surplus produce and to use all available means of increasing the acreage under cultivation and the yield of the old land, while at the same time currents of carriage, which hitherto had flowed almost entirely to the home manor of a group or the *caput honoris* of an estate, now set also towards local markets or distant towns and ports. In one department at least of the new commerce, that of the foreign wool trade, the lead had been given by the white monks and canons, but a spon-taneous movement all over the country soon showed that a new economic period was about to open.

As a natural result, clear-sighted abbots and obedientiaries began to gather into hand demesne land as leases fell in, and to cultivate grain and raise sheep and cattle with a view to market possibilities. It was the beginning of a move destined to have notable effects upon the life and economy of the religious houses and the organization and technical methods of agriculture throughout the country. For the first time since the height of the Roman Empire high farming became practicable in England; improved methods were studied,[2] and serious attempts were made to organize and pool the resources of large groups of manors. In all this the greater monastic houses played a considerable, perhaps even a leading, part, and the technique of farming, and questions of distribution of produce for market and the financial administration of a great estate, became of absorbing interest to a large number of the abler monks, while control of the general policy and regulation of the finances gave occupation to many of the seniors for an appreciable part of the year.[3]

The existing system of corn-carriage was therefore very early dupli-cated by another collecting the grain for market and delivering it either to a merchant, or to an inland market, or to the wharves of Southampton, Fordwich, Sandwich, or some other port. Soon manors containing large areas of arable were deriving very considerable annual revenues from sales

1 For the beginnings of the corn trade *v.* N. S. B. Gras, *The Evolution of the English Corn Market* (1915, reprinted 1926). The wool trade will be discussed later (*v. infra*, p. 41).

2 For a collection of treatises written at this time *v.* E. Lamond, *Walter of Henley's Husbandry, together with an Anonymous Husbandry, Seneschaucie and Robert Grosseteste's Rules.* The editor notes (p. xxv) that four MSS. once belonging to Christ Church, Canter-bury, contain Walter of Henley's treatise.

3 R. A. L. Smith has pointed out that sergeants, bailiffs and monk-wardens of the Canterbury estates are found studying such points as the advantages of bought seed corn, the number of bushels per acre to be used in sowing and the milk yield of ewes compared to that of cows.

of corn, and at Canterbury, about which we have full information, the whole schedule of food-farms was revised to stimulate production of corn, and the obligation of liveries in kind was restricted to neighbouring Kentish properties, more distant corn being grown exclusively for market. Later still, the priory even chose to purchase corn for its own use in a low-price market, while it sold all available grain where the prices soared. Every known device was employed to increase the yield of the land, wheat was sown increasingly at the expense of barley and oats, and a growing acreage under vegetable crops (the beginnings of rotation) saved land from unproductive idleness; every method then known was used to improve soil and seed; land was ploughed from pasture, assarted, reclaimed from marsh, manured and marled, and the accounts show a steep rise in cash sales of corn from almost all the Kentish manors in the last decades of the thirteenth century. It is, indeed, with justice that the historian of the house refers to the Christ Church estates as 'a capitalist concern, a "federated grain factory, producing largely for cash"'.

IV

In the new era when direct exploitation of the land became profitable, the monastic landowners had to take the initiative in several directions: to recover control of the manors previously farmed out, to regain possession here and there of the portions of the demesne more permanently alienated, to develop all the potentialities of the land, and to organize the production and sale of the crops and foodstuffs.[1]

The extent to which direct cultivation was resumed varied from house to house, and the process was never complete. Even as late as *c.* 1250 a few outlying manors were still farmed out by almost all black monk houses. But, generally speaking, by the beginning of the thirteenth century most of the monastic manors, whether liable to food farms or not, were managed by bailiffs directly supervised by the monks and accountable to them. It was far more difficult to recover the portions of demesne lost by previous sub-letting, but attempts to do so were made throughout the thirteenth century, as at Christ Church, Canterbury,[2] and notably at Glastonbury, where a series of surveys shows the change in progress.[3] Concurrently with this process a movement is discernible to increase the demesne by all other possible means; at

---

1 The recovery of demesne farming in the early thirteenth century has recently been investigated by economic historians, who were interested in ascertaining the cause of the enforcement of labour services in this period even where they had been for some time previously commuted for money payments. Landlords, it now seems clear—and especially monastic landlords—needed all the cheap labour they could get for commercialized demesne farming. *V.* E. A. Kosminsky, *Services and Money Rents in the Thirteenth Century* in the *EcHR,* v (1935), 24-45, and above all the important paper by Prof. M. M. Postan, *The Chronology of Labour Services* in *TRHS,* 4 ser. xx (1937), 169-93.

2 W. Holtzmann, *Papsturkunden in England,* ii, 374 (Alexander III, 1179): 'Statuimus etiam ut maneria vestra ulterius ad perpetuam firmam alicui non tradantur.' Cf. *ibid.* 444 (Urban III, 1187), and contrast R. A. L. Smith, *Canterbury,* 114.

3 *Liber Henrici de Soliaco,* ed. J. E. Jackson (Roxburghe Club, 1882); *Rentalia et Custumaria abbatiae. . . Glastonie (SRS,* v, 1891).

Glastonbury the chronicler records, in the mid-thirteenth century, the restitution of lapsed plough-teams, reclamation from the meres, embankments against the sea, the assarting of waste, and every kind of small addition by means of purchase and litigation.[1]

The currents of trade to markets had begun to flow briskly before 1200, and to cross the steady flow to the abbey. Soon after that date Christ Church was exporting corn to the Continent, Glastonbury was delivering cheese at Winchester and Southampton, and Ramsey was sending corn to Ipswich, Colchester, London, and even to Canterbury.[2] Besides these long-distance journeys there was a constant traffic to local markets. The process of commercializing the demesne was, however, a slow one, save in the matter of sheep-farming, where a boom period had begun at the middle of the twelfth century, and the simultaneous development of the Cistercian ranches and the cloth industries of the Netherlands and Lombardy had caused a rapid growth of mercantile organization. For other commodities trade was not considerable before c. 1200, and it was only about that time that the organization of Christ Church, Canterbury, perhaps the earliest and most complete example of the commercialized estate, was nearing perfection.

V

The new farming inevitably called for new methods of administration. In the old days of devolution and the leasing of demesne the scattered estates of each obedientiary had been overseen by him without any account being taken of their geographical situation. When demesne was being taken in hand and farmed for profit it was obvious that some other arrangement was necessary, particularly in two respects: unity of high direction, and the grouping and interlocking of manors.

The first of these two ends was achieved more universally than the second. Though no uniform method was adopted, some kind of central control almost everywhere superseded the responsibility of the several obedientiaries. At many, perhaps most, houses a steward of the estates (*senescallus terrarum*) came into prominence. He was most frequently a professional lay agent who acted for the cellarer or obedientiary concerned; sometimes, however, especially in the thirteenth century, the office was filled by a monk, though he was usually assisted by a salaried clerk. At other houses the extern cellarer and his lay steward were in charge of the exploitation, while two monks made the circuit of the estates to take the audits of the manors.[3] At others still, the complete charge of groups of

---

1 Cf. *Adam de Domerham, Historia,* ed. T. Hearne, II, *passim,* esp. 504–7 (Abbot Michael).

2 Cf. Gras, *The...English Corn Market,* 22; *Rent. et Cust. Glaston.* 108 (c. 1250) a carrying service: 'cariabit lanam vel caseum apud Winton vel apud Hanton'; *Cartul. Rameseien.,* I, 462, 476–7, etc.

3 Cf. the system at Crowland as set out by Miss F. M. Page in *The Estates of Crowland Abbey,* where the seneschal was originally a monk and later a salaried official. At Ely in 1241 and 1261 two monks perambulated the estates (*Ely Chapter Ordinances,* ed. S. J. A. Evans,

manors was given to monk-wardens who held no other office. This last was no new institution; at least as early as the first half of the twelfth century individual monks had been entrusted with a manor or a group of manors, which it was supposed that they would exploit more profitably for the house than a hired functionary. This was, however, an irregular proceeding: at the best it involved continuous residence outside the monastery; at the worst, when the wardens were allowed to take the manors on farm and live upon them for many years at a stretch, they became assimilated to lay farmers in their enjoyment of property; nor were still more serious scandals infrequent. The system, nevertheless—or the abuse—was so convenient that it showed no sign of disappearing during the thirteenth century; it was especially in favour at Christ Church, Canterbury, where its results were deplorable, and when Archbishop Pecham began his remarkable series of visitations in 1280-4 he insisted on its disappearance in favour of an organization of secular bailiffs, directed by the extern cellarer and a professional steward.[1] The wardens, however, though ejected with a pitchfork, slipped back into position immediately, and in the very next year (1282) Pecham was constrained to countenance their existence as visitors, though not as residents, for the manors.[2] Their powers were considerably extended by Prior Eastry, who in 1289 made them responsible for the returns in money and kind of the manors, and for all matters of policy and administration, and in the following decades they are found making a bi-annual tour of their custodies.[3] Monk-wardens of a similar type are found at a number of other monasteries: at Peterborough, at St Augustine's, Canterbury, and above all at Westminster.[4] They were, however, a far from universal institution.

The second great aid to commercial farming, the division, that is, of estates into groups according to locality for administrative purposes, cannot be traced at all the houses, owing to lack of records. Christ Church, Canterbury, had early divided its manors into four wards or 'custodies': that of east Kent; that of the Weald and Marsh; that of Essex, which included manors in Norfolk and Suffolk; and that of Surrey, Buckinghamshire and Oxfordshire. Some distant manors in Devon and Ireland fell

---

pp. 1 and 4), but in 1304 a chapter ordinance decreed that a monk out-steward (*senescallus forinsecus*) and a secular official should perform this duty (*ibid.* 52). At Canterbury Pecham established an extern cellarer and lay steward to oversee the manors, as also at Rochester, Bardney and elsewhere (*Reg. Epp.* II, 623 *seqq.*; III, 824).

1 For the Canterbury system before Pecham, and for other houses v. *MO*, 437-8, and R. A. L. Smith, *Canterbury Cathedral Priory*, 101; also *Reg. Epp. Pecham*, I, 89-90, 342-3; II, 545-6.

2 *V.* esp. *Reg. Epp. Pecham* II, 400-1.

3 R. A. L. Smith, *Canterbury*, 104.

4 For Peterborough v. *Historia Walteri de Whitlesey*, ed. Sparke, II, 126 (the monk-wardens, instituted *c.* 1246, were, however, replaced by three bailiffs before 1292); for St Augustine's, the *Customary*, ed. E. Maunde Thompson, *HBS*, XXIII (1902), I, 34. Westminster had two officials, the monk bailiff, who dealt with the convent's estates in general and the warden of Queen Eleanor's manors (v. E. H. Pearce, *Walter de Wenlok*, 6-7 *et al.*, and the same author's *William de Colchester*).

outside these groups, and were separately controlled.[1] St Augustine's, Canterbury, almost certainly had divisions similar to those at Christ Church, and Peterborough had at least three divisions, following geographical lines. Westminster treated the bulk of its manors as a single group, but maintained a special warden to administer the manors bequeathed by Queen Eleanor.

As centralization and business methods developed, the resources of the various manors of a group were used for mutual assistance. Thus estates on which good arable predominated sent their cattle and ewes to earn a milk-farm for the five months of the summer season on manors where the pasture was rich and extensive; seed corn was exchanged, stock agisted, and sheep concentrated on downs and marshes in the summer for milk and the wool clip, and folded elsewhere for manure and the lambing season in winter.[2] Nowhere, perhaps, was this interchange practised earlier or more systematically than on the manors allotted to an abbot's barony. On these, unity of direction and control by the supreme authority had a relatively small field over which to work, and the closest co-ordination of resources was possible. Some significant details may be noted, at the very time when Henry of Eastry ruled at Christ Church, from the manors of Walter of Wenlock, abbot of Westminster (1284–1307).[3] The estates concerned ran from Eye on Thames-side near Westminster through Laleham and Staines on the river and Denham in Buckinghamshire to Islip near Oxford and two groups in the uplands of Oxfordshire and Warwickshire between Brailes and Moreton-in-Marsh and in the vale of Avon at and about Pershore. Of these, Denham and Laleham were used as clearing-houses for stock and supplies of all kinds coming up to London from the west; seed corn was supplied from one manor to another, and if such minute transfers could be made as those of an extra hand for the wheat harvest from Denham to Bourton-on-the-Hill and of a sickly ox from Eye to Staines for a change of air and pasture, it may be assumed that resources were used for the common good where most needed in more important matters.

Over and beyond co-operation of this kind, more drastic measures were taken in the interests of commercial farming. The grain of many Canterbury manors, and the cheese and wool of others, was produced exclusively for market, often at a distance or overseas, even if the ancient food-farm from the manors concerned needed to be rearranged or forgone. Market profits in a high-price area more than compensated purchases made elsewhere at a lower price to supply deficiencies. In short, the old 'cell' economy, if, indeed, it had ever been complete, tended to disappear and to be merged in the larger group of the custody or of the abbot's manors, or even of the whole mass of an abbey's lands.

1 R. A. L. Smith, *Canterbury*, 100. For St Augustine's, *v.* last note. I am indebted to Miss Elizabeth Crittall for details of Peterborough administration.
2 R. A. L. Smith, *ibid.* 150 *seqq.* At Peterborough mutual assistance, without payment, was common on all manors of the Home and Western groups.
3 E. H. Pearce, *Walter de Wenlok*, 72 *seqq.*, with references to Westminster muniments.

VI

Some indications have been given above of the place taken by grain and dairy-farming in the economy of the black monk estate at the hey-day of demesne farming. The attention given to sheep-farming perhaps deserves a separate mention, if only because the achievements of the black monks in this respect have been thrown somewhat into the shade by the more spectacular activities of the new orders. In point of fact, sheep-farming with a view to the sale of wool was the oldest of all branches of English commercial farming. As has been noted, whereas the grain, corn, cattle, poultry and pigs of a village community might have been little more than sufficient for local needs, the yield of wool of the sheep on the commons, to say nothing of districts where down- or marsh-land was available, must always have far exceeded domestic needs. Sheep, then, when kept in any number, were at least in part a commercial asset, and it was undoubtedly from sales of wool that the small men secured the cash which they needed to pay rent or commute labour services.

As for the older religious houses, they are found possessed of large flocks before the arrival of the Cistercians. Ely Abbey had 13,400 on its estates at the time of *Domesday*;[1] the four foreign houses of St Valéry, St Ouen and the two Caen abbeys had 883 on the Essex sea marshes at the same date;[2] Peterborough had 1439 on thirteen manors c. 1125.[3] Many of the flocks, no doubt, were leased out with the manors in the course of the twelfth century, but when demesne farming became profitable and manors were taken in hand once more the flocks also increased. Glastonbury had 6717 in 1252,[4] and c. 1320 the cathedral priory of Winchester had 20,000,[5] Christ Church, Canterbury, had 13,730,[6] and Peterborough and Crowland between them 16,300.[7] Few Cistercian abbeys, save the very largest such as Fountains, Rievaulx and Strata Florida, could have surpassed these figures, though no doubt the white monks grouped their flocks in fewer units of greater size.

Nevertheless, it is precisely in their treatment of sheep that the black monk abbeys went farthest in the direction of centralization. Whereas corn-growing, however capitalized and commercialized, was necessarily tied to the manor, while the different price areas, regional needs and difficulties of transport made local rather than central collection and marketing desirable, flocks were of themselves mobile, and costs could be reduced by amalgamation, while concentration on pastures of down, moor or marsh for the summer months and the wool clipping was in every way more desirable and more economical than decentralization.

1 Power, *The Medieval English Wool Trade*, 33.
2 J. H. Round in *VCH Essex*, I, 369 and R. J. Whitwell, *English Monasteries and the Wool Trade*, 14.   3 *Liber Niger* in *Chron. Petroburgense*, 157 seqq.
4 *Adam de Domerham Historia*, II, 522.
5 Power, 34.   6 R. A. L. Smith, *Canterbury*, 153.   7 Power, 35.

Consequently, it is not surprising to find that as sheep-farming took a more prominent place as a source of the monastery's income, its organization became partly or wholly extra-manorial. Often, indeed, it was concentrated on a single manor or group of manors, and was directed by a staff of shepherds under a stock-keeper. Thus Pershore kept its flocks at Broadway on the Cotswolds,[1] Crowland pastured its sheep on the manors of Holland running down to the fens,[2] Peterborough concentrated on the large and recently reclaimed manor of La Biggin,[3] Glastonbury on its estates on the Wiltshire downs. At Christ Church, Canterbury, the flocks were never entirely amalgamated; there was no stock-keeper, and almost every manor had its quota, but great numbers were concentrated on a few large manors with sweet pasture such as Eastry and Monkton in Thanet and Agney and Welles in the Romney marshes; the former were used as a breeding ground, the latter chiefly for fattening old stock.[4] At other houses ewes, hoggets and wethers were pastured on separate estates.

In finance, the sheep farm was still more thoroughly centralized. Thus at Crowland the profits fell outside the control of the bailiffs and reeves of the manors concerned;[5] at Peterborough the sheep were accounted for by the stock-keeper of La Biggin,[6] while at Canterbury in 1288 Henry of Eastry took the sales of wool back from the manors of Kent to the priory, where the yield of the year was put for sale into the hands of the treasurers.[7]

VII

The economic organization of a great monastery can best be studied at one of the cathedral priories, where the absence of an effective abbot with paramount authority and prerogative enabled a wider and more co-operative system to flourish. This, as has been said, was particularly the case at Christ Church, Canterbury, where, in addition, the rich legacy of records has been admirably sifted and interpreted.

In the normal administration, four authorities controlled the economic policy at different levels: the reeve of the single manor, the monk-warden of the group or custody of manors, the council of seniors at the checker, and the prior. The following account is of the state of things during the epoch roughly coincident with the long priorate of Henry of Eastry, when the wardens and council of seniors enjoyed the greatest share of power.

1 R. A. L. Smith, *Pershore Abbey* (an unpublished thesis).
2 F. M. Page, *Bidentes Hoylandiae*, in *Econ. Journal* (Economic History), 1929.
3 So Miss E. Crittall, in an unpublished paper on the organization of the Peterborough estates.
4 R. A. L. Smith, *Canterbury*, 150–1.
5 Cf. F. M. Page, *Bidentes Hoylandiae*, 604: 'from the beginning there was a tendency to regard the profits of sheep-farming as a seignorial monopoly, outside the control of the bailiff or reeve.'
6 So Miss Crittall. The flocks at La Biggin were known as *Bidentes de Nasso*.
7 R. A. L. Smith, *Canterbury*, 150–1.

At the lowest stage stood the reeve, bailiff or sergeant.[1] Appointed by the warden, they were directly responsible for the day-to-day management of the manor from year's end to year's end. At the beginning of the year (that is, in the late autumn) the reeve knew what livery of money or produce he would be expected to render from the land in the coming financial year; the general policy as to the nature of the crops was also made known to him, and any extraordinary expenses, such as marling and major repairs to buildings, were met by the warden, who allowed for them in his budget. For the rest he was the man on the spot, to organize labour and direct all agricultural operations. At the end of the financial year, at Michaelmas, he and the sergeant presented their accounts to the warden on progress; they were audited on the spot, and rents and liveries carried up to headquarters.

Immediately above the reeve or sergeant stood the warden, who had in his 'custody' one-fourth of the priory's manors. For all general purposes of policy, and for estimating food-farms, acreage under corn and heads of cattle, the custody, not the manor or lesser group of manors, was taken as the component unit. Originally deputed to ascertain the state of the lands and present a report to the prior and convent, the wardens were entrusted in 1289 by Henry of Eastry with a number of more responsible duties: it was they, and no longer the sergeants, whose task it was to render the liveries to the priory; they presented the year's accounts, which they had previously audited, to the prior and seniors, and carried back to the reeve the requirements for the year to come; they collected fee-farms and lease-hold rents; they appointed the reeves, gave orders for the crops and sales, for the felling of timber, and for repairs or new buildings. Twice a year, at Easter and Michaelmas, they visited every manor: at Easter to view the new crop and be present at the 'cull' or removal of old beasts from the stock for sale and of those fattening for slaughter; at Michaelmas to audit the reeve's accounts. They were accompanied by a lay clerk, a professional expert in law, custom and finance. While, on the one hand, they decided, in consultation with the reeve, on all important or extraordinary practical measures, they acted, at the other end of the scale, as agents and advisers of the prior in general questions of estate management, purchase of land and exploitation in all branches of farming. They were, in fact, the 'linch-pins' of the whole system. Chosen from among the seniors who had had experience of responsible missions, they lived with the convent for the greater part of the year, but when the time came they set out for their lengthy tour of their manors, accompanied by their clerk and servants, reviewing, noting, issuing instructions.[2]

Above the wardens stood the seniors at the chequer. Originally an auditing body only, they came to enjoy not only the general powers given by Rome and General Chapters to the *Senior pars* of the community, but

---

1 For the relations of warden to reeve, *v.* R. A. L. Smith, *Canterbury*, 101–9. In the fourteenth century the reeve 'became largely assimilated to the sergeant or bailiff'; he 'was the *alter ego* of the sergeant'.   2 R. A. L. Smith, *Canterbury*, 104.

also special competence with regard to estate management. Counting among their number those of the community who were or had been most experienced in administration, it was natural that they should pass from auditing accounts and budgeting for the future to issuing general instructions to the wardens and reeves. In ordinances which survive from this period they are found determining food-farms and liveries of manors, regulating the sale of corn and the marling of land and the brewing of beer, and debating the purchase of land. On all these matters it is clear that the seniors as a body deliberated and decided; they were not merely a group of *fainéants* registering the decisions of the prior and the chief officials, but a senate to which the prior stood somewhat as a sole consul with the *imperium*. It was precisely Henry of Eastry, who left the impress of his personality on half a century of Canterbury history, who gave to the seniors this important share in the working of the priory. At no other house, and perhaps never before or after at Canterbury, did so large a number of monks take an intelligent share in the high farming and financial administration of great estates.[1]

At the summit of the pyramid stood the prior. What has been said will have shown that his rule was neither dictatorial nor patriarchal, but it is equally clear, both from the tenor of the conciliar decrees and from the day books and other remains of the priors, that the actual commands which translated decisions and decrees into action came from him, and that he formed his own ideas as to policy both from direct advice of the wardens and from his own circuits of the estates. Fragmentary, indeed, as the records may be, it yet seems clear that the various controversies into which the prior was drawn with the community on the one hand, and with archbishops on the other, had no repercussion upon the deliberations on estate management. In that sphere all were content to pool information and take common decision.

Almost two hundred miles away across England, open to the west, and swept by the gales and warm, wet air from the Atlantic, the wide estates of Glastonbury show the same forces at work, though differently controlled. Richer even than Christ Church, Glastonbury held a varied and not dissimilar mass of manors. There were the short, sweet grasses of the embanked shore-pastures between Brent Knoll and Burnham, the rich soil of the islands in the meres and the summer-dry fields between Banwell and Taunton, the arable on the slopes of the Poldens and the Mendips, the hillside sheep walks above Wells, or between Wincanton and Shaftesbury. Unlike Canterbury, the estates were divided between abbot and convent, and all were controlled by the abbot, but there had been a similar drift towards leasing and parcelling the demesne all through the later decades of the twelfth century.[2] In the new age of farming for profit, however, Glastonbury was ruled by a succession of able men who devoted a great

1 R. A. L. Smith, *Canterbury*, 102-5.
2 *V. supra*, p. 37, and the sources quoted in n. 3.

part of their powers to developing the land. The first of these, Michael of Amesbury (1235-52), set the duties of landowner above all other cares.[1] No previous abbot had engaged on building throughout the estates on so magnificent a scale. The value he set on plough-land can be seen by the rapidity with which he put once more under cultivation land abandoned by his predecessor, adding gradually sixteen new plough-teams to the rest on his own assarts.[2] For Glastonbury, the Brent marshes held the place of Romney, and Michael kept off the sea with embankments,[3] while elsewhere he reclaimed land from the moor or asserted lapsed rights by stripping the peat.[4] He left the abbey clear of debt with its estates admirably developed[5] and rich in live-stock, including some fourteen hundred cattle and over seven thousand sheep. His successor, Roger Ford, finds less notice with the chronicler; he ran the house into debt; but the survey and rental of his day shows a constant intake of land to demesne. Robert of Periton (1261-74) spent his great abilities in clearing the debt by means of scientific farming.[6] He left his mark everywhere about the manors, in closes and buildings; there were new cattle sheds at Glastonbury itself, offices and a dovecot at Ashbury, offices and the buildings of a bercary in stone at Winterborne, dairy farms at Domerham, Sowy and Christian Malford.[7] Meanwhile, more and more land was being taken back into demesne. Clearly the abbot was able to pay off the debts of his predecessor and yet find capital to put into the land.

The fourth and perhaps the ablest of the four, John of Taunton (1274-90), was a man of varied gifts. A scholar and a theologian, who acquired the *Summa* in the very earliest days of Thomism and who left his mark on the legislation of the province of which he was president, he enriched his church with vestments and his house with books.[8] Nevertheless, he appears as a great ruler of estates. More and still more demesne came into his hands, and a steady flow of revenue went back into the land. The chronicler notes five great barns or ranges of farm buildings and four lodgings, together with a dairy farm and its enclosure.[9] All these, he says, were on the grand scale, and he adds to them two parks and two dovecotes, together with other buildings and two chapels. All these, we may assume from previous entries, were built throughout of stone, from the quarries of Doulting or Cranmore or Somerton. There is, apparently, no record whether the manors of Glastonbury were grouped in custodies, and whether monk-

---

1 Adam of Domerham, *Hist. Glast.* 504: 'In terris autem monasterii excolendis curam gerens praecipuam, ac in aedificiis construendis omnes antecessores suos supergrediens, nullum pene locum abbaciae magnificenciae suae reliquit expertem.'
2 *Adam Dom.* 505.
3 *Adam Dom.* 507: 'Maris accessum...multis sumptibus potenter obstruxit.'
4 *Adam Dom.* 509.
5 *Adam Dom.* 522: 'Reliquit...terras suas optime cultas.' A list of stock follows.
6 *Adam Dom.* 525: 'Robertus...ingenii eminentis...monasterium exonerare...studebat, maxime per agriculturam, circa quam praecipue laborabat.'
7 *Adam Dom.* 535-6.
8 *V. supra*, pp. 13-4. For a list of his books, *v. Adam Dom.* 574-5.   9 *Adam Dom.* 573.

wardens were employed in overseeing them. There was, in any case, no committee sitting at the checker to pass ordinances on economic policy and debate the assessments of liveries. The central treasury, however, must have aided towards an efficient realization of assets.

A third centre of high farming of which record survives was Peterborough. This abbey, though never the equal of Christ Church and Glastonbury in the wealth and extent of its possessions, was throughout the middle ages among the dozen richest houses and was one of those that bettered their position between the Conquest and the Dissolution. The bulk of its estates lay between the rich arable land of the Northamptonshire uplands and the grassland bordering the Fens, which gave deep pasture for dairy herds and sheep. Near Peterborough itself the fertile river banks and islands formed by drains and creeks of the Nen could be planted with fruit-trees, vegetables and herbs.

Between 1214 and 1250—the moment of change from leases to demesne farming elsewhere—the abbey was ruled by a succession of short-lived abbots who perhaps did not hold office long enough to leave mark as individuals on the estates. Of the first, however, Robert of Lindsey (1214–22), the chronicler records that he did much assarting, both of waste and wood, a sure sign of profitable farming;[1] of the last and longest lived of the series, Walter of St Edmund's (1233–45), it is noted that he put much capital into the estates, building and repairing granges, halls, sheepcotes and cattle sheds.[2]

The great era of Peterborough's exploitation, however, came in the first decades of the fourteenth century, under Geoffrey of Crowland (1299–1320). When he treats of this period the chronicler abandons the narrative form to record under each year's date the abbot's operations on the estates, giving each year the total spent. The sum for the twenty-odd years of Geoffrey's rule he gives as £2102, or a little over £100 a year—say £3000 of our money. It was a very large sum to put back into the land, year in, year out, and one which speaks eloquently not only of the profits and expectations of commercial farming on the grand scale, but of the firm resolution of the monks to give all their surplus wealth to the development of their land, as a great industrialist of to-day puts back his profits into his spreading works and the sources of supply. Nor must it be forgotten that the process went on unchecked, though 1315 and 1316 were famine years.

Abbot Geoffrey, indeed, had work always on hand, and the value and amenities of his manors must have risen steadily under his eyes. Here he added to arable by enclosures, sometimes to the extent of creating a manor where formerly there was only uncultivated grassland;[3] elsewhere he is

---

1 *Roberti Swapham, Coen. Burg. Historia*, 112: 'Fecit quasdam magnas assartas...emit quemdam boscum...et illum fecit assartare et colere et circumfossare.'
2 *Rob. Swaph.* 120.
3 *Walteri de Whitlesey Hist.* 154 (at Eybury): 'inclusit landam quae prius jacuit velut pastura ad sustentationem ferarum.' *Ibid.* 156 (at Northolm): 'incepit manerium ubi numquam fuit prius manerium sed jacuit quasi pastura.'

seen laying out gardens, herbaries and orchards, protected with moats and dikes[1] strengthened with plantations of ash and oak; elsewhere again he is planting woods, or constructing every kind of building and appurtenance: halls, granges, stables, cattle-sheds, sheepcotes and shepherds' quarters, dairy buildings, dovecotes, windmills—hen-houses, even, and rabbit warrens. Everywhere we see him cutting drains and sluices, embanking and enclosing. Fittingly enough, the chronicler, after noting the abbot's death, gives an extent of his manors and their income, together with the receipts acknowledged by the Crown officials who held the barony during the vacancy.[2]

The early decades of the fourteenth century were indeed the golden age of monastic high farming. While Geoffrey of Crowland ruled at Peterborough, Henry of Eastry was completing his organization and realizing his highest profits at Canterbury, while at Chertsey John of Rutherwick (1307–47) was raising his house, by judicious purchases and lawsuits, to a position of economic importance without parallel in its history before or after.[3] Almost exactly the contemporaries of Rolle and Ockham, two at least of the three have left little or no trace of their personal characteristics and interests, but if a man's chief work reflects his personality, the abbots of Peterborough and Chertsey would have found, we may think, the company of Turnip Townshend and Coke of Holkham in other centuries more congenial than that of the mystic or the philosopher in their own. Not all abbots, however, were so conversant with the technicalities of husbandry as these. Only a few decades later, an abbot of Eynsham, a house deep in the fields where the novices helped with the haymaking,[4] was called upon by the Presidents to give an account of his stewardship and replied in some detail. He had, it would appear, little knowledge of the yield, either in fritillaries or weys of cheese, of the river meadows around his home. He had never been strong on farming, he said; he left these things to others who knew something about them, and did his best to keep his officials up to the mark.[5]

Few superiors of the greater houses could have afforded to make such a confession at that time. For a short century the monastic order, which at more than one period in the past had been a beneficent influence in extending and protecting the cultivated areas of Europe, stood out, in this country at least, as a nurse of intelligent and broad-minded landowners who expected, indeed, to recover with interest the capital which they sank in the land, but who nevertheless played a part which neither peasant proprietors nor great lords pushing their fortunes could have done in

1 *Walt. de Whitl. Hist.* 155: 'herbarium...quod circuivit duplicibus stagnis et pontibus.'
2 *Walt. de Whitl. Hist.* 175–216.
3 The work of John of Rutherwick has been studied in an unpublished thesis, *The manors of Chertsey Abbey under Abbot John de Rutherwyk* (London University Thesis CXLVII, by E. Toms). 4 *MC*, III, 45.
5 *MC*, III, 48: 'Dicit quod nunquam fuit agricultor; propterea habet sub se yconomos... et illos supervidet...utilius quo comode poterit.'

increasing the resources of the soil and its cultivators. By their planting, their building, their enclosing and their draining they had a large share in preparing for this country's future wealth and in determining for future ages the soft and ordered opulence of the English country scene, with its byres and farms and cottages of lichened stone or warmer brick and thatch; its hedgerows and its ditches thick with may and meadowsweet; its noble trees shading the cattle from the sun that ripens the corn.[1]

The era passed more speedily than might have been anticipated. A succession of tempests, droughts and famines,[2] though they shook the foundations of prosperity at more than one house, would not have changed a whole economy. Nor would the successive visitations of the Great Pestilence have done this if the seeds of social change had not been already in the ground. The immediate consequence of the first and most terrible plague, the decrease of rural population, resulted in the immediate disappearance from cultivation of much land, and in the partial neglect of greater areas. Its real significance, however, was as an important contributing cause of the labour shortage and social unrest which loosened the fabric of the manor and led to a rise in the cost of labour and other charges which fell heavily on the exploiters of large estates and which were not counterbalanced by an equal rise in the selling prices of wool and corn. No doubt the monks were too wealthy and too acute to be ruined or even seriously distressed; they adapted themselves to the changing conditions without losing—perhaps they even increased—their revenues. But it was at the cost of relinquishing by slow degrees the direct control of the land, and this, as will be seen, was a principal economic cause, among the many causes of different kinds, of their ultimate exclusion from the main currents of the country's life.

1 The ordered and well-timbered aspect of the typical English champaign, whether in Taunton Dean, or the Vale of the White Horse, or in the broad valleys of Derbyshire or Yorkshire, is doubtless due principally to the deliberate policy of the eighteenth-century landowners who wished to achieve a park-like landscape; nor must it be forgotten that the area of waste and unenclosed land was very great in the medieval centuries. It may well be, however, that there was notable retrogression in this respect after the fourteenth century, and in any case, as extant buildings and surviving place and field names show, the main lines of the rich landscape on, for example, the Glastonbury and Canterbury estates, were laid down in the middle ages.

2 There were great storms in 1287-8, floods in 1307, a famine in 1314-16 and a drought in 1325-6, in addition to a flooding of the sea along the south and east coasts when 4585 sheep were lost on the Christ Church estates alone. The year 1276 was marked by the appearance of the scab, which carried off as many as half the flocks in its first attack, and continued for some seven years in considerable violence. In 1327 there was a pestilence among the cattle. *V.* R. A. L. Smith, *Canterbury*, 143, 156, 189; C. E. Britton, *A Meteorological Chronology to* A.D. 1450, 121-37; and N. Denholm-Young, *Seignorial Administration in England*, 61, n. 1.

CHAPTER V

HENRY OF EASTRY
Prior of Christ Church, Canterbury, 1285–1331

I

Henry of Eastry was perhaps some thirty-five years old when he was elected prior and confirmed by Archbishop Pecham.[1] When he took over the administration the monastery was in debt to the extent of £5000—more than the average income of two years—at a time when the archbishop also was struggling to overcome a weight of debts. He speedily showed himself an economist of the first order. By a rigid curtailment of superfluous expenses at home, by a clear-sighted and total reorganization of the administration, both in deliberation and accountancy at Canterbury and in executive action on the estates, as also by a farseeing and consistent development and exploitation of the land and its fruits, Eastry raised Christ Church from a state of insolvency to what was probably the highest level of productivity in its history.

For the first thirty years of his rule the economic current of the age was flowing in his favour. During the whole of the thirteenth century the great estates of England had been increasing the acreage of demesne land exploited directly by the owner, while rising prices at the end of the century and during the first decades of the fourteenth made this the 'golden age of demesne farming'.[2] This enabled Eastry, despite exceptionally heavy losses from tempests and repeated demands, in the early thirteenth century, for loans and corrodies from the king, to sink his debts in fifteen years and inaugurate a period of sound and prosperous finance.

1 Henry of Eastry, neglected by medieval biographers and modern historians, found a discerning panegyrist in the late R. A. L. Smith, to whose work, especially his study of *Canterbury Cathedral Priory*, the following pages owe much. When no other reference is given, this book may be taken as the authority. There is a good short notice of Eastry in the *DNB* by T. F. Tout.

Eastry was traditionally ninety-two when he died. Tout is willing only to allow him eighty years. His name, unfortunately, occurs in the Christ Church profession list before the dates begin (*v.* the list of names, p. 176, in *Christ Church Canterbury, Chronicle of John Stone* and *List of... Monks*, ed. W. G. Searle, Cambridge Antiquarian Society, xxxiv, 1902), but its position suggests a date earlier (perhaps considerably earlier) than 1270.

A rich collection of documents, compiled by Eastry himself or under his direction, still exists, mainly in the library of the dean and chapter at Canterbury, but with isolated MSS. at the Lambeth Palace Library, British Museum, Cambridge University Library and library of Trinity College, Cambridge. For a list, *v.* Smith, *op. cit.* 222–4. The earliest Register is of Eastry's time, and there is a mass of his correspondence at Canterbury, while his Memorandum Book is in the British Museum (Cott. Galba E iv). Abstracts of letters to him were printed by R. L. Poole, *HMC*, VCi, (1902), 250–81, and excerpts from his Register fill much of the first volume of *Literae Cantuarienses (RS* 85), ed. J. B. Sheppard; v. also J. F. Nichols *Custodia Essexae* (London University thesis).　　2 *Canterbury Cathedral Priory*, p. 62.

Though not neglectful of other interests, and willing to advise his friends on politics and foreign affairs, Henry of Eastry found his life's work within the limited, if large, area of the Canterbury buildings and estates. Within that little world no department escaped rationalization at his hands. Economy through the avoidance of waste and superfluity was an obvious measure, to be taken at once, probably in the first year of his priorate. It was accompanied by a development of the system of central treasury and regular audit already functioning, and by a fuller use of domestic ability in the council of seniors meeting at the chequer and the increasing employment of skilled external legal advice and advocacy in the prior's council. Eastry was no doctrinaire democrat, and such slight evidence as exists shows him to have been a ruler who held the reins firmly, but he was not by temperament a monopolist of power and could tolerate colleagues, not functionaries only, and during his period of rule the number of monks who took an active share in enlightened administration, either in the house or on the manors, was probably higher than at any period before or after.

In addition to the body of senior monks sitting at the chequer he enlisted the services of the ablest practical talent in the community by regularizing the position and enhancing the powers of the monk-wardens of the manors. The function of these officials has been discussed elsewhere;[1] here we need only note that it was Eastry who made them responsible for returning the revenues of their custody and who gave them in practice extensive discretionary powers of construction and repairs of farm buildings and of choice of the particular agricultural policy to be adopted in exploiting the individual manors. At the same time, the wardens were regularly consulted and strictly controlled by the council of seniors under the prior. The system, therefore, under a competent head who could guide his subordinates along the lines of an economic policy decided by himself, was probably as satisfactory as could be wished from a material point of view. While giving a lawful outlet for practical ability, it avoided the waste and personal aggrandisement of the old obedientiary system, and secured the maximum income for the monastery.

With this machinery at his disposal, Eastry was able to show himself a master of high farming throughout the large and scattered estates of Christ Church. He increased his land wisely and unceasingly, parcel by parcel, recouping himself for the purchase by the higher rent chargeable, and by careful and persevering embankment and reclamation in the Romney marshes. He increased his liquid assets by securing payment, or the option of payment, in lieu of labour services. He improved the yield of the land by a widespread and intelligent use of marling, by a partial rotation of crops, and by a careful breaking up of unused lands.

Disposing as he did of wide estates containing arable, meadowland and coarse pasture in varying proportions, lying on a variety of subsoils and including marsh, downland, river-bottoms and well-drained, airy hillsides,

1 *V. supra*, p. 43.

all controlled by a body with capital, he was able to exploit the resources of the country to the full. The account rolls show a complicated and scientific scheme of collection and sale by which corn and cheese—sometimes the whole yield of the land—were sold on the spot or at a distance with a keen watching of the market, while produce for home consumption, whenever necessary through exhaustion of local stocks, was bought elsewhere at a lower price. In other words, the scattered estates were to a large extent treated as a single administrative *bloc* and commercialized. In a similar way, the considerable wool crop was increased and rationalized by the concentration of the flocks on a few manors, notably the fresh, open pastures of Thanet and the Romney marshes, and by transhumance to other Canterbury possessions. As for the dairy produce of cows and ewes, this too was exploited. On manors where dairy-farming on a large scale was practicable, cheese-making for the market absorbed most of the milk; on small manors, and those where arable predominated, Eastry extended the system of milk-leases, hiring out the cattle to small farmers who paid cash on the expectation of the yield for the season. On other manors still, the contrary need was felt, and cows and ewes were hired in for cheese- and butter-making. The sum of all these measures under efficient central control resulted in a very considerable betterment of Christ Church revenue. When Eastry had weathered his difficult first years, rendered still more testing by a series of calamities due to vagaries of the climate, he was able to enjoy, during the first twenty years of the new century, a space of time in which his organization found its reward and gathered a rich harvest from the contemporary 'boom' in agriculture. The gross revenue, which *c.* 1290 averaged £2050, stood in the last year of his priorate, when conditions had already begun to deteriorate, at £2540, an increase of almost 25%. The increase in the net revenue was no doubt very much greater.

II

Though Eastry's forte was undoubtedly economic administration, there is in him no trace of the bucolic. His reputation for a knowledge of the Scriptures finds little support from his correspondence, and there is no evidence that he had passed through the schools, but he was highly intelligent, with an incisive realist bent of mind, and with the assurance that often accompanies a limited outlook. His attendances in Parliament, though apparently little to his taste, and his role as host to great ones on pilgrimage to Canterbury or on the road to or from Dover, put him *au courant* with public affairs, and he was a regular correspondent and counsellor of successive archbishops.[1] He had entered the monastery in the days of Boniface of Savoy, and had had full opportunity of observing the policies and fortunes of the three distinguished men who followed him at Canterbury. Already in Pecham's day his unemotional, practical temper can be

1 *V.* e.g. letters 57, 199 in *Lit. Cant.*

seen in his tactful but firm handling of the difficult old friar whose grievances against the monks had led him to threaten to leave his body for burial among his brethren away from Canterbury.[1] Winchelsey, a determined man with a clear programme, was not a promising subject for cautious counsel, and Eastry's task was rather to ward off from his community the consequences of a respectful following of the archbishop's lead in opposition to the king and in firm adherence to the demands of Boniface VIII as set out in the bull *Clericis laicos*. In the event, Christ Church, faced with a crisis similar to, but far less desperate than, that of 1207, capitulated to the king, but Eastry guarded Winchelsey's interests and acted for a time as his vicar-general.

The weaker Walter Reynolds found in the prior an experienced and wary counsellor, firmly seated in the saddle and with advice to spare for others; consequently the archbishop turned often to him for guidance. This Eastry gave without stint: it was counsel of a piece with his character —cautious, realist, eminently level-headed. Himself unmoved by any personal or ideal considerations regarding the political and constitutional issues at stake in the last months of the reign of Edward II, he kept Reynolds trimming as best he could in awkward times, and would seem to have influenced a minor historical event by suggesting the representative deputation from parliament which urged the king's abdication at Kenilworth.[2] Though lavish of advice Eastry was fearful of publicity, and several of his letters contain cryptic datings, instructions as to silence or requests for the destruction of what he had written.[3] It must therefore have been supremely distasteful to him to learn that one of these private letters had been left lying for all to read, by some ironical accident, in the church of his native village.[4]

With Mepeham, Reynolds's successor, Eastry, now perhaps an octogenarian, adopted a still more peremptory tone, and the archbishop on more than one occasion found himself the recipient of a 'snub from old Eastry',[5] who did not hesitate to take the primate to task for his style of writing to his monks, and to outline the qualities desirable in the archbishop's officials.

III

Henry of Eastry's priorate was, in its domestic relations, one of the most peaceful Christ Church had known. The prior's efficiency, which never degenerated into fractious self-assertion or selfish domineering, commanded the respect of his community, and there is a welcome absence of the party warfare that so often marred the internal harmony of the house. What domestic troubles there were owed their existence to the aberrations of

1 Pecham, *Reg. Epp.* III.
2 *Lit. Cant.* letter 201; cf. introd. lxxxviii and Tout in *DNB.*
3 E.g. letter 191 (Oct. 1326) ends: 'Scriptum in nubibus, lator praesentium sit pro dato.'
4 *Lit. Cant.* letter 274.
5 The phrase is Dr Sheppard's, *Lit. Cant.* introd. xxviii.

a few individuals and the misdemeanour of a clique of *mauvais sujets* who were responsible for a theft of plate and a libellous missive, and who clearly deserved the punishment that was late in coming. All other indications go to show that the prior, though a firm disciplinarian, was no ascetic or reformer, and rode his community on the snaffle in all matters of diet and old custom.[1]

Eastry, like other great monastic superiors, was responsible for a number of additions to the treasure-chests and vestment-presses of the priory, and during his period of office, and presumably owing to his financial re-organization, the existing stone screen was erected round the monastic choir, together with a number of buildings in the precinct.[2] Though he had been of university age when Thomism entered upon its victorious career, and though he had seen at close quarters the controversies of Kilwardby and Pecham, he evinces no direct interest in theology. He was, however, a patron of monk scholars, and a sheaf of letters[3] has been preserved written to him by a group of young clerics connected in one way or another with Canterbury to whom he acted as patron in their university careers at Orleans, Bologna and elsewhere. It is interesting to see that these young men regarded him as a by no means inexorable friend and benefactor; it is also, perhaps, characteristic that their letters to the prior are, almost without exception, primarily concerned with money, and not at all with theology. When a direct request for advice on a theological point reached him, perhaps from the archbishop, it was at once passed on to the University of Oxford for a reply.[4]

Of spiritual or even of religious feeling there is no trace in the Eastry letters that have survived, and only too rarely does any touch of personal feeling escape the writer. He was a cool observer, not lightly to be stampeded. He had no great fears of invasion in 1325: the French, he said, would shake their fists at a man, but were slow to get their swords out of the scabbard; if they are scratched, they think all is over with them.[5] His security, however, was not derived from any patriotic illusions: the men of Kent, he said, were a poor lot; if a hostile fleet appeared they would take to the woods and leave the foreshore to others.[6] He himself forestalled false alarms with a proclamation forbidding horns and trumpets to be blown in inland towns before the warning came from the coast.[7]

Eastry, though blessed with a constitution which took him far beyond the common span of longevity, did not enjoy robust health, and there are

---

1 *V.* letters 156–7, 205, 215, 217–18.   2 *V.* his *Memorandum*, Appendix II.

3 Printed by C. E. Woodruff in *Archaeologia Kantiana*, LIII.

4 *Lit. Cant.* letters 133, 141. The question at issue was the Immaculate Conception.

5 *Ibid.* letter 165: 'Mos est Gallicorum terrorem et timorem frequentius pugno aliis incutere quam gladios evaginare, et siquis minimum digitum viderit cruentatum, statim caput suum aestimat amputatum.'

6 *Ibid.* letter 173: 'Populus Kanciae...debilis est et pauper, et dubito quod si exercitum navalem viderit ad campestria et silvestria declinabunt, et litora maritima potentioribus reliquerit, quia nemo invitus bene facit.'

7 *Ibid.* letter 132.

many references in the letters to illness and doctors. There is even one, to the physician himself, in which he reports progress and jests a little ponderously, and then thinks better of it and cancels the passage.[1] He consulted a London specialist, leaving the local practitioner to his monks. In 1321 he felt his end was near, and drew up for the benefit of posterity an account of his economic achievements.[2] He survived, however, for ten years more, and is found ordering from Flanders a little easy mule—not a great tall beast—on which he might amble down the familiar tracks and note with those keen eyes which now, perhaps, saw less clearly, how thick the stalks clustered and how full were the ears.[3]

Registers, memoranda, letters, all were kept, and almost all have survived the chances of time and the carelessness of man, but there are no intimate sheets in the Eastry files. The old prior was not a *littérateur*, nor was he, we may guess, one who received or gave affection readily or who passed through the darkness and light of a spiritual progress. It was given to him to rule Christ Church for a longer span than any other prior between the Conquest and the Dissolution; a young man when Albert the Great, Thomas Aquinas and Bonaventure were in their prime, he lived into the age of Ockham and Marsilio; he saw the papacy attain its highest flight, and lived on to the days of Avignon. While he developed his estates and organized his finances, Dante, in a world of intenser passions, found time to watch the fireflies in the vineyards of Fiesole and mark the dewdrops on the hillside grass in the starlit dawn, while Giotto was rendering imperishable the daisies and pencilled elms of Umbria. To Eastry, the primroses of the Kentish brookland, the harebells and ragwort of the downs, the whispering reeds and dazzling levels of Thanet were familiar sights, but of such things he does not speak, and perhaps did not think. He saw the pastures with the eyes of Shallow, not with those of Perdita; his thoughts worked the round of market prices, of stones of cheese, of bushels per acre, of the income from agistry, of the quality of the season's clip of wool. Stiff, dry and masterful, a great high farmer and superbly able man of business, he passes before us as he rides about the manors or sits at the chequer. He died, still active, while celebrating Mass, in April 1331.

1 *Lit. Cant.* letter 127.
2 B.M. Cott. Galba E iv, ff. 76–8. It is printed in the Appendix, pp. 335–7.
3 *Lit. Cant.* letter 285: 'Un petit muyl bien portant, nepas grant mul et haut, mes un petit muyl bien portant.'

CHAPTER VI

THE MONASTIC ADMINISTRATION

I

During the greater part of the twelfth century the administration, financial and economic, of the English monasteries had been progressively decentralized. The economy of the Rule of St Benedict, by which the cellarer controlled all temporalities under the immediate supervision of the abbot, had been dislocated both by the exigencies of the feudal system, which led to a division between the barony of the abbot and the possessions of the monks, and by a universal devolution in the course of which many of the estates and revenues, presented or allocated to particular uses, came to be administered by the officials concerned acting in complete independence and with full initiative. This state of things, which has been called the 'obedientiary system', attained its maximum of development and diffusion between 1150 and c. 1200.[1] On the material side it was largely due to the 'cell economy' of the scattered and parcelled estates held by the early Anglo-Norman landowners; on the social and monastic side it was one of the symptoms of the centrifugal, almost anarchic process which came near to dissolving the external bonds of discipline in Western christendom in the half-century before the Fourth Lateran Council.

However plausible the reasons for such devolution may have seemed, it affected medieval monasticism permanently and adversely. Economically, it rendered a uniform policy impossible and stood in the way of 'high' farming and the concentration of crops, flocks of sheep and dairy herds upon favoured areas with a view to catching the market with produce. Financially, it increased the likelihood of mismanagement, made administration more wasteful, and prevented the control and exploitation of the resources of the house as a whole; moreover, in default of any regular audit or direct, immediate accountability it opened the door to improvident spending, reckless mortgaging and even private aggrandisement. The system, indeed, common to almost all black monk houses in north-western Europe, was largely the cause of the financial straits in which an increasing number of even the potentially wealthy monasteries found themselves towards the end of the century. Equally disastrous, and perhaps responsible for still more spectacular ruin, was the absolute freedom from control enjoyed by the heads of houses, especially those exempt from diocesan control. These two abuses were, consequently, the object of direct attack

---

1 The independence of obedientiaries was probably never greater than between these dates; the *locus classicus* is the Chronicle of Jocelin of Brakelond. For a list of these officials *v. MO*, Appendix xvi. Minor officials, however, and sub-officials continued to multiply after 1200.

when Innocent III and his immediate successors attempted the task of reorganizing the old orders.[1]

Before this, a number of isolated efforts had been made to impose unity of control and accountability upon the financial organization of individual houses. These attempts took various shapes, according as those responsible differed in their aims; while some sought to withdraw the obedientiaries from the direct control of property, others wished to check or pool revenues, to control spending, and to bring abbot and officials to a regular reckoning. Leaving aside for the present the estate administration, we may recognize two main aims, ultimately associated in the ideal scheme: the establishment of a common treasury into which all receipts flowed and from which all disbursements were made, and the setting up of committees of audit, to function at regular intervals.

These ends had been secured in or before the twelfth century by the papal camera and the royal administration. In England, the establishment of the royal treasury was followed after a considerable lapse of time by that of the exchequer. The papal camera had probably been familiar still earlier with a system of audit,[2] and if the striking parallels between monastic and royal administration invite us to see in the latter the model of the former, it should be noted that all the evidence at present available points to a Roman agency behind the earlier instances of the application of the system in England.

The earliest example of the centralization of revenues would seem to be Christ Church, Canterbury, where, at least as early as 1170, all incomes were received by three treasurers who distributed them subsequently to the three spending officials, cellarer, chamberer and sacrist.[3] There were three noteworthy features in this arrangement: the treasurers were more numerous than the regular two; the income was neither pooled for distribution according to needs nor paid according to a prearranged scale, but passed on to the officials in the exact quotas received from the manors

---

1 For this reforming activity of the Papacy, which was especially remarkable on the Continent, two important articles by Dom U. Berlière should be consulted: *Innocent III et la Réorganisation des Monastères Bénédictins*, in *RB*, XXXII (1920), 22–42, 145–59, and *Honorius III et les monastères bénédictins* in *Revue Belge de Philologie et d'Histoire* (Brussels, 1923), 237–65, 461–84. In the former article he remarks (p. 32): 'La crise financière, qui entraînait si souvent à sa suite la ruine disciplinaire des monastères, était assez générale.'

2 For the papal camera, *v.* W. E. Lunt, *Papal Revenues in the Middle Ages*. It must be said, however, that though the camera had an audit in early days, the treasurer as a general receiving officer only appears in the thirteenth century.

3 In the following pages, as indeed often elsewhere in this volume, I have drawn heavily upon the researches of R. A. L. Smith, as set out particularly in his work on Canterbury Cathedral Priory and in *The Regimen Scaccarii in English Monasteries*, in *TRHS*, 4 ser. XXIV (1942), 73–94. In these, and in his other publications, the data acquired by long and patient work in the muniments of Canterbury, Winchester, Rochester, Ely and other libraries are set out with unusual clarity and judgement. Too many of the relatively few monographs on medieval economics and finance present the reader with a jungle of facts and figures of which the author neither indicates nor fully appreciates the significance. Here, by contrast, principles and conclusions, corroborated by a wealth of detailed evidence, are given to the reader in every chapter or on every page.

apportioned to each office; and the treasurers for all abnormal disbursements required the consent of the conventual chapter.[1] In the only other case known prior to 1216—that of Ramsey c. 1197–8—three monks again were appointed as receivers by Hubert Walter, the papal legate.[2]

In neither of these cases does a system of audit appear. The first occurrence of this is at Winchester cathedral priory, where Henry of Blois (c. 1163–70) established a committee of twelve monks to audit the accounts and apportion the surplus revenue as they might think fit, so as to avoid private ownership. This, it would seem, was an application of a method used at Cluny, to which monastery the bishop had originally belonged.[3]

A third type, which was to become standard with the canons, and in which for the first time appear the three elements of treasury, periodical account and auditing committee, is first met with on the English scene in the constitution of Waltham Abbey, refounded for regular canons by Henry II in 1177.[4] It had, however, so far as can be seen, no immediate imitators, and until the pontificate of Innocent III the curia had no programme to send out as common form to legates and visitors.

II

That great pope had, as has been demonstrated, a clear-cut scheme for remedying the spiritual and material disorganization which threatened to become endemic among the black monks of Italy and north-western Europe. He began at home, with the most venerable houses, and his letters to Subiaco (1202) and Monte Cassino (1215), which were taken into the decretals, served as a basis for subsequent Roman action and decrees.[5] In the material sphere the evil of dilapidation, or ruinous dissipation of monastic property, was seen to be due first to lack of any control over the abbot, who often disposed of conventual property as well as that assigned to his barony or household, and next to *proprietas*, that is, embezzlement, waste or unrestrained licence on the part of the obedientiaries. The papal remedies were threefold: the permission of the community was made necessary to give validity to large sales or expenses; a system of regular reckonings of abbot and obedientiaries was decreed; and a central board of receipt and expenditure was set up, though this did not form part of the regular papal programme under Innocent III.

Visiting legates, it seems, were allowed to use their judgement to meet the circumstances of the individual case; thus John of Ferentino imposed audits and a council of seniors on Evesham in 1206, where the abbot's

---

1 Holtzmann, *Papsturkunden in England*, II, 372.
2 *Chronic. abbat. Rameseiensis (RS)*, 342. For the case of York, *v. infra*, p. 58.
3 *Reg. Joannis de Pontissara*, ed. Deedes (C & YS, 1913–24), II, 523 and *Winchester Chartulary*, ed. A. W. Goodman (1927), p. 5.
4 Holtzmann, *Papsturkunden in England*, I, 583–4.
5 Berlière, *Innocent III*, 40–1; cf. *PL*, CCXIV, coll. 1064–6 and CCXVII, coll. 249–53.

arbitrary rule was the prime cause of trouble,[1] whereas at York in the same year he endeavoured to introduce audit and a central board of receipt, though the latter failed to establish itself in the abbey.[2]

During the first half of the thirteenth century a succession of energetic popes, several of whom were expert canonists, endeavoured by legatine visitations, local councils and Roman constitutions to put the finances of the black monks in order. A regular feature of all these methods was the double audit of abbot and obedientiaries, and these became universally binding in the statutes of Gregory IX in 1235-7.[3] They were in consequence duly embodied in the statutes of the English provincial chapter in 1277.[4] With the other part of financial reorganization, the centralized receipt, the popes were less concerned, and, speaking generally, it was only rarely that this was introduced in the first half of the thirteenth century. Indeed, the only house where the system functioned in perfection and has left adequate record was Christ Church, Canterbury. The treasury system, however, which was made the law for all English Austin canons at their general chapter of 1220[5] and which possessed such obvious advantages, was a natural corollary to the contemporary movement which was removing individual manors from the control of the chief obedientiaries, and placing them under stewards or monk-wardens directly answerable to the chapter or council of seniors. It is not surprising, therefore, to find two treasurers being appointed at Peterborough c. 1247[6] and at St Augustine's, Canterbury, before 1274.[7] It may even be that a variant of the system, first seen at Winchester, in which the treasurers received unassigned revenues with which to form a kind of reserve fund, was fairly common. The fully centralized receiving office, however, showed no signs of becoming general among the black monks until it received unexpected advertisement at the hands of Archbishop Pecham.

That energetic prelate, who continued and extended the policy of his predecessor, Kilwardby, of visiting as metropolitan the monastic and collegiate bodies throughout his province, carried with him and applied with increasing precision and enthusiasm a programme of financial reform which contained the complementary features of central receipt and disbursement and regular audit.[8] This he applied all over England and Wales

1 *Chron. Evesham.* 206.

2 The decrees are printed by C. R. Cheney in *EHR*, xlvi (1931), 449-52.

3 *Les Régistres de Grégoire IX* (ed. L. Auvray), ii, 325-6; the statutes were confirmed by Innocent IV in 1253.   4 *MC*, i, 84-5.

5 *Chapters of the Augustinian Canons*, ed. H. S. Salter (*OHS*), 22-3. The chapter, which was probably that of Bedford in 1220, also established an annual audit of the obedientiaries before a committee.

6 *Roberti Swapham, Coenobii Burgensis Historia* (ed. Sparke), 126. The treasurers, however, were for the abbot's estates, though an annual balance sheet of all the finances was simultaneously established.

7 Cf. *Customary of St Augustine's*, ed. E. M. Thompson (*HBS*, xxiii, 1902), i, 34.

8 For an account of these visitations *v.* D. Knowles, *Some Aspects of the Career of Archbishop Pecham*, in *EHR*, lvii (April 1942), 194-7, where references are given to Pecham's Register.

to the black monks and black canons, and if it appears that more than one abbey took little heed of his injunctions, it is also certain that in some houses the main lines of his system remained in force, and that other prelates, from York to Winchester, adopted his programme wherever financial chaos demanded their intervention. Pecham, while tempering his injunctions to local circumstances, aimed at obtaining as complete a centralization as possible, including both abbatial and conventual receipts. This was repugnant both to tradition and to the natural love of independence. Its introduction, therefore, at the hands of a visitor and a stranger, was not likely to be a smooth matter, and in the event, many houses retained the old obedientiary system in its entirety, while of those who adopted some kind of central control almost all allowed the almoner and sacrist, and often other officials also, to receive their revenues directly without reference to the treasurers. There is, however, some evidence that the houses where the central receiving office functioned in whole or in part were among those which attained the greatest prosperity during the agricultural boom in the half-century following Pecham's death.

III

It is remarkable that whereas regular audit was always a feature of the papal statutes the central receiving office was never imposed upon the black monks by Rome or by their own chapter and Presidents. Its introduction, when not the work of a visitor, was due to spontaneous action, principally in three or four cathedral priories, where the possessions and administration of the Ordinary who stood *in loco abbatis* were no concern of the monks, and where the acting superior, the prior, stood in a less solemn and patriarchal relation to his chapter than did an abbot. It will be well, therefore, having surveyed the stages in the reorganization of black monk finances, to take a closer view of the system as it obtained at the place and epoch of its highest competence, that is, at Christ Church, Canterbury, between 1285 and 1330.[1]

Here the treasurers, three in number, gradually came to exercise a control which reduced even the principal obedientiaries to the rank of executive officers only. Receiving all the revenues, the treasurers from their first institution distributed to the obedientiaries according to their needs, and very early came to exercise complete control over the expenditure, deciding not only upon the annual allowances, but upon the sums to be assigned to the particular purpose or work. Moreover, plurality of offices was jealously forbidden, and the major officials were compelled to devolve some of their responsibilities upon subordinates. Needless to say, the initiative in this process must have come from the prior, supported or perhaps stimulated by chapter, but the result was a state of things without parallel in monastic

1 R. A. L. Smith, *The Regimen Scaccarii*, 85–92, and still more fully in *Canterbury Cathedral Priory*.

England—a democratic or co-operative administration in which a large number of the community took a share. Alongside of the treasurers (and usually including them as members) a larger body came to assume more and more power; this was the council of seniors. In origin merely an auditing committee, meeting at the exchequer for the lengthy annual review of the receipts and accounts of the bailiffs of manors as well as of the obedientiaries, this group, which would seem to have been selected *ad hoc* on each occasion by the prior, exercised in time a general oversight upon the whole working of the priory and its estates.

The tendency of this monastic council to extend its competence was hastened by the direct action of Archbishop Pecham, who as ex-minister provincial of the Minors was familiar with the workings of committees. He ruled that the appointment of certain of the obedientiaries, hitherto falling under the control, or at least calling for the consent, of the chapter, should be decided at a meeting of the seniors at the exchequer, thereby no doubt avoiding much of the disturbance and unnecessary discussion inevitable when personal qualifications were debated by a large body of men of all ages and degrees of intelligence.[1] From this it was an easy step for the council of seniors to extend its supervision to all activities in the house, and it is, in fact, found dealing not only with personal incidents such as the future status of the ex-prior Thomas Ringmer (on which occasion Prior Eastry, dissatisfied with the advice given, 'consulted the electorate', so to say, for contrary counsel),[2] but also issuing constitutions on the domestic life of the house and promulgating a whole series of 'orders in council' defining the economic policy on the manors. Indeed, for the century that passed between the intervention of Pecham and the activities of Islip the seniors at the exchequer functioned as a board of directors of a company of which the prior was at once chairman and general manager.

In default of a detailed account by a contemporary it is not easy to recapture the atmosphere of the deliberations at the exchequer, but it seems clear that the seniors enjoyed more initiative and exercised more control than either the purely advisory group of the Rule or the auditing body set up by Roman decrees. A committee with such prerogatives, it must be said, however efficient its work, does not easily adapt itself either to the patriarchal government of the Rule or the natural inclinations of an abbot jealous of power, and its rise could scarcely have taken place outside a cathedral monastery. In the event, it was, in its fully developed form, probably peculiar to Christ Church in the fourteenth century.

1 *Reg. Epp. J. Peckham*, II, 403–4.
2 *Reg. Winchelsey (C & YS)*, IV, 373, 378.

IV

Despite legislation, great diversity of detail prevailed in the English monasteries regarding the method and frequency of the audits. Originally it was laid down in general that the abbot should give an account to the seniors (or to the whole community) once a year, while the obedientiaries gave more frequent statements either to the abbot alone or to the abbot and seniors. The former of these audits was a principal means used by the Curia to prevent dilapidation; it was taken up into the canon law, was reiterated in the Benedictine constitutions of 1336, and has remained in force to the present day.[1] As is obvious, it presupposed the economy of the Rule, that is, the prerogative and responsibility of the abbot in all undertakings. Of itself, this legislation neither included nor excluded the abbot's feudal barony with its separate estates and economy, for canon law never recognized such separation; in practice, it seems that at some abbeys the abbot accounted for all, while at others only the community's share came into reckoning. On the other hand, it remained without application at most cathedral priories, where the prior had a small fixed allowance and the chapter or the central treasurers controlled expenses. Actually, it was consistently neglected by dishonest, autocratic and incompetent superiors, and figured constantly in chapter ordinances and visitation injunctions till the Dissolution. Under modern conditions, indeed, it needs very little technical skill to deprive a balance sheet of any real significance and to conceal doubtful transactions and actual losses from all who have no direct access to the books and lack a fair knowledge of accountancy, but medieval finance was less sophisticated and in any case there was, then as now, a dislike, deeply rooted in human nature, to submit to a reckoning. In addition, a peculiar psychological difficulty stood in the way of the community when faced with the necessity of pressing for a financial account, for they had been taught from youth by their Rule to consider themselves as without possessions or rights, and as having left all to their abbot as father and master. Finally, a small and illiterate community would have scarcely any interest in accounts.

The second audit, that of the obedientiaries to the abbot and seniors, was, to judge by surviving compotus rolls, more universally taken. Originally designed to be quarterly, or even more frequent, this audit came in time to be held once a year about Michaelmas, and was usually a continuation of the annual audit of the accounts of the manorial officials. The whole process, when taken seriously in a large house, was a lengthy one, occupying a month or more of the short claustral working days. In its original form this twofold audit was concerned with two statements: the *Status obedientiarum*, or rolls of the various monastic officials, and the *Proficuum maneriorum*, or accounts of revenue and expenditure on the

1 Wilkins, *Concilia*, II, 588 *seqq.*, 591, § 4.

various manors. The last, which must be distinguished from the accounts of day-to-day expenditure of the reeves audited on the spot by bailiff or warden, were nevertheless very elaborate in the age of demesne farming, since on them depended not only the income of the house, but all budgeting for the following year. At many houses, no doubt, the auditors had to grapple with detailed rolls such as are still extant; at a few, however, such as Christ Church, Canterbury, where the centralized financial system functioned fully, a sub-committee of senior auditors digested the individual accounts and presented the whole in a summarized form which gave their colleagues a *coup d'œil*, thus enabling the larger committee to judge the past and estimate for the future with a minimum of delay and misunderstanding.

Such were the general lines of the audit at the greater houses, but unquestionably there was divergence of practice in details. For at least one house we have the direct testimony of its abbot, in the middle of the fourteenth century. The abbot of Eynsham, writing c. 1363–6 to the Presidents, outlines a threefold audit: first, he says, the bailiffs and reeves of the manors present their accounts to the seniors, who are assisted by a professional layman; next, the cellarer (who appears to have been general receiver at Eynsham) gives an account of all moneys received by him; finally, the abbot gives a statement to the whole community of receipts and expenses, and presents what would now be called a balance sheet of the whole.[1]

Gerald of Wales, long before the end of the twelfth century, had compared the numerous and independent obedientiaries of the black-monk houses unfavourably with the single cellarer of the Cistercians. The treasury system was designed to remove this reproach, and was in origin intended to apply to all revenues. In practice, however, the treasurers rarely succeeded in securing such universal control. Most of the smaller gifts of the twelfth century were made for a specific purpose, and the land or funds involved were earmarked by the donor for the obedientiary concerned, such as the almoner, sacrist or infirmarian. Sentiment worked strongly against pooling such revenues, particularly when devoted to the almonry or sacristy, where they were felt to be in the nature of a sacred trust. Even at Christ Church the almoner's income eluded the treasurers, and elsewhere he and the sacrist had favoured treatment, though Pecham's injunctions to Glastonbury admitted no exceptions.[2] Many houses struck a compromise by allowing obedientiaries to receive all income assigned to them at the source; only unassigned money passed to the treasurers. This was perhaps the most common system of treasury working; it was, in the main, that established at Winchester by Henry of Blois, and when associated with the full exchequer audit the treasurers normally received any surplus held by the obedientiaries at the end of the year's working. The sum thus accumulated was treated as a kind of reserve fund, and after meeting a

1 *MC*, III, 41.   2 *Reg. Epp. J. Peckham*, I, 262.

number of regular small charges, some of which were perhaps inherited as conditions of the original donation, it was used chiefly to meet extraordinary expenses such as building costs and fees to counsel in litigation.

Thus the period from 1250 to 1336, which witnessed the most earnest and fruitful attempt to renovate the discipline of the black monks by capitular legislation, was also that in which high farming and the centralized control of finances were practised with the greatest success. Nowhere, perhaps, were the reserves of talent in a community enlisted so fully as at Canterbury under Henry of Eastry, but at Winchester, under its different system, the auditing committee functioned regularly all through the fourteenth century, and at Ely, under yet another species of control in which the whole community in chapter took a larger share than at Canterbury, the auditors, three in number, discharged their duties punctually and wisely, and doubtless assisted in placing the finances of the cathedral priory on a firm footing which was not lost even under the strain of the extensive building schemes of priors John of Crauden and Alan of Walsingham between 1321 and 1364.[1]

All available evidence, however, goes to show that auditing committees and the central treasury attained their maximum of efficiency in the cathedral priories, where there was scope for something of a democratic spirit. At abbeys, where the abbot had the initiative and all the temptations of power, and where the old obedientiary system often prevailed, with officials accountable only to the abbot, devolution continued to shackle financial reform, or was at best overlaid and not supplanted by a treasury which received only a part of the total income.

1 *V.* R. A. L. Smith, *The Regimen Scaccarii,* 81–3. Cf. *Ely Chapter Ordinances and Visitation Records,* ed. S. J. A. Evans (Camden Miscellany, XVII, 1940).

CHAPTER VII

THE AGRARIAN ECONOMY OF THE CISTERCIANS

I

The economy of the Cistercians had been in origin professedly different from, and more simple than, that of the black monks. Topographically, the white-monk abbey was not a quasi-urban group of buildings, owning manors scattered over the neighbouring countryside at greater or less distances, but a purely monastic group lying at the heart of a large non-manorial rural area; economically, while the black monks were supported by rents, dues and the produce of the demesne on a number of manors, worked largely by the unpaid labour of villeins, the Cistercians had been able at the start to plough up the land and place their farm buildings as near the abbey as they wished, and in exactly the situation they might choose; distant properties were exploited from sub-stations known as granges, and all were worked partly by the monks, but chiefly by the lay brothers, with such hired labour as might be found necessary; as regards administration, while the black-monk property was administered by a number of different officials enjoying all but complete independence, that of the white monks was all controlled directly by a single cellarer. The result of all these differences is noted more than once by Gerald of Wales: whereas the system of the black monks would create chaos and want when applied to a group of potentially prosperous manors, that of the white monks would soon evolve order and plenty out of a wilderness.[1]

Nothing, in fact, is more certain than the success of the early Cistercians in reclaiming waste and woodland to cultivation, and the new abbeys, after some twenty or thirty years, were all surrounded with arable and pasture admirably cultivated and fertile. In the few cases where the poverty of the soil baffled every effort, the monastery was transferred wholesale to a more promising site, and the complete control of the lay-out of the fields was so profitable in itself and so essential on all land that was to be cultivated by the monks in person, that it was the habit of the Cistercians, wherever possible, to acquire all rights over a manor or village and then 'reduce it to a grange' by exiling the previous inhabitants and pulling down their cottages.[2] This free, ring-fence or enclosure type of husbandry was throughout the middle ages typical of the Cistercians and other orders modelled upon them. In ways perhaps not foreseen by its originators it decreased overhead costs, simplified administration, economized labour

---

1 Giraldus Cambrensis, *Itinerarium Kambriae*, 45.
2 The phrase was 'redigere in grangiam'. Cf. *MO*, 350 and the example there cited (the reference to the Meaux chronicle should read I, 176).

and made possible all the transferences of stock and implements, and all the specialization of production necessary for successful large-scale commercial farming. The Cistercian system of granges articulated upon the home-farm and each developing to the full local advantages, for particular types of produce was, indeed, almost as influential and as efficient an instrument in the rejuvenating of European agrarian life as was the constitutional scheme of the *Carta Caritatis* in renewing religious discipline. In the fertile and ordered, yet spacious and not wholly developed, corn-growing districts north of the Humber the grange as a unit of agriculture stood outside the normal open-field strip-cultivation.[1] Elsewhere, in the midlands, East Anglia and the south, Cistercian husbandry was perhaps less distinctive, particularly when gifts or purchases of land from among normal manors could not be adapted to any grange. Finally, the Welsh abbeys, standing outside any ordered system of cultivation, were usually free to choose sites for plough-land and granges in the open valleys of Carmarthen and Cardigan, or in the straths of Merioneth and Carnarvon. Here, especially in south and west Wales, conditions were favourable to large-scale sheep-farming, in which, indeed, the larger abbeys engaged from the start when they had peace in their borders.

II

Writers on monastic history have often given their readers the impression that the Cistercians both originated and monopolized the English wool trade. Such a view is incorrect, even for the twelfth and thirteenth centuries.[2] Large flocks were being reared by the black monks and by ecclesiastical and lay landowners before the arrival of the Cistercians, and religious orders besides the white monks continued to keep large flocks for commerce throughout the middle ages. Nevertheless, it is true that the Cistercians were the first to develop sheep-farming for the export market on a really large scale, and they, together with the other new orders who imitated their economy and settled in the same districts, remained, at least until the fourteenth century, the most powerful group of wool-growers and the producers of the finest fleeces.

1 For a full description of the Cistercian grange in arable districts *v.* T. A. M. Bishop, *Monastic Granges in Yorkshire*, in *EHR*, LI (1936).

2 All previous accounts of the English wool trade were superseded by Eileen Power in her Ford's Lectures of 1939. These were published in 1941, without any apparatus of notes, as *The Medieval English Wool Trade*. This slim volume, so graceful in form, so pregnant in matter, is in fact an epitome of fourteen years' work undertaken with a view to writing a definitive history of the wool trade. This, it is to be hoped, will be accomplished by Prof. M. Postan.

Some additional information about Cistercian sheep-farming is to be found in R. J. Whitwell, *English Monasteries and the Wool Trade in the Thirteenth Century*, in *Vierteljahrschrift für Sozial- und Wirtschaftsgeschichte*, II, i (1904), 1–34, and H. E. Wroot, *Yorkshire Abbeys and the Wool Trade*, Thoresby Society, XXXIII (Miscellanea), 1935, 1–21.

The pasturing of sheep had always been an integral part of English husbandry. The sheep, indeed, had more uses than any other animal. Besides the wool, which was carded, spun and woven in every village, the ewes gave milk for direct consumption and for cheese-making, and though it was reckoned that one cow gave a milk yield equal to that of ten ewes, the need for large quantities of milk and cheese, and the comparative ease with which large flocks could be kept, led to their multiplication. In addition, the manure of the sheep when folded on the stubble in winter was of the greatest value, while the hoof—the little 'golden' hoof—when the flocks were ranging the pasture killed the weeds and matted the roots of the grass, whereas the heavy tread of the cattle turned a soft pasture into a morass.

The precise moment at which English wool was first grown for export is difficult to mark. At the time of *Domesday* the four eastern counties (including Cambridgeshire) carried some 150,000 sheep on demesne land. A little later the nuns of Holy Trinity, Caen, had 1700 on Minchinhampton Common in Gloucestershire, and in 1125 Peterborough had 1439 on demesne in thirteen manors.[1] Even if we suppose that the milk of all these flocks was used by the religious, some at least of the wool must have gone to market, and in fact we hear of Flemish buyers, the canons of Laon, touring the country c. 1130,[2] while Henry of Huntingdon c. 1150 gives cattle and wool as among the principal articles of export to Germany.[3] There is, however, little evidence of an organized trade or large-scale sheep-farming for the wool market before the arrival of the Cistercians.

Settling as they did away from cultivation and free of the shackling organization of manor and village, with limitless pasture for their sheep on mountain, moor, wold and marsh, with abundant service and an efficient central control, they began very early to have a large surplus from the year's clip which exporters and foreign merchants were willing to buy *en masse* for the looms of the new towns of the continent. They had, at least throughout the twelfth century, heavy advantages over the black monks who in the majority of cases kept their sheep scattered over their manors and exploited by half a dozen different obedientiaries, even if they had not been leased out with the land. The estimation and collection of the crop were therefore alike more difficult, and in fact the black monks did not as a rule deliver their wool graded, as did the Cistercians, but mixed and in bulk.[4] Among the new orders, on the other hand, conditions were ideal for

1 For these figures *v.* Power, *The Medieval English Wool Trade*, 30–5; J. H. Round, *VCH Essex*, i, 360 and R. J. Whitwell, *English Monasteries and the Wool Trade*, 14.
2 *PL*, CLVI, 975–7.
3 Henry of Huntingdon, *Historia Anglorum*, 5.
4 So Wroot, *Yorkshire Abbeys and the Wool Trade*, 8. Dunstable, however, a house of Austin canons with large flocks at Bradbourne in Derbyshire, graded its wool into *bona*, *grossa et lacci*. The typical threefold grading can be seen in the Kingswood accounts (*Documents relating to the Cistercian Monastery of St Mary, Kingswood*), in *Transactions of the Bristol and Gloucester Archaeological Society*, XXII (1899), p. 200: 'For 1 sack of middle wool £6. From 5 stone of better wool 31s. From lok £24. 18s. 7d.'

large-scale buying: the woolmonger could ride up to the abbey, learn at once the number and quality of fleeces to be shorn and the probable yield in sacks of wool; he could, if he wished, ride round the sheep-walks and inspect the flocks himself; he could fix the date of delivery, settle the price and cross the moors to the next abbey. The attention of the exporting merchants was thus quickly attracted to the white monks and canons.

In all this, the Premonstratensians, whose institute was based upon the Cistercians, and the Gilbertines, who took over their system of lay brothers, were indistinguishable from the white monks. All three orders settled in Lincolnshire, Yorkshire and the north, and very soon the wolds of Lincolnshire, the pastures of Holland, and the vast moors of Yorkshire and Northumberland were covered with the flocks of monks and canons, and as foundations multiplied the downs of Wiltshire and Dorset and the valleys of Wales were adding their quota to the flow of wool from the ports of the east and south.

III

According to the spirit of their legislation the Cistercian abbeys should have remained self-sufficing families, owning enough stock and tilling enough land for their own support and that of guests and poor, and acquiring no more beyond. But when benefactors vied with one another in giving, and when, after a few decades of laborious toil, the harvests poured in and the flocks gave their increase, the problem was a difficult one. Moreover, the white monks were faced by a very real lack of ready money with which to build on the grand scale or implement their estates with substantial farm buildings. The older orders, living on land long cultivated, had a steady income from rents, leases, tithes and church dues of all kinds; the white monks, at least so long as they preserved their original purity, had no cash income. Three forces, therefore, joined at the same moment to make a breach in the simple economy of the early Cistercians: the possession of surplus wool, the desire to build on the grand scale, and the woolmongers present at the gate with attractive offers of cash. It was still an era of free trade, and wool prices were rising steadily. There is no evidence that the white monks made any kind of stand against the forces that drew them back into the world, and they were soon knots in the great web of commercial life that had its centres in Flanders and Brabant, Tuscany and Lombardy. First, perhaps, came the small middlemen, carrying the wool to a port; then came the great merchants of Flanders and their agents; finally, when the floodgates of the south were opened at the end of the reign of John, came the still greater merchants of Venice and Florence.

To the straightforward selling of the year's yield to a woolmonger other transactions were soon added. The first of these was the undertaking of a selling agency for small proprietors. As soon as large-scale buying became common, the great landowners had begun the practice of sending round their neighbourhood to buy in the wool of the multitudes of small growers and peasant sheepowners in order to add it to their own in the bargain with the great merchant; this, at least in the first century of the trade, was to the advantage of all parties. The miscellaneous freight so gathered was known as *collecta*. The larger abbeys of white monks and canons in the north naturally attracted to themselves as focal points all the wool of the neighbourhood, and there is very early evidence that *conversi* were sent round to gather it in. This traffic, which was in direct contradiction to the spirit of Cîteaux, was explicitly forbidden by general chapter, but it was the common practice all over England with the great sheepowners, and far too lucrative to be dropped. Moreover, under the system of forward selling, greater bulk gave greater bargaining power, while a deficit in the home crop through pestilence or climatic vagaries could only be made good by putting in bought wool.

Next came the wholesale forward sale. Faced by the need of raising cash, either for buildings or to sink a debt incurred through misfortune or mismanagement, or simply attracted by a broker's offer, the abbey contracted for two or three or even twenty years ahead to deliver a specified number of sacks to the exporter, receiving spot cash either for the first year, or for several years of the period. In the latter case the sum received was in reality a loan on the security of the wool, and the merchant did not fail to take a hidden interest by a slight lowering of the price below market rates, or the exaction of an extra sack or two when collecting. Already as early as c. 1165 Louth Park was making a six years' contract with William Cade,[1] who had most of the celebrities of the day, both ecclesiastics and laymen, on his books, and the procedure soon became general. Such contracts, when the money had been paid in advance, hung like millstones about the necks of successive abbots; when the money had been spent, the contract remained, and if the clip fell short, the amount had to be made up from other sources without any profit.

Finally, when the merchants found from past experience or present distress that an abbey's contracts were not fulfilled, they insisted on some security besides the wool. Perhaps an extreme instance was the mortgaging of the abbey of Fountains in 1276 on the receipt of four years' advance payment for the wool crop.[2] Such a transaction was humiliating in the

---

1 H. Jenkinson, *William Cade*, in *EHR*, xxviii (1913), 221.
2 Wroot, 14–5. An unpublished MS. in Bodley's Library (Rawl. B 449, f. 9), quoted by Denholm-Young, *Seignorial Administration*, 55, n. 8, gives a list of English monasteries in debt to the Italians in 1291–4. Fountains had a debt of £6473 in 1291 and £3533 in 1294. At about the same time Glastonbury owed £801 to the Riccardi (1279) and Westminster 800 marks to merchants of Siena (1291). The period 1280–90 was one of great depression for the sheep-owners, owing to the first and most virulent outbreak of scab, which had a devastating effect comparable to that produced early in the present century by the Isle of Wight disease among English bees.

extreme to any who might recall the circumstances which had given birth to their abbey little more than a century before, but in practice it perhaps affected the rhythm of the normal life of the place little more than does the modern paper transaction by which a bank takes a lien on stock when allowing an overdraft to a well-secured firm or institution. The Italians were hanging thickly on England at the time; only three years later they were taking out a bull of excommunication against John Pecham for the costs of his election and enthronement, and almost all the great monasteries were in their hands for large sums. The great financiers of Florence and Siena had appetites like cormorants for deals and loans of every kind in England; they all failed early in the next century, and even at the height of their power they would have found it impracticable to sell up the premier Yorkshire abbey. In the sequel, the king took charge.

The Cistercian general chapter had from the first endeavoured to stop these irregular dealings. In 1157 the purchase of wool for resale had been forbidden,[1] and in 1214 the abbots of Fountains and Whitland had been deputed to investigate the conduct of the lay brothers, who were on the agenda of chapter for buying wool to sell at a higher price.[2] The practice, however, was too simple and too profitable to be allowed to cease, nor were the endeavours of the merchants of Lincoln in 1262 and 1275 more successful in preventing it, despite petitions to the king.[3] In the matter of forward selling, the chapter had pronounced in 1181 by a formal prohibition of any agreement for more than a year ahead; in no case was payment to be accepted before the wool had been delivered.[4] This, though completely disregarded, remained unrepealed and was re-enacted in 1277, but in the following year sales in advance for one year only were allowed. This was apparently felt as too rigid, and in 1279 the statute was modified to allow of anticipatory payments when the money was needed to pay off debts.[5] In the event, the peculiar circumstances of the time did not long continue. The Italian houses failed, and when lesser men, of whom many were English, took up the trade they were not eager to put up the necessary cash, and take the inevitable risks, connected with advance sales of wool.

1 *Statuta Capitulorum Generalium Ordinis Cisterciensis* (ed. J. M. Canivez), I, 61.
2 *Statuta*, I, 426 (1214), n. 45.   3 *Rot. Parl.* I, 156–7; *Rot. Hund.* I, 317.
4 *Statuta*, I, 89.
5 *Statuta*, III, 169, 175, 184. For examples of forward selling *v.* Denholm-Young, *Seignorial Administration*, 54, 56.

IV

Although the new orders had not originated the wool trade, the excellence of their produce and the ease with which it could be viewed and collected rapidly swept them to the top of the market, and from *c.* 1170 onwards for almost a century they were undoubtedly selling the bulk of the finest wool in the country. As no figures are available for the export trade in the early thirteenth century, it is not possible to say what fraction of the total wool crop of the country was monastic, but at the end of the century, when the production for the foreign market was approaching its peak, the whole monastic output can scarcely have been a tenth of the 32,743 sacks exported in 1273, or of the 35,509 sacks of 1310–11.[1] Long before then, the easy money to be found in large-scale sheep-farming had become visible to all, and the great landowners, ecclesiastical and lay, were throwing themselves into the business *à qui mieux mieux*. Already round about 1220 Thomas of Lancaster was pasturing 5500 sheep on his ranches in the Peak; in 1259 the bishop of Winchester's estates carried 29,000; in 1300 those of Winchester cathedral priory held 20,000; in 1303 Henry Lacy, earl of Lincoln, owned 13,400, while Peterborough and Crowland abbeys between them had 16,300; in 1322 the four custodies of Canterbury cathedral priory, at the height of its prosperity under Henry of Eastry, carried 13,730.[2]

Despite all competition, however, the northern houses of monks and canons were still the most distinguished group of wool-growers, and save for the small knot of sheepowners in Shropshire who clipped the finest wool of all—the famed 'Lemster ore'—the numerous monasteries of Lincolnshire offered the finest quality on the market. Valuable evidence of this exists in two lists, compiled by merchants of Flanders and Italy *c.* 1280 and 1315 respectively, which give the religious houses supplying wool to their market, together with the annual number of sacks available and in some cases the price demanded.[3] These lists are unfortunately treacherous unless used with great caution, as they do not tell us whether the number of sacks is the total available for export, or the number allowed to the mercantile house with which the compiler is connected. Isolated figures, in fact, from other sources show houses producing for other contracts far more wool than the total given by the Italian list, and in yet other cases the size of the abbey's flocks is known, and would give a larger yield than that of the lists. Some of the wool may well have been bespoken by brokers acting for English clothiers; this might account, for example, for the very low total of fourteen sacks credited to the large abbey of Waverley in

---

1 Power, *The Medieval English Wool Trade*, 37, calculates the latter figure; for the earlier *v.* Schaube, *Die Wollausfuhr Englands von Jahre 1273* in *Vierteljahrschift für Sozial- und Wirtschaftsgeschichte*, VI (1908).

2 For these figures, *v.* Power, 33 *seqq.*

3 A conflated version of these lists is printed as Appendix I by W. Cunningham, *The Growth of English Industry and Commerce*, I.

Surrey. In addition, the lists are far from complete, and omit such large sheep-owning houses as Glastonbury, Shaftesbury and Wilton abbeys.

Nevertheless, they are of the greatest interest as showing the preponderance of the Cistercians, Premonstratensians and Gilbertines. Of these three orders about four-fifths of the then existing houses are registered, whereas of the autonomous black-monk monasteries only a quarter appear, and of the Austin canons a smaller proportion still. Where quantities are given the figures, whatever their absolute value, suggest a relative strength of the same kind.[1] Fountains heads the list with seventy-six sacks, almost a third more than its nearest rival, Rievaulx, with sixty. Jervaulx comes third with fifty, which was the figure reached by Christ Church, Canterbury, as its absolute total at the peak of its productive drive, and by the largest owners among the Austin canons of the north, Bridlington priory. To what an extent comparatively small houses specialized in pastoral farming can be seen from the output of the Gilbertine priory of canons at Old Malton, which with forty-five sacks fell little short of Jervaulx and Canterbury, or from that of the still more undistinguished house of St Catherine's, Lincoln, whose thirty-five sacks surpassed the thirty of the large and wealthy abbey of St Mary at York.

It would materially assist in comparing the data from the various sources if a rough equation could be evolved between the number of sheep owned, the number of sacks of wool produced, and the profit made. The *Reules S. Roberd* of Grosseteste[2] calculates that a thousand sheep on a good pasture should give fifty marks ($£33. 6s. 8d.$) a year income, while from other sources it would appear that an average yield in sacks was in the neighbourhood of 4–5 per thousand sheep. The equation would therefore be 10,000 sheep = 45 sacks = $£336$. But such figures, it need scarcely be said, are of the roughest; they are in any case valid only for the period 1250–1300; both weight and price would vary greatly with quality, and an understanding would have to be reached as to whether the manure and milk of the sheep and ewes, which were each worth about a third of the price paid for the wool-clip, should be counted into the figure of the profits.

V

Large-scale sheep-farming was possible to the new orders largely because of their access to vast unenclosed sheep-walks. It was thus easy for them from the start to order their pastoral economy free of all conflicting interests and claims, and the sheepfarm could be an autonomous part of the establishment without the employment of any delicate manorial adjustments. In summer the flocks could roam the moors and wolds and marshes, under the care of shepherds supervised by lay brothers; on the Yorkshire

1 The output in sacks of the various houses is tabulated by H. E. Wroot, *Yorkshire Abbeys and the Wool Trade*, 9–10.
2 *Reules S. Roberd*, ed. Lamond, p. 145.

fells and the Welsh mountains they were no doubt based on shielings where milk was collected and cheese made, and the sheep themselves dipped and shorn; in the winter they could be driven down to sheepcotes near the grange and folded on the stubble. Few, perhaps, of the monks or even of the *conversi* spent the long summer days with the flocks in the pure air of the fells near the springs of Wharfe, or beneath the gullies of a Welsh crag, where the silence of the high places was broken only by bittern and curlew, by the mountain torrent and by the intruding sheep, but this, the daily life of the flocks, must have been familiar to some, at least, of the religious as a more constant reality than the rare bargaining with the Italian woolmonger.

Not all the Cistercian abbeys, however, lay in the folds of the hills, and many lowland houses kept their sheep in small flocks on village commons, or concentrated on a piece of marsh or rising ground. Such arrangements can be seen in some detail in the chronicle of the abbey of Meaux in the East Riding. The original holding of the abbey was in the river flats along the Hull, and the bulk of the flocks were concentrated in the marshland of Wawne and Sutton, where at one time eight sheepcotes held 2000 sheep.[1] The low ground in Holderness was in demand by sheepowners, and Sutton and its neighbourhood supported also the flocks of Isabella de Fortibus; from the sources of information that remain regarding the Aumâle and Meaux estates an interesting outline could be drawn of the two great sheep farms that marched in Holderness.[2] In addition, the abbey had sheep on a number of common pastures about its estates.

The chronicle of Meaux is also of value as showing the fluid character of even a large Cistercian abbey's economy; directed as it was by the abbot and his cellarer without intermediaries, its structure could be modified to suit the needs of the day; sheep could be sold and leases granted by one abbot, in need of cash, and the policy reversed by his successor.[3] As the bulk of the abbey's land was in long-cultivated districts, Meaux at first devoted its attention to arable and dairy-farming. Towards the end of the twelfth century, however, dairy produce proved less profitable than wool, and the monks changed over from cattle to sheep as the main stock, though their herds were never allowed to disappear entirely.[4] Some decades after the change, the chronicler inserts the interesting calculation that as five sheep could find pasture where only a single ox could feed, and as pasture for twenty oxen went with each bovate in Sutton, though only two were needed to plough its arable, ninety sheep could be put on the land in the place of eighteen cattle.[5] Meaux accordingly adapted its holding in Sutton to this formula, and *c.* 1270 owned there and elsewhere about 11,000 sheep;

---

1 *Chron. Mels.* (RS), II, 171, where there is a full and interesting description of the capacity of the marshland commons.

2 For this, *v.* Denholm-Young, *Seignorial Administration*, 58 seqq.

3 *Chron. Mels.* II, 175, 183, 222 et al.

4 *Chron. Mels.* I, 219: 'Cum vaccariae deficere incepissent, vaccariae in bercarias sunt conversae.'

5 *Chron. Mels.* II, 171.

abbot Robert at this time was able to bargain with merchants of Lucca for 120 sacks of wool.[1] The money, however, was long in coming, and when he resigned in 1280 the abbot left a debt of £3678, of which £2500 was to foreign merchants and moneylenders; his successor, Richard, leased land, sold wool in advance and reduced his flocks by lease and sale to 1320 sheep in order to bring the debt down to £1443.[2] This was to retrench too far, and in 1318, though the debt still stood at £1169, many of the leases had been recalled, and the stock had regained a total of 5406 sheep, 606 cattle and 120 horses.[3]

VI

The Cistercian grange, especially in the north and west, has often been considered as primarily a sheep station. No doubt some of the isolated granges among the fells of the West Riding or on the moors of Radnor were mere centres of assembly for the flocks, just as the farm of to-day in those districts lies among the stone walls behind a clump of sycamores without an acre of ploughland or a row of green vegetables between the kitchen door and the moor, but the Cistercian grange, even in Yorkshire, was more often a centre of agriculture, taking the place, in the economy of the white monks, of the manor in more settled land, and providing for sheep only as a part of its function.[4]

Originally, indeed, the grange had been instituted as a centre of husbandry of all kinds where the land to be cultivated was too far from the monastery for the monks and *conversi* to make the journey out to work and back each day.[5] It was not, on the other hand, to be too distant for constant supervision, and its inmates were even expected to return to the abbey for great festivals; the original plan was certainly for shifts to relieve each other, so that all might have periods of residence at home, while the grange itself contained a chapel and refectory, and was supervised by one of the monks who was a priest, and staffed by a team of *conversi*.

A grange of this kind can be seen in action as late as the beginning of the fourteenth century at Faringdon in Berkshire, through the fortunate accident of the survival of a custumal of Beaulieu giving rules for its conduct.[6] The large manor of Faringdon, the site of the original foundation which migrated to Beaulieu, was indeed situated at a greater distance from the abbey than was allowed by the Cistercian statutes, and in some ways resembled a black monk cell rather than a grange. It was kept by two choir monks and four *conversi*, all of whom were apparently permanently in residence, and lived on its own income and produce, sending up each year very considerable profits to Beaulieu.

1 *Chron. Mels.* II, 156.
2 *Chron. Mels.* II, 175.   3 *Chron. Mels.* II, 238.
4 For the Yorkshire granges *v.* the article of T. A. M. Bishop (*supra*, p. 65, n. 1).
5 *Consuetudines*, ed. Guignard, 72.
6 It is printed as Appendix III by Denholm-Young, *Seignorial Administration*.

A somewhat less elaborate, but not dissimilar, system can be seen from the financial accounts that have survived of the granges, apparently ten or eleven in number, of the Wiltshire abbey of Kingswood between 1240 and 1290.[1] Here a monk-warden had charge of one or more granges, apparently without permanently residing outside the abbey; to each was allotted a team of lay brothers, but the routine work of the farm and fields was done by hired labour; ploughmen, carters, cowherds, foresters and cooks appear on the wage-sheet, which is an extremely heavy one, containing well over a hundred regular labourers in addition to thirty-five shepherds and a number of hands to deal with the harvesting and storing of grain; the sheep for all the granges seem to have been dealt with apart, in some such way as the sheep farm with the black monks was often a seignorial, not a manorial concern.

More often, however, in the thirteenth century, as granges were multi-plied and the primitive zeal was lost, it became common to put *conversi* in charge of granges, and in command of the hired shepherds and labourers; the grange thus became a purely agricultural unit without religious significance. This system was open to grave criticism, and Cistercian history abounds in instances of *conversi* who betrayed their trust. Thus the Meaux chronicle records the destruction by fire of a valuable granary during a carouse of the lay brothers;[2] it also records the wholesale with-drawal, *c.* 1225, of the *conversi* from positions of trust in charge of granges, and their relegation to duties of carting and herding, and to the work of masons, carpenters, glaziers and plumbers.[3] Such a heroic measure, how-ever, was only possible while the religious life was still tolerably fervent and plastic; the more general practice was to give a grange to a lay brother, as to a bailiff, with the charge of producing a fixed yield of grain and other produce. Finally, a grange could be put under the care of a lay bailiff or reeve, and thus become equivalent in status to the normal manor of the black monks. Of this, again, the Meaux chronicle gives an example. The grange of Croo—so named, it would seem, from the most vocal of its tenants—lay in the open, wind-swept country by Beeforth near the sea. Despite its exposed position, it was completely sheltered and hidden by a thick grove of oak and ash and other trees which harboured a large colony of rooks. A certain villein who was administering the grange found the crying and calling of the birds so exasperating that he approached the abbot and obtained permission to deal with the nuisance. His method, effective if drastic, was to fell every stick of timber in the place, so that the farm buildings, now visible from afar, lay open to the four winds. Nothing could more clearly show the complete control exercised by one in charge of a grange of this kind.[4]

1 *V.* the account rolls in *Documents...of...Kingswood* (*supra*, p. 66, n. 4).
2 *Chron. Mels.* II, 109.   3 *Chron. Mels.* I, 432.
4 *Chron. Mels.* II, 48–9.

VII

As has been said, the Cistercians were by no means exclusively devoted to pastoral farming. Save perhaps for a few of the remoter Welsh abbeys, such as Kimmer and Cwmhir, the houses of white monks grew corn for the market as well as for their own needs. In the building up of their arable the grange took an important place. This, whenever it was established in open country[1] or on a manor or village of which the monks had complete control, resembled a large farmhouse in East Anglia or the dales of Yorkshire rather than the lord's hall of the medieval manor. The buildings contained quarters for the permanent staff and were made up of byres, cattle-sheds, dairies, sheepcotes and shelters for poultry; the grange was the administrative centre of the property which was delimited by a boundary often consisting of a dike, hedge or wall, and was divided into large areas of arable and meadow with no intermingling of strips or intercommoning on pasture. In Yorkshire in particular, where the monks had a freer hand owing to the regional, social and economic conditions and to the abundance of unclaimed land, the grange became a distinctive unit in the countryside, a self-contained demesne farm, worked by religious or hired labour with implements belonging to the owners, anticipating thus in the midst of the manorial economy the establishment of the gentleman farmer or prosperous tenant of an enclosing landlord of the late seventeenth century. Granges of this type were being formed in the Yorkshire dales in considerable numbers during the second half of the thirteenth century; they were held by monk wardens or *conversi* and exploited largely for the corn crop. Waste was eliminated by the consolidation of arable, and costs were relatively low; profits from sales could be correspondingly high. It is, therefore, not surprising that the white monks endeavoured wherever possible to reduce to the simplicity and order of a grange the tangle of strips and claims that made up the fields of a village, and to effect a total or partial consolidation by purchase and exchange. The large enclosures of the dales were perhaps peculiar to the north, but a typical south-country house such as Kingswood, lying in country where the Cotswolds fall steeply to the Severn valley, lived on its granges as well as its flocks, and in the middle of the thirteenth century sold corn to the value of some £50 a year, or about one-fourth of the value of its wool.[2]

In many cases, however, especially in less pastoral areas, the holdings that came to the Cistercians by gift did not permit of absorption in a grange, and in such cases they were worked by villeins or hired labour just as any other lord's land.

1 For the formation of several fields by assarting *v.* T. A. M. Bishop, *Assarting and the Growth of the Open Fields*, in *EcHR*, VI (1935).
2 *Documents...of...Kingswood*, 200–1.

VIII

The Cistercian financial system was in many ways simpler than that of the black monks. In the early days, when they held rigidly to the Rule, the cellarer alone under the abbot had any business or financial dealings. Such an arrangement, as modern experience has shown, works well even when a religious house has many points of contact with the world around it, but the preference, so marked in the twelfth century, for devolution and division of administrative powers, brought about a multiplication of officials and purses even among the white monks. Thus in one of the earliest sets of accounts that has been preserved, that of Kingswood *c.* 1240, the cellarer appears as paying the daily expenses of the house out of a lump sum received from the bursars;[1] the number of these is not specified, but it is they who present a complete account of the house's finances and make all extra-ordinary payments, as well as some regular ones. All receipts for the sale of wool, corn and stock, as well as all rents, passed directly to them, and besides handing over lump sums to cellarer and sub-cellarer they paid for stock and fodder and apparently also for all the regular, as opposed to the casual, labour employed on the estates. The year was divided into two unequal parts, running from St Peter in Chains (1 August) to St Andrew's Day (30 November), but accounts were rendered annually for the year ending on 1 August.

At Beaulieu *c.* 1300 the system was somewhat different. Here the financial responsibility lay with the warden of the *camera* (an official, it would seem, identical with the warden of the rolls elsewhere referred to)[2] who received all surplus moneys from the officials and wardens of the granges and paid out an allowance to them, save in the case of certain granges which were self-supporting. A treatise has survived which gives a series of elaborate rules for accounting and for arriving at a statement of profits; care is taken to eliminate from the final balance-sheet all cross-payments and cross-deliveries of goods between officials. According to this document Beaulieu had a threefold audit. Every Monday morning the warden of the rolls, together with the *custos ordinis*, sub-cellarer, porter, monk-baker, monk-cellarer, infirmarian (a lay brother), lay marshal and guest master, examined the weekly expenses of the infirmary, guest-house, marshalry, cellarer, office of works and sub-cellarer. Four times a year the warden of the *camera* himself stood audit before the abbot, while once a year, at or about Michaelmas Day, all officials and wardens of granges submitted their accounts.

The institution of the *camera* was so bound up with financial methods at Beaulieu that not only was there a lesser *camera* at the abbey itself, of

---

1 *Documents...of...Kingswood*, nos. XII and XIII.
2 Denholm-Young, *Seignorial Administration*, 169; where the *monachus camere* is apparently the *custos rotulorum qui pro tempore fuerit.*

which the functions are not clear, but a miniature *camera* was established at the large grange of Faringdon.[1] Beaulieu had been founded directly from Cîteaux; its arrangements therefore were doubtless a replica of those obtaining at the mother-house *c.* 1200.

IX

The typical white-monk economy underwent a number of changes during the fourteenth century.

In the first place, the gradual establishment of a monopoly at the wool staple and the failure of the great Italian merchant houses ended the days of long forward contracts, and the monks, like others, sold to lesser English middlemen, either for export or for the home cloth trade. The days of great profits and overseas debts alike came to an end.

Secondly, the rise in value of a labourer's hire, the gradual emancipation of the villein class, and the growing prosperity of the small leaseholder and peasant cultivator towards the end of the century combined with the visitations of pestilence to dry up the resources that supplied *conversi* to the white monks and canons, just as in the present century the rise in wages, the betterment of living conditions and the ease of access to cities and industrial districts has lessened the supply of lay brothers to the farming abbeys of Central Europe and the United States.

Thirdly, the Cistercians, like the older orders, found costs rising without a corresponding advance in market prices, and tended to realize their assets by leasing land and even stock to small men. When, in the following century, they had lost their *conversi* almost entirely and had become in large part *rentiers*, they retained little save their larger flocks and surviving grange economy to differentiate them from the older monastic orders to which at first they had stood in such notable contrast.

---

1 *Seignorial Administration*, 169: 'Unam (*sc.* cameram) in manerio de Farend' cuius curam habet socius custodis dicti manerii, et in omnibus habet modum et formam camere abbatie.' The grange of the monks was not at the modern Faringdon, but at Great Coxwell, less than two miles distant, where the tithe barn, perhaps the most splendid example of its genus in the country, still exists.

CHAPTER VIII

THE SYSTEM OF VISITATION

I

If historians must deplore the lack, from the death of Matthew Paris onwards, of chronicles and other biographical and literary works comparable in fullness and intimacy to those illustrating English monastic life immediately after the Conquest, they command, as some compensation, for a great portion of the later middle ages, a source of information both detailed and unexceptionable, which was not available for earlier centuries. The voluminous records of the episcopal visitations of religious houses are indeed incomplete in many respects; numerous orders and individual houses were wholly exempt from the bishop's surveillance and, while many episcopal registers have disappeared, others which survive retain their records only in a fragmentary or abbreviated form. Nevertheless, sufficient material exists and has already been printed to enable the historian, at least at fairly regular intervals throughout the centuries concerned, to gain a tolerably clear view of significant cross-sections of English religious life.

The black monks of the twelfth century were, as has been seen, almost entirely immune from visitation. Within the body itself, no machinery for the purpose existed, and with a few rare exceptions towards the end of the period no bishop exercised his ancient canonical right in the matter. An occasional legate and, later in the century, an archbishop with legatine powers were the only authorities who made a few sporadic visitations in this country. Meanwhile, the success of visitation in all the new orders, and some flagrant examples of misconduct never brought to book till too late, caused a demand for visitation to be a leading feature of the programme of reformers and critics.[1] This demand was met in full by the Lateran Council, and during the thirteenth century, an epoch that might well be called the golden age of visitation, the monasteries received attention from no less than five classes of visitors.

The great Council, when establishing provincial chapters, set up also a system of visitation modelled on that of the Cistercians, while at the same time it proclaimed the right of bishops to visit non-exempt houses, and demanded that this right should be exercised. Furthermore, reforming popes such as Gregory IX and Innocent IV organized on occasion a special visitation to be executed either by the Ordinary or by delegates appointed

---

1 For visitations before the Lateran decrees and for the desires of reformers, *v. MO*, 649–54, 670. For a detailed account of the development of visitations in the thirteenth century, *v.* C. R. Cheney, *Episcopal Visitation of Monasteries in the Thirteenth Century*.

for the purpose. In addition, papal legates *a latere*, who visited England from time to time, had powers of visitation, while during this century metropolitans all over Europe were endeavouring to vindicate their rights of visitation throughout their province, and several exercised this right at the expense of the monasteries of the land.

The Lateran decrees, enlarged somewhat by the decretal *Ea quae* of Honorius III, established the visitation of all houses of monks and nuns by visitors elected by the provincial chapter.[1] The duty was not entrusted to the presidents of the chapter, perhaps because the Council envisaged the presidential office as concerned merely with the conduct of the chapter; in any case, the great number of houses to be visited in the southern province would have made the task too great for them. At first, then, it was the practice to elect or appoint in chapter two visitors, who were usually, but not always, abbots or the priors of cathedral monasteries, for each diocese; later, visitors were assigned to groups of dioceses, and were instructed to set out in the spring of the year following the September chapter. Later, it was decreed that the visitors must be prelates with jurisdiction, not simple members of a community or priors of a dependent house, but this rule was not strictly kept.[2]

Records of these visitations are singularly meagre. No articles survive; there are few allusions in the chapter documents and surprisingly few in contemporary monastic chronicles. In all probability the *acta* of visitation were destroyed when the visitors had made their report to the subsequent chapter, for there was no standing presidential chancery, as there was for the bishops, where archives might be preserved.[3] With this dearth of evidence it is not easy to judge how effective the system may have been. No doubt the periodical examination of all houses by officials charged with the promulgation and enforcement of the decrees of chapter helped to maintain and standardize discipline and observance, but the visitors had no powers before or after their visit, nor had they the power of deposing an unsatisfactory superior, and an acquaintance with the working of a similar system in more recent times would suggest that such men, visiting houses of their own order, and keenly aware that in due course their own measure would be meted to them by others, would rarely act in a very drastic or revolutionary manner. Certainly, in the relatively few cases of serious decadence in the thirteenth century of which records survive, it is the bishop who acts with energy, and there is no mention of the purely monastic visitation which must have preceded the bishop's. In theory these capitular visitations were triennial, like the chapter meetings; no information exists as to their actual frequency.

---

1 The decretals *In singulis regnis* and *Ea quae* (Decret. Greg. IX, Lib. III, tit. xxxv, cc. 7 and 8) are in *MC*, I, Appendix I.

2 Cf. *MC*, I, 24, 51, 54, 87; II, 9. For all details see the very full index.

3 At the present day the visitor's decrees (often of a purely formal nature) are preserved and read in public on stated occasions, but the *procès-verbal* is not usually kept.

The second visitor was the diocesan bishop. The Lateran Council, indeed, set the Ordinary in his old canonical position as the authority principally responsible for the supervision of monastic discipline. It is he who is to reform the monasteries, so that the visitors from the chapter may find nothing to correct, and it is he, not they, who has the power of deposing a superior. In practice, also, it was soon seen that a strong and zealous bishop such as Grosseteste of Lincoln or Walter Cantilupe of Worcester could exert a very powerful influence, and it is the bishops who are found dealing with the really relaxed houses. Many of the bishops, however, were absent for long periods or lacked the personal interest or moral superiority needful in a reformer. Moreover, half a dozen of the most important abbeys were exempt. Speaking generally, also, it was not until the middle of the century that episcopal visitation became normal. In 1233, therefore, and again in 1251 a reforming pope felt it desirable to give personal orders for a general visitation by the diocesans, with the view of promulgating a set of statutes. In the earlier of these, under Gregory IX, the work was done with some thoroughness, and three visitors—the Cistercian abbot of Boxley, a distinguished man who later became abbot of Cîteaux, the Premonstratensian abbot of Bayham, and the precentor of Christ Church, Canterbury—were appointed to deal with the exempt houses. The thorough nature of the reforms proposed by them, and especially by the abbot of Boxley, who is said to have been violent in his methods, led to the formation of a league to appeal to the Holy See.[1] In the later papal visitation, when the Gregorian decrees were again enforced, visitors were appointed as before for the exempt houses, but this time, since they were all black monks themselves, they were less obnoxious. Nevertheless, attempts were once more made to set up a league of the abbots of the exempt houses concerned.[2]

From the middle of the century onwards, records of episcopal visitations become more common, and for its later decades documents survive from a number of dioceses; this evidence will be considered more fully below.

The third and by far the rarest visitor was the legate a latere. In the years immediately preceding the Lateran Council, visitations by legates in England had not been uncommon, and in 1234 papal delegates assisted the enforcement of the Gregorian decrees in this way,[3] but after his time the legate Ottoboni, though making some visitations in person and by commissaries, was in general content to promulgate his decrees and leave their enforcement to the normal agencies of bishop and provincial chapter.[4]

The fourth visitor was the metropolitan. Throughout the century,

---

1 *Ann. Dunstapl. s.a.* 1233.

2 *MPChM*, v, 208, 226, 258.

3 *V.* R. Graham, *Visitation of Bury St Edmund's and Westminster in* 1234, in *EHR*, xxvii (Oct. 1912), 728–39.

4 Ottoboni in 1265–8 visited exempt monasteries such as Westminster and Sempringham, and attempted to visit the Cistercians by deputy. *V.* R. Graham, *Cardinal Ottoboni and the Monastery of Stratford Langthorne*, in *EHR*, xxxiii (April 1918), 213–25.

archbishops all over Europe were asserting their right to visit all institutes, bodies and churches in the dioceses of their province. This claim naturally aroused the ordinaries, and was equally distasteful to secular chapters and religious bodies, but when cases were referred to Rome the decision, given for the first time in broad outline by Innocent IV in the decretal *Romana ecclesia*, was generally in favour of the metropolitan, and only the exempt houses were able to maintain complete immunity.[1] The first comprehensive visitation was that made by Boniface of Savoy in 1250–1; coinciding with the general visitation ordered from Rome, it had repercussions among the monks, while the bishops, who had assembled in strength for the dedication of Hayles abbey at which Grosseteste officiated, adjourned to the neighbouring abbey of Winchcombe in November 1251, to draw up an appeal to Rome, which proved fruitless.[2] In 1253 Boniface made a still more extensive tour in East Anglia;[3] his example was followed by Kilwardby and still more thoroughly by Pecham, who visited houses of monks and nuns in nearly every diocese of southern England and Wales.

II

The common form taken by the visitation records has often been described; only a brief summary will be given here. The procedure, minutely established by canon law and the rubrics, was unchanging throughout the centuries between the Lateran Council and the Dissolution. The bishop's visitation, in theory annual, was in practice made at irregular intervals which were determined by the energy and other commitments of the Ordinary, the extent of his diocese, and the needs of particular houses. Its frequency, even under the most zealous prelate, rarely exceeded a quadriennial incidence, and if an average were to be struck over a long period for a considerable number of houses the interval would be found to be much greater than this. As the episcopal visitation was the type and original of all others, it will be sufficient to give in broad outline the procedure followed by the Ordinary. The visitors from chapter proceeded upon the same lines, though with somewhat less solemnity of ceremonial.

A set form was prescribed for every stage of the visitation.[4] The bishop's arrival was preceded by his mandate and a citation of all to appear before him on a fixed date. After his ceremonial reception, the receipt of this mandate was acknowledged and the superior presented his credentials

1 *MPChM*, VI (Additamenta), 188; Cheney, *Episcopal Visitation*, 135–6.
2 *Ann. Dunstapl. s.a.* 1250; *MPChM*, V, 120–5, 186.
3 *MPChM*, V, 382; *Ann. Wig. s.a.* 1260; Cheney, 142–3.
4 The best brief account of the visitation procedure is that by A. Hamilton Thompson in his introductions to vols. I and II (pp. ix–xiii and xliv–lxix respectively) of *Visitations of Religious Houses in the Diocese of Lincoln* (Lincs Rec. Soc. 1915, 1919), where the interpretation of the evidence also is fully discussed. The conclusions are substantially those arrived at independently and almost simultaneously by Dr G. G. Coulton, *The Interpretation of Visitation Documents*, in *EHR*, XXXIX (Jan. 1914); cf. also Cheney, *Episcopal Visitation*, 54–103, where the different stages of the visitation and local variations are fully dealt with.

of appointment, together with evidence of the canonical foundation of the house and a statement of its financial position. The visitor then proceded to the chapter-house, where in larger monasteries a sermon was preached, and then either in person or by deputy gave private audience to every professed member of the house, beginning with the superior. The information given, the complaints lodged and the accusations made were entirely voluntary and personal; the religious were asked, in a long and elaborate questionnaire, if, in their opinion, the Rule, constitutions and customs of the house were observed, and whether discipline and administration were satisfactory. They might answer that all was well, and so depart, or that certain matters stood in need of reformation and that certain persons were culpable. While there was a strong moral obligation to expose abuses, no one was examined as to his own conduct, even if this had been the object of criticism. Notes were taken of all that had been said, and the schedule so compiled furnished the *detecta*, or facts revealed. From these the visitor formed his conclusions as to the matters to be dealt with; these were officially known as the *comperta*, or information gathered, and the basis of his subsequent action, which might include an examination of those accused, or their admission to compurgation or clearance from the charges on the sworn testimony of a fixed number of persons. Both these processes might be adjourned. The visitor then departed, unless some unusually drastic step was to be taken, such as the removal of a superior, and when occasion served—sometimes after a considerable interval of time—he forwarded his injunctions or series of decrees for the better conduct of the house. These, if the visitor were a man of energy and method, translated into statutes of general application measures directed primarily against individual shortcomings, and the measure of success achieved in this is a fair indication of the intelligence and efficiency of the bishop and chancery concerned.

When a bishop or his notary had to deal regularly with a large number of visitations, certain formulae were inevitably beaten out which were used again and again. This has led some writers to put forward the opinion that many or most of these sets of injunctions are mere common form having little or no relation to the state of things in the house concerned. Such a view has been shown to be quite untenable. When a large number of contemporary injunctions are compared, as they can be in the York registers of our period, or in those of Lincoln a century later, where every stage of their manufacture can be examined, it is seen at once that though they are largely permutations and combinations of similar elements, they vary in number and wording from place to place in a way that can only imply an attempt to deal with concrete cases within the framework of a formula designed for repeated use. If we find that even the most vehement and scathing denunciations could be stereotyped and filed, so to say, against a future need, this is an example, not of thoughtless and perfunctory treatment, but of that formalism which is typical of the later medieval centuries. Nevertheless, in some of the southern and midland sets it is clear that we are presented simply with a set of religious constitutions, or a repetition of previous decrees, or a rehearsal of important points of discipline, rather than with injunctions based directly on *comperta* elicited in the visitation. Consequently, here as in all other questions of the interpretation of these documents, judgement and experience are necessary, and it is precisely this that makes of these dry and formal records matter worthy of the historian's attention.

III

Visitation records, the majority of which have been published only within the last fifty years, have taken their place as a principal source of evidence in all recent estimates of the state of religious discipline in England. Dealing as they do directly with the morals and religious behaviour of individuals, and affording of necessity innumerable glimpses of everyday life, they are certainly, within limits, a most valuable source of knowledge. At the same time, they can be used with profit only if their limitations are clearly grasped.

Of these limitations, the most obvious is a direct consequence of the purpose of all visitations, which is the detection and punishment of failure, whether moral, disciplinary or administrative.[1] The specific information given to the visitor by the religious had to do with faults; if the examinee had neither accusations nor complaints to make he used the colourless phrase 'all is well'. Occasionally, indeed, an exceptionally devoted bishop would praise an abbot's or a prior's administration, but as a general rule the positive achievements of a house receive no mention, still less is any place found for a record of the strivings, successes or holiness of the individual; while the harshness, incompetence and moral delinquencies of superiors are freely canvassed we have no picture of conscientious devotion to duty.

This determinant is indeed common to all visitations, medieval and modern; others are peculiar to the middle ages. One such is the absence of any lawful, and often also of any physical, means of escape from the obligations of the religious state. At the present day those who have mistaken their vocation, or who have developed psychological illness or even failed seriously in morals, can in more than one way—by transfer, by special employment, by secularization or by dispensation—find a respectable *modus vivendi*, while those who frankly break with their obligations and abandon their profession can at least mingle unrecognized with their fellow-citizens and make for themselves what career they may. In the medieval world this was not so. Lawful means of relief were few; mental and psychological illness was often, and that not only in religious houses,

---

1 For a contemporary questionnaire, *v. Ann. Burton.* pp. 484–6 (*s.a.* 1259). For Archbishop Winchelsey's articles of inquiry for bishops, chapters, secular canons, nuns and monks (these last more than fifty questions), *v.* B.M. Cott. Galba E, IV, fos. 61–5.

treated as moral delinquency or at least as liable to coercive treatment; if a subject abandoned the habit he was an apostate who might be recaptured by episcopal or royal agents and either imprisoned by them or returned for punishment to his monastery. In consequence, rebels, fugitives and apostates who in modern times are, if the phrase may be used, written off the books of an institute, remained then as a kind of running sore in the visitation records. Moreover, in the modern world, at least in many countries, there is an *esprit de corps* in all societies, whether hospitals, regiments, colleges or religious bodies, which shuns, whenever possible, even a quasi-public washing of soiled linen. In the middle ages, where denominational rivalry did not exist, and where purely conventional reasons for reticence were almost universally absent, complete frankness prevailed in all cases where the parties were not interested in preserving silence for strictly personal motives.

Yet the apparent frankness of the visitation documents must not be allowed to lull the reader's critical faculty to sleep. They were spoken in secret, and it may be with warmth and without reflection, in the perturbation of the moment and behind closed doors; they must now be surveyed coldly upon the printed page. It is not easy to separate honest denunciation of real evil from the irresponsible gossip of the malevolent or the neurotic, or to decide whether collusion or torpor, rather than the true peace of charity, has prompted the *omnia bene* of deponents in a house where fervour is not likely to have been present.

The visitation records may be studied for more than one purpose: to ascertain the methods, aims and efficiency of the bishops and the system; to obtain an intimate knowledge of the daily life of the monasteries; and to collect material for a judgement on the state of the religious life of the age. All these topics may receive some illustration in the pages that follow, but before ending these words of introduction a historian may be allowed to express a regret that it should be necessary to make any use at all of such intimate documents. They were not compiled or preserved for his eye or indeed for the eyes of any outside the chancery of the bishop. The information that they contain was given in private and in confidence to a lawful authority charged with a grave spiritual responsibility. The dead as well as the living have a right to their good name, and the accidents of time which have made public property of the visitation dossiers do not of themselves entitle the historian to bruit abroad the failings and weaknesses, the vagaries, the quarrels and the recriminations of those long since gone to their reckoning, and to present them as a fit subject for the strictures or the flippancies of another age. It is, however, no longer possible, even were it desirable, to treat these records as if they did not exist. They have been published and commented upon, and since the silence of a single writer would no longer avail to protect the dead, it seems to be rather the historian's task to use this copious source of information as fully as may be for his lawful purposes.

CHAPTER IX

THE FIRST CENTURY OF VISITATION: (I)

I

The systematic visitation of such religious houses in England as were not exempt from the jurisdiction of the Ordinary began, as is well known, soon after the Fourth Lateran Council of 1215. Prior to this, visitation by those of their own habit was unknown among the black monks and black canons, and the right and duty of the diocesan to visit, though it was an ancient practice sanctioned by early canons and decretals, was in fact rarely exercised in this country before the pontificate of Innocent III. In contrast to this, among the new orders, such as the Cistercians and the Premonstratensians, regular visitation had from the first been an integral part of their constitution. They were, however, exempt from episcopal surveillance, and therefore experienced no change in the thirteenth century. For the two older bodies, still the most numerous in England, the black monks and the black canons, together with the nuns who followed their Rules, the years immediately after the Council saw the opening of two series of visitations: the triennial visitation by two religious of their own habit appointed in provincial chapter, and the less regular visitation by the diocesan undertaken in the course of his periodical tours through the diocese.[1] In addition, the regulars who did not depend immediately upon the Apostolic See were liable from the middle of the century onwards to receive a call from the archbishop of Canterbury when he visited the dioceses of his suffragans.

The full records of these visitations, if all or most had been preserved, would enable the historian to form a fairly adequate judgement upon the state of discipline and observance of the religious from decade to decade, as also to ascertain what were the common or most serious faults of each generation and what measures were taken (and with what success) by superiors to remedy them. Actually, however, the necessary documents do not exist. For the period 1215–1350, during which each house must have been visited some forty times by the Order, not a single set of injunctions from the monastic visitors has survived, and only one set has been accidentally preserved from the Austin canons.[2] Nor is the case better with episcopal visitations in the early years. Probably bishops did not become

---

1 Throughout these pages each episcopal register is noted in full on its first occurrence; thenceforward it is quoted by the bishop's name only.

2 For this, a visitation of Newstead in 1261, v. infra p. 90. From the black monks a few scattered sets of injunctions survive from legates or papal visitors commissioned by Gregory IX; two such have been printed by Dr Rose Graham in EHR xxvii (Oct. 1912), 728–39, Visitations of Bury St Edmund's and Westminster in 1234.

generally active for a decade or two after the Council.[1] Registers do not survive in any number before c. 1270, and the earlier ones, such as those of Hugh de Wells (1209-35) and Grosseteste (1235-53) of Lincoln, contain no visitation dossiers, and this is the case also of some later ones, such as those of Lichfield. Even when, from 1270 onwards, registers are available and are more ample in scope, the visitation records are far from complete; indeed, it may be said that no register of the thirteenth and fourteenth centuries contains details of half the visitations which the bishop is known to have made, and that before 1400 instances of the occurrence of the first two out of the three pieces—detecta, comperta and injunctions—making up the dossier can be counted on the fingers of one hand;[2] all that is usually recorded, even in the best of registers, is the set of injunctions and notes of punitive measures.

Nevertheless, when all these reservations have been made, a plentiful supply remains for analysis. Between c. 1270 and 1350 some twenty-five of the surviving episcopal registers contain visitation injunctions, and three more have records of metropolitan visitations. In addition, a few scattered documents from earlier days are preserved in the latter registers, while the diocese of Worcester has also the record of visitations undertaken by the prior during the vacancies of the see after 1300. When set out side by side for the decades immediately before and after the year 1300 these records of visitation cover the diocese of York and almost the whole of the province of Canterbury save for the large midland and eastern bloc of Lincoln, Ely and Norwich. They contain in all particulars of more than 150 visitations, made up from ninety-odd houses of Austin canons, some forty black-monk houses and some twenty-five dependent or alien priories, and to them may be added the summary notices of the state of more than thirty Cluniac monasteries during the period.[3] From all these it should be possible to construct a composite picture of the condition of the older bodies of religious houses shortly before and after 1300, and to note at least the most common weaknesses and the changes (if any) during the period. Such a synthesis is all the more desirable since visitation records have never been used to present a coup d'œil of the religious life during a single limited period.

1 For an account of the beginnings v. C. R. Cheney, Episcopal Visitation of Monasteries in the Thirteenth Century.

2 A fragment of the notes of detecta, i.e. evidence given by the religious, from a visitation of Battle by Pecham in ?1283 is preserved on the back of a notice inserted in his register (Registrum J. Pecham (C & YS, 1910), 198-9. An example of comperta, i.e. a list of faults based on the evidence and drawn up by the bishop, is seen in a visitation of Bolton in 1267 in Register of Walter Giffard (Surtees Soc. 109 (1904)), I, 145-6. V. also A Visitation of St Peter's Priory, Ipswich [c. 1327-36] by C. R. Cheney, in EHR, XLVII (1932).

3 The publication of episcopal registers, long neglected, has gone forward sporadically during the last sixty years under the auspices of a number of archaeological or learned societies and through the devotion of private individuals. The circumstances of the appearance of these volumes account for the widely different methods adopted by the editors in dealing with great masses of matter, consisting largely of documents in common form. Some of the earlier editors were content to give an abstract in English amounting to little more than

II

Of all the collections, the series most important in virtue of duration and fullness is that of York, a diocese which in the middle ages included the county of Nottingham, the northern part of the modern Lancashire, and parts of the modern Westmorland, not to speak of the isolated peculiar of Hexham. In all this vast area, the archbishop had under his supervision only three large abbeys of black monks, together with two smaller but important priories. He had, however, a host of Austin canons, some twenty houses in all, and for these one or more sets of injunctions exist in the case of all but five, rising to a maximum of seven for Newstead and six each for Bridlington and Thurgarton. This is certainly very different from the profusion of records existing for the tours of Archbishop Rigaud of Rouen, but it is enough to give matter for fair general judgements.

The earliest extant register is that of Walter Gray for the last thirty years (1225–55) of his long rule; it contains only one full set of injunctions.[1] After this, there is a gap till 1266, when the very full register of Walter Giffard[2] begins the series which continues with only very short intervals during vacancies till the death of Melton in 1340. The earliest injunctions that have survived, are those of Gray at St Oswald's, Gloucester, in 1250, and at Newstead in 1252;[3] they are followed by some of Godfrey Ludham also at Newstead in 1259.[4] The two sets of Gray contain detailed instructions as to the receipt of money; it is remarkable that the two financial systems outlined differ widely; in view of this, and of the dates, more than

a calendar of the contents; later publications have tended to be fuller, and the Canterbury and York Society, founded in 1904 for this precise purpose, has issued a most valuable series of Latin transcripts complete save for the purely formal parts of routine documents. This method, adopted also by some editors for the Hampshire Record Society, is indeed the only satisfactory one, and however impatient medievalists may be to have all extant registers in print, most would prefer to suffer the inevitable delay if a full transcript were finally to result. In addition to two or three given in the Rolls Series, the following regional societies have printed registers: the Cantilupe Society (Hereford; in conjunction with the Canterbury & York Society); the Hampshire Record Society (Winchester); the Lincolnshire Record Society (Lincoln); the Somerset Record Society (Bath and Wells); the Staffordshire Historical (orig. William Salt) Society (Lichfield and Coventry); the Surtees Society (York and Durham); the Sussex Archaeological Society (Chichester); the Worcestershire Historical Society (Worcester); and, for Wales, the Hon. Society of Cymmrodorion (St David's). For Exeter, the late Prebendary F. C. Hingeston Randolph devoted himself for more than twenty years to the publication of the series of Exeter registers, which has been continued since his death. A description of the registers and a summary list of those printed to date (1916) was given by R. C. Fowler in his booklet *Episcopal Registers*. For the Cluniacs Sir G. F. Duckett published records in his *Visitations and Chapters-General of the Order of Cluni.*

1 *Register of Rolls of Walter Gray*, ed. J. Raine, SS, 56 (1872). The injunctions are those to Newstead in 1252 (app. p. 210) and a single decree for Marton in 1234 (*ibid.* 261).

2 *Register of Walter Giffard*, ed. W. Brown, SS, 109 (1904).

3 *Reg. W. Giffard*, DCCVI, pp. 203–6 (Gloucester); *Reg. Gray*, 210 (Newstead).

4 *Reg. W. Giffard*, DCCXV, pp. 212–13.

thirty years after Gray had succeeded to York, it would seem probable that the pertinent injunctions reiterated those given previously, and that the archbishop in both cases accepted the domestic arrangements of the houses concerned.

With Walter Giffard (1266-79) more data become available: his injunctions follow no set pattern: sometimes he endorses those of a predecessor, elsewhere he issues sets, long or short, to suit the particular circumstances. Under William Wickwane (1279-85), an able administrator with monastic family connections who had come north with Giffard and was familiar with York business, the injunctions become fuller, but still show no tendency to formalize.[1] Certain items recur constantly—the cloister doors are to be better kept, there is to be no drinking after compline —but the variety of the injunctions shows the personal care of the archbishop, who was clearly a conscientious, if not a spiritual, man. Many details of the life of the canons appear: the office is hurried and there is a tendency to feign illness in order to avoid the lessons at matins and the strain of singing;[2] the canons of Newburgh and Cartmel have been hunting;[3] those of Bridlington are keeping and boarding horses and hounds.[4] At Kirkham they have been shouting each other down when intoning the chant, and idiots, clowns and vagabonds make use of the refectory.[5] At Healaugh Park they wander too freely in the forest, and at Bolton they follow young Romilly up Wharfe and over the moors.[6] Often there is a personal touch: at Drax the prior has taken unwise advice from hangers-on, while the sub-prior has avoided trouble by keeping his bed; Hugh de Rykhale is docked of Sunday meat as a punishment for past indulgence, and must go last in the community for quarrelling; Elias, hitherto sub-cellarer, has clouted John of Lincoln: he is sent back to the cloister and must ask pardon of his victim daily for two months.[7] In the ordinary matters of discipline one or two points out of half a dozen recur in almost every list: drinking after compline must cease; carols are to be inspected frequently for private property; the cloister doors must be better kept; miscellaneous arrivals must not stray into the refectory; the amenities of the infirmary must not be abused by malingerers, nor used by healthy canons who feel the need of a fire and a drink. At a few houses there are more serious disorders: Marton in 1280, Thurgarton in 1284 were faced with financial ruin. The canons of Marton, irregular as they were, had only themselves to thank, but the archbishop, nevertheless, took time from his hours of sleep

---

1 *Register of William Wickwane*, ed. W. Brown, *SS*, 114 (1907). Wickwane came from Child's Wickham near Evesham; his brother was abbot of Winchcombe.

2 *Reg. Wickwane*, n. 184, p. 55 (Newburgh); n. 302, p. 87 (Bridlington, where office is recited *sincopando*).

3 *Ibid.* n. 184, p. 55 (Newburgh); n. 440, p. 148 (Cartmel).

4 *Ibid.* n. 302, p. 87.

5 *Ibid.* n. 303, pp. 88-90 ('simplices, viles, scuriles et vagi in refectorio...altercatio et strepitus in prosis et cantibus inchoandis').

6 *Ibid.* n. 427, p. 130 ('in boscis nimis spaciose'); n. 428, p. 131 ('per moras et nemora').

7 *Ibid.* n. 430, pp. 134-6.

to devise means to relieve them; this he achieved by sending them a prior and three efficient canons from Newburgh in exchange for three of their own number.[1] At Thurgarton, after careful consideration, he ordered all revenues to be pooled till the debt sank; he had previously issued an earnest exhortation, unique in the series, that fit religious instruction be given to the lay brethren.[2] Unique also is his confirmation of a grant by prior John of Warter, who had assigned thirty shillings a year for sweet-meats to his community as a reward for their agreeing to chant the office more slowly and reverently.[3]

Wickwane was followed by another diocesan official, John le Romeyn (1286–96), who showed himself an equally conscientious visitor, giving particular attention to financial arrangements.[4] Romeyn's successor, Newark, left no injunctions, and Thomas Corbridge (1300–4) was not long in office, though records survive of his treatment of two depressed houses and of his readiness to allow impropriation as a remedy for want.[5] William Greenfield, the next archbishop, a Gloucestershire man with experience in York administration (1306–15), is chiefly remarkable for the detailed and personal attention he gave to those convicted of serious faults, and for a consistent policy in rearranging the finances of the canons.[6] The series ends with the hitherto unpublished register of William Melton (1317–40), which has been used by regional historians and which shows the archbishop carrying on the tradition of painstaking supervision.[7]

The Yorkshire visitation records are thus very numerous, but they are so widely distributed over time and space that it is difficult to reduce their evidence to order. Perhaps the readiest way to grasp the problems that faced the diocesan is to consider the records of the three houses of canons that were visited six times or more during the period.

Newstead in Nottinghamshire provides the only set of injunctions found in Walter Gray's register. It is remarkable that this, one of the earliest recorded visitations, should contain the warmest praise given by any archbishop. Gray, in 1252, testified that he found the canons fervent religious, lovers of peace and concord both among themselves and in relation to others. He left no injunction of any significance save a precise

1 *Ibid.* n. 442, p. 151 (Marton): 'Misere et vix reparabili ruine cui vos et domum vestram impellentibus lasciviis et demeritis vestris supponi conspicimus, pro reparacione vestra sollicitas cumulavimus vigilias.'

2 *Ibid.* n. 752, p. 313; cf. n. 437, p. 146: 'Injungimus priori et conventui firmiter coram Deo, quod conversos suos circa devotionem et opera meritorum fideliter instruant et informent, ne eorum sanguis in extremo examine a nostro vel eorum manibus requiratur.'

3 *Ibid.* n. 306, p. 90: 'Quia dilecti filii Johannes subprior et conventus noster jam solito devocius Deo serviunt et psalmodizantes pausas longiores in medio cujuslibet versus ad exhortacionem nostram benigne faciunt.'

4 *Register of John le Romeyn*, ed. W. Brown, SS (2 vols.), 123 (1913) and 128 (1916).

5 *Register of Thomas of Corbridge*, ed. W. Brown, SS (2 vols.), 138 (1925) and 141 (1928).

6 *Register of William Greenfield*, ed. A. H. Thompson, SS (4 vols,), 145 (1931), 149 (1934), 151 (1936), 152 (1937).

7 *V.*, for example, the articles on religious house in *VCH, Yorks*, III, by T. M. Fallow for Selby, 97–8, Whitby, 102–4, York, 109, Bolton, 197–8, Bridlington, 202–3, etc.

ordinance as to the compilation and auditing of the accounts.[1] Seven years later, in 1259, Godfrey Ludham reiterated Gray's statutes, adding a few of his own: the prior is to study how to win the love of his brethren and is to take their advice.[2] Two years later, in 1261, the visitors of the Order were at Newstead and their injunctions are preserved; no others of the kind survive from the thirteenth century. They are concerned entirely with small points: the sick are to have a good servant, with his boy; suitable food is to be provided for them, and they are to have the services of a canon to say Mass and the Hours for them; the diet of the community is to be improved; all income is to go to the receivers.[3] Twenty years later, in 1280, Wickwane found things less satisfactory. The prior neglected his religious duties; the sub-prior was equally slack and often out of the house; three canons were penanced for serious moral faults.[4] Thirteen years later, in 1293, Romeyn found the place in debt with two quondam priors on its hands; the sacrist was deposed and a decree issued against dicing.[5] Nine years later, in 1302, Corbridge found Newstead in still worse case; numbers and assets were shrinking, and in spite of past injunctions no accounts of any kind were kept. He appropriated two churches, and brought in the prior of Felley to form, with the prior of the house and two canons, a committee of management.[6] Two years later he complained that his injunctions had not been obeyed: the canons were to frequent the cloister and pray, not wander abroad; to remedy the insolvency no novices were to be taken, the staff was to be cut down to three stableboys, a porter and an infirmary servant, and only two horses were to be kept—at grass when not working, the careful archbishop added, and on corn only when at work.[7] With this Newstead passes from view.

Bridlington in 1280 was small and poor and could afford no novices; the office was scamped, and canons were habitually absent on manors or at home or malingering in the infirmary; horses and hounds were plentiful, some kept and others boarded by the canons and lay brothers. The root of the evil was the prior who ruled by favourites with no second in command.[8] Seven years later, in 1287, Romeyn found the place still unsatisfactory; six canons were confined to the cloister for varying periods and a long set of injunctions was issued, including precise financial regulations. Among the prohibitions was the entertainment of Jews (perhaps creditors); there were too many servants and the town was full of pedlars and hucksters who brawled about the place; the stables were still too full.[9] In 1311 Greenfield, before coming to reform the house, sent a canon to do penance at Hexham

---

1 *Reg. Gray,* 210: 'Per examinationem singularem comperimus tam Priorem quam canonicos in religione fervidos, et tam in invicem quam ad alios pacis et concordiae amatores.'
2 *Reg. W. Giffard,* 212–13. 3 *Ibid.* 213–15.
4 *Reg. Wickwane,* n. 435, p. 143. 5 *Reg. Romeyn,* n. 903, pp. 317–19.
6 *Reg. Corbridge,* DCXLII, p. 228, where he requests the presentation of a balance-sheet *sine quo et male vixistis hactenus.*
7 *Ibid.* DCCLI, p. 280. 8 *Reg. Wickwane,* n. 302, p. 87.
9 *Reg. Romeyn,* n. 561, pp. 199–202.

and confined another at home. On his visitation in 1314, however, he had nothing very severe to say, though the place could still support no novices and long financial regulations were reissued.[1] It was still in debt at Melton's arrival in 1328, and hounds and horses were still in evidence. Three years later the prior resigned, and the sub-prior and cellarer were deprived of office. Three years again passed, and the archbishop had little to reprehend.[2]

Thurgarton in Nottinghamshire was visited by Giffard at an unknown date previous to 1276, when he left a series of injunctions covering the ordinary shortcomings, together with a detailed financial scheme. In 1276 he found these were not observed; he repeated them with special emphasis against wandering abroad, and with a decree of imprisonment against a canon who had written an abusive pamphlet against him.[3] Four years later Wickwane found an inefficient prior who had given responsibility to unsuitable lay brothers; after a few commonplace injunctions he added the solemn exhortation already referred to regarding the converses.[4] Four years later the place was in dire straits, and Wickwane ordered all revenues to be pooled.[5] In 1286 there were serious accusations against the prior, and though he succeeded in canonically purging himself of a charge of incontinence, he was apparently replaced by a canon of Nostell who, after some years of unquiet rule, asked to be allowed to return home.[6] In 1304 Corbridge found things in a desperate condition. Gross carelessness had produced chaos and poverty; the fault was the prior's, and the archbishop, after endeavouring to mend matters by removing his opponents, finally deposed him.[7] It was not long before the feckless sub-prior and community were petitioning for his return; they already had two other quondams on their hands they said, and neighbours had it that they were so bad a lot that no prior could cope with them. The archbishop, however, stood his ground, and after quashing an election which was apparently intended as a *reductio ad absurdum* appointed a new prior.[8] From these depths there appears to have been a certain recovery; in 1308 the house is still in debt, but the injunctions are conventional.[9]

III

The trouble that might be given by a single house, and the pains that bishops were willing to take, is nowhere better shown than at the small priory of Blyth in Nottinghamshire belonging to St Katherine's at Rouen and manned chiefly by Norman monks. Godfrey Ludham was there in 1261; he republished the decrees of Gray with routine additions. In 1276 Giffard sent some injunctions: there was irregularity at office; the

1 *Reg. Greenfield*, III, n. 1539, p. 194; n. 1618, pp. 223–6.
2 *VCH, Yorks*, III, 202.   3 *Reg. W. Giffard*, DCCCCXV, pp. 316–18.
4 *Reg. Wickwane*, n. 437, pp. 145–6.   5 *Ibid.* n. 752, p. 313.
6 *Reg. Romeyn*, n. 711, p. 245; cf. n. 278, p. 104.
7 *Reg. Corbridge*, DCCXLII, pp. 272–3. He comments bitterly: 'Vos et illi de Novo loco de eodem calice jam bibistis.'   8 *Ibid.* pp. 274–9.   9 *Reg. Greenfield*, IV, n. 1736, p. 28.

obedientiaries were unsatisfactory and no accounts were available.[1] In 1280 Wickwane approved some regulations of the abbot of St Katherine's and added a few of his own.[2] In 1287 Romeyn sent a criminous monk back to Rouen and ordered the prior to treat his subjects kindly and provide an inventory and accounts. In the years that followed the archbishop was often troubled by Blyth. Early in 1288 he sent back an undesirable monk to France with a request for reinforcements of a better type. A few years later he suggested that French monks should never stay more than four or five years; it was natural, he said, that they should be homesick. Shortly after, he returned the impossible Robert de Angeville home for the second time, together with another whose health was the worse for the climate of the Trent valley, while remonstrating with the abbot for recalling useful men.[3] Corbridge in 1303 found the prior old and sick; at his request the abbot appointed another.[4] Archbishop Greenfield in 1307 issued a conventional set of injunctions with some financial items: the prior had never presented accounts; he must do so and appoint a bursar and cellarer.[5] Before anything could be effected the place was reduced to the brink of ruin by a visit from the king and his entourage on their way to Scotland. In spite of this, the abbot of St Katherine's sent out two more monks to come upon the strength; Corbridge riposted by returning a couple of nostalgic Normans.[6] His troubles were not yet ended: the next year he was forced to send back another misfit and ask for a replacement for the old and paralysed prior.[7] With the new appointment Blyth disappears from sight.

From the mass of York injunctions for the canons three particular evils stand out; all are endemic to religious bodies and indeed to all organized groups of men: personal immorality, weak and unspiritual government, and poverty seeking refuge in debt. Perhaps the surest rough test of a visitor's earnestness is an examination of his success in dealing with bad superiors. Judged in this way, none of the archbishops showed himself a reformer of the type of Grosseteste; on the other hand, none was prepared to let a scandalous situation develop indefinitely. Giffard deposed an unsatisfactory prior at Bolton and an immoral one at Felley;[8] Wickwane acted firmly, though certainly not prematurely, at Selby, and Corbridge at Thurgarton.[9] The most disquieting case is one of Greenfield's. Shortly before his death he was faced by several difficult situations. At Worksop,

---

1 Both these are in *Reg. Greenfield*, IV, 1754, p. 40–1.

2 *Reg. Wickwane*, n. 439, pp. 147–8.

3 *Reg. Romeyn*, n. 730, p. 253; n. 757, p. 269; n. 762, p. 272. It is significant that the clerk noted this letter for future use as common form: *forma scribendi quando mittuntur intolerabiles monachi de Blida abbati suo et ut mittantur meliores ibidem. V.* also n. 842, pp. 298–9 ('cum natale solum, racione originis, quisque diligit ex natura'); n. 844, p. 300; n. 853, p. 302.

4 *Reg. Corbridge*, DCCXV, p. 262.   5 *Reg. Greenfield*, IV, n. 1697, p. 11.

6 *Reg. Greenfield*, II, n. 775, p. 48 ('qui natale solum sciciunt et aere proprio desiderant recreari').   7 *Ibid.* IV, n. 1807, p. 61; n. 1828, p. 67.

8 *Reg. W. Giffard*, DCCCCIII, pp. 302–4; DCCCCXII, pp. 313–14.

9 *Reg. Wickwane*, n. 75, p. 22. *Reg. Corbridge*, I, DCCXLII, p. 273.

in a visitation of which no record remains, the prior had been found guilty of incontinence and dilapidation. Nevertheless, he was allowed to remain in office. He did not improve and was deposed.[1] A month later the archbishop deposed the prior of Newstead.[2] In the same summer he visited Newburgh, where less than two years previously he had deposed the sub-prior and found a cellarer who had been in office for thirty years without rendering accounts. Now, the prior John de Foxholes admitted immoral relations with several women, married and single. Nevertheless, the bishop considered that the interests of the house and the prior's own deserts warranted his further tenure of office.[3]

IV

The York registers give very full information regarding the punishment of private religious. If a canon or monk was diffamed (that is, notoriously suspected) of immorality he was given the opportunity (if he did not confess) of purging himself canonically by the support of a number of his fellows, and the impression given by the York records is that such purgations, at this period, were generally *bona fide*, though it is probable that in most cases the accused had acted in some respects reprehensibly. If he failed to produce compurgators, or confessed, he was invariably punished either at home or in exile. The penance took the form of confinement to church and cloister for a fixed period, together with restrictions of diet, disciplines in chapter and sacramental confession at regular intervals. In extreme cases close confinement was imposed, though it was rare at this period, and was usually accompanied with the proviso that the culprit should receive frequent friendly visits. These penances are detailed with care, and in their severest form were certainly formidable. William de Wadworth, for example, a peccant monk of Monk Bretton, was sent to Whitby with the following sentence: he was to take the lowest place in choir, cloister, dormitory and refectory; on Wednesdays and Fridays he was to fast on bread and vegetables; he was to follow the strictest observance, not to go out, and not to celebrate Mass. Bretton allowed Whitby fifty shillings a year for his keep.[4] This was a penance of Romeyn's; a few years previously he had sentenced a repentant lay brother of Newburgh who had apostatized: he was to be placed at the grange of Hood where he was to work on the land and follow the plough-tail in place of a hired labourer; twice a week he was to fast on bread and vegetables, and thrice a week was to receive the discipline from the canon in charge of the grange.[5]

---

1 *Reg. Greenfield*, IV, n. 2000, p. 149. This *déposé* has given his name to the Tickhill Psalter, of which he was the scribe; *v. infra*, p. 303.   2 *Ibid.* IV, n. 2011, p. 154.

3 *Ibid.* III, n. 1291, p. 71; n. 1325, p. 80 ('ponderata utilitate monasterii...attentisque persone sue meritis').

4 *Reg. Romeyn*, n. 505, p. 178; cf. n. 361, pp. 131–2.

5 *Reg. Romeyn*, n. 447, pp. 161–2 ('ubi agriculture vacet et caudam aratri teneat loco cujusdam mercenarii').

The reluctance of houses to receive penitents who might or might not give edification may be readily understood, but the Ordinary had canonical powers in the matter, and in a large diocese such as York there was a wide choice of hosts. The financial difficulty was sometimes met by an exchange, sometimes by the settlement of a pension, and occasionally by the relatives of the culprit.[1] Isolated references in the registers appear to indicate that the treatment was more successful than might have been expected, and that the bishops took a genuine interest in the welfare of their convicts. The penances were exactly performed, as is seen by their relaxation or cancellation after a term of good behaviour, or their commutation when health was impaired.[2] Greenfield was particularly careful, and on one occasion is recorded to have sent his official to ascertain the dispositions of a culprit, in order that his mother, who was in distress at her son's plight, might see that he was in good health.[3] No doubt much depended on the root cause of the moral failing: the pervert or the psychopath rebelled under correction, broke prison and apostatized, while a young man who had fallen through yielding to a sudden passion was often truly penitent.[4] If the record of the register has a formal, legal ring, it must be remembered that any personal advice or sympathy that may have been given would necessarily escape all record.

V

The canons bulk large in the York registers. Of the three black-monk abbeys Whitby does not appear at all, save for a word of praise,[5] before the time of Melton, and St Mary's York only figures twice, when it was in debt. Selby, however, a house with a peculiarly bad record, gave trouble more than once. When Giffard visited the parish in 1275 he heard the worst reports of the abbey. The abbot was said to keep mistresses in the town and on his manors, and similar accusations were made against three of the

---

1 Thus the friends and relations of a canon of Hexham put up 5 marks *p.a.* during his stay at Bridlington (*Reg. Greenfield*, III, 1613, pp. 220–1). This was considerably above the pension to Whitby noted in the text, and the 4 marks noted in *Reg. Greenfield*, II, n. 695, p. 13; it is to be hoped that the increase was reflected in the quality of the canon's *maigre* fare.

2 Cf. *Reg. Greenfield*, IV, n. 2013, p. 156; n. 2042–3, pp. 174–5.

3 *Reg. Greenfield*, II, n. 704, p. 20 ('ut eum sanum videat quia mesta').

4 Cf. *Reg. Greenfield*, II, nos. 695, 706, 808 (pp. 15, 21, 55) for the downward progress of a monk of Selby, and *ibid.* nos. 982, 1005, 1030, pp. 140, 153, 169, where William de Appelton, confined to cloister at Bolton, indulged in nocturnal poaching and was reduced to a single kind of fish; five months later he was up for battery of a secular cleric, and in consequence lost his fish on Fridays and gained another day's discipline; four months later still his brethren got rid of him by exchange against a canon of Thurgarton. Cf. also the case of the incorrigible canon Leonard of Marton (whether lunatic or cracksman does not appear) whom Wickwane passed on to the priors president, *cum nulla serura ferrea eidem possit resistere quia eam infirmet ad libitum et dissolvat.* (*Reg. Wickwane*, n. 445, p. 153.) For a case from the west, where a monk of Peterborough, sent to Athelney, escaped twice *v.* Drokensford's register (*v. infra*, p. 102, n. 1), I, 8.

5 *Reg. Romeyn*, n. 505, p. 178 (1293): 'ubi regula monachilis salubriter et stricte, sicut confidimus, observatur.'

monks, the worst of them, black Alexander, having a particularly unsavoury reputation.[1] We are not told what steps, if any, Giffard took; they were certainly not effective, for when, five years later, Wickwane visited the abbey he heard a list of charges without parallel even in the York registers. After the cautious statement that Abbot Thomas did not observe the Rule of St Benedict, his accusers went on to explain that he never celebrated Mass, was rarely in choir, chapter or refectory, and remained in bed while his chaplains recited Matins; he ate meat publicly with layfolk on his manors and when at home did not abstain even on Wednesdays. He had alienated and lost property of the house, and had given manors to relatives, and minions; he was incontinent with two women, and excommunicate on a series of counts, including that of drawing blood from three monks, one of whom he had hauled out of choir. Finally, he had spent much money on a sorcerer in an attempt to get the corpse of his drowned brother out of the Ouse. The register qualifies him as quite incorrigible; he was deposed, and accepted the verdict.[2] No other visitation of Selby is recorded for fifty years, but there are indications that the house was constant to its traditions. In 1306 Greenfield sent two of the monks for penance: the one went to Whitby with what may be called the maximum sentence, which after six months told upon his health; the other's exile was at St Bee's, whence, after a year, he apostatized.[3] When Melton visited Selby in 1324 he found nothing remarkable, but ten years later the pest had broken out again, and six monks were accused of incontinence, and of spending the monastic funds on women.[4]

VI

The most common fault with which the archbishops had to deal was mismanagement. During the seventy years covered by the York registers very many of the houses were in financial distress, some of them chronically. It was a time of prosperity for intelligent high farmers, but it was also a time of rising prices, and few if any of the Austin priories benefited so much by the first condition as they lost by the latter. Apart from isolated calamities, such as the floods that periodically devastated the banks of Ouse and Derwent, and the advent of royal armies or of Scots, the cause of distress was usually sheer bad management, aggravated by the reckless granting of corrodies and the maintenance of superfluous dependents and miscellaneous guests. All the archbishops reiterate their commands for the establishment of a financial system which was, after all, common law for the church and expressed in the current statutes of monks and canons. From a comparison of various injunctions we can construct the framework of the system as it should have been: the bailiffs or sergeants on the manors

1 *Reg. W. Giffard*, DCCCCXIX, pp. 324–6 ('et fetidissimus est').
2 *Reg. Wickwane*, n. 75, p. 23 ('et est incorrigibilis omnino').
3 *Reg. Greenfield*, II, n. 695, pp. 13–14 (at Whitby); for the other exile, *v. supra*, p. 94, n. 4.
4 *VCH, Yorks*, III, 97–8.

are to give accounts in spring and autumn to the cellarer or obedientiaries concerned, who tour the estates at Easter taking an inventory of the stock and receive the year's yield at home in the autumn; the bursars or receivers in the monastery take in all moneys and issue funds against tallies to the cellarer and principal officials. Between October and Christmas each year all account: the bailiffs to the obedientiaries, the latter to the bursars, and these in their turn to an auditing body of prior and seniors, who have before them extents, rent rolls and the balance-sheet of the previous year. Finally, the prior gives to all in chapter a summary statement of the year's profit or loss.[1] Such was the system: but the reiterated injunctions, now on this point, now on that, show the difficulty of keeping this or any other rational scheme working in small houses where happy-go-lucky methods were preferred. The bursars or receivers in particular were constantly dropping out of commission, and often no yearly account was given and no inventory of stock taken. This, when once an extravagance or misfortune had upset the forecast, landed the superior in debt with no certain knowledge of his assets for the coming year or of the best means of retrenchment.

1 Interesting economic injunctions are in *Reg. Gray*, p. 210 (Newstead, 1252); *W. Giffard*, DCCCCXI, pp. 316–9 (Thurgarton, 1276); *Romeyn*, n. 561, p. 200 (Bridlington, 1287); *Greenfield*, III, n. 1618, pp. 224–5 (*ibid*. 1314). That Giffard's injunctions are for Thurgarton, not Felley, as the editor suggests, appears from the reference to Hugh of Farndon there and in *Reg. Romeyn*, n. 946, p. 330 (*v. supra*, p. 91, n. 3).

CHAPTER X

THE FIRST CENTURY OF VISITATION: (II)

I

Away in the west midlands the registers of the neighbouring dioceses of Worcester and Hereford can be surveyed over the same half-century. Hereford, it is true, had only three houses of canons and three small houses of monks, but several of these were perpetually in trouble and provide copious information. Worcester for its part was rich in monasteries, with five major black-monk houses and several communities of Austin canons ranging from the abbeys of Bristol and Cirencester in the south to the small priory of Studley in the north. Both sees had able bishops: at Hereford the well-connected Thomas of Cantilupe, the future saint, was succeeded by his loyal official Richard of Swinfield, to be followed in turn by the energetic Adam of Orleton. At Worcester the long reign of Godfrey Giffard, brother of the archbishop of York, was followed after an interval by the distinguished 'good clerk', Thomas de Cobham.

Godfrey Giffard (1268–1301), like his brother, was a good administrator, at least till years told upon him, and it is unfortunate that only a few of his injunctions survive.[1] Generally speaking, there is little difference between those to monks and to canons. Indeed, he occasionally served identical lists on large houses of both orders. In one of such pairs the two abbots are accused of dilapidation and of supporting unnecessary servants; the office is neglected by the community and there is a failure at every level of the administration to render accounts, with the result that no one knows what they have or what they spend. The specific remedy proposed is the familiar one of two treasurers.[2] At almost every house there is the same insistence on financial reorganization, together with familiar points of discipline: houses in the town must not be frequented; the doors of the monastic buildings must be kept shut; meat-eating must be regularized and hunting discontinued. Sometimes the bishop found nothing to reprehend.[3]

None of Giffard's injunctions for the smaller houses survive, but he was troubled with two disorderly priories, each of which exemplifies the causes of the worst irregularity. The one, the alien priory of Wootton Wawen, a dependency of Conches, shows well enough the unsatisfactory conditions of a small house composed chiefly of foreigners. Lasting friction between the prior and one of the monks ended in a disgraceful

---

1 *The Register of Bishop Godfrey Giffard*, ed. with introduction and appendices by J. W. Willis Bund for the Worcestershire Historical Society (2 vols 1902).
2 *Reg. G. Giffard*, II, 100 (St Augustine's, Bristol) and 104 (Tewkesbury).
3 E.g. II, 233 (St Augustine's, Bristol) and 243 (Worcester) in 1284 and 1286 respectively.

fracas in which the prior used his fists upon his subject.[1] More important was the case of Great Malvern, a replica in miniature of that of Evesham eighty years before and, like its predecessor, one of the most familiar of medieval monastic scandals. Malvern, originally a colony of hermits from Worcester, became c. 1100, for reasons which have never been fully investigated, a dependency of Westminster, a house that owned a number of manors in Worcestershire. When the abbey in due course from being a royal *eigenkirche* became an exempt house depending directly on the Apostolic See, its members claimed similar liberty, though it is not clear that Malvern consistently refused admission to the bishop. There is no record of any friction till 1282, when Giffard had already been fourteen years bishop of Worcester, only a few miles away, and the presumption is that Malvern had not been disorderly for long. Now, however, the prior William de Ledbury, a local man, was the object of the most serious accusations; the charges included fornication, adultery and incest with no less than twenty-two women. Giffard, in the autumn of 1282, visited the priory and deposed the prior, apparently without encountering serious opposition from the community.[2] A new prior, William of Wickwane, a namesake of the contemporary archbishop of York and a nephew of Cardinal Hugh of Evesham, was appointed and sent up to Westminster for confirmation. On arrival, however, he was thrown into prison by the abbot, who claimed sole jurisdiction at Malvern,[3] whereupon the deposed prior came to the surface again and took control, while Giffard, after excommunicating him and his followers, informed the cardinal of his nephew's plight, appealed to Pecham for support and wrote to Cardinal Hugh and to Robert Burnell of Bath and Wells, then chancellor, asking him to make things clear to the king, to whom Westminster was peculiarly a matter of concern. Before any action could be taken the metropolitan, Pecham, on tour in the west, arrived at Great Malvern to visit the place. Like Giffard, he broke his teeth on the privileges and departed, adding his excommunication, renewed at short intervals, to that of the diocesan.[4] Meanwhile, Westminster had appealed to the pope, and though judges delegate were in favour of the bishop, a direct confirmation of Westminster's exemption was obtained from Rome. Peace was then made by the king's good offices, one of the manors of Malvern was transferred to the bishop as compensation for the loss of jurisdiction, and the excommunications were lifted, leaving Ledbury, on whom the searchlights had ceased to play, *in situ*.[5] It was only some four years later that he was deposed by the abbot.

The register of Thomas de Cobham (1317–27) contains fewer injunctions

1 *Reg. G. Giffard*, II, 129–33.   2 *Ibid.* II, 164.
3 *Ibid.* II, 178. *Reg. Epp. Peckham (RS)*, II, no. cccxxix.
4 *Reg. Pecham*, nos. ccccix (first excommunication, 23 March 1283), ccccxxi (repeated, 11 May), ccccxl (and again, 18 June). Later, Pecham wrote to Cardinal Hugh, 23 Feb. 1284 (ep. dxvi). Cf. *Reg. G. Giffard*, II, 170, 178, 181–210.
5 *Reg. G. Giffard*, II, 219. *Ann. Wig. (AM*, IV, 494) *s.a.* 1287.

than that of Giffard.[1] The longest set is to the small priory of Little Malvern, where numerous decrees are followed by the statement that the bishop found much more worthy of commendation than demanding correction.[2] Cobham's sense of responsibility appears most clearly at Studley, where the small house of canons, after wasting its income and admitting more recruits than it could support, was suffering also from internal discord. The bishop appointed a local rector to manage the place, and the series of letters, in which this reluctant parson was brought up to the scratch and his path smoothed by the temporary removal of the prior, shows the bishop at his best.[3]

The diocese of Hereford has an unusually complete set of registers which have fortunately been printed in extenso. In area one of the smallest in medieval England, it had no autonomous monastery, and only three houses of canons, but such religious as existed were able to give successive bishops an amount of trouble out of all proportion to their numbers.

The earliest register, that of Thomas of Cantilupe[4] (1275–82), contains injunctions only for the priories of Wormesley and Chirbury. Both were in debt, and were forbidden to receive novices while poor; at both, also, a prohibition was necessary against admitting women and guests into the precinct.[5] At Leominster Cantilupe came up against an obstacle similar to that encountered by Giffard at Great Malvern. The priory was a cell of Reading, and a previous bishop, Hugh Foliot (1219–34), had renounced all claims of jurisdiction over it. The people, however, had rights over part of the monastic church, and a visitation of the parish naturally flushed game from the neighbouring cover. In 1275 Reading was heavily in debt, and the preoccupations of the mother-house led to slackness; all was not well at Leominster, and in 1281 the prior had been deposed by the abbot. A year later Cantilupe heard of serious charges against the sub-prior, who failed to answer the bishop's citation and appealed to Canterbury. Friction between the bishop of Hereford and Pecham had recently broken into flame, and the archbishop inhibited Cantilupe from proceeding.[6]

Richard of Swinfield (1283–1317), Cantilupe's confidant,[7] took up the Leominster case, but after all relevant documents had been produced was compelled to confirm its exemption. There were then nine monks, including the prior, but three years later the numbers had fallen and the liturgy

---

1 *Register of Thomas de Cobham*, ed. E. H. Pearce (Worcs. Hist. Soc. 1930). This has been transcribed in greater fullness than previous Worcester registers, and is supplemented by Bishop Pearce's painstaking biography *Thomas de Cobham* (1926).

2 *Reg. Cobham*, 153 seqq.

3 *Ibid.* 33–42. On p. 224 there is a curious example of the interplay of lawlessness and legalism: a canon of Studley, who had taken a hand in the capture of a gang of local free-booters, is sent to Rome for absolution.

4 *Registrum Thome de Cantilupo*, ed. R. G. Griffiths (C & YS, 1907). The introduction by W. W. Capes contains some inaccuracies and in general is without historical perspective.

5 *Reg. Cantilupe*, 144, 147.

6 *Ibid.* 37, 46–8, 88, 95, 116, 265, 296.

7 *Reg. Ricardi de Swinfield*, ed. W. W. Capes (C & YS, 1909).

suffered; the bishop asked the abbot to send reinforcements. Reading itself was in a bad way and nothing was done; when the bishop visited the parish at the end of 1286 he found the liturgy still curtailed, the prior defamed of promiscuous incontinence, and of entertaining a household of boon companions with whom he hunted and hawked and hallooed in the woods.[1] With this, Leominster disappears from view.

Meanwhile, Chirbury and Wigmore continued their traditional misbehaviour. Both were small houses in the broken, wooded country of the marches, subject to incursions from the roving hillfolk. Chirbury was a nest of quarrelling and gossip;[2] at Wigmore no very scandalous disorders came to light, but the canons were making money as middlemen, a swarm of relations was living on the place and unsuitable novices were being received.[3] Six years later the abbot resigned, against the bishop's wishes, who perhaps saw in him the only capable inmate of the abbey.[4] In any case, his successor followed him three years later in search of a quiet life,[5] and the next abbot was soon at loggerheads with the prior and the majority of the community.[6] Swinfield decided against another change, but gave the abbot a committee of seven, including the prior and an ex-abbot, with powers of advice and veto that must have effectively shackled all initiative, and in the sequel the bishop himself is seen taking an active part in supervising the affairs of Wigmore.[7]

Swinfield was succeeded by Adam of Orleton (1317–27), an able king's clerk who had held a diplomatic post at the Curia.[8] Whatever his antecedents and outlook, his recorded actions at Hereford show him second to no bishop of his day in energetic enforcement of discipline. It was about twenty years since the affairs of Wigmore had been put into commission, and the house was now decayed almost to perishing. Orleton procured the resignation of the abbot, appointed another, and published a set of injunctions. These bore chiefly on the common life and diet: besides the customary prohibition of clothes-money, the canons were to keep no private horses, pigs, sheep, greyhounds or pages; they were to have no breakfast and eat but twice a day in the refectory; when blood-letting they were to forgo the consolations of song.[9] A week later Orleton endeavoured to rid the house of disorderly members by boarding canons at Keynsham and Bristol. When the two prelates of these abbeys returned a *non possumus* Orleton demanded of the respective ordinaries that they should issue

---

1 *Reg. Swinfield*, 14–5, 100, 131, 149–50 ('cum canibus, avibus et personis inhonestis indifferenter venacionem saltuosam exercuit et clamosam').

2 *Reg. Swinfield*, 102 ('ipsi fratres...sunt vani, litigiosi, garruli, vagi et profugi super terram').

3 *Ibid.* 132–3.   4 *Ibid.* 301–2.

5 *Ibid.* 335 ('cupiens vite contemplative de cetero in majori quiete vacare').

6 *Ibid.* 362–3.

7 *Ibid.* 363–4, 371–3, 382–3.

8 *Register of Adam of Orleton*, ed. A. T. Banister (*C & YS*, 1908). There is a good introduction by the editor.

9 *Reg. Orleton*, 85–6, 90, 99–102 ('sine disolucione et cantilenis inhonestis').

commands. Cobham of Worcester, a friend of Orleton whom he had probably met at this time in London, duly obliged, but Drokensford of Wells demurred. He did not know his Orleton; the bishop of Hereford followed up another warning by an application to Canterbury and an appeal to the pope, who knew him well. This took time, but a year after the first move John XXII stirred up Reynolds, who passed the message on to Drokensford, and the transfer to Keynsham was no doubt effected.[1]

Chirbury caused less trouble, but in 1322 a defaulting prior was called up *ad audiendum verbum*. His defence was insufficient; he had wasted his possessions by dilapidation and incompetence; warnings had proved useless, and he was removed.[2] Meanwhile Orleton had been deputed by John XXII to visit the priory of Abergavenny, a dependency of St Vincent, Saumur. His account of what he found there is remarkable. The house was potentially well-to-do, but alienations and dilapidations had confused the finances and only half a dozen monks remained. They were far from all control and had not been visited for forty years; by now, all religious observance had gone down the wind. The office was neglected, silence was not observed, abstinence and fasting had ceased, and the monks diced and gamed at home, or spent their time in dissolute company with friends. They appear, indeed, to have reached lower depths of perversion, and were in the habit of entertaining their guests with nocturnal travesties of the Crucifixion; it is not surprising that they were reputed to be addicts of the worst vices. The prior, guilty of adultery with several partners, had levanted after embezzling the valuables.[3] Here also Orleton acted with decision. On the morrow of his visit, in which he was accompanied by the bishop of Llandaff and the abbot of Dore, he wrote to Cobham for a prior in the person of the eminently respectable Richard de Bromwich, sometime precentor of the cathedral priory of Worcester and a doctor of divinity.[4] The register is silent as to the experiences of this staid theologian with his debauched community of foreigners.

---

1 *Reg. Orleton*, 92–5, 98–9, 103, 107.
2 *Ibid.* 212, 215–6.
3 *Reg. Orleton*, 151, 190–4 ('aliquociens...nudi extensis brachiis cum baculis et ligatis ad modum crucifixi, stramine vel alio aliquo ad modum corone capitibus eorum superposito de ipsorum dormitorio nocturno tempore descendentes et sic incedentes ac ludentes coram sociis suis').
4 *Reg. Orleton*, 154. For Richard de Bromwich *v.* Pearce, *Thomas de Cobham* and *Register* of Cobham, indices *s.v.*

II

In Somerset the register of Orleton's contemporary, John de Drokensford (1309–29), gives little information.[1] We find the bishop complaining that the monks of Bath and Glastonbury have conspired to maintain silence during visitation; there is the usual story of inefficiency among the canons and of irregular life at a cell.[2]

Farther west, the register of Stapeldon of Exeter (1307–26) is scarcely more informative;[3] the bishop gives a coadjutor to the prior of Bodmin, who is aged, blind, infirm and weak in the head, sets up a chamberlain at St Germans, and endeavours to repair the buildings of windy Hartland, where the dormitory is collapsing, the lavatory ill-appointed and the church dark, while the lantern leaks in the gales and swine root in the garth and make free of the offices.[4] The register of Stapeldon's great successor, John de Grandisson (1327–69),[5] becomes useful only in 1332, but there is no reason to suppose that conditions had changed rapidly. The picture given is not bright. There was only one large black-monk house in the diocese, the abbey of Tavistock. There, Grandisson had deposed abbot Bonus in 1333 for waste and misconduct, and had himself chosen a member of a great Devon house in his place.[6] John Courtenay, however, was a disappointment. He lived expensively, while his monks were on short commons and the buildings decayed. Grandisson sent commissioners, who set up administrators and ordered the abbot to live apart from the community on an allowance.[7] This was in 1338; seven years later Courtenay was still keeping hounds and doubtful company, and wearing secular dress. His high connections protected him for three years more; he was then suspended and the revenues sequestered.[8] Nor were the smaller houses more prosperous. The administration of Barnstaple, deserted by its prior, was in commission in 1332; so was that of Exeter, St James, in 1338, where a lunatic prior had brought things to ruin; so also was that of Totnes in

---

1 *Register of John de Drokensford*, ed. Bishop Hobhouse (Somerset Rec. Soc. vol. I, 1887). This was one of the earliest essays in publishing a register and in consequence leaves much to be desired; it is little more than a calendar, and the translation is sometimes clearly at fault when there is a question of technical terms in medieval Latin.

2 *Reg. Drokensford*, 153, 158 (coadjutors for prior of Taunton); 261 (incontinence at Stogursey).

3 *Register of Walter de Stapeldon*, ed. F. C. Hingeston-Randolph (1902). The series of printed Exeter registers is a monument to the persevering labour and enthusiasm of their editor, and as such deserves all praise. The method, however, by which documents are summarized or merely calendared in English according to the judgement of the editor is often far from satisfactory for the historian.

4 *Reg. Stapeldon*, 48–50 (Bodmin); 331 (St Germans); 171 (Hartland, where the bishop notes the *discursus porcorum intra septa monasterii* as the cause of *inhonesta*).

5 *Register of John de Grandisson*, ed. F. C. Hingeston-Randolph, vol. I, 1327–30 (1894); vol. II, 1331–60 (1897).

6 *Reg. Grandisson*, II, 716–17, 741. For this, *v.* H. P. R. Finberg in *Devon and Cornwall Notes and Queries*, XXII, 341–7.

7 *Ibid.* II, 882, 886–90.   8 *Ibid.* II, 996–8, 1050–2, 1071–3.

1348, where a weak and worldly prior had allowed his relations to live in the priory with their horses, hounds and hawks.[1] Lower down the scale Tywardreath was desolate in 1333, and St Michael's Mount badly in debt three years later.[2]

Among the canons the two rival houses of Bodmin and Launceston take up the most space in the register, resembling in this respect Chirbury and Wigmore at Hereford. Launceston was already in trouble in 1337; the prior was absent, living irregularly and probably incontinently with seculars. Five years later Grandisson attempted to set its finances in order by getting rid of hounds, hawks and spare servants and importing some needy boys accounted towardly at grammar. It was to no purpose: the prior, weak in health, incompetent, wasteful and probably impure, was too much for the bishop; he was at last given a coadjutor and removed from administration. Infirm and incompetent as he was, however, he did not take his quietus gladly, and he and his friends, intent on continuing their carousals, set upon the administrators and restored the *status quo*; it was not till 1346 that he was induced to resign, when Grandisson endeavoured to reduce the canons to reasonable discipline by closing their private establishments, which were fully equipped with rooms, horses, dogs, boys, herb gardens and dovecotes.[3] Meanwhile, Bodmin claimed attention; it was disorderly and in debt, and in the same year, 1346, the prior was removed and private apartments and kennels suppressed. Here the canons affected the more sedentary pursuits of dice, draughts and chess.[4] What would have been the issue we can only guess; in the event, Bodmin, its season of grace past, met with a visitation of another kind, for a year later all the canons but two, one of whom was sick and the other simple, were carried off by the Black Death.[5] The two survivors, each unable to control the other, petitioned Grandisson for a superior; he sent a canon of Launceston, but when the affairs of Bodmin are again on the *tapis* the prior has been suspended and a commission set up, but things have gone no better.[6]

III

When we pass from the north and west to the parts of England nearer to the centre of national life we find the bishops of Winchester systematically ordering the economy of the canons. Thus John of Pontoise[7] (1282–1304) drew up a scheme for Newark in 1301: an external cellarer or seneschal was to be appointed; he, together with the internal cellarer and a third canon appointed by the prior and convent, were to receive and distribute all

---

1 *Ibid.* 658–9, 670–2 (Barnstaple); 883 (Exeter, where the *fatuum et incautum regimen* is stigmatized); 1073–4 (Totnes).
2 *Ibid.* 695–6 (Tywardreath); 813 (St Michael's Mount).
3 *Ibid.* 837, 955–6, 989–92, 1002–8.   4 *Ibid.* 1009–11.
5 *Ibid.* 1076–8 (the two canons are characterized respectively as *aeger* and *simplex*).
6 *Ibid.* III, 1238 (March, 1362/3).
7 *Registrum Johannis de Pontissara*, ed. Cecil Deedes (*C & YS*, vol. I, 1915).

moneys and give accounts quarterly.[1] This was a noteworthy variant of the regular system in which the two receivers were not in charge of the spending departments, and it was presumably never established, as seven years later Henry Woodlock[2] (1305-16) found the prior old and weak but apparently still handling the cash; he was given two wardens, one to receive, one to disburse all moneys.[3] Woodlock's injunctions for Southwick follow familiar lines,[4] but a visitation of Tandridge opened up abysses of confusion. No accounts of any kind had ever been given since the foundation c. 1200; the cellarer had no idea what the year's income was, nor did he know what each grange brought in, nor how many bushels of the various grains were sown each year, nor what a rick of corn was worth, nor what amount of grain went each year to the bakehouse, brewery and servants' liveries. The prior and all the other canons were equally innocent of all knowledge of these things.[5] Woodlock was content to issue a normal set of injunctions, but four years later, when a visitation had disclosed general mismanagement due to the prior's stupidity, he gave him a local parson as coadjutor.[6] At the more important Merton, where there had been scandals and disturbances nine years before, things were still unsatisfactory in 1314; numbers had fallen, the choir was badly kept, accounts were never audited, and the canons took longbows and crossbows with them for all to see on their strolls.[7] Woodlock had himself been prior of St Swithun's; his injunctions for that house in 1308 are general, but include directions to the prior to give yearly accounts and to visit his manors.[8] The decrees for Chertsey are more interesting since the abbot at the time was the great high farmer John de Rutherwyk, who was also at the time and for long after one of the abbots president of the black monks. As the articles contain a detailed scheme of accounting and directions for preserving the records it is possible that Woodlock was acting as mouthpiece of the abbot rather than correcting faults.[9]

At London Woodlock's contemporary, Ralph Baldock (1304-13), compiled an interesting register[10] in which he filed a number of Winchelsey's injunctions in addition to his own. His diocese in the middle ages included Essex and Hertfordshire, with the abbey of Colchester and several large

1 *Reg. Pontissara*, 119-21.
2 *Registrum Henrici Woodlock*, ed. A. W. Goodman (C & YS, 2 vols. 1940-1). An admirably edited publication.
3 *Reg. Woodlock*, 523.   4 *Ibid.* 524.
5 *Ibid.* 315-16: 'Nesciebat [celerarius] valorem domus, summam redditus anni nec exitum cuiuscumque grangie nec summam seminis seminati per annum in quocumque genere grani nec exitum cuiuscumque tasse bladi nec summam bladi ad furniendum per annum nec ad bracinam nec liberaciones famulorum, nec aliud sciebant prior celerarius vel alii quod ad statum domus pertinere debuit.' The clerk's Latin was perhaps affected by the chaos he reveals; had Henry of Eastry been the visitor his comments would doubtless have done fuller justice to the situation.   6 *Ibid.* 598.
7 *Ibid.* 751. For the earlier trouble at Merton, *v. infra*, p. 109.
8 *Ibid.* 507; cf. 747.
9 *Ibid.* 533-5; the set on p. 754 is a doublet of this.
10 *Reg. Radulphi Baldock* (C & YS, 1911).

houses of Austin canons. His injunctions to the abbey of St Osyth's are typical: they are almost entirely concerned with economics, and a double system of accounting is established: two receivers accept and disburse all moneys, giving a yearly account to the abbot and seniors, and a financial statement to the community; in addition, the obedientiaries account yearly to abbot, receivers and seniors. Any surplus is for the uses of abbot and community.[1] The injunctions for the smaller priories of Leighs, Blackmore and Royston follow a different pattern; they are almost entirely disciplinary, and are clearly drawn up to meet individual circumstances; they include the dismissal of defaulting servants, but they do not disclose any grave disorders.[2] The decrees for Colchester follow traditional lines: the rules for meat-eating are put out; no clothes-money is to be given; the abbot is to give accounts for the past years of his rule.[3]

As regards the rest of East Anglia, the diocesan registers of Ely and Norwich have not yet been printed, but items have been published relating to the cathedral priories of the two sees.[4] Both were in a tolerably flourishing condition. At Ely we have the injunctions of three bishops, the late subprior Hugh of Balsham in 1261, Ralph of Walpole in 1306 and Robert of Orford, another ex-prior, in 1307. The fullest of these is Walpole's, and he notes that he has been through a mass of past legislation in order to make a selection. As a result, he has compiled a set of injunctions which includes most of the familiar items: prohibition of clothes-money and of meat-eating save in the appointed places; the institution of two treasurers and the abolition of purely recreative conversations in the cloister. Orford reiterates the prohibition of clothes-money.[5] At Norwich a few years later, in 1347, the ordinances of Bishop Bateman are chiefly concerned with the constitution of the many dependent cells and with the financial organization of the priory, but once again meat-eating and clothes-money figure on the list.[6]

IV

Our knowledge of the state of religious life in the country during this period can be supplemented by the decisions of the chapters-general of Cluny on the reports of the visitors of the English province.[7] The Cluniac houses were exempt from episcopal surveillance save for those such as Monk Bretton, Barnstaple and Exeter, noted above, which made attempts

---

1 *Reg. Baldock*, 57–60.
2 *Ibid.* 112 *seqq.* (Leighs); 120 *seqq.* (Blackmore); 174 *seqq.* (Royston).
3 *Ibid.* 131.
4 *V. Ely Chapter Ordinances and Visitation Records*: 1241–1515, ed. Seiriol J. A. Evans in *Camden Miscellany*, XVII (*CS*, 3rd ser. LXIV, 1940), pp. 1–74, and *Norwich Cathedral Priory in the Fourteenth Century*, by C. R. Cheney, in *BJRL*, vol. 20, 105, January 1936 (and reprinted separately).
5 *Ely Chapter Ordinances*, 6–21, 31–4.
6 *Norwich Cathedral Priory*, 16, 202.
7 *Visitations and Chapters of the Order of Cluni*, by Sir G. F. Duckett (1893).

to free themselves from Cluny. They were, however, visited from the beginning of the thirteenth century by monks appointed in the yearly chapter-general at Cluny. Some records of these visitations have survived, and the resolutions of the chapter, based upon them, often give summary information of the state of the houses. Thus the largest priory, Lewes, may be seen at intervals from the year 1273, in which all houses were reported to be spiritually in a good condition.[1] In 1288 the same verdict was given of Lewes and Lenton, but four years later they were so deeply in debt that the visitors feared they might sink altogether unless assisted. The debts of Lewes persisted in 1293, 1294, 1299 and 1301, when wool as well as money was in default. In consequence, both numbers and the giving of hospitality have declined, and in 1306 the place has only thirty-odd monks in place of the ancient number of sixty.[2] Even before the chapter had taken cognizance of Lewes, Pecham, who had loved the priory from boyhood, had remarked that numbers, hospitality and care of the poor were all dwindling. He attributed this state of things primarily to the inefficiency of the priors appointed by Cluny, some of whom could not speak English.[3] As the above notes show, Pecham's appeal had little immediate effect, but in 1314 the visitors could report that a careful prior had reduced the debt by a third to £2000.[4] Early in the fourteenth century the visitors become more critical; few of the English monks have been regularly professed owing to inability to meet the abbot of Cluny, and the priors fail to attend chapter; when they cross the Channel they are in no hurry to return. In fact, the Cluniac monks of England as a body are not edifying, and few of the monasteries are in a really satisfactory condition.[5] Thetford was a peculiarly unfortunate house at this time, and it is noted that at Lenton, as elsewhere in England, monks receive money in lieu of clothes.

V

The activities of the diocesan in this period were controlled and supplemented by those of the archbishop of Canterbury. The right of metropolitical visitation, established by ancient practice, had long been canonically recognized; it was apparently first asserted in England by Edmund Rich, but not exercised on any scale before the time of Boniface. That prelate visited several dioceses, including London, Lincoln, Winchester and Exeter, but no detailed account or set of injunctions remains to show his policy in regard to religious houses.[6] His successor, Kilwardby, trained in the

---

1 Duckett, *Visitations*, 226: 'Omnes domus in spiritualibus sunt in bono statu.'
2 *Ibid.* 239, 246, 248–9, 259, 267, 279.
3 Peckham, *Registrum Epistolarum* (*RS*), III, *ep.* dcxlvi (1 June 1285).
4 Duckett, *Visitations*, 301–2.
5 *Ibid.* 303–4, 316–7 ('paucae domus de Anglia, prout visitatores referunt, sunt in bono statu').
6 For this *v.* C. R. Cheney, *Episcopal Visitation of Monasteries in the Thirteenth Century*, 133–48, and Miss I. J. Churchill, *Canterbury Administration*, I, 288–94.

religious life and of firm principles, was far more thorough. As he perhaps took his register with him to Rome when created cardinal, and as it has certainly vanished, no complete record exists, but it is possible from incidental references to trace his presence at at least a dozen religious houses situated in seven or eight dioceses, and at least one set of his injunctions has been preserved intact, while others survive in a revised form. He was active during the greater part of the five years of his rule; he deposed the abbot of Faversham in 1275 and the abbot of Bardney a year later; he made serious efforts to restore order at Waltham and Reading, and notes of his action at such small houses as Wormesley (Hereford), Little Malvern (Worcester) and Boxgrove (Sussex) show that he was thorough.[1] It is from Boxgrove that a set of his injunctions survives; the situation there was not grave, and the archbishop's decrees are concerned with the normal dangers and shortcomings of a mediocre community, but there is individuality in the drastic attempt to check meat-eating by pulling down the misericord, in the abolition of recreative conversations in the cloister, and in the exhortation to silence and stability.

Kilwardby's policy was developed by his successor. Pecham was a man of austere personal habits and tireless energy, and in the years 1280–4 covered almost all England and Wales south of the Danelaw. Injunctions have been preserved in some quantity in his register of letters from houses in almost every district, and though by no means complete, they are sufficient to indicate very clearly Pecham's policy. Nicely varied to suit local needs they show that the archbishop, besides a firm faith in the ideals and possibilities of the religious life, brought to his task a sincere desire to benefit each house and individual, and a detailed analysis of these ordinances would throw vivid light on the daily life and organization of the monasteries and nunneries of the day. Two features of his policy may be noted here: his method of dealing with unsatisfactory superiors, and his endeavour to standardize financial arrangements.[2]

Although most of his visitations were at halting-places on his long journeys through districts never seen before or after, he did not hesitate to remove priors and obedientiaries when the *comperta* pointed to them as the cause of serious misbehaviour. Thus he deposed the priors of Luffield, Rochester, Southwick, Pembroke and Kidwelly, and requested the bishop of Chichester and the abbot of Séez to do the same by the priors of Boxgrove

---

1 Churchill, *op. et loc. citt.* makes no mention of Kilwardby, perhaps because his register is wanting at Lambeth; Cheney refers to some of his visitations, *op. cit.* 142–3, and others are noted by E. M. F. Sommer-Seckendorff, *Studies in the Life of Robert Kilwardby, O.P.*, 90–101. For his efforts at Reading, *v.* Peckham, *Reg. Epp.* I, *ep.* clxxxix. The *Register of Robert Winchelsey*, ed. R. Graham (*C & YS*), part viii (1939), has references to Kilwardby at Little Malvern (p. 864), Worcester (p. 873), and Boxgrove (pp. 852–3). Cantilupe's *Register* (p. 144) discloses a visit to Wormesley; for Ely *v.* Seiriol Evans, *Ely Chapter Ordinances*, introd. p. xvi.

2 For Pecham's visitations *v.* Cheney, *op. cit.* 142–3; Churchill, *op. cit.* 295–304, and the present writer's article in *EHR* (April, 1942), pp. 191–8.

and Arundel.[1] When inefficiency rather than misconduct was discovered, Pecham, canonically unable to proceed to extreme measures, sometimes took the course of setting up a commission of management, as at Christ Church in the days of Ringmer and at the nunneries of Wessex.[2] His usual procedure, however, was to enforce the canonical system of treasury and account. Some such arrangement, as we have seen, was urged or decreed by a number of bishops, but the emphasis laid by Pecham on the merits of the system, and the clear-cut scheme of economics and finance which he dealt out to houses great and small entitles him to a place among the financiers and high farmers of the golden age of English medieval commerce.[3]

For the rest, he notes the usual shortcomings. At Coxford the prior and canons hunt on foot, dine out, and indulge in chess and the like disreputable amusements.[4] These they must abandon, and if the prior follows the hounds he must be mounted. At the nunneries in particular, which do not fall within the scope of these notes, the details of domestic life and the foibles of aristocratic ladies receive careful attention.

Pecham's successor, Winchelsey, was equally active during the few years that were free for touring in his troubled rule.[5] Though without Pecham's personal experience of religious life, he was a man of zeal and entirely fearless in asserting what he deemed to be his rights. The questionnaire with which he provided himself for examining the various types of community is still extant,[6] but his usual procedure was first to inquire if any previous injunctions were available. If so, he might republish them, or promulgate an amended form; if not, he issued a new set based on the answers to his questionnaire, though his injunctions by no means follow the order of his questions. In some cases, as at Gloucester and probably also at Christ Church, he took up old chapter ordinances which amounted to a full set of domestic constitutions.[7] In general, Winchelsey's injunctions are less of a pattern than Pecham's, though the obligation of giving audits and of a common treasury is often repeated; at three houses, Christ Church, Rochester and Lesnes, decrees of both prelates have survived, and it is noteworthy that the later sets bear no resemblence to the earlier.[8] Though

---

1 Peckham, *Reg. Epp.* I, *ep.* lxxxvi (Luffield), II, *epp.* ccccxxvii (Boxgrove), ccccxxxiii (Arundel), cccclxxxvi (Rochester), dx (Southwick), III, dlxxiv (Pembroke) and dlxxxviii (Kidwelly).

2 *Ibid.* I, *ep.* cclxii and II, *ep.* cccviii (Christ Church), div (Wherwell) and dvii (Romsey).

3 These activities of Pecham have been described at length in an article in *EHR*, LVII (April, 1942), 191 *seqq.*

4 *Ibid.* I, *ep.* cxxxvii ('scaccorum autem ludum et consimilia scurrilia solatia vobis omnibus...perpetue inhibemus').

5 Churchill, *op. cit.* 305–7; R. Graham, *Metropolitical Visitation of the diocese of Worcester* (*TRHS*, 4 ser., vol. II, 1919; reprinted in *English Ecclesiastical Studies*, 330–59).

6 It is in Brit. Mus. MS. Cott. Galba E IV, f. 61 *seqq.* Dr Rose Graham has a transcript, which she kindly allowed me to consult.

7 *Reg. Winchelsey*, part viii, 813–26 (Christ Church); 856–63 (Gloucester).

8 Peckham, *Reg. Epp.* II, cccviii, ccccxxxvii, ccccxxxviii. Cf. *Reg. Winchelsey*, viii, 813–26, 838–41, 842.

less personal in his appeal, Winchelsey often lets a remark fall on the discipline of the house. Thus at Leeds he notes that Pecham's decrees are badly observed; at Boxgrove that Kilwardby's injunctions and the Rule are transgressed; at Gloucester that they do not keep their own ordinances, at Worcester that the honourable estate of the monastic life is in abeyance.[1]

Both Pecham and Winchelsey provide instances of co-operation with the ordinary in setting a house to rights. Reading had for some time been mismanaged in Kilwardby's day. It was one of the few great abbeys where the establishments of abbot and monks had never been separated, and the archbishop at his visitation endeavoured to remedy the existing trouble by ordaining that the abbot's expenses of whatever kind, public or private, were to be received from the chamberlain and accounts given. When Pecham arrived in 1281 the debts were worse. He decreed that three receivers were to be appointed for all revenues; they were to pay the obedientiaries what was needed and all surplus was to go to relieve the debt.[2] Nevertheless, the debt increased; funds were short even for maintenance of the monks, and the community was threatened with dispersal. News of this came to the newly consecrated Walter Scammell of Salisbury, and he visited Reading. Rather than suffer disbandment the monks agreed to put into operation a scheme of radical retrenchment drawn up by themselves, by which one-fifth of the debt would be paid off every year, the bishop keeping close watch over the obedientiaries. Six months later Pecham confirmed this arrangement, and agreed that his treasury system should remain in abeyance for five years till the debt was paid off.[3]

The second case is typical of the energetic methods of Winchelsey. When Henry Woodlock of Winchester had been consecrated a bare month, the archbishop commanded him to execute corrections at Merton, which he himself had visited during the vacancy, and to report results. Eight weeks later the bishop's commissaries visited the priory, deposed the sub-prior, penanced some guilty canons and laid the prior under sentence of removal, adjourning the visitation till the arrival of the bishop. Next month Woodlock duly appeared, refused the prior's offer to resign subject to a declaration of his innocence, and deposed him; he nevertheless allowed him the private establishment normally given to quondam superiors. For some reason report of this never reached the primate; he therefore revisited Merton, found the ex-prior intriguing against the election of an opponent, and reduced him to the ranks. He ended the letter giving this information with another command to Woodlock to visit and report. The bishop replied that he had already acted, and sent a distinguished monk of Winchester to

---

1 *Reg. Winchelsey*, 873 *seqq.* ('religionis honestas apud vos exulans').
2 Peckham, *Reg. Epp.* I, *ep.* clxxxix.
3 The relevant documents are preserved in the Hereford *Reg. Swinfield*, 149-50, 165-9, where they form part of the Leominster dossier.

explain more fully.[1] Rarely, if ever, after Winchelsey's death did a primate keep so watchful an eye over his neighbours, and act so speedily.

It is remarkable that in all the mass of documents upon which these notes are based there is scarcely a single reference to the parallel series of visitations by the authorities of the order, still less any notice of action taken by them.[2] Indeed, a casual reader of these registers might be excused for failing to realize that such visitations existed. It is possible, indeed, that had we the full records, we might find a similar absence of all reference to episcopal visitation on the part of the representatives of the chapters. The latter, however, lacked the final power of deposition, and it is probable that in many cases, especially among the canons, they left difficult situations to the bishop. Certainly, there does not seem to be a single instance of their applying to him for the deposition of a superior.

VI

Visitations can be an effective instrument to safeguard religious perfection only if a number of conditions are verified. First, the visits must be made regularly and frequently by visitors able to act on the spot with full powers. Next, the visitor must be concerned to apply a rule and constitutions that are clear, practical and adequate. Thirdly, and most important of all, he must himself be a spiritual man and he must have at his disposal, either within or without the house, a reservoir of spiritual fervour upon which to draw. Neither administrative efficiency, nor the stern allotment of punishment, nor the punctilious care of a martinet can take the place of the love of God. When that is absent the watchman waketh but in vain. *Nemo dat quod non habet.* And unless there is in the community to be visited some focus of good will, or the possibility of importing it from elsewhere, all disciplinary regulations are in the end useless; water will not rise above its head. Medieval critics and modern historians alike, by making too great a demand upon the institution of visitation, have often been led to blame too severely those concerned with its working.

When all the necessary conditions are present, visitation can be the most powerful of all external agencies in maintaining or reforming discipline. It can kill germs of decay before they do irreparable harm; it can rid the body of a cancer; it can graft a new life upon the old stock. Never in the history of the Church has this been seen more clearly than in the first century of the life of the Cistercian order. There, the annual visitation was conducted by abbots who had behind them the moral and judicial power of

1 The documents are in *Reg. Woodlock*, I, 65, 96, 106.

2 The present writer has noted only three references in all the registers quoted in these pages, viz.: the articles for Newstead in 1261 (*supra*, p. 90); the reference by Archbishop Wickwane of an incorrigible canon to the priors president (*supra*, p. 94, n. 4) and a disparaging reference of Pecham (*Reg. Epp.* III, *ep.* dcxcv) when urging Faversham's claim to exemption from capitular visitation: 'nec credunt plurimi prudentum quod vestra visitatio semel in triennio inibi impendenda...nostrae visitationi annuae quicquam facile possit superaddere fructuosum.'

a general chapter to which they gave account; they had before them the Rule and *Consuetudines* to be literally applied; they could depose or penance any official from the abbot downwards, and they could, if necessary, infuse new blood from some other and fervent house. The Cistercian visitation ceased to be powerful only when political and ecclesiastical changes had weakened the cohesion of the order, and when the constitutions were no longer kept according to the letter.

Judged in the light of the above principles, episcopal visitation in the late thirteenth and early fourteenth centuries cannot be said completely to have fulfilled its function. The visitations could only be made frequently and regularly under optimum conditions and when unusually zealous men were at work, and though in theory the bishops had full powers, they were in practice limited by the medium in which they worked. Worse still, they had no clear-cut code to apply. Even in their heyday two centuries earlier the black monks had made no claim to follow the Rule *ad litteram*, while the basic code of the black canons was short and vague; in both orders constitutions and local customs of considerable variety existed, while the relevant decrees and decretals were so numerous and often so general in their terms as to be unfitted for rigid and universal enforcement. Finally, the bishop, even if himself a spiritual man, had no reserve on which to draw. In extreme cases he could advise or even compel a community to receive a superior of his own choice, but in practice the field of choice did not as a rule extend outside his diocese, and the resentment and party feeling aroused in a large community by the imposition of a superior from outside might usually be expected to outweigh the advantages.

Nevertheless, episcopal visitation had a real value, and this was never greater than in the century under review. On the whole, the bishops of that period were men of ability and principle, and long vacancies and absences from the diocese were probably rarer than in the troubled twelfth century or in the last two centuries before the Reformation, when so many bishops held offices or fulfilled missions of state. The impression of painstaking fulfilment of duty grows upon the reader as he passes through one register after another, and while it is nowhere more strong than in the great series of York archbishops, it is equally present in the records of Orleton of Hereford, Grandisson of Exeter, and Woodlock of Winchester. In short, within the limits imposed by contemporary circumstances and by human nature, the bishops of the time did all that could reasonably be expected of them. They toured the diocese, they took considerable pains to punish delinquents and straighten out finances; they interested themselves in individual religious, and nowhere do they show lack of respect for the religious ideals or the perfunctory manner that comes from indifference to spiritual issues or from a despair of doing good.

Of the religious houses, also, it is possible to form a general judgement. Certainly, the registers give no more than a cross-section, and that of two great families only, but it is a cross-section that runs from Carlisle[1] to Bodmin, from Wigmore to Dover, and there is no reason to suppose that the the missing and unprinted registers would modify its characteristics. The period, as can be ascertained from sources of every kind, was one neither of fervour nor of widespread decadence. The registers bear this out. While it is hard to find in the records a house with zeal above the ordinary, the examples of thorough corruption, among the houses of any size, are few. The majority show a decent mediocrity. Secondly, it is clear that there was very little to choose, or even to distinguish, between houses of comparable size of monks and canons. They have the same shortcomings and the same embarrassments. Thirdly, it is equally noticeable that the monasteries of the west midlands beyond Severn, and still more those of the west country beyond Exe, were more irregular than those of the north and probably, also, than those near London and in the eastern counties. Finally, the small dependent priories and those belonging to foreign abbeys were almost without exception lax in discipline, if not positively corrupt.

The chief sources of decay that distinguished the period, as opposed to those weaknesses, small and great, that are part of the human heritage in all ages, appear to have been two: an improvidence which, either by failing to meet changing economic conditions, or by allowing miscellaneous dependents and casuals to live upon the house to an unconscionable extent, caused expenses and waste greater than the fixed income could bear; and, secondly, an independence on the part of superiors of all accountability and a lack of consideration of the counsel of others. This last, of course, is a failing common to all ages, but it was rendered peculiarly harmful in the late middle ages by the feudal conception of the head of a religious house as the owner of the property and as entitled to a private establishment on retirement. The number of defaulting or immoral priors is relatively large in these visitations, and is without doubt partly to be attributed to the excessive administrative freedom which the medieval superior enjoyed. The evil custom of setting up a kind of dower-house for the quondam, especially when there were more than one, was a serious addition both to the liabilities and opportunities for waste; it also operated as a deterrent to the bishop when there was a question of resignation, forced or free. It had been the endeavour of the reforming popes from Innocent III onwards to counteract this independence by giving to the community the right of veto, of counsel, and of audit, and the dowering of an ex-abbot or prior never had any place in canon law, but the injunctions of these registers show how difficult it was to bring all parties to a just sense of their responsibilities.

1 A visitation of Carlisle cathedral priory of Augustinian canons in 1300 is the only one recorded (vol. I, pp. 119–21, II, 224–6) in the *Register of John of Halton*, bishop of Carlisle, 1292–1324, and himself an ex-canon of the house, printed by the Canterbury and York Soc. 1913, with an introduction by T. F. Tout.

Part Two

The Friars, 1216–1340

CHAPTER XI

THE FRIARS MINOR

I

While Innocent III and the more earnest members of the Curia were elaborating measures of reform and preparing for a general council which should knit together and envigorate the languid members of the Church, two spiritual agencies of another kind, but of incalculable power, whose birth could by no clairvoyance have been foreseen and whose unfolding followed no ascertainable law, were coming to maturity, the one in Languedoc, the other in the heart of Italy. While the Canterbury election, and the troubles of Evesham, and the claims of Gerald of Wales were occupying cardinals and canonists at Rome, and while the Interdict and the vagaries of John were paralysing life and growth in England, Dominic Guzman was finding his true vocation in the land of the Albigenses, and Francesco Bernardone of Assisi was passing from one stage to another of his conversion to the perfect following of Christ.

Probably no canonized saint of the Christian centuries has been the object of such widespread and enthusiastic admiration outside the circle of the devout as has Francis of Assisi. His cult, formerly purely religious in character and confined to Catholics, became during the latter half of the nineteenth century a great wave of enthusiasm which made of him one of the most familiar and admired figures in the history of mankind, while at the same time the chronological and other problems presented by the events of his life and the enigmatical circumstances surrounding the labours of his early biographers gave rise to a branch of medieval studies abounding in religious, historical and critical problems of great complexity, which attracted to itself eminent scholars of many nations and gave birth to a vast technical literature of its own.[1]

[1] As the subject of Franciscan origins has no direct connection with the present study no detailed bibliography will be expected. For a short list, v. A. G. Little's *Guide to Franciscan Studies* (1920); the most recent treatment is by Dr J. R. H. Moorman, *Sources for the Life of St Francis*, which contains a short bibliography. For the comprehension of the character and teaching of Francis his own brief writings are of the first importance; they are quoted in the text from the edition of H. Böhmer, *Analekten zur Geschichte des Franciscus von Assisi*. To these should be added the two Lives by Thomas of Celano, the *Documenta Antiqua Franciscana* (ed. Lemmens) and the *Legend of the Three Companions* (for the editions of these quoted, v. Bibliography). The best fully documented biography in English is that of Fr Cuthbert, O.S.F.C., *St Francis of Assisi*, which, though written more than a quarter of a century ago, retains its original value. Of it Paul Sabatier wrote in 1926 that of all recent lives: 'il y en a une qui vient se placer au tout premier rang....Peut-être même est-elle la meilleure de toutes' (*St Francis of Assisi*, 1226–1926, preface, p. vii). Studies of various aspects of Franciscan history will be found in *Franciscan Essays, I* and *II* (British Society of Franciscan Studies. Extra Series, vols. I and II), and in *St Francis of Assisi, 1226–1926*, edited by W. W. Seton.

The causes of what has been somewhat incorrectly described as the re-discovery of St Francis are to be sought not so much in the religious life as in the later phases of the romantic movement in France and England. The new interest taken by so many in the early literature and primitive art of Italy, and the revived appreciation of medieval architecture, became during the fifty years that followed the battle of Waterloo a part of the culture of the upper classes in all countries north of the Alps, while the number of those from the northern countries who visited, or even took up residence in, Italy grew steadily in the second half of the century. Among these were not a few of the most eminent poets, critics and *littérateurs* of the period, and their writings and personal influence in society carried into all educated circles an enthusiasm for medieval Italian life and art and a familiarity with the soft and lucent landscape of Tuscany and Umbria. To all thus affected, steeped as they were in the liberal and humanitarian atmosphere of the age, the story of Francis, handed down in the majestic verse of Dante and the fragrant vernal prose of the Fioretti, and outlined in the exquisite frescoes and altar-pieces of Giotto and the primitives, made a powerful appeal; the children of the nineteenth century seemed to recognize in the saint's feeling for the poor and the sick, and in his love of flowers and living creatures and all the forces and beauties of nature, something akin to their own sentiments, while they found a still deeper appeal in the delicacy and tenderness of his human relationships with those nearest to him. The new cult gathered force and inspired several notable works of literature; these in their turn led scholars to investigate the sources of knowledge, and it was found that the literary monuments of early Franciscan life presented critical and spiritual problems curiously similar to those connected with the earliest records of Christianity which were then being canvassed with such eagerness by the higher criticism; the methods and outlook and fashion of interpretation already in use in the earlier field were in consequence transferred to the later, in some cases by the very scholars who had already employed them in work upon the New Testament. Here, as there, the findings of the early workers, who were for the most part not members of the Catholic Church, aroused both interest and a certain sense of resentment among the members of St Francis's order, and a rival school of historians made its appearance among the friars, stimulated by the reorganization of the Franciscan order by Leo XIII and the contemporary revival of interest in all schools of scholastic philosophy.[1]

With the opening of the twentieth century something of a fusion began to take place between the various groups. Critical work of great value had been accomplished by all parties, and all had contributed to the common store newly discovered documents of great significance together with fresh light on the personality of Francis; the cruder antagonisms faded away and something of a *rapprochement* was reached which, while leaving a number of purely critical problems open to discussion by all, recognized as authentic

[1] See n. 1 on p. 206.

certain broad outlines of the life of Francis and his first companions, and a certain definite character in his aims and in his order. Indeed, it may be said that by 1914 the bulk of the purely critical and historical work had been done, and though not a little of value has been achieved during the recent past in the presentation and interpretation of Franciscan sources, a certain slackening of interest in Franciscan studies has made itself apparent in the learned world, and the passing of some of the foremost scholars of the movement, of whom Paul Sabatier may be reckoned the chief, has deprived the subject of the interest lent it by the distinction of mind and personal enthusiasm of those who debated it most keenly in the last generation.

II

The critical work of the past fifty years has given to the world for the first time something approaching to a genuine text of the principal monuments of Franciscan tradition and has established with some certainty the sequence of events in the early history of the friars.[1] It has also, as has been said, placed Francis in the forefront of the historical scene as a figure whom all salute as one of the most significant and lovable in the annals of Christianity. It has not succeeded, nor could it be expected to succeed, in fully comprehending, still less in adequately presenting, the deepest spiritual aspirations and achievements of St Francis. Even among those who would readily hail him as one of the greatest of saints and as reflecting, to an uncommon degree, the life and mind of Christ, there is the widest divergence as to the meaning to be attached to such phrases, as indeed there is in the understanding of the personality and message of Christ Himself. In the present volume there is no need to repeat the story of Francis's life, or to do more than recall some of the critical problems presented by Franciscan literature, but it is impossible to consider the early history of the English province of the Friars Minor without some appreciation of the new focus of spiritual energy developed by the life and teaching of Francis, and without some acquaintance with the ideals and anxieties of his early followers in Italy, which influenced directly and deeply the lives of the first friars in England.

The new vigour that St Francis gave to the life of the Western Church had a very different character from the stimulus given by the measures of the reforming legislators of the age. These latter sought to impose an order and a discipline upon the discordant and flaccid elements in the body of the Church by means of a legal code and measures of administration; learning, law and organization were to be the instruments of their policy; they followed a rationally calculated method of action, based on a careful study of the discipline of the past, the conditions of the age, and the external ends

---

[1] No attempt need here be made to summarize the results of this work; one such summary, by the late Prof. F. C. Burkitt, will be found in the volume edited by Dr Seton; but Dr Moorman's work has in large part replaced all previous studies. Cf. also the articles *Francesco, San* in the *Enciclopedia Italiana* and *François d'Assise* in the *DS*.

to be attained. Though the goal they aimed at was a spiritual rebirth, and though many of them were, like Grosseteste, men of evangelical zeal, they thought and acted as rulers and legislators in a world of men and things. St Francis moved upon another and a far deeper plane. With him, the new birth came first to his own soul; he had begun to know Christ in the reality of living by a supernatural light, not through the words of theologians and the formularies of law; he saw and followed the life of the gospel, the life of the perfect Christian, in its true simplicity and fullness, not as an ideal, not as a goal, but as the only way of life. This way he gave to others: to his first companions, to Clare, to all his friars, to all the world. Francis had the mind of Christ, he lived in Him, and it was an agony and ultimately an impossibility for him to divide, to adapt, and to accommodate for others the unity and fullness of his vision. Christ Himself gave His teaching to the world and to the apostles with a simplicity, an elevation and a comprehensive plenitude that few or none of His hearers were capable of accepting; He left it to His followers to codify, to divide and to economize. So it was in a measure with Francis, but he was unable to give, as Christ had given, in a few strong germinal words and with the promise of divine guidance, the basis of an organization that should preserve and propagate his teaching. He stands thus in a position apart from other founders of religious institutes in the Church; while it is true of all the saints that they have themselves lived on a different plane from others, seeing man's life *sub specie aeternitatis* with a simplicity and directness of vision withheld from ordinary men, they have as founders and legislators given to the world codes and constitutions which do not so much translate their own experience as point towards and safeguard a certain type of life. Such was the achievement of a Benedict, a Bernard, a Teresa, an Ignatius; the achievement of Francis was at once greater and less. He saw only Christ's life, in a vivid light and from a single point of view. When called upon to give to others a Rule he could only isolate certain of Christ's own words; he wrote and spoke on the spiritual, not on the forensic plane; he gave a life, not a code; and though, to those who asked in all sincerity for direction in the concrete happenings of life, he could give direct and lucid personal guidance, he was not capable of expressing in general and external legislation the principles by which his followers were to live. It was this directness and simplicity of sight and aim that at once attracted, baffled and at times exasperated those who lived and had dealings with him; the early history of the friars shows the inevitable conflict and impoverishment that took place when men of more ordinary mould strove to express his teaching in their own idiom; and modern literature, with its repeated endeavours to interpret *Francescanismo* in terms of art, of poetry, of social reform or of romance, 'still clutching the inviolable shade', bears witness to the perplexity of the human mind when confronted with one who, while intensely receptive of all beauty and sensitive to the needs of the world of creatures around him, nevertheless had bread to eat which they knew not, and walked by a light other than theirs.

III

The aim of Francis, which in intension was so deep and comprehensive, was in extension also simple and wide. The leaders of monastic reform in the past had either addressed themselves only to a small band of *âmes d'élite* or had proclaimed that all who sought salvation in its full security must seek it within the shelter of a monastic rule. Francis was convinced that his message was for all, for the whole world, like the message of Christ Himself. He preached repentance first,[1] and then the gospel in all its depth and purity. To this he had himself been called; this was the way which Christ Himself had taught him to give to those who had been given as his followers from the world;[2] this he gave to Clare and her sisters;[3] this he offered to all Christians in his preaching, in the Order of Penance and in the letter which, with sublime and simple confidence and directness, he addressed 'to all Christians, religious, clerics and lay, men and women, all who lived in the whole world'.[4] It is, however, very noteworthy that there is no trace in his sayings or writings of the tendency, which can be seen in such earlier reformers as Peter Damian, to equate the Christian life with the monastic or the eremitical. Francis, who distinguished in his own life between the stage of penance, the turning, that is, from evil, and the perfect following of Christ with its abandonment of merely human standards,[5] made something of the same distinction between what he demanded of his friars and what he proposed to those who had no call to join him.

But of those who were so called he demanded what no religious legislator hitherto had asked, and it is this quality of intension which sharply divides his Rule from the previous monastic and canonical Rules: it is neither an external code nor a propaedeutic to perfection, but an enunciation of the pure and full imitation of Christ in certain aspects of His life. It is this insistence on purely spiritual, supernatural action, this

---

1 The preaching of penance by laymen and the members of fraternities such as the *Humiliati* of Lombardy was common during Francis's youth, cf. H. Grundmann, *Religiöse Bewegungen im Mittelalter*; hence the original instructions of Francis: 'annunciate simpliciter poenitentiam' (*Leg. 3 Soc.* ed. Marcellino da Civezza, c. x, p. 62), and the commission of Innocent III in 1210: 'omnibus poenitentiam praedicate' (*ibid.* c. xiii, pp. 84, 86), and Francis's description of his first brothers as: 'viri poenitentiales de civitate Assisii oriundi' (*ibid.* c. x, p. 64).

2 Cf. *Regula Prima*, proem (ed Böhmer, 1): 'Hec est vita evangelii Jesu Christi, quam frater Franciscus petiit a domino papa Innocentio'; *Testamentum*, §4 (Böhmer, 25): 'Et postquam Dominus dedit michi de fratribus, nemo ostendebat michi, quid deberem facere, sed ipse Altissimus revelavit michi, quod deberem vivere secundum formam sancti Evangelii.'

3 Cf. the words of the *Forma vivendi sororibus data* (Böhmer, 24): 'vivere secundum perfectionem sancti evangelii'; and the *Ultima voluntas quam scripsit sororibus* (*ibid.*).

4 Cf. *Epistola quam misit omnibus fidelibus* (Böhmer, 33–8), and Francis's words to Ugolino in *Speculum Perfectionis* (ed. Sabatier), c. 65, p. 183: 'Dico vobis in veritate quod Dominus elegit et misit fratres propter profectum et salutem animarum omnium hominum hujus mundi.'

5 Cf. *Testamentum*, §§ 1, 4 (Böhmer, 24–5).

elimination of all but the highest, not only in the framework of his institute, but in all relations between his friars and the authorities of the Church, and with men at large, that makes of the Rules and Testament of St Francis something unique among the Rules of religious orders. The founder himself saw clearly that many of his followers would fail to live on the purely spiritual plane and that authority, within and without his order, would seek to modify his demands or translate them into legal formulae. Even when full allowance is made for the embroidery of the generation after his death which, able to prophesy from the event, may have put point and clarity into some of his words, his genuine writings and the incidents of his last years make it clear that Francis foresaw that few would follow the form of perfect living that he wished to give.[1] Hence it was that he felt called to assert, not only to individuals in private, but to all in the text of his Rules and Testament, that the right of the individual friar to follow the perfect way was indefeasible, and that obedience should not be given to commands running contrary to spiritual perfection, even if persecution at the hands of superiors were to ensue.[2] This, as few were slow to see, was capable of misinterpretation at the hands of those who claimed licence in the name of spirituality, and Francis had perforce to make something of a verbal compromise.[3] But from the doctrine itself he never receded; others might see and speak forensically, he could only write, as he saw, with spiritual simplicity.[4]

Besides this note of intensity, the institute of Friars Minor came, even before the death of Francis, to have two essential characteristics which separated it from all previous orders, though they were shared to a greater

1 *V.* esp. *Speculum Perfectionis*, c. 71, above all § 13, p. 205: 'Postquam consideravi quod...ipsi (fratres) propter tepiditatem et inopiam spiritus incipiebant declinare a via recta et secura...recommendavi religionis praelationem et regimen Domino et ministris.' This is one of many important passages which cannot be used with complete confidence until the problems connected with the *Speculum* are solved. To the present writer it seems essentially authentic. Cf. also *Speculum*, c. 39, pp. 101–3.

2 *Regula Prima*, § 5 (Böhmer, 4): 'Si quis ministrorum alicui fratrum aliquid contra vitam nostram vel contra animam suam preciperet, frater non teneatur ei obedire'; this absolute liberty was later somewhat modified in *Regula Bullata*, § 10 (Böhmer, 23): 'ministri ...non praecipi[ant] eis aliquid, quod sit contra animam suam (= eorum) et regulam nostram...fratres...obediant...in omnibus, quae...non sunt contraria animae et regulae nostrae'; *Verba admonitionis*, § 3 (Böhmer, 29): 'Si vero prelatus precipiat aliquid subdito contra animam suam, licet ei non obediat, tamen ipsum non dimittat (i.e. let the subject not depart). Et si ab aliquibus inde persecutionem sustinuerit...vere permanet in perfecta obedientia,' etc.

3 If an early testimony, attributed to Brother Leo, is genuine, Francis, in the Rule submitted to Honorius III in 1223, ordered friars who found themselves unable to keep the Rule *pure et simpliciter et ad litteram et sine glosa* to apply to their minister for facilities to do so. If he refused, they were to do it nevertheless, *quia omnes fratres tam ministri quam subditi debent regule esse subditi*. The Pope, apprehensive of the misunderstandings that might arise, himself softened the passage, while assuring Francis that the essential permission stood. Cf. *Regula Bullata*, § 10 (Böhmer), and Brother Leo's account quoted by Angelo da Clareno (*ibid.* ed. 1, 86–8).

4 Cf. the words of Francis, *Speculum Perfectionis*, c. 3, p. 8, apropos of a request to possess books: 'Nec volo, nec debeo, nec possum venire contra conscientiam meam et professionem sancti evangelii quam professi sumus.'

or less degree by the other bodies of friars. While he made full and explicit allowance for a contemplative and solitary element in the body of his followers,[1] Francis was always clear in his declaration that it was their vocation as a body to preach to all men, faithful and heathen alike, both by the example of a life of service lived among men, and by direct, formal, widespread evangelization.[2] From this there followed the second distinguishing note of the friars. They formed from the first one great body, not an aggregate of communities; they were not bound as individuals to perpetual stability in a particular home, nor even to continual residence in any home; in the eyes of St Francis, the friar, like his Master, had no home, and must be prepared to spend much of his life on the road or as a pilgrim lodger; he might be sent, or might volunteer to go, anywhere in the world where souls were to be found needing to hear the gospel preached.[3]

Besides these two characteristics, which were in a sense external, the Rule of St Francis made three essentially spiritual demands which were from the first to cause the keenest controversy and searching of heart, and which have never ceased to attract and to perplex both friars and historians throughout the centuries. These were absolute poverty, implying incapacity for even corporate ownership and a refusal of all physical contact with money as a possession; refusal to solicit or accept ecclesiastical privilege; and the renunciation of all human learning. Those who have studied the history of the religious orders in the twelfth century will have no difficulty in recognizing the accuracy with which Francis's intuition had hit upon the three great contemporary sources of spiritual corruption. The avarice and capitalization of all religious bodies; the litigation and chicanery that accompanied the struggle for privilege and exemption; the desiccation of theology, and particularly of those branches of theology concerned with Scripture and the spiritual life, and the prevalence of an arid and heartless ingenuity among the class of clerics who still held almost a monopoly of learning—these are, and must continue to be, the commonplaces of all who consider the life of the Church in the fifty years following the death of St Bernard. It is easy to see in these three demands a psychological result of the conversion and call of Francis himself, from traffic to poverty, from class warfare to the common life, from illiteracy (in its contemporary sense) to evangelization. But the practicability of these demands, as made of an organized body of men counted by many thousands, and even their desirability in all circumstances, were not so easy to grant. Ownership, and the holding of money, a position of chartered independence, a command of the learning of the centuries, these were not of themselves

---

1 Cf. the opening words of the little treatise *De religiosa habitatione in eremo* (Böhmer, 46): 'Illi, qui volunt religiose stare in heremis,' etc., and the reference to such friars in *Speculum Perfectionis*, c. 72, § 14, pp. 213–14: 'Isti sunt fratres mei milites tabulae rotundae qui latitant in desertis et remotis locis ut diligentius vacent orationi et meditationi', etc. These words are surely authentic.

2 *V. supra* p. 118, n. 4, and *Regula Prima*, §§7, 14 (Böhmer, 5, 9).

3 Cf. *Regula Prima*, §16 (Böhmer, 10).

evil, or inconsistent with perfection of soul. As regards the first, the example of Christ Himself could be, and was in the event, alleged victoriously;[1] for the others, such recent examples of sanctity as Thomas of Canterbury and Anselm of Bec might have been put forward. Material possessions, the advantages of privilege, and the riches of the mind, though often the occasion of spiritual loss, are not in themselves evil or the cause of evil; it is not the material presence of creatures, but the desire for them, that separates from God. Yet Francis demanded of his followers these three material renunciations with inexorable reiteration,[2] and the early history of the Friars Minor is in large part a record of the mental strife which was the outcome of attempts to reconcile departures from the letter of the Rule and Testament with fidelity to the profession of a friar.

IV

The spontaneity, the independence and the freshness that radiate to such a unique degree from every recorded act and word of Francis have been remarked by all who have studied the sources of our knowledge of his life. They have, indeed, often been misinterpreted as if they were a shaking off of the established order of the Church, or a novel restatement of the spirit and ideals of Christianity. Such a view, in itself without any historical basis, fails to take reckoning of the spiritual, supernatural power which made Francis what he was. Free as was his spirit and antipathetic to formalism and Pharisaism of all kinds, spontaneous and original as were all his words and works, they were so because he lived and moved by a light and love simpler than law, of which Christ's teaching in the gospel record and the tradition of the Church were expressions in human words. To most men, the doctrines of the Church and her sacraments appear as means of attaining to Christ; Francis knew Christ more directly, lived in Him and His sacraments, and saw in the Church the reflected beauty of God's authority. His freedom was not the freedom of revolt or escape, but of eminent simplicity, and confident self-possession.

For this very reason, the absolute freshness and originality which were characteristic of his mind had full scope. Perhaps they can be appreciated adequately only by those long familiar with the religious literature of the early middle ages and of the renaissance of the eleventh and twelfth centuries. Francis is, indeed, spontaneous and original on a double count; he has neither the outlook nor the culture of the early middle ages. The *Weltanschauung* common to all minds in the Western Church between Augustine and Gregory VII, which is seen alike in St Benedict and Gregory

---

1 In the Bull *Cum inter nonnullos* of John XXII (12 Nov. 1323) declaring heretical, as against the Fraticelli and others, the assertion that Christ and His Apostles: 'non habuisse aliqua (bona) nec in communi etiam' (cf. Denzinger-Bannwart, *Enchiridion Symbolorum*, no. 494).

2 Cf. *Testamentum*, §§7, 8 (Böhmer, 26).

the Great, in Bede and in Peter Damian, and which was in part the outcome of the collapse of the ancient civilization and the impotence of the new nations to attain mental self-possession—the outlook which saw the forces of evil as all but visible and tangible, and which regarded catastrophe and judgement as always impending upon the world—this has given place, for Francis, to a more personal, direct view, in which the human life of Christ on earth is the centre of the world's history and the model of all lives. Together with the old outlook has disappeared also the emphasis on the need for a flight from the world to the desert or at least into the bosom of a monastic society apart from the rest of men; for Francis solitude is something entirely spiritual.

Nor is there with him any trace of that literary culture which clothes even the most intimate utterances of such wholly sincere voices as those of Anselm, Bernard and Ailred. Compared with the limpid freshness of Francis, the letters and dialogues of the abbots of Clairvaux and Rievaulx seem artificial and rhetorical; they are of a school and of a date; the most characteristic utterances of Francis have something of the dateless purity of the gospels. Anselm and Ailred consciously, Bernard perhaps unconsciously, speak to the mind as well as to the spirit; Francis speaks directly to the soul.

V

Francis had by nature a mind exquisitely sensitive and keenly receptive of all beauty, whether of earth or sky, of colour, sound or taste, and as readily repelled by every manifestation of deformity or squalor.[1] That this keen and unstudied love of all beauty grew throughout his life and was greatest during the last months when his body was one wound and every sense ached is a commonplace among his biographers; it extended to all creation, flowers, trees and animals, and was most characteristic when it found a new joy in the elemental clarity and beauty of the most familiar things, sun, moon and stars, earth, air, cloud and water. In its simplicity, its purity, this faculty of Francis to seize upon the central beauty of all creation inevitably recalls the similar, but still purer and more comprehensive, faculty in Christ Himself, which so often passes unnoticed by reason of its extreme directness and simplicity. Along with this went a delicacy and intuition of sympathy hard to parallel even among the saints. Perhaps the most revealing of all traits in Francis's nature is his expression in terms of a mother's love of the tireless tenderness of care which all should have for those under their charge. His ministers are to be

1 The indications abound in the biographies, e.g. *I Celano*, 2: 'in jocis, in curiosis...in cantilenis, in vestibus mollibus et fluidis...prodigus; *II Celano*, 7: 'sumptuosum praeparat prandium, cibaria sapida duplicat'; *I Celano*, 3: 'pulchritudo agrorum, vinearum amoenitas, et quicquid visu pulchrum est, in nullo eum potuit (*sc.* amplius) delectare'; *Testamentum*, § I (Böhmer, 24): 'nimis michi videbatur amarum videre leprosos'; *Leg. 3 Soc.* 8, 12, 14 (rich clothes); III, 20 (affection for others); IV, 26 (horror of lepers); VII, 42 (rich foods); III, 22, VII, 46 (thrice), IX, 58 (references to Francis singing in French, *gallice*).

as mothers to their friars; in the minute treatise on brethren in the hermitages the term 'mother' occurs no less than six times in this sense, and Francis, who allowed and encouraged those nearest him to address him thus, assumes the title in his most intimate address to his beloved disciple.[1] In this, as in all things else, he was no doubt following the exemplar and echoing the expressions of Christ,[2] but it was also the revelation of a new age in Europe of which Ailred of Rievaulx had been a harbinger half a century before; to Francis, rather than to the centres of contemporary learning, must we look for the fruit of the promise that had been given by the flowering of the renaissance of humanism a hundred years before.

A similar freshness appears on the deeper, more spiritual plane, and in nothing, perhaps, is this seen more clearly than in Francis's use of Scripture. It has often been remarked that Bernard's writings are a mosaic of sentences, phrases, words, allusions and reminiscences drawn from the inspired books, and though a familiarity with Scripture almost as great is found in all the lettered ecclesiastics of the day, such as Peter of Blois, Baldwin of Canterbury, and the rest, there is a sincerity and a reality in Bernard's quotation which the others lack. Yet, when compared with Francis, Bernard in his turn appears frigid, artificial and unreal. The most characteristic writings of Francis are little more than centos of passages from the gospels, but the quotations have in them nothing of art; they present the direct, not the allegorical meaning of the words; they are, indeed, not quotations from a book, however sacred, but words of life and power, words which are works, truths that have been lived. To a superficial reader it might seem that the sentences which follow one another have been assembled almost perfunctorily by a memory which had no other store of wealth, but the more thoughtful will realize very speedily that the choice of texts, their order, and the illustration that they give, reveal a spiritual vision of marvellous clarity and penetration.

And because he was conscious alike of his vision and of its clarity Francis never ceased to assert the originality of the life that he had found for himself and his friars, and to resist all attempts that were made within and without the order to pour the new wine into old bottles. When we remember how faithfully each new monastic reformer of the early middle ages from Benedict to Lanfranc had copied the model of the past, and how even the most clear-sighted and drastic legislators of the revival had staked their all upon reproducing as nearly as possible the practice of distant antiquity, Italian or Egyptian, the resolution of the unlettered deacon

---

1 *Regula Prima*, §9 (Böhmer, 7): 'et quilibet diligat et nutriat fratrem suum, sicut mater diligit et nutrit filium suum'; *De religiosa habitatione in deserta* (Böhmer, 46); *II Celano*, 137, where Fra Pacifico twice addresses Francis as *carissima mater*; above all Francis's *Epistola ad fratrem Leonem* (Böhmer, 46): 'dico tibi, fili mi, et sicut mater', etc.

2 E.g., Matt. xxiii. 37: 'Jerusalem...quoties volui congregare filios tuos quemadmodum gallina congregat pullos suos sub alas.' Allowance must also be made for Francis's memory of the love he had himself received from his mother. Sabatier (*Speculum Perfectionis*, p. 82, note *d*), justly remarks the presence in Francis's utterances of a 'bonté d'une délicatesse qui n'a jamais été surpassée.'

Francis, who reverenced all priests and religious as his masters,[1] to have nothing to do with the Rule and regulations of Augustine, Benedict or Cîteaux,[2] but to initiate a new way of following Christ in lowliness and simplicity, becomes all the more striking in contrast.[3] To this resolution he held to the end, not only in private conference among his sympathetic disciples, but in crowded general chapter and in presence of Cardinal Ugolino.

VI

The Friars Minor, then, according to the mind of their founder, were a new model in Christendom. The novelty of their way was to be found in its simplicity and lowliness, and also in the fact that their way of life was to have the full liberty of Christ's human life on earth. The friars were not to live, like the early monks and the later eremitical orders, wholly apart from men, nor were they to live the segregated lives of the corporate bodies, as did the black and white monks of the twelfth century, and the canonical orders in general. They were to live and work as Christ had lived and worked, now in the hidden labourer's life of Nazareth, now alone in the desert and mountains, now on the highways and in the market-places of Galilee and Judea. And this life was to be lived, this work of evangelization was to be done, as Christ had lived and preached, in actual poverty, without assured means of livelihood and without any aid from the training and learning of the schools; the friars were to be at once more free and more strictly confined than the new orders of the previous century, which had vied with each other in devising constitutional safeguards for poverty, seclusion and abstinence. The followers of Francis had the gospel freedom of eating what was set before them, and of choosing, now to preach to the infidel, now to retire to the mountain hermitage,[4] and they were relieved of the heavy choral and ceremonial observances of a great abbey. Their superiors, in Francis's original scheme, were to be neither the permanent heads of families and the great prelates such as were the abbots, black and

---

1 *Regula Prima*, §19 (Böhmer, 12): 'Et omnes clericos et omnes religiosos habeamus pro dominis; *Testamentum*, §3 (Böhmer, 25): 'Et si...invenirem pauperculos sacerdotes... ipsos...volo timere, amare et honorare, sicut meos dominos.'

2 'Et nolo quod nominetis mihi regulam': *Verba S. P. Francisci*, in Lemmens, *Documenta Antiqua*, I, 104. Cf. also his denunciation (*Speculum Perfectionis*, c. 41, §3, p. 105) of the *praelati quidam* who lead the friars away from his teaching, *proponentes illis antiquorum exempla*.

3 *Documenta Antiqua*, ed. Lemmens, I, 104: 'Dominus...volebat quod essem unus novellus pazzus (= *Ital.* pazzo, fool; an allusion to *I Corinth.* 1–3) in hoc mundo: et noluit nos ducere Dominus per aliam viam.'

4 *Regula Prima*, §16 (Böhmer, 10): 'quicumque fratrum voluerint ire inter saracenos et alios infideles vadant de licentia sui ministri'. This permission reappears, somewhat more cautiously worded, in the *Regula Bullata*, §12 (Böhmer, 24): 'quicumque fratrum divina inspiratione voluerit ire inter saracenos et alios infideles petant inde licentiam a suis ministris provincialibus (who are only to allow suitable applicants to proceed). For the hermits, *v. De religiosa habitatione in eremo* (Böhmer, 46): 'illi qui volunt religiose stare in heremis', etc.

white, nor the impersonal directors of a vast army of effectives, but the servants and 'mothers' of groups of friars, whose only responsibilities were to be spiritual.[1] At the same time (and only so could such freedom exist) every friar, by his act of surrender to God, committed himself to a literal and complete observance of the words of Christ commanding trust in God and the perfect following of Himself; he was held also to an absolute obedience to the letter and spirit of Francis's Rule, to the commands of superiors within that Rule, and to absolute poverty. Abandonment once and for all of all material possessions; a life without care for the present or provision for the future; a readiness and desire to imitate Christ in His Passion and death—these were the three words that Francis and Bernard, his first friar, had heard before the order of Friars Minor was born,[2] and Francis continued throughout his life to realize them more completely in himself and to demand that his followers should accept them not merely as an ideal, but as the practical guiding principles of his new way for all.

VII

This brief outline of the teaching of Francis has been given as an aid towards an appreciation of his significance in the religious history of Europe and to an understanding of some of the controversies and ideals of the English friars in the first decade of the province. Too many, by using of Francis and his words such terms as 'mystical', 'ideal' and 'romantic', have escaped not only from the task of setting his most earnest and intimate utterances alongside the later history of his order, but also from the deeper effort involved in the comprehension of his own mind and life.

As all who have read the history of Francis know, his friars did not as a body accept, even during his lifetime, the way of life he wished to give them in all its purity. Failing for breath in the rarified air, they fell back into the broader ways that he had of set purpose abandoned. They would not live in the complete poverty of resources, material and constitutional, which he required of them, and they adopted, to some extent at least, the organization and practices of earlier religious institutes. In things of the spirit elasticity and tension increase and decrease conjointly; only the heroic can be free; and thus the Friars Minor, unable to accept in full Francis's Testament, were caught up in the more complex and more rigid network of disciplinary and constitutional regulations. Yet although something of

1 Cf. the words used by Francis of himself (*Documenta Antiqua*, ed. Lemmens, I, 97; cf. *Speculum Perfectionis*, c. 71, p. 206): 'meum officium est spirituale, videlicet praelatio supe- fratres, quare debeo dominari vitiis et ea emendare...nolo carnifex fieri ad percutiendum.'

2 *II Celano*, 15; *Leg. 3 Soc.* c. 8, p. 52. The texts were Matt. xix. 21: 'Sell all thou hast', etc.; Luke ix. 3: 'Take nothing for your journey, neither...bread nor money', etc.; and Matt. xvi. 24: 'If any man will come after me, let him deny himself, and take up his cross, and follow me.' For the *ultima voluntas* of Francis, *v. Speculum Perfectionis*, c. 2, pp. 4-5.

sadness hangs over the history of the Friars Minor of the second generation, the new life that Francis himself had lived and shown to others remained and remains in the Church, and has in all centuries inspired individuals and groups within his Order as the model for a type of sanctity which all recognize as Franciscan. It has, besides, enriched the spirit of all Europe, not only, or even principally, as a new manifestation of the brotherhood of all men and of the share of all creatures in the beauty and beneficence of God, but as a showing forth of the Gospel lived in its fullness with a detail and a clarity rare to equal in any age, and as a revelation of the imitation of Christ crucified, in love and suffering, which though present in essence in all Christian sanctity, appeared in Francis in a new form to which the growing mind of Europe responded at once, and which was to prove the prototype of much that was to come in the religious life of the West.

CHAPTER XII

THE COMING OF THE MINORS

I

The characters and antecedents of the first followers of St Francis to arrive in England, and the events of their first years of residence, give a peculiar interest to the early history of the English province of the Friars Minor,[1] and we are fortunate in possessing, in the chronicle of Brother Thomas, a record which, though far from being as full as could be desired, is nevertheless more complete than any which remain from the other northern countries, and is, indeed, a valuable source of information concerning the early history of the order in general and of several of its most distinguished members.[2] It has often been remarked that the early Minors, apostles of poverty and simplicity of life as they were, have yet left more intimate record of their doings than any other contemporary religious body. Besides the literature directly connected with St Francis and his companions, at least three friars of the second generation have given vivid accounts of the order and its luminaries as they saw them. Perhaps the very simplicity they were taught to prize, and a sense that they were a new leaven in the Church, together with a real appreciation of the saintly and remarkable personalities of their brethren, combined to inspire these compositions. In any case, the three Franciscan chroniclers Jordan of Giano, Salimbene of Parma and Thomas of Eccleston have, for all their differences of character, a striking family resemblance in their love of personal detail

---

1 English Franciscan studies, as all conversant with the subject are aware, owe an inestimable debt to the late A. G. Little who, during a long scholar's life of more than half a century, succeeded by patient research, careful editing, luminous exposition and wise inspiration, in creating a literature, the work of himself and his friends, which, as regards the first century of the province, and in particular of Oxford, leaves little to be desired for accuracy and completeness of information. Most of his works will be cited in subsequent notes; a list (which does not aim at being exhaustive) will be found in the Bibliography.

2 The chronicle of Brother Thomas 'of Eccleston' (the convenient eponym has apparently no more reliable authority than a note by Bale) was first edited, with many imperfections, by J. S. Brewer in the Rolls Series as vol. I of *Monumenta Franciscana* (1858). Brewer's text served as basis for other editions during the nineteenth century, including that in *Analecta Franciscana*, I (1885) and extracts by F. Liebermann in *MGH, SS*, xxviii (1888); a definitive edition was published by Dr Little, making use of a MS. (Cheltenham Phillipps, 3119) which he was the first to examine with care (*Tractatus Fr. Thomae vulgo dicti de Eccleston, De adventu fratrum Minorum in Angliam*: Collection d'études...du Moyen Age, Paris, 1909). The author, who had spent twenty-six years in collecting his information, finished his work, c. 1258-9. For all that can be known of his methods, etc., v. Dr Little's introduction, xx-xxii. Despite the time given to the preparation of his materials and a superficial appearance of order in arrangement, Eccleston is in fact extremely disorderly and confused in method; the reader will find Dr Little's excellent index invaluable.

and anecdote, and in the direct, individual and unaffected style of their writing.[1]

Of the Englishman nothing is known save the little he tells us. He introduces himself as Brother Thomas *tout court*; the surname 'of Eccleston', by which he is commonly known, is due to the Tudor antiquary Bale. Brother Thomas himself tells us, by implication, that he entered the order in 1232–3, and wrote his chronicle in 1258–9; from passing allusions we gather that he had studied at Oxford, that he had visited London and other places, and that he had known several eminent English friars.[2] That is all, and his book is singularly free from egoism. In addition, whenever it can be controlled by contemporary documents, it appears to be remarkably sober and accurate; it is, indeed, with all its simplicity, one of the last examples of that genius for historical writing that distinguished the countrymen of Bede for five centuries after his death.

II

Before approaching the history of the English province it is necessary to understand something of the situation of the young order at the time of the English mission.

Innocent III had given his verbal approval to the original simple outline of Francis's Rule in 1210,[3] but for several years after that date the work and government of the growing body had kept to the informal, unorganized character of its beginnings. An important step forward took place at the Pentecost chapter at the Porziuncola in 1217, when the office of provincial minister was instituted, the first provinces divided, and the first great missions of friars to countries outside Italy and across the Alps despatched. Two years later, in 1219, the first movements of discontent came to a head in the spring chapter, when a number of those friars who had never lived in intimacy with Francis and who, before their entry into the brotherhood, had passed through the schools or lived in ecclesiastical circles, demanded a formal organization for their body and the adoption of the main disciplinary and constitutional framework of the old orders, to which the Fourth Lateran Council had recently given such precision. Francis refused to make any compromise; the chapter effected a further division of provinces, and Francis set out for the East.

In his absence, and in the lack of direction and administration which

---

1 For an account of all these chronicles, *v*. A. G. Little, *Chronicles of the Mendicant Friars*, in *BSFS*, II, 85–103, reprinted *FP*, 25–41. For Jordan, *v*. *Chronica Fratris Jordani*, ed. H. Böhmer, in *Collection d'études*, VI (1908); for Salimbene, *Chronica fr. Salimbene de Adam*, ed. O. Holder-Egger, in *MGH, SS*, XXXII.

2 *Eccleston*, introd. xx; 2, 14, 65 *et al*.

3 This, the original Rule, has not survived. For references to its contents, *v*. Böhmer, *Analekten*, Appendix, 83–9; for a critical reconstruction *v*. Fr Cuthbert, *St Francis of Assisi*, Appendix I and Moorman, *Sources*, 51–4.

ensued, the vicars whom he had left in control of the fraternity returned to their previous designs and obtained from Honorius III a decree[1] making a year's novitiate obligatory, binding professed friars for life to the order, and forbidding brethren to journey about without letters of obedience from a provincial minister. Simple and inevitable as were these enactments, they transformed the Friars Minor from a brotherhood into a religious order of the Church, and marked the first stage in the history of the long and painful struggle between the purely spiritual conception which Francis had of his friars as followers of Christ in perfect poverty and simplicity, a new leaven to the world, and the legal, external conception of the body as a new order, to be organized and exploited for the needs and with the weapons of the thirteenth century.

Francis, on his return from the East, realized that a parting of the ways was at hand. He resigned the direct, external government of the brotherhood, appointing Peter Cathanii Vicar,[2] but devoted himself, with assistance, to composing a Rule which should maintain the spiritual principles and way of life for which he stood, while allowing for a certain degree of organization to harmonize with the common canonical discipline of the Church. He thus completed, early in 1221, the so-called *Regula Prima*. On 10 March of that year Peter Cathanii died, and his office was filled by the friar whose character has proved an enigma so baffling to historians, Elias, called of Cortona. In May of the same spring Francis laid his rewritten Rule before the chapter; once more the opposition broke out, led by the ministers, who desired both a greater latitude in matters of property, and a closer following of tradition on points of organization and observance. Francis held to what he had written, and externally his will prevailed, but the opposition remained, and thenceforward the three parties appeared in outline which were to play so great a part in the years that followed: the intimate companions of Francis and those who stood with them for the simplest, most spiritual and most literally evangelical conception of their life; those of the original opposition, who wished for a powerful, active, strongly governed order at the sacrifice of absolute poverty and simplicity; and a third body, which came gradually to the fore, composed largely of men of learning and zeal, but differing in character and outlook from St Francis, who wished for a strict observance of the Rule with the fewest possible changes, and with no concessions to worldliness or luxury, but who desired to take a full part in the intellectual and ecclesiastical and even the political and social activities of the age. As for Francis, he retired more and more from the direct government of his order; he gave as his ostensible reason the ever-increasing maladies which had begun in the East and continued to develop, reaching a climax after his reception of the stigmata; on the deeper level, however, it is clear that he

---

1 This was the Bull *Cum secundum consilium* of 22 September 1220 (in Sbaralea, *Bullarium Franciscanum*, I, p. 6).

2 Or, possibly, General, *v*. Sabatier, *Speculum Perfectionis*, ed. 1928–31, II, 92.

desired to be away from mere routine contacts in order that his life of conformity with the suffering Christ might have free scope. Henceforward, as he said, he was to be a living example of his Rule rather than the ruler of his friars. He did, nevertheless, once more rewrite the Rule, making it more formal and concrete, though preserving the essential notes of poverty and simplicity. The first draft of this revision disappeared in the hands of Elias and the ministers. A second draft, after undergoing some modifications at the hands both of the ministers and of Honorius III, was finally approved by the pope at the end of November 1223, though the opposition was never wholly reconciled by its provisions.

Such was the constitutional position of the Friars Minor when, in the June chapter of 1224 at the Porziuncola, the decision was taken to despatch a mission to England, and Fra Agnello of Pisa, then minister in Paris, was appointed by Francis himself as minister provincial. He and his eight companions, who had received hospitality and means of transport from the monks of Fécamp, landed at Dover on Tuesday, 10 September 1224.[1] On Saturday of the same week, the feast of the Exaltation of the Cross, Francis, in solitude on Monte Alverna, received the stigmata.

II

The little group, like all those that went out in the early days on new ventures from Assisi, was composed of the most diverse elements and might be cross-divided in half a dozen different ways; probably several, if not almost all, were volunteers. The chronicler notes that four were clerks and five lay; of the four clerks only one was a priest, and he was not the leader; the provincial, like Francis, was a deacon. Three only were English by birth, and of these two were young men: one came from Norfolk, the second from Northamptonshire, the third from Devon. Of the rest, the minister was from Pisa, one from Florence, another from Lombardy, and yet two more were Italians. Three at least had drunk of Franciscan tradition near the source: Agnellus had probably been received into the order by Francis himself in 1211; Richard of Ingworth, the doyen of the party, had joined the brotherhood in Italy and had been among the first band to cross the Alps in 1217;[2] Laurence of Beauvais, who had apparently known St Francis in the past, returned to visit him in 1225–6 and was one of the two to whom the saint, on request, gave his tunic;[3] the subsequent careers of several are, in their variety, typical of the primitive individuality of the order: thus Richard of Ingworth, after holding important office, made the petition to which the Rule invited all friars and died a missionary to the

1 *Eccleston*, 3–11.

2 *Eccleston*, 4: 'qui primus extitit qui citra montes populo praedicavit in ordine.'

3 *Eccleston*, 7: 'ad beatum Franciscum regressus, ipsum videre frequenter et ejus colloquiis consolari meruit; tunicam denique suam sibi pater sanctus liberalissime contulit benedictioneque dulcissima laetificatum in Angliam remisit.' For the gift of the tunic *v. Speculum Perfectionis*, c. 34 (ed. Sabatier, 1928, pp. 92–3).

Saracens; Melioratus returned to Italy and William to France; Richard of Devon, after passing to a number of provinces, spent the last eleven years of his life in retirement at Romney, which was perhaps the English friary most resembling the hermitages of the Abruzzi and the March of Ancona.[1]

But though few in number and including three youthful members, the band had not been chosen at random. Several of the friars were of exceptional holiness of life. Agnellus the minister was celebrated for his sanctity during his ten years of office; he died at Oxford after a long and painful illness, during the last three days of which, like Ailred of Rievaulx sixty years before, he called continuously and with joy for Christ to come to him; his tomb became a place of pilgrimage, and he is at the present day venerated as *Beatus* in his order.[2] Of the others, Eccleston characterizes one as supremely holy[3] and three others as exemplars of virtue.[4] Laurence of Beauvais passed among the companions of St Francis for a saint,[5] and Melioratus, who returned to Italy, had a reputation as worker of miracles.[6] Nor were they without natural ability. Agnellus, who had been custodian of Paris, was a man of charm, judgement and tact which made him the friend and agent of the king and of magnates ecclesiastical and lay; Richard of Ingworth later became first minister provincial of Ireland from 1230 to 1239, and William of Ashby was in turn guardian of Oxford, custodian of Oxford, and visitor of Ireland. But to those who saw them arrive at Dover they did not appear men of distinction. Nine wayfarers of all ages, clothed in rough and patched tunics, without visible means of support, who had crossed the Channel by charity and sought lodging as beggars, seemed to those unfamiliar with the friars to be mere vagabonds, and according to one account they were actually treated as such soon after landing.[7] At Canterbury, however, whither they at once proceeded, they were received hospitably by the monks of Christ Church, and remained in the cathedral monastery for two days as guests.

III

The rapid decision with which the nine made three important settlements within six weeks shows clearly that their policy had been settled before the arrival in England. For this Agnellus was probably responsible; he would, during his residence at Paris, have had every opportunity of informing himself as to conditions across the Channel. The procedure adopted differed considerably from that of Francis and his first companions in central Italy ten years previously. The climate of the country, its sparse

---

1 Romney, which appears in *Eccleston* (p. 5) as Romehale, had ceased to exist a century later and the only other known reference to the house is an entry in the Liberate Roll of 1241 (*Eccleston*, 5 note *b*). Cf. A. G. Little in *Archaeologia Cantiana*, L (1939), 152.

2 *Eccleston*, 4, 55, 94–6.

3 *Eccleston*, 4: 'eximiae sanctitatis praeclara exempla praebuerat' [Ric. de Ingewurde].

4 *Eccleston*, 5–6.   5 Celano, *Vita Secunda*, ch. 181; 'magnae sanctitatis.'

6 *Chron. XXIV Generalium*, in *Analecta Franciscana*, III (1897), 268: 'vitae sanctissimae et clarus miraculis.'   7 So *Chronicon de Lanercost* (ed. Stevenson), *s.a.* 1224.

agricultural population, and the scarcity of towns and large villages would in any case have made hermitages unpractical and long missionary journeys unfruitful, but Agnellus, as his later actions showed, intended from the start that his friars should have a part in the intellectual life of the country and had decided to strike out at once for the great centres of life and population and occupy them one by one as speedily as might be. Thus within a few weeks steps were taken that were to determine the character of the English province and its work for the three centuries of its existence.

Remaining himself at Canterbury with four others as guests at the Poor Priests' hospice,[1] he sent the two senior Englishmen, Richard of Ingworth and Richard of Devon, with two Italian friars, to London; there, after staying a fortnight with the Preaching Friars, they hired a house in Cornhill,[2] which done, the two Englishmen pressed on to Oxford, where they arrived before 1 November, and once more stayed with the Preaching Friars for a week until they obtained the hire of a house in the parish of St Ebbe's.[3] This, too, they left within a few months and journeyed to Northampton, William of Ashby, the third Englishman of the party, who was still a novice, being summoned from Canterbury to become guardian at Oxford. Thus within some six months of their landing at Dover the nine had established friaries at the three centres—ecclesiastical, civil and intellectual—of national life, and at the important town which, by reason of its position between north and south, east and west, was so often the scene of meetings of those in authority in Church and State. Nor did the growth cease there, for within the next five years a dozen more houses had been founded at Norwich (1226), Worcester, Hereford (c. 1227), Bristol, Gloucester, Cambridge, Leicester, Nottingham, Stamford, Salisbury (-1230), Lincoln and King's Lynn (1230). This list, including as it does almost all the principal towns of the central parallelogram of England, is a sufficient indication of Franciscan policy; by 1240 another twenty friaries had been added by the occupation of the towns of southern and eastern England, and by plantations north of the Humber at York (c. 1230), Carlisle (1233), Newcastle (1237), Durham, Scarborough and Hartlepool (c. 1239); by the last date, indeed, the Friars Minor had penetrated into Scotland and were established at Roxburgh (1235), if not also at Berwick.[4] The names of these thirty-four friaries, when contrasted with a similar number of early Cistercian foundations a little less than a century before, cannot fail to strike the observer with a sense of the profound difference in aim between the white monks and the friars. The sites of the Cistercian abbeys, with

1 For this, and early days at Canterbury, v. C. Cotton, *The Grey Friars of Canterbury* (*BSFS*, 1924).

2 For the beginnings of London, v. C. L. Kingsford, *The Grey Friars of London* (*BSFS*, VI, 1915).

3 For the history of the Oxford convent, v. A. G. Little, *The Grey Friars in Oxford* (*OHS*, xx, 1892); for the Oxford school, v. infra p. 207.

4 For a list of friaries with dates of foundation v. Little, *FP*, 217–29, and D. Knowles, *Religious Houses*, 109–12.

scarcely an exception, were unknown to the world before their arrival, and are familiar to it to-day only when the accident of time has left enough of the ruined arches of the monks to attract the antiquary or the sightseer. The friars, on the other hand, had within twenty years settled at the two university towns, and fifteen out of the nineteen existing cathedral cities,[1] and at no less than twenty-five of the towns which were already, or which subsequently became, the county towns of England.

IV

It goes without saying that a settlement of friars, and above all one of the Friars Minor, needed far less resources and occupied far less space than even the smallest and most primitive house of monks or canons. This was especially true of the earliest settlements, often made by a group counting no priest among its members and in any case not counting a private church or chapel among the first *desiderata*, but even later wherever there was a question of a simple friary nothing more was needed than an ordinary house, situated among the other houses of a town and not accompanied by any area of open land. To this essential simplicity of demand, the first friars added a rigid observance of their founder's call to actual and absolute poverty and to his provisions against ownership. By establishing themselves in towns which in most cases had no public connection with existing religious houses, and by their avowed object of working for those among whom they lived, they immediately enlisted the sympathy and help of a class of the population now rising to importance and outside the ranks of the benefactors to the old orders: the class, that is, of wealthy merchants, shopkeepers and artificers who were just beginning to control the municipal administration of the young towns. In almost every case the list of benefactors to a friary includes among its early names those of mayors, sheriffs and leading citizens of the town concerned, though gifts were not wanting from feudal families who happened to own land or house property there, and many friaries enjoyed regular or occasional gifts of fuel, clothes, leather and foodstuffs from the king.

As they were forbidden by rule to own property, and as it was scarcely practicable for the small gifts of buildings and gardens made by a number of citizens to remain radically in the possession of the original owners, a procedure was often adopted by which the community of the town held the property for the use of the friars. Such was the case at Canterbury, London, Oxford and elsewhere, though when the crown or great landowners were concerned the donor retained radical ownership.[2] Whatever

---

1 The four without friaries were Bath, Ely, Rochester (small towns largely controlled by monks) and Wells (also as yet unimportant).

2 E.g. *Eccleston*, 25 (Canterbury): 'et quia fratres nihil sibi omnino appropriare voluerunt, facta est propria communitati civitatis, fratribus vero pro civium libitu commodata.' For a further discussion of this and other points, v. A. G. Little, *Studies in English Franciscan History*, pp. 6 *seqq.*

the arrangement, the property in question was, at least during the first half-century of the province, insignificant in value. Beginning with a small house, the friars added a few necessary buildings, or acquired adjacent tenements as need arose, but any additions, not excluding the chapel, were for many decades low, wooden erections run up in a few days or hours. At first, free land was refused or returned to the donor, but it soon became customary to obtain space for a garden and orchard, and at a few houses, of which Oxford is a notable example, the numbers in residence demanded considerable space for accommodation, together with a hall in which lectures might be given.

It has frequently been asserted that the first friars chose of set purpose insecure and insanitary sites in the purlieus;[1] closer examination has found no evidence that any principle lay behind their choice other than that of obtaining a lodging among the people, but as the site was usually the gift of public authority or small benefactors cheapness was always a consideration, and it is an undoubted fact that very many friaries lay in undesirable situations near the city walls, exposed to floods or surrounded by cesspools or shambles, and in several cases it was ultimately necessary to transfer the convent elsewhere. It must, however, be remembered that a fair-sized community, including a number of the old and infirm, living decade after decade upon a particular site, would be more sensitive to its disabilities and more vocal in the expression of their feelings than would the changing, illiterate families of the poor.

The minute groups of the first settlement were soon supplemented by recruits from all quarters. The chronicler, looking back over thirty years, has singled out a number of names for mention; he divides them into four groups, and the division would seem to have been made from a mixture of local, chronological and social considerations.[2] The first small group, apparently of some who joined the London house while Agnellus was in charge, contains a priest and two clerics, thus showing that the appeal of the friars was recognized immediately in ecclesiastical circles, and at least two of the novices came from City families of note, one, Joyce, of Cornhill, being a son of Joyce fitzPeter, sheriff in 1221, and another a skilled tailor in the household of the justiciar, Hubert de Burgh.

Of more significance is the second group, that of university-trained *magistri* who became friars, for the most part at Oxford, in the first years. Eccleston gives six names, of which the last is that of the celebrated Adam Marsh, an Oxford graduate who took the habit at Worcester between 1226 and 1232;[3] to the names of *magistri* he adds John of Reading, abbot of the Austin canons of Oseney (1229-35), who became a friar in 1235, but he

1 This view was propounded by J. S. Brewer, in his important introduction to *Monumenta Franciscana*, I, p. xvii; it is examined by Little, *Studies*, 10-13.

2 Eccleston, *Collatio III*, 'de receptione Novitiorum.'

3 For Adam Marsh, *v.* his letters in *Monumenta Franciscana*, I, ed. J. S. Brewer, and an essay by Fr Cuthbert, O.S.F.C., in *The Romanticism of St Francis* (2 ed. 190-235); also *v. infra*, pp. 209-10.

does not add, as he might well have done, that of Ralph of Maidstone, bishop of Hereford (1234-9), who resigned his see to become a friar. Eccleston's third division contains the names of four members of noble or knightly families who took the habit; one of these was the owner of a castle and land at Northampton who had given the friars the site of their convent and whose son had joined the new arrivals against his father's will;[1] taken as a whole, this class of recruit was sufficiently large and distinguished to attract comment from the king. Finally, the chronicler gives the names of a number of eminent English scholars, trained in the university of Paris, who had become friars abroad but returned to England in the early years and were of great influence in the order. Among these Haymo of Faversham must take pride of place; after a few years in England he held a number of important posts abroad and finally, in 1240, became sixth minister general of the Friars Minor, the only Englishman to attain to that high office.

The names given by Eccleston are those of a few representative or distinguished men only. An immense stream of recruits flowed into the friaries in the first decades, and Eccleston's pages become a kind of litany of simple English names—William Joiner, Robert Mercer, Richard Pride and Lawrence Cox. Fortunately, the chronicler provides us with a total, which may be received as accurate, of those actually living in the forty-nine houses of the province in 1256. It is the very large figure of 1242.[2]

V

Agnellus came from Paris, where he had seen many well-known teachers and scholars joining the Friars Minor, and he fixed his eyes from the first on Oxford, but he can scarcely have foreseen, nor would he perhaps altogether have desired, the bent that was to be given to the character of the English province by its connection with the university and the peculiar influence that the Franciscans were to exercise over Oxford thought for a century to come.[3] Certainly, he could not have foreseen two circumstances which contributed very materially to the linking of the destinies of the two bodies of men. The first of these, the great Paris dispersion of spring, 1229, by sending to Oxford numerous eminent *magistri*, many of them English by birth and not a few already friars of Paris, both permanently increased the prestige of the English university and supplied the friars with recruits; some eight years later the most celebrated master of Paris, the Englishman Alexander of Hales, became a Franciscan. It is significant that it should have been in the year of the dispersion that the

1 The father was Richard Gubiun; he had been a justice of assize for Northamptonshire in 1227. Cf. *Eccleston*, 24, 29–30, with Little's notes.

2 *Eccleston*, 14. The names in the text are of benefactors, not friars.

3 The *Chron. XXIV Generalium*, copied by Bartholomew of Pisa (*Eccleston*, Append. Ib, 139–40), says of him: 'sollicitus fuit de studio. De quo aliquando postea doluit, quando videbat quod fratres studebant in vanis, necessariis pretermissis.'

friars of Oxford moved into a larger house purchased for them by public subscription, and that Agnellus should have added the building of a school.

The second circumstance was the intimate connection between Robert Grosseteste and the Friars Minor.[1] The friendship of that eminent man, who had been chancellor and *Magister scholarum* of Oxford since 1214, was probably given to the Franciscans on their first arrival, for he was keenly interested in every movement that could give new life and discipline to the Church; he and Agnellus would have a mutual esteem for each other; but though Eccleston tells us that it was the provincial who, probably between 1227 and 1229, invited Grosseteste to become lecturer to the friars, the initiative must in reality have lain with the chancellor.[2] It has been remarked with justice that his undertaking of the duty shows alike his faith in the Franciscans and his humility; it should not, however, be forgotten that by 1229 the province already counted a number of very distinguished *magistri* among whom may well have been Grosseteste's friend, Adam Marsh, and that a number of young Oxford scholars had become friars, and we may suppose with some degree of confidence that the chancellor's action was a piece of fixed policy. Grosseteste, *nulli secundus* among both the teachers and reforming prelates of his age, might also be taken as their type. His zeal was great, and he was a whole-hearted imitator, as well as a generous admirer, of the laborious life and austere simplicity of the early friars. At the same time, his own career and writings, and a number of his *obiter dicta* that have been preserved, show that he conceived of reform in terms of law, discipline and reason, in the calculated employment of means to the end; mature wisdom, a just observation of possibilities as seen by experience, a love of order and organization—these qualities are always in evidence in Grosseteste. They are the qualities which, under favourable circumstances, can carry great designs to a successful issue, and are by no means incompatible with a deep and fervent religious spirit; but they are not the qualities that made Francis of Assisi what he was, nor are they those which he sought and praised in his most intimate disciples.

On no point, perhaps, is the contrast of outlook between the two men, who, born within a few years of each other, so excited the attention and admiration of their contemporaries, more striking than on that of learning. Grosseteste's words to the English friar, Peter of Tewkesbury, have often been quoted: Unless, he said, the friars encourage study, and devote all their energies to divinity, it will certainly be with them as with religious of other orders who, as we see with such sadness, walk in the darkness of ignorance.[3] Only a few years previously Francis had said that a great scholar when he joined the order ought to resign even his learning, in order that, having stripped himself of such a possession, he might offer

---

1 For Grosseteste, besides particular studies to be quoted later, *v. Roberti Grosseteste Epistolae*, ed. H. R. Luard (*RS*, 25, 1861) and *Robert Grosseteste*, by F. S. Stevenson.

2 *Eccleston*, 60: 'Agnellus...impetravit a...Grossesteste, ut legeret ibi fratribus.'

3 *Eccleston*, 114.

himself naked to the arms of the Crucified.[1] In the event, Grosseteste's action in going as *Magister scholarum* to lecture in the friars' new and simple school in St Ebbe's had results, both in the immediate sequel and in the distant future, more vast than he could possibly have foreseen, for it not only gave an impetus to the growth of the Franciscan faculty at Oxford, but did much to determine the character of the thought that evolved there between the days of Adam Marsh and Roger Bacon, and those of Duns Scotus and William of Occam.

VI

The settlement in towns and, still more, the rapid and universal diffusion of theological studies in the English province very soon made of the Friars Minor in England something very different as a body from the early companions of St Francis and from their contemporaries in central Italy who lived in small groups and remote hermitages. Simplicity, by which term he would seem to understand both a lack of intellectual formation and a spiritual innocence of mind, is often noted by Eccleston as a characteristic of the first brethren.[2] Their lack of letters was soon to give place to a refined subtlety of intellect. Spiritual simplicity, however, a spirit of prayer, of frankness, of poverty and of fidelity to the Rule did not go so early, and for some fifty years at least there were among the Friars Minor in England many examples of unusual fervour and sanctity.

Thomas of Eccleston, in the course of his disjointed memoirs, loves to record the names and virtues of his predecessors and contemporaries in the order, from Agnellus and his first companions to William of Nottingham, who ceased to be provincial in 1254, and others who were still alive when he wrote. He tells us that in the first communities the devotion was such that it was possible at any hour of the night to find one or more engaged in private prayer in the oratory; assiduity in the divine office was as great, and even if only three or four friars were available they chanted all the parts solemnly, so that on principal feasts, mattins and lauds continued throughout the night, as in the palmy days of Cluny. To bear out his general statement, he gives a particular example from Cambridge, where William of Ashby and Hugh of Bugton, assisted only by a lame novice Elias, sang the whole of the office on the Feast of St Laurence.[3] In view of Eccleston's words, it is perhaps significant that an Italian chronicler should have noted a zeal for the divine office as one of the marks of the Englishman Haymo's tenure of office as general.[4]

Almost all the friars whose holiness is praised by the chronicler held

---

1 *II Celano*, 194. 2 E.g. *Eccleston*, 16, 22, 31, 35, 45 (five times), and index, *sub voc.*
3 *Eccleston*, 31, 28 *et al.*
4 *Chronicon Peregrini de Bononia* (*Eccleston*, Append. II, p. 142: 'Hic [Haymo] habuit magnam curam de divino officio celebrando.' Cf. the saying attributed to another prominent English friar, Henry of Reresby: 'si fratres dicerent bene officium divinum, essent oves apostolorum' (*Eccleston*, 39).

important office. If such were the rulers, it may be assumed that there were many among the simpler and more hidden who equalled or surpassed them. Eustace de Merk, guardian of Oxford and custodian of York; Robert of Thornham, guardian of Lynn and custodian of Cambridge; Stephen of Belassise, likewise guardian of Lynn before becoming custodian of Hereford; Salomon, guardian of London, friend of Bishop Ralph Niger and court confessor—these are among those whom Eccleston selects, and the fact that more than one of his group volunteered for the mission to the East or retired from office to a life of prayer and silence shows that there was much of the spirit of the Rule in England.

The province was happy in its first provincial ministers. Something has already been said of Agnellus. When he died, probably in 1236, he was succeeded after an interval by another Pisan friar, Albert, who had already been minister of half a dozen provinces. Like Agnellus, he was a friar of the first days; he had even been privileged to live in intimate companionship with Francis himself. His beginnings were stern, but he soon grew to love the English province, and if he was rigid in his insistence that the Rule should be observed to the full, he had much also of Francis's sympathetic liberty of spirit.[1] Albert became minister general at the deposition of Elias in 1239; his successor was Haymo of Faversham, whose affectionate and peaceful disposition endeared him to all,[2] but he remained in office for a year only, being elected minister general in 1240. He was followed by his vicar, William of Nottingham, chosen by the provincial chapter. Under his guidance the English province reached what was probably the zenith of its first and purest celebrity. It had recently given a general to the order; it counted among its members some of the most distinguished *alumni* of Paris and Oxford, who joined to an exacting zeal for poverty an exquisite capacity of devotion to others,[3] and several of whom, such as Adam Marsh, were celebrated alike for theological learning and for the practical wisdom which made them the friends and counsellors of bishops such as Grosseteste of Lincoln, Ralph of London, and Roger of Coventry; the numbers both of friaries and friars was large and still on the increase, and the reputation of the body for fervour and observance was European in its extent. Their representatives were able to exercise decisive influence in the interests of the primitive purity of the order, and they were praised in the warmest terms by the most eminent of the bishops of England when writing to the pope.[4] It is not surprising that John of Parma, the general who succeeded Haymo, should have held up the English province as an

1 *Eccleston*, 106.

2 *Eccleston*, 57: 'dicebatur anima sua [i.e. eorum] a nonnullis fratribus.'

3 *Eccleston*, 107, where we are told of Haymo who: 'fratres, sicut erat benignissimus et dulcissimus, in omni pace et caritate tenere curavit.'

4 Grosseteste, *ep.* lviii (? of 1238) to Gregory IX: 'sua [= illorum] sancta conversatio vehementer accendit ad mundi contemptum et spontaneam paupertatem, ad humilitatem... obedientiam...patientiam...abstinentiam.' Cf. his letter xxxiv of 1236 to Alexander Stavensby of Lichfield, where he alludes to the *sancta caelestisque conversatio* and *devotio jugis orationis* of the Friars Minor.

example to all and sundry, and should have expressed a wish that it were situated at the centre of the world for all to see.[1]

As is almost invariably the case in things spiritual, the moment of the purest fervour probably preceded by a number of years the moment of recognition and praise. As with Cluny, as with Cîteaux and Clairvaux, so in a lesser way here also the best was perhaps past when John of Parma was uttering his encomium. Eccleston more than once allows a note of apprehension to be heard in his narrative, and the later letters of Adam Marsh are full of sadness.[2] But in Adam, if not in Eccleston, the sadness may have been caused as much by the trend events were taking in Church and State as by any decadence within the order of Friars Minor.

VII

Eccleston is a valuable and indeed a unique witness, not only to the achievements of the first English Minors, but also to the existence of a world of sincere and simple English piety of which neither the chronicles of Paris nor the treatises of Bacon and Pecham give a hint. He alone shows us the leaven of Francis at work in a distant country, and among men who could have had no conception of the background of Umbrian life. His narrative may warn us against making a sweeping or *a priori* judgement unfavourable to all who accepted the *Quo elongati*.

Brother Thomas, like Jordan of Giano, is happiest when telling of the simplicity and purity of the early friars, but there is in his pages no trace of the bitterness of strife or nostalgia for the bright dawn in Umbria. The stories he tells, the enthusiasm he records, are such as form part of the birth of every true religious venture; there is no trace in them of party spirit or apologetic. Eccleston himself is remarkably self-effacing; there are none of the vanities of Salimbene or the occasional naïvetés of Jordan; he gives no personal details, and when he relates incidents which he has heard of one of the actors he earns our respect by making no comment or reflection.

The most attractive parts of his narrative are, as might be expected, those that tell of the simplicity and poverty of the first friars. There is the well-known account of the first days of all at Canterbury:

Soon after this they were granted the use of a small room underneath the schoolhouse. In this they sat almost all day with the door shut, but when the boys had gone home in the evening they went into the schoolroom, made themselves a fire, and sat by it, and sometimes when they were going to have their evening drink in common they put a crock on the fire with lees of beer in it, and then dipped a porringer in the pot and drank a round, while each said something to rouse devotion. One who had the good fortune to share this holy poverty related that their drink was sometimes so thick that they poured in water and so drank it joyfully.[3]

---

1 *Eccleston*, 91–2, 123.   2 *V*. especially his *ep*. ccii.
3 *Eccleston*, 8–9. *Cerevisia* of this kind was more like porridge than modern beer.

There is the equally familiar anecdote of the young novice Salomon fitzJoyce who, as he told Eccleston, used, when returning from a begging tour, to carry flour and salt and a handful of figs for a sick brother in his cape and a bundle of wood under his arm, and who never accepted anything that was not of rigid necessity. His self-denial was such

that it happened once to him to suffer such extremity of cold as to believe that he was then and there about to die. As the brethren had not the wherewithal to make him warm, their brotherly love taught them a remedy; they all gathered round him and pressing close to him, like a litter of pigs, they made him warm.[1]

Touches of this kind abound in Eccleston. There is his vivid account of the first recruits at Oxford, eager and high-spirited in their new adventure, with boyhood's keen sense of the ridiculous and the contagious laughter of the novitiate:

As the young friars at Oxford laughed unceasingly, a command was given that one particular brother should receive the discipline as often as he laughed in choir or at table. Now it happened, when he had received the discipline eleven times in a single day, but still could not contain his laughter, that he dreamt one night that the whole community was in choir as usual, and as usual the friars felt an inclination to laugh, when lo, the image of the Crucified which stood by the door of the choir turned to them as if alive, and said: 'These are the sons of Korah who laugh and sleep when I am on the cross', and it seemed to him that the Crucified strove to loosen his hands from the cross as though fain to come down and be off. . . . When this dream was told, the brethren were dismayed and bore themselves with greater dignity and without excessive laughter.[2]

As a pendant to this picture of Oxford may be set another from Cambridge, where in the friars' minute chapel on the feast of St Laurence,

although there were only three friars who were clerks, that is to say, Br William of Ashby and Br Hugh of Bugton and a novice called Br Elias who was so lame of his legs that they had to carry him into the chapel, they nevertheless chanted the office solemnly with plainsong, and the novice wept so copiously that tears ran openly down his cheeks as he sang. And when he had died a holy death at York, he appeared to Br William Ashby at Northampton, who asked him how it went with him, and he answered that it went well.[3]

So all-pervading was the comradeship of early days

that the only thing that could sadden them was the necessity of parting. For this reason they often accompanied departing brethren a long way on their journey, and showed their faithful and affectionate regard by tears shed on both sides as they parted.[4]

1 *Eccleston*, 16: 'Suis sinibus, sicut porcis mos est, eum comprimendo foverunt.'
2 *Eccleston*, 32. The restraint of Eccleston's narrative is to be noted; by the time Bartholomew of Pisa got hold of the story the wooden figure of the crucifix was turning itself *fragore stupendo*, and many of the friars died soon afterwards (*Liber Conformitatum*, VIII, printed by Little, *Eccleston*, Append. I. B, p. 140).
3 *Eccleston*, 28.   4 *Eccleston*, 33.

From Eccleston's pages a whole series of vignettes can be cut: that of Agnellus, 'crying through three whole days before he died, "Come, sweetest Jesus"', who, at the last, having absolved his community and ordered them to begin the prayers for a passing soul, 'closed his eyes with his own hands, crossed his hands on his breast', and so died; or that of Vincent of Worcester, 'the father of his native city, who, stern and self-denying to himself, was so gentle and generous to others that he was loved by all as if he were an angel'; or that of the friars in general 'so assiduous in prayer that there was hardly an hour in the night when there were not some of the brethren at prayer in the chapel'.[1]

The picture of the English province given by Eccleston is indeed a very pleasing one; no doubt he was a patriot, but his story rings true; he is telling of the examples which inspired and warmed his own endeavour, and he writes that others may share the warmth. He tells how Agnellus, going through the petty expenses of the London friary with the abstemious Salomon, became suddenly appalled at the mounting sum and threw down the rolls and tallies with a cry of anguish, though Eccleston himself, when a guest at London, then a large convent of fifty or more, had seen the brethren drinking beer so bitter that water was preferable, and eating unbolted bread.[2] Even bread had been lacking there for a long space during his stay. At Oxford, the scene of such intense intellectual activity, and in its custody, the friars wore no shoes and were without pillows; in the custody of Cambridge at the same date they went without mantles through lack of money, and the first chapel at Cambridge, built before 1238, was of the simplest model, a few days' work for a single carpenter;[3] in the custody of York it was never permitted for more friars to live in a house than could be supported by alms of food without incurring debts. At Gloucester, John of Malvern, visitor c. 1231, proceeded severely against the guardian and the friar who had painted a screen in the chapel; Oxford was for ten or fifteen years without a guest-room, and the walls of its infirmary were only six feet high; stone took the place of clay in the walls of the dormitory at London c. 1238.[4] The last change took place in the days of Albert of Pisa, who caused the stone cloister at Southampton to be destroyed, despite the protests of the burgesses of the town who had presumably built it.[5] William of Nottingham, provincial 1241-54, was unremitting in his efforts to preserve the original poverty. At London he ordered the roof of the church to be altered and decorations in the cloister to be erased in the interests of simplicity, and at Shrewsbury he replaced the stone walls of the dormitory with walls of clay.[6] In default of any chronicle to take up the story after Eccleston it is difficult to trace the development of domestic building among the friars, but the authority best qualified to pronounce has given it as his opinion that they remained

1 *Eccleston*, 95-7, 76, 31.   2 *Eccleston*, 10-11.
3 *Eccleston*, 28, 43 et al.   4 *Eccleston*, 47, 55.
5 *Eccleston*, 99.   6 *Eccleston*, 57, 29.

unassuming for long, and that until 1270, if not after, the churches of the friars in England remained small and of the simplest construction.[1]

The Franciscan vow and glory of poverty affected the whole economy of life. The *Regula Bullata* enacted that no friar was under any circumstances to receive money, either himself or by means of a third person; the minister and custodian might secure the provision of clothing and necessaries for the sick from spiritual friends, but they were never to receive money for this purpose.[2] As early as 1230 the general chapter inquired of Gregory IX, formerly Cardinal Ugolino, whether trustees might be appointed to receive benefactions in money and apply them for the needs of the friars; the pope replied that they might name a go-between to receive money from benefactors and make payments, and that this agent might use a 'spiritual friend' of the friars as a depositary of money to be used for immediate necessaries.[3] Innocent IV in 1245 extended this permission to cover all reasonable expenditure, and in 1247, by reserving to the Apostolic See the ownership of the friars' possessions, he made of the spiritual friend a legal representative or procurator with full powers of attorney in all business and money matters under the control of the friars.[4] The full establishment of the legal procurator was closely connected with the question of incurring money debts of any kind, since whereas no credit would be given to a friar *in propria persona*, reference could be made with security to a substantial trustee who had, or expected shortly to have, a deposit of money. The permission of Innocent IV, therefore, cut at the roots of the primitive Franciscan ideal.

In the controversy to which the papal decisions gave rise the English province had an honourable share. Agents or procurators as allowed by Gregory IX had been employed from the first; an example may be seen at Oxford in 1232, when at the request of Haymo of Faversham the king granted letters of quittance of tallage to William the Cutler, a merchant, the friars' proctor.[5] Previous to this, William de Colville, who had returned from Paris with Haymo and who made a visitation of the province in 1229, disapproved of the contracting of debts and of the appointment of proctors altogether,[6] and Martin of Barton, as has been said, refused to allow any debts to be incurred in the custody of York. It is therefore not surprising to learn that in 1249–51 the English provincial, William of Nottingham, together with his companion and John de Kethene, sometime guardian of London and provincial of Scotland, and then provincial of Ireland, took

---

1 Little, *Studies in English Franciscan History*, 68, and *BSFS, Franciscan Architecture in England*, by A. R. Martin.

2 *Regula Bullata*, ed. Böhmer, § 4, p. 21.

3 This was the Bull *Quo elongati*, Sbaralea, *Bullarium Franciscanum*, I, 68. For a discussion of the development of Franciscan theory on poverty, *v.* F. Ehrle in *ALKG*, II; Little, *Studies*, 27–34 and III, 553 *seqq.*; *Catholic Encyclopedia* art. Francis, St, Rule of; Wetze und Welte, *Kirchenlexicon* (2 ed.) arts. *Armut* and *Franciscaner Orden*; Herzog, *Realencyklopädie* (3 ed.), art. *Franz von Assisi*.

4 The Bulls *Ordinem vestrum* and *Quanto studiosius* (*Bull. Franc.* I, 400, 487).

5 *Eccleston*, 46 note c.   6 *Ibid.*

a firm stand against the relaxations of Innocent IV and, though at first almost alone, finally persuaded the general chapter to reject them and retain only the permission of Gregory IX.[1] It was precisely at this moment that the most distinguished member of the English province, Adam Marsh, restored to the giver a bag of money which had been deposited in his cell, on the grounds that it would be inconsistent with his profession to accept it.[2] This decision was reasserted at subsequent chapters and in the General Constitutions of 1260, and appears in its main lines in the decretal *Exiit qui seminat* of Nicholas III in 1279, which reflected the teaching of St Bonaventure. Before this decision of the chapter, it would seem that the English friars had, at least on occasion, taken advantage of the decision of Innocent IV, for in 1246 the king is found making gifts of money to the friars' procurator at Shrewsbury; possibly, however, nice customs curtsied to great kings, and to them alone, or the money may have been considered as given for 'urgent necessity'.[3]

VIII

The stand made by William of Nottingham on the point of poverty was only an incident in the long controversy concerning the character and government of the order which had begun before Francis's death and was to become secular; in this also the early English friars took a leading part.

As regards the Rule, the English province held by the so-called *Regula Bullata*, that is, the revision made by Francis and approved by Honorius III in 1223, together with the later directions of Francis; these were introduced in 1224 and observed without alteration or addition.[4] The Bull *Quo elongati* of 28 September 1230, which declared that the Testament of the saint had no constitutional binding force and gave certain other permissions modifying the Rule, reached England with the visitor John of Malvern in *c.* 1231.[5] This the province accepted, but when *c.* 1241 the chapter of definitors at Montpellier ordered delegates from each province to forward doubts and queries concerning the Rule to the minister general, the English committee, of which Adam Marsh and Peter of Tewkesbury were members, proceeded personally to the general, Haymo of Faversham, bearing an open letter from the province imploring him by the Precious

---

1 *Eccleston*, 52: 'fere contra totum capitulum generale causam feliciter obtinuerunt, ut privilegium indultum a domino papa de recipienda pecunia per procuratores penitus destrueretur, et expositio regulae secundum dominum Innocentium, quantum ad ea in quibus laxior est quam Gregoriana, suspenderetur.'

2 *Ep.* 79, ed. Brewer, p. 195.

3 Cf. *Eccleston*, 28 note *d*. The gifts date from 1246 and 1247.

4 *Eccleston*, 30–1: 'regula tantum contenti et paucissimis aliis statutis' (of St Francis himself, probably).

5 *Eccleston*, 47: 'tunc primo portavit expositionem regulae secundum dominum Gregorium nonum.'

Blood of Christ to let the Rule stand as written by Francis under divine inspiration—an action which, according to Eccleston, greatly impressed both the continental friars and the cardinal protector, Raymund of Ostia.[1] The protagonist of the later struggle against the proctors, the provincial William of Nottingham, is quoted by Eccleston as saying that in questions of the Rule regard should always be had to the mind and intention of St Francis, and that when opposing the influence of the world and the growth of superfluous possessions the friar should act like a ferryman who aims at a point above that which he desires to reach, since otherwise the current will carry him down far below it.[2]

Friars with these pronounced views on primitive simplicity were naturally not among the supporters of Elias, and Eccleston, who in such matters certainly reflects the spirit and tradition of his countrymen, is as hostile in his references to him as he is laudatory of Giovanni Parenti, general 1227–32, who held more closely to Franciscan ideals. The conduct of the visitors sent by Elias in 1238 is severely criticized, and according to the chronicler the provincial chapter appealed successfully to the pope against Elias and his emissaries, obtaining a decree that in future visitors should be appointed by general chapter.[3] Indeed, it would seem certain that Haymo of Faversham, and probably also Adam Marsh, were the spearpoint of the revolt against Elias and spokesmen of the order in the attack on him before the pope. Elias, nevertheless, left his mark on the province, not only by separating from it for a time the administration of northern England and Scotland, and by sending English *magistri* to lecture abroad, but also by appointing, after some delay, Agnellus's own candidate to succeed him as provincial. Albert of Pisa was of the primitive school and is consistently praised by Eccleston both as provincial and later as general; his successor Haymo, the active opponent of Elias, who also had been provincial in England, naturally receives equal praise, as does Crescenzio, general 1245–7, and a passing reference would seem to show that the chronicler was no friend of the *zelanti*.[4] It is possible, however, that the course of the struggle in Italy was imperfectly known in England, for Eccleston, if indeed he can be classed as a 'moderate' at all, stood well upon the extreme right wing of the party, and allots to the Zealot John of Parma, general 1247–57, a still higher meed of praise than that given to his predecessors, and the general, on his visit to England, would appear to have overcome all opposition to

1 *Eccleston*, 88–9: 'obsecrantes per aspersionem sanguinis Jesu Christi ut regulam stare permittat, sicut a sancto Francisco, dictante Spiritu Sancto, tradita fuit.'

2 *Eccleston*, 125.

3 *Eccleston*, 48–9.

4 *Eccleston*, 90. For a fuller account *v. infra* 173. Haymo's share is made clear by Eccleston. That chronicler does not mention Adam's name in this connection, but the late and unreliable *Speculum Vitae S. Francisci et sociorum ejus* makes 'sanctus Antonius et frater Adam' leaders against Elias. Adam may be taken, with some certainty, to be Adam Marsh, and Sabatier's suggestion (*Examen de la Vie de Frère Elie*, 168 note 1 *et al.*) that a late copyist substituted the familiar, but chronologically impossible, name of Antonius for the less familiar Aimo is very probable. The whole question, however, is still very uncertain.

the strict observance of the Rule, for it was he who praised the purity of the English province above all others.[1]

On the whole, therefore, the English province, while giving birth to no fanatics and showing little inclination towards the eremitical life, was not far distant in spirit from the *zelanti* and was probably, as a province, more united than any other in its resolve to preserve the first purity of the Rule, even if the English *magistri*, of whom Adam Marsh may be taken as type, were animated by a spirit more rigid and legal than that of the joyful liberty and abandonment of St Francis.

Note. The chronicle of Eccleston is now available in an edition with notes in English and a translation by the late Dr A. G. Little. The book, which has the same title as the French edition, was published at Manchester in 1951. More recently Dr J. R. H. Moorman has, in his study of *The Grey Friars in Cambridge* (1952), provided a pendant to Dr Little's early work on the Oxford Friars Minor.

1 *Eccleston*, 91: 'praecipuus zelator ordinis...et fratres ad unitatem revocaverat.' I take the last clause to refer to dissensions on the question of poverty, arising out of the decisions of Innocent IV.

CHAPTER XIII

THE ORDER OF PREACHERS

I

An early Franciscan, writing when controversies from within and from without were agitating his order, compared the two original bodies of friars to the twin brothers Jacob and Esau, whose quarrels began while they were yet in the womb of their mother.[1] The comparison has become a commonplace, and the black friars, by tacitly assuming the name and rôle of Jacob,[2] may perhaps be said to have given an excuse to the historian for treating the Friars Minor as the firstborn. Actually, indeed, Dominic was the senior to Francis by more than ten years, and though his order came formally into being only in the year of the Lateran Council, when the Friars Minor also received approval, he had been for many years the leader of a group of priests dedicated to combating heresy, and the Friars Preachers were in England three years before the Franciscans came. Nevertheless, the life history of Francis, and the peculiarly vivid and vivifying quality of the new blood with which he enriched the veins of Europe, make it inevitable that he should take precedence of Dominic in any general account of the religious renaissance in which both shared, and though it may well be argued that in course of time the life and institutions of the grey friars were profoundly modified by the influence of the black, it is all but unquestionable that the Dominicans changed their style of canons for that of friars owing to the example of Francis. It was, indeed, Francis who gave the friar, as distinct from the monk and the canon, to the Church, and it is to Francis that the friar as such must always look back as to his spiritual patriarch.

The history of Dominic's life is undoubtedly far less arresting than that of Francis, and his human personality less markedly original. Moreover, devotion to his person and memory never became a battle-cry, and his words and precepts never became the nucleus of legends and *legendae* as did those of Francis, and though he gave to his order that strongly marked character to which it has been singularly faithful throughout the ages, his name and ideals, true or supposed, have never become a shibboleth or a heart-ache among his sons, and his successors were able to develop methodically the organization and scheme that he had devised with no

---

1 Cf. *Interpretatio praeclara abbatis Joachim*, the work of an anonymous Friar Minor *c.* 1250 (ed. Venice, 1528 f. 24b), referred to by Père P. Mandonnet, *Siger de Brabant*, 1 ed., cxi, n. 1.

2 Mandonnet, *Siger de Brabant*, cxii, of the Dominicans: 'Jacob, conscient d'une supériorité,' etc.

more internal friction than that which is inevitable in the expansion of all human institutions.

Dominic was perhaps some fifty years old when he died. He may have been a cleric at fifteen and a priest at twenty-four. Yet at his death his order had existed for but six years and had assumed its final shape only two years before its founder passed away. These facts, and the lack of any formal body of spiritual doctrine, whether oral or written, descending from him, have brought it to pass that his order has taken for guidance, beyond its constitutional documents, the writings of the great early theologians, and especially of St Thomas, who has come to occupy a position comparable, but not truly similar, to that held by St Bonaventure with respect to the Friars Minor. In consequence, the personality of St Dominic has been thrown somewhat into the shade, at least for the general reader of devout or historical literature, and it has been left for his sons, and for students of religious constitutional history, to comprehend and to demonstrate that the Order of Preachers owes to its founder not only its peculiar character and aims, but also its elaborate, original and singularly efficient machinery of administration.

The life of Francis was in a sense a series of conversions, moral and spiritual, in which the intellectual element entered scarcely at all; though in the deepest sense he lived for others, and especially for his friars, he remained in a very real sense alone, and his power lay not so much in his activity as ruler and guide as in the deeper life of his soul, seen in glimpses by those who had contact with him; in those contacts it might truly have been said that heart spoke to heart, for mind, if by that we understand the *ratio ratiocinans*, had no part in Francis's life and achievement. With Dominic, on the other hand, there was no spectacular change or conversion; his life, so far as it can be seen, went steadily forward directed by a single purpose, and though he showed himself to the end singularly flexible and sympathetic to the needs of circumstance, all the changes and developments of his own life and that of his institute were the result (at least on an external view) of patient observation and the adaptation of many means to one primary end clearly seen. It may even be said that in his last great decision at Bologna by which he allowed his sons to assimilate themselves to the friars he saw the life of a friar as a means to the end of preaching the truth rather than as the simple and inevitable expression of Christ's life on earth.

Dominic, the first in time of the four great Spaniards who in their different ways have exercised such a prodigious influence over the religious life of the Church, passed in early life through all the schools of intellectual and spiritual formation that were open to men of his class and age. In turn a student, a priest and secular canon, and a member of a reformed chapter which had adopted the Augustinian Rule and the discipline of Prémontré, he was distinguished from others only by his gifts, natural and supernatural, and by a consuming desire to work for the salvation of souls. His earliest biographer,[1] who knew him well, though for less than two years and at the end of his life, was himself a student and a bachelor before becoming a Preacher, and gives us all too few glimpses of his master's early life. He has, however, preserved two traits which throw a vivid if momentary flash of light: he tells us that Dominic's inner life was formed and nourished by the repeated reading of Cassian's *Conferences*,[2] and that his constant and most characteristic prayer in early life was that he might have a true love of souls and the ability to help others.[3] In these two precious indications we can see in germ the twofold character of his order—monastic and apostolic—winning its sons and others to the perfect following of Christ by reasoned asceticism and earnest petition. The contrast between the calculated employment of means in moving towards a clearly seen end, so characteristic of Dominic,[4] and the incalculable, bewildering movements of Francis, that *esprit primesautier*, is obvious and has often been stressed, sometimes unduly.

Dominic's zeal for souls found scope as a result of a series of tasks which took him from Spain and set him among the Albigensian heretics of Languedoc. Here, *c.* 1205–7, his first companions grouped themselves around him; with them, in a way strangely similar to that taken by another illustrious Spaniard three centuries later, he attended school at Toulouse; his first foundation was a convent of nuns formed by converts who had followed him, and it was not until ten years later that Innocent III instructed him to choose a rule for his institute and present it for solemn approval. The Fourth Lateran Council had recently decreed that no new orders should come into being, but that all in future should choose one of the existing rules; hence the charge to Dominic to choose, not to compose. In the event, however, his institute, like that of Francis, was something wholly new. Himself a black canon, he naturally took the so-called Rule of St Augustine as the basis of his order's life, but in giving to it the precision and austerity which he desired he made use of the constitutions of the white canons of Prémontré, which in their turn drew much from

---

1 This was B. Jordan of Saxony, second master-general. His brief *Vita S. Dominici* (*MOPH* xvi, 1935, pp. 25–88) is the only account of the saint written by a contemporary who knew him. It has been published, together with the early *legendae*, in a volume from the Instituto Storico S. Sabina, Rome, with the title *Monumenta S.P.N. Dominici*. For all the problems of his life and the genesis of his order, M. H. Vicaire's *Histoire de S. Dominique*, is indispensable.

2 *Vita S. Dominici*, 546, § 11: 'Hunc [librum] legens et diligens, in eo salutis rimari semitas et easdem tota animi virtute studuit imitari.' St Thomas Aquinas, it will be remembered, read the *Collationes* daily.

3 *Ibid.* 546, § 10: 'Fuit...ei frequens et specialis ad Deum petitio quaedam, ut ei largiri dignaretur veram caritatem atque curandae et procurandae saluti hominum efficacem.' H. Denifle, in *ALKG*, i, 183 and notes, assembles a most impressive array of witnesses to this apostolic zeal as the *leitmotiv* of Dominic's life.

4 Those who knew him noted that he always looked to the end before he spoke and therefore seldom if ever consented to change a decision (*MOPH* xvi p. 74 no. 103).

Cîteaux.[1] Thus the Order of Preachers was in origin a canonical institute with a markedly monastic character, though from the first they had taken an important step which set them midway between canons and friars, for Dominic's experience in Languedoc and his realization of the spiritual liberty necessary to a Preacher had led him to consent to a break with religious tradition by renouncing the possession of lands and properties, though retaining at first the use of revenues.[2] In origin, therefore, his followers held to the style of canon, and Dominic himself endeavoured to escape from office by causing one of his companions to be elected abbot, the first and last to hold that title among the Preachers.[3] These arrangements were solemnly confirmed by Honorius III in the last days of 1216, and the *raison d'être* of the order and its intimate dependence upon the papacy were defined for all time by the words in which the pope addressed them as champions of the truth and lights of the world.[4] It was during this visit to Rome that Dominic met Francis; the two saints, so different in mind and natural character, met at once on the deeper plane of the spirit, and it is remarkable that the meeting was the occasion of one of the few examples of impulsive action of which there is any record in Dominic's life.[5] He offered, it is said, to merge his order with that of the Friars Minor under Francis's leadership. Francis refused; though both aimed at the same goal their ways were very different and could not merge; yet in the sequel each order profoundly modified the other's character in a process of assimilation of which they were only half aware. One such movement took place three years later, at the first general chapter held at Bologna in 1220, when the Preachers relinquished revenues and adopted the strict poverty of mendicants[6] without, however, taking upon themselves as individuals the ideal of absolute material poverty as expressed in Francis's Rule and Testament; they also abandoned the distinctive dress of canons

1 *Vita S. Dominici*, 550, §32: 'Beati Augustini...regulam elegerunt, quasdam sibi super hoc in victu et jejuniis, in lectis et laneis arctiores consuetudines assumentes.' Diego of Osma, Dominic's bishop and first companion in Languedoc, had, it may be noted, taken the Cistercian habit in 1206, though perhaps only as 'un geste symbolique et passager'[!] (Mandonnet, *S. Dominique*, I, 40, note). The same writer (*ibid.* I, 49–56) brings forward arguments to show that the prohibition of new orders was the work of regulars among the fathers of the Council, and that it never had the whole-hearted approval of Innocent.

2 *Ibid.* 550, §32: 'Proposuerunt...non habere possessiones, ne praedicationis impediretur officium...sed tantum redditus recipere.'

3 *Ibid.* 550, §35: '[Fr. Matthaeus] primus atque novissimus abbas.'

4 *V.* second Bull of Honorius, 22 December 1216 (Potthast, 5402–3): 'futuros pugiles fidei et vera mundi lumina confirmamus ordinem tuum.' The words *vera mundi lumina* are applied to the college of Apostles in the hymn of the Office of Apostles.

5 The earliest authorities for this are *II Celano*, 150, *Speculum Perfectionis*, c. 43 and *Vitae Fratrum*, I, i, but the tradition is doubtless correct as to the fact, though not necessarily as to the words used. They may well have met earlier, in 1215; they certainly met later, at Assisi and probably also in Rome. As another example of impulse, we may recall Dominic's offer, earlier in life, to sell himself as a slave to redeem a widow's son.

6 *Vita S. Dominici*, 554, §64: 'Ordinatum est ne possessiones vel redditus de cetero tenerent Fratres nostri.' It is impossible not to see in this step the influence of the example of the Friars Minor.

and the title of abbey for their houses, thus to all appearances joining the ranks of the friars, though the title of *canonicus* was never wholly expunged from the constitutional documents and the Preachers remained by definition clerics.[1] At this chapter, we are told, Dominic urged upon the body his wish that all material administration should be entrusted to the lay brethren.[2] If this was indeed the case, it is somewhat surprising to find him reverting to an expedient which had been employed by several canonical and monastic bodies in the previous century, and had been found to imply grave disabilities; had the proposal been adopted, it could not have long endured. In other respects, the chapter approved and completed the founder's elaborate scheme of organization for the order which has from that day continued in all its main lines to function unchanged and with conspicuous success.

II

The Friars Minor came into being as a body by a kind of spontaneous generation; their Rules and constitutions were the result of a series of endeavours from without to impose a regular form upon a living and exuberant organism. In strong contrast to this, the legislation of the Preachers was a piece of carefully pondered and eclectic constitution-building which marked an important stage in the development of the religious life within the Church and which formed a link between the monastic and canonical bodies of the early middle ages and the wholly non-monastic orders and clerical congregations of the modern world.[3] The monastic bodies had pursued the contemplative life (to use that phrase in the sense made classic by St Thomas); the friars, and especially the Preachers, adopted a 'mixed' life.[4]

---

1 The Dominicans, in fact, still strongly maintain this. Cf. Père H. Denifle in *ALKG*, I, 168–72, and Père Mandonnet, art. *Preachers* in *Catholic Encyclopedia*, 357a. The prologue of the Constitutions speaks of the Preachers as *uniformes in observantiis canonice religionis*.

2 This was stated by John of Navarre in the process of canonization; *v. Acta SS.*, August, I, 638, 30.

3 For the original constitutions of 1220 and the revised version of Raymond of Pennafort *v.* the editions of Denifle in *ALKG*, I, 165–227 and v, 530–64. Denifle's introduction to the early constitutions is a masterpiece of critical thought, and remains by far the best analysis of the genius and aims of the Order of Preachers; it has, however, been conclusively shown by Père M. Vicaire that the legislation of the Preachers was completed in all essentials during Dominic's lifetime at the chapters of 1216 and 1220, not, as Denifle suggested, at that of 1228. There is an exceptionally full and valuable article on the *Preachers* by Père Mandonnet in the *Catholic Encyclopedia* (1907) which is, however, a little difficult to absorb on account of errors in translation and the inclusion in the text of numerous bibliographical details. For a full and excellent analysis of the original Dominican system *v. The Constitution of the Dominican Order*, 1216–1360, by G. R. Galbraith; cf. also *The Dominican Order and Convocation*, by E. Barker; some of the conclusions and hypotheses there expressed, should, however, be received with caution.

4 Cf. *Summa Theologica*, IIa IIae Q. clxxxviii art. 2, ii: 'monachorum religio est instituta ad vitam contemplativam,' etc. It must be added, however, that St Thomas does not use, and would indeed have repudiated, the term 'mixed life'; in his scheme, the 'activity' of the Preacher flows from the abundance of his 'contemplation'; they are not co-ordinates: the former is subordinated to the latter.

As has been said they were in origin quasi-monastic, and that not merely because all the regular canonical families were quasi-monastic, but especially because they were modelled upon the family of Prémontré, itself by far the most monastic body among the canons, which had tended to become not less, but more monastic in the century between Norbert and Dominic. Consequently, in their regime within their convents and in the strictness of their original dietary and domestic arrangements, the early Dominicans were far more traditional than the first Franciscans, and the monastic element has always remained a marked characteristic of their life, especially at certain epochs and in certain provinces. On the other hand, Dominic broke away at once from the monastic and canonical tradition in a number of important respects, apart altogether from questions of constitutional organization. With the monks and the black canons work *ad extra* had been incidental, almost accidental; with the white canons it had been an integral part of their life, but equated with the traditional tasks of liturgical service and manual work. For the Dominicans the defence and preaching of Catholic truth was an essential part of their life, the *raison d'être* of their order, and to this all other employments were sacrificed or subordinated.[1] Manual labour, which even among the early Friars Minor was an alternative to apostolic work, vanished altogether, within and without doors, for the clerics; all necessary work was to be done by lay brothers. Liturgical prayer was retained, but kept within strict bounds; it was to be performed briskly, and from the first dispensations for purposes of study and preaching were explicitly countenanced by rule.[2]

The Preachers, therefore, existed for a single great purpose, indicated by their name, and whereas for the original Franciscans the moral conversion of their hearers was the primary aim, and the means employed were an unschooled simplicity and the example of a life of absolute poverty, for the Dominicans ignorance and intellectual error were the direct objects of attack, to be confronted with all the resources of a trained mind. Consequently, every Dominican convent was a school, and the presence of a doctor of theology was a *sine qua non* for its foundation.[3] Within its walls study, regarded as a religious, ascetic exercise, took pride of place among all employments. To allow of ample time for this the Office, as has been said, was chanted without elaboration, manual work was abandoned and purely meditative *lectio divina* disappeared from the horarium; the daily chapter might be omitted, fasts broken, and every kind of dispensation given to save interference with study.

1 Cf. the words of the preface to the first Distinction of the Constitutions: 'cum ordo noster specialiter ad predicationem et animarum salutem ab initio noscatur institutus fuisse;' on which Humbert of the Romans (*Opera*, II, 38–9) comments: 'in quo excellit alios ordines cum ipsi statuti fuerunt solum ob salutem ingredientium.'

2 *Ibid.* cap. 1: 'Horae omnes in ecclesia breviter et succincte taliter dicantur ne...studium ...impediatur,' etc.

3 *Ibid.* Dist. II, cap. i: 'Conventus...absque priore et doctore non mittatur.'

From the first an elaborate scholastic system was organized.[1] Each convent had a school of theology under a doctor. Above these, in larger priories which later came to be called *studia particularia* or *solemnia*, were schools to which friars of promise were sent from the neighbouring convents of the province; in these, besides the doctor or lector, there was a master of the students and a sub-lector, often a bachelor of divinity. Finally, the convents at the chief university towns of Europe housed *studia generalia*, to which friars could be sent from any province of the order. In these were a master or regent and two bachelors; regular disputations, ordinary and solemn, were held, and degrees conferred within the framework of the university. Paris was the first of such schools to be formally erected in 1228;[2] Oxford, Cologne, Montpellier and Bologna followed in 1248. Cambridge became a *studium generale* only c. 1350

At first the only subject taught in the convent schools was theology, understood in the traditional sense as embracing *summae* of Scripture, divinity, church history and morals; a knowledge of grammar and elementary 'logic' was presupposed in recruits. Soon, however, schools of 'arts', that is, philosophy, and of the natural sciences as understood by Aristotle were erected in certain convents, and thus the educational system of the Preachers became complete and self-contained, assuming only an elementary knowledge of letters in recruits at one end of the scale, and at the other the association of the *studium generale* with a university. Dominic had laid down the general outlines of this system solely in order to ensure that his sons should master the theological learning of the age before beginning to preach; as the curriculum of the schools was widened by the inclusion of the whole *corpus* of Aristotle's writings on philosophy and the sciences, the Dominican schools inevitably developed from lecture-rooms of traditional teaching into homes of disputation, speculation and research; finally, when the order came to include many of the first intelligences of the age, the convents of the Preachers became centres of dynamic power, extinguishing or at least eclipsing for the time all other founts of philosophical and theological light, and serving as sources whence all Europe drew the waters of doctrine.

III

Although the establishment of the first preaching and student order in the Church was Dominic's principal achievement, his consummate ability and striking originality as a legislator are seen most clearly in the constitutions he devised for the government of his order. These mark an epoch in the history of religious institutional legislation, and exerted an influence within

---

1 *V.* Mandonnet in *Catholic Encyclopedia*, 360b–363a; A. G. Little, *Educational organization of the mendicant friars in England* (*TRHS*, New Series, VIII, 1894, 49–70). Denifle (*ALKG*, I, 188–92) made it clear that the emphasis on study, and its organization, was part of the original work of Dominic, not (as with the Friars Minor) a later development.

2 Paris had been chosen by Dominic himself as the centre of the order's intellectual life, and St Jacques as early as 1224 held over 120 friars; cf. Denifle, *ALKG*, I, 188–9.

the Church from 1220 till the Reformation as profound and as pervasive as had been that of the *Carta Caritatis* during the twelfth century and as was to be that of the Constitutions of the Society of Jesus from the middle of the sixteenth century onwards. It is, indeed, true that the Friars Minor evolved a somewhat similar scheme of government at about the same time; there is, however, a great difference between the two schemes, for whereas the Dominican system came all but complete from the mind of the founder, the Franciscan organization, rudimentary as it long remained, was accepted piecemeal and *à contre-cœur* by Francis and his first followers, and in it the most original and characteristic features of the Dominican scheme had no place; it was only later, and especially under Haymo of Faversham, that the Minors assimilated their organization to that of the Preachers.

All historians of monasticism have noted the gradual evolution of the organized religious order from the original conception of the *ordo monasticus* as a number of autonomous houses united by no bond save that of the common Rule. The Cluniac system, so often considered as the first stage in the process, was so chronologically rather than logically, for it was in essence a feudal rather than a 'rational' organism. Nevertheless, it had a share in the evolution of the order, as showing to all at once the possibility and the dangers of a vast federation. In contrast to the scheme of Cluny, the *Carta Caritatis* of Cîteaux may stand as the first great achievement of scientific constitution-building. In a few brief sentences it linked in indissoluble bonds the abbeys, existent and to come, of the new family, secured the observance of a uniform discipline by regular visitations, safeguarded internal autonomy while ensuring external surveillance, and gave, in the general chapter of abbots, a body with plenary powers of legislation and correction in which every house, through its head, had a voice.

The Cistercian family, however, was not strictly speaking an order. Each abbey was self-sufficient and self-governing, the individual monk was subject to no external interference or control, and the abbot of Cîteaux was a primate rather than a general. The white canons of Prémontré, while modelling their system upon Cîteaux, moved a little in the direction of centralization and articulation by slightly strengthening the position of the abbot of Prémontré and by dividing the order regionally for purposes of visitation. The twelfth century, in which so many of the finest minds were devoted to the study of law, was a period of luxuriant growth in religious constitutions. Especially noteworthy were those of the military orders, in which two essential features of the centralized order make their appearance —the grand master, whose only *raison d'être* is to be the administrative head of the body, and the general chapter, the sovereign legislative, executive and disciplinary body, regarded as possessing a competence distinct from, and even opposed to, that of the master.[1] In the many institutes that

1 For a comparison between the system of the Preachers and those of the military orders *v.* E. Barker, *The Dominican Order*, 18–21, and G. R. Galbraith, *The Constitution of the Dominican Order*, 17–21.

pullulated in the twelfth century—Gilbertines, Grandimontines, Fontev-
rault and the rest—the most liberal eclecticism was shown, and constitutional elements and titles were borrowed from far and near. None of these
institutes, however, made any serious step forward in the direction of
centralization, for all took as the essential unit not the whole order, but the
individual house, possessed of property and lands.

With the Friars Minor and the Preachers a novel situation at once arose.
They were not small families of men who had retired from the world to
enclose themselves within a ring-fence and bind themselves to the soil, but
an army of individuals eager to be sent out among men to teach and preach,
directed originally by the initiative of a single leader, and regarded from
the first as an instrument to be used by the supreme authority in the
Church. Here, for the first time, local stability was unknown; the whole
body was the unit, and precisely because external activities were essential
to the life of the order centralization and devolution of authority were indispensable. The problem was to ensure the maximum of efficiency and
flexibility to the administration while establishing safeguards against arbitrary change and despotic action, either on the part of permanent superiors
or on that of a majority swayed by a passing excitement or acting on the
mandate of a party caucus.

This problem Francis neither solved nor wished to solve. He held to
the last unswervingly to his simple, spiritual conception by which each
friar, secure in the possession of his Rule and the model of Christ, troubled
not at all about matters of administration and organization. In so far as he
remained true to his vocation, his work would be fruitful, and he himself
would be at peace; if he failed, no machinery could repair the failure. To
Francis, the general chapter (originally of all the friars, but soon limited to
wardens of custodies and provincial ministers) was a meeting for mutual
encouragement, where unity and charity might be confirmed and important
new enterprises undertaken. Under Elias the government of the order
became frankly monarchical and autocratic, and despite a serious attempt
to remould the constitution after the model of the Preachers, it remained
distinctly monarchical in character throughout the middle ages.

IV

The government of the Order of Preachers, on the other hand, was from
the first extremely democratic in constitution. Modern historians, very
naturally, have considered Dominic's legislation, which is so original as to
be all but revolutionary, purely from the constitutional point of view. It is,
however, equally remarkable in the history of religious thought, as implying a conception of authority very different from that traditional in the
monastic order. Of this something will be said in the sequel; for the
moment, attention must be confined to the formal organization of the
preaching friars.

This is distinguished from all the earlier monastic and canonical institutes by two fundamental characteristics: first, the place given to election in the constitution of all authority, and consequently to the element of representation or delegation throughout, and, secondly, the singularly important function in the order entrusted to commissioners elected *ad hoc* rather than to those holding office as religious superiors. This organization has been described, both by Dominicans and by modern historians, as democratic.[1] The term is perhaps misleading, for whatever may be its strict meaning, it has been currently used in both ancient and modern times to denote the kind of government that is devoted primarily to the interests of the many and that in every way reflects the interests of the majority, however unenlightened, rather than the wisdom of the best elements among its constituents. Of this—of the democracy of Cleon or of the cruder Socialism—there was nothing in the mind of Dominic. His aim, perfectly in harmony with the emphasis laid upon the intellectual element in the life and work of the order, was to secure power to the most prudent and alert; it was assumed that the aim of the administration, however constituted, would be to secure the fulfilment of the purpose of the order, not the interests of its members considered as individuals. In effect, however, the Dominican government was in every part elected and representative, not only because all the superiors of the order were elected, directly or indirectly, by the body of friars, and held office at the discretion of elected boards, but also because the supreme legislative and executive power in each province and in the whole order was, for a short, regularly recurring period, vested in small bodies of men of whom the majority had been recently elected *ad hoc* by their fellows and were in a few days to be merged once more with the great body of friars in private place.

It would exceed the scope of this book to give an account in detail of the Dominican polity, the more so as more than one excellent monograph on the subject is in existence. A brief outline, however, will be in place, if only that some idea may be given of the machine of which the English province formed a component part, and of the scheme of government, novel in more than one respect at the time of its origin, with which the English friars became familiar.

Hitherto, whether at Cîteaux or Prémontré, all direct power of rule had lain with the numerous heads of houses elected for life and directly responsible to no higher authority on earth. The general chapter, which could legislate, judge and set in motion processes of discipline, was composed of the total number of these superiors and of no others. Historically speaking, such a scheme represented a fusion of the original patriarchal, purely spiritual conception of the office of abbot with the electoral and deliberative machinery sanctioned by the ancient canon law. In it, a number of

---

1 Thus Mandonnet, *art. cit.* 368 E, speaks of the 'democratic constitution' of the Preachers, E. Barker, *op. cit.* 17, writes that 'we may call the friars [*sc.* Preachers] democratic', and G. R. Galbraith, *op. cit.* 30, says that 'it remained for Dominic to create a democratic...body'.

monarchs assembled annually for a few days as a senate, their houses forming a great family of autonomous confederates.

With the Preachers, federation gave place to subordination within a single family, of which the members were divided into many regional and local groups. The convent formed part of the province, the province part of the order, and for each of these three bodies there was a single permanent executive officer, and for the two last a deliberative and legislative body meeting at regular intervals. For the house there was the conventual prior; for the province the provincial prior and the annual provincial chapter; for the whole order the master-general and the annual general chapter. All these persons and bodies were constituted in power by similar methods.[1] The conventual prior was elected by his chapter, composed of all those in the convent of a certain seniority; he held office (in the thirteenth century, at least) for an indeterminate period, until he resigned or was elected to higher office or was 'absolved' by one of the several competent superior authorities. The provincial prior was elected by the representative element in the provincial chapter, viz. the conventual priors and two delegates elected by each house, for the preachers-general of the province, who were *ex-officio* chapter-men, had no vote; he also held office for an indeterminate period, subject to the will of general chapter and the master-general. The master was elected by an electoral general chapter constituted *ad hoc*, consisting of the provincial priors and two representatives from each province; he held office originally for life, subject only to the decision of general chapter to 'absolve' him or permit his resignation.[2]

The annual legislative general chapter, when there was no master to be elected, was constituted by two alternative bodies: for two years in succession the master was joined by a board of delegates, one from each province; in the third year he sat with the provincial priors.[3] No legislation affecting the whole order could take effect until it had been approved by three successive chapters. By this alternation of representative and administrative bodies Dominic clearly intended to balance the claims of progressive, independent minds and of the supposedly more conservative and cautious holders of office; an early gathering thought it well to decree that neither body should propose legislation affecting the interests of the other, but in the sequel no clash of policy would seem ever to have manifested itself between the two types of chapter. Finally, provision was later made for an extraordinary chapter, called *generalissimum*, consisting of master,

1 In what follows complicated details and controversial points have been omitted, e.g. at all chapters the regular chaptermen soon came to be accompanied by *socii* either chosen by themselves or elected by their constituents; these had certain consultative rights, but did not enjoy full voting power, etc. For all this the work of G. R. Galbraith may be consulted. It may be remarked, that while the general chapter was primarily a legislative body, the provincial chapter was largely concerned with discipline.

2 The master-general held his office for life until the Napoleonic era.

3 When the legislative general chapter followed immediately upon the election of a master-general it took yet a third form, consisting of provincial priors and *one* of the two electoral representatives of each province.

provincial priors, and two delegates from each province. This could only be summoned on the demand of a majority of the provinces and, combining as it did the elements of both types of ordinary general chapter, had the power of passing legislation which took effect at once and of altering certain fundamental constitutions which were intangible at the annual general chapters. Actually, however, this member of the constitution was not found to be necessary; only two such *capitula generalissima* were held, both in the early years of the order, in 1228 and 1236.

As will have been noted, the three normal chapters formed something of a pyramid. In the conventual gathering was the wide base of universal attendance and suffrage; in the provincial meeting there was still a very large body present, as the preachers-general, never limited in number by any legislation, might be very many; at the summit was the very small general chapter, having its peak in the master-general. One striking feature, however, remains to be mentioned. The apparently disproportionate size of the provincial chapter, which for England might consist of as many as two hundred friars, was wholly corrected by Dominic's provision that all the deliberative and legislative business should be accomplished by a small committee consisting of the provincial prior and four *diffinitores*[1] elected by the whole chapter. Indeed, the function of the full chapter would seem to have been only to elect this committee and (when necessary) a representative for general chapter and electors of the master, and to register a formal acceptance of the decisions of the *diffinitores* and of any judical committees that might have been set up. All powers of initiative and decision, in both administration and legislation, lay with the provincial and the four *diffinitores*.

The most striking characteristic of the Dominican legislation is its bestowal of supreme authority on small groups of men not necessarily at the moment holding important positions as ruling superiors,[2] who were elected directly or indirectly by the whole body of friars and met together at a board for a few days only, never so to meet again. It is natural to see in this provision a reflection of the idea, peculiar to Dominic and his school, that when decisions, speculative or practical, are to be made, the reason alone is to be consulted, all considerations of seniority, dignity and custom being set aside as impertinent. That this is not a mere figment of modern criticism may be seen from the words of Humbert of the Romans, fifth master-general, who had entered the order as early as *c.* 1224. He states explicitly that among the Preachers, as opposed to other orders, not only superiors but ordinary friars become the supreme legislators, because the

---

1 The term *diffinitor* in the Dominican documents is ambiguous, as it is applied both to the four friars elected as a committee by the provincial chapter and to the whole body of provincial representatives elected to attend general chapter; in both cases, however, the name (= legislator) corresponds to the function of the persons concerned.

2 Conventual priors were of course eligible as *diffinitores* at both provincial and general chapters, and no doubt were often so elected. Their election, however, was due to their merits, not to their office.

order commands such a supply of excellent judgement from among its subjects.[1] It may, however, be suggested that it is anachronistic to find in the Dominican predilection for elected officers a recognition of the principle of representation in government. Election, and that often of an indirect, complicated kind, was adopted as the only rational method of arriving at a selection of those best qualified to serve, not as a means of securing a representation of the views of the constituencies. The whole conception of a legislator as one representing an interest or holding a mandate was indeed wholly foreign to the mind of Dominic and still more to that of the Aristotelian Dominican of the succeeding generations.

But if it is misleading to see in the Dominican constitution a conscious movement towards democracy and representative government, Dominic did nevertheless, and probably with full deliberation, bring into being a religious family with a conception of authority wholly different from that traditional among the monastic bodies. The fundamental characteristic of personal obedience among the monks, from the early days of the desert until those of Cîteaux, had lain in the total submission of the disciple to the master, of the son to the father, in every department of life, spiritual and temporal. To the primitive, purely personal relation of two individuals St Benedict had added the subjection of both to the Rule, and circumstances had transformed the celebrated master of the desert whose disciples had often no direct relation one with another into the common father of a large family, but the root idea remained of submission to one whose authority (under God) was personal and monarchical, enduring for life and existing for the spiritual and temporal welfare of his sons considered as individuals. Much as this simple and pure idea had been disfigured by developments and changes in the monastic order; it had nevertheless remained as the only conception of religious government until the middle of the twelfth century, and it may be suggested that Francis aimed at simplifying it and reducing it to its primitive and purely spiritual form rather than at creating a new model.

With Dominic, however, the whole aim was different. All his superiors and legislators outside the individual convent existed primarily for the direction of the whole order or its regional divisions towards its end of work for souls, not to guide the individual friar towards the perfection of the life of the gospel *in foro interno*. Efficiency, therefore, in the truest sense of the word—promptness, that is, and energy in action directed by far-sighted and prudent judgement in council—was the ideal to be aimed at, and for this purpose temporary, elected superiors and chosen committees of the most active and alert formed the most desirable body of gover-

---

1 Humbert of the Romans, who was master-general 1254–63, remarks that with the Cistercians and other orders 'tota discretio est fere in praelatis majoribus', whereas among the Preachers there is: 'abundantia discretionis etiam in subditis...et ideo fiunt diffinitores apud nos non solum praelati majores, ut provinciales, sed etiam subditi quicunque per electionem in majore numero' (*B. Humberti de Romanis Opera de Vita Regulari*, ed. J. J. Berthier, II, 61).

nors. The obedience of the friar to these was not that of a son to his spiritual father, but of a subject to his ruler and lawgiver, and it has been noted that the term 'subject' is current in some of the early Dominican literature, with its correlative 'prelate', whereas Francis spoke always of a brother and his 'minister' or 'guardian'. This formal change in the conception of the function of authority, which was a necessary consequence of the 'active' character of the institute of Preachers, was as important a development in the history of the religious life as any of Dominic's constitutional innovations; it was the first overt step towards the formal division of the single repository of authority into two—the external, administrative and legislative authority falling to the superior or committee in office, and the internal, directive authority to the spiritual father and guide. If the monastic obedience was ideally that of the disciple to the master, and the monk could find an analogy to his life in the patriarchal family ruled by its father as head, the obedience of the Preacher, outside the formative life of his convent, was that of a subject to law and the holders of office, for which the friar might find an analogy in the subordination of all the faculties of the human microcosm to the will directed by the reason. Yet a third step, it may be suggested, was taken by St Ignatius of Loyola and his many imitators, who put before their sons an ideal of absolute obedience, within certain agreed limits, to the free initiative of the supreme and subaltern authorities, who were to be concerned solely with the prosperity and exploitation, under the direction of supreme authority, of their institute.[1] To this obedience an analogy was from the first found in the obedience of the private soldier to his captain and generalissimo—an obedience blind by contract—who in their turn care for their men and employ their resources with their eyes fixed on the purpose for which an army exists, that is, to defend the possessions and assert the rights of its sovereign at whatever cost in wastage and sacrifice that may be justified by the laws of strategy and tactics. Though the Dominican system was devised before the full discovery of Aristotle, it was nevertheless singularly well adapted to a mental climate in which the leading idea of Greek rationalism —a conviction of the power of the unaided human faculties to attain to a certain and adequate possession of metaphysical and moral truth— coloured the whole *Weltanschauung* of the best minds, just as the system of St Ignatius was well calculated to make an immediate appeal to a society which had lost its grasp of the body of revealed and metaphysical truth, and of the sovereignty of rational law, and which exalted to such a degree the personal prerogative of the prince.

1 It goes without saying that in all cases the religious, supernatural *motive* of obedience is the same, viz. the will of God as the source of all lawful authority, and the will of Christ as seen in His representative, however set in office: 'He who heareth you, heareth me.'

V

In the preceding account, mention has been made of the older sources of religious legislation whence Dominic drew, and attention has been called to the originality of much of his work. This originality will in no sense be called into question if it is suggested that, had we fuller record of Dominic's life, it might be possible to find in contemporary institutions a further model for some of his electoral and capitular dispositions. Besides the Rule of St Augustine and the constitutions of Prémontré, themselves deriving from the Uses of Cîteaux and the Rule of St Benedict, the organization of the military orders has been noted as a possible influence. It is very possible, also, that the organization of the guilds, especially as seen in a developed and federal form in the nascent universities, may have supplied more than one idea to the legislator.[1] Neither Palencia, where he studied as a boy, nor Toulouse, where he went to school as a mature man, had, so far as is known, developed as a university at the epoch of Dominic's residence, but Bologna, which he knew well in the years when he was devising the constitutions for the Preachers, had an efficient organization of which some of the main lines are not unlike those of Dominic.[2] There was the whole body of students, there were the elected and very powerful councillors, there was the rector, severely limited in power, and the relationships of the nations and 'universities' of the various faculties to each other and to the supreme control must have given rise, in a sophisticated legal society, to endless discussion of theory and practice. Unfortunately, no statutes of Bologna exist of a date earlier than Dominic, and in their later form they may well have been themselves 'contaminated' by the influence of the friars, but the method of government by elected committees and checks on the executive was a favourite one throughout the thirteenth century, as can be seen from the history of urban and guild development, above all in Italy, and in particular from the series of constitutional experiments in England inspired by Simon de Montfort. Schemes similar to that of Dominic were therefore in the air at the time, but if his achievement were no more than to have produced a model of such excellence that it functioned smoothly from the start and has continued ever since to operate with scarcely any change, he would have done what few legislators in the course of the ages have shown ability to do.

The founder of the Preachers left but the scantiest memorials of purely spiritual doctrine for his sons. The saint must not, however, be suffered wholly to elude observation behind the legislator. To his contemporaries, Dominic was primarily a leader and an inspiration, not a thinker; they

1 Cf. H. Rashdall, *The Universities of Europe* (ed. Powicke and Emden), I, 163: 'In fact, the whole organization of the university was exactly parallel to that of the guilds... while the organization of the guilds was in Italy largely a reproduction of the municipal organization of the cities.'

2 *V. ibid.* I, 176–89.

emphasize his severe penances, his exquisite charity, the nights spent in prayer and the spiritual power that radiated from and even seemed to inform his physical frame.[1] Yet we may wonder whether his order would have attained the full definition of character and spirit that are now recognized as Dominican had not Aristotle and Thomas Aquinas given to the Western Church a new intellectual fabric. Dominic had in a sense built better than he knew. He had created an order of Preachers and given to it an organization superbly 'rational' in all its parts, but in the early years their preaching was indistinguishable in tone and accent from that of others. Only when two eminent sons of Dominic saw in the teaching of Aristotle not the tenets of a school but the *philosophia perennis* of mankind, and built upon its foundations a great edifice of truth did the Order of Preachers find its full vocation. Since that discovery, the peculiar task and glory of the Dominicans has been, not only to preach the traditional gospel of the Church, but to cherish and maintain as certain, indivisible and inviolable a massive fabric of autonomous metaphysical and theological truth against the attacks of every kind of agnosticism, illuminism, eclecticism and opportunism. In so doing they have found, not only their work, but their nourishment, for Aquinas and his greatest disciples have given to their order its spiritual doctrine by transmuting and elevating the ethics of ancient philosophy to the level of the virtues of Christ and the inspiration of the Holy Spirit.

The Order of Preachers was never shaken by controversies or rent by divisions in any way comparable to those which continued to agitate the Friars Minor throughout the middle ages. The clearly defined purpose of the order, and the full and all but dryly legalistic expressions of its constitutions left no scope for interpreters abounding in their own sense and made schism impossible. Indeed, the only schism that has ever affected the Dominicans was the purely external and vertical division caused by the division of Western Christianity by the rival claimants to the papacy. One element of stress there was, however, intrinsic to the institute. This was the combination of the monastic and apostolic elements within a single life and code; the Preacher in the daily life of his convent was all but a monk; outside it, and in time, also, even within it, he tended to become a student, a teacher and a missionary. Thus there remained, and still remains, a stress between the current of retirement, silence and austerity and that of activity and a greater external latitude of life, and at certain times, and in certain regional divisions of the order, one element has gained ground upon the other.[2] Above all, in the first decades, the movement towards intensive study and public teaching of theology aroused

1 Cf. the descriptions of Dominic's compelling attraction given by Jordan of Saxony, and above all the letter of the nun of Toulouse.
2 Père Mandonnet, *art. cit.* 357, in an interesting passage, speaks of a 'sort of dualism in the interior life' and of 'the difficulty of maintaining the nice equilibrium' between the monastic and the apostolic elements.

apprehension among a section of the friars, full of the memories of the first simple beginnings and enamoured of the ideal set up by the unlearned Friars Minor. It is to this trend of sentiment that we owe the composition of the Lives of the Brethren, that precious and indeed unique picture of life among the first Preachers, which throws into high light the unworldliness and simplicity of the early friars, and concentrates attention upon the domestic life of the convent rather than upon that of the schools. Twenty years after the composition of the *Vitae Fratrum*, a more speculative question divided the order for a while, but only to weld it more firmly and permanently into a single whole.[1]

In this process, and in the growth and working of the Dominican body politic as a European organization with an intellectual life of unparalleled vigour the friars of the English province were to have a share, never preponderant, but not wholly insignificant.

1 *V*. Mandonnet, *Siger de Brabant*, xlviii–xlix.

CHAPTER XIV

THE PREACHERS IN ENGLAND

It is a remarkable fact that in almost every centre of new religious life in Europe between 1066 and 1250 there may be found an Englishman. Stephen Harding was a leader at Molesmes and Cîteaux; William, later of Rievaulx, was among the first disciples of St Bernard; another William of England was, if not the first, at least one of the most fervent and faithful of Francis's companions at Assisi; and, as we shall see, a singularly elusive Englishman was at the heart of the movement that led to the establishment of the Carmelite friars in this country. No surprise, therefore, can be felt at the presence of an Englishman, Brother Laurence, among the small group of six around St Dominic at Toulouse. There, as it happened, they attended the school of another Englishman, Alexander of Stavensby,[1] and from him the founder would have become familiar with the religious and intellectual conditions in England, though at the moment these were extremely abnormal and Oxford in particular can have shown little promise *c.* 1216 of what it was so shortly to become. Laurence of England was one of the first two Preachers to be sent to study at Paris in 1217,[2] but when, at the second general chapter of the order held at Bologna in 1221, it was decided to send a mission of the friars to England, the leader of the band chosen by Dominic was not Laurence, but Gilbert of Fresney, who may or may not have been a native of the country.[3]

The Preachers, unlike the Friars Minor three years later, arrived in England under distinguished protection, travelling with Peter des Roches, bishop of Winchester, who took them to Canterbury and presented them to Stephen Langton.[4] The archbishop straightway commanded Gilbert to justify his calling by giving an impromptu sermon; the result was satisfactory, and henceforward Langton was one of the order's most enthusiastic supporters. For the moment, apparently, no colony was

---

1 Trivet, *Annales*, ed. Hog, 224.

2 *Vita S. Dominici*, in *Acta SS.* Aug. I, 550, §39.

3 *Ibid.* 554, § 65. He was probably a brother of William Fresney, also a Preacher, titular archbishop of Edessa, whose tombstone still exists in the ruins of the Dominican priory at Rhuddlan (Gumbley, *Flints. Archaeol. Journal*, I (1915), 31–41).

4 Trivet, 209. There is no contemporary chronicle of the early black friars; the fullest notices are in Trivet, who wrote more than eighty years later. Scattered references abound, and were first collected more than sixty years ago by Fr C. F. R. Palmer, O.P. All previous work has now been outdated by Fr W. A. Hinnebusch, O.P., whose *Early English Friars Preachers* (Rome, 1952), a monument of exact and laborious scholarship, is definitive in its field. His conclusions, however, do not necessitate any great modification in the summary account given above.

left at Canterbury; the friars reached London on 10 August and immediately pushed on to Oxford, the goal of their journey, whither they arrived on 15 August, the Feast of the Assumption of the Blessed Virgin. Three years later, while the first Friars Minor were halted at Canterbury, Francis received the stigmata on Monte Alverna; while the first Preachers were in the same city Dominic, on 6 August, had died at Bologna.

In following the story of the black friars we have, unfortunately, no chronicler to give us, like Eccleston, a living picture of the first simplicity and enthusiasm. Oxford and the Holborn convent in London appear to have been the first two foundations;[1] recruits came in large numbers; the Preachers spread rapidly over England and by c. 1260 had some thirty-six houses, to which eleven more were added before 1272.[2] All these, with very few exceptions, were in the cathedral cities and important market towns, and ultimately reached a total of some fifty-three, as compared with the forty-eight of the Friars Minor. It is significant that there were settlements of both grey and black friars in no less than thirty towns, and nothing in the character or regional situation of the places chosen by one order alone affords any ground for supposing that the two bodies had different motives for choosing a site. Both clearly aimed at occupying the greater towns and, after them, the lesser ones as opportunity might arise. The history of the Preachers in England followed a course strangely similar to that of the Minors.[3] Just as the conversion of the English Parisian masters Haymo of Faversham and Alexander of Hales was of decisive importance to the latter, so the reception of the learned Englishman, John of St Giles, a master of divinity at Paris and of medicine at Montpellier, was of moment in the history of the former. It was not he, however, but another physician, John of St Albans, sometime medical adviser to Philip Augustus, who became owner of the hospital of St Jacques; this he presented to the Preachers in 1218, thus linking his memory with the most famous convent of the order, which gave its name first to the friars and then, in a later age, to a brotherhood of another kind. John of St Giles took the habit with something of a flourish at Paris, in September 1230; his conversion, which preceded and may have influenced that of Alexander of Hales, had a similar result, as he continued his lectures in the friars' convent, thus inaugurating the second chair of theology there. In England the centre of the life of the province was at Oxford, as it soon became for the Minors. Jordan of Saxony, the saintly and inspiring second master-general, who was in England for the first provincial chapter in 1230, wrote

1 V. the very full articles in VCH, Oxford (A. G. Little), II, 107 seqq., and VCH, London, I, 498.

2 V. list in Religious Houses of Medieval England.

3 Short biographies of many of the leading friars may be found in J. C. Russell's Writers of Thirteenth Century England and (in the case of Masters of Paris) in P. Glorieux Répertoire des maîtres en théologie de Paris au XIIIᵉ siècle. These often (as with John of St Giles) correct in important particulars the articles in DNB.

from Oxford that he had hopes of a rich haul there.[1] It is possible that among those who answered his call was Robert Bacon, who continued his lectures as a friar as the first regent master of the Preachers in the Jewry school. He was followed by Richard Fishacre, his pupil, the first Preacher to incept at Oxford, and already in 1238 and 1244 a black friar, Simon de Bovill, was chancellor of the university.

It may have been on his visit to Oxford in 1230 that Jordan first met Grosseteste. Whatever the ills of the time, it was an age, like that of St Teresa in Spain and of Bérulle in France, when spiritual leaders of whatever allegiance were working in company. Though Grosseteste was so closely linked in friendship with prominent Minors he welcomed Jordan's advances,[2] and his letters show that he made equal, if not greater, use of the Preachers in his *entourage*. He is found in 1235 begging John of St Giles to come to England, to join him, and to preach; this is followed by a letter to the English provincial, Alard, asking that he may have John and a companion for at least a year as confessors and companions to himself and his household.[3] This in turn is followed by a third letter to the provincial chapter at York asking for a third Preacher skilled in civil and canon law, who may indicate and hold fast by the truth among the shifting currents of worldly jurisprudence. Apparently these requests were not granted, for two years later the bishop of Lincoln is asking Jordan of Saxony to give him John. Whatever the immediate success of this request, a letter of 1242 shows that two Preachers were then regularly with the bishop, and the well-known account by Matthew Paris of Grosseteste's last hours, whatever may be the exact degree of its authenticity, is at least a witness to the intimate friendship with the bishop to which John of St Giles was admitted.[4]

Indeed, the reforming bishops as a group seem to have had closer relations with the black than with the grey friars. Alexander Stavensby had them always with him; Robert Bacon, once a fellow-student with Edmund Rich, remained his friend, and the two other canonized bishops of the age were in close contact with the Preachers. Richard of Chichester had a Brother Ralph as his confessor, and later as his biographer, and thirty years later Thomas of Cantilupe, pupil, penitent and friend of Robert Kilwardby, delayed his inception in theology at Oxford until the newly-

---

1 B. Altaner, *Die Briefe Jordans von Sachsen*, ep. xvi (shortly before 2 Feb. 1230), 20: 'Apud studium Oxoniense, ubi ad praesens eram, largam spem bonae capturae Dominus nobis dedit.' Historians have been disposed to see in the phrase a suggestion of craft, but Jordan doubtless had in mind the words of the gospel (Matt. iv. 19; Lk. v. 4, where the word *captura* occurs in the Vulgate). In any case, he had a name for fishing of this kind, cf. *Cronica ordinis* in *MOPH*, I, *s.a.* 1233, p. 529: 'Jordanus se totum dabat ad attrahendas personas bonas ad ordinem et ideo morabatur quasi semper in locis in quibus erant scolares.'

2 *Ep.* xl (1237): 'Quanta familiaritate, cum fuistis Oxoniae, vestra dulcis affabilitas ad privata nos suscipit frequenter colloquia.'

3 *Epp.* xiv ('ut mores meos et familiae meae corrigant, errata deprehendant,' etc.), xv, xvi.

4 *Epp.* xl (1237), c (1242); *MPChM*, v, 400–7.

appointed archbishop could be present at his vesperies.[1] Long before that time Walter Mauclerc, bishop of Carlisle and a benefactor to the Preachers of Oxford, had left his see to take their habit in that house; almost a century later Richard de Bury had friars of both orders always in his household.[2]

The English province was quick to organize itself. The first provincial chapter was at Oxford in 1230;[3] twenty years later the general chapter was held in London, when four hundred friars met in the Holborn convent and received a day's provisions from the king, queen and abbot of Westminster in turn.[4] Yet at both universities the Minors took the lead in development. Oxford was early recognized by them as a school to which friars from the continent might frequent, but it was not till 1263 that it became a *studium generale* for the Preachers. The deepest reasons for this delay are not apparent, but we can trace in the official records the stages and mischances of the affair. As early as 1247 England, along with three other provinces, was charged with selecting a convent as the site of a *studium generale*, whither friars might be sent from every province; the decree was repeated in the following year, but in 1250, at a general chapter held in London, the prior provincial of England was penanced for extravagance in building, and nothing had been done. In 1261 the project was still hanging fire, the *studium* was once more decreed and the prior provincial absolved from office; in addition, those diffinitors who had refused to allow foreign students to be placed at Oxford were severely penanced. It has been suggested that Kilwardby was elected to carry through the plan; certainly, it was not till his day, in 1263, when the general chapter was again held in London, that Oxford became an international school for the black friars.[5] It is difficult to suppose that pecuniary considerations, or merely personal sentiment, were alone causes of the delay. Perhaps public difficulties, and the current prejudice against foreigners, had a large part in the matter. At Cambridge, also, the Minors, who had preceded the Preachers by almost a decade, took the lead, and by 1250 their school there was on an equality with that of Oxford. For the Preachers it did not become an international house till the Bull of John XXII in 1318.[6]

But if the Preachers were somewhat less prominent in the universities they had equal, if not greater, influence in the counsels of the great. Some-

---

1 Trivet, 228. [S. Edmundus] 'in comitiva sua fratres Praedicatores habebat continue'; 228–9 (Bacon and Fishacre; Robert Bacon was probably uncle to Roger); 242 (Richard of Chichester); 306 (Thomas of Cantilupe).

2 *Philobiblon* (ed. Thomas), 77: 'Ad statum pontificalem assumpti nonnullos habuimus de duobus ordinibus, Praedicatorum videlicet et Minorum, nostris assistentes lateribus nostraeque familiae commensales.' 3 Trivet, 217. 4 *MPChM*, v, 127.

5 The story may be traced in *Acta Capituli Generalis* (*MOPH*, III), i, 38, 41, 54, 110–1. The alleged visit of St Thomas to London in 1263 is disproved by Hinnebusch, *Early English Friars Preachers*, 31 n. 69.

6 Cf. *The Friars and the Foundation of the Faculty of Theology in the University of Cambridge*, by A. G. Little, in *FP*, p. 137.

what paradoxically, perhaps, while the Minors excelled in speculative theology, the Preachers were distinguished by their excursions into diplomacy.[1] One of the earliest in this field was Brother John of Darlington. In his early days as a friar he was a prominent member of the group of Englishmen who, as editors of a new edition of the biblical concordances of Hugh of St Cher, were responsible for the collection known thenceforward as the *Anglicanae Concordantiae*.[2] In 1256 he became a councillor and confidential adviser (and then or later confessor) to the king, and had a prominent position among the royal partisans in the following years, being one of the king's representatives in drawing up the Provisions of Oxford. Subsequently he acted as representative at Rome of Edward I and as collector of the papal crusading tenth in England, a vexatious employment that brought him into collision with a number of prelates and heads of religious houses. Meanwhile he had been appointed by the pope archbishop of Dublin in 1279, shortly after the appointment of Pecham to Canterbury, but his office as collector kept him employed in England, and when he died suddenly in 1283 he had just started upon his first journey to Ireland.

During the reigns of the three first Edwards the Preachers came to occupy something of the position filled by members of the Society of Jesus in the castles and palaces of the Counter-Reformation. They are found acting, by special dispensation, as household chaplains and confessors to the great,[3] and for some two hundred years without a break the post of royal confessor was given to the friars.[4] In this office the Preachers all but held a monopoly; from the reign of Henry III to the fall of Richard II they were the sole royal confessors, and although the house of Lancaster, beginning with John of Gaunt, favoured the Carmelites, who held office throughout the reign of Henry IV, when Stephen Patrington died in 1418 Henry V returned to the Preachers,[5] and they continued to fill the post under his son. The king's confessor who, accompanied by a *socius*, had lodging in the palace and followed the court on tour, was a natural choice

1 A very full account of these is given in an unpublished thesis for the London University M.A. degree (1930), *Some secular activities of the English Dominicans during the reigns of Edward I, Edward II and Edward III*, 1272–1377, by R. D. Clarke.

2 Trivet, 230; cf. also Glorieux, *Répertoire*, and *DNB*.

3 Jarrett, *English Dominicans*, 125, gives examples, with references, mostly from the fourteenth century.

4 For a fairly complete and accurate list of Preachers who were royal confessors v. the articles, *The King's Confessors*, by Fr C. F. R. Palmer, O.P., in the (now defunct) periodical *The Antiquary*, vol. 22 (1890). A vast amount of painstaking and useful work on the English Dominicans was done by this writer in the last quarter of the nineteenth century; it has been absorbed by Hinnebusch, *op. cit.*, who gives a full list of Palmer's articles. He also rightly emphasizes the importance of early Dominican theologians; Robert Bacon and Simon of Hinton are especially remarkable, as has been shown by Miss B. Smalley, *The Study of the Bible in the Middle Ages* (2 ed., 1952), 318–23, and *TRHS* 4 ser. xxx (1948), 1–19.

5 *V.* H. Ellis, *Original Letters (CS)*, 1st ser. vol. 1, no. 2, where Archbishop Chichele writes to Henry V that he has chosen Thomas Dyss, O.P., as his confessor to succeed Stephen Patrington, O.C. (*ob.* 22 Nov. 1417).

when an agent was wanted for either confidential or public negotiations at home or abroad.

The prior provincial, who had often to be at court on his order's business, and who was constantly travelling overseas to a general chapter or to the Curia, had similar qualifications for the functions of a confidential envoy, and as in fact the two offices were not infrequently held in succession by a distinguished friar, the king had often at his disposal two competent agents who were also *personae gratae* at the papal court and familiar with French notabilities through previous residence at the convent of St Jacques. Consequently, for more than a century Preachers are found constantly on diplomatic missions or residing as envoys at the Curia: declaring war, arranging peace, negotiating alliances, carrying representations to the papal court or to Scotland, and engaging in every kind of diplomatic business.[1] Thus as early as 1277 the provincial William of Southampton was an agent for peace in the Welsh war, a field to which the contentious Welsh Preacher, Anian the black friar of Nannau, attracted attention during his long tenure of the see of St Asaph.[2] A little later, in 1294, the ex-provincial, Hugh of Manchester, joined on this occasion to his 'opposite number', William of Gainsborough, ex-minister-provincial of the Minors, was charged with the declaration of war on France. The ablest of all these Dominican diplomatists, however, was probably William of Hothum, twice prior provincial, of whom we catch a welcome glimpse at close quarters as the tactful, if not wholly ingenuous, protector of his flock against the attacks of Pecham. Though his relations with the highest powers of his order were not always peaceful, his tact in dealing with awkward situations, and the amiable character to which his confrère Trivet bears witness,[3] stood him in good stead, and from 1289 till his death in 1298 he was in constant employment by the king, first at the papal court, then in the Scottish negotiations at Norham and Berwick, and finally in Flanders. In 1298 he was provided by Boniface VIII to the archbishopric of Dublin, but died before taking possession.

While several of the leading black friars were thus eminent in secular diplomacy, others during the same period, when the *éclat* of their order was greatest in the schools and administrative circles, were attached to the Curia as penitentiaries, sent as papal collectors, employed as inquisitors, and chosen for the college of cardinals. The first English Preacher so honoured, Robert Kilwardby, did not long survive his promotion which

1 R. D. Clarke, in the thesis referred to, gives a long list of such employments; other cases will be found in Jarrett and articles in *DNB*.

2 By a strange error Anian has often passed (as in *DNB*) for Dutch under the name Schonaw. His biography has been set out correctly by R. Easterling in *Flints. Historical Society Journal*, 1 (1915). His native village Nannau (which R. Easterling places near Caernarvon), lies high upon the slope facing Cader Idris in Merioneth; it has been replaced by the trees and gardens of the Georgian country house of the Vaughans which looks across the beautiful vale of Dolgelley.

3 Trivet, 364: 'Cum esset vir acutissimi ingenii...erat jucundus in verbis, in affatu placidus, religionis honestae, in omnium oculis gratiosus. *V*. also the article in *DNB*.

was, indeed, a veiled form of superannuation, but between 1303 and 1310 three Englishmen of the habit succeeded each other in the title of Santa Sabina. Two were unfortunate: William of Macclesfield was created cardinal in December 1303, but died before the news reached him; his place was immediately filled by Walter of Winterbourne, but he in turn died within a year. The third, who survived his appointment for five somewhat stormy years, was Thomas Jorz.[1] Jorz was a member of a well-to-do London family; five of his brothers were, like himself, Preachers, and two of them were in succession provided to the metropolitan see of Armagh, which each in turn resigned in order to act as auxiliary bishop in England. Thomas, after teaching at Paris, London and Oxford, succeeded Hothum as provincial in 1296 and was confessor to the king. Relieved from office in 1304, he was sent by Edward I on a mission to the pope. There he was created cardinal, and for the next few years combined an attention to English interests with an active share in papal administration, being a member of the commission in the Poverty dispute and of that appointed to give judgement on Olivi. He died in 1310.

With his death the series of English Dominican cardinals came to an end. Their significance should not be exaggerated; two were the creations of a Dominican pope,[2] and had William of Macclesfield survived for ten years, he would probably have been the only English friar of his day to receive the supreme mark of papal favour. Moreover, the controversies and schisms which were rending the rival order at this time made of the Preachers a more trustworthy source of assistance to the Curia. Nevertheless, the English Preachers, at least during the reigns of Edward I and Edward II, had, so to say, a tone of social distinction not found in the other three mendicant orders, even though as many individuals in these may have been recruited from the higher classes of society, and though the fame of the Minors, and even of the Carmelites, stood as high in the schools. Never, perhaps, did they stand higher in favour at court than under Edward II, who became in effect founder of the convent, used as a novitiate for the province, of King's Langley, where a splendid, quasi-monastic range of buildings with a church capable of accommodating a hundred friars, was lavishly furnished and endowed as a memorial of Piers Gaveston. It is not surprising that the Preachers regretted the loss of their benefactor, and that a number of them went into rebellion in 1327, led by the versatile adventurer Thomas Dunhead, who had previously engaged in a series of escapades at home and abroad in which he was alleged to have posed as a papal chaplain in England and as a royal ambassador at the Curia. He certainly appears, along with some confrères

---

1 Trivet, 400, 404, 406. For Jorz and Winterbourne, cf. also the (somewhat meagre) articles in *DNB*, and Fr W. Gumbley, O.P., in *Analecta Ordinis Praedicatorum*, 1925–6. Jorz's family came from Burton Jorce (now Joyce).

2 It should be noted, however, that Benedict XI only created three cardinals in all: they were three Preachers, two were of the English province, the third an Italian.

and a Cistercian from Hayles, as assaulting Berkeley Castle in 1327 with a band of mutineers, and as employing the black arts in order to prove the continued existence of the murdered king; Edmund of Woodstock, earl of Kent, was among his confederates. The earl paid for his support with his life; as for Dunhead, his disreputable career came to an end when he was in the act of breaking prison at Pontefract.[1] This episode, the long series of entries in official documents of the time of vagabond Preachers 'wanted' by government, and the sequence of riots at Boston, in the last of which, in 1376, the bishop of Lincoln was barricaded out of the friars' church by two hundred of the brethren furnished with a supply of stones,[2] reminds us that the Minors were not the only order to be embarrassed at times by the unruly conduct of some of its members, but the Preachers were never seriously threatened with a schism or inordinately troubled by parties of relaxation or reform.[3]

Émeutes such as this, however, though attaining wide publicity, were abnormal, and we have no intimate account of the private life of a friar Preacher of the thirteenth or fourteenth century. Lacking an Eccleston, we are also without any adequate account of the province in its early days, when the order was rich in hidden sanctity. The compilation of edifying stories by Gerard of Frachetum can be no real substitute for the picture given by the Franciscan chronicler, but it is worth noting that the English province contributes its full share of examples. We read of the holiness of Brother Lawrence, of the young friar Gerard of Derby, of the saintly Brother William, lector at Cambridge, and of the edifying death of Brother Walter of Norwich.[4] These are but glimpses, which we catch or seem to catch, before the mist falls again, never to rise; but they may serve as a warning that there was at first, and perhaps for long, a hidden life among the friars that was not wholly overlaid by the business of courts and the disputations of schools.

1 Dunhead's adventures are noted by the Friar Minor who composed the latter part of the *Chronicon de Lanercost*, pp. 254, 260, 265; they have left traces also in official documents. Cf. *The conspiracy of Thomas Dunheved*, 1327, by F. J. Tanquerey in *EHR*, XXXI (1916), 119–24.

2 *Reg. Bockingham*, f. 142, cited in *VCH, Lincs*, II, 214. The bishop had attempted to attend a funeral without asking permission.

3 F. Ehrle, in his article on the Franciscan Spirituals in *ALKG*, III (1887), 612, has some interesting lines on a movement for reform within the Dominican body, clearly influenced by contemporary happenings among the Minors, though remaining domestic and orderly.

4 *V. Fratris Gerardi de Francheto Vitae Fratrum O.PP.* ed. B. M. Reichert (*MOPH*, I), 164–5; 267, 276 et al. Gerard was not an original chronicler like Eccleston; he was deputed to work over materials collected from all parts of the order in response to a decree of the general chapter of 1256. His work was published in 1260, and cannot therefore have influenced Eccleston, though it is possible that the Minor was put on his mettle by hearing of the capitular resolution.

CHAPTER XV

THE EVOLUTION OF THE FRANCISCAN IDEAL

I

While the Order of Preachers received from its founder an organization complete in every detail and so perfectly devised that it has functioned with little change to the present day, the peculiar genius of St Francis, which was concerned not at all with laws and regulations, left to future generations the task of constitution-building, and in consequence the Friars Minor were slow in evolving a machinery of government, nor did their organization ever equal that of the Preachers in perfect poise, in clarity of outline, and in nice balance of elective and administrative responsibility. Yet here, also, the two first orders of friars interacted upon each other; for while it was without doubt the example of the Franciscans that led the Preachers to become mendicants and allow their early canonical character to fall more and more completely into the background, the Minors still more clearly borrowed from the Dominicans several of the elements of their strong system of government.

The order of St Francis, therefore, took a considerable time in finding that constitutional equilibrium which the Preachers had from their first beginnings, and it was not until the great legislative chapter of Narbonne in 1260, by setting its seal upon the labours of St Bonaventure and his predecessors, had gathered up and codified the experience and decrees of the past, that the Minors had a framework of constitutional law that was fully adequate to their needs, and that guided their destinies throughout the remaining centuries of the medieval period. In the preceding and crucial half-century of change three periods may be clearly distinguished, and as these changes deeply affected Franciscan life in England, and were in part due to the initiative of two or three English friars, a brief account must here be given. The three periods were: the lifetime of St Francis (1206–26); the terms of office of Giovanni Parenti and Elias (1227–39); the phase of experiment and gradual settlement between the deposition of Elias and the legislation of Narbonne and Bonaventure (1240–60).[1]

1 Of all that has been written on early Franciscan constitutional history, the account which best combines a full presentation of the documents with a balanced and luminous judgement is, in my opinion, that of Ehrle in his contribution to *ALKG*, VI (1892), 1–138, *Die ältesten Redactionen der Generalconstitutionen des Franziskanerordens*. Though over half a century old, this study needs correction only on a very few points of detail by the works of Dr Little and others. Of all recent works, perhaps the best is that of Père Gratien, *Histoire de la Fondation et de l'Evolution de l'ordre des Frères Mineurs au XIII* siècle*. It is a full account, admirably documented, the work of a trained historian. But for a certain hesitancy of judgement, particularly where Bonaventure is concerned, and occasional omissions of important facts, it would be in all respects a satisfactory guide.

The 1260 constitutions of Narbonne are printed by Ehrle, *op. cit.* 87–138.

The original conception of Francis was that of a brotherhood working with an evangelical liberty of spirit under his personal guidance. When the office of minister was created to meet the needs of a growing body, it was to be held by appointment from him, and was to be, as the full title of *minister et servus* implied, one of service rather than of government or administration. Every year all the brethren were to meet together at Santa Maria degli Angeli to discuss and settle problems of the past and work of the future. The last of such meetings was that of 1221; the numbers and dispersion of the friars made anything of the kind impossible for the future; Francis therefore reduced the annual chapter to one of the ministers only: those of Italy were to meet each year; those from beyond the Alps and overseas were to come every third year; the ministers in their turn might if they saw fit, summon their brethren to a meeting in their own district in the autumn. Hitherto there had been mention only of the head of the brotherhood and of ministers; in the Rule of 1223 three grades of office appear: the minister general, the ministers provincial, and the wardens (*custodes*); these last had charge of the friars within a subdivision of the province; they were not merely the domestic superiors of a convent, for in Francis's lifetime the flexibility and fluidity of movement remained, together with the primitive simplicity of housing.[1] In this Rule, also, the general chapter is fixed to every third year, and is composed of general, provincials and wardens; the latter may hold provincial chapters in the autumn following the general chapter. Concurrently, the office of general is outlined with greater precision and the holder acquires many of the powers formerly held by the ministers; he is to be elected and may be judged by the general chapter. This Rule of 1223, together with the writings and actions of Francis, show clearly that he conceived of the government of his order as in a real sense monarchical; the minister general, not the chapter, was the pivot of the system. In the sequel, this simple arrangement was subjected to various stresses and strains by the arbitrary conduct of Elias as general, by the new needs of the friars, and by the influence of the Preachers.

Under Giovanni Parenti (1227–32), who followed the tradition of the founder, little was changed,[2] save that by decision of Gregory IX in the bull *Quo elongati* of 1230 the whole body of *custodes* were no longer to assemble for general chapter, but were to elect in each province one of their number to accompany the provincial. No doubt this arrangement was made with an eye upon the constitution of the Preachers, but the primary aim was not to secure representation, but to limit numbers. The few other indications that survive of his activity show Parenti as exercising

---

1 In other words, the *ministri* and *custodes*, as conceived by Francis, were responsible for the spiritual welfare of groups, not for the government or administration of local communities.

2 Cf. the judgement of Eccleston (ed. Little), 79: 'vir sapiens et religiosus et summi rigoris.' It should be added that the recorded actions of Parenti do not bear the impress of great wisdom or strength.

the full powers of a general, as in the matter of the visitors sent by him to the various provinces.[1]

The troubled career of Elias does not directly concern us here; it is unquestionable that he made of his monarchical position something wholly despotic, and reduced, if indeed he did not altogether suspend, the meetings of general chapter. In the movement which led to his removal two English friars took a leading part. One of these, whose name appears frequently enough in these pages, was Adam Marsh.[2] The other, during the few years of life that remained to him, was to play an extremely important part in moulding the future of his order. That Haymo of Faversham, a secular master of Paris who knew nothing from experience of the early life of the friars in the cradle of the order, should pass rapidly from the offices of warden and lecturer to that of minister provincial of England, should act as agent in diplomacy for the Curia, and should, within fourteen years of the death of St Francis, come to be the order's general, is an astonishing sign of the rapidity with which the institute grew and changed; Haymo, indeed, is one more to be added to the group of Englishmen of the middle ages, almost unknown to their countrymen of modern times, who left an indelible mark on the religious history of Europe. He, more than any other single man, fixed the constitutional and social lines along which the order was to travel during the thirteenth century, and he showed himself throughout, as was to be expected, completely free from any sense of confinement to the primitive aims.[3] An Englishman, trained in the schools of Paris and with a love of order, free from the personal ambition and self-indulgence of Elias, he proceeded energetically against the two tendencies in the latter's method of rule which he conceived to be most baneful—despotic, uncontrolled government, and the entrusting of office to the unlettered lay members of the order. The powers of the general and other officials were therefore curtailed, and a corresponding increase of power given to the chapters. Provincial ministers were to be appointed by general chapter, wardens and guardians[4] were to be elected by their subjects. As for the chapters,

1 For the visitors in England in 1229 and 1230, v. Eccleston, 45–6.

2 Haymo's share is clear from Eccleston, 36, 82–3. That chronicler does not mention Adam's name in this connection, but the enigmatical Speculum vitae S. Francisci et sociorum ejus makes sanctus Antonius et frater Adam leaders against Elias (cf. also Chron. XXIV Gen. 229), and Sabatier's suggestion that a late copyist substituted the (chronologically impossible) name of Antony for Haymo is very probable, but the whole question is still very uncertain (v. P. Sabatier, Examen de la Vie de Frère Elie, 168, note 1, et al., and Eccleston, 23 note b.)

3 It is noteworthy that as early as 1230 Haymo was one of those who approached Gregory IX to ask for an exposition of the Rule, cf. Eccleston, 81. The DNB does not do justice to Haymo, but there is a good brief article on him by Fr Cuthbert in the CE. P. Gratien remarks, very justly (Histoire...des Frères Mineurs, p. 155): 'Frère Aymon...après le saint fondateur et après Grégoire IX, apparaît comme le principal auteur de sa législation.'

4 Guardians (guardiani), the domestic superiors of convents, had by this time become normal. They are not mentioned in the Rule, and for this reason there was a movement to abolish the office of custos as superfluous, and to transfer the name to the local superior; thus the magistri of Paris put forward in 1241 a proposal that these latter should be called housewardens or house-ministers (custodes sive ministri domus). In the event, they retained their original name, and the custodies with their superiors fell into abeyance.

they also were partially remodelled under the influence of Dominican practice. Under the Rule of 1223 the general chapter consisted solely of those who held important office, and the subsequent exclusion of the wardens, save for a nominee of each province, had intensified this official character. Haymo introduced a third group, that of the *discreti*, to be elected, one from each province, at the provincial chapter. Indeed, he wished to go still further in following the model of the Preachers, and to fix a rotation of chapters made up of provincials and *discreti* or *diffinitores* in turn. One chapter of *diffinitores* was in fact actually held at Montpellier in 1241, but it showed signs of driving the order still further along the road to democracy; there was a reaction, and no attempt was made after Haymo's day either to repeat the experiment or to make the chapter annual in order to facilitate a rotation of meetings differing in composition.[1] Haymo's third great administrative act was to incapacitate those who were not clerics from holding official position in the order, and to limit most severely the number of lay recruits.[2] No information is available as to the reception this met with; the measure must have passed through general chapter, but this was now made up largely of the university trained masters, and in the northern provinces, at least, the lay element had been almost from the first sharply cut off, socially and mentally, from the clerics. The change in outlook, however, which this measure implied and perpetuated, was drastic; the simple, solitary brethren of the hermitages and by-ways of Umbria and the Marches, who to Francis had been the heart of the order, became a regional survival or an aching memory, while the lay brethren of the rest of the world rapidly became, what they were already among the white monks and Preachers and have since been with all other orders, the labourers and servants for the clerics, without any influence upon the external history of the body.

These epoch-making measures were not the only achievements of Haymo during his short term of office. In it he published the results of his work in revising the breviary of the Roman Curia for his order, and this subsequently became, with a few changes, that of the whole Latin Church.[3] He also reduced the number of provinces from seventy-two set up by Elias to thirty-two, a figure maintained, with only two additions, throughout the middle ages. He died in 1243 or 1244, and the ashes of this man of Kent, like those of so many of his restless and indomitable countrymen

1 For this, a crux to historians by reason of the fragmentary and conflicting evidence, *v.* Ehrle, *ALKG*, vi, 21–9, and Little, *Eccleston*, 86–9 and notes. The one chapter of *diffinitores* certainly held was that of Montpellier, probably in 1241. The term *diffinitor* is ambiguous among the Minors after 1241, being used (*a*) of those present at general chapter with the *vox deliberativa et consultativa*, and (*b*) of the four friars elected by the provincial chapter to inquire into the administration of the province.

2 For the exclusion of the lay brethren from office *v. Chron. XXIV Gen.* (cited by Ehrle, *ALKG*, iii, 581 n.). Both Ehrle (*loc. cit.*) and Fr Cuthbert in his article in *CE* state that this affected important offices only, but give no authority for this. As regards recruitment, *v.* Salimbene, *Chronica*, 103: 'Eorum receptio quasi totaliter est prohibita.'

3 Cf. Batiffol, *Histoire du Bréviaire romain*, 203 (Eng. trans. pp. 160 *seqq.*).

before and since, found a grave under skies not English; the epitaph[1] on his tomb remains to catch the eye, but scarcely to attract the imagination, of those Englishmen and women of to-day who stay more than a moment by the stone that marks the resting-place of Elizabeth Barrett Browning or John Keats. Haymo's work endured, and the constitutional changes made between his death and 1260 were few; among them was, perhaps, a reduction of the elective element by transference of the appointment of wardens and guardians from the vote of their future subjects to the choice of the provincial.[2] Finally, the chapter of Narbonne in 1260, held under Bonaventure as general, by approving the code of constitutions compiled by him from decrees of past chapters and ministers general, fixed once and for all the constitutional organization of the Friars Minor. This code, though different in emphasis and in many details from that of the Preachers, does in fact set out the scheme of a religious order similar in all its main lines of government; the stamp of monarchy and individual authority, clearer in the one than the other, did little to differentiate them in practice, for the tendencies of the times, and the strong sense of corporate interest, made of both orders highly centralized and strongly governed bodies, save where political isolation or spiritual relaxation intervened to loosen bonds; and the more troubled, uneasy history of the Franciscans in the sequel was due, not to any peculiarities of constitutional machinery, but to the glimpses seen and the echoes heard across the years of the voice of Francis, and to the ever-reawakened longing to return

ad patrios montes et ad incunabula nostra.

II

The constitutional development of the Order of Friars Minor was accompanied by changes of aim and of practice which continued to cause unrest within the body throughout the medieval period. The history of these movements is so intricate and so controversial, and their repercussions in England so occasional, that no full account is demanded here. A brief outline is, nevertheless, needful if the action of individual English friars, and parallel currents in this country, are to be at all comprehended.[3]

The vocation of Francis, which he wished to transmit to his friars, had been to poverty, simplicity, and complete renunciation of the security that comes

---

1 *Hic jacet Anglorum summum decus, Haymo, Minorum | Vivendo frater, hosque regendo pater.|Eximius lector, generalis in ordine rector.* Haymo's tomb is at Anagni. *V. Chron. XXIV. Gen.,* 255.

2 Cf. the constitutions of Narbonne, *ALKG,* VI, 127. But this also may have been a change of Haymo's; cf. *Eccleston,* 87.

3 Here again the most judicial and penetrating study known to me is that of Ehrle in *Die Spiritualen, ihr Verhältniss zum Franciscanerorden und zu den Fraticellen,* in *ALKG,* III (1887), 553–623. The emphasis on the influence of the Preachers upon the Minors, and the sharpness of the antithesis between their ideals should, however, be a little softened. Other good accounts will be found in Fr Cuthbert, *The Romanticism of St Francis* and P. Gratien, *Histoire...des Frères Mineurs.*

from ownership and position. Stripped of all, naked following the naked Christ, he might then call others to a change of heart by example rather than by words, and by direct appeal rather than by formal preaching and dispute. Himself a deacon only, he continued to the end to regard his friars as a body distinct from, and more lowly than, the priesthood; clerics and laymen were on an equality among them, and it was his desire that some should live in lonely hermitages, in unbroken prayer and praise, while others preached, and that all should in a measure share the lives of Martha and Mary.

Such a way of life, we may think, could only have endured if it had been restricted to a small number, and had been lived in the cultural and climatic conditions of central Italy, that land of mountain valleys and small enclosed cities, which has always been also a land of hermits and wayfaring preachers. In the event, the growth of the order, especially beyond the Alps, the success of the rival body of Preachers, the devotion of the populace to all the friars and the favour shown to the Minors as well as the Preachers by the most zealous of the bishops and above all by the papacy, led to a rapid extension of apostolic work at the expense of simplicity and obscurity, and the hermitages of Italy were not reproduced beyond the Alps. Already, in the third decade of the century, within a few years of the death of Francis, the influx of *magistri* in England, France and south Germany, and the policy of Elias had made a student order of the Minors; ten years later these same *magistri* were at the head of the government and, through the initiative of Haymo the Englishman, had made it an order of clerics. Henceforward, at least north of the Alps, the difference of vocation between Minors and Preachers was specific, not generic; it was a difference of emphasis and tone, not of instrument and theme.

Few, perhaps, of the recruits in northern lands between 1230 and 1260 realized how great had been the development in the scope and vocation of the order. Many of them had been brought up in the schools, had been welcomed by the friars as learned masters and had been set almost immediately to teach or to govern. They had never known Italy and the simple life of the hermitages; they had no access to the writings of the early companions of Francis; they knew only the convent schools of Paris and Oxford, and the urban friaries of England, France and the Rhineland. Soon, they were attacked by the same enemies as were the Dominicans, and protected by the same privileges; indeed, it became the common practice of the Curia to issue all new indults to both orders simultaneously. In a short while, again, they found themselves vindicating for their order the right of preaching and teaching as against the privileged position claimed by the black friars, and adopting, almost unconsciously, the aims of their rivals. These had in their early days regarded poverty and simplicity as means to the end of study and preaching; Francis had wished all apostolic activity to be the overflow, the surplus only, of the inner life.[1] Gradually, this

---

[1] For an excellent, though possibly too schematic, exposition of the differing ideals *v.* Ehrle, *ALKG*, III, 555 *seqq.*

primitive conception of the friars' preaching as the occasional, spontaneous revelation of his inmost self was changed into the more comprehensible one by which it became his professional life-work, his normal occupation, for which he must be prepared and trained by study. Manual work was altogether abandoned, intensive study encouraged, and the Minors became, like the Dominicans, an established division of the army of the Church, the auxiliaries and often the successful rivals of the parochial clergy in all their ministrations, and the directive force in the life of the theological schools.

III

The changes in the Franciscan vocation and the relaxations of the Rule led gradually to a division of sentiment within the order and at length to a series of open attempts at secession which, after a long story of controversies, disasters and lapses into revolt and heresy, issued in the fifteenth and sixteenth centuries in the formation of independent provinces following a stricter observance than the bulk of the order. The history of the *Spirituales* or *Zelanti*, as they came to be called, has often been traced.[1] In the days of strife at the beginning of the fourteenth century the leaders of the various groups of Spirituals claimed to inherit the spirit and traditions of those early companions of St Francis who, persecuted by Elias and perhaps also by Crescentius for fidelity to their master, had continued to live a hidden and austere life in the mountains of central Italy and the March of Ancona, and had handed on to their disciples by word and writing the precious legacy of literal observance of the Rule. Much of the early Franciscan literature does, indeed, bear out the claim that such a stream, half hidden, had always flowed with waters unpolluted from their mountain source.[2] But besides these, there was in the early days a large body, and in some provinces a majority, of the friars who, while accepting to the full the orientation of the order towards theological study and external activities, held at the same time to a full observance of the spiritual counsels of the Rule and to a literal acceptance of its poverty. Beyond all others, the English province would seem to have held an honourable position in this respect, as has already been seen. The narrative of Eccleston, which emphasizes the simplicity of life and adherence to the Rule, and notes the repeated commendations of the minister general, John of Parma, has already been quoted at length.[3] John of Parma, indeed, both in his

1 Above all by Ehrle, in the study of the Spirituals in *ALKG* referred to above, p.175, n. 3, and in other volumes of the same periodical.

2 For the persecution under Crescentius, *v. ALKG*, II, 256 *seqq*. Almost all the early sources for the life and teaching of Francis, especially Thomas of Celano's *Vita Secunda* and the *Speculum Perfectionis* and the *Scripta Leonis* have affinities with the later 'Spiritual' literature, and critics are still divided as to how much of this is a true reflection of Francis, and how much is tendencious party propaganda.

3 *V. supra*, pp. 139 *seqq*.

personal virtues and in his striving to maintain primitive purity of obser-vance, as also in his misfortunes and equivocal relationships, might well have been hailed as archetype by all later Spirituals; he was the first and last of his race to hold supreme power in the order, and the difficulties which led to his resignation, and his designation of Bonaventure as his successor showed clearly enough that the majority even of the most obser-vant friars no longer shared his ideals.[1]

St Bonaventure, himself a character of limpid clarity whose spirit is mirrored to perfection in his voluminous writings, left an indelible stamp upon the Franciscan order, and will always remain something of a crux for its historians.[2] Born, as many would say, like the sister of Polyneices in the Greek play, to join in love, not strife,[3] he ranks for them as a second founder, one who, pre-eminent in holiness and prudence alike, in-terpreted in lofty and yet practical terms the soaring ideals of St Francis; a leader sent by Providence to bless the new direction of the order's activity and to prove for all time that it was possible to combine the spirit of Francis with the practical needs of life. To others he has seemed, for all his personal holiness, as the leader chiefly responsible for the conversion of the Friars Minor from their unique vocation into a religious order indistinguishable in character from the rest, and for a policy of compromise between the spirit and the world; in other words as one mentally and spiritually alien from Francis, as no true Franciscan.

Whatever may be thought of such views, the legislative and adminis-trative work of Bonaventure, and his great personal prestige as a theologian and saint, confirmed the order irrevocably in the direction it had already taken in the intellectual life of the Church, and established as official the policy of following a *via media* between the extremes of austerity and with-drawal on the one hand and relaxation and worldliness on the other. Yet though he fought with energy and constancy against laxity and irregu-larity, and could give utterance to his celebrated wish to be ground to

1 Ehrle writes of him (*ALKG*, III, 591) as the 'Typus eines Spiritualen: die gewaltigen Reisen zu Fuss, die Übung der Handarbeit, der Joachimismus, die strenge Beurtheilung reicher Prälaten, das Bestreben die Brüder zur ursprünglichen Strenge zurückzuführen.' Raymond Godefroid ultimately gave his adherence to the Spirituals, but as minister-general (1289–95) he was not openly of the party.

2 Several of the fullest and best documented modern accounts of St Bonaventure (e.g. arts. in *DTC, DHG* and *DS*) are by Franciscans, who are not unnaturally preoccupied with the need of presenting the saint as a theological luminary of the first magnitude; they tend, for this and other reasons, to burke the very real contrast between his aim and that of St Francis. Some modern scholars, on the other hand, exaggerate the contrast so as to obscure the considerable spiritual possession held in common by both. Fr Cuthbert who, as usual, is very just in his estimate, refers (*The Romanticism of St Francis*, 149) to the 'attempts' made by St Bonaventure 'to effect a compromise' which 'satisfied neither party'. *V*. also P. Gratien, *Histoire*, 266–320, but here again the critical historian is sometimes lost behind the loyal Franciscan.

3 Sophocles, *Antigone*, 523: οὔτοι συνέχθειν ἀλλὰ συμφιλεῖν ἔφυν. Ehrle, *ALKG*, III, 516–17, prints an exceedingly interesting estimate of Bonaventure, written by the celebrated Spiritual leader Olivi, *c*. 1279.

powder, if so be the order might regain its pristine purity,[1] he remained aloof from those who cherished the fondest memories of the days of primitive simplicity, and remains, when all is said and done, a contrast to, not a complement of, Francis.

Bonaventure died early, and henceforward the rift in the order steadily widened; a succession of general chapters and ministers did, indeed, maintain for a time not only his policy but much also of his spirit of energy and fervour, but authority was fatally embarrassed in its fight with laxity by the repeated papal privileges and by a radical lack of sympathy with many of the primitive ideals. Wholeheartedly in favour of intensive study, of large urban churches, of a moderate use of privilege, and of activity of all kinds, they were, for all their personal excellence, in an equivocal position when combating a lax interpretation or practice on other points of the Rule.[2] The last quarter of the thirteenth century, in fact, saw a steady movement on the part of the *communitas ordinis* or, as it came to be called, the conventual body, away from any sympathy with the simplicity and solitude of the hermit life. Simultaneously, the party of reform, which *c.* 1300 acquired the name of Spirituals began to take visible shape round nuclei in Italy and Provence, and a period opened which was to be marked by strife and recrimination, leading inevitably to persecution, revolt and schism.

1 Quoted by Olivi (Ehrle, *ALKG*, III, 517): 'Parisius in pleno capitulo [i.e. that of 1266] me astante dixit, quod...vellet esse pulverizatus, ut ordo ad puritatem beati Francisci et sociorum ejus et ad illud, quod ipse de ordine suo intenderat, perveniret.'

2 As Ehrle excellently remarks (*ALKG*, III, 597): 'Andererseits lässt es sich doch nicht leugnen, dass [the better Conventuals] sich nicht wenig von den Einrichtungen und in etwas auch vom Geiste der ursprünglichen Stiftung mit Wissen und Willen entfernt hatte und eine Rückkehr zu derselben nicht für erspriesslich hielt.' For the later history of these controversies, *v.* D. Douie, *The Fraticelli*.

CHAPTER XVI

THE APOSTOLIC WORK OF THE FRIARS

I

St Francis, in his latest Rule, supposed two forms of work as the employment of his friars: the manual work of a craft, or its equivalent in domestic duties, and the preaching of the gospel in its simplest form.[1] The first of these two employments soon ceased to exist as an alternative to the second, especially in the transalpine provinces, where recruitment and training were from the first predominantly clerical. Eccleston, indeed, relates that one of the first friars in England practised a craft in accordance with the Rule,[2] but his language shows that by the time he wrote the fact had become something of a curiosity. The early friars no doubt long continued to do the simple domestic and garden work for themselves, but very soon this, too, passed to the remaining lay brothers and even to servants.

With the disappearance of craft or garden work as a regular employment preaching, with its accompaniment, for those in priest's orders, of hearing confessions, remained alone in the field as work for the rank and file of the Friars Minor, and this was throughout the middle ages their distinctive employment, though in the case of many, during the heyday of scholastic theology, its place was taken by study and lecturing. Unfortunately, no contemporary document gives any detailed account of the preaching journeys and experiences of the first English friars. Eccleston, however, and other chroniclers give incidental anecdotes which show the brethren going about the country two by two, especially in the penitential seasons of Advent and Lent, under conditions of what was at first truly evangelical simplicity, their bare feet cut by the frozen ground and leaving a blood-stained impress on the snow of winter.[3]

St Francis had presupposed that the initiative and the choice of destination for their preaching journeys would come from the friars themselves; if the bishop and local clergy received them, well and good; if not, they might pass elsewhere. In England, their activities were directed almost from the first by the action of a group of enlightened bishops of which Grosseteste was the most eminent member, who, working energetically for a moral and disciplinary reform in their dioceses, saw in the two orders of friars a most powerful instrument for their ends. Grosseteste, already the intimate friend and patron of the Minors, became bishop of Lincoln in 1235, less than nine

---

1 *Regula Bullata*, c. v; *Regula Prima*, c. vii.
2 *Eccleston*, 7: 'Frater Laurentius...qui laboravit in principio in opere mechanico secundum decretum regulae.'
3 *Chronicon de Lanercost*, 31 (cf. *Eccleston*, ed. Little, 135); 107–8.

years after their arrival in England, and immediately began to solicit the help of the superiors of both orders of friars. Having temporarily failed to secure the services of the Preachers, he applied to his friend Adam Marsh for Minors and was apparently successful, for in a letter to Alexander Stavensby of Lichfield in 1236 he speaks as if from experience of the spiritual profit and assistance that the Friars Minor bring with them wherever they go; by their preaching, and still more by their example they are a shining light in England and serve to atone for a bishop's failings.[1] The bishop of Lichfield, who had received the Preachers as old friends, had shown himself reluctant to allow the Franciscans to settle at Chester, on the grounds that the alms of the town would not suffice for two bodies of mendicants. Grosseteste told him that experience had shown that bene- factors multiplied with the friars; he need therefore have no fear. A year later he is imploring Elias to send him two or three friars, for they have no equals as confessors; later still, he is writing to Gregory IX that they bring inestimable benefits to England and that he wishes the pope could but see how all flock to them to confess or to be instructed, and how clergy and other religious profit by their example.[2]

Grosseteste's letters refer to the Preachers as his companions more often than to the Minors, but Adam Marsh was his close friend throughout life, and on at least one return journey from the Curia he had Friars Minor with him;[3] besides this, the many references of Eccleston show the bishop in constant relations with the friars, among whom Peter of Tewkesbury would seem to have been his most intimate friend after Adam Marsh. After Grosseteste, Roger Niger of London (1229–41) was perhaps the warmest supporter of the Minors,[4] but we hear of Adam Marsh assisting the archbishop of Canterbury on his visitation, and of a bishop of Salisbury, probably William of York (1247–56), who was anxious to obtain the services of Henry of Syreford. Marsh, indeed, was in such demand that he ulti- mately found it necessary to obtain letters from the pope inhibiting bishops from calling upon him for help.[5]

Besides work on these regular lines, individual friars were from the first selected as counsellors or confessors at court or by magnates. Here again Adam Marsh stood in a place apart. His influence with Henry III has already been recorded; he was twice used on foreign diplomatic missions,[6] and was in demand at other times; he enjoyed the confidence also of Queen Eleanor, who was among his correspondents.[7] His relations with the Earl and Countess of Leicester are well known; twenty-seven of his letters are

1 *Epp.* xiv, xv, xvi, xx, all of *c.* 1235. Also *ep.* xxxiv. More than sixty of Marsh's letters are addressed to Grosseteste.
2 *Ep.* xli of 1237; *ep.* lviii of ?1238; cf. *ep.* lviii: 'apud nostrates per dictos fratres inaesti- mabilia perveniunt bona.'
3 *Ep.* cxiv of 1245.
4 *Eccleston*, 75.
5 Adam Marsh, *Epp.* clxxxii, ccix, ccxxv, clxxiii.
6 In 1247 and 1257; *v.* the *Liberate Rolls* cited by Little, *The Grey Friars in Oxford*, 307–8.
7 *Ep.* clxxxv.

addressed to Simon de Montfort. But Adam did not stand alone. Other letters show that the queen had another friar in her household,[1] and in 1250 there is a royal order for the construction of a chapel for the Minors near the queen's lodging at Clarendon.[2] Benefactions of Henry III to almost all the houses of England are recorded in the Liberate and Close Rolls, and both the queen and Richard king of the Romans left their hearts to be buried with the Minors.[3]

II

The simple, individual methods of the first followers of St Francis in Italy had given way, even in the saint's lifetime, though against his desires, to a reliance upon letters of introduction and protection and other privileges from Rome which had enabled the friars, when once accepted by a bishop, to establish their own chapels where they and their clientele might administer and receive the sacraments. In England the Minors had from the first a policy which altered scarcely at all and developed logically with events; as it differed little from that of the contemporary Preachers, and as the Carmelites and Austin Friars when they arrived fell naturally into line with the older bodies, the relations between mendicants and the secular clergy in England can best be studied as a part of the history of the Minors. This is the more appropriate because they, who began by having aims somewhat different from those of the Preachers, were greatly influenced by the practice of the Curia in issuing almost simultaneously and as a matter of routine to the one order privileges demanded by or granted to the other.

Agnellus of Pisa who, by his patronage of study at Oxford, was responsible more than any other individual for the development in this country of an intellectual activity which St Francis had not desired, was responsible also for a departure from the letter of the Founder's injunctions against obtaining papal privileges. The exhortations of Francis were directed primarily against friars who might wish to force themselves into a diocese or parish against the wishes of bishop and clergy; he would appear never to have foreseen a contingency that he would presumably have feared no less, the attempt, that is, on the part of a bishop to assert complete jurisdiction over the life of the friars. Perhaps even to the end he regarded his order as lying outside the clerical body; in any case, central Italy, with its numerous city-bishops and small, ancient, and clearly defined dioceses, had witnessed none of the fierce struggles for jurisdiction and exemption of all kinds that had become so familiar in northern France and England. Even in this country it was not till 1231 that a crisis arose. Few of the first friars were priests; for many years they had no churches of their own, but were content with domestic oratories. But c. 1230–1 Ralph Niger of London, an energetic disciplinarian and friend of the friars,

---

1 *Ep.* clxxxv.
2 *V.* extracts from the *Liberate Rolls* printed by Little as Appendix 9 to *Eccleston*, pp. 177–8.
3 Trivet, *Annals*, 279, 323.

claimed complete jurisdiction over them, and demanded an oath of canonical obedience. Agnellus straightway applied to Gregory IX and obtained an exemption which the pope made complete and extended to all countries by the bull *Nimis iniqua*.[1]

Canonically speaking, this did no more than give the friars power to order their own way of life without interference, like the Cistercians; it did, indeed, establish papal *conservatores privilegiorum*, but it left the bishop free to use or refuse their services as he might wish. In practice, the anxiety of the English bishops to employ the friars gave them very great freedom of action, and it was a considerable time before this was openly resented or resisted by the parochial clergy. These latter, indeed, in the early decades of the century, were often without either the competence or the desire to preach and administer the sacrament of penance on the scale now made normal by the Lateran decrees. Encouraged as the friars were by almost all the bishops, two of whom were soon appointed conservators of their privileges, and courted by the leading citizens in the towns, they were at first content to give spiritual ministrations without depriving the secular clergy of their regular dues. They thus offered no direct target for attack, and the private resentment, where it existed, of the older generation of the clergy, formed in pre-Lateran days and content to do no more than dispense sacraments and rites on demand, had no canonical foundation on which to find a foothold. Gradually, however, as the country began to receive a leaven of university trained priests, conversant with canon law and encouraged by many of the bishops to observe the Lateran decrees, and as at the same time the friars began to trespass upon their preserves in ways that implied a loss of clientele and of income, a conflict became inevitable. In the learned world, this took the form of the celebrated attack upon the mendicants opened by William of St Amour *c.* 1250, continued at the Council of Lyons in 1274, and lasting until the bull *Super cathedram* of Boniface VIII in 1300 and beyond. In the administrative circles of the Church the counterpart of this pamphlet and conciliar warfare was found in a vigorous effort on the part of the secular clergy to provoke a reversal, or at least to impose a limit, to the papal policy of concession of rights.

This effort was stimulated by a growing sense of the power of the new orders. For several decades the Preachers were alone in posing as a fully clerical body; many of the Minors were not in orders, or at least not priests, and the early Carmelites and Austin Friars were at their first arrival retiring and uninfluential. But when, after the middle of the century, the friars had multiplied, when the Minors had become a clerical body, and when the Carmelites and Hermits were assimilating themselves more and more to the others, the secular clergy, themselves becoming more 'class conscious' and having often received a careful theological training, began to realize that a serious rivalry had developed in their field of work,

1 21 August 1231; *v. Eccleston*, 75; Sbaralea, I, 74–5.

and that the friendship and material support of numerous and influential layfolk would daily pass under their very eyes from the parish church to the friary. The contest which ensued was fought out in form, so to say, on the continent and above all in the University of Paris and at the papal court. In this country the fighting was largely between irregulars, who were inspired by developments abroad and by the various and often mutually contradictory pronouncements of Rome. The details of the struggle must be sought in monographs and dissertations; only a summary will here be attempted.[1]

When once the domestic status of the friars *vis-à-vis* the Ordinary had been regularized by *Nimis iniqua*, the potential field of conflict was restricted to the relationship of the friars to the bishops and parish clergy in the exercise of their sacerdotal functions. Here, the principal heads of contention were preaching, confessing and the reception of dues usually considered parochial; chief among these were the payments made by custom at a burial. In all these matters, owing to the absence of any competition in the past, the need for minute legislation had not been felt and the terms of the decrees were vague: this was especially the case with regard to the sacrament of penance, in itself one of the most obscure points in the discipline and theology of the Church prior to the later middle ages.

The friars, and especially the Preachers, had been sent from Italy with a papal commission to preach, and had been welcomed and employed by many of the bishops. There had therefore at first been no question of any abstract right to preach or to confess; both tasks were no doubt usually executed in early years by mendicants engaged in specific missions or acting with the full cognizance of the bishop. The difficulties arose when the friars, established in all the large towns and no longer the immediate instruments of the diocesan, acquired a clientele among the well-to-do as well as among the poor, and attracted penitents by their more expert knowledge of theology and ethics, and by their more sympathetic attitude which, so their enemies alleged, sprang from easily comprehensible motives of self-interest. Many of their penitents wished to lie in death within the precinct of the friary, so as to share in the daily suffrages of the brethren; this inevitably deprived the parish clergy of the customary burial dues, as also of the normal accompaniment of legacies and foundations for Masses. The parish clergy put up a resistance, claiming the right of burying all parishioners, and to overcome this Innocent IV issued in 1250 the bull

---

1 The gradual evolution in the practice and ideals of the Minors, and their reaction to the parallel but not exactly coincident evolution of their juridical status achieved by the papacy, has exercised the analytical powers of a number of able historians. The most penetrating and suggestive is still perhaps that of F. Ehrle, *Die ältesten Redaktionen den Generalconstitutionen des Franziskanerordens* in *ALKG*, VI (1892), 1–138; an excellent summary is given by Père Gratien, *op. cit.* 110 *seqq.* English readers will find a sketch in Dr A. G. Little's *Franciscan Studies*, 92–122. As regards England in particular the ground is well covered in a London University M.A. thesis by Miss J. L. Copeland, *The relations between the Mendicant Friars and the secular clergy in England, during the century after the issue of the bull* Super cathedram (1300).

Cum a nobis petitur,[1] which permitted the friars to bury in their own churches or cemeteries all who might ask this favour.

The bull was not the outcome of mature policy, and its issue coincided with the unfolding of the main secular attack upon the ideals of the mendicants; it provoked strong and widespread protests, and the protagonist of the secular clergy, William of St Amour, who found himself on a mission in Rome shortly after, was active in agitation. In consequence, Innocent IV reversed his policy with the bull *Etsi animarum*[2] in 1254 which, though ostensibly no more than a reiteration of established canonical principles in the demarcation of parochial jurisdiction, did in fact deprive the friars of the absolute freedom of preaching and administering the sacraments in their own churches which they had hitherto enjoyed, and put all their external activities under a control which in friendly hands might not have been oppressive but which could become a strangle-hold when employed by enemies. They were not to hear confessions, or to preach in parish churches without the invitation or permission of the curate, nor were they to admit the laity to their own churches on Sundays and holy days. If they buried a parishioner, the full canonical dues were to be paid to the parish priest.

Innocent died a few days after the bull had been issued, and the event was attributed by many to the efficacy of the litanies recited by the Preachers in defence of their rights.[3] His successor, Alexander IV, straightway annulled Innocent's action by decreeing, in the bull *Quasi lignum vitae* (14 April 1255), that the consent of the curate was not necessary for the friars who intended to hear confessions or to preach; the permission of the Ordinary, though not expressly mentioned, was still tacitly assumed as necessary. The good understanding or *laissez-faire* of earlier days, however, which alone could have made such an arrangement feasible, had now gone beyond recall, and friction and hostility became general and were openly accepted by all as inevitable. In the fifty years of controversy that ensued the friars had, in the main, the papacy on their side, and by this time the centralized orders commanded an influence in the Curia which even the most powerful diocesan could not hope to rival. In addition to the minister or master-general, who was often at the side of the pope, and to the cardinal protector of the Order, the friars from *c.* 1250 onwards had an official procurator of their habit who followed the Curia to watch over their interests and expedite business,[4] while in each country or province one or more of the episcopate held appointment from Rome as conservator of the privileges and rights of the mendicants. In addition, there were between 1250 and 1320 probably more friars appointed to bishoprics and

1 Sbaralea, I, 537.
2 *Bullarium Franciscanum, Supplementum*, ed. Eubel, p. 259.
3 Cf. *Eccleston*, 118.
4 Humberti de Romanis, *Opera*, ed. Berthier, II, 186–7, and R. F. Bennett, *The Early Dominicans*, 138–9.

cardinalitial churches than at any other period. Consequently, though the secular opposition succeeded so far as to prevent the growth of all mendicant bodies save the four greatest at the Council of Lyons in 1274, the personal actions of the popes were almost always in favour of the friars, and a series of bulls, of which the most comprehensive was the *Ad fructus uberes*[1] of Martin IV in 1281, added steadily to their privileges. In these bulls the doctrine of the papal plenitude of power was pushed to its logical extreme in the sphere of ecclesiastical administration as it had been in the realm of politics by Innocent IV; *Ad fructus uberes* in particular cut through all canonical tradition: the friars were commissioned directly by the pope, in virtue of hi; immediate jurisdiction over all Christians, to exercise all sacerdotal functions alongside and independent of the secular clergy. Neither parochial nor diocesan consent was needed.

Such a liberty was excessive, and had the papacy maintained this policy the Church would have exhibited the spectacle of a great body of clergy acting at variance both with ancient law and with the most cogent reasoning of the great scholastic theologians—the spectacle, in fact, of two parallel and unco-ordinated jurisdictions—and the result would have been disastrous. Even the friars were chary of using the liberty thus given them to the full. On the continent, and especially in France, the hostility of the bishops and clergy was widespread. In England, though the literature of the quarrel was less, Pecham and Godfrey Giffard of Worcester, respectively conservators of the Minors' and Preachers' privileges, were kept fully occupied in intervening to protect their clients. At length in 1300, Boniface VIII, who a few years earlier as legate in Paris had defended the friars with some intemperance, intervened to strike a compromise with the equitable and justly celebrated *Super cathedram*[2] of 18 February in the jubilee year of Dante's vision.

By this pronouncement he ensured an adequate status to the friars while safeguarding the traditional rights of the diocesan and the parish clergy. The mendicants were free to preach in their own churches and in public; they were forbidden to appear in parish pulpits without invitation. For confessions, the provincials were to choose a number of their subjects in each diocese proportionate to the population; these were to be presented to the bishop for licence; he might reject individuals, but was not free to reduce the agreed numbers; should he refuse to grant any licences the requisite faculties were supplied from the plenitude of the Apostolic power. The friars were at liberty to bury all who might wish, but a fourth part of all dues and legacies were to go to the parish clergy.

It was now the turn of the friars to pose as the injured party, and in four years' time the successor of Boniface VIII, Benedict XI, himself a Preacher, revoked *Super cathedram* by the bull *Inter cunctas*.[3] This restored com-

---

1 Sbaralea, III, 480.
2 *Bullarium Franciscanum*, IV, 498–500.
3 *Inter cunctas* in *Extrav. Commun.* Lib. v, tit. 7 De privilegiis, c. 1.

plete freedom of action to the mendicants by transferring the licensing of confessors from the bishops to the provincials; free rights of burial were conceded, and no part of the gifts or legacies need be surrendered; half only of the actual funeral dues was to be paid.

This retrograde step, however, provoked from the bishops signs of an indignation too strong and (it may perhaps be added) too just to be resisted, and the next pope, Clement V, reissued *Super cathedram* in 1311 without change. It endured in its main features until the end of the middle ages, and even the modern discipline of the Church preserves its general outlines.

The papal legislation subsequent to the Council of Lyons of 1274, though issuing at last in an equitable settlement by which the centralized orders were inserted as a new part into the existing machinery of the Church's life without dislocating the older portions of the engine, nevertheless gave final confirmation to the change which had taken place among the friars as to their conception of their work. Their churches were given a quasi-parochial status, and the initiative in their external activities rested with their own superiors. Both Minors and Preachers had been at first the itinerant, occasional auxiliaries of the bishops and resident clergy; their convents had been as purely domestic as the houses of the monks. Soon, however, the Preachers had come to confine their activities to the neighbourhood of their houses; next, the Minors did the same, and as each friary attracted to itself a clientele of wealthy townspeople the tendency to occupy central sites and build large churches became more and more irresistible. Both in England and abroad the decades between 1270 and 1320 have been noted by historians as those which witnessed the construction of spacious convents and churches with no corresponding increase in the number of friars;[1] in short, by 1300 the four great orders of mendicants had become, at least among the organized nations of western Europe, localized and conventual bodies, devoted to theological teaching, popular preaching and the administration of the sacraments.

In England, where official records have survived in greater abundance than abroad, it is clear that the bishops proceeded at once to honour the dispositions of *Super cathedram* with regard to the licensing of confessors. In 1300 and the years immediately following, and again after 1311, when *Super cathedram* was finally approved by the Council of Vienne, the episcopal registers show the system in full operation.[2] Generally speaking, the bishops appear to have shown generosity in their acceptance of the

---

1 Thus Ehrle in *ALKG*, III, 575: 'Daher dann in den letzten Jahrzehnten des 13 Jhs... die Erbauung der grossen Convente und Kirchen mitten in der volksreichsten Vierteln.' Cf. Little, *Studies*, 68, 73: 'It was about 1270 or soon after that the great building period began in England, and it lasted about fifty years....I have noted evidence of enlargement or rebuilding of church or houses in thirty-four of the English friaries between 1270 and 1320.'

2 Miss Copeland, in the thesis mentioned *supra*, p. 184 n., after a careful search through the episcopal records, has analysed the licences very thoroughly, with a complete list of friars' names found.

candidates proposed, and the auctioneering tactics of the provincials, who in early days at least showed an insistence in pressing their candidates which resembled that of Abraham when pleading for the cities of the plain, were usually successful.[1] Several bishops were also ready to agree that doctors of divinity should be *ex officio* licensees, in addition to those presented, while the licence, once given, was taken to hold good even after the death of the granting prelate. Recent research has gone to show that shortly before the middle of the fourteenth century about three hundred Minors and as many Preachers—that is, about one-fifth of the total number of their habits in the English province—held licences to absolve. Such a number would represent perhaps a little less than a half of the priests of the province.

III

The emergence of the friars as an official preaching and absolving body, the stages of which have been outlined above, brought them into a collision with bishops and parish priests which issued often in mutual recrimination, sometimes in lawsuits, and occasionally in acts of physical violence. The forensic struggle had its counterpart in intellectual controversy, which as early as the middle of the thirteenth century rose to its height on two principal issues: the validity of the spiritual ideals of poverty and mendicancy, and the theological justice of the friars' claim to exercise the apostolic functions of preaching and administering the sacraments. The conflict was destined to endure for more than a century, but its first phase was at once the most distinguished and decisive. It was fought out mainly in France and at the papal court, and the fierce challenge made by William of St Amour[2] and his friends was countered by the decisions of Rome and answered for all time by St Bonaventure and St Thomas Aquinas.[3] Leaving aside for a moment the question of poverty, a brief outline may be given of the theological debate on apostolic work.

The right of the friars to preach was denied by William of St Amour on the grounds that bishop and curate were the only divinely appointed

---

1 Thus Bishop Dalderby of Lincoln originally licensed five Preachers temporarily, when approached by a proctor of the vicar-general of the prior provincial. A little later twenty-two were licensed. Three days later (5 August 1300) Thomas Jorz, the provincial (later Cardinal) appeared with eight more friars from Oxford; on 10 August with seven more from Northampton, on 15th with seven from Leicester; all of these received licenses from the patient Dalderby. On 11 November he returned with seventy-three names, of which the bishop licensed twelve; the total was thus fifty-six. The Minors, by similar tactics, secured fifty in the same diocese.

2 For a summary account of William of St Amour, together with a full bibliography, v. *MU*, I, 370–97 and Gratien, 217 *seqq*. See also M. Bierbaum, *Bettelorden und Weltgeistlichkeit an der Universität Paris* (Münster-i-W., 1920).

3 St Thomas's most direct contribution to the controversy was his tract *Contra impugnantes religionem*. St Bonaventura wrote many treatises on the subject, v. *Opera*, ed. Quaracchi, vol. VIII, also *Quare Fratres Minores praedicent et confessiones audiant, ibid.* 375–85.

pastors and rulers of souls. To this, St Thomas replied that a bishop, having general jurisdiction over all the faithful of his diocese, could delegate other priests in addition to curates to preach and absolve when the need existed; while St Bonaventure laid emphasis rather on the supreme jurisdictional and directive powers of the pope over all the members of the Church. This main controversy had as a corollary the debate as to the need of repeating to the parish priest confessions made to a friar; as has been seen, a fresh actuality was given to this point by the bull *Ad fructus uberes*. The secular doctors of Paris, and in particular Henry of Ghent, who maintained the affirmative, found a convenient foothold for their argument in the Lateran decree *Omnis utriusque sexus*, which Martin IV had declared to be still in force notwithstanding the privileges granted to the mendicants in *Ad fructus uberes*, and started an old hare of unusually long wind: the decree, they submitted, implied the necessity of confessing for a second time all sins confessed to a friar during the previous year. Their deeper reasoning was, however, based on an insistence upon the inalienable rights of bishop and priest over their subjects.[1] It is for historians of dogma to pronounce upon the true origins of Gallicanism, but it may be remarked in passing that it was in the controversies with the mendicants that the secular doctors of Paris, a university which owed everything to the papacy, became as a body interested in maintaining the jurisdictional rights of bishop and clergy against what appeared in practice to be encroachments from the papacy in the name of universal jurisdiction. The question was settled as a matter of discipline in 1290 by the legate in Paris, Benedetto Gaetani, later to be Boniface VIII, but it continued to be debated theoretically by Jean de Pouilli and Pierre de la Palu, his adversary among the Preachers, the secular insisting upon the jurisdiction divinely bestowed on bishops and curates, the regular laying emphasis on the position of the pope as universal ordinary.[2] In the event, Jean de Pouilli was condemned in 1321. There are few traces of any active interest taken by the English seculars or friars in the earlier phases of this controversy. Later, a number of minor treatises were written, and the great Baconthorp would seem to have entered the lists against de Pouilli.[3] Friction in this country developed on more material grounds; thus a petition drawn up in 1309 against the friars by the London curates was occasioned by an alleged claim on the part of the mendicants to powers of absolution from 'reserved' cases, and by the resentment felt by the seculars at the conduct of friars who shrived the dying and received legacies, and who refused to hand over the burial dues.

1 Henry of Ghent and Geoffrey of Fontaines led the seculars; *v.* P. Glorieux, *Prélats français contre religieux mendicants*, in *Revue d'Histoire de l'Eglise de France*, xi, no. 52 (1925); for the friars' position, *v. Fratris Richardi de Mediavilla Quaestio disputata*, ed. Père Delorme.

2 For this controversy *v.* esp. J. G. Sikes, *Jean de Pouilli and Peter de la Palu* in *EHR*, XLIX, 219–240.

3 Miss Copeland, in the thesis already mentioned, discusses this and gives references to some unprinted MSS.

IV

In an earlier chapter we have followed the rise and full expansion of the intellectual activities of the mendicants at Oxford and Cambridge. Drawn out of their own orbit by that compulsive magnetism which drew all the mental life of the age to the schools, both Preachers and Minors, by attracting to themselves in their turn many of the keenest minds of Europe, came in a few years to be an integral, and even a uniquely important, element in university life, while remaining as aloof as possible from the closely knit professional union of teachers which formed the university and which was engaged, especially at Paris, in asserting its rights against ecclesiastical and civil interference.[1] It was inevitable that a struggle should sooner or later take place between two organizations which existed for very different purposes and whose interests coincided over only a very small field. At Paris the main engagement took place in the middle of the thirteenth century, when an attack on the mendicants was being made all along the line by the secular clerks. The academic contest turned on the claim of the university that full admission to membership of their body, an undertaking to observe the statutes, and a regular examination should be precedent conditions to the grant of a magisterial licence in theology. The friars for their part (and above all the Preachers, upon whom the brunt of the attack fell) wished to be able to teach as hitherto by personal licence from the chancellor, and to be free of any obligation of obedience to the university, in particular when it was a question of the 'suspension of studies' ordered by the university as a tactical move in any contest that might seem to touch its vital interests.

The friars, warmly supported by ecclesiastical authorities at Rome and by royal favour in France, won the day, and the bull *Quasi lignum vitae* of Alexander IV in 1255 made them practically independent of the university as a governing body since their masters' degrees were to be obtained directly from the chancellor, while at the same time they had all the rights of masters in university congregations and were sufficiently numerous to be able to veto any obnoxious decree. Actually, however, their victory was only partial, as henceforth their schools were attended almost exclusively by members of their own body, and at a later date they were compelled to take an oath of obedience to the university statutes.

In England the clash was long in coming. The cordial relations between mendicants and the secular doctors, the mutual assistance rendered in early days, and the absence in this country both of opposition to the friars by the secular clerks and of any serious hindrance to the activities of Oxford by authorities in Church or State postponed the conflict beyond the end of the century. When it came at last it was no doubt embittered, if not occasioned, by the contemporary discord between friars and the secular

1 For the Paris controversies *v. MU*, I, 344–97, and bibliography there given.

clergy arising from the issue and subsequent annulment of the bull *Super cathedram*. The Oxford contest of 1303–20[1] was conducted almost entirely by the Preachers and turned chiefly on their demand, resulting from more than half-a-century's experience of dispensations granted almost as a matter of course by graces of the university, that friars should proceed to the doctorate in divinity without having previously graduated in arts or taken the bachelor's degree in theology. The secular masters desired at once to exercise their authority and develop their opposition to the mendicants in these and other matters, and in order to ensure their control of university legislation passed a constitutional decree by virtue of which a majority vote of the faculties was to be binding upon the theological faculty, in which alone the friars were represented in force. After a number of hearings before delegates and arbitrators in the Curia and in England the decision was given in the main against the friars.

At Cambridge a similar, though somewhat less comprehensive, struggle broke out simultaneously; it was clearly inspired by what was happening at Oxford.[2] In this case the university endeavoured to secure that its statutes should be ordained by the *major et sanior pars* of the regent and non-regent masters, thus putting legislative power into the hands of the masters of arts, among whom the friars had few if any representatives. The challenge was taken up by the friars, who appealed to Rome, and after a number of proposals agreement was reached before arbitrators at the Dominican house in Bordeaux, whither representatives of the university proceeded; among the arbitrators was the English Dominican Cardinal Thomas Jorz, the late provincial. The decision, given on 17 June 1306, though it saved the face of the university by accepting the obnoxious statutes, was in practice in favour of the friars, since riders were added to the statutes ensuring personal arrangements and dispensations.

V

Although the friars, by attracting large numbers from among the ablest and most fervent of the youth of England, tapped at the source, so to say, the stream of life for the monks, the ensuing loss was invisible and hypothetical, and therefore little felt. In the normal course of their respective activities the interests of the friars, who were neither holders of real property nor landowners with a farming connection, would not collide with those of the monks as they did with those of the secular clergy. Relations between the two great families of religious were, however, none of the best, though there are numerous instances of personal friendships and mutual services rendered between individuals.

1 *V.* H. Rashdall, *The Friars Preachers v. the University* in *OHS Collectanea*, 2 ser. (1890), 193–273, and the sections in the same writer's *Mediaeval Universities*, III, 66–78.
2 For the Cambridge controversy *v. The Friars v. the University of Cambridge* in *EHR*, L (1935), 686–96 by A. G. Little, and *The Cambridge Dominicans*, by W. Gumbley, O.P.

At the first appearance of the friars, penniless, friendless, and with the glamour of Francis and Dominic about them, they met with a generous welcome. The monks of Christ Church gave hospitality to the first Minors[1] and even Matthew Paris, who was later to become more bitter, devoted several pages to the stigmatized Francis and treated with unusual reverence the work of his companion, Brother William of England.[2] At first, too, any beginnings of jealousy were forestalled by the humility of the Minors who, as at Reading, obeyed literally the directions of their founder by accepting an unenviable site for their house and by refusing to tie the hands of the owning abbey by any legal instrument.[3]

The newcomers, however, could not long be treated with a tolerant charity. Their new fervour, as that of the Cistercians a century before, drew off from monks and canons several individuals of distinction, who made use of the canonical principle that transference to a stricter religious order was always permissible, besides attracting restless undesirables.[4] Their ideal of poverty, however modestly and sincerely it might be preached and practised, involved at least a tacit comparison with the wealthy older orders which enthusiasm or indiscretion might easily make more explicit. Their presence in a monastic town, where the monks were acutely sensitive to trespass and dreaded a focus of opposition to their privileges,[5] or on parishes where they might draw off some of the revenues appropriated to the monastery;[6] the protection given them by the king or by magnates who had been none too favourable to the monks; their vindication of the common

1 *Eccleston*, ed. Little, 8. At Abingdon, however, they are said to have been less charitable; cf. the story printed by Little in *Eccleston*, 136–40.

2 *MPChM*, III, 133 *seqq.* For discussions of the relations of monks and friars, *v.* Little, *Studies in English Franciscan History*, 92 *seqq.*, and Moorman, *Church Life in England*, 373 *seqq.*

3 *Eccleston*, 99–100: 'Cartam seu compositionem quae fuit inter monachos Redyngiae et fratres, quod scilicet pro voluntate sua non possent eos expellere, ferventissime eis restituit [fr. Albertus of Pisa, the English minister-provincial, *c.* 1236] et obtulit se fratres amoturum si vellent.'

4 Among the recruits were John of Reading, abbot of Oseney (*Ann. Osn. s.a.* 1235; *MPChM*, IV, 163–4), 'qui nobis omnis perfectionis exempla reliquit' (*Eccleston*, 24) and the abbot of Walden (*MP, loc. cit.*), who joined respectively the Minors and the Preachers, and a number of monks and canons (*GASA*, II, 416; *Ann. Dunstapl.* 133). As early as 1223 the Cistercian general chapter had declared that all monks or *conversi* who crossed to the friars were to be considered *fugitivi* (*Statuta*, ed. Canivez, II, 24, n. 12).

5 For the case of Bury, *v. MPChM*, III, 332–3 (1235), where the Minors and Preachers are taxed with arriving with specious promises *in territorio aliquorum nobilium coenobiorum* and then staying, having sent a clandestine messenger to Rome; also *GASA*, I, 385 (1257, another composition by Paris) where the entry at Bury *invitis abbate et conventu* is retailed, with the sequel *arridente fortuna, expulsi sunt extra muros* (i.e. to Babwell), and *ibid.* 386, for the Preachers at Dunstable (1259): 'qui profecto cunctis religiosis de secta sua non existentibus onerosi sunt, molesti penitus et infesti'; cf. *Chron. Burien.* in *MSE*, III, 28, and *Ann. Dunstapl.* pp. 134, 213, 336. In the last passage (1287) the canons forestall the Preachers by causing their porter to buy up a house next to the friars to prevent them extending their premises *nobis invitis.*

6 Cf. *Ann. Theok. s.a.* 1230 for the unavailing protest of the monks of Bristol priory against the Preachers taking offertories, etc., at their oratory in the parish of St James, and *MPChM*, IV, 511–12, 514–16 (1245) for the opposition of the monastic archdeacon in synod to the Preachers as confessors.

rights they had at first been ready to waive; their novel privileges and ready access to the popes, who issued bull after bull in their favour: all these gave cause for suspicion and friction.[1] These, in early days at least, would seem to have been needlessly fostered by many of the monks and canons, both black and white, who yielded to the irrational, if not unnatural, resentment felt by an old concern in face of a competition claiming to make use of improved methods; they were aggravated by the language held by some of the friars who, like the Cistercians a hundred years before, criticized the older orders where they were most vulnerable and sensitive.

Here, as in so many other matters, the attitude of Matthew Paris, familiar and well defined as it is, has often been presented as typical of the feeling of the mass. Paris, who did not take over from Roger of Wendover till 1236, incorporated in his fair copy of the *Chronica Majora* Wendover's laudatory account of St Francis under the year 1227, and added the *Regula Bullata* in full.[2] By 1241, however, he is found animadverting upon monks and canons who become friars,[3] and three years later he denounces the friars in the severest terms: they are luxurious, yet show contempt for the older orders; they call the Cistercians ignorant boors, and the black monks haughty gluttons.[4] In the following year it is the wide faculties of absolution enjoyed by the Preachers that provokes him;[5] in 1247, the insolent and luxurious ways of two Minors engaged in raising money for the papacy.[6] Paris, however, continued to show warm appreciation of the holiness of individual Minors, and of the learning of eminent Preachers,[7] and he has a good word to say of the Minors who interceded for the persecuted Jews in London,[8] though he tells at length of the alleged violence used by the friars to intrude themselves into monastic towns at Bury and Dunstable.

Generally speaking, the two bodies of religious gradually settled down into an uneasy equilibrium which lasted for nearly a century, and was marked by a number of instances of both hostility and co-operation, such as quarrels over parish rights and burial dues on the one hand, and on the other, the engagement of friars as preachers in the monastic cathedrals, and as lecturers in theology to the monks. It was only in the middle of the fourteenth century, when the controversies on Dominion and Grace reached their height, and the opprobrious term 'possessioners' became current, that the monks and friars were openly ranged in opposition, to be reconciled in part by the unexpected turn given to events by the polemics of Wyclif.

1 *V. Ann. Dunstapl. s.a.* 1233, p. 134, for Bury and Reading, and *ibid.* (1259), p. 213 for Dunstable: 'Nobis invitis villam de D. ingressi sunt et per dominum regem et reginam et aliquos magnates moram ibidem a nobis impetraverunt.'
2 *MPChM*, III, 133 *seqq.*   3 *Ibid.* IV, 163–4.
4 *Ibid.* 279–80: 'Rudes reputant, simplices, et semilaicos, vel potius rusticos, Cistercienses monachos; nigros vero superbos et epicuros.'
5 *Ibid.* 511–12.   6 *Ibid.* 599–600. Cf. also *GASA*, II, 385–6.
7 *MPChM*, IV, 655, for praise of Anselm, Minorite bishop of Menevia, and v, 16 (1248) for praise of R. Bacon and Richard Fishacre: 'Qui egregie...legerunt et populis gloriose praedicaverunt verbum Domini.'
8 *Ibid.* v, 546: 'ut pie credendum arbitror, spiritu ducti pietatis.'

CHAPTER XVII

THE CARMELITES, AUSTIN HERMITS AND LESSER ORDERS

I

In the history of the Church it has repeatedly happened that a dynamic idea, taking shape in a great religious institute, has found numerous admirers who have modelled new and similar families upon the first exemplar or who, originally members of a separate but kindred establishment, have come into the magnetic field of the more powerful agent, and have been drawn to merge with it, or at least to take their colour from it. Thus in the early twelfth century the congregation of Savigny, originally an independent growth of the same spiritual movement that had driven Stephen Harding and his fellows into the wilderness, merged its own individuality in that of Cîteaux; thus also, though in a different way, Cîteaux gave much of its spirit and outward organization to the institutes of Norbert of Xanten and Gilbert of Sempringham. Four hundred years later, in a manner still more striking, the Company of Jesus not only served as a close model for innumerable independent congregations of men and women, but also attracted and was imitated by not a few of the older monastic bodies, in whose constitutions features borrowed from the Jesuits may still be recognized to-day.

So, in the early thirteenth century, it was with the friars. The two original institutes of Francis and Dominic had each given something entirely new to the religious world. The gift of the former had been in the main spiritual: the ideal of poverty and simplicity added to that of apostolic service of the poor; all, in fact, that the world associates with the name of friar. The legacy of Dominic to the world was seen most clearly in the sphere of organization: the firmly knit, fully centralized order, strongly governed, pivoting upon Rome, perfectly organized for study and for work, not on the monarchical or patriarchal lines of all previous monastic and clerical orders, but by a finely adjusted system of elected bodies and nominated, temporary superiors. Before many years had passed, as has already been seen, the orders of Minors and Preachers had each taken something of the other's peculiar property: the Preachers, beginning as quasi-canons, professedly clerks, became friars and mendicants; the Minors from a loosely knit, unconventional body became a centralized order and a student order, whose machinery was modelled closely upon that of the Preachers.

It was not long before other bodies of religious, hitherto unorganized and now swollen by the mysterious impulse which impelled multitudes to join the friars, were forced by circumstances to take shape and define their aims both to themselves and to the Church. Two of these, humble in origin and with no novel or even very definite policy, soon grew in numbers and influence to a position little short of that of the Minors and Preachers, and became two of the 'four orders' of the later middle ages. These were the Carmelite Friars and the Augustinian Friars or Hermits.

The origins of both these great bodies are exceedingly obscure, and since on the one hand each lacked a commanding figure of a founder to match Dominic and Francis, and on the other each had a certain antiquity and was in no sense an upstart imitation of the Minors, there was an inevitable temptation for later, uncritical historians and apologists of the medieval period to eke out a real but scanty tradition with a generous admixture of legend or improvisation.[1] In the case of the Carmelites, as the preamble to the Constitutions somewhat naively informs us, the origins of the body were set out in order to satisfy the younger generation, which found itself unable to give any information as to when, how or why their institute came into being;[2] with the Hermits of St Augustine it was a somewhat later collision with the Augustinian canons that rendered it imperative for them to make clear their direct descent from the community founded by the great doctor. The amalgam of fact and fancy thus created by labours as unremitting as those of Hercules or Tantalus,[3] which was accepted in all sincerity by subsequent generations, came in time to serve

[1] Very little critical work has been done upon early Carmelite history; for the pre-scholastic period almost the only studies of value are those of the Swiss-born English Carmelite, the late Fr Benedict Zimmermann, O.C.D. The results of his research, which covered all periods of his order's history, are scattered in a number of articles and booklets, for the most part published abroad and written in German, French and Latin; some of them are extremely hard to come by in England. Though possessed to the full of a scholar's critical acumen, and with an unusually wide knowledge of European languages, Fr Zimmermann possessed little detailed knowledge of English history and had had no direct training in scientific methods. He never, unfortunately, produced a large work embodying his many discoveries and revisions of Carmelite history.

The Carmelite Order, like the Franciscan, has in the past been divided by acute controversies, and remains at the present day split into two bodies. Though the controversies are now ancient history, the authorities of the order have often shown themselves peculiarly jealous of tradition, and if the flames of the past have subsided, 'ev'n in their ashes live their wonted fires'. Fr Zimmermann, therefore, often gives an impression of treading delicately *supposito cineri*. Recently, however, especially in France and Spain, much excellent historical work has been achieved by Carmelites.

For the earliest years of the order the fullest collection of sources and comments is *Monumenta Historica Carmelitana*, vol. I (Lérins, 1907), the work of Fr Zimmermann; for articles by the same writer and others on the university activities *v. Analecta Ordinis Carmelitarum, Analecta Carmelitarum Discalceatorum* and (since *c.* 1920) *Études Carmélitaines*; *v.* also H. Denifle, O.P., *Quellen zur Gelehrtengeschichte des Carmelitenordens im 13 und 14 Jahrhundert*, in *ALKG*, v, 365–86 (where, however, some points need correction in the light of subsequent research).

[2] Cf. preamble to the first constitutions (after 1247) in *Mon. Hist. Carm.* I, 20: 'Cum quidam fratres in ordine nostro juniores quaerentibus a quo quando vel quomodo ordo noster sumpserit exordium, vel quare dicamur fratres ordinis Beatae Mariae de Monte Carmeli juxta rei veritatem nesciant satisfacere, pro eis in scriptis formam talibus relinquentes volumus respondere.'

[3] The phrase is Zimmermann's in *Mon. Hist. Carm.* I, 266: 'Herculeum ne dicam tantaleum laborem.'

as a basis which supported the most vital provisions of the Rule and the essential features of the order's ideal and observance; when, therefore, it came to be challenged it was defended *à corps perdu* in its totality, and that none the less desperately because it was instinctively felt that if criticism once breached the dyke the floods might sweep away no one knew what familiar landmarks. Consequently, what may be called the prehistoric period in the life of these orders has scarcely yet been critically examined, and floating wraiths of legend, venerable only in name, make their appearance in unexpected places or are allowed to pass in respectful silence through the first chapters of otherwise critical works in some such way as a relative of enfeebled mental power is admitted to the fringe of a ceremonial family reunion.

II

The congregation of hermits that grew into the Order of Our Lady of Mount Carmel first appears as existing without any organization on the slopes of Mount Carmel in Palestine at the middle of the twelfth century.[1] It had probably been formed by those in the train of the Crusades, and by later pilgrims who had remained in the Holy Land to live the eremitical life which even in northern Europe was such a feature of the age, and for which the climate and the surface of Palestine were peculiarly suitable. Their leader was probably Berthold, a European if not an Italian by race. They were in character and ideals very similar to the eremitical congregations of the Chartreuse and of Calabria which ultimately developed into the Carthusian order. While still *in situ* they received a Rule *c.* 1210 from Albert of Vercelli, Patriarch of Jerusalem; it was extremely strict in point of abstinence, silence and retirement, like that of the Camaldolese; the brethren met together only at certain moments, and not for meals; it was prescribed that they should live only in places remote from human habitation.

Originally, there had been a single community on Carmel. Later, there were several offshoots in Palestine, but not long after receiving their Rule the Hermits of Carmel were disturbed by the incursions of the Saracens, and *c.* 1238 migrated in groups to Cyprus and continental Europe. Some went to Italy, Sicily and Spain, while a few, among whom were the Englishmen Simon and Ralph Freshbourne, patronized by English crusaders such as the barons de Vescy and Grey returning from the expedition of Richard, earl of Cornwall, were transplanted to this country and established at remote spots in Kent, Northumberland, and elsewhere. Thus hermitages came into being at Hulne, near Alnwick (*c.* 1240–2), at Aylesford and Losenham, in the Weald of Kent (1241–2), at Burnham Norton in Norfolk (1241) and at Chesterton, near Cambridge (*c.* 1247). These English foundations were among the first in Europe; the English

1 For the sources of what follows *v. Mon. Hist. Carm.* I, 212, 266, 364 *seqq.*, and B. Zimmermann, *De Sacro Scapulari Carmelitano* in *Analecta Carm. Disc.* II, f. 2 (1927), 70–99.

province appears third in the Order in early lists, preceded only by those of the Holy Land and Sicily, and this fact no doubt accounts for the important part played by English Carmelites in determining the fortunes of their institute.[1] Meanwhile, in 1229, as a result of an appeal to Rome by a house in southern Italy, the Carmelites had been recognized by Gregory IX as mendicants, and thus slipped almost unperceived into the ranks of the friars.

From their first arrival in Europe, when recruits began to join in some numbers, the Carmelites found it hard to preserve both union and their original vocation. Their Rule was strict and eremitical, but had no legislation for a large and centralized order. Among those who had come from the East the old traditions were strong; among the new recruits, on the other hand, the spirit of the age was at work. They wished, like the other friars, to preach and, in preparation for this, to receive a theological training at the universities. Before the middle of the thirteenth century a crisis had gradually arisen which threatened not only the prosperity, but even the bare existence of the order, and this came at the very moment when the hostility of the secular clergy to the mendicants was coming to a head, and when the enemies of the friars, unable to defeat the two most powerful orders, turned all their efforts against the minor organizations. In the case of the Carmelites, some bishops refused to recognize the order, on the score that it had come into being contrary to the decree of the Lateran Council forbidding new rules, while others endeavoured, as with the Minors a few years before, to treat the friars as their subjects and issue commands under obedience. Meanwhile, the strictness of diet and silence continued to put a severe strain upon the Carmelites living under northern skies and familiar with the ways of life of the other orders of friars. In this crisis of their history the lead was taken by an Englishman who, like his contemporary and fellow-countryman Haymo of Faversham, was destined to determine the whole future scope and policy of his order.

St Simon Stock is without doubt the most elusive personality in a group of eminent Englishmen of his time, which includes Haymo and Roger Bacon, of whose life and character we know almost nothing save that they were endowed with talents of the highest order. His very title of saint was purely domestic in origin and tardy in arrival; he has never been formally canonized or recognized by the universal Church; not only his surname but his very name also is traditional, the latter being used by no contemporary, while the former first occurs a century after his death; and the incident with which his name has been linked in Catholic devotion rests upon no ascertainable basis of fact. All that is known with certainty is that an English general, called Simon by the next generation, effected certain radical changes in the order's constitutions.[2]

According to the traditional account, this man, an English hermit, joined

1 For the English province as third v. Regula in Mon. Hist. Carm. I, 21; cf. also Eccleston, 130.
2 For Simon, v. Zimmermann, Mon. Hist. Carm. I, 317 seqq. and De Sacro Scapulari 3 seqq.

the brethren of Carmel in Palestine, and it is a very probable conjecture that identifies him with the historic Simon found as their prior *c*. 1237. Returning with others to Europe and to England he was elected general at a chapter held at Aylesford in 1247. Almost immediately he secured a provisional approval of the Rule from Innocent IV, and two Dominican prelates, the celebrated Cardinal Hugh of St Cher and William, bishop of Anthère, were charged with its revision and the framing of constitutions; the latter were naturally modelled very closely upon those of the Preachers, and this similarity of organization was ever after retained.[1] As regards the Rule, the general obtained a number of important changes: the strict abstinence was relaxed, meals were to be taken in common, the absolute silence hitherto enjoined from Vespers to Terce (that is, perhaps, from 4 p.m. to 9 a.m.) was altered to the normal monastic *summum silentium* from Compline to Prime (6–7 p.m. to 6–7 a.m.) and, finally, foundations were to be allowed in and near towns.[2] The constitutions thus compiled date from *c*. 1250.

The way was thus cleared for active work, whether intellectual or apostolic, and the general did not shrink from following his programme to the limit. The Carmelites, who had moved from Chesterton to Newnham in 1249, began to attend the schools at Cambridge, and Simon established them likewise at Oxford (1256), Paris and Bologna. The English prior-general had thus brought his order into line with the two great student orders, and no reaction of sentiment could undo his work. It is significant that, while the first settlements prior to 1247 had been in nameless and remote localities, all subsequent foundations were in cities and towns. The term of office of Simon was not, however, one of unbroken progress and concord. What have been called the 'fat' years of his success (1247–56) were followed by a series of 'lean' years of strife and distress (1257–65). Some of the older members of the order felt that their vocation had been betrayed; others of the younger school contrasted their own inchoate system with the excellent organization of the Minors and Preachers. Apostasies and transferences to the Franciscans, Dominicans and even Cistercians were numerous.[3] There was, indeed, a deep moral truth behind the tradition that looked to Elijah and his disciples as the founders of Carmel, and when Simon died his successor, the Frenchman Nicholas, was an ardent advocate of the primitive, eremitical life. To defend his views he composed an impassioned encyclical with the title *Ignea sagitta*, in which he spoke his opinion so boldly and sounded so clear a call to the desert that the work was from the start suppressed in many places, and has not hitherto been printed.[4]

1 *Mon. Hist. Carm.* I, 3 (Zimmermann): 'Maximam videre est similitudinem inter nostras constitutiones modumque gubernandi in eis descriptum et ejusdem naturae ordinationes apud Fratres Praedicatores.'

2 *Bullarium Carmelitanum*, I, 8–11.   3 Zimmermann, *de Sacro Scapulari*, 12 seqq.

4 Zimmermann, *Les Carmes aux Universités* in *Études Carmélitaines* (April 1932), 88, and *Analecta Ord. Carm.* III (1930), 165.

Nicholas resigned in 1271, but his successor, Ralph Freshbourne, late provincial of England, though a peacemaker, was of the same school, with an especial devotion to the liturgy,[1] and he too resigned in 1276, having obtained final approval for his order at the Council of Lyons in 1274; he retired to Holne, which he had founded, and died there in the odour of sanctity. The new prior-general, Pierre de Millaud, the first master of theology to hold the office, guided the Carmelites firmly along the lines laid down by Simon, and at the chapter-general held in London in 1281 the studies of the order were organized on the lines established first by the Preachers, and *studia generalia* were appointed, of which London was one. Henceforward, the Carmelites took an even larger part in the work of the schools; in particular, they sent many of their most brilliant men to Cambridge, as will be seen on a later page. It is nevertheless noteworthy that twice more within forty years a prior-general resigned on account of his love of the eremitical life,[2] and the order, as is well known, has preserved throughout the centuries a nostalgia for the desert and the mountain that has operated, like a similar longing among the Franciscans for the pure poverty of the Rule, to distinguish the Carmelites from their brother friars and served to prepare them for the renewal of their spirit which took place under the two great Spanish apostles of the contemplative life in the sixteenth century.[3]

III

The fourth order of friars had an origin even more obscure than that of the Carmelites; in its final form, indeed, it sprang from a number of separate roots.[4] The title officially given to the body—Friars Hermits of St Augustine—is itself an indication of their beginnings; it does not, of course, imply that the history of the order is to be traced back to the great doctor's personal influence, though writers possessed of an intrepidity sufficient to nerve them to this task have not been wanting either in medieval or modern times. In fact, the Austin Friars sprang from a number of semi-eremitical or penitent communities such as modern research has shown to have existed in profusion in Italy shortly before the lifetime of St Francis. Chief among them were the hermits of Tuscany, Lombardy and the Romagna, and some were early united in groups such as those at Cesena

1 Cf. documents printed by Denifle in *ALKG*, v, 378: 'Eratque pacis singularis amator, divini officii specialis zelator.'

2 Sc. Raymundus de Insula (1294–7): 'quia vitam anachoreticam superne (?) diligebat'; and Johannes de Alerio (1312–30) who: 'tantum dilexit vitam contemplativam' (Denifle, *ALKG*, v, 379).

3 For the hermitages throughout the centuries till modern times *v.* Zimmermann, *Les Saints Déserts des Carmes déchaussés*.

4 For the 'pre-history' of the Hermits, *v.* H. Grundmann, *Religiöse Bewegungen im Mittelalter*; for the early years of the order E. A. Van Moé, *Recherches sur les Ermites de Saint Augustin*, in *Revue des Questions Historiques*, CXVI, 275–316; above all, the series of studies by Fr F. Roth, O.E.S.A., in *Augustiniana* II and subsequent vols., which herald a history of the order. Fra Salimbene, *MGH, SS*, XXXII, 54 (*s.a.* 1248) distinguishes five congregations of hermits, and states that all were joined to the Bonites, which became the head of the body.

and Brittino, the Williamites of Siena and the Bonites of Mantua. A few had sent out colonies to Spain, Germany and southern France early in the thirteenth century; almost all used as a basis of their life the so-called Rule of St Augustine, which ever since the reforms of Gregory VII had been common property to all non-monastic bodies. Living as they did for the most part in Italy, they fell under the direct observation both of the papacy and of the two elder orders. The papacy, which was yearly becoming more concerned with the organization and centralization of the friars, was rendered more prone to action by the lack of any rule on the part of certain congregations of the hermits, while others, originally of purely local influence and as yet without solemn approbation, were sending offshoots beyond the Alps.

In 1243 Innocent IV, soon after his election, united the hermits of Tuscany under the Rule of St Augustine and took what proved to be a decisive step by giving them into the charge of Cardinal Richard Annibaldi. From 1243 until his death more than thirty years later this eminent man proved a steadfast friend to the Hermits, and to him, more than to any other man, the order owes its existence, its prosperity and its form.[1]

Under his tutelage the young institute grew steadily. In 1248 it was established with headquarters in Rome at the church of Santa Maria del Popolo whence the Minors had migrated to the Ara Coeli, itself recently vacated by the black monks. In 1253 the hermits of Lombardy and the Romagna were united at the pope's command, and in 1256 Innocent's successor, Alexander IV, published the bull of fuller union which has since been held to mark the birthday of the Austin Friars as a fully established order. By it they were constituted friars and mendicants, but mendicancy was permissive not obligatory for them and the corporate possession of necessities was permitted; thus they, like the Preachers, escaped the distressing controversies which tore at the vitals of the Minors. They still lacked, however, approved constitutional legislation; they also lacked any outstanding leaders, and in consequence they came nearer than the Carmelites to shipwreck at the Council of Lyons in 1274 where, if a lively chronicler is to be believed, they were saved from the destruction intended by Gregory X only by the efforts of Cardinal Annibaldi.[2] This need for close dependence on their protector, together with their origin at the papal bidding and their prolonged uncertainty of status gave to the Hermits of St Augustine an even closer bond with the Holy See than that existing for the other friars; in the controversies of the near future this was to have important results.

The Austin Friars were long in achieving legislation. Their constitutions, in preparation from 1284 onwards, were ratified by the general chapter of Ratisbon in 1290, but they received only a modified recognition at Rome, and were altered by successive generals. Like those of the Carmelites

---

1 Salimbene, *MGH*, XXXII, 255: 'Voluit etiam Gregorius X cassare et ad nihilum redigere Heremitarum ordinem; sed interventu domini Ricardi Romane curie cardinalis...abstinuit se ne faceret quod volebat.'   2 Van Moé, *art. cit.* 290, and *v.* last notes.

they were modelled very closely upon those of the Preachers in all matters of organization;[1] so, too, the Hermits came to imitate the Preachers in the whole trend of their life; they became a 'preaching' order, and their theological teaching, largely owing to the influence of Giles Colonna, a brilliant pupil of St Thomas, was strongly Thomist in colour. The Austin Friars, indeed, appear to have lost more rapidly and more completely than the Minors and the Carmelites their original characteristics and aims; though they retained the name of Hermits they became in effect academic and urban. Yet the hermitages of Italy continued to exist, and we shall see more than one English Austin friar seeking to live again the life of the first fathers of the order.

The Hermits had been introduced into England before the definitive union of 1256, probably from the English territory of Gascony.[2] The first foundations due, like those of the Carmelites, to wealthy patrons and the king himself, were in remote districts, at Stoke Clare in Suffolk (1248), at Woodhouse near Cleobury Mortimer in Shropshire (1250) and Shamele in Kent. For a short space of years hermitages continued to be founded in the depths of the country, as at Shuttington in Warwickshire and Whittle-seamere in Cambridgeshire, but soon the Austin Friars followed the three other orders to the cities and the towns, and entered university life with a foundation at Oxford in 1268. Between the death of Simon de Montfort and 1300 they made at least thirteen settlements; all were at centres of population, and many were in towns already occupied by two or three of the other orders.[3] Almost the only feature of interest that characterizes the list of Austin friaries is the importance given to the west country house of Ludlow, a town having no other community of religious, which became the head of the small group of western houses including Cleobury Mortimer, Droitwich, Newport and Shrewsbury.

IV

The Carmelites and Austin Hermits, though ultimately assimilated to the friars, already existed as religious bodies in their own right, though unorganized, when the Minors and Preachers came into being as orders. The same may be said of another body, the Trinitarians, who had actually arrived in England a few years before the friars.[4] Though often confused

---

1 The only work dealing at all with the order in England is *The English Austin Friars in the Time of Wyclif*, by Aubrey Gwynn, S. J. (Oxford, 1940).

2 For English houses and dates *v. The Religious Houses of Medieval England*, 115–16.

3 There were houses of all four orders at London, Oxford, Cambridge and eight other towns.

4 For the Trinitarians *v.* R. von Kralik, *Geschichte des Trinitarienordens* (Vienna, 1919), In the early sixteenth century the royal visitors and commissioners more than once confused Trinitarians and Crutched Friars (e.g. Wright, *Three Chapters of Letters*, CS, xxvi (1843), 235); more recently Dr J. C. Cox (*VCH, Berks*, ii, 92) has endeavoured to establish an identity. The first Trinitarian foundation was at Hounslow, *c.* 1200, cf. Lieut.-Col. H. F. Chettle, *The Trinitarian Friars and Easton Royal*, in *Wilts Archaeological Magazine*, li, 365.

with them both by their contemporaries in the middle ages and by later antiquarians, their domestic life, especially in later centuries, approximated closely to that of the Augustinian canons, though they resembled the friars in being an international order divided into provinces. They had been founded at the very end of the twelfth century at Cerfroy, near Château-Thierry, by John of Matha and Felix of Valois; their mother-house remained that of Cerfroy, though their convent of S. Maturin in Paris was more famous, and earned for them the name of Maturins. They existed for the purpose of ransoming Christian captives from the Saracens, and achieved this end in the last resort by personal substitution, but the normal method was that of a pecuniary transaction at a relatively stable tariff, and the houses established in northern Europe were in the nature of centres for recruitment and the collection of funds, though some were hospitals, at first for the maintenance of rescued captives, and later for more general purposes. When the end for which they had come into being ceased to hold its place in the popular imagination, the Trinitarians sank gradually into a way of life little different, as has been said, from that of the Austin canons. They continued to exist, but made no mark.

Another small institute, of undiscoverable provenance, which established itself somewhat later, was that of the Bonshommes of Ashridge in Buckinghamshire; they also followed the Augustinian Rule.[1] The name had earlier been given in France by popular consent to the Order of Grammont, and was to be used much later of the Minims of St Francis of Paula, but the religious of Ashridge were unconnected with any other body, and seemingly purely English. After a considerable interval, they sent a colony to Edington in Wiltshire.

Apart, however, from these independent bodies the extraordinary successes of the early mendicants led inevitably to a series of imitations, especially in northern Italy and Provence, and several new orders made their appearance, distinguished from their great models by little more than peculiarity of dress and lack of organization. As they were soon officially condemned to extinction by the Council of Lyons in 1274, leaving few material or literary traces, the history of these shifting groups cannot easily be reconstructed; historians may perhaps take comfort in this from Matthew Paris who himself was, or affected to be, unable to see clearly in the matter.[2]

Nevertheless, a few groups stand out with some distinctness. Chief among these were the Friars of the Sack, of whose origin Salimbene gives a lively and probably fairly accurate account.[3] Their founder, a Provençal, had first tried his vocation among the Minors, had left them for reasons of health, and had subsequently appeared as a free-lance in northern Italy. They were, it would appear, one of the groups intended to fall within the

---

1 For these, v. art. by H. F. Chettle in *DR* (1944), LXII, 40–55, and *VCH, Bucks*, I, 386.

2 *MPChM* v, 612, (1257), 'Quidam novus ordo fratrum...apparuit et incognitus'; cf. *ibid.*, 621 and 631: 'Totque jam apparuerunt ordines...ut ordinum confusio videretur inordinata'.

3 Salimbene, *Chronica*, ed. Holder-Egger (*MGH, SS*, XXXII), 254–5.

scope of the union of 1256 which gave birth to the Augustinian Hermits, but as a body they refused to merge, alleging a papal bull forbidding any member of their body to join a less austere order.[1] Their constitutions, which have been preserved, were modelled closely upon those of the Preachers,[2] and their life in general, which soon lost its fluid character and gave much attention to study, differed little from that of the Minors of Bonaventure's day in north-western Europe. Their formal name was Brothers of Penance of Jesus Christ, but they were generally known as Friars of the Sack from their dress, which consisted of a mantle of sack-cloth over a tunic of better material. They arrived in England in 1257 and soon had a dozen or so places of residence, including a house of studies at Oxford. The order was doomed to extinction in 1274, as Salimbene relates with some satisfaction,[3] but the English houses lingered on till the inmates passed away in the early years of the fourteenth century.

Another group, the Friars of the Cross or Crutched Friars, were more fortunate.[4] At least four families of *cruciferi* existed in the thirteenth century, all following the Rule of St Augustine, but unconnected with each other. The English Crutched Friars derived from a group founded near Huy in Belgium in 1211 which spread all over north-western Europe; they were organized under a Master-General with constitutions resembling those of the Preachers, but their work was chiefly in hospitals, and they had little resemblance to the Minors and Preachers in their way of life. They first arrived in England in 1244 and received royal protection;[5] the bishops, however, were not so cordial, and Eccleston notes with approval that Grosseteste would have none of them[6]—a statement not easy to reconcile with the known fact of their establishment in 1247 at Whaplode in his diocese, even though the house was abandoned in 1260.[7] Shortly after the settlement at Whaplode their first permanent establishment was made at Colchester. They were unfortunate in a number of their ventures. Archbishop Greenfield succeeded in ejecting them from Kildale, where they had settled,[8] and their projected foundation at Oxford was thwarted by Gynewell of Lincoln; London was the only house which maintained a fairly prosperous existence throughout. Nevertheless, they survived till the end, an exiguous and undistinguished body.

1 So M. Heimbucher, *Orden und Kongregationen*, I, 541, and R. W. Emery, *The Friars of the Sack*, in *Speculum*, XVIII, 3 (July 1943), 323–34.

2 Printed by A. G. Little, *EHR*, IX (1894), 121 *seqq*.

3 Salimbene, ed. Holder-Egger, 255: 'Papa Gregorius decimus...cassavit hunc ordinem, illustratus inspiratione divina.'

4 M. Heimbucher, *Orden und Kongregationen*, I, 419–22; H. F. Chettle, *The Friars of the Holy Cross in England*, in *DR*, LXIII (Sept. 1945). Their habit bore a cross on the breast; they did not carry a crossed stick, as is sometimes said.

5 *MPChM*, IV, 393–4; *CPR*, 1237–47, 435.   6 Eccleston, 130.

7 Miss K. Major, *An Unknown House of Crutched Friars at Whaplode*, in *Assoc. Archit. and Archaeolog. Soc. Reports*, vol. LXI, ii, (1933), 149–54.

8 *Guisborough Chartulary*, II, (*SS*, 1891, 388–90); for details of other houses, see H. F. Chettle, *The Friars of the Holy Cross*, (*supra*, n. 4).

Besides these sizable groups a few scattered visitants, like birds of an exotic species, appear fitfully in the records. Such were the friars De Ordine Martyrum, apparently far-ranging individuals of an order whose chief scene of activity was in Poland;[1] they arrived in England in 1256–7 and made a settlement, of which nothing further is known, at Guildford. Others are still more elusive, and it is possible that their names conceal religious better known under another style.[2] But indeed England, which had received so readily the new monastic orders of northern France, was far from Italy, the nursery of orders in the later middle ages, and national characters and loyalties were developing fast.

[1] Eccleston, 131, with Little's note. Heimbucher, I, 422, gives *ordo paenitentiae sanctorum martyrum* as one of the names of the Polish *cruciferi*.

[2] The Pied Friars of London and Norwich (*VCH, London, Norfolk*) and the Friars de Domina at Cambridge and London (*Rot. Hundred*..., II, 360 and *VCH, Norfolk*, II, 433) are very probably Carmelites. The Cambridge Bethlehemites referred to by Matthew Paris (*ChM*, v, 631), if really existent, may have been stray *cruciferi*; there was more than one order of Bethlehemites but of a later date (Heimbucher, I, 60. *seqq.*). Sections xv–xvii (pp. 119–21) of D. Knowles, *Religious Houses*, should therefore be deleted.

CHAPTER XVIII

THE EARLY ENGLISH FRANCISCAN SCHOLASTICS

I

The process by which the brotherhood, founded by the unlettered Francis as a new manifestation of the folly of the Cross, became in less than fifty years one of the two 'student orders' of the Church,[1] whose policy was directed by a group of the most celebrated teachers of Europe, began at Paris and developed almost exclusively there and at Oxford. In this transformation it may be claimed that Englishmen played a predominant part, for it was the conversion of eminent English teachers at Paris that began the movement north of the Alps; some of them, remaining in France, became the spokesmen of the French province; others migrated to Oxford, where they were joined by recruits of the same stamp, and together they gave immediate *éclat* to the school of the Friars Minor; finally, in the century that followed, almost all the Franciscan doctors of the first rank were Englishmen, with the eminent exception of Bonaventure.[2]

The Friars Preachers had arrived in Paris in 1217; the Friars Minor came three years later. To the outward view there was probably little difference between the types of men and of mind at the two convents; both groups preached, and both lived lives of striking simplicity and fervour. But if both also attracted to themselves the more earnest of the masters and scholars, the most brilliant recruits of the early years went to the Franciscans. Among the first was Haymo of Faversham, who entered the order with three companions in 1224.[3] His conversion, more than that of any other, *momentum fuit rerum*, but the most spectacular change of life, which had important consequences in the history of European thought, was that of the most celebrated doctor of his time, the Englishman Alexander of Hales,[4] who took the habit in 1238. By that date the stream had begun to flow in England also, and there it reached a high-water mark with the entry *c.* 1232 of Adam Marsh who became, after Grosseteste, the most eminent master of England. The aggregation of such a number of teachers, of mature mind and formed outlook, gave to the life and policy of the friars in the infant provinces of France and England a new colour and direction. Men such as Haymo, Adam Marsh and Alexander of Hales inevitably became leaders

1 The phrase 'two student Orders' is Bacon's; cf. *Opera inedita*, ed. J. S. Brewer (*RS*), pp. 398, 426, 427. In this chapter, contrary to general practice in this book, the terms Franciscan and Dominican have been freely used, since many of the modern works quoted employ them.

2 Dr Little, *Studies*, 193, quotes the modern Franciscan historian, Fr H. Felder: 'The English nation has given to the Franciscan Order a greater number of eminent scholars than all the rest of the nations put together.'

3 For Haymo, *v. Eccleston*, 34, where his choice of the Franciscan habit is attributed to the Dominican general Jordan of Saxony.

4 For Alexander *v.* Bacon, *Opera inedita*, 326, where his taking of the habit is noted as the moment when the obscure Friars Minor entered into fame. There is a valuable bibliography of Alexander by I. Herscher O.F.M. in *Franciscan Studies*, vol. 26, no. 4.

of any body to which they belonged, and the grey friars at once embarked upon a distinguished career in the schools.

No aspect of medieval history was more neglected half a century ago than the rise and development of the schools of theology and philosophy in the thirteenth century, and in no province of history has more significant research been achieved in recent years. Summary generalizations which had become stereotyped have been challenged and abandoned or modified, and though very much still remains to be done, many of the complicated lines in the descent of thought can now be perceived. The old attitude, which was primarily that of a zealous adherent of a school of theology turned historian, who looked at early facts and characters in the light of later or modern developments, has given place to that of the trained 'positive' historian, not immediately concerned to be the champion of a system or a school, who unravels the web of the past piece by piece, uninfluenced by later events which were as yet in the womb of time.[1]

In these pages no attempt, not even the most superficial, can be made to analyse the philosophical and theological speculation of the English friars. A word must, however, be said of their share in building up the great fabric of scholastic thought, for this was their work, no less than were the chronicles and illuminated manuscripts the work of the black monks a century before.[2]

Of all the summary classifications of medieval theologians made in the past, none perhaps was more misleading than that which, basing itself on later controversies and systems, assumed the existence from the first among the friars of schools of thought typically Franciscan or Dominican. In fact,

[1] The pioneers of this research, to which the original impulse was given by the action of Leo XIII in recalling Catholic theologians to Thomism, were Père Denifle, O.P., Émile Chatelain, and the long-lived Fr Ehrle (later Cardinal), S.J. A little later came the epoch-making studies of Père Mandonnet, O.P., and Mgr Grabmann; they have been followed by a host of scholars in Rome, Munich, Louvain, Paris and elsewhere. Adequate bibliographies to date of publication will be found in M. de Wulf, *Histoire de la Philosophie médiévale*, 6 ed. trans. E. C. Messenger (1938), and F. Ueberweg, *Grundriss der Geschichte der Philosophie*, ed. B. Geyer, 11 ed. 1928, but the output of articles, papers and monographs far outstrips all attempts to arrive at a reckoning, and many are scattered in periodicals and collections peculiarly difficult to come by in England; this is of course particularly the case with all continental work of the years 1939–45. As regards the English scholastics, the field was until very recently entirely virgin, save for a few attempts to assess Roger Bacon, but much good work has now been achieved by Mandonnet, Grabmann, Ehrle and others, and still more recently by Père Ephrem Longpré, O.F.M., Fr Pelster, S.J., Père M. D. Chenu, O.P., Dom O. Lottin, O.S.B., and Mgr A. Pelzer. Finally, English scholars have at last begun to devote their attention to the great English scholastics; the tireless Dr Little has investigated the careers and work of a number of the theologians among the friars, Prof. Powicke, Mgr G. Lacombe and Miss B. Smalley have studied Stephen Langton, and the first serious attempt to assess the philosophical significance of the English school has appeared in the notable work of Dr D. E. Sharp, *Franciscan Philosophy at Oxford*. Dr Little's achievement, in which the threads of many years' labour are gathered up, may be seen in his articles on the schools at Oxford and Cambridge (*v.* Bibliography) and especially in the volume produced in collaboration with Fr Pelster, *Oxford Theology and Theologians* (*OHS*, 96, 1934). For bibliography, *v. MU* (new ed.), and the lists given in Sharp and de Wulf.

[2] In default of a full account the reader may consult the relevant sections in de Wulf and Ueberweg-Geyer. But before a final judgement can be made much more work remains to be done of the type inaugurated by Dr Sharp.

both Friars Minor and Friars Preachers fell into place in the succession and tradition of the teachers of their time; not until the last decades of the thirteenth century did the Preachers as a body begin to form a school which identified itself with the teaching of St Thomas, and the official adoption by the Friars Minor of systems deriving from St Bonaventure and Scotus was a still later and more irregular development. The historian of theology in England, therefore, when he traces the life of the Franciscan and Dominican schools prior to c. 1280, considers a succession of masters, of the most varied antecedents and provenance, who did indeed often influence one another as teacher and disciple, but who can scarcely be said to have composed a closed school of thought, still less to have been animated by a single *esprit d'école*. Moreover, it must never be forgotten that the majority of the early Franciscan masters took the habit late in life, when their reputations were made and their minds formed, and that it is therefore wholly misleading to point in the *corpus* of their doctrine to anything specifically Franciscan. The first Franciscan theologians were, intellectually speaking, the product of contemporary Paris and Oxford, differing not at all in outlook from the secular masters of their time.

The history of the Franciscan school at Oxford during the first half-century of its existence has often been retailed.[1] The predominant influence of its early years, which impressed certain characteristics upon a long succession of masters and pupils, was that of the massive intelligence of Robert Grosseteste, Chancellor of Oxford, who was its first regent from 1229 until his election to Lincoln in 1235.[2] All recent study upon Grosseteste has gone to confirm his title to the eminent position accorded to him by his contemporaries. As a thinker, he was the first Englishman to absorb a great part of the philosophic system of Aristotle[3] and though he had been previously and profoundly influenced by the doctrines of Augustine and his medieval followers, he faces in his writings many of the great metaphysical and psychological problems that were to be debated throughout

1 Especially by Dr A. G. Little *à plusieurs reprises*, each surpassing its predecessor in penetration and completeness: *v. The Grey Friars in Oxford*, c. iii Franciscan Schools at Oxford, with invaluable biographical notices; *Studies in English Franciscan History*, c. vi The Franciscan School at Oxford (pp. 193–221) and the sketch of the career of John of Wales (pp. 174–192); *St Francis of Assisi* (ed. W. Seton), *The First Hundred Years of the Franciscan School at Oxford; The Franciscan School at Oxford in the Thirteenth Century* in *Archivum Franciscanum Historicum* (1926), XIX, 803–74; and a paper with the same title in *FP*, 55–71 (the most complete); *Oxford Theology and Theologians*. Besides these, Dr Sharp's *Franciscan Philosophy at Oxford* is in a place by itself.

2 Until they had Oxford Masters of their own both black and grey friars had perforce to employ seculars as lecturers; at Paris the same situation arose at the beginning. For Grosseteste's achievement as a thinker *v.* Sharp, 10–46; L. Baur, *Der Einfluss des Robert Grosseteste auf die wissenschaftliche Richtung des Roger Bacon* in *Roger Bacon: Commemoration Essays*; and Little, esp. in *St Francis*, 171–5; S. H. Thomson, *The Writings of Robert Grosseteste*, and E. Franceschini, *Roberto Grossatesta e le sue traduzioni latine*. Cf. also Fr D. Callus, O.P., *Introduction of Aristotelian Learning to Oxford*, and *The Oxford Career of Robert Grosseteste*.

3 The judgement of de Wulf, *History of Medieval Philosophy*, § 227, p. 57, who cites with approval Bacon's statement that Grosseteste 'neglexit omnino libros Aristotelis et vias eorum' (*Opera inedita*, ed. Brewer, 469) needs revision in the light of recent investigation. Cf. Sharp, *Franciscan Philosophy*, 10–11, and the important bibliographical note on Grosseteste's translations in *MU* (new ed.), III, 240.

the century, and shows the first traces of the clash between the two great traditions, together with the first attempts to make harmony. As a scholar and a teacher he did more, perhaps, than any of his contemporaries to grapple with the immense task that faced all those devoted to the higher learning between 1200 and 1270, the task, that is, of mastering the whole content of ancient science as transmitted by Latins, Greeks, Arabs and Jews, and of using it as a positive basis upon which to rest the structure of philosophy, theology and biblical exegesis. His significance as a philosopher and the nature of his influence in questions of pure thought upon later English Franciscans has recently been set in a clear light. In his works it is possible to trace a number of those doctrines, such as the hylomorphic conception of all substance, the plurality of forms, and the divine illumination of the intellect as part of the normal cognoscitive process, which were common property to the majority of thirteenth century thinkers before St Thomas, and which were in a modified form retained by the later Franciscans after they had been abandoned by the Dominicans. In the realm of more positive studies, he left an even more recognizable mark; it is noteworthy that while the great Parisian masters, and especially those of Latin race such as St Bonaventure and St Thomas, regarded positive studies as doing no more than to provide data for the philosopher and theologian, the early English doctors gave much attention to perfecting the matter and methods of the sciences for their own sake, and in order to enlarge and perfect positive knowledge of all kinds. In this their great standard bearer was Grosseteste. The characteristics of his teaching, as has been pointed out by more than one careful historian, were a close attention to the study of the Bible, read textually and critically, as the basis of theology; the study of languages especially of Greek; an interest in securing faithful translations of all ancient works as a necessary part of the equipment of a scholar; and, above all, an attention to mathematics.

Grosseteste, like all the scholastic masters of the early thirteenth century, lacked humanism. Both his treatises and his private letters are wholly without beauty of form and language, and not only want the warmth of feeling, the delicacy of sympathy and the breadth of interest that are shown by an Abelard or an Ailred, but are also wholly lacking in that sense of form or ordered presentation which gives dignity and cohesion to the letters of almost all the great ecclesiastics of the twelfth century. Indeed, the element of charm and the impress of personality are almost entirely absent from his correspondence; it is not easy to instance any other man, as equally and as justly celebrated for his mental and moral qualities, of whom such a judgement can be made.[1] In this, however, he was the child,

1 It is difficult to think of any other character in English history so lavishly and unanimously praised by near and remote posterity, who has left so little of intimate record behind him; he found no biographer of his age, and Grosseteste 'the man' remains an elusive, veiled figure. As regards his aesthetic perceptions, it may perhaps be worth noting that while his predecessors at Lincoln built the nave and west front, and his successors the Angel choir, work would seem to have been almost at a standstill during his tenure of the see.

for all his eminence, of his age; the educational curriculum of the thirteenth century, so bracing and stimulating to the pure reason, starved many of the other powers of the mind, and deprived it of the ability and of the desire to give expression in words to its perceptions of beauty and of emotion. Magnificently eloquent in stone and painted glass and coloured page, it was an age in which the most cultured were, in the exercise of more than one of the mind's activities, the least possessed of a flexible and living speech.

Grosseteste was followed in the friars' school at Oxford by three other secular masters: Peter, later bishop of Aberdeen, Roger Wesham, subsequently bishop of Lichfield, and Thomas the Welshman, highly praised by Roger Bacon, who soon became bishop of St David's. Not until 1247 did a friar hold the post of regent, though many fully qualified had long been available; in default of any positive indication we cannot say whether this was due to the readiness with which distinguished secular masters proffered their services, or whether, as has been suggested, the early friars shrank from taking the degree (and therefore the style) of master, which was an indispensable qualification at Oxford for a regent in theology.[1] Meanwhile, however, a succession of students had gone forth from the school, in addition to the Oxford scholars who continued to join the friars; as will be seen, lecturers were established in all the important English houses, and Oxford-trained friars were appointed to lectureships abroad.

When in 1247 Thomas the Welshman was elected bishop, he was succeeded by a friar who had long been regarded as one of the most remarkable in the province and who, like Grosseteste, is in every way a type of that class of which he was an eminent member.[2] Adam Marsh, a wealthy secular clerk and nephew of Bishop Richard Marsh of Durham who possibly beneficed him at Wearmouth, had been a noted master in arts of Oxford and the close friend of Grosseteste for many years before he took the Franciscan habit.[3] As with Grosseteste, so with Marsh it is impossible to say whether he had ever studied at Paris. The final impetus in his progress to religion was given by his namesake and secretary, Adam of Oxford, who became a friar and subsequently, having volunteered for missionary work, died on his journey to the East in 1232. The other Adam took the habit c. 1232 at Worcester, whither the poverty and simplicity of the house had attracted him,[4] but he was soon sent back to Oxford, and that convent remained his headquarters for the rest of his life, though absences became more and more frequent in proportion to the demands made for his spiritual and diplomatic good offices by the order, by

---

1 Little, *The Franciscan School at Oxford* in *St Francis*, 169 (*FP*, 58).

2 Of the many accounts of Adam Marsh the fullest perhaps is that by Fr Cuthbert, O.S.F.C., in *The Romanticism of St Francis* (2 ed. only), 190–235.

3 He had known Grosseteste *ab annis juvenilibus* (*Monumenta Franciscana*, ed. Brewer, I, 145).

4 The precise date cannot be ascertained. Fr Cuthbert, *op. cit.*, 192 n. 1, and Dr Little, *Archiv. Francisc. Hist.* XIX, 833 show that it was probably late in 1232.

bishops, by influential laymen and by the king. Of some of these activities a word will be said later; for the moment we are concerned with Marsh as a teacher.

On his return to Oxford, he would have taken up the threads of his friendship with Grosseteste, and their constant intercourse, unbroken till the bishop's death in 1253, was maintained by letter when they were apart. The two men were peculiarly alike in mental and moral temper. Adam Marsh was all but Grosseteste's equal as scholar and teacher, and the two men are frequently coupled as ornaments of the same branches of learning by that stern critic, Roger Bacon.[1] Both were ardent reformers and defenders of the privileges of the Church; both were friends and counsellors of Simon de Montfort and his party; both were men of personal austerity of life. The resemblance goes even deeper, for the letters of Marsh, though perhaps a shade more individual than the bishop's, have the same characteristics of formlessness and dryness, and are wholly wanting in personal charm and all indications of a sense of beauty in life, nature or letters.[2] Adam Marsh, indeed, shows himself, like Grosseteste, a zealous friend and an exemplary spiritual adviser, full of consideration and mercy for repentant defaulters, but there is in him, though perhaps less than in the bishop, a touch of hardness and formalism, and an overtone of bitterness in his reactions to the external changes in the order and in the nation during his later years—qualities which, it may be remarked, have been noted in some other eminent friars in other centuries, though signally absent from the zeal and from the sadness of Francis of Assisi. The written treatises of Adam Marsh have not survived; they included a commentary on Genesis and a *Summa de Penitentia*, and all the evidence goes to show that his intellectual interests were in the main similar to Grosseteste's. Both were expert in mathematics, to which their devotion was lifelong, to natural philosophy, and to languages; Roger Bacon names them together as the two luminaries of his age who could equal or surpass the philosophers of any epoch, and Marsh's learning receives the highest praise from contemporaries as different in character and outlook as Matthew Paris, Bocking, the biographer of Richard of Chichester, Nicholas Trivet the Dominican and the Minorite chronicler Salimbene.[3]

Marsh was regent at Oxford only until 1249; after that date he continued to lecture when in residence, but his place as regent was taken by Ralph de Colebruge, who had been a master in Paris before taking the habit; and he in turn was soon followed by Eustace de Normaneville, who had been Chancellor of Oxford shortly before becoming a Franciscan.

The fourth Franciscan lector was a still more eminent man. Of Thomas

---

1 Cf. *Opus Majus*, ed. Bridges, I, 108; *Opus Tertium*, ed. Brewer, 88; *De communibus mathematice*, ed. Steele, cited in *Roger Bacon*, 164 n. 2.

2 Fr D. Callus has suggested to me the possibility that Marsh had a hand in the composition of some of Grosseteste's letters.

3 *V*. references in Fr Cuthbert, *The Romanticism of St Francis*, 190 notes.

of York's life little is known,[1] save that he was the protégé and friend of Adam Marsh, and possessed the complete confidence of William of Nottingham, the great provincial. His great work, the *Sapientiale*, a kind of *Summa* of metaphysics, has however, survived; it has been described by a competent judge as 'the only great presentation of the system of metaphysics produced in the best period of scholasticism', and has recently been made the subject of careful analysis.[2] Thomas of York, while resembling Grosseteste in the main lines of his thought, shows a particular familiarity with the great Arab and Jewish philosophers; in him, as in Grosseteste, appear the doctrines of hylomorphism and of the divine illumination of the intellect.

Thomas of York passed to Cambridge as regent in 1256; his successor, Richard of Cornwall, was a master at Paris before receiving the habit; he had immediately taken a prominent place in the order, though it was not he, but Rigaud, who was one of the four masters to propound questions on the Rule for the General in 1242.[3] Like his predecessors, Richard was a metaphysician, and his fame among contemporaries was great; his reputation with posterity has suffered from the repeated attacks made upon him by Roger Bacon, who alludes to him, probably unjustly, in the most slighting language as 'an absolute fool', and accuses him of sowing a crop of tares at Oxford which were still flourishing hardily forty years later.[4] Adam Marsh, on the other hand, praises alike his character, his learning, his orthodoxy and his abilities as a teacher.[5]

John of Wales, his successor, who became a Franciscan when already a bachelor of divinity, was regent at Oxford before 1260; he afterwards passed to Paris, where he became celebrated, and was employed both on diplomatic

1 *V.* esp. the pages (49–112) devoted to him by Dr Sharp; *Die Metaphysik des Thomas von York*, by Mgr Grabmann, in *Festgabe ʒ. 60 Geburtstag C. Baeumker*, 1913; *Frère Thomas d'York, O.F.M.* by Père Ephrem Longpré, O.F.M., in *Archiv. Francisc. Hist.*, 1926; and the bibliographies in Sharp, Ueberweg-Geyer, and de Wulf.

2 P. Longpré writes, *art. cit.* 895: 'Incontestablement les livres III–V, consacrés à la métaphysique générale de l'être et à l'étude des catégories, les chapitres sur la démonstration de l'existence de Dieu...appartiennent aux meilleures pages dont puisse s'honorer la pensée médiévale. Ainsi l'école franciscaine d'Oxford a donné au siècle d'or de la scolastique les deux grands noms qui illustrent la métaphysique médiévale à son apogée: Thomas d'York et le B. Duns Scotus.' And again (p. 905): 'Thomas d'York s'est révélé comme une personnalité philosophique de premier ordre, que l'histoire des idées mettra un jour fort près de S. Bonaventure et du B. Duns Scotus.' The reader who feels that another Frater Thomas might well have received mention among the luminaries of medieval metaphysics must remember that Père Longpré is himself a Friar Minor; he may find something of a *correctorium* in Fr Callus's paper to the British Academy (XXIV, 1944); Callus writes (p. 35): 'It is not Aristotle but Avicebron who gives the tone to the whole work.'

3 Little, *AFH*, XIX, 841 n. 11.

4 *V. Fr Rogeri Bacon Compendium Studii Theologiae*, ed. H. Rashdall (*BSFS*, III, 1911), 52–3. Richard Rufus was something of an obsession to Bacon, who refers repeatedly to his 'opinio damnabilis' and to its author as 'insanus' and 'stultissimus'. Some of his 'errors' were merely questions of logic (*v.* Little in *Archiv. Francisc. Hist.*, 1926, p. 842); others, however, were in metaphysics (*v.* Sharp, *Franciscan Philosophy*, 158 n. 3.). For more balanced estimates of Richard *v.* *MU* (new ed.), III, 248 n. 5, and Callus, *Introduction of Aristotelian Learning to Oxford*, 35–6.

5 *V.* Little, *The Grey Friars in Oxford*, 143 n. 8.

missions in England and on theological commissions at Paris.[1] In contrast to his predecessors, he was a theologian interested in ethics and matters of practice and history rather than metaphysical speculation. His writings were voluminous; among them were a *Summa de Penitentia*, a number of moral and philosophical treatises, and a collection of Lives of ancient philosophers; all show a wide and varied learning, and the many manuscripts which survive throughout Europe and were repeatedly printed in Italy, France and Germany between 1470 and 1520, are a witness to his great and permanent popularity.

Thomas Docking, a Norfolk friar, who followed John of Wales, was a biblical scholar of repute; like Thomas of York, he had been helped in his student days by Adam Marsh, and, as will be seen later, took part in the controversy at Oxford between the Minorites and the Preachers. He ceased to be regent some time before 1270.[2]

This brief list will at least have shown something of the calibre of the men whom the authorities of the Friars Minor were able to dispose of in the first forty years of the Oxford school. Until recently, little was known of them save the titles of some of their works, which appeared to historians of yesterday to lack all interest and significance; the more sympathetic and discerning treatment of scholars of the present moment has begun to show us the early English Franciscans as men of keen and powerful intelligence, able to seize and to develop the fundamental questions of pure metaphysics with a certainty and a penetration that had not been known in Europe since the days of Parmenides and Aristotle, and to have a part in that great work of adapting the thought of the Philosopher to the needs of Christian speculation which was carried to perfection by St Thomas.

II

Meanwhile, the organization of studies throughout the whole English province had gone steadily forward. In the words of the chronicler, the gift of learning so overflowed in those days that it reached to all the houses of the friars,[3] and the same writer shows us clearly that the task of organization was accomplished thoroughly and almost solely by William of Nottingham, provincial from 1240 to 1254.[4] As has been well noted, studies had no place in the original scheme of a Franciscan house or province, whereas each Dominican convent was from the first and professedly also a school of theology, constitutionally incomplete without

1 For John of Wales, *v*. Little, *Studies*, 174–92; for printed editions of his works *v. ibid.* Appendix IV, pp. 231–2.

2 For Docking *v*. Little in *Essays presented to R. L. Poole: Thomas Docking and his relations to Roger Bacon*, reprinted in *FP*, 98–121.

3 *Eccleston*, 62–3: 'Ita inundavit in provincia Anglicana donum sapientiae,' etc.

4 For the organization of the Franciscan schools *v*., in addition to Dr Little's other work, his paper *The Educational Organization of the Mendicant Friars in England* in *TRHS*, new ser. VIII (1894), 49–70, and his article *The Friars and the Foundation of the Faculty of Theology in the University of Cambridge* in *Mélanges Mandonnet* (Bibliothèque Thomiste, XIV), 389–401, reprinted *FP*, 122–43.

a doctor. It is therefore most probable that the Franciscans, who at Paris, Oxford and elsewhere were moving in the same circles and with the same problems as the black friars, took from them much of the framework of their schools. In any case, William of Nottingham had ample material with which to work, and by the end of his term of office the English province of Friars Minor had a system almost as complete as that of the Dominicans. At Oxford and Cambridge there were schools under regent masters forming a part of the university; in them were assigned students to take up lectureships in the various houses when these should fall vacant, and the figures given by Eccleston show that already more than thirty out of the forty existing friaries possessed qualified teachers. So far as can be gathered from the chronicler, there was in his time no mean between the two universities and the individual houses; later, however, there appear the three grades of school common among the Dominicans: the *studia generalia* of the two university convents, to which students might be sent from all over the province and even from abroad; the 'higher schools' or *studia particularia*, of which one existed, it would seem, in each custody; and the ordinary schools of the individual convents, sufficient to give a general and practical knowledge to the rank and file of the friars who were not capable of benefiting by an advanced course of philosophy or divinity. Indeed, by *c.* 1270 the grey friars in England were a 'student order' as fully, perhaps even more fully, than were the contemporary Dominicans.

III

The name has yet to be mentioned of the most generally celebrated Franciscan thinker of this period in England. Unlike his more sober and perhaps more substantial masters and fellows, Roger Bacon has never, at least since the sixteenth century, been suffered to rest in oblivion, though his celebrity has at times been of the most equivocal nature, while the interest taken in him has been due to the association of his name with mechanical or chemical discoveries which, even if not wholly mythical, form no real part of his true and significant achievement.[1]

---

[1] For Bacon's significance as thinker, *v.* esp. *Roger Bacon: Commemoration Essays*, ed. A. G. Little, 1914. This important collection, in which the contributions of the editor, of Ludwig Baur and of François Picavet are especially valuable, made comparatively little impact upon contemporary studies owing to the accident of its publication a few weeks before the outbreak of the Great War. Dr Little has also treated of Bacon at some length in *Studies in English Franciscan History*, 193 seqq., in *Archiv. Francisc. Hist.* XIX (1926), and in a lecture *Roger Bacon* in *Proceedings of the British Academy* XIV (1928), reprinted in *FP*, 72–97. *V.* also the works referred to in *MU*, III, 242 n. 2, in Ueberweg-Geyer, and the voluminous though far from exhaustive bibliography in de Wulf's *History of Medieval Philosophy*. For a careful analysis of his metaphysical and psychological thought *v.* Sharp, *Franciscan Philosophy at Oxford*, 115–71; for his epistemology *v.* three essays by R. Carton in *Études de philosophie médiévale*, ed. E. Gilson, II, III, V (1924); for his contribution to biblical studies, *v.* B. Smalley, *The Study of the Bible in the Middle Ages*, 241–5. His works have been edited by J. S. Brewer, *Opus Tertium, Opus Minus* (*RS*, 1859), J. H. Bridges, *Opus Majus* (1897–1900), J. H. Rashdall, *Compendium Studii Theologiae* (*BSFS*, III, 1911) and R. Steele and others, *Opera hactenus inedita* (1905–).

Roger Bacon, like almost all the great schoolmen from Alexander of Hales to Duns Scotus, eludes every attempt on the part of posterity to obtain a clear sight of his life's history and of his personal environment and intimate character. Apart from the autobiographical *obiter dicta* which are scattered all too rarely about his chaotic treatises, we know next to nothing of his life; the date of his birth, the date of his master's degree, the date of his reception to the habit and the date of his death are all uncertain. Yet it would be an error to imagine Roger Bacon (or, indeed, Adam Marsh and many other leading scholastics) as a friar of obscure and poor parentage and a narrow horizon bounded by the walls of his convent and the pronouncements of his masters in the schools. He was, it would seem certain, the son of an Anglo-Norman family of note, branches of which were settled in Norfolk, Essex and Dorset; he was possibly a nephew of the celebrated Oxford Dominican, Robert Bacon, and an elder brother held the family estates. He was born probably *c.* 1214, and certainly spent all his life from boyhood in study at Oxford and Paris; as in all likelihood he did not become a friar till *c.* 1255 no specifically Franciscan character is to be sought in his writings,[1] though many date from after his reception and it is certain that he was influenced deeply by Grosseteste and to a less extent by Adam Marsh, Thomas of York and others of the Oxford school. There is no evidence that he ever became a doctor of theology or that he was in priest's orders.

Almost all the forty odd years of his life as a friar were spent abroad, ten of them in retirement owing to frail health accompanied, we may suspect, by some kind of neurotic disability. He had his day of glory, when he was requested to set out his programme for the reform of learning for the benefit of Clement IV, but the pontiff died before he could implement the scheme or reward its author, and Bacon's lack of self-control continued to alienate sympathy. The later decades of the century were electric with theological disputes, with upheavals among the Minors and with tense feeling between Minors and Preachers. The generals of the two orders met in Paris in 1277 to negotiate a truce, and it is probable that Bacon was thrown to the wolves he had infuriated. In any case, he seems to have spent more than ten years (1278–*c.* 1290) in confinement.[2] His death probably occurred in 1292, and at Oxford.

The extraordinary reputation which Bacon acquired as a necromancer within a century of his death, and which endured for nearly three hundred years, his equally undeserved fame as a martyr to the cause of free thought, and his (probably also unmerited) celebrity as the inventor of gunpowder and the telescope, and the prophet (as Leonardo da Vinci in a later age) of

1 *V*. Dr Little's lecture to the British Academy, *supra* p. 213 n. In other words, Bacon's metaphysical doctrine dates from his secular days.

2 In his article on Bacon in *DHG* (1932), Père B. Vandewalle, himself a Franciscan, casts doubt upon the evidence for this imprisonment, viz. the single account in the *Chron. XXIV Gen.* 350, which in its present form dates from the next century. Probably, however, the fact is to be accepted, though the confinement may well have been briefer and more mild than is usually supposed.

many scientific and mechanical discoveries of to-day, have in the past attracted to him the attention, often misplaced and almost always undiscerning, which his countrymen have failed to give to his greater contemporaries in the schools of Oxford and Paris. This is not the place to attempt a survey of his achievement or to assess his mind and character, which would seem to have been vitiated by some deep psychological flaw, and by a restlessness and lack of control that prevented his brilliant talents and intuitive genius from attaining full realization. In his extreme sensitiveness, in his intolerance of the obscurantism, real or supposed, of those in high place, and in the jealous, critical temper which prevented him from receiving what his great rivals in the schools had to give, he has affinities with Abelard, with Lorenzo Valla, and with de Lamennais. Here it is only to the purpose to note that it was as a Franciscan and as the heir of the Franciscan traditions at Oxford that Bacon turned from speculative thought to pursue his encyclopaedic investigations into mathematics, natural science and the conditions of society around him. His work is at once the culmination and the last 'uncontaminated' manifestation of the peculiar characteristics of the school of Oxford—an interest in positive studies, both for their own sake and as forming a basis for theology, a close attention to observation and experiment, and an independence of outlook with regard to all the conventions of contemporary thought.[1] The developments of later ages and the desire which few have been able to resist to compare him with his later namesake, whose position as thinker and reputation as reformer are strangely similar, and almost equally equivocal, have made Roger Bacon an object of interest to many who have known little of, and cared less for, scholastic philosophy and theology. Recent and more careful investigation has suggested that his deepest significance in the history of thought is rather the promise that his work holds, and the possibility that had other and more sober thinkers followed in his footsteps medieval philosophy might have retained that contact with the actual, the concrete and the individual which alone can keep the speculations of the pure reason living and fruitful, and might in consequence have avoided the decay that took place when thought came to be increasingly isolated from life and from the changing conditions of society.

Roger Bacon had without doubt a mind of singular intuitive genius and rare critical power. He seized with precision the basic faults in the foundation of the later scholastic method which did in the event bring about a fossilization. He deplored the divorce of pure thought from life and experience, the insecurity of the positive basis of uncritical texts, jealous tradition and bookish science on which it rested, and the neglect of the ancient heritage of form and beauty.[2] Though he himself had few or

---

1 Various departments of Bacon's thought have been analysed, and important revisions made, by D. E. Sharp, R. Carton (v. supra p. 213 n.) and others; v. also W. Singer, *The Alchemical Writings of Roger Bacon* in *Speculum* (1931), 345–91, and Prof. L. Thorndike in *American Historical Review*, XXI (1916), 237–257.

2 For these, v. Brewer, introd. to *Opera*, lvi–lxviii.

no gifts as an artist in words, and was in no sense a literary or aesthetic humanist, he could pass a true judgement on the arts, and his criticisms of contemporary tendencies in music and his regret at the abandonment of classical prosody and metre by hymn-writers of his time are just, and have been echoed by modern judges. Moreover, when all legends have been excluded, there are still in his writings a number of remarkable anticipations of the discoveries of the Italian renaissance, and also of the general temper of mind of the humanists of the fifteenth century. It has even been said that Bacon stood for a religious culture, embracing science, philosophy and theology, which might have preserved the breadth and unity of intellectual life within the Church, and rendered the causes of the Reformation inoperative.[1] Such an opinion is unquestionably at once an exaggeration and an undue simplification. One powerful bond of cultural union had already disappeared before Bacon's birth with the decay of the classical and literary humanism of the century between 1050 and 1150. But beyond this, when all acknowledgement has been made of Bacon's powers, as also of his fundamental orthodoxy and sense of tradition, it must be confessed that he moves altogether on a lower plane, and breathes another atmosphere from that of the greatest scholastics.[2] *Non omnia possumus omnes*, and it may be that Bonaventure, Albert and Thomas Aquinas made little account of some of the mental activities essential to a full human culture; but they, and especially the great Dominicans, had a sense of the majesty and reality of the body of metaphysical truth which is quite absent from Bacon; they were a summit of attainment; they were able with luminous clarity to harmonize in due subordination human truth with divine, and to see all things in a lucid order in which nature and grace, knowledge and love, action and contemplation filled up the rich whole of man's life.

Of this there is nothing in Bacon, and he had no group of disciples, and neither his philosophical nor his scientific opinions had any influence on the generation that immediately followed him at Paris though later masters of the Franciscan school at Oxford drew inspiration from him. In the history of the religious orders of England his significance lies chiefly in the evidence his career and writings give of the wide gulf that separated the purely 'student' Friar Minor from the first brethren of Francis of Assisi fifty years before.[3]

1 Thus F. Picavet in an article in the *Revue des Deux Mondes* for 1 June, 1914, pp. 643–75, wrote (p. 644) of Bacon as: 'l'un des créateurs de la direction théologique qui aurait rendu la Réforme inutile et maintenu l'union étroite de la science, de la philosophie et de la religion.'

2 There is a personal, shallow quality in many of Bacon's observations such as is conspicuously absent from the judgements of St Thomas, e.g. his assertion that 'twenty years ago all philosophers held' the plurality of forms, and that 'this is still the view of all the English, who are and have been distinguished among others for their learning'. *V*. Bacon's *Communia Naturalium* in *Opera hactenus inedita*, ed. Steele, cited by Little in his Academy Lecture, pp. 281–3.

3 The most reliable authority for the chronology of Bacon's life and work is now [1955] Fr T. Crowley's *Roger Bacon*. His account of Bacon's later thought, and that of Dr Easton Stewart of his scientific outlook in *Roger Bacon* (Oxford, 1952) are stimulating, but open to criticism on certain points.

CHAPTER XIX

DOCTRINAL AND MORAL CONTROVERSIES: KILWARDBY AND PECHAM

I

The Friars Minor and Preachers, the double birth of a single hour, had at first taken paths that did not cross, and the mutual affection and admiration of Francis and Dominic had been shared by their first disciples. As we have seen, the Preachers at London and Oxford gave ready hospitality to the first Minors, and Grosseteste laid it down as a principle that the establishment of both orders in a city drew down a double blessing. When, however, each had adopted from the other an essential element in its life— when the Dominicans had become mendicants and the Franciscans students —the similarity of occupation and interests foreboded rivalry between Jacob and Esau, and significant records appear in the acts of general chapter of the Preachers enjoining mutual charity and endeavouring to forestall friction by submitting cases of difference to the judgement of arbitrators of the other habit.[1] Community of interest, indeed, while it ultimately led to collision was also a cause of delaying rivalries, for the violent attacks on the mendicants in France closed the ranks of the friars, and all alike were shielded by the apologetics of St Bonaventure and St Thomas. Yet even thus early a bitter opponent could liken the alliance to that of Pilate and Herod, and when the immediate danger to both lessened, disputes broke out between the two on those points precisely in which each had imitated the other. The Preachers challenged the claim of the Minors to be alone in imitating the poverty of Christ, and questioned both the theory and practice of their ideal, while the Minors resented the claim to a monopoly in truth and its presentation claimed by the Preachers, asserting themselves to be as learned and as authorized as their rivals, and endeavoured to vindicate for themselves the possession of the authentic science of the saints.

In England, as abroad, the latter decades of the thirteenth century witnessed a number of such controversies upon points of doctrine or asceticism, and the history of these disputes is so intimately linked with the life's history of two distinguished friars, each the first and last of his habit to hold the primatial office in England, that it will be well to sketch in outline the careers of the two before considering the issues with which they were occupied.

---

1 *Monumenta Ordinis Fratrum Praedicatorum Historica*, III. *Acta Capitulorum Generalium*, ed. B. M. Reichert, vol. I [5], 1234; [9] 1236.

II

Robert Kilwardby and John Pecham, whose lives followed courses so strictly parallel and whose outlook was so characteristic of their epoch and of their profession, seemed destined by a kind of fatality to cross each other's paths again and again and to be involved in the same controversies, now united against the same opponent, now pitted one against the other. Each belonged to what may be called the third generation of their order. The history of great religious movements has repeatedly followed a particular rhythm. At the beginning, the founder, moving on a plane purely spiritual, communicates his ideals and something of his spirit to his followers, who comprehend his teaching and live in its strength. To this succeeds a generation of which the leaders, while true in the main to the spirit of the founder and themselves often examples of true sanctity, find the need of an elaborate framework, legal and theoretical, and put out, on a less intense note, a programme and defence of their institute. To them in turn succeeds a generation of men of influence, at once more numerous and more mediocre, who echo the phrases of their predecessors without a full appreciation of their depth, and who press the claims and the interests of the body to which they belong with an eagerness that at times lapses into the violence and bitterness of *esprit de corps*. Thus to Francis and Dominic and the simple beginnings had succeeded the more sophisticated age of Adam Marsh and Haymo, Humbert of the Romans and St Raymund of Penaforte; then had come the rivalries and attacks, at first from the seculars upon the mendicants in general, and then in the form of friction between the two great orders themselves. To this period belong the careers of Kilwardby and Pecham.

Born perhaps *c.* 1210, Robert Kilwardby[1] studied arts and taught at Paris before taking the Dominican habit; he became a friar *c.* 1240, and studied theology at Oxford under Robert Bacon and Richard Fishacre. These two had, as regent masters, laid the foundations of a flourishing school.[2] Of this, external evidence is provided by the decree of the general chapter of 1247 ordering the erection of a *studium generale* in the English

---

1 The life of Kilwardby, like that of almost all the great scholastics, is known to us only in skeleton; for the events, *v.* art. by T. F. Tout in *DNB*, and *Studies in the Life of Robert Kilwardby*, O.P. by E. M. F. Sommer-Seckendorff. The latter is a careful and exhaustive piece of work, especially valuable as a book of reference; the reader unacquainted with its subject will perhaps note a certain lack of emphasis and clarity, especially in the section dealing with Kilwardby as a thinker. Other articles touching upon him will be mentioned below.

2 Cf. the judgement of Matthew Paris, *ChM*, v, 16, when recording their death: 'quibus non erant majores, immo nec pares, ut creditur, viventes in theologia et aliis scientiis...qui egregie plurimis annis in eadem facultate legerunt et populis gloriose praedicaverunt verbum Domini.' Cf. also the notice of Nicholas Trivet, *Annales*, ed. Hog, 228–9, *s.a.* 1240. For what is known of Fishacre and his teaching, *v.* F. Pelster, *Das Leben und die Schriften des Oxforder Dominikanerlehrers Richard Fishacre*, in *ZfkT* 54 (1930), 518–53, and literature cited in *MU*, III, 251.

province; but before this could be accomplished both Bacon and Fishacre died, and although the decree was repeated in 1248 nothing was done.[1] In view of later events it is natural to put much of the responsibility for this delay upon Simon of Hinton, Fishacre's successor as regent at Oxford, who probably occupied the chair until his election as provincial in 1254, for when in office he would seem to have opposed the reception of students from abroad at Oxford. In this he was not alone, but was supported by a number of the *diffinitores* of his provincial chapter; unfortunately, we are given no hint as to whether this opposition was due merely to fear of financial loss, or whether national feeling or even dislike of the policy of development in the studies of the order were motives. In any case, Humbert of the Romans, a strenuous advocate of intensive studies, succeeded as Master at the important chapter of 1261 in deposing, penancing and banishing the English provincial and in penancing and rendering ineligible for the future his *diffinitores*, while constituting at Oxford a *studium generale* which might not be removed without leave of general chapter.[2] Simon's successor in the provincialate was Kilwardby, at the time regent at Oxford, and his election at such a moment may be taken as evidence that he stood for a reversal of his predecessor's policy. His provincialate was marked by energy, at least in external affairs, and some eleven new friaries were founded during his decade of office.[3] It was also distinguished by his controversies within and without his own order. Of one of these, that on the question of poverty with Pecham, something will be said later. Another, in which Kilwardby found himself at variance with no less a person than Thomas Aquinas, was the first occasion on which the English Dominican stood forward as champion of the traditional philosophy of the schools, as against the new Aristotelianism of Albert and his pupil.

John of Vercelli, master general of the Preachers, had in the course of his visitations in north Italy in 1270 collected a number of philosophical propositions of doubtful orthodoxy.[4] Before these should be discussed in general chapter he wished to obtain the best available theological opinion on them, and therefore submitted them to St Thomas and Kilwardby. St Thomas, who had been requested to answer immediately in the midst of other work, replied briefly, treating most of the questions as unimportant philosophical speculations which might safely be left to the test of reasoned debate and trial. Kilwardby, who had clearly seen the other's answers, took the points more seriously, even ponderously, and adopted at times a position directly contrary to St Thomas, not without sharpness. In the

---

1 *MOPH*, III, *Act. Cap. Gen.* 1 [38], 1247; [41], 1248.

2 *Ibid.* [110], 1261; [111]: 'Diffinitores vero qui non assenserunt ut fratres studentes aliarum provinciarum reponerentur Oxonie suspendi mus usque ad vii annos ab officio diffinicionis,' etc.

3 *V.* Sommer-Seckendorff, *Studies in the Life of Robert Kilwardby*, 46.

4 For this *v.* esp. M. D. Chenu, O.P., *Les Réponses de S. Thomas et de Kilwardby à l consultation de Jean de Verceil*, in *Mélanges Mandonnet* (Bibliothèque Thomiste, XIII), 193' 191–222.

sequel, the chapter at Montpellier in 1271 accepted the answers of Aquinas, and it can no longer be maintained that the fathers honoured Kilwardby by referring to him publicly in his presence as *magnus magister in theologia*.[1] The incident, of no great importance in itself, is, however, significant as showing that the English provincial was regarded as one of the most eminent members of the order.

This reputation, together, perhaps, with the favour in which Kilwardby stood at the court of Henry III, led to his appointment as archbishop of Canterbury by Gregory X after the disputed election of 1270–2. He received the papal notification in October of the latter year, and was consecrated in the following February. Of his general activities as primate, something has been said in another chapter; his incursions into the theological field will be discussed in the course of a few pages.

The career of John Pecham had, during the same decades, been following similar lines.[2] Born *c.* 1220 he appears first as a young man of promise and tutor to the son of Henry d'Angers in a letter of Adam Marsh, whose protégé he was; this was probably before he became a friar. He probably studied at Oxford some time before 1250 and subsequently also at Paris, where he made the acquaintance of St Bonaventure and his doctrines, though it is not certain that the relationship was that of master and pupil. Becoming regent at Paris *c.* 1269–71 he knew well, and came into collision with, Thomas Aquinas, the Dominican regent master during these years; he returned as regent to Oxford *c.* 1272 and in *c.* 1276 became minister provincial. From this office he was called, in 1276 or 1277, to be lector in theology at the papal court. He thus held a position in his own order similar in all respects to Kilwardby's among the Dominicans, and when the latter was recalled to Rome, and disputes again arose over the election of a successor, it was natural that the pope should turn to Pecham. His energy in visiting the religious houses of the Canterbury province has already been noted; his disciplinary action in matters of theology will be discussed later.

1 *MOPH*, III, *Act. Cap. Gen.* I [156]. It has been shown by J. Destrez, *Robert Kilwardby, O.P.*, '*magnus magister in theologia*' (*Bulletin Thomiste*, III, 1933, 191–3) that the words hitherto taken as a capitular eulogium of Kilwardby are a gloss added to one manuscript in or after 1279.

2 For Pecham *v.* art. by C. L. Kingsford in *DNB* and the very full art. by Père Teetaert, O.S.F.C. in *DTC*; some of the judgements of the latter are, however, to be received with caution. Pecham's writings are also discussed by C. L. Kingsford, A. G. Little and F. Tocco in *Fratris Johannis Pecham Tractatus Tres de Paupertate* (*BSFS*, II); where there is a bibliography; his thought is analysed by D. E. Sharp, *Franciscan Philosophy*, 175–207, who may perhaps be thought to attribute too much significance to him. Reference may also be made to an article by the present writer, *Some aspects of the career of Archbishop Pecham*, in *EHR*, LVII (January and April 1942), henceforward referred to as *Pecham* by page number. Miss D. L. Douie has in hand a more thorough study.

III

The controversy between the mendicants and seculars on the Continent was revived in the years following 1265, when William of St Amour sent to Clement IV his treatise *De antichristo et ejusdem ministris* and Gerard of Abbeville, his supporter, published a reply to the Minorite work *Manus quae contra omnipotentem erigitur*. Gerard's challenge received replies from both Bonaventure and Thomas Aquinas, and Pecham also contributed to the literature of the dispute with his poem *Defensio fratrum mendicantium* and his prose *Tractatus pauperis*, written *c*. 1269 against an attack which cannot now be identified.[1] The verses are not lacking in a certain vigour, though they have no poetic value; the treatise has no great worth either as literature or as spiritual doctrine, and cannot be ranked with the writings of the two saints; it is a formal, dialectical reply which takes the arguments of the adversary point by point; it would doubtless satisfy the writer's colleagues, but can certainly have neither convinced nor attracted an opponent. That Pecham, however, should have taken upon himself the task of replying for the Minors shows that his reputation stood high in the order.

Meanwhile disputes had broken out in England between the two bodies of friars regarding the comparative excellence of their theory and practice of poverty. Originally, as has been seen, the call of Francis to absolute and naked poverty, reinforced by his own consecrated example and informed as it was by an exalted and chivalrous enthusiasm, exercised an unrivalled appeal. In time, however, when the Minors had sensibly departed as a body from their founder's ideal, and were receiving papal privileges, solicited or not, which bore at least the appearance of allowing them to evade the consequences of their profession, the Preachers found themselves in a more advantageous position. Neither their rule nor their practice of mendicancy committed them to the Franciscan position which set the essence of poverty in the absence of material things and which forbade physical contact with money. They were therefore able to adopt without uneasiness or apparent hypocrisy the doctrine of spiritual poverty elaborated by St Thomas, and to take their stand on the traditional canon law of the Church interpreted strictly indeed, but not mystically. This position, while lacking the charm of a devotion to the Lady Poverty, gave them a defence no less secure, if more sober, than that of the Minors. Yet the Franciscan claim to utter poverty, supported as it still was by a real simplicity of life, was clearly an attractive force to friends and recruits; the Preachers were therefore impelled to throw the searchlight of their keen logic over the

---

1 For a critical text of these with historical introductions, *v. Fratris Johannis Pecham Tractatus Tres de Paupertate*, ed. C. L. Kingsford, A. G. Little and F. Tocco (*BSFS*, II, Aberdeen, 1910). Bonaventure's treatise was his *Contra adversarium perfectionis christianae*; that of Aquinas his *De perfectione vitae spiritualis*. Cf. also P. Glorieux, *Les polémiques 'Contra Geraldinos'* in *Recherches de théologie ancienne et médiévale*, VI (1934), 5–41 and VII (1935), 129–55.

ideal and observance of their rivals, and its beams threw into high relief the 'third person' or 'spiritual friend' of the Minors, who acted as depositary of all gifts of money and who might well seem in practice to be little better than a banker.

An indication of the uneasiness of the Minors on this point of the *interposita persona* is provided by a curious incident that occurred at Oxford in the spring of 1269.[1] It was not the first occasion of friction between the two orders in the city; already the Minors had found it more than once advisable to remove lecturers out of deference to the suscepti-bilities of the Preachers.[2] Rivalry between the two bodies was keen, and it was clearly the fashion to institute comparisons of all kinds between them in the set form of the schools. In these, the Preachers inevitably suffered on the point of poverty, and it was a temptation for them to reply by passing from the plane of theory to that of apparent facts, and to assert that in practice the Minors enjoyed all the benefits of gifts of money, and that their 'third person' was little more than a legal fiction.[3]

The Oxford dispute took its rise from some words uttered in a moment of heat by one of the Dominicans, friar Solomon by name, who, in the course of a visit of business to the Minors, connected, it may well be supposed, with some transaction in which the Franciscans had not been the losers, exclaimed that the Minors received money just as much as the Preachers, adding that he was a plain man and no scholar, but would stand to his words in face of the pope himself;[4] the Franciscans therefore were unfaithful to their vows. Another Preacher still further embittered the quarrel a day or two later by asserting that he had never found two Minors who agreed in the explanation they gave of their 'third person'.[5] The negotiations that followed lasted some three months; they were conducted by deputations from the convents concerned who waited upon each other and after a formal crossing of swords in set logical form proceeded to make their demands or counter allegations. The chronicler records a whole series of such meetings, which have more than a touch of the ludicrous in their solemnity and might well seem puerile were it not remembered that both parties consisted of men whose life was spent in a society that breathed an atmosphere of disputation by syllogism, and who would have been as profoundly distressed to admit a flaw in their premises as would a Scots Lord Justice-Clerk of the eighteenth century to acknowledge

1 The contemporary account by an Oxford Franciscan is printed by A. G. Little in *The Grey Friars in Oxford*, Appendix C, 320-35.

2 *Ibid.* 329. At this date there can scarcely have been any question of attacks on Thomist doctrine by the Minors.

3 *Ibid.* 323: 'Veniunt ad nos [*sc.* the Preachers] diversi seculares et religiosi compara-cionem inter statum et statum facientes, statum vestrum extollentes, et nostrum in hoc deprimentes, quod nos pecuniam recipimus, vos autem non recipitis.... Nos modo in... status nostri exaltacionem, dicimus vos hoc facere per interpositas personas quod nos facimus in propriis personis.'

4 *Ibid.* 321: 'Ego non sum magnus clericus nec homo magne litterature, et tamen constanter hec affirmo et in presencia pape, si necesse fuerit, affirmabo.'

5 *Ibid.* 323.

ignorance on a point of law. The circle of those affected gradually widened as the matter became more public; the offer of the Preachers to impose a penance on friar Solomon for the past and perpetual silence for the future was rejected by the Minors, who demanded a formal retractation or removal. Thomas Docking, the well-known theologian, became spokesman for the Franciscans; for the Dominicans, Kilwardby as provincial refused for some time either to force Solomon to speak against his conscience or to remove him from Oxford, and the services of the Chancellor and other distinguished masters were enlisted by the Preachers. These, however, were eventually won over by the legal arguments of the Minors and the matter was ultimately settled by Solomon's formal statement that he had had no thought of implying by his words what in fact he had clearly intended to say.[1] In the legal and logical sphere, no doubt, the Minors had a strong case, for they had on their side the precise statement of Gregory IX, together with the pope's declaration that he knew the mind of Francis.[2] Against this reef of law and authority the *ad hominem* arguments of the Preachers, cogent as they were to the ears of the plain man, were doomed to make shipwreck, for the Franciscans could either deny their allegations outright or reply that the transgressions of individuals could not affect the canonical position of the order as a whole.

It was probably shortly after this incident that Kilwardby as provincial felt called upon to address the novices of his province in a short letter in which he put out the claims of their order to veneration.[3] Like all Kilwardby's writings, it is a careful, painstaking piece of argument: his theme is that the Preachers alone have by profession, whatever others may say, the glory of following the apostolic life of preaching; their poverty also is truly apostolic, and if others choose to make prouder claims for themselves the Dominicans may well let them abound in their own sense, remembering that in the last resort it is not material want, but poverty of spirit, that counts before God. In all this Kilwardby shows himself a follower of Humbert, though in his exposition of interior poverty he exactly anticipates (if, indeed, he is not following) the line taken by St Thomas in the *Summa*; the undertone of apologetic is perceptible throughout, but the language is measured and impersonal, and cannot be called provocative. The letter was perhaps intended to have readers outside the Dominican novitiate; in any case it became public property, and Pecham countered with a reply of some warmth, in which he quoted Kilwardby line by line and dealt with each point at length. His tone,

---

1 *The Grey Friars*, 335.

2 *Ibid.* 324: 'Nos habemus regulam qua utimur secundum declaracionem domini pape qui eam juxta mentem beati francisci declaravit.'

3 The letter is known only from Pecham's full, if not entire, quotation in his treatise *contra Kilwardby* (ed. F. Tocco in *Tractatus Tres*, 121–47). Kilwardby's disclaimer of any intention to challenge the Franciscan theory (136: 'contentionibus inservire nolumus nec debemus; unde bene concedimus talem eorum professionem esse qualem asserunt', etc.) and Pecham's allusion to the awkward case of pecuniary legacies (139: 'obicies forte de testamentis') appear to echo, rather than to anticipate, the Oxford dispute.

unlike that of his opponent, is personal and petulant; he takes up the two questions of preaching and poverty as a controversialist. Whereas the Rule of St Augustine, followed by the Dominicans, says nothing about preaching, that of St Francis expressly enjoins it; it was divinely revealed as a duty to the founder and imposed on the Minors by Popes Innocent, Honorius and Gregory; there is therefore no question of their having imitated the Dominicans, and if comparisons must be instituted the Friars Minor can show a more illustrious company of doctors than the Preachers.[1] As regards poverty, its perfection is to be found only among the Minors, who alone follow Christ perfectly in having neither money nor possessions of any kind. Pecham then proceeds to answer the charges brought against Franciscan observance and ends with a prayer that Kilwardby may be given the spirit of compunction. The whole composition, it must be said, was calculated to exacerbate, rather than to assuage, any soreness of feeling that existed, but Pecham continued to regard his order as the aggrieved party, and ten years later wrote of Kilwardby's harsh and inconsiderate action.[2]

IV

The period of office of each of the mendicant archbishops of Canterbury was marked by disciplinary action on a question of theological teaching. In order, therefore, to grasp the significance of the dispute in which both Kilwardby and Pecham became involved, it is necessary to review briefly the main lines of development in the schools during their years of academic life.[3]

Until the sixth decade of the thirteenth century, the philosophical and theological outlook of the schools of both orders of friars had been identical. Each had originally gone to Paris and Oxford to receive, not to give, and both had found recruits among the most distinguished masters. The traditional discipline of the schools, therefore, was their common possession. This was in its main outline Augustinian, or what was conceived to be such, but there was no complete philosophical synthesis, no system of thought logically and coherently ordered, and as an ever greater proportion of the Aristotelian *corpus* and of the works of his Arabian and Jewish commentators were subjected to scrutiny at Paris and Oxford,[4] it became the task of every gifted theologian to construct a whole out of the materials

---

1 Pecham, *contra Kilwardby*, 128: 'Quibus nulli equales tuum ordinem sunt ingressi', etc.

2 *Registrum Epistolarum*, ed. Martin, I, 118 (a letter of 11 April 1280, to the Dominican prior of Oxford): 'Frequenter stupui qualiter de tam benigno, tam sapienti pastoris domicilio potuit tanta crudelitas tantaque inconsideratio provenire', etc.

3 What follows is based on the *Pecham* articles in *EHR*, with the kind permission of the editors and publishers.

4 For a summary of the process of translation *v.* the valuable note of the editors in *MU*, I, 360–2. The account of the intellectual revolution of the thirteenth century given by Mandonnet in *Siger de Brabant et l'Averroïsme latin* (1 ed. Fribourg, 1899) has not been superseded; it needs, however, to be supplemented both by the parallel studies of F. Ehrle, S.J. (later Cardinal), and others referred to below, and more particularly by the

to hand. For several decades, however, all such work was eclectic; all were engaged in forging a system of thought from an alloy in which were elements from Plato and neo-Platonism, from Augustine, from Aristotle, and from his Arabian and Jewish commentators. In all this there was no divergence at Oxford between the series of Franciscan masters who followed Grosseteste, and the Preachers such as Robert Bacon and Fishacre.[1]

At Paris, on the other hand, the currents of thought were by c. 1250 beginning to flow along three divergent channels. The Franciscan school, which at first had followed Alexander of Hales and now had in Bonaventure a doctor of first rank who gave the Minors a coherent body of teaching, tended to make little use of the new Aristotle, to distrust all who attempted to follow him implicitly, and to accept as a standard what they took to be the teaching of Augustine, but which was in fact a complex fabric made up of the elements mentioned above. The Franciscan school at Paris was therefore somewhat freer from Aristotelian doctrines than was that of Oxford.

At the other extreme, a group of masters of arts led by Siger of Brabant and Boethius of Dacia not only adopted the peripatetic system *en bloc*, but accepted it and interpreted it as handed down, with additions, by Averroes. These commentators made of the silences and obscurities of Aristotle an occasion for additions to his teaching which ran counter to fundamental Christian doctrine on such points as the creation of the world, the separate existence of each human soul during life and after death, and the personal freedom and responsibility of the individual. To avoid, or at least to evade, the consequences of holding such opinions, Siger and his friends had recourse to the expedient of putting them out as the teaching of Aristotle or of natural philosophy, while at the same time doing verbal homage to revealed truth.[2]

---

results of the investigation of Oxford theology by A. G. Little, D. E. Sharp, F. Pelster, S.J., and D. Callus, all of which show the absorption and eclectic use (as opposed to the exclusive adoption) of Aristotle by theologians to have been both earlier and more general than is suggested by Mandonnet. The literature of the subject is too vast to be mentioned here; a selection may be seen in M. de Wulf, *History of Medieval Philosophy*, and in Gilson, *Philosophie du M. Age* (2 ed.), 377–90.

1 The convenient label *Augustinismus* has been currently applied to the traditionalists largely owing to its use by Ehrle; *v. Der Augustinismus und der Aristotelismus in der Scholastik gegen Ende des* 13. *Jahrhunderts*, in *ALKG*, v (1889), 603–35, and *L'Agostinismo e l'Aristotelismo nella Scolastica del secolo XIII* (*Xenia Thomistica*, III (1925), 517–88), and the writings of Mandonnet, Pelster, and others. As a label it is useful, and perhaps indispensable, but Ehrle himself was the first to recognize that Augustinism contained many elements not to be found in the writings of St Augustine. Research in the present century has shown clearly: (a) that much of what medieval theologians claimed as the thought of Augustine came in fact from neo-Platonist, Jewish and Arab sources, and (b) that even among the Augustinians the penetration of Aristotle was considerable. For a brief analysis of 'Augustinian' doctrine *v.* M. de Wulf, *History of Medieval Philosophy*, 321; for a discussion of particular points the same writer's *Le traité 'de unitate formae' de Gilles de Lessines* (*Les Philosophes Belges*, I, Louvain, 1901), pp. 16–32.

2 *V.* Mandonnet, *Siger de Brabant*, Gilson, *PhMA*, 550–68, and F. Van Steenberghen, *Siger de Brabant d'après ses œuvres inédites*, in *Les Philosophes Belges*, XII–XIII.

Midway between these two schools in their attitude to the philosopher stood Albert the Great and his pupil Thomas of Aquinum. Of these Albert, by means of his encyclopaedic commentaries, made use of the whole *corpus* of Aristotle as a basis for science and philosophy, without treating his doctrine as the sole foundation of metaphysical truth. St Thomas, as is well known, went further, and adopted the peripatetic teaching in all its main lines as the sole rational basis in his construction of a great synthesis embracing all truth, rational and revealed; nevertheless, he reserved to himself the freedom of interpreting Aristotle in a Christian sense, of supplying what was wanting in his system, and even of contradicting what appeared to be false. As all recognize, no small part of the strength and beauty of the Thomist synthesis comes from the intimate connection between all the parts, and this unity is achieved largely by the adoption of a small number of fundamental theses from which all the rest flow as necessary conclusions, and which reappear as guiding lights to illustrate objects in appearance the most diverse. More than one of these theses was pure Aristotle and therefore came as a novelty, and even as a scandal, to the current 'Augustinian' opinions; others, which gave a Christian, or at least a neutral interpretation to Aristotle, were opposed as false by the Paris Averroists. Thomism, therefore, in the first decade of its publication, came under fire from both flanks; it was attacked at once by the traditionalist theologians—for the most part Friars Minor—and by the secular, quasi-heretical masters of arts at Paris. St Thomas, indeed, found his most inveterate opponents among the mendicants, many of whom believed, or allowed themselves to be persuaded, that his system was closely allied to that of the Averroists, if indeed it were not the fountainhead of Siger's errors, and thus subversive of faith and morals.[1] For Thomism could not be ignored; the twofold assumption of Aquinas, that a true and complete system of thought could be constructed, and that the essential elements for this were to be found in the writings of Aristotle, made his teaching something new and challenging in the intellectual world.

Among those who took up the challenge from the start was Pecham, and the precise point at issue between himself and Aquinas would seem to have been what came to be known as the thesis of the plurality of forms in man—a question that was to haunt the archbishop for the rest of his life.[2]

The controversy was not a new one. In the past, it had been common in the schools to regard the body and soul as two independent entities: this view was derived immediately from Augustine and remotely from Plato, and found expression in such comparisons as that of the soul and body to

---

1 As Mandonnet wrote (*Siger de Brabant.* p. 177): 'Les augustiniens réputent erreur dans le Péripatétisme ce que l'école albertino-thomiste considère comme des théories scientifiques rigoureusement établies.' Some of these were common to both Aquinas and Siger.

2 The best account of the philosophical issue at stake is that of M. de Wulf in *Giles de Lessines*; cf. also, G. Théry, O.P., *L'Augustinisme médiéval et le problème de l'unité de la forme substantielle* (Acta Hebdom. aug.–thomisticae), Rome, 1931, pp. 140–200. For numerous references to Pecham's opinions, see Sharp, *op. cit.*, especially pp. 186–92.

a rider and his horse, or to a pilot and the ship he steers. Such a theory, while fully accounting for the struggle between the lower and higher self, had grave moral and theological drawbacks, and disappeared with the introduction of the full Aristotelian doctrine of matter and form as the metaphysical components of all being; this was partially adopted, so far as words went, by all schools, but the concept of a single substantial form for each being was obscured by the lack of a clear distinction between 'substantial' and 'accidental' forms, which opened the door to the admission of an indefinite number of forms of equal metaphysical significance. Similarly, the application of the doctrine to man, also made by Aristotle, by which the intellective soul was regarded as the substantial form of the body, received insufficient attention. Jewish philosophy had left a legacy in its doctrine that spiritual substances were composed of 'matter' and 'form', while to the body, considered apart from the soul, a *forma corporeitatis* was attributed. In opposition to such views St Thomas set his thesis, which developed and clarified that of Aristotle, that the soul, as pure form, actualizes the body as its matter from the first moment of its creation.[1]

This proposition gave a clear, but unfamiliar, answer to the problem with which all the keenest minds of Europe had been wrestling; to accept it, therefore, was in the case of mature men to abandon the habits of thought of a lifetime. Furthermore, the philosophical postulate from which it is an immediate deduction is one of the essential half-dozen foundation stones upon which the whole Thomist fabric rests.[2] It was not to be expected that those who looked upon the new school as fundamentally unsound would let such an important thesis pass unchallenged. Moreover, it might well be thought that the peripatetic concept of the soul was inadequate: it is merely a substantial form, an intellective principle; it is something, to all appearances, very different from man's soul as seen by Christ in the gospels, or even by Plato. Aristotle, indeed, was concerned little or not at all with the separate or endless existence of the soul. The first opponents of Aristotelianism felt this dimly, and it has remained ever since a great practical difficulty, while for more shallow minds the issue was confused and shifted from the realm of pure thought to that of dogmatic theology by the supposed conflict of the new doctrine with a whole mass of religious facts and truths, among which the resurrection of the body and

1 It has recently been shown that the pluralist theory was not so universally held as hitherto asserted. As early as *c.* 1230 John Blund was teaching the pure Aristotelian doctrine at Oxford (*v.* D. Callus, *Proc. Brit. Acad.* XXIV (1944), 26. See also Dom O. Lottin, O.S.B., *La pluralité des formes substantielles avant S. Thomas d'Aquin. Quelques documents nouveaux,* in *Revue Néoscolastique de Philosophie,* XXXIV (1932), 449–75; the same writer's *Psychologie et Morale aux XIIᵉ et XIIIᵉ siècles*; and D. Callus, O.P., *Two Early Oxford Masters on the Problem of Plurality of Forms. Adam of Buckfield and Richard Rufus of Cornwall* (*ibid.* XLII (1939), 411–45). Hence Pecham's assertion that St Thomas originated the theory of unity of form, or that he learnt it from the Averroists, is still more against the evidence of fact than was thought.

2 Cf. *Summa Theologica,* I, Q. lxxvi, art. 3, *corp. art.*: 'Nihil enim est simpliciter unum nisi per formam unam, per quam habet res esse; ab eodem enim habet res quod sit ens et quod sit una.'

the veneration of relics were only the chief.[1] Once the question had been transferred to this level, the strain of following high metaphysical reasoning was avoided, heresy hunters could pick up the scent, and purely personal considerations were allowed entry.

What has been said may help to explain the important place which the question of the unity of form came to hold in Pecham's mind, and the heat which it generated there. When St Thomas proclaimed his doctrine publicly at Paris, Pecham, like his master Bonaventure, certainly opposed him strenuously, maintaining, it would seem, that the Preacher had learnt it from the Averroists.[2] Shortly after, the authorities endeavoured to silence Aquinas as a teacher of error. Pecham, writing fifteen years later, when St Thomas had been dead for more than a decade, and when the archbishop was concerned to disclaim any private hostility, states that he defended his opponent so far as was consistent with the service of truth. The circumstances are not clear, but according to Pecham himself it was only when Aquinas submitted his teaching to the masters of Paris for judgement that he stood forward to defend him from extreme measures.[3]

Almost immediately afterwards, on 10 December 1270, the bishop of Paris, Étienne Tempier, condemned a number of Averroist propositions. No Thomist thesis was included in the list, either explicitly or by implication, but it is probable that the doctrines of St Thomas on the unity of form in man and the simplicity of purely spiritual beings came near to being stigmatized.[4] In the following year the great Preacher left Paris, never to return, and a quarrel broke out between the university and Tempier which interrupted studies for a number of years.

Meanwhile, Pecham had returned to England as regent master at Oxford, and at about the same time Kilwardby, the prior provincial of the Preachers, was appointed by the pope to the see of Canterbury. His period of rule lasted for five years only, but it was marked both by energetic disciplinary action and by an important decision on a speculative point. Early in 1277 Pope John XXI ordered Bishop Tempier to make a doctrinal enquiry as to the teaching of Paris university, and the bishop in consequence condemned a long list of propositions; most of these were Averroist, but a number of key Thomist theses were explicitly proscribed.[5] Among these the unity of form did not figure, though it was closely connected with more than one of the doctrines condemned.

The omission was shortly made good elsewhere. Ten days after

1 It was argued that if the body apart from the soul had no 'form', then at death it ceased absolutely to be A's body or B's; this, of course, raised particular difficulties with regard to the dead body of Christ and the Resurrection.

2 Pecham, *Reg. Epp.* III, 842: 'Nec eam [*sc.* unitatem formarum] credimus a religiosis personis sed saecularibus quibusdam duxisse originem.' This is a clear reference to Siger.

3 Pecham, *Reg. Epp.* III, 866.

4 Cf. M. de Wulf, *Giles de Lessines*, introd. p. 64. Giles wrote to this effect to Albert the Great; his letter was edited by Mandonnet in *Siger de Brabant*.

5 For a discussion see Mandonnet, *Siger de Brabant*, 248.

Tempier's decree, and almost certainly through collusive action, if not also in response to a monition from Rome, Archbishop Kilwardby 'visited' the University of Oxford. The eminent theologian of the old way of thinking had doubtless followed with interest the development of the Preachers' school there, of which he had been regent before becoming prior provincial, and he cannot have been unaware of the gradual infiltration of Thomist opinions among the younger friars, one of whom, Richard Knapwell, had recently signalized his conversion from the traditional teaching to the new Aristotelianism, above all on the point of the unity of form in man.[1] This thesis, therefore, along with other important Thomist doctrines, was specifically condemned by Kilwardby.

The action, however, proved to be the archbishop's undoing. Early in the following year the pope, probably at the instigation of the prominent Dominican Pierre de Conflans, recalled Kilwardby to Rome to receive 'promotion' to the cardinalate.[2] Shortly before, a Paris disciple of St Thomas, Giles de Lessines, had addressed to the archbishop a long, moderate and dignified exposition of the Thomist doctrine of form,[3] and at the chapter-general of the Preachers in 1278 two distinguished French friars were commissioned to proceed to England, in order to discover and punish all who might have attacked the writings of Aquinas, which received a still warmer commendation at the following chapter.[4] From this moment the *positio de unitate formarum*, as it came to be called, became the topic of a pamphlet warfare. The treatise of Giles de Lessines had been an objective, scientific presentation; subsequent publications were frankly polemic.[5]

Of these the first was that of an English Minor, probably resident at Paris, William de Mara, who in his *Correctorium fratris Thomae* (1278) grappled with the doctrine of Aquinas point by point. His work was found so useful that the chapter-general of the Minors in 1282 prescribed it as a species of antitoxin to be absorbed *pari passu* with the *Summa* by the exceptionally intelligent friars who alone were to be exposed to the risk of

---

1 For Knapwell see the biographical notice by A. G. Little in *Oxford Theology and Theologians* (*OHS*, xcvi, 1934), pp. 90–1; and M. D. Chenu, O.P., *La première diffusion du Thomisme à Oxford: Knapwell et ses 'Notes' sur les Sentences* (*Archives d'Histoire doctrinale et littéraire du moyen âge*, III, 1928). For the condemnation by Pecham at Oxford cf. P. Glorieux, *Comment les thèses thomistes furent proscrites à Oxford* in *Revue Thomiste*, XXXII (1932), 259–91.

2 For this episode v. A. Birkenmajer, *Der Brief Robert Kilwardbys an Peter von Conflans* (*Vermischte Untersuchungen zur Geschichte der mittelalt. Philosophie*, Münster, 1922, pp. 36–69).

3 First published by M. de Wulf in 1901 as tome 1 of *Les Philosophes Belges*. It was written in the spring of 1278.

4 Mandonnet, *Siger*, 252; *Acta capitulorum generalium*, ed. B. M. Reichert (*MOPH*, III), I, 199.

5 For this literature see F. Ehrle, *Der Kampf um die Lehre des h. Thomas von Aquin in der ersten fünfzig Jahren nach seinem Tod*, in *ZfkT*, XXXVII (1913), pp. 266–318; P. Mandonnet, *Premiers travaux de polémique Thomiste* (*Rev. des sciences phil. et théol.* VII (1913), 46–70, 244–62); and the more recent *La littérature des Correctoires* of P. Glorieux in *Revue Thomiste*, XXXIII (1928), 69–96. See also the bibliographical note in *MU*, III, 252.

infection incurred by readers of Aquinas.[1] The Preachers naturally did not let the last word rest with the *soi-disant* corrector of their doctor, and a whole flight of pamphlets in reply to de Mara issued from their houses. Of this band of pamphleteers the English friars formed no inconsiderable contingent, and William of Macclesfield and Richard Knapwell, besides writing directly against their opponents, composed treatises dealing explicitly with the unity of form.[2]

Thus the Paris and Oxford condemnations of 1277 had had precisely the opposite effect to that intended by the two prelates concerned. Instead of strangling the infant Thomism in the cradle, they had brought about a new solidarity among its adherents; it had been officially adopted by the Order of Preachers, and its leading doctrines were no longer mere opinions freely circulating and trying their fortune in the world of thought, but were rapidly becoming the *corpus doctrinae* of an order. Yet the permanent influence of the condemnation was considerable. It undoubtedly did much to confirm thinkers of the traditional school, and in particular the Minors, in their distrust of peripatetic thought, a distrust which the later history of Averroism and secular Aristotelian thought at Paris and in northern Italy must have seemed to justify. More than any other external cause, the condemnation of 1277 helped to put an end to the attempt at a synthesis of theological and philosophical truth which had been the aim of all schools at the middle of the thirteenth century, and which had in the system of St Thomas gone so far to achieve its aim. Henceforward, save in the relatively small school of the strict followers of Aquinas, distrust of rationalism grew, and the great Minors of the next generation became less and less convinced of the possibility of demonstrating by the unaided human reason what had seemed to St Thomas to be the truths of natural religion.

For the moment, however, the *positio de unitate formarum* continued to be the 'neuralgic spot' in the prevailing soreness of mind in academic circles. Kilwardby's disciplinary measures of 1277 may be assumed to have had no effect whatever upon the Thomist sympathies of the younger generation of friars. Of these the most vocal was Richard Knapwell, whose activities had very possibly provided the immediate occasion for Kilwardby's interference. It is in any case almost certain that his noisy propaganda on behalf of Thomism brought about further action on the part of authority in 1284, for in that year he incepted as regent master of the Preachers' school in the university.

---

1 Cf. the command of the minister-general to the provincials in 1282, ed. Van Ortroy in *Analecta Bollandiana*, XVIII (1899), 292: 'Non permittant multiplicari summam fr. Thome nisi apud lectores notabiliter intelligentes, et hoc nisi cum declarationibus fr. Willelmi de Mara.' This is pehaps the most striking testimony in existence to the reputation of the *Summa* at this early date.

2 Bernard Gui (printed by Denifle, *ALKG*, II, 238–9) attributes treatises *de unitate formarum* to Richard Knapwell, Thomas of Sutton, William Hothum, and William of Macclesfield.

Pecham, who had been called out to Rome as the first *Lector sacri palatii* in 1277 by Nicholas III, a friend of the Minors, was appointed to Canterbury by the pope early in 1279. His first years in England were largely occupied with his own administrative difficulties and with public business, but in 1284 he acted once more in the controversial field of theology. Early in November of that year, either following out a routine or, as is more probable, acting with special design, the archbishop announced his intention of 'visiting' the university of Oxford; he made no secret of his intention of proceeding while there against supporters of the Thomist doctrine on the unity of form. News of this had reached the Preachers of Oxford,[1] and they applied for help to the prior provincial, William of Hothum,[2] hitherto on cordial terms with the primate, who travelled across England in haste to save the situation. Pecham's letters[3] enable us to reconstruct in some detail the conversations that took place, but the archbishop was not to be put off; he not only renewed his predecessor's decree, but added to it an express condemnation of the thesis of unity of form.[4] This elicited a formal appeal from the Preachers, and both parties put their case, and an account of the previous negotiations, before the university and the bishop of Lincoln. It is in the two long apologias composed by Pecham that occur his accounts of the old disputes with Aquinas at Paris, and of the revolution in current thought brought about by Thomism.[5] His words throw such a vivid light on the warmth of feeling of both parties, that they may be quoted once more:

We are far [he wrote] from condemning philosophy, in so far as it serves the cause of theology; what we condemn are the unsanctified and novel terms that have these last twenty years been introduced into the treatment of high theology, to the manifest contempt and rejection of the tradition of the saints of old. Which of these two doctrines, we ask, is the more sound and solid, that of the sons of St Francis, Alexander of Hales and Bonaventure of blessed memory and their like, who in their treatises take for authorities saints and philosophers who are above criticism, or that newfangled system opposed to this at all points, which strains every nerve to demolish the teaching of Augustine...thus filling the whole world with the strife of words? Let the doctors of old, the truly wise, regard this; let God in heaven regard it and punish it!...May God but grant opportunity to the supreme pontiff and incline his mind to root them up, that we may see where be those stout defenders of a dead man's opinions [i.e. those of Aquinas]...and since the doctrine of the one order is in almost every particular the contrary of the other, save in the fundamentals of the faith, and since the

---

1 Pecham, *Reg. Epp.* III, 865: 'Fratres sui Oxonienses pluries ei scripserant, nos in partes Oxonie properantes intendere ipsorum ordini et ordinis opinionibus derogare.'

2 For Hothum see his bibliography in *Oxford Theology and Theologians*, pp. 83–7.

3 Especially nos. dcviii, dcxxii, dcxxv, dcxlv, dclxi, dclxxxi; cf. also *Reg. Johannis de Pontissara* (*C & YS*, I, 1915), pp. 307–8. For a fuller account *v.* Pecham.

4 *Reg. Epp.* III, p. 841: 'Unum vero illorum expresse notavimus articulum quorundam dicentium "in homine esse tantummodo formam unam".' *V.* also p. 871.

5 Nos. dcviii and dcxxii.

contrary of the true is false, consider well [he is addressing the bishop of Lincoln] the danger of allowing such a body of false doctrine to have its importunate defenders all over the world, some of whom reject both doctrinal and disciplinary authority.[1]

A little less than a year after this letter Pecham took solemn action against Knapwell, and, together with three bishops and the chancellor of Oxford, anathematized, at St Mary Arches, London, a batch of Dominican propositions; the last on the list was that asserting a single substantial form in man; this was characterized as the source of all the others. This time the condemnation was more formal: the 'errors' were described as heresies, and their supporters were declared excommunicate and *vitandi*.[2] William Hothum at once lodged a formal appeal on behalf of Knapwell, but by the time the case reached Rome Nicholas IV, a Minor, was pope. From him Knapwell could scarcely expect sympathetic treatment, and in the event he was condemned to perpetual silence.

With Pecham's letter of 1285 the controversy disappears from sight on English soil, and it is pleasant to find the archbishop writing a few months later to the provincial and chapter of the Preachers, thanking them for prayers they have offered for him.[3] Pecham was by nature a kindly man, and this very fact makes his bitterness of tone in the theological controversy the more noteworthy. The whole episode, indeed, is of an interest greater than its intrinsic importance might imply, for it throws valuable light on an otherwise too obscure moment in the history of thought.

Pecham was an eminent and typical example of the English Minors of his day. Diligent, correct, learned, hard-working, austere of life and eminently devout, he took his stand, with Bonaventure, on the *Regula Bullata* as interpreted by the bull *Quo elongati* of Gregory IX and the constitutions of the order. This, he asserted, was a secure way of life wholly consonant with the perfect following of Christ.[4] Strict in discipline, an energetic reformer of the religious houses of his province, he has left behind a rich collection of *acta* and correspondence which allows us to see in some fullness the good qualities and the limitations of one of the most distinguished of the friars in the epoch of their greatest outward glory.

---

1 *Reg. Epp.* dcxlv (III, 901–2). Pecham here defines the essential doctrines of Augustinism: 'Quidquid docet Augustinus de regulis aeternis et luce incommutabili, de potentiis animae, de rationibus seminalibus inditis materiae.'

2 *Reg. Epp.* III, 921–3 (no. dclxi). All eight articles refer to the unity of form.

3 *Reg. Epp.* III, no. dcxciv (22 August 1288).

4 *Reg. Epp.* I, p. 67: 'Hoc enim sentio, hoc toti mundo profiteor, quod vivere secundum Beati Francisci regulam, ut a Gregorio declaratam et constitutionibus ordinis munitam, non solum omni caret scrupulo, verum etiam est securissimum et sanctissimum et exemplo Salvatoris simillimum.'

CHAPTER XX

THE FRIARS FROM THE COUNCIL OF LYONS TO WILLIAM OF OCKHAM (1272-1340)

I. THE SCHOOLS

I

In the years immediately following the condemnation of Thomist theses by Tempier and Pecham disciples of the new school, which had been officially adopted by the chapter-general of the Preachers in 1278-9, multiplied at Oxford.[1] If some of the older generation, such as the provincial, William of Hothum, and his successor, Thomas Jorz, were willing to temporize, while a number of the younger friars, for whom Richard Knapwell was spokesman, were importunate in their propaganda, a small body of masters came into prominence, at once convinced Thomists and thinkers of weight, who, while defending and expanding their system, did not hesitate to make additions or modifications of detail in the scheme of St Thomas. The most notable of these was unquestionably Thomas of Sutton, who taught at Oxford at the end of the century.[2] Sutton had absorbed Thomist doctrine in its entirety, including the metaphysical basis, and himself composed a treatise on the unity of form in which he gave precision to controverted points. He also entered the lists with a direct attack on Scotus. He is one of the few English Thomists of the golden age of scholasticism, when the discipline was still a living force, drawing its strength from tradition and Scripture and passing from acquired conclusions to new developments without departing from the pure principles of the system.[3]

[1] V. supra. p. 229 n. 4. The final adoption of Thomism by the order was at the chapter of Saragossa in 1309.

[2] For Sutton v. Ehrle, *Thomas de Sutton, sein Leben, seine Quodlibet und seine Quaestiones disputatae* in *Festschrift Georg von Hertling*, 1913 (Kempten-München), 426–50; also some work of his printed by Denifle in *ALKG*, II (1886), 167–240, *Quellen zur Gelehrengeschichte des Predigerordens*, and D. E. Sharp, *Thomas of Sutton, O.P.* in *Rev. néoscolastique de philosophie*, XLI (1934), 332–54. For his work against Scotus v. F. Pelster, *Thomas von Sutton, ein Oxforder Verteidiger der thomistischen Lehre*, in *ZfkT* (1922), 223 seqq. He wrote three treatises on the question of Forms, cf. Pelster, *Thomas von Sutton, O.P., als Verfasser zweier Schriften über die Einheit der Wesenforms*, in *Scholastik*, III (1928), 411–13. For his work against Scotus v. M. Schmaus, *Der 'Liber Propugnatorius' des Thomas Anglicus und die Lehrunterschiede zwischen Thomas von Aquin und Duns Scotus (BGPM*, XXIX). For the question of free will v. Dom O. Lottin, *Psychologie et Morale aux XIIe et XIIIe siècles*, I, 339–77, where he discusses also the question of 'le thomisme de Thomas Sutton'. I owe the last three references to Fr D. Callus, O.P.

[3] Ehrle, *Thomas de Sutton*, 441, remarks: 'So können wir ihn den besten Denkern und Lehrern der goldenen Zeit der alten Scholastik zurechnen.' There were other English Thomists: Robert of Orford (fl. 1280–90), who defended Aquinas against Henry of Ghent, Giles of Rome and William de la Mare; cf. P. Bayerschmidt in *Divus Thomas*, XVII (1939), 311–36, and F. Pelster in *Gregorianum*, XXIV (1943), 135–70. In the last quarter of the thirteenth century there were also at Oxford three secular Thomist masters: Robert Winchelsea, Simon de Guant and Simon of Faversham. I owe the matter of the last two sentences to Fr Callus.

Sutton was a theologian *pur sang*, and his best work was done by 1300. His younger contemporary, Nicholas Trivet (*c.* 1258–1330), was perhaps the most versatile and widely read writer ever produced by the province.[1] The son of a distinguished judge, he was an able and orthodox Thomist theologian, twice regent master at Oxford and later lecturer in the priory of London; he was even more celebrated in at least four departments of literary activity: as a biblical exegete he stands above any other English friar of the middle ages; as a student of classical literature, and annotator of Aristotle, Seneca, Ovid, Livy and Juvenal he is almost alone in England in the fourteenth century; as a chronicler of his own age he produced the most reliable and individual piece of work since Matthew Paris; finally, as a controversialist he wrote an exposition of the theory of poverty as held by his order which two contemporary Minors, at least, felt called upon to answer. His literary work, indeed, enjoyed a reputation abroad; Pope John XXII supplied him with funds (presumably for his polemic against the Minors) in 1317, and some years later wrote to ask for a copy of his notes on the Psalms; Cardinal Alberti di Prato, a friend and fellow Preacher, solicited a copy of his commentary on Seneca, and he wrote a French chronicle for the Princess Mary, daughter of Edward I.[2] Perhaps it would not be altogether fanciful to see in Nicholas Trivet a medieval example of the type of friar-scholar embodied in recent years in a Denifle or a Mandonnet, combining a solid theological training with a wide literary and historical culture.

II

Distinguished though they were, Sutton and Trivet were altogether eclipsed in intellectual brilliance by the contemporary Minors. While almost everything (not excluding his name) connected with Richard of Middleton[3] is still a matter of debate, it is at least highly probable that he was an Englishman, and that he studied at Oxford *c.* 1278–80; it is certain that he taught at Paris from 1280 to *c.* 1295. Though sometimes regarded as a harbinger of Scotus, Richard may with greater justice be classed with the scholastics of the golden age who joined to an acute sense of the worth of tradition a conviction (that hall-mark of the classic age) that metaphysical truth and revealed truth were parts of a great whole which the

1 For Trivet *v.* Ehrle, *Nikolaus Trivet, sein Leben, seine Quolibet und Quaestiones ordinariae*, in *Festgabe Clemens Baeumker* (Münster-i-W. 1923), 1–63. His commentary on Seneca has been discussed by E. Franceschini in *Studi e Note di Filologia Latina Medievale* (Milan, 1938); that on Livy is discussed by Ruth J. Dean, *Medievalia et Humanistica*, III (1945), 86–98. His Scriptural work is considered by Miss B. Smalley in *The Study of the Bible in the Middle Ages*.

2 For full references *v.* Ehrle, *Nikolaus Trivet*, 4–9 and for the later Crathorn *v.* J. Kraus, *Die Stellung des Oxforder Dominikanerlehrer Crathorn zu Thomas von Aquin*, in *ZfkT*, LVII (1933), 66–88.

3 For him *v.* Sharp, *Franciscan Philosophy*, 211–76, where a bibliography is given. While the general impression given by Richard's work is continental, he has a number of characteristics in common with the Oxford school, and may well have been English. For his nationality, *v. MU*, III, 266 n. Cf. also E. C. Hocédez, S.J., *Richard de Middleton*.

human intellect was capable of integrating and harmonizing. Though he stood in the tradition of his school and borrowed largely from Pecham and Bonaventure, Richard of Middleton modified the extreme Augustinian doctrine of the divine illumination of the intellect and of the *rationales seminales* in matter; and though he remained a convinced opponent of Thomism on a number of essential points of metaphysics and psychology he approached perhaps more nearly in spirit and method to Aquinas than did any other doctor of his habit. Like his predecessors in the order he is eclectic, and his system therefore lacks the coherence and unity of the *Summa* of Aquinas; like the earlier Oxford theologians he refers constantly to the facts of experience as checks and subordinate proofs for abstract reasoning. Richard of Middleton had a mind far more virile and profound than Pecham; had the Minors produced a third doctor to succeed him and Thomas of York they might have been put in possession of a coherent system differing from Thomism and yet wholly traditional in spirit.

This was not to be. The next great master whom the Oxford Minors gave to Western thought possessed what was perhaps the most finely tempered intellect of all the theologians of his order, but his short life and his bent for criticism frustrated in part the promise that his genius had given.[1] John Duns the Scot, one of the first and perhaps the greatest of the many philosophers who have given lustre to his native land, was born *c.* 1266 at Maxton in Roxburghshire between Melrose and Kelso, in the beautiful valley that in after years was to become the scene of so much bloodshed and rapine, and the theme of ballad and romance. He took the habit with the Minors at Dumfries in 1281 and was at Oxford before 1290. Later, after four years at Paris, he returned to Oxford to lecture for two years on the Sentences; this in turn was followed by three years of teaching at Paris. Banished in 1303 for supporting the pope against Philip IV, he was nevertheless in Paris again the next year, and received the Master's licence in 1305. In 1307 he was sent to Cologne, and there he died in the following autumn. His outstanding gifts were appreciated by his superiors even during his brief lifetime, and almost the only contemporary reference to him is that of the minister-general, Gonsalvo, who writes of his honourable life, admirable knowledge, and most subtle mind.[2]

---

1 For the few facts known about Scotus *v.* Little, *Chronological Notes on the Life of Duns Scotus* in *EHR*, XLVII (1932), 568–82. For his thought *v.* C. R. S. Harris, *Duns Scotus*, 2 vols. (Oxford, 1927), P. Minges, *Joannis Duns Scoti doctrina*, etc., 2 vols. (Berlin, 1930), the section in Sharp, *Franciscan Philosophy*, 279–368, Ueberweg-Geyer, 507–9, and Gilson, *PhMA*, 591–610.

2 Wadding, *Annales*, I, 9; Little, *Grey Friars in Oxford* (*OHS*, xv), 219. This reference, and the internal evidence of his works, which everywhere reflect a devout religious spirit, should be borne in mind when any attempt is made to estimate the character of Scotus, whatever may be held as to the logical consequences of his opinions. His title of *beatus*, however, which some recent writers have shown signs of exploiting, rests only upon a local cultus of great antiquity which cannot be corroborated from any existing record of his life. In the case of St Thomas, contemporary evidence of his sanctity exists, and his works have a spiritual depth and wisdom which is not found in Scotus.

As a Minor, Duns stands in the main by the traditional 'Augustinian' doctrines of his order, but in his eclectic use of Aristotle he goes far beyond Bonaventure and Pecham; his interest in mathematics and the value he assigns to experience show him as one of the Oxford school.[1] His critical powers were unrivalled, and his attacks on some of the positions of Aristotelian Thomism were probably the most damaging that the system has ever received from within the ranks of orthodox thinkers. The principal significance of Duns, however, and the essential difference that separated him from earlier doctors among the Minors, is his sense of the need of basic principles on which to rest the superstructure of his thought. His critical genius, great as was its destructive power, did not hinder him from positive and original speculation. In contrast to all his predecessors in the order, he cut himself loose from several of the fundamental doctrines of both the traditional Augustinian and the strict Aristotelian schools; his was therefore a personal system, and therefore in contrast both to that of Bonaventure, who claimed to follow the saints and doctors of old, and to that of Aquinas, who professed to follow reason as set out by the Philosopher; and though in a broad history of thought Scotus must be counted among those who aimed at making a synthesis of metaphysics and theology, reason and revelation, he is from another point of view the first great medieval thinker to construct a metaphysical fabric of his own. His presentation of realism, with its peculiar notion of nature and form and the individualizing *haecceitas*, is perhaps an example of the method, so familiar to the modern world, by which a thinker constructs, not only a new system of thought, but the technical terms in which his opinions are expressed. Scotus is in this respect the first stone in the bridge which connects the golden age of scholastic philosophy with the systems of the modern world descending from Descartes.

He showed equal originality in his depreciation of *a posteriori* demonstration in natural theology. In contrast to Aquinas, whose classical proofs of the existence of God and of His principal attributes are evidence both of his belief in the validity of an argument from effect to cause and of his conviction that that order of creation is a direct reflection of the divine reason, Scotus, though no sceptic, held that all such *a posteriori* demonstration gave no more than relative proof, while for divine providence and the immortality of the soul no argument could be advanced of more than probable force. In other words, Scotus reduced the number of those truths of the faith that could be established by purely natural reasoning, and here

---

1 For expositions of the main features of Scotus's philosophical system *v.* Sharp, *Franciscan Philosophy*, 279–368, Ueberweg-Geyer, 504–17, and C. Balić, O.F.M., *Ratio criticae editionis operum omnium I. D. Scoti.* Gilson, *PhMA*, 591–609, has an illuminating discussion, now [1952] supplanted by his full-length study *Jean Duns Scot.* No account has been taken in the above account of the *Theoremata*, sometimes ascribed to Scotus; if accepted as genuine, this work would show him to have gone much further in denying the possibility of a rational demonstration of the truths of natural religion.

again he began a movement which his successors were to continue.[1] Similarly, while showing himself an Aristotelian rather than an Augustinian in his analysis of the process of understanding, he was influenced by traditions of the Oxford school and Roger Bacon in his selection of the individual rather than the abstract concept as the principal object of the mind's operation. Finally, as a Franciscan as well as a reactionary against Averroism he sought in the will of God rather than in His reason the key of all; the universe did not develop as it were necessarily from the divine Ideas; it was called into being by the will of God free from all limiting conditions. Here again theology gained at the expense of philosophy; what we know of God and His works we know because faith has told us what His good will is, not because reason tells us how the God of Law and Reason must act.

Though Scotus did not live to formulate an all-embracing system comparable to that of Aquinas, his marvellously keen mind was able to fortify every position and meet every objection with a logical and coherent mass of arguments, proofs and *obiter dicta* from which patient commentators were able later to construct a whole which could be set out question by question in opposition to that of St Thomas. Within a few years of his death Ockham could refer to him as *doctor ordinis*, and he was later officially adopted as such in the schools of his order. Unfortunately, he found it necessary to express himself in novel technical terms, and to create a forest of metaphysical forms which make it next to impossible for a reader to comprehend his thought unless he is willing to 'bolte him to the bren'. To the humanists and reformers of the sixteenth century, therefore, he was regarded either as the type of Gothic stupidity or, in curious contrast, as a nonpareil of super-subtle ingenuity. To strict Thomists he was from early days *bête noire*, the standard-bearer of the great revolt that led from Ockham to Descartes, Kant and Hegel. His direct influence was indeed great. Some at least of his teaching was inherited by Ockham, more by Wyclif and Hus, and some formed part of the Oxford tradition till the Reformation. Though pure Scotism, like pure Thomism, was eclipsed for more than a century by victorious Nominalism, it revived with its rival in the sixteenth century, and was perhaps even more powerful in the schools of the counter-Reformation. It has in our own day received a new lease of life.

The hostility of the English reformers to John Duns, which has been perpetuated in a strange freak of etymology,[2] could only have arisen from a conviction that his teaching was wholly conservative. The great Minor was indeed in every way orthodox, whatever may be thought of his

---

1 Gilson remarks of St Thomas (*PhMA*, 607): 'Son œuvre est une victoire de la théologie dans la philosophie'; whereas Duns Scotus 'a désespéré de la philosophie pure...son œuvre ne pouvait être qu'une victoire de la théologie sur la philosophie. Les deux œuvres sont donc d'une espirit essentiellement différent.'

2 The followers of Scotus in the fifteenth century were known as Dunsmen or Dunses; later, when scholastic theology was in disfavour, the name was adopted for a 'cavilling sophist' and then for a 'blockhead' (*N.E. Dictionary*). The earliest quotation for the word in these senses is 1577.

influence as a metaphysician or natural theologian. The same cannot be said of the last great English friar of the first rank as a thinker, William of Ockham,[1] who taught at Oxford for some years before 1324, when he was summoned to Avignon to answer a charge of false doctrine, probably arising from his new logic as applied to theology. Much work still remains to be done before his philosophical position and the development of his thought can be fully understood, but it is now seen more clearly than before that he was primarily a logician, not a metaphysician, and that many of the modern expositions of his system rest upon a misunderstanding of this point. Ockham was not a sceptic, either philosophically or theologically, as that term is understood in the modern world. As a logician, he held that the mind was capable of intellection, though he denied that it could abstract the intelligible essence from extramental being or attain to its *haecceitas* by a perception of the Scotist type; rather, the mind in understanding expressed itself in a language of its own which was an unreflective consequence of its contact with its object, the individual thing. Ockham did in effect destroy metaphysics by concentrating all interest upon logic and by regarding universals as no more than terms or symbols, while in other respects, by his appeal to Scripture rather than to tradition and authority, and by his virulent attacks on the papacy, his influence in disrupting the medieval religious synthesis was very great. He does, indeed, mark an epoch in medieval thought even more clearly than St Thomas, for his system, both logical and political, contained in germ almost all the tendencies that were to mould the thought of Europe after the Reformation.

Ockham went beyond Scotus in the stringency of the conditions he required for a demonstration, accepting no proposition that did not flow as a necessary consequence from a self-evident truth. All arguments *a posteriori* were no more than probable. On the other hand the individual, which to Aristotle and St Thomas had been little more than the starting-point for a process of abstraction, became for Ockham the only entity truly existing outside the mind, and the intuitive perception of the individual became the only perfect knowledge. Natural theology is therefore no more than a series of probable arguments; the real authority for all the truths of religion is faith alone.[2] Similarly, all attempts to deduce morality

---

1 The most recent and complete accounts of Ockham are by R. Guelluy, *Philosophie et théologie chez Guillaume d'Ockham* (1947) and L. Baudry, *Guillaume d'Occam*, vol. i (1950). *V.* also G. de Lagarde, *La Naissance de l'esprit laïque*, vols. lv–vi, the excellent arts. *Occam* and *Nominalisme* by P. Vignaux in *DTC*, the same writer's *Nominalisme au xive siècle* (1948), Fr Ph. Boehner, 'A recent presentation of Ockham's philosophy' in *Franciscan Studies* ix (1949), 443–56, and the volume of *Franziscanische Studien* (vol. 32, Münster, 1950) devoted to Ockham on the sexcentenary of his death. But indeed Ockhamist literature at the moment outstrips all bibliographical agility.

2 Ueberweg-Geyer, 576–82, give the following quotations with references: 'Nullum universale est extra animam existens realiter. Nihil potest naturaliter cognosci in se nisi cognoscatur intuitive. Articuli fidei non sunt principia demonstrationis nec conclusionis, nec sunt probabiles.' Universals are, in Ockham's view, 'purum figmentum intellectus.'

or the working of Providence from the nature of God are futile; God is absolutely free, and all is as it is because He wills it so, not because our reason, as a reflection of God's, sees that God acts thus since He is true to His own nature.

Like his elder contemporary, Marsilius of Padua, Ockham was ruthlessly and dauntlessly thorough, and when he had finished his critical attack there remained, for those who lacked artillery strong enough to withstand him, no rational foundation whatever for faith. With the existence of God and the immortality of the soul no longer demonstrable, and all essential difference between good and evil removed, so that the worst crimes were evil, not because they were of themselves repugnant to God, but because God had freely decreed to forbid them, while all future rewards and punishments were regarded as deriving from the sheer free disposition of God without any reference whatsoever to the inherent goodness or evil of the actor and his act, there was clearly no room for natural theology or morality of any kind. At the same time, if cause and effect were to be considered as mere names, without any philosophical or scientific meaning,[1] and if all general concepts and 'natures' were likewise mere names, there had ceased to be any room for metaphysics.

Scotus, as we have seen, had a very deep faith and reverence for tradition in theology, but in Ockham we can see clearly the dual tendency that was to develop in both Nominalist and Scotist circles: a distrust of the reason as an instrument for attaining to abstract truth, and a consequent reliance upon the immediate, uncontrolled statement of authority, whether Scriptural or ecclesiastical, on every point of doctrine. This in turn led often to what has been called 'fideism', and a readiness to embrace a number of opinions—on the Real Presence in the Eucharist, for example, or on the Immaculate Conception—which were, or at least at that time appeared to be, less susceptible of reasoned explanation and defence than the views of the Thomists. For this, and for much besides, the *venerabilis inceptor*[2] must be held in great part responsible. His adventures after departing from Oxford in 1324 are scarcely part of English religious history, but the influence of this English friar upon the intellectual history of Europe can scarcely be exaggerated.

With Ockham the series of eminent scholastics given by Britain to European thought terminated in one whose public and intellectual activities were precisely those which the founder of the friars had sought most earnestly to exclude from the lives of his followers. The series, opened by Alexander of Hales and continued through Adam Marsh, Thomas of York, Pecham, Thomas of Middleton and John Duns, presents

1 Gilson, *PhMA*, 642, cites: 'Quod aliquod creatum sit determinate causa efficiens, non potest demonstrari vel probari, sed solum per experientiam patet hoc, scilicet quod ad ejus praesentiam sequitur effectus, et ad ejus absentiam non.'

2 Ockham had qualified to incept at Oxford, but had not proceeded to the degree of D.D. (*v*. Little, *Oxford Theology and Theologians*, 93–4), hence his title of *inceptor*. This, when later admirers had added the adjective *venerabilis*, came to be understood of his position as originator of the school of Nominalism.

a succession of men of speculative powers which can scarcely be paralleled in any other epoch of English history. They have long remained most unjustly neglected, while men of far lesser genius in other centuries have become familiar to all. Within recent years they have received more notice and greater justice. A beginning has been made of printing their works, and it is to be hoped that in course of time the whole corpus of their writings will be published.

There is, however, a danger that the *amor operis incepti* may carry English critics and editors to indiscriminate praise.[1] It may well be true that in the realm of pure metaphysics and psychology the English Minorite scholastics detected real weaknesses in the peripatetic system, and by laying stress on the facts of experience, on the significance of the perception of the individual by the mind, and on quasi-intuitive knowledge supplied a valuable corrective to Aristotelian psychology, and touched the Thomist epistemology at its weakest spot.[2] Nevertheless, there are vast fields of Thomist doctrine, and those among the richest in harvest, to which the English Minorite school did not advert, but which their criticism, if ultimately successful, would have sterilized for ever. The profound doctrine of analogy, so truly Christian, which preserves the likeness of God in varying degrees on every level of being in the universe without a trace of either pantheism or anthropomorphism; the account of the process of cognition which gives full validity within the proper sphere to every faculty of man while safeguarding alike rational certainty and the potentiality for divine action,[3] without a trace of scepticism or illuminism; the assertion of the essentially supernatural character of the life of grace, the light of faith and the love of God; the doctrine of the theological virtues, the gifts of the Holy Ghost and the Christian sonship to God issuing in a divine illumination of the intellect and movement of the will, made possible only by an elevation of all the powers of the perfect follower of Christ; the profound articles which treat of the Eucharist, the Incarnation and the indwelling of the Holy Trinity in the soul of the just man—all this, which is not only an integral part of the Thomist system, but the crown of the fabric for which all the foundations are laid, has no real counterpart in the writings, as we know them, of the Oxford school of the Minors, and could not fully exist within the framework of Scotist teaching, to say nothing of

1 E.g. C. R. S. Harris, *Duns Scotus*, I, 303, speaks of 'a system which in many ways is more suited [*sc.* than Thomism] to serve as the speculative basis for the Catholic faith', and (306), 'it is manifest that Scotus' teaching [*sc.* on the nature of the soul] is more in harmony with the Christian faith' and D. S. Sharp, *Franciscan Philosophy*, 283: 'the most important differences between Scotus and St Thomas, if we except the views of the latter condemned by Bishop Tempier in 1277, concern purely speculative problems.' It should, however, in fairness be remembered that neither of these two writers is concerned with pure theology.

2 Its failure, that is, to reckon with the rich intellectual and emotional life which has its seat not in the *ratio ratiocinans*, but in the quasi-intuitive appreciation of individual persons and things and includes within its scope so much of poetry and art—the whole province of *Anima* who (in Paul Claudel's parable) is silent when *Animus* is speaking.

3 That is to say, the *potentia obedientialis*, not the natural potency.

the wholly destructive principles of Ockham.[1] Though the lives of men, for good as well as for evil, may often give the lie to the speculative opinions they profess, yet there is truth in the axiom of the schools that the heart can only love what the mind knows,[2] and the victory of Nominalist thought, with all its implications, cannot be left out of the reckoning when assessment is made of the spiritual life of the friars in the later middle ages.

III

The third order of friars, that of Carmel, reached the universities and organized its studies later than the Minors and Preachers. The English province produced no master of note till the beginning of the fourteenth century, when it gave to the order its most distinguished theologian of the middle ages in the person of John Baconthorpe.[3] Taking his name from the village of Baconsthorpe near Sheringham in Norfolk, and perhaps belonging to the family that had already given a mind of genius to each of the two older orders, he took the Carmelite habit at Blakeney, a house founded by his near relatives, and studied at Oxford, where he was the friend of Bradwardine, and at Paris, where he was the sixth regent master of the Carmelite house in 1324. Throughout his life as a friar he was an assiduous writer on philosophy, theology and Scripture, and left a reputation for holiness of life equal to his learning. From 1327 to 1333 he was English prior provincial; resigning office to devote himself to study he spent some years at Cambridge, dying at the London priory in 1346. Almost the only personal trait that has been recorded is his diminutive stature.[4]

Baconthorpe was influenced to a certain degree by Scotus, but recent

1 The theologians concerned were no doubt entirely orthodox in their adherence to defined doctrine, but they made no complete synthesis of all the departments of their science, and their teaching on, e.g., faith and grace would, if logically drawn out, imperil some of the most sublime portions of the traditional Christian moral and mystical life. In fact, the Franciscan school has drawn its inspiration in these matters from St Bonaventure, a source very different from Ockham and even from Duns, but this has inevitably caused something of a dyarchy in the system. The Thomists, on the other hand, have had the advantage of a single comprehensive source of teaching, and their greatest theologians in every age— a Cajetan, a Bañez, a John of St Thomas, a Gardeil, a del Prado and a Garrigou-Lagrange— have joined speculative to moral and mystical theology in a harmonious union.

2 *Nil amatum quin praecognitum.*

3 The best account of the life and characteristics of Baconthorpe is the article in *DHG*; the fullest analysis of his doctrine is by P. Chrysogone du Saint-Sacrament, *Maître Jean Baconthorpe*, in *Rev. néoscolastique de philosophie*, xxv (1932), 341–65, where his divergencies from Thomist principles are shown to be less than has been supposed. B. M. Xiberta, O.C., has also done valuable work in this field.

4 Cf. the notice in the fourteenth-century list of Parisian masters printed by Denifle in *ALKG*, v, 365–86, *Quellen zur Gelehrtengeschichte des Carmelitenordens im 13 und 14 Jahrhundert* p. 371–2 :'Johannes de Bachone...qui magnis virtutibus et optimis studiis preditus fuit... fuitque minimus in persona sed maximus sapiencia et doctrina.' Further information about the Carmelites in England can be found in *Les Carmes aux Universités du Moyen-Age*, by Fr B. Zimmermann, O.C.D., in *Études Carmélitaines*, 17 ann. vol. 1 (April, 1932), 82–112, and *La vie intellectuelle des Carmes* by Fr Elisée de la Nativité in the same periodical 20 ann. vol. 11 (April 1935), pp. 93–157.

criticism has shown that in the main lines of his doctrinal synthesis he was a Thomist, and that his reputation as an Averroist is totally undeserved. He was widely read in scholastic theology and his work is critical, complicated and abounding in quotations. From the first he took his place as an authoritative teacher, but he never became the sole *doctor ordinis*. Another Englishman, Thomas Netter of Walden a century later and the strictly Thomist Michael of Bologna disputed the field, and all attempts to give Baconthorpe a position equivalent to that of Aquinas or Scotus failed, though his works were repeatedly printed in the sixteenth century, and as late as 1560 he remained the doctor of the Italian province.

IV

The fourth order, that of the Augustinian Hermits, made even less mark in the English schools.[1] The *doctor ordinis*, Giles of Rome, was in the main a Thomist and he was the ablest supporter of the most extreme papal claims under Boniface VIII; the most brilliant theologians of the order were Italians. The Augustinians were firmer than any other order in their stand against the first onset of Nominalism, especially under the prior-general Thomas of Strassburg (1345–56); thus the chapter-general of 1345 prohibited Ockham's teaching in general terms, and that of 1348 stigmatized his teaching explicitly as 'strange and useless'. It was under Thomas of Strassburg that the extraordinary step was taken, for which the reasons are not clear, of reducing the *studia generalia* of the order to three only, Paris, Oxford, and Cambridge. The decree, made in 1355, was repealed ten years later, when the eminent Nominalist Gregory of Rimini was prior-general, but it had the effect of directing a stream of foreign students, many of them Italian, to England, and of acquainting the English friars with Italian conditions; doubtless it was this circumstance that led to the departure of William Flete and his companions for Italy, as we shall see later.

V

With the disappearance from the English scene of William of Ockham in 1324 the succession of eminent teachers in the school of the Minors at Oxford came to an abrupt end. It was almost exactly a century since Grosseteste had first lectured there, and in that period, little longer than a long lifetime, scholastic thought had put forth its most perfect bud, broken into full flower, ripened its fruit and fallen into the sere leaf of decay. Throughout that century there had passed through the school at Oxford a series of distinguished friars to which the annals of no single province of their own or any other order can offer a parallel. More than once, indeed, the British Isles have given birth to a sequence of great thinkers, but it may

1 For an account of the Augustinian theology in general and in England *v.* Gwynn, *The English Austin Friars*, 26–73.

be doubted whether any such has surpassed in speculative powers and in influence over posterity the line of Friars Minor which culminated in Duns Scotus and William of Ockham.

Though certain characteristics mark every thinker among the Minors who can be proved to have studied at Oxford, the group does not form a homogeneous whole; some of the earlier masters fall into the common stream of English thought of their day; others, such as Pecham, belong rather to the tradition of continental Europe. Three, however, stand apart from all their contemporaries in virtue alike of their original genius, their self-confidence, their powers of incisive criticism and their foreshadowing of the modern world. Of these the first, Roger Bacon, though in many ways the most audacious and the most prophetic, had little influence on those who came immediately after; the two others, by contrast, must rank for better or for worse among the most powerful disruptive agencies in the history of medieval thought. If the achievement of a philosopher is to be judged not by his approximation to the standard of an assumed body of absolute truth, but purely historically by the degree of mental power exhibited and of influence exerted upon later generations, then Duns Scotus and William of Ockham deserve a far higher place in the estimation of their countrymen than has hitherto been accorded to them. It was they who indirectly exposed the fatal flaw in Augustinian epistemology, the assumption, that is, of at least some kind of direct and not extraordinary divine illumination of the human mind as essential for the attainment of at least some kinds of natural certainty, an assumption which implied a denial of autonomy to the human reason, and of separate powers and degrees of knowledge to the natural and supernatural orders.[1] Led to abandon such a position alike by their keen critical sense and their reliance on individual experience, and unwilling to accept the Aristotelian doctrine, perfected by St Thomas, of the capacity of the senses to receive from the external world true impressions from which the intellect may frame concepts of general validity, they fell back upon the intuition of the individual and upon the assent of faith. Scotus certainly, and Ockham possibly, retained the truths of natural theology and ethics in this way fully and sincerely, but their system of metaphysics afforded no basis for so doing and their followers and successors were left to supply the deficiency by a reliance on mystical knowledge, or emotional experience, or an acceptance of all certainty regarding the existence of God and his attributes on the authority of Scripture or tradition.[2] If none of these was acceptable, there remained no escape from a doubt or a denial of all knowledge of God and of the divine nature and providence.

The study of the doctrines and fortunes of the schools of medieval

---

1 Cf. Ueberweg-Geyer, II, 505: 'Das natürliche Licht der Vernunft wird [bei Scotus] zur Erkenntnis der natürlichen Wahrheit für ausreichend erklärt.'

2 *Ibid.* 571: 'Auch das Dasein, die Einheit und die Unendlichkeit Gottes wird ihm [*sc.* Ockham] zum blossen Glaubensartikel.'

thought has too long been neglected, and in this country, perhaps, longer than elsewhere. The writings of the schoolmen, treating of unfamiliar matters in a technical language of forbidding density and subtlety, make the task of absorbing their teaching laborious in the extreme. With none is this more true than with Scotus and Ockham; acute and subtle to a fault,[1] they proceed slowly, eliminating obstacles, weaving entanglements, sheltering their thought with a quilt of finespun distinctions. The grace of a Berkeley, the cadences of a Bradley, the luminous clarity of an Aquinas, have no place with them. It is only when the great significance of their thought has been appreciated that a detailed examination of its processes becomes tolerable or profitable. For in fact these two critical minds did more than any others to determine the course of future speculation.

It is still very commonly supposed that Thomism was the typical system of medieval philosophy, and as such the direct object of attack for the Reformers; it is also assumed that scholastic philosophy, as an intellectual force, was extinct in northern countries from the time of Luther. Neither supposition is correct: in England and north-western Europe in general Scotist, and still more commonly Nominalist, thought held the field almost universally in the fourteenth and fifteenth centuries,[2] and when, a century after Luther, humanism and dogmatic controversy ceased to absorb all minds, and the sequence of philosophers began again in the modern world, Scotists dominated the seminaries north of the Pyrenees[3] and Nominalism reigned in the old universities of the north. In consequence, though the new thought was given its peculiar cast by ideas unknown to the medieval world—the system of Copernicus, a mechanical view of the universe and an outlook in which the thinking human being, not God, was the centre from which all radiated—the minds of the age were not, like some in more recent times, *tabulae rasae* in metaphysics; they had been fed upon late scholastic thought and trained in its logic rather than in the pure sources of Greek philosophy.[4] Continuity with the past was thus maintained, but this

1 Cf. Ueberweg-Geyer, II, 509: 'Duns Scotus ist wohl der scharfsinnigste Denker des ganzen Mittelalters gewesen. Den Beinamen Doctor subtilis trägt er nicht mit Unrecht.'
2 For the spread and extent of Nominalism in the universities *v.* Ehrle, *Der Sentenzenkommentar Peters von Candia*, 239–44.
3 For the influence of Scotism *c.* 1650 *v.* Sharp, *Franciscan Philosophy*, 282. In England in the early sixteenth century 'Scotist' denoted 'scholastic theologian', as may be seen, e.g. in Erasmus's description of the Prior (Goldstone) of Canterbury as *neque Scoticae Theologiae rudis* (*Colloquiae*, ed. Amsterdam, 1693, p. 434) and in the familiar passage where Dr Layton relates how he 'sette Dunce in Bocardo', *Letters relating to the Suppression of the Monasteries* (*CS*), ed. T. Wright, 71.
4 Hobbes was brought up at Magdalen, *c.* 1603–8, on scholastic philosophy, and 'ausserlich betrachtet, gehört [his logic] dem englischen Nominalismus in seinen terministischen Zuspitzung an' (Ueberweg-Geyer, III, 255). For Leibniz, cf. *ibid.* 316: 'In der...Disputatio metaphysica de principio individui...behauptet Leibniz die nominalistische Thesis: omne individuum sua tota entitate individuatur, als deren erste Vertreter er Petrus Aureolus und Durandus [predecessors of Ockham] nennt. Endlich prüft Leibniz die Haecceitas, die Scotus behauptet habe....Der Behauptung [*sc.* von Scotus]...setzt Leibniz die nominalistische Doktrin entgegen....Hierdurch ist schon die Richtung des späteren leibnizischen Philosophierens angedeutet, namentlich die Betonung des Individualismus.' For Locke, *ibid.* 355:

past was not the golden age of scholasticism, but the sceptical, individualistic age of Ockham. While it would thus be wholly misleading to regard William of Ockham as the source or seminal agent of all the systems from Descartes to Kant, the two basic assumptions upon which almost all the modern schools agree—the absence of any adequate connection between the thinking mind and external reality, and the lack of causal or analogical relationship between creatures and the Creator sufficient to serve as basis for a natural theology or theodicy—these are to be found in outline in the works of Ockham, whose system of logic must be reckoned the most powerful single instrument that prepared the ground for the scepticism and agnosticism that was to come.[1]

It is an irony of history that the agents who in their piercing subtlety did most to destroy the bridge linking matter with mind and mind with God should have been members of that order of friars whose founder, with his *mens praesaga mali*, had wished to interdict his followers for ever the entrance to the schools of human wisdom.

II. THE PAPAL COURT

The second and third decades of the fourteenth century were marked by two theological controversies of note which had their focus at Avignon and were due in large part to the personal characteristics and initiative of John XXII. The first was the celebrated debate on the Poverty of Christ and the Apostles; the second that on the delayed Beatific Vision; in both, English friars were involved.

The long and deplorable struggle between the two parties among the Minors, the Zealots or Spirituals and the Conventuals, had for more than thirty years been a running sore in the ecclesiastical life of southern France and Italy. In England it had had few direct repercussions; as has been noted on a previous page, the English province was from its origin noted for a combination of strict observance with a devotion to study; few English friars, therefore, would have felt a pressing need for reform or a

'Die scholastische Philosophie, mit der er sich eingehend beschäftigen musste [i.e. at Christ Church, Oxford, from 1651], liess ihm unbefriedigt, wenn sie auch namentlich in der nominalistischen Fassung des Wilhelm von Occam, dessen Summa zu Lockes Zeit noch viel in England studiert wurde, auf seine spätere Lehre nicht unwesentlichen Einfluss gehabt haben mag.' For Hobbes cf. also M. Oakeshott, *Leviathan*, introd. *passim*.

1 Rashdall, *MU*, III, 263, quotes with approval the dictum of Dean Milman (*Latin Christianity*, IX, 148): 'Ockham's Philosophy is that of centuries later.' When, however, he writes (*ibid.* 262): 'On its purely logical, its purely intellectual side, Ockhamism represents the culmination of all scholastic thought; and so far scholasticism supplied the weapons by which it was itself destroyed', he is misleading. St Thomas, Scotus, and Ockham do not stand in a succession as do, e.g. Albert the Great, St Thomas, and Giles of Rome. The Thomist school stood entirely apart from and opposed to the followers of both Scotus and Ockham, even if individual Preachers absorbed Nominalism. It did indeed suffer an eclipse, owing to the lack of genius among its teachers, but it possessed a logical discipline capable of opposing Nominalism as it had opposed and refuted the earlier Nominalism of Abelard; the bow hung, as it hangs still, for an Odysseus to bend.

desire for solitude. Abroad, the long strife was at least outwardly composed by the drastic action of John XXII, which gave the victory to the Conventuals and drove the extreme Spirituals into confinement or the wilderness.[1]

The Minors, however, were to enjoy no long period of peace. Within two years, at the end of 1321, an accidental spark set light to an old store of inflammable material. A Beguin of Narbonne, brought before the Dominican Inquisitor, was about to be condemned as a heretic for maintaining that Christ never owned property either in person or in common with the apostles when one of the judges, a Minor, objected that such a proposition, far from being heretical, was an article of faith; he quoted the Bull *Exiit qui seminat* of Nicholas III in which, as he alleged, the pope had not only stated the belief of the Church but had prohibited any further discussion of his words. The Inquisitor's reply was to demand a recantation from his colleague; the Minor thereupon appealed to the Holy See. John XXII, whose sympathies lay entirely with the Preachers, suspended his predecessor's ban and threw the matter open to discussion in consistory and by theologians at large.[2]

The Minors, who saw that the most precious and distinctive claim of their order to absolute poverty and a unique approximation to Christ, which had seemed beyond the reach of question, was about to vanish downstream, met in general chapter at Perugia in the spring of 1322 and drew up two letters, the one addressed to the Pope, begging him not to alter the decrees of his predecessors, the other, in the form of an encyclical to Christendom, stating that the doctrine of Christ's poverty as condemned by the Inquisition at Narbonne was sound and orthodox.

This action was to prove the first step in the lamentable progress that led to schism in the order and the rebellion of the general, Michael of Cesena. John XXII, in his bulls *Ad conditorem canonum* (1322) and *Cum inter nonnullos* (1323), renounced the ownership of the Minors' property, which had been vested in the Holy See for eighty years, and declared it heretical to assert that Christ and the Apostles were not the owners of the property which Holy Scripture represented them as possessing, thus cutting the ground from under the Minors' feet on both the legal and the theoretical level.[3] The details of the controversy and its sequel form no part of English religious history and no considerable section of the English friars went into schism. The English provincial, however, William of

---

1 The extreme complexity of the subject, the fragmentary nature of the sources and the controversial topics involved have combined to deter scholars from dealing with this period of Franciscan history. The best English account is in D. L. Douie, *The Nature and the Effect of the heresy of the Fraticelli* (Manchester, 1932); P. Gratien's study, often referred to, may also be consulted for the origins of the struggle. Indispensable documents and illuminating comment are to be found in the articles of Denifle and Ehrle in *ALKG*, i–iv.

2 Douie, *op. cit.* 165, referring to *Bull. Franc.* v, 520, p. 259.

3 Douie, *op. cit.* 153 *seqq.*, with references. The Pope's definition was based on the teaching of St Thomas, whom he was to canonize in the following year (1323): 'Perfectio vitae christianae principaliter et etiam essentialiter in charitate consistit.' Cf. Denzinger, *Enchiridion*, 494.

Nottingham, and the two English doctors of theology, Hugh of Newcastle and William of Alnwick, signed both letters at Perugia, and in the following year the last-named preached at Bologna against the pope's doctrine in *Cum inter nonnullos*. Alnwick was not the only Englishman in a pulpit at Bologna. Thomas Waleys, O.P., of whose chequered career more will be said, preached often in the city against the Minors.[1]

Meanwhile, a furious pamphlet war had broken out, which the successive pronouncements of John XXII rendered more bitter among the rebels and failed to end among the orthodox. To this at least three English friars contributed.[2] Richard of Conyngton had already as provincial put out a long treatise on Franciscan poverty from the standpoint of the moderate Conventual.[3] He had been answered by the Italian Zealot Ubertino da Casale who, so it was asserted by his opponents, had once come within an ace of trampling under the hoofs of his unpermitted mount the English provincial as he picked his way, like a true Minor, on foot through the miry streets of Vienne.[4] Now, ten years later and in retirement at Cambridge, Conyngton took up his pen once more in defence of the ideal of poverty, though expressing his complete submission to the pope. A younger member of the English province, Walter of Chatton, took a bolder if less ingenuous line in an endeavour to give the go-by to *Ad conditorem*. Treating it as a legal formulary, and entirely abstracting from the intentions of its author and the circumstances of its issue, he maintained by a dexterous *petitio principii* that as the followers of St Francis at their profession completely renounced all possession, whether personal or corporate, of all temporal goods, any subsequent imputation of ownership was a mere form of words without significance.[5]

Besides the pope, both the English apologists had on their hands a distinguished countryman from among the Preachers. Nicholas Trivet, who after the death of Thomas Sutton was the leading English theologian of his order, had written a treatise on evangelical perfection in which he had expounded the Thomist position, approved by John XXII, and had put forward the usual arguments from the gospel narrative to show that Christ and the Apostles disposed of property. Trivet's labours, as has been noted, were most probably subsidized by the pope. In addition, yet another Preacher was in the field against the Minors, the pugnacious Thomas Waleys.[6]

---

1 Cf. Waleys, *Epistola* (ed. Käppeli), 241: 'Predicavi eciam Bononie sepe contra heresim illam.'

2 *Three Treatises on Evangelical Poverty*, ed. D. L. Douie, in *Archivum Franciscanum Historicum*, XXIV–XXV (1931–2). The third (anonymous) piece was too fragmentary to publish; it is discussed introd. xxiv, 347–8.

3 It has been printed in *Archiv. Franc. Hist.* XXIII, 57–105, 340–60.

4 *ALKG*, III, 104: 'Si opponens [*sc.* Olivi] ivisset nuper in Vienna peditando, non posuisset cum pedibus equi, cui insidebat, magistrum theologie peditantem per lutum fratrem Rycardum ministrum Anglie in tanto periculo sicut fecit.'

5 The style and matter of Chatton's treatise make the exasperation of Waleys with the author, when the latter was one of his judges, very comprehensible (*v. infra*, p. 251).

6 Waleys, *Epistola*, 240: 'Contra eorum [*sc.* Minorum] errores scripsi.'

Whatever might be their feelings, the English Minors as a body remained firm in their allegiance to the pope, though retaining strong personal sympathy for the rebellious Michael of Cesena. Only four English friars, so far as is known, withdrew from regular obedience to join the dissidents and preached against the pope; the provincial was commanded to secure them and convey them to Avignon.[1] The official position, then or a little later, was set out in a public sermon at Oxford by an Italian master.[2] The province, however, was to contribute to the schism the acutest mind of the age. William of Ockham, regent-master at Oxford, had been summoned to Avignon in 1324 to answer a charge of false doctrine, and had been in confinement there pending the decision of a court of inquiry. If we may believe his statement, Ockham had of set purpose refrained from acquainting himself with the facts and documents of the Poverty question until commanded by the minister-general, Michael of Cesena, to study the matter. In any case, his situation and the adverse decision upon his teaching which had probably become known to him, would, when added to the influence of his general, tend to dispose him for revolt, and on the night of 26 June 1328, he absconded from the papal city in company with Michael of Cesena and two companions. For the intellectual and political development of Europe in the near and remote future the moment was fraught with consequence; it would not be easy to name any other thinker of the century, not excluding Marsiglio and Wyclif, who as philosopher, theologian and political theorist acted as a more powerful solvent of the amalgam of ideas upon which the higher life of the middle ages rested.

In the last months of 1331 the aged and opinionated pope embarked upon a course of sermons at Avignon in which he put forward with a perverse energy the view that the sight of God face to face, the Beatific Vision properly so called, was not granted to the souls of the just, even when wholly purified, until after the general resurrection and the last judgement. A novel opinion of this kind, reiterated with obstinate emphasis by a pope who was not a trained theologian and who had already set influential sections of Christendom by the ears, naturally aroused passions in minds both interested and disinterested. The view of John XXII was a godsend to the schismatical Minors, and was violently attacked by them as heretical; the Preachers, with the traditional teaching of St Thomas in mind, were unfavourable, but as an order refrained from action; the university of Paris, stirred up by the King of France, was hostile. The main body of the Conventual Minors, on the other hand, defended the pope's thesis; it was sponsored also by a mass of interested ecclesiastics in the papal city who hoped (as the event showed, with reason,) for rewards of a tangible kind for their good offices. It was at this juncture that the English

---

1 *Bull. Franc.* v, 806–7, 809, 849. *Cal. Papal Lett.* (1305–42), 492.

2 *Archivum Franc. Hist.* III, 277–8, and Douie, *Fraticelli*, 198 n. 1, where the authority is quoted.

Preacher, Thomas Waleys, found himself at Avignon as chaplain to Cardinal Matthew Orsini, himself a friar of the order.

Thomas Waleys,[1] a master in theology and a biblical commentator of note, would have been recognized as a kindred spirit by his elder confrère, Richard Knapwell. Previous to his exploits on the continent he had been regent-master at Oxford, having attained the rank, appropriately enough, only after prolonged opposition on the part of the chancellor during the feud between the university and the Preachers.[2] Retiring after the regular term, he was apparently transferred to Bologna, where he resumed his lectures; he certainly preached there often against the Poverty of Christ, a topic on which he had also composed a treatise; he subsequently (if his own account may be believed) routed a gathering of malcontent Minors in conclave at Arezzo by silencing them in public debate.[3]

To his lasting misfortune, and for reasons that do not appear and perhaps need not be sought elsewhere than in his own propensity to have a hand in any controversy that was toward, Waleys saw fit to enter the lists against the pope at a public sermon in the church of his order on Sunday, 3 January 1333. His discourse, ostensibly a panegyric on St John the Apostle (it was the octave day of his feast) was framed on the text, singularly inappropriate to the matter of the sermon: 'The Lord shall fill him with the spirit of wisdom and understanding.'

After an innocent opening in which the gifts of the Evangelist were extolled, the preacher had a passing fling at the pride and vanity that had inspired the Minors in their heretical exaltation of poverty, and in their preposterous doctrine of the freedom of God.[4] He then resumed his consideration of the virtues of the apostle, only to break off, à propos de bottes, into a frontal attack on the proposition of the delayed Vision of God, dealing in a series of paragraphs with the arguments of Cardinal Annibaldo Gaetani de Ceccano, who had supported the opinion of John XXII. Particularly rough treatment was then dealt out to an argument devised by the pope himself,[5] of which its author was extremely proud. By this

---

1 All previous accounts of this affair have been supplanted by the analysis and collection of documents printed (in some cases, for the first time) by F. Th. Käppeli, O.P., *Le Procès contre Thomas Waleys, O.P.* (Inst. Hist. FF. Praedic.; *Dissertationes Historicae*, fasc. VI, Rome, 1936) but this can still be supplemented from Denifle-Chatelain, *Chart. Univ. Paris.* II, nos. 970–87. The theological issue is well treated by X. Le Bachelet in *DTC* and there is a remarkable study of John XXII by N. Valois in *Hist. Litt. de la France*, 34 (1914), 391–630. Other participants in the controversy are treated of in the same or a subsequent volume (37) of the same work.   2 Waleys, *Epistola*, ed. Käppeli, 244.   3 *Ibid.* 241.

4 Waleys, *Sermo*, ed. Käppeli, 96–7: 'Heresis enim, que ponit Christum...nichil habuisse ...unde processit, nisi ex appetitu inanis glorie...vel quia volunt apparere singularis sciencie, ut patet de paupertate Christi, et quod Deus potest precipere homini quod odiat deum, vel quod homo sine caritate vel gracia possit mereri.' The reference (which is not noted by the editor) is presumably to Ockham, e.g. *In Sentt.* I, dist. xvii, *q.* 1: 'Aliquis potest esse Deo acceptus et carus sine omni forma supernaturali inhaerente.'

5 *Ibid.* 103: 'Quantum ad istum argumentum dico, quod si haberem causam arduam coram aliquo judice, quam nollem judici esse suspectam, ego nullo modo producerem testem ita viciosum sicut est istud argumentum.' The Paris MS. Bibl. Nat. lat. 6731 has a marginal note: *ratio domini pape.*

time the audience was no doubt thoroughly excited,[1] and the preacher, like others of his class before and since, stimulated by the electricity in the atmosphere, launched out into an extempore attack[2] on the mercenary motives of those who supported the pope's views, and brought the house down with a devastating reference to the formula used in the papal dispensation of favours, in which the solemn scriptural imprecation employed by a rival Minor, preaching a week or two previously, was reiterated with ludicrous emphasis.[3] The words of Scripture which really supported his opponent's view, he said, were the Psalmist's 'Fiat, fiat!' 'Your devoted son begs your Holiness for such and such a benefice.' 'Granted! Granted!'

It was the preacher's last success. Within a few days he received a summons from the regional inquisitor, a Minor, and after a series of interrogatories was lodged in that official's prison. The head and front of the friar's offending, his opposition to the novel opinions of John XXII, did not figure in the indictment, nor did his criticism of the Minors, which undoubtedly inspired their unrelenting efforts to undo him. At one moment his case was made to coincide with that of the eminent but erratic Durand de Saint Pourçain, also a Preacher, and now bishop of Meaux, who had recently been requested to give his views to John XXII on the question of the Beatific Vision, and had responded by demolishing the pope's position.[4] Waleys, unluckily for himself, had not been content to state in bare terms the traditional doctrine, but had treated of the manner of the resurrection and last judgement in some detail, and propositions were extracted from his sermon which formed a basis for endless cross-examinations in which the unfortunate friar's explanations served as material for fresh charges, while Waleys himself, with a doctor's *amour propre*, added fuel to the fire by writing in his prison a long eschatological treatise[5] which his enemies were not slow to use in their attacks. The case was prolonged, interruped and neglected of set purpose, and there can be no doubt that Waleys, whatever his indiscretions, was the victim of unjust treatment. Besides the inquisitor, a number of his examiners and referees were eminent Minors, including an archbishop and two provincials; it is interesting to

1 A Cluniac monk, replying to Waleys a fortnight later, refers to this, quoting *Quare fremuerunt gentes* and *Ne forte tumultus fieret in populo*. Cf. *Hist. Litt. France*, vol. XXXIV, p. 580.

2 *Acta Processus*, ed. Käppeli, 119: 'Illud invectivum de "fiat, fiat" se dixisse absque precedenti intencione.'

3 Käppeli, 14, was the first to indicate the reference to a previous sermon which inspired the sally. *Fiat, fiat* are the last words of Psalm lxxi in the Vulgate.

4 For Durand, *v.* J. Koch, *Durandus de S. Porciano: Forschungen z. Streit um Thomas von Aquin zu Beginn des 14 Jahrhunderts*, and the article by Paul Fournier in *Hist. Litt. France*, XXXVII (1938), 1–38. The incident in the text is noted on pp. 14–15. Durand, who controverted the teaching of St Thomas on a number of points, was before becoming a bishop repeatedly in trouble at the hands of the general chapter of his order. The commission which examined his doctrine and that of Waleys met in the apartments of Cardinal Annibaldo (Denifle, *Chartul. Paris.* no. 975), whose views had been the ostensible target of the friar's criticism.

5 The *Epistola de instantibus et momentis*, is printed by Käppeli, 157–83.

find Walter Chatton in the party; he was the object of his countryman's peculiar animosity, for Waleys had some time before composed a treatise attacking his opinions on the Beatific Vision, and he now complained that there was no end to his cavilling and quibbling, and that he was clearly fishing for a mitre.[1] Every effort was indeed made to tire Waleys out or to trap him into rash statements on points which were of no intrinsic importance and had no direct reference to either of the two major controversies in which he had interfered.

His enemies, however, did not have it all their own way. Although it does not appear that he received official support from his own order, which stood in high favour with John XXII and which certainly disapproved of the pope's speculations in eschatology, his cause was taken up by the king of France, who convoked an influential body of theologians to assert the traditional doctrine. Although the pope was at some pains to explain that Waleys was not in trouble for opposing the papal opinions, and was in any case kept in very easy captivity, Philip VI continued to agitate, and his interest probably saved Waleys from incidental hardship.[2]

Finally, in despair of getting justice or even activity from the inquisitor, Waleys decided to escape from Charybdis by running upon Scylla, and appealed to the pope, remarking that all the devils in hell could not have surpassed the inquisitorial court in malice.[3] He thus exchanged the inquisitor's prison for the pope's; his spirit was not yet broken, for he complained to John XXII at a personal interview that he would have received fairer treatment from the king of Tartary or the Soldan than he had met with at the hands of the inquisitor.[4] A commission of cardinals was appointed to go into the case, but they showed no greater expedition, and the business dragged into its second year. Meanwhile, a small literature of sermons and pamphlets, for and against Waleys, gradually formed around the original incriminating documents; an attack on the friar was answered by a treatise in his favour, probably by a confrère, and Waleys himself continued to write.[5] No document that has hitherto come to light tells of the issue of the matter. Probably Waleys was neither acquitted nor condemned. In any case he continued to languish in prison for some years after the death of the

---

1 Waleys, *Epistola*, 246: 'Sciatis quod Chattonensis additus est aliis ex magna malicia, ut videlicet retardet alios magistros suis cavillacionibus.' Another English doctor, formerly Chancellor of Oxford, John Lutterell, a cleric of illegitimate birth, was one of the judges; he was a master of theology. An unprinted letter of his is extant in MS. Ii. III 10 fol. 91 v. in the University Library, Cambridge. Waleys' conjecture as to Chatton's hopes, whatever the prospects in 1333, proved correct ten years later, when he was provided to St Asaph by Clement VI, but died almost at once before consecration.

2 Valois, *Jean XXII* in *Hist. Litt. France*, XXXIV, pp. 588 *seqq.*

3 Waleys, *Epistola*, 241.

4 *Ibid. loc. cit.*: 'Dixi domino pape in presencia duorum cardinalium [one of whom was Jacques Fournier, later Benedict XII] quod si fuissem in curia regis Tartarorum vel soldani, credo firmiter quod majorem justiciam invenissem.'

5 The *Libellus famosus*, written by an anonymous opponent in reply to Waleys' *De instantibus*, is printed by Käppeli, 184–94. It was answered by both Waleys himself and a friend, perhaps at Paris, in a *disputatio* (Käppeli, 71).

pope, and even after Benedict XII had solemnly defined the doctrine of the Beatific Vision in the sense upheld in the notorious sermon. He was still alive, and presumably at liberty, in 1349; the last words of his that survive are those of an old and broken man, abandoned by his friends, but there is some evidence that he was ultimately provided to a bishopric.[1]

The affair of Thomas Waleys, though of no intrinsic nobility, serves like similar incidents in other ages, such as the trials of Sacheverell and Dreyfus, to throw into light and shade the currents of sentiment of the times. The rivalries of the two great orders of friars, the European activities of English theologians and controversialists, the acrimonious strife at the court of Avignon, the trend of theological speculation, are all mirrored in the documents of the Waleys case. The friar himself, though the immediate cause of his tribulations was his defence of the traditional doctrine, arouses little enthusiasm as a confessor of the faith and, to do him justice, he never, in his many apologies, demands sympathy for himself as a martyr. His incurable pugnacity and the virulence of his gratuitous attacks on all around him, which seem to have alienated so many of his contemporaries, prevent any warmth of feeling in his regard.

    [1] Denifle, *Chartularium*, no. 971 n. 3: 'Senio confractus aliisque graviter percussus ac amicorum subsidio destitutus.' But a Thomas Waleys, O.P. appears as bishop of Lycostomium in 1353 (*Handbook of British Chronology*, 188).

Part Three

The Monasteries and Their World

CHAPTER XXI

THE CATHEDRAL MONASTERIES

I

The cathedral monasteries, with the peculiar constitution which made of them a class apart among the black monks, deserve a brief separate treatment.

As has been shown elsewhere, they owed their origin to the peculiar circumstances of the English Church in the tenth century and again after the Norman Conquest, when monks were in the forefront of ecclesiastical reform, and when the Primate and other influential bishops were monks.[1] The intention of both Dunstan and Lanfranc and their colleagues was undoubtedly to establish in perpetuity a monastic community which should serve the cathedral and take the place of a chapter, and which was to be presided over by a bishop, himself a monk, who should stand in all things *in loco abbatis*. Of this scheme one part was realized, the other speedily proved unworkable. Before the end of the eleventh century secular bishops ruled more than one important monastic cathedral, and by 1150 the succession of monastic bishops had everywhere been interrupted.

This had inevitably dislocated the primitive harmony between head and members: while the monks strove to emancipate themselves in domestic affairs from the control of one who was not of their profession, secular bishops were rarely willing explicitly to abandon ancient rights, while monastic bishops, appointed after an interval, made every attempt to resume powers that might have fallen into abeyance. In the event, emancipation was achieved by the monks in various degrees and at different times, and when, at the beginning of the thirteenth century, Innocent III set up a commission to report on current practice at cathedral monasteries as a basis for a proposed constitution for Glastonbury, no kind of uniformity was to be found.[2] In the new age of diocesan and monastic reform that followed the Lateran Council a series of collisions occurred, resulting in compositions of every kind, nearly always in favour of the monks, which regulated the priory for the remainder of the medieval centuries.

First among the matters in controversy was the appointment of the prior. The original scheme, in which the bishop took the place of abbot, allowed for his election by the monks; naturally, therefore, he enjoyed the rights of an abbot in the appointment of prior and officials. When, however, the prior came to replace the bishop as effective superior it was equally natural for the monks to wish to elect the head of their house, and to have

---

1 *MO*, 619–31.

2 The commission and its findings are described by Adam of Domerham, *De rebus gestis Glastoniensibus*, ed. T. Hearn, 1727, pp. 395–408.

the management of their own affairs. At Christ Church, Canterbury, where the archbishop always retained a measure of control, the monks obtained as early as 1174 the right of electing a prior *sede vacante*;[1] fifty years later, under Gregory IX (1227–41), they were given the right of free election, but as the archbishop presided as scrutator he could doubtless exercise indirect influence.[2] At Winchester the monks were involved in a series of vexatious disputes with bishops and the king throughout the thirteenth century over episcopal and domestic elections and the wardship of the house during vacancies, and as late as 1280 the bishop was appointing the prior,[3] but the ex-prior Henry Woodlock in 1305 confirmed the right of free election with formal permission obtained from the bishop.[4] At Durham, where no monk had reigned since William of St Calais, the convent had in the reign of John secured a charter giving freedom of election.[5] This was confirmed by the agreement of 1231 known as *le Convenit*,[6] which reduced the bishop's right to a formal grant of permission which, if refused, could be dispensed with. As the elections were presided over by the subprior, and the bishop put in no appearance, Durham enjoyed absolute freedom of choice, and an account of an election in the fifteenth century conducted by way of majority vote shows the system working without a hitch.[7] Not all the cathedral priories achieved freedom so easily. Worcester, where there was a long dispute from 1221 onwards over the removal of a prior, got no further in a composition with William de Blois in 1229 than the right of presenting seven (or five) candidates to the bishop, and this was still in force half a century later.[8] Of the others, Bath received licence of free election in 1261, Rochester somewhat later, and both Ely and Norwich were enjoying it before the end of the thirteenth century.[9]

A still greater diversity appeared in the appointment of obedientiaries which, by a natural anomaly, remained a part of the bishop's prerogative even after the more essential post of prior had become elective. The commissioners of 1203 reported that in most cathedrals the bishop had the right of appointing sacrist, cellarer, chamberlain and almoner.[10] At Christ Church, however, it was the subprior, precentor, sacrist and chamberlain,

1 *Papsturkunden in England*, ed. W. Holtzmann, II, p. 323.

2 Hist. MSS. Comm., App. to VIIIth Rep. p. 317. An example may be seen in 1263, when the monks held a free election and sent the votes to Boniface in France; he did not appoint the candidate with the most votes (Gervase Cant. II, 226–7).

3 *Ann. Waverl.* (*Ann. Monast.* II), s.a. 1279. *Reg. Johannis de Pontissara*, ed. C. Deedes (*C & YS*, 1915), II, 655, 693 *et al.*

4 *Reg. Hen. Woodlock*, ed. A. W. Goodman (*C & YS*, 1940), I, 39.

5 The charter is in *Feodarium Prioratus Dunelmensis*, ed. W. Greenwell, 93.

6 *Feodarium*, 212–17.

7 *Durham Obituary Rolls*, ed. J. Raine, 91–102 (election of J. Burnby in 1456).

8 *Ann. Wigorn.* (*Ann. Monast.* IV), s.a. 1221–4. The final agreement is in *Registrum Prioratus B.M. Wigorniensis*, 27*a*–29*b*. The number there is seven.
Cf. *Reg. Bishop Godfrey Giffard*, ed. J. W. Willis Bund (Worcs. Hist. Soc. 2 vols. 1902), II, 304, 325.

9 *Two Chartularies of Bath Priory* (*SRS*, 1893), II, nos. 251, 808.

10 Adam of Domerham 418.

together with three of the most important lay functionaries; the convent often contested this right unsuccessfully, though they established the custom of presenting three names for the archbishop's choice. An endeavour to reduce the three names to one was frustrated after a long struggle by Archbishop Winchelsey, but friction continued for many years.[1] At Norwich the monks had apparently at some time or other brought off the feat attempted in vain by Christ Church, for in the award of Archbishop Arundel in 1411 the convent were confirmed in their practice of sending up a single name to the bishop for each of ten important offices,[2] and at Durham, at least from early in the thirteenth century, the prior had the right of appointment to all offices; this was confirmed by the *Convenit*.[3] At Winchester, on the other hand, where the long rule of Henry of Blois had perhaps shackled early developments, the bishop as late as 1270 was appointing a dozen obedientiaries besides the prior, despite the convent's protests; here again, however, Henry Woodlock gave over the right to the prior.[4] At Worcester the bishop appointed the sacrist, and one of the keepers of the shrine.[5]

The third power originally possessed by the abbot-bishop was that of admitting candidates to the monastic habit and of subsequently receiving their profession. Here again there was diversity of practice. At Christ Church the prior and convent obtained from Gregory IX the right of clothing and professing novices *sede vacante* but attempts to get the privilege when the see was occupied failed, and the archbishop retained in perpetuity at least the formal right of examination and refusal.[6] At other houses his control was reduced to a legal fiction: thus at Durham would-be novices, after having been passed by prior and chapter, had a formal examination before the bishop; at the end of probation they made two professions, one in chapter and the second before the bishop, who gave the prescribed blessing;[7] at Norwich, the prior and chapter examined and admitted the postulant, who was presented to the bishop, who blessed the novice without more ado; when the time came for profession the convent admitted the candidate and the bishop was bound to solemnize the profession at request.[8]

While the bishop thus lost ground to the monks they held firmly to their

---

1 For a brief account of this, *v.* R. A. L. Smith, *Canterbury Cathedral Priory*, 33–6.

2 E. H. Carter, *Studies in Norwich Cathedral History* (Norwich, 1935). Cf. no. 3 in the articles of adjudication of Archbishop Arundel in 1411.

3 *Feodarium Dunelm.* 93: 'Priores...omnes fratres officiales ipsi libere statuant vel amoveant.'

4 *Reg. J. de Pontissara*, II, 655; *Reg. Hen. Woodlock*, I, 39.

5 *Reg. B.M. Wigorniensis*, 137b.

6 The long history of the struggle may be traced in *Literae Cantuarienses*. For references, *v.* Smith, *Canterbury*, 7 n. 3.

7 *Feodarium*, 212–13. To avoid confusion it may be noted that the postulant was clothed with the novice's habit with appropriate prayers and blessings; when the novice made his profession he and his monk's habit were more solemnly blessed.

8 E. H. Carter, *op. cit.* Arundel's adjudication, nos. 1 and 2.

right of electing the occupant of the see. This had been in origin the indefeasible right of the monastic community to elect its head; as such it had lost much of its *raison d'être* when the bishop ceased to be the effective superior, and would scarcely have survived the storms and stresses of time but for the importance of free capitular election in the programme of later Gregorian reform; the monks, and they alone, formed the chapter of the cathedral monasteries, and it was therefore impossible, without uncanonical revolution, to deprive them formally of their right to elect the bishop. Historians have used hard words of this arrangement,[1] and a case might perhaps be made against a scheme which put the choice of the Primate of England into the hands of a miscellaneous body of private individuals who were biased in favour of one of their own house and profession. In practice, however, the Canterbury monks, if impervious to reason or persuasion, could always be dragooned or disregarded by a piece of legal chicanery, and although throughout the thirteenth century they made obstinate attempts to put one of their own house into the see,[2] they were never successful, and in later periods were usually willing to elect the royal candidate. In other cathedrals, similar attempts were made to elect a domestic candidate, usually a prior or sacrist; they were not always unsuccessful, and at Rochester, Ely and Norwich in particular several monk-bishops ruled.[3] It might, indeed, be argued that a man capable of governing or administering with success a great house such as Durham or Ely would possess most of the qualities needed in a bishop, and in fact the monastic bishops of the whole period were as a class capable and edifying men, if not remarkable for genius and sanctity, while many of the monastic candidates rejected by pope or king for reasons of policy were to all seeming better qualified for spiritual rule than their successful rivals.[4]

Actually, the potentially evil results of the monastic control of election were neutralized in various ways throughout the three centuries with which we are concerned. In the thirteenth century, when the newly complicated canonical procedure was carefully supervised by Rome, it was often possible to find a flaw in the process which allowed the pope to quash an election and make his own choice, nor was it unknown for the king to use extreme pressure or even downright violence. Later, when the papal claims to immediate and universal jurisdiction were being pushed to the uttermost limit, elections were often anticipated or nullified by papal provision.

Besides the right of election, the monks and their prior claimed the right of a dean and chapter to administer the see during a vacancy, and as a jealous and undying corporation were able to exploit their powers more

1 E.g. Stubbs, *Epp. Cant.*, introd. xxix–xxxi.
2 *Gervase of Canterbury (Gesta Regum*, continuation), II, 122 (Walter of Eynsham, 1228); 129 (John of Sittingbourne, 1232); 253 (Adam of Chillenden, 1270).
3 For a list of monastic bishops, *v.* Appendix II.
4 The judgement on monastic bishops in Gibbs and Lang, *Bishops and Reform*, 5–10, is a little too harsh.

freely than their secular counterparts. The monks of Christ Church, in particular, claimed the right of exercising both diocesan and provincial authority during a vacancy, and thus of receiving profession of obedience from the suffragans and arranging for the consecration at Canterbury of the elect; this made them in a sense arbiters of the election, and in the thirteenth century they did not hesitate to excommunicate bishops, while ready, on other occasions, to defy an archbishop's ban in virtue of papal privilege.[1] At Worcester, where the traditions of Wulfstan died hard, and an unusual number of vacancies occurred, the prior of the day frequently embarked upon a tour of visitation among the numerous and important religious houses of the diocese.[2] At Durham the prior was recognized as first in the diocese after the bishop, and sat during a vacancy with the archdeacons.[3] Elsewhere, and notably at Ely, Norwich and Winchester, where relations with the bishop were usually cordial in the fourteenth century, the prior often acted as sole or joint vicar-general during absences of the ordinary from the diocese.[4] Conversely, the bishop was visitor to his cathedral priory, with a peculiar domestic interest in the service of his cathedral. This right could not be, and was not, denied, for an exempt cathedral priory would have been almost a contradiction in terms, but the monks jealously preserved as much privacy as possible by papal privileges or compositions limiting the number of secular clerks the bishop might bring with him. Indeed, they tried to exclude all except those of their habit, but the bishops stood out for at least one disinterested witness as a safeguard against any claims the monks might make of concessions obtained.[5]

In other respects, also, each cathedral monastery was brought into contact with its bishop in a host of incidents of daily life. At Worcester, by old agreement, the prior acted as dean of the city churches and the precentor took the place of the archdeacon;[6] at Norwich the churches on the manors in Norfolk had a species of exemption;[7] at Canterbury and elsewhere the jurisdictional boundaries of the archbishop's barony and the convent's liberty were only settled after controversy.

As the bishop withdrew by successive stages from the position of effective superior, the prior came to acquire something of the status of an abbot. Originally no more than a resident second-in-command, he now took the place of a prelate with jurisdiction, and the change was marked externally by the erection of a lodging, with chapel, hall and offices complete with staff, resembling the separate establishment of an abbot.

---

1 *V.* Smith, *Canterbury*, 9, with ref. to Gervase, vol. II.

2 Cf. the Worcester *Reg. Sede Vacante*, ed. J. W. Willis Bund (Worc. Hist. Soc. 2 vols. 1895 and 1897).

3 *Feodarium* (le Convenit), 212–13: 'Sit Prior secundus ab Episcopo, scilicet, major persona post Episcopum in Episcopatu Dunelmensi in omni dignitate et honore Abbatis.'

4 E.g. Prior Crauden of Ely.

5 The best example of this particular type of quarrel is perhaps that at Durham in 1300. *V. Gesta Dunelmensia*, ed. R. K. Richardson (*CS*, 3 ser. XXXIV).

6 *Ann. Wigorn. s.a.* 1288.

7 *V.* arts. 4 and 5 of Arundel's adjudication, in Carter, *op. cit.*

Like the abbot, also, the prior during the thirteenth and early fourteenth centuries spent much of his time on his manors or absent on official business,[1] and in some cases he was even summoned to parliament.[2] Indeed, the independent position of the prior received in time the somewhat curious recognition of the grant of *pontificalia*, which, first appearing at Canterbury in 1221 and Winchester in 1254, became almost universal in the next century.[3] He thus resembled an abbot in all respects, save only for the title and the abbatial benediction, which did not in fact confer jurisdiction or any spiritual powers. There were, nevertheless, some circumstances which, although not essential, had a profound psychological effect. In the first place the priors never resembled the abbots in holding groups of lands and revenues apart from the community and forming a feudal barony. The knight-service of the church was always borne by the bishop, and the prior received his income from community sources and usually through a monastic official. Next, the name and consecration of an abbot, to which the Rule and tradition had attached a peculiar reverence, were never his. Consequently, the priors of the cathedral monasteries were less separated from the body of the community in interests or sympathy, and, real as was their authority, it is possible to see in these houses a co-operative and almost democratic spirit which contrasts with the more monarchic constitution of the abbeys. The free election of the prior, and the appointment of officials by the bishop, tended alike to throw the prior and his monks together, and the numerous conflicts with the bishop strengthened the ties. In the discussions issuing in the disciplinary ordinances of chapter, which are more numerous in the cathedrals than elsewhere, and in the work of the council of seniors in auditing accounts and directing policy, we see the prior working with his monks almost as a chairman with his board. This aspect of sentiment and practice must not be exaggerated, and it had no further results in monastic history, but it cannot be omitted from any full survey of medieval conditions.

Two of the cathedral monasteries stand somewhat apart from the rest. The monks of Bath and Coventry did not originally serve cathedrals; they were independent abbeys absorbed by powerful bishops who had, at Wells and Lichfield respectively, churches and secular chapters of their own. If this made it easier in time for the monks to secure a degree of autonomy, it also made their claim to act as electors less reasonable. In both cases, however, the claim was pressed home, and after prolonged controversy compromises were effected. In the western see it was

---

1 E.g. in 1310–11 the prior of Durham spent 241 days on his manors (*Durham Account Rolls*, ed. J. T. Fowler, II, 507).

2 E.g. in 1265 the priors of Canterbury, Coventry, Ely and Norwich were summoned.

3 The prior of Christ Church obtained the use of the mitre on great solemnities in 1221 (*Ann. Dunstapl., s.a.*), but a century later is found asking for staff, tunic and sandals, as the prior of Worcester has them and he fears loss of prestige (*Lit. Cant.* 810–15; cf. 708). The prior of Durham did not get the mitre and staff till 1381 (*Scriptores Tres*, 136). The prior of Winchester received the ring, mitre and staff in 1254 (*Ann. Wint. s.a.*).

arranged that the chapters should elect jointly, meeting alternately at Bath and Wells. In the midlands the two bodies agreed to elect separately in turn.[1]

As a result of all these circumstances, the cathedral monasteries preserved certain characteristics to the end. All (if we except Bath and Coventry) were very wealthy, and their position at a centre of ecclesiastical and civil affairs gave them advantages in recruitment and in variety of interests over all save a few of the abbeys. Certainly, they were, as a group, distinguished for their intellectual activities: Christ Church, Durham, Worcester and Norwich were in the forefront of the university movement, and produced between them most of the distinguished monk-graduates. As a group they preserved their numbers relatively high, and even if the ease with which they accepted the new order and settled into comfortable positions argued no very obstinate devotion to monastic ideals, it must be allowed that as a group their record during the century before the dissolution had been on the whole a clear one. They were certainly worthy custodians of the great churches they served; it is perhaps largely accidental that we should have so many of their books to enjoy, but it is owing directly to the energies and large views of a dozen great priors and their officials that we can see such magnificent pieces of late medieval building as the naves of Winchester, Canterbury and Norwich, the central towers of Durham and Canterbury, and the Lady chapel and lantern of Ely.

II

The story of the cathedral monasteries is chequered with the quarrels between the monks and their bishops. Speaking generally, three periods may be observed: in the thirteenth century, when the disputes were most common and most bitter, they were usually concerned with important points where legal issues had yet to be settled. Many instances have already been noted; two of the most deplorable, and seemingly most avoidable, were those at Winchester and between the monks of Christ Church and St Edmund Rich. Both were prolonged yet both were historically insignificant. In the next period, which covers the greater part of the fourteenth century, disputes were less frequent, and were commonly brought about by the overbearing or unreasonable conduct of one of the parties: that between the monks of Durham and Antony Bek is perhaps the most notorious, but the history of Christ Church abounds in minor incidents between archbishop and monks. Finally, the fifteenth century is almost wholly free from great quarrels; institutions had become static, and neither party had anything to gain from litigation; moreover, the disappearance of the papacy, for all practical purposes, as a powerful and independent third party of appeal, automatically lessened litigation. Such quarrels as occurred were personal matters, and the Norwich dispute settled by

1 *Two Bath Chartularies*, ed. W. Hunt (*SRS*, 1893). *Mag. Reg. Album Lich.* (Will. Salt. Soc., 1924), 198–203.

Arundel in 1411 was, as the composition showed, something of a fossil.

Of all these controversies perhaps the most deplorable was that between the monks of Christ Church and St Edmund Rich.[1] Despite the length of the existing narratives of the course of the quarrel, its origins are never clearly stated, but apparently the claims of the archbishop's officials to receive return of writs in the Christ Church liberty, and the old question of the right to the customary *exennia* from certain of the monastery's manors were at the root of the trouble.[2] In the sequel, both sides appear to have trespassed; the archbishop by demanding to view the accounts of the monks, and the monks more gravely by denying the undoubted right of the archbishop to appoint the prior of Dover and the major obedientiaries. It must not be forgotten that the see of Canterbury had been vacant over long, and that two *bona fide* elections had been quashed at Rome somewhat arbitrarily. The moral tone of the community, long regarded as factious and obstructive, must have suffered from this repeated frustration, and when Edmund Rich, an unworldly scholar, was elected in deference to papal wishes, a party of the monks may have decided to exploit his supposed inexperience to the utmost.

When all attempts at understanding and arbitration failed, a papal commission of no great strength was set up.[3] A series of vexatious delays and adjournments ensued, for the archbishop, though far more amenable to argument and equable in temper than his great predecessor, had much of Becket's tenacity and fearlessness when what he conceived to be justice

1 The fullest account is by the continuator of Gervase of Canterbury, printed by Stubbs in vol. II of the *Opera* of Gervase (*RS*, 73); he naturally favours the convent. Several lives of St Edmund exist, and a completely critical edition of the whole group is greatly to be desired; for some *prolegomena* to the problem of their authorship and interdependence, v. H. W. C. Davis, *An early life of Edmund Rich*, in *EHR* XXII, 84–92. Three lives are printed by Dom Wilfrid Wallace, in his valuable *Life of St Edmund of Canterbury* (1893), which also contains interesting documents from the Canterbury archives; the reader should not be unduly prejudiced by its pietistic tone. One *Life*, which is clearly by one who was with the archbishop, is probably the work of the monk Eustace, the chamberlain and chaplain of the archbishop (*Gervase*, II, 145–6), who was in Rome and later at Tonbridge with him (*ibid.* 131, 155). Stubbs, who differs from most English historians in showing partiality for St Edmund, is severe towards the monks, but few will wish to reverse his judgement that it was an impossible task for 'the best of archbishops to manage his captious and litigious chapter'.

2 The Christ Church annalist says nothing of this, but the writer (?Eustace) of the *Vita B. Edmundi* has: 'Monachi...quasdam suas libertates ipsum, ut dicebant, conventum specialiter contingentes, quas archiepiscopales occuparant, constanter reposcebant', while the archbishop considered that he 'de rei familiaris cognitione merito debere certificari'. The monks, as it seems from the report of the commissioners in 1237 (Wallace, Appendix IX), were trying to recover 22,000 marks stolen by King John and alleged to have been restored to Langton, and the archbishop may have wished to see their account rolls, which were always jealously kept private (cf. *Litt. Cant.*, *RS*, II, 869). The return of the king's writs was allowed to archbishop Edmund (*Close Rolls, Henry III*, 1234–37, pp. 117, 149), and this may well have precipitated the controversy settled by the composition with Boniface in 1259 (for which see Smith, *Canterbury Cathedral Priory*, 95–6).

3 For the commission (the abbots of Boxley, St Radegund's and Lesnes) and a valuable statement of the points ultimately at issue, v. Wallace, Appendices IX, X, pp. 488–98.

was at stake. When at last the commission decided rightly in the archbishop's favour the prospect of peace was shut out on the one hand by the king's claim to take cognizance of the matter and on the other by the conduct of the professional advocates of both sides at Rome. The monks' lawyers urged a continuance of the struggle, while the archbishop's friends, among whom his archdeacon Simon Langton took the part of an Achitophel, made capital out of two pieces of sharp practice by the monks among the muniments[1] and revived the fatal scheme for a large prebendal college in the neighbourhood of Canterbury which might rival or supplant the cathedral monastery. The issue was further embittered by a rift within the community, a minority being in favour of a reconciliation with the archbishop, while the monks, though successively suspended and interdicted, proceeded to elect a prior without reference to St Edmund. Eventually, a complete *impasse* was reached from which monks, archbishop and king were all equally unable to escape, and no glimpse of a way out had been seen when St Edmund died overseas. The dispute died with him;[2] the issues at stake had been purely private and personal, and subsequent disagreements over these and similar matters were discussed and settled in a less violent temper.

To set against these painful quarrels there are records of more friendly relationships. The letters of Henry of Eastry, soothing, advising and chastening successive archbishops, are well known, as are the benefactions of Bishop Hatfield to the Oxford house of the Durham monks, and at almost every house there are notices of gifts on this side and on that, and evidences of respect and friendship between the community who never ceased to have something of a filial regard for their bishop, and the prelate who hoped to lie at last in the church of the monks.

1 One monk had forged or (as he put it) rewritten, a charter of St Thomas in favour of the monks, while another had burnt a bull of Alexander III, entrusted to Christ Church by the archbishop and presumably telling in his favour (*Gervase*, II, 131-3).

2 The attempts of Simon Langton to prolong it ceased with his death. The relations of Archbishop Boniface with the monks were comparatively amicable.

CHAPTER XXII

THE MONASTIC BOROUGHS

I

Among the assets and interests of a number of the larger monasteries and houses of black canons the control of a borough held an important place. The history of these towns belongs strictly to that of municipal, not of monastic institutions, and though they differed in several important respects from royal boroughs and those of secular mesne lords they do not form a homogeneous group. Their origins, growth and organization were so varied and so gradual that a series of monographs would be necessary before any attempt could be made to regard them as a class.[1] Certain characteristics can, however, be seen in many, if not in most, and almost without exception they failed to achieve the complete independence and autonomy for which they struggled, and which the other towns of England had less difficulty in securing.

The control of the monastic boroughs normally resided with the prior or abbot concerned, who was in all cases the feudal lord, but at some houses the town had in early times been allotted to the convent's share in the division of property and was therefore immediately controlled by one of the obedientiaries: thus at Bury the sacrist was in power, at Coventry the cellarer, and at Faversham the cellarer and chamberlain. In any case, the effective duties of administration and exploitation were in the hands of a secular official, the reeve, bailiff or steward, who collected the rents, taxes and fines and presided over the courts as the representative of the abbot and convent. In early times, the bailiff usually farmed the profits for a fixed sum from the convent, but later he became a steward pure and simple, receiving and accounting for all revenues. For the greater part of the medieval period he was chosen from among the burgesses, but in the last hundred years before the dissolution he was generally a local landowner, while in early Tudor times the post was usually held (often in plurality) by one of the leading gentlemen or noblemen of the district. Besides the bailiff, the convent also appointed the coroner, who was the keeper (and sometimes also the holder) of the pleas of the crown, and the constables. Not infrequently the bailiff himself was coroner and chief constable.[2]

The income from the town to the monastery, in addition to the rents, was made up of taxes (and particularly the house or tenement tax of a shilling a year), and of tolls, customs, dues, small imposts such as the tax on ale, and the profits of courts.

1 The only satisfactory monograph hitherto published is the wholly excellent *Borough of Bury St Edmund's* by Mrs M. D. Lobel. Prof. N. M. Trenholme's *The English Monastic Boroughs* is a careful and useful work, but fuller study of individual boroughs is needed before a final synthesis can be made. For some paragraphs on the monastic town in the twelfth century *v. MO*, 444–7.   2 *V.* the section *Borough Officers* in Lobel, 59–95.

The organization of the townspeople took two forms: there was the universal association of the burgesses under an alderman or mayor, and the gild merchant.[1] This latter did not exist in all the monastic boroughs;[2] in a few the monastic overlords had encouraged its formation in the twelfth century, when its commercial advantages were obvious and its potentialities as a union for agitation were not so clear; later, when it was being used elsewhere as an instrument in the struggle for self-government, monks and canons were not as a rule prepared to allow its establishment. Where no gild merchant existed, it was natural that the burgesses should form a union with a head—alderman or mayor—who might lead them in the fight for self-determination, act as their representative to the abbot and as go-between in the abbot's dealing with the townspeople. At Bury and a few other boroughs both organizations existed, overlapping but not absolutely coincident;[3] here the alderman of the town was also head of the gild, though not all burgesses were members; originally, he was elected as head of the town by the burgesses and presented for confirmation to the abbot; later, the abbots claimed the right of appointment and deposition. Once appointed the alderman was opposite number to the bailiff; the presence of both was necessary at the portmanmote and market court; he was responsible for the actual maintenance of order within the town, while on the other hand, he could in some cases deputize for an absent bailiff. His position, like that of the bailiff or steward, rose in the social scale and in the later medieval period the alderman came from the urban aristocracy. Despite this, and despite the volume of wealth controlled by the burgesses in the fourteenth and early fifteenth centuries, the monastic boroughs were held firmly in the grip of the abbot and convent, whose supervision extended even to the conditions of trade. As the author of the most careful study of the subject observes of one of the largest of the class: 'Bury was extremely closely controlled by its lord. The powers of the bailiffs and their subordinates were all pervading, and the right to appoint and dismiss these officers lay with the sacrist and was never acquired by the burgesses.'[4]

II

The relations between the monastic bodies and the townsfolk at their gates were in general troubled. Such friction was by no means confined to monastic boroughs; it was common throughout north-western Europe from the end of the eleventh century onwards wherever the lord of a

1 For this last the indispensable work is still that of C. Gross, *The Gild Merchant* (1890).

2 Trenholme (p. 90) states that six possessed the gild, but his own data and those of Gross (1, 9–16) to which he refers show at least seven.

3 For Bury, Lobel (p. 79) corrects the opinion of Gross and Trenholme that the gild and borough had entirely separate organizations. The town, she writes, 'presents a case of an elaborate fusion of the functions of merchant guild and borough community'. At Reading alone 'the gild became identified with the *communitas* of the borough', and 'no borough organization existed outside the gild' (Trenholme, 92).

4 Lobel, 72.

growing town desired, and was strong enough to put barriers in the way of urban autonomy; it was most marked in towns which had an ecclesiastical overlord, because a monastery or a resident bishop was more anxious and more able to maintain his hold than was a distant sovereign or a secular lord, and in northern France, in Flanders, and in south-western Germany, the most violent and most successful risings were in the bishops' towns. In England the monasteries were more important holders of boroughs than were the bishops,[1] and the struggle came later than abroad; in the twelfth century the monastic boroughs, many of which owed a large part of their trade to the monastery and its pilgrims, and enjoyed a freedom and good order superior to that common elsewhere, were content to remain in tutelage or confined their revolts to refusing services or imposts that were peculiarly irksome or out of date. From the thirteenth century onwards, however, a series of attempts, usually due to a communal movement and accompanied by violence, aimed at securing complete self-government. These failed, almost without exception, for the townspeople were fighting against a resident deathless body which had the support of the crown. When recourse was had to violence the concessions extracted by force or terror were almost always repudiated, and when these or other matters came before the royal courts these invariably gave judgement for the monastery.

Until the materials for the history of all the monastic boroughs have been fully analysed only the main features of the struggle can be seen, but it is noteworthy that the outbreaks of general violence usually occurred at moments of disorder or weak government in the country at large.

The first period of disturbance was in the second half of the thirteenth century, when political conditions were unstable owing to the activities of de Montfort and his party. In some cases the agitation took the form of a demand for recognition of the gild merchant; at Reading, in 1252–6, the burgesses achieved this, though the abbot succeeded in obtaining a virtual control of the gild.[2] At Bury, a few years later, a group of younger townsmen, relying on the support of de Montfort's party, formed a gild and endeavoured to set up a commune. Riots took place, the abbey gates were assaulted and the abbot shut out of the town; but when the day of reckoning before a royal inquiry came, the gild, which had nothing to do with the gild merchant, and was in reality a political association, was dissolved.[3]

---

1 For the struggles of the continental towns *v.* H. Pirenne, *Camb. Med. Hist.* VI, 517 *seqq.*, and authorities given by him in bibliography. An English example may be seen in Lynn in Norfolk, belonging to the bishop of Norwich, which never succeeded during the medieval period in obtaining the liberty which Norwich itself, a royal borough, enjoyed from early times.

2 Trenholme, pp. 19 *seqq.*

3 Lobel points this out (p. 131); many previous writers, including Gross (II, 30 *seqq.*), Arnold and Réville, confused the *gilda juvenum* with the *gilda mercatoria.* Trenholme (p. 23) took a more correct view, citing B.M. Add. MS 14847, f. 102: 'Quaedam multitudo...qui se Bachelarii vocari fecerunt, per conspirationem mutuam quandam Gildam levaverunt, quam Geldam juvenum vocaverunt.' Gross (II, 31) had quoted the passage.

Coventry was the scene of *émeutes* at the same time; here the town was divided between the prior and the earl of Chester and the monastic burgesses had a gild merchant which was the object of jealousy among the earl's men.[1] Finally, the first recorded serious disturbance took place at St Albans in these years. Here the immediate *casus belli* was the abbey's monopoly of milling corn and fulling cloth; the townsmen therefore installed handmills in private houses, and were for setting up a commune.[2] As always, a royal inquisition restored the *status quo*, while the abbot made a few concessions, such as the abandonment of the tax on ale.

The next season of disturbance was in 1327, after the inefficient government of Edward II. The revolts, which were widespread, were in some cases at least encouraged by emissaries from London, which was in a state of upheaval. At St Albans[3] a commune was set up which demanded two burgesses to go to parliament, rights of common, power to grind corn in private houses, and a town bailiff free from the abbot's jurisdiction. While preparations for a discussion in London were pending the townspeople assaulted the abbey, but failed to carry the gates; they were, however, more successful in London, where their appeal to alleged ancient rights was upheld by arbitrators and a letter obtained from the king ordering a composition. This was forced upon the chapter by an irresolute abbot amid universal protest. The town enjoyed its freedom for seven years, when another abbot, the energetic Richard of Wallingford, decided upon action after his spiritual jurisdiction had been resisted. In the brawl which followed both the abbot's marshal and the burgess on whom he was serving a summons were killed, and in the series of lawsuits which ensued the townspeople lost all the liberties they had won in 1327, largely owing to the mixture of persistence and conciliation employed by the abbot, though he was so seriously affected by leprosy as to be scarcely intelligible when speaking.[4]

At Bury events followed a very similar course. Here the rising took place in January, 1327.[5] Three thousand tenants and villeins revolted; the

---

1 Trenholme, 25–6.   2 *GASA*, I, 410.

3 For this *v*. Trenholme's article *The Risings in the English Monastic Towns in 1327* in *American Historical Review*, VI (1901), 650–70. Much of this was embodied in Prof. Trenholme's book.

4 Trenholme, 31 *seqq*.; *GASA*, II, 149 *seqq*. The editor (H. T. Riley) of the *GASA* in the *RS* places the death of Abbot Hugh on 7 September 1326, and consequently puts this rising in the first months of that year. As, however, it is clearly stated (p. 155) that the trouble began 'circa annum Domini 1326 postquam Dominus Edwardus Karnervan adjudicatus fuisset a regno...post festum Epiphaniae Domini', the date must be January 1326/7, and the abbot's death in September 1327.

GASA, II, 255–6: 'Ipse Abbas, propter detestabilem leprae morbum...nec aspectu placidus nec sermone gratiosus naturaliter potuit apparere...vix distincte poterat concipi prae raucitudine loquela sua.' The millstones of offence were brought into the church by the people (*ibid*. 255) and were used by the monks, *ad perpetuam rei memoriam*, to pave the parlour, whence they were removed by the rioters of 1381, and subsequently returned with apologies.

5 *MSE*, II, 329 *seqq*., *Depraedatio abbatiae*.

abbey precinct was invaded and plundered, and the abbot was forced to sign a charter giving Bury the full rights of an autonomous borough.[1] On the pretext of ratifying this document he visited London, where he canvassed the lords and prelates at Westminster for sympathy and advice. They advised repudiation, but news of this caused a second outbreak of rioting and pillage which was only stopped by the king taking the abbey into his hands. When he withdrew to Scotland in the autumn a third outbreak took place; this was the most serious of all: the gates were stormed and a whole range of outbuildings, offices and guest halls torn down and burnt, while on the monastic manors stock was driven off, fodder and grain plundered, and buildings fired;[2] meanwhile, the monks, barricaded in a section of the conventual buildings, had armed their servants, who had frequent and fatal brushes with the insurgents. Peace was only restored by force of arms by the sheriff of Norfolk; executions and heavy fines followed. A group of the outlaws, bent on revenge, made a descent upon the abbot in his manor at Chevington. Overpowering the servants they seized the abbot in his room, from which his chaplains had escaped by sliding down a towel tied to the window, and haled the unfortunate prelate to London, where, after his head and eyebrows had been shaved, he was passed from house to house in the city, and thence to Brabant, where he was maintained in wretched durance for three months. Two years later, after a succession of royal commissions and courts, the *status quo ante* was once more restored.

Meanwhile, similar scenes had been enacted at Abingdon,[3] where early in May 1327, after an ineffectual attack on the abbey gates, the insurgents invoked and obtained the assistance of the mayor of Oxford. A mob of townsmen and scholars took the road to Abingdon, stormed the gates, sacked the abbey, imprisoned some of the monks and pursued for a distance another band of the brethren, of whom more than one had adventures in the Thames while endeavouring to get clear.[4] On the next day three of the senior monks were brought into the presence of a great crowd of three thousand rioters under the greenwood tree[5] and forced by threats of death to grant a charter, which was soon after signed in chapter, giving autonomy and indemnity to the revolutionaries. The abbot, however, had escaped to court, and as at Bury royal protection was given and the sheriffs of Oxford and Berkshire detailed to quell the revolt. This they succeeded in doing, and for three years suits, indictments, condemnations and

1 *MSE*, II, 333: 'Unam cartam de communitate et de communi sigillo, gilda mercatoria, et aldermanno perpetuis habendis.'

2 *MSE*, II, 340–7 (long list of losses on manors). According to the editor's computation, the total estimate of loss on the manors alone is £1118.

3 Trenholme, 41–4, gives a full account of this, using several manuscript sources. The most detailed printed account is in the *Chronicle Roll of the Abbots of Abingdon*, ed. H. E. Salter in *EHR*, XXVI, 727–38.

4 Trenholme (p. 42) writes 'several of these were drowned', but the *Chronicle Roll*, 732, says merely *fere submersis*.

5 *Chron. Roll*, 733. 'In sylva de Baggele' (Bagley).

executions continued, and the townspeople were forced to surrender their charter and accept liability for damages. The abbey had indeed sustained severe damage and losses, many of which could not be made good,[1] but the monks had learnt their lesson, and fortified their precinct and the neighbouring buildings.

These do not exhaust the list of risings in 1327; Canterbury, Coventry, Plymouth, Dunstable, Barnstaple and Cirencester saw trouble,[2] but everywhere, save at Coventry, where the non-monastic half of the town, falling into the hands of the queen mother, Isabel, secured self-government and was joined by the greater part of the prior's half, the insurgents were uniformly unsuccessful in setting up a commune.

The monastic lords of boroughs had yet another storm to weather, that of the Peasants' Revolt of 1381. In this the burgesses exploited in their own interests the revolutionary and anti-monastic animus of the rebels. At Bury[3] the abbey was attacked by the insurgents; the prior, captured at Mildenhall, was beheaded out of hand, and another monk, the warden of the abbot's barony, was executed at Bury and all charters and muniments establishing rights over the town were seized. The situation was only restored by the arrival in East Anglia of the warlike Henry Despenser of Norwich.

On the day after the attack on Bury a spontaneous rising took place at St Albans, where the townspeople opened negotiations with Wat Tyler and aroused the villeins of the neighbouring villages.[4] The abbey was attacked and Abbot Thomas de la Mare, after lengthy parleys, bowed to the storm like the monks of Bury and surrendered his charters, granting also a new one, dictated by the insurgents; this reflected the old grievances, without giving a clearly cut autonomy to the town: the people were to have certain rights of common and game, they were to enjoy the use of handmills, and the bailiff of the abbot's liberty was not to enter the town without a writ from the king. No doubt de la Mare knew that his surrender would not be permanent, and in fact soon after the death of Wat Tyler armed forces, followed by the king himself, arrived and overpowered the burgesses; the charters, old and new, were given up, and executions and penalties followed, which the abbot was able in part to mitigate.

Other monastic towns in the district affected by the rising took the opportunity of pressing their claims. Dunstable, not far from St Albans,

---

1 The *Chronicle Roll* (p. 734) gives a list of the losses. Besides precious articles of every kind, including the monks' drinking mazers, the loot included 100 psalters, 100 graduals, 40 missals and 10 decretals. These, it is to be supposed, were picked up by Oxford *stationarii* in the crowd.

2 Trenholme, 44 *seqq.* For Barnstaple, *v.* R. Graham.

3 The fullest and most accurate account of this rising, and of the troubles at Bury and St Albans, is in *Le Soulèvement des Travailleurs d'Angleterre en* 1381, by André Réville, which has as preface an equally valuable discussion (pp. i–cxxxvi) of the rising by Ch. Petit-Dutaillis. It is based on original and manuscript sources, some of which have not yet been printed.

4 For the voluminous documents of this episode *v.* Trenholme and Réville.

took its cue from its neighbour and the customary process took its course: a charter of liberties was extracted by force from the prior, to be later annulled by the king. At Peterborough the monks were saved at the very moment of an attack by the mob by the arrival of Henry Despenser on his way to Norwich.[1]

The Peasants' Revolt of 1381, like its successors throughout England for almost two centuries, was a simultaneous rising of many classes and groups with varied grievances and aims. It is clear that the inhabitants of the monastic towns exploited a rising in which they had no originating share in order to reiterate their old demands without any definite or thorough-going programme. The organized forces of conservatism were everywhere victorious here, as in the contemporary struggle against Lollardy, and they were strong enough to preserve the *status quo* for more than a century. They were indeed assisted in the following generations by the economic changes of the time and by the consequent decay and decline in importance of the lesser towns of England. Only Reading bettered its municipal position during the fifteenth century; at Bury and other monastic towns the troubles were on a small scale and indecisive in their results, and it is noteworthy that most of these towns allowed a considerable period to elapse, even after the Dissolution had removed their masters, before obtaining royal charters of incorporation.

Thus the lords of boroughs among the monks and canons succeeded, save for two or three cases where special circumstances existed, in preserving their control substantially intact, even if they abandoned their claim to various rights and revenues that had fallen out of date. This control, while in some cases it may have fettered commercial development, was not in itself tyrannical or unjust, nor did it have the bitterness of seignorial rule that characterized some of the lay and ecclesiastical liberties of the Continent. This, however, was not the chief reason for the lack of success in the English revolts. Abroad, in the case of the great ecclesiastical towns, the bishop had found himself alone and distracted by many cares, while the town was large, powerful, and well organized. In England, the monastic overlord was powerful and deathless. Abroad, the king or emperor often supported the town against a dangerous vassal; in England, the king always supported the monastery. But the state of tutelage was not a pure loss to the town; the monks were often closely related to the burgesses of the town, and the presence of the abbey secured to them a constant flow of income which may have been small in comparison with the profits of large-scale merchant ventures, but was at least visible. To later eyes the conduct of the monks may seem illiberal and obstructive and even financially unwise, but privileged groups of men, deliberating and voting as a corporate body, have rarely been liberal save upon the brink of a precipice.

1 *Ann. Dunstapl.* in *Ann. Mon.* III, 417; Trenholme, 65; Réville, 41–2. For Peterborough *v.* Knighton, *Chronic.* II, 140–1.

CHAPTER XXIII

THE ABBOT

I

The feudalization of the abbot and his household had, as we have noted,[1] very serious consequences in monastic history, and was invariably accompanied, to a greater or less degree, by a profound change in relationships between abbot and community which on the continent culminated in the virtual extinction of the abbatial office in favour of commendatory place-holders. Even where, as in England, matters did not come to such a pass, the abbot became an autocrat rather than a father: he was in office for life; he disposed without any control of a large revenue and a numerous household; and even where the finances of the convent were concerned, a domineering or unscrupulous abbot did not in fact need to fear any effective opposition.

When, therefore, the papal Curia under Innocent III and his immediate successors turned its attention to the reform of the old orders, it was concerned to put a check on the abbot's power of ruining a house unhindered. Legates of the period laid down or confirmed regulations limiting the abbot's establishment and putting all revenues, even those of the abbot's chamber, under the control of treasurers, from whom the abbot's chaplains were to draw funds as need arose, and to whom the abbot himself must give account. In addition, all leases and grants, even when the Abbot's lands were concerned, were to be submitted to the community, one of whom, chosen from and by his brethren, was to keep the abbot's seal.[2]

Innocent III in his personal directions went a stage further, and endeavoured to bring the abbot back into the common life of the monastery, and Gregory IX carried this attempt over into his decretals.[3] In the first issue of his statutes (May 1235) he decreed that abbots should take meals in the refectory. This was softened in the definitive issue (1237), but the recommendation appears that the abbot should stay in the cloister. All this was confirmed by Innocent IV in 1253, and there is an interesting record of a capitular discussion in which the community of St Albans 'received', with a few exceptions, these decrees which were in fact already observed by the house.[4] No reforming legislation, however, was able to stem the

---

1 *MO*, 404–6.
2 Cf. decrees of Council of Oxford of 1222 in Wilkins, *Concilia*, I, 590, and subsequent English councils, legatine and otherwise; also *MC*, I, 9, 35 *et al.* For monastic seals, *v. Monastic seals of the thirteenth century*, by Gale Pedrick.
3 Cf. letter of Innocent III, *Quum ad monasterium*, adopted as a decretal by Gregory IX in *Corpus Juris Canonici*, ed. Friedberg, Lib. III, tit. xxxv, c. vi and *Les Registres de Grégoire IX*, ed. L. Auvray, II, 327–30. Cf. *MC*, I, 8, 35, 65.
4 *MPChM*, Addit. VI, 238 *seqq.*, 244.

tide of the times, and all attempts to give a constitutional character to the abbot's office were bound to founder upon the rock which since St Benedict's day had formed the basis of the monastic life: the doctrine, that is, that a monk had no will or rights of his own, but had yielded himself up entirely to the abbot. This was assumed by the canonists, and gradually accepted by the common lawyers: a monk could not sue or be sued without his 'sovereign'; he had died a civil death on the day of his profession, and the abbot from being regarded as the head of a corporation aggregate gradually came to be looked upon as a corporation sole. He was the representative of the abbey, the *persona ecclesiae*, and it was natural for the common law to regard him as an absolute monarch. All psychological influences, therefore, from the side of church and state alike, exalted the absolute, unlimited power of the abbot, and against them no constitutional movement could make any headway.[1]

II

One important consequence of the abbot's position as a great landlord was a need of technical advice on points of ecclesiastical, feudal and common law, as well as a need of influential persons in general to watch over and forward his interests. In smaller houses this may have remained for long a mere unofficial taking of counsel from friends or professional lawyers, but a group of occasional advisers soon crystallized into a permanent body of men, retained by an annual payment and bound by oath to advance the interests of their employer. In consequence, the practice of engaging counsel for isolated suits seems to have developed, in the latter half of the thirteenth century, into the retention of a permanent group of counsellors; they are seen in action at about the same time at St Albans and Canterbury, and resemble the council to be found in the households of lay landowners.[2] As has been pointed out, this council was made up of four different elements: a small group of permanent officials, including the abbot's steward and perhaps one or two monks; a number of neighbouring landowners, whose local knowledge and social influence would be of value; a small number of professional lawyers, civil and ecclesiastical; and, finally, one or

---

1 'It is not as a specially holy person, but as a property-less and a specially obedient person that the law knows the monk. He has no will of his own (*non habet velle neque nolle*, Lyndwood, *Provinciale*, 168) because he is subject to the will of another.' (F. Pollock and F. W. Maitland, *History of English Law*, 2 ed., I, 433.) 'As to torts or civil wrongs, the rule was that the monk could neither sue nor be sued without his "sovereign".' (*Ibid.* 435; cf. also 436–8.) 'The abbot and his monastery were halfway between the corporation aggregate and the corporation sole; but nearer to the latter than to the former. The rules of law applying to this particular corporation thus paved the way to the recognition by the common law of such a conception as that of the corporation sole.' (W. S. Holdsworth, *History of English Law*, 3 ed., III, 481; cf. also *ibid.* 473–4.)

2 Cf. N. Denholm-Young, *Seignorial Administration in England*, 25–31; E. Levett, *The Courts and Court Rolls of St Albans Abbey*, in *TRHS*, 4 ser. VII (1924), and *Studies in Manorial History*, 26–7, 31–4, 153 *seqq.*; F. M. Page, *The Estates of Crowland Abbey*, 45–9; and, above all, R. A. L. Smith, *Canterbury Cathedral Priory*, 68–82.

two of the leading judges or itinerant justices of the day.[1] The first and third of these groups made up a body that could be easily assembled, and that often followed the abbot or prior on his journeys; the second contained neighbours and friends who could be consulted on specific points; the fourth consisted of a few eminent men who could watch the interests of the house at Westminster, or help in tipping the scales of justice in the courts. The domestic circle of counsellors who, like lawyers in every age, erred always on the side of caution and prescriptive right, can occasionally be seen in action as a repressive force and consequently incurred the dislike of the tenants and townspeople of the abbey. At St Albans in 1381 they were among those who fled from the insurgents, and the latter called vainly for them, and above all for the seneschal, when they arrived at the gates of the abbey.[2]

This council advised the abbot on all matters of weight, particularly where the canon or common law might be doubtful, and in general in all cases where a corporate body would to-day seek advice of counsel. It is not always easy to distinguish in the records between this council and the council of seniors which, according to canon law as well as the Rule of St Benedict, the abbot was obliged to consult on matters of moment.[3] At the beginning of the thirteenth century, when the decretals were being codified and enforced, there was a noticeable movement on the part of the Curia to assert the rights of the seniors; as has been said, such attempts always foundered upon the indefeasible rights allowed to the abbot by the Rule, but it was a general and natural procedure to consult the senior monks— a consultation which, when an autocratic abbot was concerned, often took the form of winning individuals over in private interviews.[4] Where technical advice, however, and not domestic policy was in question, the abbot turned to his sworn council. Its activities can be traced down to the middle of the fifteenth century, and the group of lay notabilities from the neighbourhood can sometimes be seen acting in the interests of the abbey even in matters where their advice had not been solicited by the abbot.[5] By the opening of the sixteenth century, however, the council had ceased to be a force in the changed times, and its place had largely been taken by the group of lay magnates who, in growing numbers, were coming to fill the honorary posts of steward, receiver and the like.

1 Smith, *Canterbury*, *loc. cit.*
2 *GASA*, I, 441 (1279), 'cum consilio suo'; II, 165; III, 6, 'consuluit igitur abbas justiciarios regionis et jurisperitissimos'; 287, 'nonnulli de consiliariis et jurisperiti' are compelled by insurgents to flee to Tynemouth; 294, rebels call for seneschal and *autres de son conseil*; cf. also Amundesham, *Annales*, I, 314 (1433), 'viri solidi temporalis concilii'; II, 267. For the opposite case of a monk in a magnate's council, cf. *Reg. Whethamstede*, II, 218, where prior of Tynemouth in 1480 serves on council of earl of Northumberland.
3 Thus, e.g. E. Levett seems occasionally to confuse the two.
4 E.g. *MC*, III, 51.
5 E.g. at Glastonbury in 1408 during archbishop Arundel's visitation (*Reg. Bekynton*, *SRS*, II, 554).

III

The separation of the abbot's household from that of the convent had been completed in most cases during the twelfth century. A primary motive for the change in the case of abbots holding in chief was a desire to save their house from falling into the hand of the king at each vacancy of the barony, but the separation was rendered all but necessary owing to the numerous commitments and activities of the head of the house. Convenience, indeed, was served so well by the existence of two households, that abbeys which were not baronies, cathedral monasteries and all large priories came to have two establishments, even if the revenues were not formally allocated in division.[1] Although the separation had in most cases been effected in the twelfth century, several abbeys found it necessary to have this confirmed in the thirteenth, and even as late as 1298 the convent of Ely paid a thousand marks to ensure that their revenues should not be confiscated on a vacancy of the bishopric.[2]

Separation of revenues and activities carried with it separation of lodging and staff, and by the end of the twelfth century the greater abbots had quarters of their own, with a private chamber, hall, chapel and the rest, and as the century wore on a similar move was made by the priors of cathedral monasteries and others.[3] In early times the abbot often had his lodging in or adjacent to the range of the cloister nearest to the outer court and great gateway; later, separate houses were built communicating with the outer court. The prior's lodging at Much Wenlock, still extant, shows how far this process went even in houses of mediocre importance.

At first the abbot's household had been organized simply, with steward and chamberlain and one or two other officers on the lines of the contemporary magnate's household. Later, again following the fashion of the great lay establishments, the structure became more complicated. The stewardship split into two—the steward of the hall and the steward or procurator of the estates—and the chamberlain, either alone or with the marshal, fuctioned as a major domo with servants and guests.[4] There was, however, one important official who had no exact counterpart in the

---

1 Cf. Dom Ph. Schmitz in *DHG*, VII, 1103; for confirmations *v. Reg. J. de Pontissara*, II, 683 (Winchester, 1284); *MSE*, III, 34 (Bury, 1281); *Cart. Glocestr.* III, 103; *Reg. Malmesbur.* I, 192–4 (1300).

2 James Bentham, *History and Antiquities of the Church of Ely* (1771), 153; cf. *HMC*, Append. to VI Report, 290.

3 At Canterbury before 1165; *v.* contemporary drawing in Willis, *History of Conventual Buildings of Christ Church*, 196. *V.* also H. Brakspear in *Archaeologia*, LXXXIII.

4 For the development of the royal household, *v.* T. F. Tout, *Chapters in the Administrative History of Medieval England*, especially vol. 1; for private households, Denholm-Young, *Seignorial Administration*. For the lay-out of the abbot's and prior's lodging, A. Hamilton Thompson, *English Monasteries*, 121–5, and T. D. Atkinson, *The Monastic Buildings of Ely*, 66 *et al.* The fullest single account of an abbot's household is perhaps that of St Augustine's, *temp.* abbot Nicholas de Spina, 1273–83 in *Customary of St Augustine's*, ed. E. M. Thompson, *HBS*, 1902; cf. also *Register of St Benet, Holme*, ed. J. R. West, *Norf. Record Soc.* 1932, vol. II; and *Norfolk Archaeology*, XIX, 268–313.

household of the king and nobles: this was the chaplain (or chaplains), who came to combine the functions of secretary and bursar to the abbot with the daily activities of liaison officer between abbot and convent. Originally appointed solely for devotional and honorific services, to sleep in the abbot's room and say office with him, the chaplain gradually became, not only a kind of private secretary or confidential clerk, but also the official responsible for the abbot's finances, thus taking the place in abbatial households of the treasurer or receiver-general of lay lords. Many monasteries assigned two chaplains to their abbot, lest fear or favour might be too much for a single monk's honesty, or, as an alternative, chose a monk from among themselves as assessor to the chaplain. The position of chaplain was naturally one of great delicacy; besides his financial responsibilities he had human contacts of importance; like a parliamentary private secretary he was expected to canvass opinion in the community and report upon it to his chief, while on the other hand he could use his position at the ear of the abbot to further or mar the fortunes of his confrères. Consequently it was felt that fair play was a greater good than efficiency, and every effort was made to prevent a favourite entrenching himself. Common practice, and ultimately papal and visitatorial decrees, insisted that the abbot's chaplains should be changed yearly.[1]

Within the circle of household officials the greatest variety prevailed in the assignment of duties. In one abbey the steward, at another the marshal or chamberlain had the greatest part in the internal administration; at some the chamberlain, at others the chaplain, performed the routine secretarial duties, while the financial oversight, usually the task of the chaplain, was in some instances committed to the chamberlain or the procurator. The cathedral priory of Norwich stood apart from all others with its office of master-cellarer, a kind of super-obedientiary who had a finger in every dish, besides acting as procurator to the prior's household.[2] Normally, however, the chaplain held the strings of the abbot's privy purse. He drew money from the convent's treasurer, with whom he accounted monthly; he checked the outgoings of petty cash every evening with seneschal, steward and cook, and gave a full statement every year to the abbot.

Beneath the principal officials came a whole retinue of a dozen to twenty minor functionaries, each with a man at arms or page, and one or more horses.[3] It was these trains, with their numerous hangers-on, which were docked of superfluous members by visitatorial injunction or by abbots and communities bent on financial retrenchment.[4]

1 Cf. Council of Oxford, 1222, in Wilkins, *Concilia*, I, 591: 'Ut abbates annuatim capellanos suos mutent'; two hundred years later the regulation was being repeated (*MC*, II, 193, in 1445). For the chaplain's assessor at Peterborough v. Whitlesey's *Historia Coenobri Burgensis*, ed. Sparke, 126.

2 H. W. Saunders, *Introduction to the Rolls of Norwich Cath. Priory*, 76 seqq.

3 There is a full and interesting list for St Augustine's in 1275 in the *Customary*, 69; for Christ Church in 1377 v. Smith, *Canterbury*, 31.

4 For early attempts, cf. *MPChM*, III, 503 (legate Otto in 1238); *A papal visitation of Westminster in* 1234, by R. Graham in *EHR*, XXVII, 737; *MC*, I, 9 (often repeated, e.g. 36, 65 and v. infra. p. 276).

IV

When first the division of estates was made the abbot, ostensibly the greater beneficiary, often undertook to find from his portion a number of food-farms, or a fixed quantity of meat and drink for the community. Even as late as the middle of the thirteenth century some abbots, as at Westminster and Glastonbury, were still responsible for part of the catering expenses. The abbot also regarded it as his duty to defend the convent in lawsuits at his own expense.[1] Gradually, however, as the activities and expenses of the abbot increased, his contributions to the upkeep of the community diminished. Some of the great abbots of the thirteenth century, indeed, continued to give manors or lands to their convents for specific purposes, including that of finding provisions; these lands were sometimes part of the abbot's original share, but more often they were new acquisitions; in general, the food-farm estates fell back to the monks, and often became part of the cellarer's endowment.[2] Ultimately, however, the roles of the two parties were reversed, and the abbot received regular food allowances, cash payments and exennia or presents from the monks. This was notably the case in the cathedral priories, where the income of the prior was largely made up of regular subscriptions from the obedientiaries.[3]

The unassailable pre-eminence of the abbot, and the natural tendency which made of the obedientiaries an official class unfavourable to democratic views, effectually thwarted the efforts that had been made in the late twelfth century by the communities of a few great abbeys to assert their voting powers and to govern the monastery on democratic lines, and the practice of putting the abbot on the carpet, attempted at Bury in the days of Jocelin and continued more effectually at St Albans in the next century, ceased to be common as the decades passed. At certain houses, however, the conventual chapter long continued to promulgate regulations for the whole house or, as at St Albans, to register abbatial arrangements for satellite priories. Such domestic legislation was, for reasons that have been mentioned already, most commonly employed at cathedral priories, where the ordinances of the conventual chapter were treated as the governing code.

Both the Curia and the provincial chapters did their best to check irresponsibility and dilapidation on the part of abbots by making necessary the consent of the community for the reception of novices, leases, aliena-

---

1 E.g. *Chron. Mon. de Abingdon* (*RS*), II, 306–7, 312, 352 (*c.* 1190); *GASA*, I, 73–6 (*c.* 1140); *Reg. of St Benet, Holme*, II, 247. For the abbot assigning revenues to the convent kitchen *v.* Flete's *History of Westminster*, 101, and *GASA*, I, 370–3 (1257).

2 *Annales Theokusb.* p. 129; *GASA*, III, 390; *Chron. Joh. Glastoniensis*, ed. T. Hearne, I, 209–10, 212, 221; *Chart. Mon. de Ramesey*, II, 212–18.

3 For payments to abbot, *v.* J. Amundesham, *Annales*, II, 316–21 (St Albans); *Accounts of the Obedientiars of Abingdon Abbey*, ed. R. E. G. Kirk, *CS* (1892), 2–4 and *passim*; *Whitby Cartulary*, ed. J. C. Atkinson, 600–20. For payments to prior *v. Durham Household Book*, 1530–4, ed. J. Raine, *SS* (1844), 142 *et al. Obedientiary Rolls of St Swithun's, Winchester*, ed. G. W. Kitchin, 37–8; *Ely Chapter Ordinances*, 54; Smith, *Canterbury*, 23–4.

tions and the negotiation of large loans;[1] in addition, the provincial chapters repeatedly attempted to enforce the old custom that obediences (*i.e.* offices) should only be imposed or withdrawn in open chapter, and to re-enact what may be called the monastic *habeas corpus*, that no monk should be sent away from the house to a cell without at least the cognizance of chapter.[2] In the twelfth and early thirteenth centuries Jocelin of Brakelond, the *Gesta Abbatum* and narratives of lawsuits show the chapter functioning as an active and often critical parliament; in default of intimate chronicles it is hard to say how long this continued, but there are indications that by the middle of the fourteenth century, save perhaps at the cathedral monasteries and a few greater abbeys, the official group of abbot and obedientiaries ruled without effective criticism, and that the 'constitutional movement' of the twelfth century bore no fruit, despite the example of free speech and representative government given by the mendicant orders.

V

In the thirteenth century the abbots of the greater houses continued as before to take part in public life, though as individuals they were consulted less by the king, and filled fewer administrative and diplomatic posts.

The abbots and priors in very large numbers received summons to attend, and often in fact attended, the meetings of the council that gradually became the meetings of parliament, and were held with great and on the whole increasing frequency in the latter half of the thirteenth century. The later history of this will be noted in another place; here it is sufficient to remark that at this period a very large number of white monk abbots and priors of Augustinian houses were summoned, as well as the abbots of the older monasteries.[3]

In the mid-thirteenth century abbots were frequently employed as itinerant justices; thus the abbot of Ramsey was a justice in 1217 and 1236;[4] the abbot of Croyland in 1239;[5] the abbots of Colchester and Peterborough in 1254, and the latter again in 1257.[6] This employment roused the wrath of Grosseteste, who is repeatedly found urging the archbishop or legate to action against a practice which was to him an infringement of the liberties of the Church and a sin against the canons and the Rule.[7] In addition, individual abbots were caught up into administrative life by royal appreciation of their character or talents. Chief among these,

---

1 *MC*, I, 255.   2 *GASA*, I, 255; *MC*, II, 52.
3 Thus, for example, in 1265 about a hundred religious superiors were summoned: fifty black monks, twenty white monks, and some thirty canons of various orders (W. Dugdale, *Summons... to Parliaments*; H. M. Chew, *Ecclesiastical Tenants-in-chief*, 171).
4 *Ann. Dunstapl. s.a.* (p. 53); Grosseteste, *ep.* xxvii.
5 Grosseteste, *ep.* lxxxii.
6 *Ann. Dunstapl. s.a.* 1254 (pp. 192, 195); *s.a.* 1257 (p. 206).
7 Grosseteste, *ep.* lxxii (1236).

in the reign of Henry III, were Richard le Gras of Evesham (1236–42), who served the king in a number of ways at home and abroad and who, from 1239 to 1242, had unofficial control of the Seal,[1] and abbot Crokesley of Westminster (1246–58), who in 1251 was abroad on the king's business and in 1254 was one of the papal executors of the crusade and tenth, and two years later went to Rome as royal envoy.[2] When, from about the middle of the century onwards, Westminster was used as a Treasury for part of the Wardrobe, the abbot of Westminster became responsible; it is in this sense that Crokesley and Ware and Wenlock are called Treasurers, though the chronicler, writing more than a century after the event, draws upon the phraseology of his own age in his description.[3]

VI

The great contests between monks and bishops, whether they took the form of struggles for exemption or were reactions against absorption, as at Glastonbury, had without exception passed their climax before 1216, and the work of centralization and formalization carried on by the popes from Innocent III to Innocent IV, together with the emergence of the totally exempt orders of friars, helped to make the equilibrium permanent. Such activity as took place, therefore, was in the nature of tidying up the loose ends of quarrels. Thus at St Albans abbots William of Trumpington and John of Hatfield negotiated a whole series of small arrangements settling the relations between the bishops of Lincoln and Norwich and the cells and parishes of the abbey;[4] at Westminster a final attempt of the bishop of London to challenge the abbey's exemption was defeated by a papal commission in 1222;[5] at St Augustine's, Canterbury, a final settlement was made with Archbishop Edmund in 1237, though it was challenged again unsuccessfully as late as 1397.[6] At Glastonbury the final agreement with Bishop Jocelin had been made still earlier at Shaftesbury on 1 July 1218, when the monastery and bishopric were finally cut apart, the monastery recovering its independence and leaving the bishop with some churches and the bare title of patron of the abbey.[7] At Malmesbury

---

1 He is called *cancellarius* by the Dunstable annalist, s.a. 1240 (p. 152), and by the Tewkesbury annalist, s.a. 1241. Matthew Paris notes that he held the Seal for three years (*MPChM*, III, 629 and IV, 191); the Evesham chronicler merely notes his services to the king (278–9). Actually, he only held the Seal unofficially, cf. T. F. Tout, *Chapters*, VI, 4 and L. B. Dibben, *Chancellor and Keeper of the Seal under Henry III*, in *EHR*, XXVII (1912), 42–3.

2 Cf. *Ann. Burton. s.a.* 1258 (p. 447); *Ann. Dunstapl. s.a.* 1254 (p. 191) and 1256 (p. 199); *MPChM*, IV, 586 and V, 228 (1251) and Flete, *Hist. Westminster*, 109.

3 Flete, 114, 116; cf. Tout, *Chapters*, II, 52.

4 *GASA*, I, 275–7, 350–4.

5 Flete, *History of Westminster*, 101; *MPChM*, III, 75. The commissioners were a strong team: Stephen Langton, Peter des Roches of Winchester, Richard Poore of Salisbury, and the priors of the two leading Augustinian houses, Merton and Dunstable.

6 W. Thorne, 1882–4; cf. 1966, 2199 *seqq.*

7 Adam of Domerham, II, 466–7.

the question of exemption, so often moved by the bishop, was committed to judges-delegate and decided in favour of the abbey, which duly received papal bulls in confirmation in 1221.[1] The freedom of Battle and Bury had been definitively settled long before in the twelfth century, though as late as 1345 Bishop William Bateman of Norwich made a courageous attempt to get Bury's exemption revoked.[2]

The exempt abbeys, however, were quick to find that their privilege was not an unmixed blessing. As no bishop had the right to check or confirm their elections, a journey to Rome on the part of the elect became necessary, and when there, the ingenuity of canonists could often disappoint him by finding a technical flaw in the election. This put the whole matter into the hands of the pope, who could either refer the elect back to England for another and better attempt, or graciously provide the pretender to his post.[3] As may be imagined, the whole process, with the journey and its delays, and the business of smoothing a passage through the Curia, was an extremely expensive one. Thus abbot Simon of Bury gave 2000 marks for his confirmation in 1257, when he was excused from going to Rome;[4] at St Albans, papal confirmation cost £800 in 1263, and in 1302 abbot John de Maryns was forced to put up some 3000 marks at Rome alone.[5] Even as early as 1229 Thomas of Marleberge who, thirty years before, had been most eager to go before the Curia, was fittingly enough caught in the toils himself, and saw his election quashed by Gregory IX whom in earlier days he had briefed in the case against Bishop Mauger; his expenses kept him for several years in difficult straits with his creditors.[6] It was not till the fourteenth century was far advanced that the Curia was willing, for a consideration, to forgo its right of confirming the elect in person.

Fees and presents to Rome, however, were by no means the only expenses incident upon a demise of the abbacy. Although the separation of the revenues of abbot and convent protected the latter from losing their own estates to the escheator, the king claimed the custody of the barony during a vacancy, thus depriving the house as a whole of a considerable part of its revenue. Gradually the practice arose of holding the estates and paying the king a fixed sum per month or year. Thus at Bury in 1304 an arrangement was made by which the convent compounded with the Exchequer for an annual charge of 1200 marks;[7] at St Albans in 1301 it was agreed that the convent should have the barony (exclusive of advowsons and knights' fees) during a vacancy for 1000 marks a year;[8] at Evesham in

1 *Reg. Malmesburiense*, I, 378 *seqq.*
2 *VCH, Suffolk*, II, 63.
3 For the former procedure *v. Chron. Evesham.* 272 (Marleberge, 1229); for the latter, *GASA*, II, 189–90 (Richard of Wallingford, 1326).
4 *VCH, Suffolk*, II, 61.
5 *GASA*, II, 56–8, where the list of *douceurs* and the recipients is given in full.
6 *Chron. Evesham.* 272.   7 *VCH, Suffolk*, II, 62.
8 *VCH, Herts*, IV, 384–5; *GASA*, II, 32–3.

1309 the sum was 600 marks, with the same reservations, and nine years later the price was fixed at 240 marks for the first four months and thenceforward 200 marks for each period of four months;[1] at Hyde in 1319 the price was 200 marks for a two months' vacancy.[2]

Later, it became common to take out a form of insurance against frequent vacancies by paying a fixed annual premium. This was set at fifty marks at St Albans, which would profit the abbey if a series of abbots ruled for less than twenty years;[3] St Augustine's, Canterbury, likewise put the matter on an actuarial basis in 1392.[4] At almost the same time the Curia allowed similar policies to be taken out by exempt houses; thus St Albans, for an annual premium of twenty marks, were excused from sending their abbot out to Rome and he might receive confirmation from a bishop of his choice.[5] Evesham received a similar privilege in 1363.[6] It will be noticed that while the premium paid to the king did no more than put the recurring large expenses upon an actuarial footing, the annual payment to the papacy was advantageous to all parties: to the Curia it gave a fixed annual rent with which to budget, while to the abbey it was a considerable saving to pay no more than the Curial fee, with none of the expenses of travelling. At the same time, for one of the large exempt houses these two regular charges, added to the smaller inescapable ones connected with an election, must have amounted to an annual expense of something like one thousand pounds of our currency, for which the abbey received absolutely nothing in return. In a simpler age, and even in 1300 among the white monks, an election cost nothing at all, save perhaps the travelling expenses and hospitality of a visiting abbot or two. This heavy charge of later times, of which the greater part was payable by all houses, whether exempt or not, which held in chief, must be borne in mind when we feel disposed to wonder where all the monastic revenues went.

1 VCH, Worcs, II, 123.
3 GASA, III, 135; CPR (1362–1404), 545.
5 GASA, III, 146–84, 398; CPL (1396), 293.
6 Chron. Evesh. 297; VCH, Worcs, II, 124.

2 VCH, Hants, II, 118.
4 W. Thorne, 2196–7.

CHAPTER XXIV

THE DAILY LIFE OF THE MONASTERY

I

THE HORARIUM

When we attempt to reconstruct the monastic horarium we are baffled, in the later as in the earlier middle ages, by a lack of reference to hours of the day. Generally speaking, however, few changes were made during the period under review.[1] One such may have been an advancement of the hour of the night-office to midnight in large houses, consequent upon the practice, now becoming general, of retiring to the dormitory for sleep in the interval between Mattins and Lauds.[2] As the latter office began before dawn a difficulty was caused by the length of the night office on great feasts in the early summer, and a solution was found by throwing Mattins back to the previous evening,[3] thus giving on those nights a single period of rest after the office, supplemented by the normal summer siesta. The only other change was in the morning, where at some houses the morrow or chapter Mass was advanced from 9 a.m. to c. 7.30 or 8 a.m. in order to provide students of theology with a longer unbroken period of work.[4] On the very eve of the dissolution the course of the day at Durham appears before us in its main outlines: the midnight Mattins, the sung Chapter-Mass at 9.30 followed by the chapter; the High Mass at about 10.30 followed by dinner and reading till Vespers at 3; supper at 4.30 followed by a conference, and Compline followed by the Salve at 6.[5]

In the day's general arrangement the two most troublesome questions continued to be the number of meals and the eating of meat. A difficulty had long been felt in the enactment of the Rule, which in England had little climatic justification, by which the regime of two meals ran only from Easter to September, thus leaving between four and five months before

---

1 For a fuller review of the monastic horarium, v. *MO*, ch. xxvi.

2 The few but explicit references make it quite clear that midnight was zero hour, e.g. *Customary of St Augustine's, Canterbury*, 188 (c. 1275): 'In media nocte pulsandum est ad matutinas, juxta illud... "media nocte surgebam"'; *Rites of Durham*, 19 (referring to c. 1535): 'The bells were rung ever at midnight... for the Monkes went evermore to theire mattens at that houre of the night.' Cf. also *Reg. Joh. Amundesham*, I, 11 (1427) where Sopwell nunnery is robbed *circa horam undecimam noctis*, when the nuns rise for Mattins. For the second period of sleep v. *Consuetudines Mon. S. Petri Westmonasteriensis*, 143–4, *Customary of St Augustine's*, 189, and for Christ Church, Canterbury, *Reg. Winchelsey*, 818.

3 *GASA*, II, 424 (1351) for Mattins immediately after Compline; a still more extreme course had been adopted by Cluny earlier, v. *MO*, 150.

4 *GASA*, II, 306 (c. 1340).

5 *Rites of Durham, passim*. The tendencious nature of this work does not affect precise data as to hours, etc.

the beginning of Lent, and those among the coldest and darkest of the year, in which no supper was allowed save on Sundays. The custom of relaxing this rule during the Christmas season and on numerous feasts had long been common,[1] but it was part of the Curial monastic reform of the early thirteenth century to enforce the letter of the Rule on this point. The early chapters, indeed, stood out for 1 November as the limiting date (for October was, and still is, something of a liturgical No Man's land), but at St Alban's abbot William of Trumpington enforced the more rigid observance.[2] Despite Roman action, most houses would seem to have kept, or reverted, to the customary modifications which reduced in practice the number of supperless days in the winter by a third or more, but St Albans at least seems to have kept to the supperless winter regime from 14 September till very near the end.

Meat-eating was a still more perplexed question. The clear prohibition of the Rule for all save the sick who needed a fortifying diet was in 1216 so far honoured that no meat was ever served in the refectory, but invitations to the abbot's table and permissions to join the sick in the infirmary were normal, and a new practice was establishing itself everywhere of setting up a second dining-hall (known as the *misericord* in most houses, but by a special name, such as the *oriole*, at St Albans, or the *deportus* as elsewhere) where meat might be served to the weak or to those with special permission, while in many houses it was customary for monks taking meals in the guesthouse or with the cellarer to eat meat. The misericord was in a manner legalized in the first meetings of the Canterbury and York chapters, in which a place of recreation for the monks of the cloister was appointed,[4] but the reforming Curia tried to put a stop to this by promulgating the decretal *Quum ad monasterium* from a letter of Innocent III,[5] whereby meat was allowed to be eaten only by genuine invalids in the infirmary or by a somewhat strained interpretation at the abbot's table. Accordingly the chapter of 1237, no doubt stimulated by the imminent action of the legate Otho, put a total inhibition on the misericord,[6] and was commended by the cardinal for its pains, while the

---

1 Thus at Peterborough, between 14 September and Lent, two meals were taken: (a) till 1 October, (b) on all feasts of twelve lessons, (c) during the octave of St Martin, (d) from Christmas till the octave of the Epiphany.

2 Swapham, *Coen. Burgensis Historia*, 111; *MC*, I (1218–19). In October, e.g., the ferial hymns follow the winter scheme, whereas the lessons at Mattins are as in summer.

3 *MC*, II, 112 (1421) and *Reg. Whethamstede*, 460.

4 *MC*, I, 11–2 (1219), where a *locus juxta refectorium* (i.e. not in infirmary) is to be used by those *qui pondus diei portaverunt at aestus*. Cf. *ibid*. 17.

5 *Corpus Juris Canonici*, ed. Friedberg, II Decret. Gen. Lib. III, tit. xxxv, c. vi. Innocent's letter dates from 1202; it prescribes (a) that meat shall never be eaten in the refectory, (b) or in a second refectory, but that (c) the weak and sick are to eat meat in the infirmary, while (d) the abbot may on occasion invite monks to his table where better fare may be given (*melius et plenius exhibere*). The last phrase does not necessarily imply meat (which the context would seem to demand), neither does it categorically exclude it. The decree is given also in *MPChM*, III, 507. *V. supra*, p. 19.

6 *MC*, I, 24 (1237): 'Misericordiis et aliis recreacionibus...penitus interdictis.'

drastic Grosseteste did not fail to enforce the ban in his visitations.[1] The prohibition was repeated at intervals till the end of the century, and Archbishop Kilwardby in 1275 went so far as to order the monks of Box-grove to pull down their misericord, but he was fighting a losing battle.[2] At the very moment of his visitation Abbot Nicholas of St Augustine's, Canterbury, was hesitatingly admitting the misericord as an appendage of the infirmary, thus saving the letter of *Quum ad monasterium*, and it was becoming clear that the system of recreations had come to stay, whether in the Christmas holidays, as at Whitby, or at regular intervals, as at Durham, Christ Church, Winchester, and other houses.[3] Finally, in 1300 the chapter did its best to give verbal legality to an irregular situation by declaring that prelates had power to dispense their subjects,[4] and within a few years the misericord, long a feature at Gloucester, Worcester, Norwich and elsewhere, was allowed by the most exigent visitors.[5] The practice, if not the precise shape it had taken, received a blessing from the highest quarters in 1316, when meat-eating in the infirmary by the healthy was allowed by Benedict XII. The Bull *Summi Magistri* went further than previous decrees in allowing half the community at a time to be absent from the refectory, but even this benign ruling caused difficulties, as many were always absent from the house on business, and the decree was therefore often interpreted somewhat casuistically as applying to half the number actually available on a given day.[6] Elsewhere a rotation of three groups was observed, and soon it was the common practice on all days save Fridays (and Wednesdays also in some houses) for meat to be served in a room contiguous to the refectory, where reading and the other regular ceremonies might be observed,[7] but for long there was something furtive about the business; no seculars were to see the brethren taking their ease; at most some trusty servant might wait upon them. As this duplication of refectories sadly depleted communities which even when assembled in strength had shrunk considerably in numbers, it was often found con-venient to use a smaller refectory for both groups, and thus in the last centuries of the middle ages the original refectory might remain unused save on the greater feasts. By the fifteenth century the custom of meat-eating had hardened so much that even the reformers of 1421 let it stand

1 *MPChM*, III, 432–3; Swapham, *Hist. Burg.* 110–11 speaks of *tam arta inhibitio...tam importabile onus.*

2 *MC*, I, 37 (1249), 56 (1256), 78 (1277); *Reg. Winchelsey*, 853 (Kilwardby's injunctions).

3 *Customary of St Augustine's*, 39–40: 'Ad tempus, licet cum timore, permittimus.' *MC*, I, 258 (1287, Whitby); *Hist. Dunelm. SS* 3, Appendix XLIV; *Reg. Winchelsey* (Christ Church, 1298), 819–20; *Reg. Pontissara*, II, 641–2 (Winchester, 1276).

4 *MC*, I, 143 (1300): 'De esu carnium quilibet praelatus...potest cum suis subditis dispensare.'

5 *Reg. Winchelsey*, 859 (Gloucester, 1301); 876 (Worcester, 1301); *Studies in Norwich Cathedral History*, E. H. Carter, 21 (1308/9).

6 Wilkins, *Concilia*, II, 588 seqq. par. 27 (summarized *MC*, Appendix II).

7 Swapham, *Hist. Burg.* 110–11; *GASA*, II, 304 (1338); *Reg. Winchelsey*, 859; Flete, *Hist. Westmon.* 130 (Simon Langham). For the secrecy, cf. *Reg. Winchelsey*, 859 (Gloucester, 1301).

in their programme, even adding economic to moral arguments in its favour.[1] Meat was served in the misericord at supper also, though towards the end of the medieval period there was a reaction on purely hygienic grounds from such Homeric fare.[2] There is no evidence to show whether in Tudor times the stage had been reached when meat was served publicly in the refectory. Doubtless every kind of meat figures on the later provision lists, but this does not exclude the possibility that a regular meal was served to one section of the monks, particularly when it is remembered that birds of all kinds—capons, chickens and pigeons—were not considered as flesh-meat.[3]

When a single meal was the norm for more than half the year the need was naturally felt for a refreshing drink which, in an age before tea and coffee, could be no other than beer or wine. The evening drink was of very early institution, as was also the *caritas* of wine at the *Mandatum*; an afternoon drink in summer at what is now tea-time was likewise recognized even by the exacting Pecham.[4] There was, however, a tendency, as in all large establishments of every age, for one refreshing drink to succeed another, and reformers were busy at the upas-tree.[5] Their efforts were directed above all to the after-compline drink; this was a time consecrated by the Rule to absolute silence, but obedientiaries dropping in after a day's travel were justified in taking refreshment, and there were always friends eager to hear the latest news. Statutes were made and repeated against the practice, but visitations show with wearying iteration that an ineradicable human weakness was at odds with the law.

Recreational conversation had never found a place in early monastic codes; its introduction since the fifteenth century into the horarium of the strict and enclosed orders is perhaps a consequence of the greater mental activity of the modern world. Conversation 'on business' had always been allowed in the morning in a special part of the cloister and among the novices.[6] As time went on it was found peculiarly difficult to prevent social conversation when the community broke up from the procession after the midday meal; many direct attempts were made to regulate this;[7] a more indirect approach was tried by banning English in the cloister in favour of Latin or French, the latter tongue having become obsolete for colloquial purposes between 1290 and 1350.[8] Yet another means of ensuring silence in the cloister was the provision of an adjacent parlour, where officials and others could meet.[9]

1 *MC*, II, 112.

2 *Reg. Joh. Amundesham*, I, 28 (1428): 'Complexiones praesentium juvenum non adeo fortes ut ante nos fuere.'

3 They appear in Tewkesbury suppers in 1378 (*VCH, Glos*, II, 63).

4 *Pech. Epp.* I, ccxiii (Glastonbury, 1281).

5 *GASA*, II, 103 (c. 1305): 'Quoniam...inter unum potum et alium vix medium spatium intercessit.'   6 *MC*, I, 73 (1277).

7 *MC*, I, 37 (1249), 257 (1287); *GASA*, II, 434 (1351); *Reg. Winchelsey*, 839 (Rochester, 1298), 874 (Worcester, 1301).

8 *MC*, I, 260 (1290), II, 46 (1343); *Custom. Westmon.* 164.   9 *Custom. Westmon.* 18.

Failing daily periods of conversation several alternatives for relieving the mind remained. There was, earliest of all, the regular seyney, which implied freedom for two or three days from all community acts save the principal Mass, and gave to a group an opportunity for relaxation. Originally, in intention at least, a piece of personal hygiene, the seyney came to be taken by all in turn three times a year, with dispensations and diet that varied from house to house. Next, there was the practice of taking the air in country walks; this at many monasteries remained an affair of individual permission, but later a weekly walk was customary here and there.[1] As the general life of the country became more civilized and the monastic life less self-sufficient the need for a complete holiday was voiced, and all the larger houses set aside a manor for *villegiatura*; in several cases the place became a miniature monastery with chapel and refectory. Thus Christ Church had Caldecote, Durham Bearpark, whilst at St Augustine's, Canterbury, the wardens of manors were apparently charged with providing accommodation for relays from the abbey.[2] Nowhere was the routine more elaborate than at St Albans, where a house at Redburn was used as a rest hostel from early times. More than one set of constitutions for it have survived. The earliest dates from the time of Abbot Richard Wallingford (*ob.* 1335); at that time three monks of the cloister spent in turns a month there, thus perhaps giving each monk a biennial holiday. They were to say office together and take the air in the fields of a morning, but this was not to tempt them to the chase, or even to the more innocent indulgence of vaulting the hedges.[3] Forty years later, under the great Thomas de la Mare, the numbers at Redburn had increased, for there was question of singing Mass on Sundays and feasts. The abbot himself loved to stay there rather than alone on his manors, and though he insisted on punctuality at meals his presence was never felt to be irksome.[4] Sixty years later again Abbot John Amundesham found it necessary to ban late hours; his ordinances suggest that Redburn was now not only a holiday house but also the venue of reading-parties in the vacation.[5]

Finally, there was the holiday at home, with parents or friends. This was noted as a possibility as early as 1221, and there are a few references which show it to have been normal;[6] a century later at Bury we learn that at the time of the rising of 1327 no less than thirty-two of the brethren were scattered over the countryside on holiday and a contemporary letter

1 At Christ Church in 1298, the monks walk in the fields *propter aerem graciorem* (*Reg. Winchelsey*, 825), at Ely in 1300, 1314 there are walks *causa recreacionis* (*Ely Chapter Ordinances*, 13, 38); at Durham, 1384–93, it is something of a grievance that only a short, hurried weekly walk is allowed (*MC*, III, 84).

2 *Memorials of Canterbury* (Woodruff and Danks), 142; *Chron. Will. Thorne*, 1937 (*c.* 1280).

3 *GASA*, II, 202–5.

4 *GASA*, II, 398–401.

5 *Reg. Joh. Amundesham*, II, 204.

6 *MC*, I, 241 (1221); cf. *Ann. Wig. s.a.* 1283, where there is mention of the keep of two horses *qui specialiter intitulantur claustralibus spatiaturis*.

mentions frequent visits *en vacances* of Bury monks to St Benet's of Holme.[1]
A century later still, there was a regular system of visits home, with servants
and a fixed allowance of money;[2] it was also customary to allow a monk to
visit his near relations *in extremis*.

II

THE NOVICIATE

The noviciate in the thirteenth century was the object of several canonical
decrees. The children of the monastery had long since disappeared; it was
now laid down that the time of probation was not to begin before the
eighteenth birthday, and that a year's trial, neither more nor less, was to be
followed immediately by profession.[3] No dower might be demanded,
though money or lands were no doubt often freely given, and a little later
the large sum of £5 was fixed as payable by a novice for his outfit.[4] In
addition, he helped at some houses to support useful functionaries by a
small contribution.[5]

The principal task of the teacher or master was to instruct the newcomers in all the customs of the house and the ceremonies of choir and
altar. The elaborate directory, drawn up by the presidents in 1279 for
general observance, gives some idea of their complexity. Purely spiritual
instruction was less in evidence, though there is a reference to a manual,
Hugo de institutione noviciorum.[6] When customs had been learnt there
began the long task of absorbing liturgical texts, during which the novice
learnt by heart an amount of chant and Latin text that seems prodigious to
us, though perhaps not larger in bulk than the amount of repetition
demanded of a boy at Eton or Westminster in the days of Pitt. It must,
however, have been a wearisome business for those who, like many
religious women of the present day, had little or no idea of what the Latin
meant. Actually, there was a practical reason for all this memorizing, for
until the fourteenth century the choir was in darkness save for candles on
the lectern, except on great feasts; it was therefore essential that the monks
should know by heart not only the whole psalter with the customary
canticles and the hymns, but the versicles also, the anthems and the whole
of the 'common' office of saints.[7] No doubt a kind of mass-memory helped
to keep the psalmody going, but this relied ultimately on the familiarity of
all with the phrases and cadences. Consequently the novice had to pass an
examination in all this before he was allowed to leave the custody of his

---

1 *MSE*, III, 39, 48; the number seems large, but the context implies this.
2 *MC*, II, 114: 'Hoc semel in anno ad maius fiat.'
3 *MC*, I, 99 (1277).   4 *MC*, II, 50 (1343).
5 E.g. at Athelney in 1455 (*Reg. Bekynton*, 936) the barber and tailor depended for salary
partly upon sums coming from novices at profession.
6 This is printed at the end of the *Customary of St Augustine's*. For Hugo *v. ibid.* 402.
7 For the list *v. MC*, I, 73–4 (1277), and *Chron. Will. Thorne*, 1935.

master and proceed to ordination or to take office.[1] This arid mental drill, hard enough for a dull-witted boy of eighteen, was intolerable in a different way to the agile and mature mind of a university graduate, and throughout the thirteenth century efforts were made to lighten the task by omitting all save the night office, and in other ways.[2] Early in the fourteenth century lights were provided in choir at Mattins for the first time;[3] this led to less rigid demands, and less careful fulfilment, and towards the end of the middle ages the discipline of repetition would seem almost entirely to have fallen out among the black monks and canons.

III

LAY BRETHREN

A word must be said about a somewhat elusive element of the population in some of the great abbeys. As has been seen elsewhere, the original community of the Rule had no horizontal division; the majority of the monks were not in orders, and the farm work was done in the main by *coloni*. This arrangement remained in general unchanged, save that monks in growing numbers received orders, while serfs and lay servants multiplied within and without the monastery, especially in the Cluniac houses; in the pre-Conquest English monasteries there is no trace of lay brethren as distinct from choir monks. In the Norman abbeys, however, as in those of Lorraine and Switzerland, a small class of illiterate *conversi* came into being made up largely of 'late vocations', not necessarily of lower social standing than the rest. Special manual or administrative duties were assigned to them, but they were in the full sense monks of the house. How far they accompanied Norman monastic ways to England cannot be said with certainty, but there is virtually no trace of them in the records between 1100 and 1200.[4]

Meanwhile, the Cistercians, Gilbertines and others had given a prominent place in their economy to lay brothers with separate quarters, work and religious duties, and recruits had flocked to join them. The convenience of this form of co-operation, and the plentiful supply of such men cannot have escaped the black monks, but no word of any new departure has survived either in the records or the statutes, and it is certain that no great influx of any kind took place. Nevertheless, during the thirteenth century passing references to lay brothers occur at many, but by no means all, of the great abbeys. Thus at St Albans there is mention of a lay brother as steward, and another as painter,[5] as also of lay brothers working at a building, and as an obit roll of the period contains the names of eight *conversi* out of some

---

1 *MC*, i, 38 (1249).
2 *MC*, ii, 50 (1343), where *literati* need learn no more than the *nocturnum servitium*.
3 *GASA*, ii, 106 (c. 1305); *MC*, ii, 35 (1343).
4 *MO*, 6; cf. 419–20, 439.
5 *MPAddit.* vi, 270, 276 ('senescallus'), 277 ('Alanus pictor').

two hundred and fifty monks it may be concluded that if there have been no omissions of style only two or three *conversi* were in the house at a time and that at St Albans at least admission was restricted to an occasional gifted artist or craftsman or foreman. At Gloucester, a little later, a lay brother is recommended as the most suitable waiter for the brethren eating meat, and there is a casual reference to the lay brothers' refectory.[1] At Evesham, at almost the same time, there is a tantalizing statement of the chronicler that lay brothers, hitherto in charge of the manors of the house, had been recalled as having mismanaged their charge.[2] The presence of *conversi* is noted also in documents from Bath and Durham, and one of the queries for transmission to Rome *à propos* of the code of 1277 is whether *conversi*, where they existed, might be used as cooks.[3] Most illuminating of all is the section dealing with *conversi* in the customary of St Augustine's, where a distinction is made between the educated and illiterate; they have different daily prayers, but it is laid down that lay brethren as a rule are to be employed only as porters and cooks.[4] At Westminster, on the other hand, the small group of *conversi* seem to resemble more the oblates of the modern world—devout layfolk, that is, who live in a monastery and follow its religious exercises under no obligation to remain and who do work suitable to the gifts and training of the individual.[5] On the whole, it seems clear that the *conversi* were few in number, and, so far as has been noted, there is no trace of them in the voluminous records of some of the largest houses, such as Christ Church, Glastonbury, Bury and Ely. Few or many, they disappeared almost entirely with their Cistercian and Gilbertine fellows when economic conditions changed in the fourteenth century, though a few lingered on, as at Winchcombe in 1428.[6] There would seem to be no record of *conversi* at any black monk house in the narratives of the dissolution or in the pension lists.

IV

THE PECULIUM

Throughout the three last centuries of the middle ages reformers and visitors were concerned to preserve the personal poverty of the religious or, to use the technical phrase of the time, to extirpate the vice of *proprietas*. This appears in two forms which ultimately merged into one. From early times monks had been allowed to receive small gifts in cash to distribute to

1 *Reg. Winchelsey*, 859. All fragments from everywhere are to be collected, including the *refectorium conversorum*, to go as alms.

2 *Chron. Evesh.* 285: 'Quosdam fratres vocatos conversos.' The phrase suggests that the species was extinct when the chronicler wrote.

3 *Bath. Cartulary*, II, 811; *Hist. Dun. SS* 3, ccx; *MC*, I, 116, cf. II, 41 (1343).

4 *Custom. St Augustine's*, 275 *seqq.* 400.

5 H. F. Westlake, *Westminster Abbey*, II, 377-9.

6 Cf. Royce, *Landbok* of Winchcombe, II, 5.

the poor or needy relations; later, between 1150–1250, the custom grew up in some monasteries that various officials should contribute small sums to be divided amongst the monks of the cloister for alms, medicines, spices and holiday purposes.[1] Meanwhile, another practice of obscure origin was growing up, that of giving a fixed allowance of money to each monk in lieu of clothes. In the old English and Anglo-Norman monasteries clothes were issued as required by the cellarer or chamberer, as laid down by the Rule; often certain revenues from land were ear-marked *de vestitu mona-chorum.* Why such a system, which works simply and which obtains almost universally in modern religious houses, should have been so universally superseded is not clear. Possibly the original sources of revenue became confused, or appreciated or depreciated so as to bear no direct relation to the needs of the case; it may even have been found, as in some modern institutions, that thrift is greater and costs are less when a fixed sum is put under individual control than when all can draw wastefully upon the establishment. In any case, the custom arose early and became all but universal. Throughout the latter half of the thirteenth century and onwards visitors and chapters reprobated it, and it was duly condemned in the *Summi Magistri.*[2] Nevertheless, it persisted, save at a few houses.[3] Its abolition was one of the leading points of the reform programme of 1421, when it was suggested that a single monk should receive all the funds and distribute clothes and other necessaries according to need, but obstruction and inveterate custom proved too strong.[4] The amount given annually was in the neighbourhood of £1 (Ely, £1. 2s. 6d. in 1403; St Albans, after a rise, £1. 7s. 8d. c. 1425; Durham, £1 in 1535);[5] at Ely clothes money and pocket money (*gracie*) are mentioned separately,[6] but it was more customary to allow a fixed inclusive sum known in English as wages, in Anglo-French as *le apaye* and in Latin as *stipendium.* Immediately before the dissolution the tariff of each monastery was so well known as to attract or repel recruits,[7] and it was a common practice of the commissioners when dissolving a house to give a year's wages and sometimes even to pay off arrears.

1 For early alms-money, *v. MO*, 484; for pocket-money *v. Ely Chapter Ordinances,* 9 (1300): 'quas quidem gracias vocant.' For money for spices and medicine, *v. Ann. Wig. s.a.* 1300 (1s. 6d. p.a.).

2 *MC*, I, 11 (1219). Eighty years later there is a prohibition in the statutes of Bishop Ralph de Walpole (*Ely Chapter Ordinances,* 9), and Winchelsey tried everywhere to stop the practice (*Register*, 813, Christ Church; 840, Rochester, etc.); it was common also in Cluniac houses (e.g. *Visitations and Chapters General of Cluny*, 308) and among the Austin canons (e.g. *Reg. York Giffard*, 214, Newstead; *Reg. York Wickwane*, 130, Healaugh Park). Cf. *Summi Magistri*, cap. 17 (*MC*, II, 231).

3 The list of annual clothes rations at certain houses would seem to imply that there was still distribution from the common store, e.g. Tewkesbury in 1243 (*Ann. Theok. s.a.*); Gloucester in 1301 (*Reg. Winchelsey*, 861).

4 *MC*, II, 114–16; cf. the objections and the final articles, 131–2, where custom is allowed as excuse for receiving money *partim pro necessariis, partim pro recreacionibus.*

5 *Rites of Durham*, 81; *Ely Chapter Ordinances*, 55 (1403); *Reg. Whethamstede*, I, 459.

6 *Ely Chapter Ordinances*, 9.

7 Cf. *Visitations of Archbishop Warham*, 28–30 (Faversham).

Petty as were the sums in question and reasonable as were most of the purchases and expenses, the custom of issuing money, and in particular clothes-money, had a demoralizing effect; the dignified spiritual conception of common property and common care was lost, and the monk, from being a son of the house, became the petty pensioner with a small allowance.

V

Within the precinct of the monastery, buildings and furnishings in the thirteenth century began slowly to take the shape that was to set them, during the late medieval period in England, in the forefront of the gradual process which substituted for the large and comfortless halls and open arcades of the Norman period smaller, warmer and more comfortable apartments, and the glazed windows and wainscoted walls of the fourteenth and fifteenth centuries. In this evolution the monasteries, and in particular the abbot's and prior's lodgings, led the way. From being a collection of large halls surrounding a cloister, the buildings of the typical great black monk abbey grew slowly into the rich, irregular mass of which the great gatehouse, the oriel or mullioned windows, the well-lighted gallery and the built-in fireplace and chimney were familiar features.

One of the first steps in the process was the provision of warmly wainscoted cubicles in the dormitory. This was done at Peterborough at the very opening of our period, and at the same time the monks of St Albans were being provided with oaken bedsteads.[1] In the cloister a corresponding advance was made by glazing the windows and constructing panelled carrells with reading desks, a double defence against the climate which became common in the thirteenth century and must have made work in the cloister during the winter a physical possibility.[2] Eighty years after the dormitory at Peterborough, the return of students from the newly opened college at Oxford called for provision of quiet places for study giving more space than a carrell for books, and in the early years of the fourteenth century St Albans, Glastonbury and Evesham are found building a range of studies, for which a site was often found above the cloister and near to the dormitory.[3] In the church, the choir stalls were becoming more elaborate, with canopies to break the down draughts, while the mechanical clock, a new invention that found favour in church after church, served at once as a convenience, an ornament and a source of interest for the monks.[4]

1 Swapham, 108 (c. 1220); GASA, I, 280 (also c. 1220).
2 Chron. Evesham. 301.
3 Chron. Evesham. 286 (c. 1310, studii); GASA, II, 302 (c. 1330, studia juxta dormitorium); Johann. Glaston. ed. T. Hearne, 271 (aula with four camerae); also Christ Church, infra p. 336.
4 For Abbot Wallingford's interest (c. 1330) in illud nobile opus horologii in ecclesia, v. GASA, II, 281; for the Glastonbury clock, c. 1295—magnum horologium, processionibus et spectaculis insignitum, v. Johann. Glaston. 263; for the Christ Church clock of 1292 v. infra p. 335.

VI

There remains from the thirteenth century no life of a saintly abbot or monk bishop comparable to those which were so numerous a century earlier, the work of a Coleman, an Eadmer, a Walter Daniel or an Adam of Eynsham; there are not even any biographical notices such as the early chroniclers give, of edifying lives or holy deaths. There are, however, a few entries in the records which show that lives of unusual holiness were still not unknown.

The series may open with John Denis of Evesham, whose tomb Thomas of Marleberge built, who for thirty years and more had lived a life of prayer and penance;[1] a little later, c. 1230, the sacrist and precentor of Bury, Gregory by name, left a reputation for sanctity and wonder-working after death.[2] A few years later we hear of Peter, a saintly prior of Westminster c. 1240;[3] at Tewkesbury Abbot Robert (ob. 1254) was said to work miracles;[4] at Croyland in the same year died Abbot Thomas, distinguished by the severity of his self-inflicted penances, as also by his custom of preaching to the people, and whose tomb had a similar reputation.[5] Three years later Paris records the death of the holy prior Simon of Norwich who, like the saints of an earlier age, daily recited the Psalter in its entirety.[6] Nor were abbots alone in their fame. In 1273 died Adam of Emly, a monk of Gloucester, whose fame for holiness was so great that the people of the city demanded that he should be buried before the altar of the Holy Cross, in the nave of the church in a place accessible to them; the chronicler adds that many miracles occurred at his tomb, and twenty years later the Worcester chronicler notes their continuance. St Mary's had an exemplar of holiness in Prior Philip, who died in 1296; eleven years later the annalist pays tribute to John de Gamages, the great abbot of Gloucester, who had passed sixty-two years of holy life in the monastic habit.

The precise degree of credence and shade of meaning to be given to these passages may be uncertain; they show at least that alongside of other and more material activities and interests, individuals were still to be found, even in high places, who put before all else that endeavour to enter by the narrow gate which has always been the end of the religious profession.

---

1 *Chron. Evesh.* 271. The passage is quoted in full in *MO*, 342, note 6.

2 *MSE*, II, 294.

3 *Flores Historiarum*, II, 321.

4 *Ann. Theok. s.a.* 1254: 'Pro quo piisimus Jesus multa pandit miracula.' Cf. also entry on following page.

5 *Hist. Croyland. Continuatio* (ed. Fulman), 479–80. In addition to his fasts and watchings we are told that *lorica cilicioque vicissim quasi vestibus mutatoriis assidue induebatur.* His body was said to have been found incorrupt. The *Historia* in its present form is the work of the fifteenth century, but it clearly rests on older material.

6 *MPChM*, V, 41: 'vir eximiae sanctitatis…piissimae recordationis.' For an earlier example of the daily psalter *v. MO*, 471; cf. also *Reg. S. Benedicti, c.* XVIII.

CHAPTER XXV

INTELLECTUAL LIFE

I. HISTORY

I

The monasteries of England, which at the close of the eleventh century had been the sole focus of a highly developed literary culture, humane in spirit and seeking its models in the Roman past, did not long retain this position. The growth of a more complex society, the development of education in the cathedral and urban schools, the rise of a court circle of literary and legal clerks, and above all the magnetic power of the nascent universities, which drew to themselves all young talent and immersed it in the study of law or dialectic, entailed the transference of cultural leadership from the monasteries to the schools and the still more essential change from a literary culture to one that was primarily legal or dialectical. Already in the reign of John the race of great monastic chroniclers, biographers and letter-writers had died out, and though the monasteries with their rich libraries continued to nourish receptive minds with the classical literature and encyclopedic learning of the past, they were never again centres of purely intellectual life.

An exception, however, to the general decay of literary activity must be made in the case of St Albans. This great abbey, though neither the wealthiest nor the most populous in the country, could undoubtedly in the reign of Henry III vindicate its claim to be the premier monastery of England.[1] Situated on the great North Road, near the capital, but not embarrassed by its business and unrest, the house had ever since the Conquest been fortunate in a succession of enlightened abbots and distinguished recruits, many of whom came from abroad, or had received their education on the continent. Though it had not yet given birth to a historian of the calibre of Malmesbury or a chronicler of the vivacity of Jocelin of Brakelond or Richard of Devizes, it had kept some domestic records and nourished something of a democratic spirit. The first appearance, however, of historical writing on the grand scale at St Albans dates from the moment when Wendover began to compile his ambitious chronicle in the early years of the thirteenth century. Roger of Wendover, whose career in office had been terminated by incompetent administration of the priory of Belvoir, c. 1219, compiled, as precentor, the *Flores Historiarum*, which from the beginning of the thirteenth century at least gives an original account of contemporary history. Wendover is always a partial and rarely

---

1 At the coronation of Queen Eleanor in 1236 the abbot of St Albans took precedence of all other abbots *sicut ejusdem ecclesiae autentica privilegia protestantur*. (*MPChM*, III, 337.)

a trustworthy writer, but he deserves well of students of English history both for his own contributions to our knowledge and for the patronage and inspiration he gave to a brilliant pupil and continuator of his work.[1]

Matthew Paris is without question the most familiar figure among the monastic writers between the Conquest and the Dissolution.[2] His fame, which was established in his lifetime, has never suffered a serious eclipse among historians and antiquaries.[3] He has been fortunate both in his literary remains, which have survived in magnificent manuscripts readily accessible to students, and in his critics, who have in the past almost without exception treated him with remarkable indulgence. The reasons for his popularity are not far to seek. His copious chronicles provide a mass of information about contemporary Europe and the near East which is not to be found elsewhere; they contain numerous personal details about celebrities derived from direct conversations or first-hand information,[4] and extracts from original documents which are not known to have survived elsewhere; they are discursive and yet extremely readable. In the past, when the sources of medieval history were hard to come by and all except a very few scholars relied upon writers of a later date, historians were delighted to be able to follow, for an important period, an honest and extremely well-informed contemporary, upon whom they might rest their narrative in some such way as historians of Greece may rest it upon Thucydides. Moreover, the prejudices of Paris—his violent criticism of papal exactions, his obstructive resentment towards reformers, and even his jealousy of the friars—were precisely such as to appeal to Protestant,

1 As Prof. V. H. Galbraith well observes (*The St Albans Chronicle*, xxvii): 'Roger Wendover and Matthew Paris left behind them a tradition of historical writing at St Albans which lasted for about two centuries.'

2 Apart from notices in the *DNB* and similar collections, there is no study of Paris which does justice to all his activities and attempts a critical appreciation. For his purely historical work, *v.* C. Jenkins, *The Monastic Chronicler*, V. H. Galbraith, *Roger Wendover and Matthew Paris* and F. M. Powicke, *The Compilation of the 'Chronica Majora' of Matthew Paris*, in *Proc. Brit. Acad.*, xxix.

3 His obituary in *GASA*, I, 394 speaks of him as: 'vir quidem eloquens et famosus, innumeris virtutibus plenus, historiographus ac chronographus magnificus, dictator egregius, corde frequenter revolvens *Otiositas inimica est animae*' (*Reg. S. Ben. c.* xlviii). The continuator of the *Chronica Majora* is alluded to as (v, 748 note): 'Tanti praedecessoris opera praesumens aggredi...cum non sit dignus ejusdem corrigiam solvere calciamenti.' Modern writers have taken the same tone: thus the author (W. Hunt) of the article in *DNB* speaks of his 'manly temperament' and of 'his wide knowledge, acute intellect and perfect truthfulness', while Professor W. Jones in the *Cambridge History of English Literature* sees in him 'a thoroughly patriotic Englishman...animated by a transparently honest fervour of moral indignation and by a patriotic jealousy for the honour of England'. Almost the first to disturb the harmonious chorus was A. L. Smith in his Ford lectures of 1905 (published 1913), *Church and State in the Middle Ages*. 'The loftier side of medieval thought', he writes (pp. 168–71), 'hardly appears at all in him...all that is on the surface he reflects so that it stands out before us, but he is no magician to make us see what lies beneath, for he does not see this himself.... In robustness, in industry, in eagerness, in strong language, he is a Macaulay minus the style. He is also a Macaulay in prejudice...in lack of spirituality.'

4 Lists of Paris's informants, ranging from Henry III and Haakon IV to travellers and confidential servants, will be found in Dr Luard's introductions to the Rolls Series volumes.

liberty-loving historians who nevertheless had a warm corner in their hearts for the monks.

In consequence, he has often been followed uncritically, or at least too exclusively, and it is only in recent years that something of a reaction has set in. Great, indeed, as are the services he has rendered to posterity, Paris, as a critical historian, is inferior, not only to Bede, but also to William of Malmesbury. Unlike his two predecessors, he is concerned almost exclusively with contemporary events; he never makes a critical examination of the sources of an earlier time. Nor does he, like Bede and Malmesbury, submit his material to complete digestion. His pages consist of a succession of separate topics, any number of which could be removed without affecting either the context or any other part of the book. He remains, in fact, a chronicler rather than a writer of history. It must be added that the mass of information he provides often creates the illusion that his account is exhaustive; this has led writers to follow him alike in his emphasis and in his silences. Finally, his judgements, though freely and fearlessly given, often lack both dignity and finality, and show a certain irresponsibility and a failure to co-ordinate the data he himself provides.[1] Paris, indeed, has the defects of his qualities; his curiosity, wide interests and love of incident imply a certain lack of spiritual depth and of a sense of the true values of things. *Non omnia possumus omnes*: but a monastic historian whose time of manhood overlapped the last years of St Francis and the early maturity of St Thomas Aquinas cannot escape judgement by the highest standards of moral and intellectual achievement.

These shortcomings, however, must not be allowed to obscure the very great merits of Matthew Paris. His tireless energy, upon which his friends remarked, maintained a copious output of literary and artistic work of a very high quality. When we set ourselves to imagine the labour of collecting, sifting, arranging, copying and illustrating the mass of material from which the final narrative was constructed, and the wide interest which rejected no happenings, however distant; when we consider the self-restraint needed to preserve a balance between the acquisition of information and its embodiment in literary form, the prevailing self-effacement of the historian and the absence of personal bias against individuals or of flattery of the great, we cannot in justice withhold our admiration for the talents and practical intelligence of the monk of St Albans. There is in Paris none of the morbid vanity of Gerald of Wales or the bitter cynicism of Richard of Devizes. His prejudices are largely those of his class and his age; they are not without a historical value of their own, for they show how a typical

1 Paris, like Malmesbury before him, went through his work striking out or softening down some of the more violent passages and expressions. His editor in the Rolls Series, while noting this in his introduction, prints the full text and does not always make it clear where these rejections occur. In spite of afterthoughts, not a few pages remain uncancelled which do little credit to Paris's good sense, e.g. the wholly incredible account of Grosseteste's proceedings in visitation (*ChM*, v, 226–7) and the *fabliau* of the pope's nightmare in which he is prodded in the ribs by the dead bishop's crozier (v, 429–30).

mind in a great and active monastery reacted to events and movements of which we can see the implications more clearly than could a contemporary. Perhaps it is not fanciful to see in Paris, not only a typical conservative of the age, but a medieval embodiment of many of the elements that have always distinguished the national character—a love of old custom and a fear of being dragooned into the unfamiliar; an instinctive dislike of foreign ways; and an interest in persons and events rather than in principles and movements.

Matthew Paris was clothed as a novice at St Albans on 21 January 1217; probably, therefore, he was born *c.* 1200. His name does not imply foreign birth or provenance, nor is there any suggestion of this in his writings. Gifted and versatile, he is one of the last of the monks to include within his scope, like a Dunstan, the whole range of letters and art. His primary interest was contemporary history, and here he had the good fortune to meet with Roger of Wendover, the first great chronicler of the house. Him he succeeded in 1236; thenceforward till his own death he was engaged on his great work, the *Chronica Majora*, together with a briefer account and a collection of additions and *pièces justificatives*. He also put together and refashioned the existing materials for domestic history, adding an account of his own times in the monastery and thus launching the series of *Gesta Abbatum* which was to be continued for a century and a half after his death.

He soon became celebrated. Henry III when visiting St Albans sought him out, and on a well-known occasion at Westminster was at pains to call him up from the crowd and bid him write what he saw.[1] Other public men, also, realized that their share in events could best be preserved for posterity by judicious conversations at St Albans.[2] Nor were his gifts those of the student and artist alone. He had won the esteem and friendship of Haakon IV of Norway (*reg.* 1218–64) a personal friend of Henry III and a patron of English artists. When, therefore, the abbey of St Benet Holm on the island Niderholm near Trondhjem was in financial embarrassment owing to the fraudulent action of an abbot who had absconded with the convent's seal and subsequently died, Haakon, *c.* 1246, sent the prior to England for help with a letter to Paris, through whose good offices the Cahorsin money-lenders in London agreed to a composition.[3] When, a little later, the same abbey was at issue with the archbishop of Trondhjem, a papal legate advised the monks to solicit the pope for one to reform the obser-

1 *MPChM*, IV, 644. The occasion was the procession of the Holy Blood at Westminster in 1247.

2 St Louis must have been in contact with Paris before 1248; he heard in that year of his intended journey to Norway and asked him to convey to King Haakon a letter offering hospitality to Norwegian crusaders *MPHA*, III, 40–1. With Haakon the friendship must have been an old one, as the king turned for help to Paris in 1246 (*v.* text and notes *infra*) and the Norwegian envoys could speak of him to the pope in 1247 as *familiarissimus regi nostro et amicissimus*. Later, the king, *pro amore ipsius*, replaced the splintered mast of the ship which had carried him to Norway, and made him a gift of rich cloths (*ChM*, VI, 391).

3 For this episode *v. ChM*, IV, 651–2; V, 36; 42–5, and *Hist. Angl.* III, 40–1.

vance of their house. This they did, and when Innocent IV ordered them to choose whom they would they asked for the dispatch of Matthew Paris.[1] The pope assented, and in 1248 Paris duly accomplished his mission. With remarkable self-effacement he tells us nothing of his sojourn in Norway save for an escape, while saying Mass on shore at Bergen, from a stroke of lightning which struck the ship in which he had arrived a few hours before, but his visit has very reasonably been connected with an impulse given to Norwegian painting in the style of the school of St Albans. He remained less than a year, and his task was doubtless simply to pass on to the Norwegian monks the observance, domestic and liturgical, and the general tone of St Albans, rather than to act as disciplinary reformer and ruler, a position for which he had neither official authority nor temperament. He returned to his *scriptorium*, from which he was never again summoned by the duties of any other office; he died, while still at work, probably in 1259, leaving behind him a tradition of historical writing which endured at St Albans until the end of the fifteenth century.[2]

II

The writing of history did not immediately cease at St Albans. The pen of Matthew Paris was taken up at once, probably by the monk, so conscious of his own indignity to succeed the great man, who paid the well-known tribute to his memory. For six years the great chronicle continued in a manner which an exacting critic has judged to be not unworthy of its past.[3] After that there is a gap of more than forty years before a succession of smaller works covers the early decades of the fourteenth century. St Albans did not give birth to another historian of the first rank till the days of Thomas of Walsingham eighty years later.

Elsewhere, the writing of literary history, as opposed to annalistic or purely domestic chronicling, is almost unknown. The important group of monastic annals which helped to give the background to the story of the twelfth century are still running at the beginning of the reign of Henry III, but they drop off one by one as the century advances, and only two survive the reign of Edward I.[4] In most of them the entries grow briefer long before the end and the place given to monastic affairs is small. Two, however, the annals of Burton and Dunstable, are exceptions; though

1 Paris (*ChM*, v, 44) alleges him to have asserted that English monks surpassed all others in observance, so St Albans excelled all other English houses. The Norwegian monks refer to Paris's prudence and reliability, and Innocent's letter speaks of him as *probatae vitae et religionis expertae*.

2 A laudatory account of Paris, by his continuator is in *GASA*, I, 394–5. For a suggestion that he lived beyond 1259 *v*. Powicke, *Proc. Brit. Acad.*, XXIX, 14.

3 Galbraith, *The St Albans Chronicle*, XXIX: 'Nor is the text of the *Flores*, 1259–65 inferior either in scale or quality to what precedes it.'

4 The monastic Annals give out as follows: Margam, 1232; Tewkesbury, 1263; Burton (save for isolated entries), 1263; Winchester, 1277; Waverley, 1291; Osney, 1293; Dunstable, 1296; Worcester, 1307. The Bermondsey annals continue briefly till 1400 but are of little value.

unimportant in their original parts, they both embody numerous transcripts of contemporary documents which make them authorities of the first importance for the political history of the century. Perhaps the most typical monastic compositions of the age are the purely domestic chronicles, impersonal and objective in manner, which record the doings of an abbot and the fortunes of the house, especially upon its estates and in the courts, often with a number of official documents. The most elaborate of these is the history of the abbots of St Albans, originated and completed to date by Paris, and continued, no doubt from material supplied by abbatial registers, by unknown hands;[1] of a somewhat different type are the chronicle of Evesham, which had owed so much of its bulk and interest in earlier days to Thomas of Marlberge, and the continuation of the chronicle of Gervase at Canterbury. At Durham, also, which, St Albans apart, was the house with the most continuous tradition of historical work, a number of writers told the story of the priory without ever touching the level reached by Symeon. More typical of the time are such chronicles as that of Adam of Domerham and his continuator John of Glastonbury in the West, and the slightly earlier Robert of Swapham and Walter of Whittlesey at Peterborough. Other houses, such as St Augustine's, Canterbury, Croyland and Westminster had to wait till the following century was all but over, or even longer, before a chronicler arose to give unity, or at least continuity, to the scattered records.[2]

II. ART

I

The latter years of the reign of John had not been propitious to artistic enterprise. Under the new king, himself a connoisseur, the admirer and patron of native talent and devoted to the contemporary French work, the new style in architecture, sculpture and painting blossomed all over the country under the stimulus of the vigorous rule of a number of enlightened bishops. The manifestations of the new art-form were many and various. The large-scale, 'heavy' arts of architectural engineering and sculpture were, as a general rule, in the hands of professional masons. So also, for the most part, were the 'medium' arts of metal and wood work, and wall and panel painting. Here, however, a number of executants, and those among the most gifted and celebrated, were, or subsequently became, monks. The most notable group of these was connected with St Albans.

That great monastery had long been a centre of artistic activity, and it is probable that for a long time artists within and without the community had worked together; there had also been cases of professional artists

1 The *Gesta Abbatum* is at its fullest for the reigns of Abbots Wallingford, Mentmore, and de la Mare (1308–96); of each of these three abbots valuable biographical notes are given.

2 The rebirth of historical writing at St Albans, and elsewhere, and the interest shown in domestic antiquities early in the fifteenth century will be noted in another place.

becoming monks.[1] In the early thirteenth century a small family party, hailing from Colchester, established themselves near the abbey: Master Walter the Painter, his brother Master Simon, and the latter's son, Richard.[2] Walter soon became a monk and sacristan of the abbey. He was the most gifted English artist and craftsman of his day, and under his direction the monastery and church received additions on a magnificent scale to their furniture and decorations. Matthew Paris, himself an artist of outstanding talent, extols without a trace of jealousy this 'incomparable painter and sculptor', this 'marvellous craftsman', whose equal in every kind of work had not hitherto been seen, nor would be seen hereafter.[3] The High Altar, with the story of St Alban in carving or painting; the great statue of Our Lady, and above all the rood screen with its figures were among his principal achievements.[4] The screen, indeed, attracted such notice that Henry III ordered a replica for Westminster, and a whole *atelier* of craftsmen went into residence at St Albans to execute the commission.[5] An even more striking proof of fame was the choice of Walter by the monks of Christ Church, Canterbury, to design and erect what was to be the most celebrated shrine of England, if not of north-western Europe, that of St Thomas the martyr. The body of the saint was translated to its new resting-place on 7 July 1220, the day which, three centuries later, was to prove 'very convenient' for the martyrdom of another Thomas, and the artist was present to supervise the function.[6] Of this, and of all the other gorgeous monuments of his genius, not a fragment has survived the spoiling of the centuries. He died on 2 September 1248.

Walter was assisted by his brother, Simon. The latter was not a monk, but his son Richard, the third artist of the family, was received into the community. He was working before 1240 and continued for some thirty years. The guest hall with its decorations was one of his works, and we may perhaps identify him with the chamberer who supplied the dormitory with oak beds, roofed the aisles of the church with oak, and completed the tower.[7]

The Colchesters, though possibly the most eminent of their school, did not stand alone. Matthew Paris, a monk of the cloister who had never

1 E.g. Anketil, *c.* 1120; *v. MO*, 537.

2 For the Colchesters *v.* W. Page, *The St Albans School of Painting*, in *Archaeologia*, LVIII (1902), 275–92, and W. R. Lethaby, *The English Primitives*, in *The Burlington Magazine*, XXIX (1916) and subsequent vols.; also *English Medieval Painting*, by Tancred Borenius and E. W. Tristram (Paris, 1927), pp. 7–8 and Plates 12–16. The Colchester provenance seems to be established by the mention of *Walterus pictor*, at an uncertain date after 1192, in the *Cartularium Monasterii S. Johannis Baptiste de Colecestria* (Roxburghe Club, 1897), II, 587.

3 *GASA*, I, 280: 'Cui [*sc.* Mag. Waltero] in artificiis quamplurimis comparem non meminimus praevidisse, vel aliquem credimus affuturum.' *Ibid.* 281: 'Pictor et sculptor incomparabilis.'

4 *GASA*, loc. cit.   5 *Rot. Claus.* 33 Hen. III, m. 3.

6 *MPChM*, III, 59: 'Walterus monachus et sacrista ecclesiae S. Albani... cujus documento omnia tractabantur.'

7 *GASA*, I, 280: 'Conquaestu et industria Ricardi de Thidenhanger, monachi nostri ac camerarii.' For a list of Richard's works *v. MPChM*, VI (*Additamenta*), 202.

been a professional craftsman, was a worker in metal, a sculptor and a painter.[1] No work of his larger than the page of a book has been preserved in England, but it has been suggested that in an oak panel of St Peter, originally in Faaberg church in Norway, we have a memorial of the sojourn of the artist in that country. Whoever may have been the artist, it may without doubt be reckoned among the works of the school of St Albans, and English influence from the same source may be seen in a number of works still preserved in Norway.[2]

Other members of the school remained laymen. Craftsmen of St Albans not only worked in the town on the Westminster screen, but also joined the team of the king's workmen at Westminster. Henceforward large-scale painting, sculpture and metal work was to become almost exclusively the occupation of lay professionals. The last monastic artist at St Albans was perhaps Alan the painter, a converse who was working between 1260 and 1270.[3]

It is impossible to say how many other great monasteries harboured artist monks early in the thirteenth century; probably very few. There is, however, one notable instance, that of William of Winchester, the most favoured artist of Henry III.[4] He would seem to have begun his career as a lay craftsman of the Winchester art school, and as such was appointed by the king in 1240 to the office of painter in the cathedral church.[5] Whether he became a converse there is not clear, though it is probable; he was soon transferred to the king's work in the abbey church and palace of Westminster and at Windsor;[6] he was by 1248 at latest a monk of Westminster. Between 1248 and Henry's death in 1272 there is a constant stream of allusions in the royal accounts to the king's beloved painter

---

1 Cf. B. M. Cott., MS Nero D VII, f. 50 v–51 (quoted by M. R. James, *La Estoire de Seint Aedward*, 28): 'Religiosus monachus, incomparabilis cronographus et pictor peroptimus ...excellens in doctrinis et pictura.' Also *GASA*, 1, 395: 'Inerat ei tanta subtilitas in auro et argento caeteroque metallo, in sculpendo et in picturis depingendo ut nullum post se in Latino orbe creditur reliquisse secundum.' This, if referring to Paris as an artist alone, would be extravagant praise, but if taken to refer to his attainments as an Admirable Crichton is perhaps justifiable.

2 For this, *v.* Borenius and Tristram, *English Medieval Painting* pp. 13–14 and Plates 28–9. There is a good reproduction of the Faaberg St Peter there and in Lindblom (*v. infra*), pl. 7. Prof. A. Lindblom, in *La Peinture Gothique en Suède et en Norvège* (Stockholm, 1916), p. 128–32, possibly minimizes the direct influence of Paris in Norway, but he remarks (p. 131]: 'la venue de Mathieu Paris en Norvège est de la plus haute importance pour l'histoire de l'art.'

3 For *Alanus pictor, conversus, v. MPChM*, VI, 277.

4 Almost all the references in Liberate Rolls, etc., to William and other royal painters were diligently collected and printed more than a century ago by J. Gage Rokewood in *Vetusta Monumenta*, vol. VI, *Memoir on the Painted Chamber*. They have recently been reviewed by W. R. Lethaby in the *Burlington* articles referred to on p. 297, n. 2, and elsewhere.

5 *Rot. Claus.* 24 Hen. III, m. 13 (*Vet. Monumenta, art. cit.* 29, n.): 'Rex contulit magistro Willelmo pictori officium pictoris prioratus Sci Swithuni Winton. ratione Episcopatus Winton. vacantis et in manu Regis existentis, et mandatum est priori Sci Swithuni Winton. quod de officio illo cum liberationibus ad idem officium pertinentibus saisinam ei habere faciat.' The date is 1240, and the expressions seem to make it clear that William was not a monk at the time.

6 Cf. Lethaby, *English Primitives*, II (*Burlington Magazine*, 1916, pp. 281–9).

Master William.[1] The fruits of these years of work, in which he was only one among many artists, have perished almost entirely, but in the impressive contemporary figure of St Faith at Westminster and in the Crucifixion beneath it we can see painting which, if not from the master's hand, argues an extraordinary fecundity of talent in his assistants.[2] The celebrated altar piece, which even in its present lamentable condition shows a technical skill and an emotional delicacy not unworthy of comparison with Simone Martini, is still a subject of controversy; critics have assigned it to William, to a nameless monk of Westminster, and to a French master.[3] Excellence in another genre has been more convincingly claimed for Master William; the encaustic tiles from the floor of the chapter house at Westminster, and the still more interesting series from Chertsey, illustrating the romance of *Tristram and Iseult*, are very possibly from his designs.[4]

II

While the large-scale arts had passed or were passing from monastic to lay hands, the basic art of the early medieval period, that of manuscript illumination, was still at the end of King John's reign mainly a monastic pursuit, though a professional class of illuminators was already in existence. The thirteenth century, indeed, was to be in the realm of manuscript painting what the twelfth had been in the realm of thought and letters; in each the monopoly, or at least the dominating position, in an important field of cultural life passed from the monks, but whereas the intellectual focus shifted from the monasteries to another group of corporate bodies, the universities, the inheritors of the artistic legacy of the cloister were private artists, and the scriptorium still remained a potential studio for a monk with talent.

During the whole of the thirteenth century manuscript painting in the traditional religious style, dignified in tone and gorgeous in execution, continued in certain houses. From Peterborough, where two hundred years earlier Wulfstan's master Erwin had delighted kings, the fortunate survival of a number of psalters shows that a succession of artists was continuing to produce magnificent work. The earliest of these books was decorated for Abbot Robert de Lindesey (1214–22), and its exquisitely balanced designs and cool tones are in the monumental style that was passing.[5] Almost a hundred years later the Peterborough scriptorium

---

1 E.g. *Rot. Liberate*, 40 Hen. III, m. 9 (1252): 'Dilecto nobis magistro Willelmo pictori monacho Westmon.' The reference in one roll to him as a *monachus West. nuper Winton.* leaves it uncertain whether his status or place of residence is in question.

2 *English Medieval Painting*, Pls. 19–21.

3 *Ibid.* Pls. 22–4. On p. 12 the authors cautiously observe that 'it would seem that the balance of probability favours the theory of English origin'.

4 Lethaby, *English Primitives*, v (*Burlington Magazine*, 1917, pp. 133 *seqq.*) Borenius and Tristram, *op. cit.* p. 12, n. appear to agree.

5 London, MS. 59 of the Society of Antiquaries. Millar, *English Illuminated Manuscripts from the X to the XIII Century* (cited as Millar, 1), p. 47 and Pls. 69–70.

could still give birth to a masterpiece, this time in the delicate, mannered Gothic style that had been developed in both France and England. This psalter, presented by the distinguished Geoffrey of Crowland to the visiting cardinal Gaucelin d'Euse, c. 1320, ultimately found its way to Brussels, where it remains to-day.[1] A marvel of colour and design, it is in the full tradition of religious dignity, in contrast to the more secular and fanciful style of the contemporary school of East Anglia.

Yet another fine Peterborough psalter has survived,[2] and from the middle decades of the century there is a splendid Bible, which can be assigned with some confidence to St Augustine's, Canterbury.[3] Meanwhile, a new style, having some affinity to the outline drawing of the Utrecht Psalter and the Old English period, was being developed by Matthew Paris at St Albans, to have a considerable vogue there and elsewhere. That gifted artist was responsible for a very large number of small drawings in the margin of his works. He did not sign his sketches, and there has been a controversy over his drawings, as there has been over his handwriting, but judges well qualified to pronounce have accepted as his the drawings in the autograph manuscripts of the *Chronica Majora* and the *Historia Anglorum*, as also the illustrations in the *Lives of the Offas*, the *Life of St Alban*, and the *Life of St Edward the Confessor*.[4] The sketches are for the most part illustrations of the narrative, and the vivacity of treatment and tricks of style have invited imitation and reproduction; in recent times they have been taken as the models of numerous imaginative or burlesque reconstructions of medieval scenes. As works of art they cannot compare with the more elaborate contemporary designs or with the more sensitive line drawings of the Old English period or of the Guthlac roll. Paris, indeed, was perhaps a gifted illustrator and cartoonist rather than a master

1 Brussels Royal Library MSS. 9961–2. Millar, I, 66–7, gives an interesting account of its travels from Avignon to Paris and Brussels, and a reproduction in Pl. 100. The Psalter was executed c. 1290–1300; the pictures, as M. R. James pointed out, were derived from a series of paintings formerly in the choir of the abbey church at Peterborough.

2 Cambridge, Fitzwilliam Museum MS. 12 (a page is reproduced in M. R. James's *Catalogue*); Millar, I, 48, Pls. 71–2.

3 Brit. Mus. Burney MS. 3, the Bible of Robert de Bello, abbot of St Augustine's, 1224–53, and 'certainly executed at that house' (Millar, I, 51–2). It may be added that the output of Bibles, often with pictures and script of extreme beauty, was still large in the thirteenth century, and that most of them were probably monastic in origin. For the pictures in these and other Bibles, v. M. R. James, *Illustrations of the Old Testament*, an introduction to Sir Sydney Cockerell's *A Book of Old Testament Illustrations* (Roxburghe Club, 1927).

4 For an excellent critical discussion, v. M. R. James, *The Drawings of Matthew Paris* (Walpole Society, 1926), where reproductions are given of a great number of Paris's illustrations, and the same writer's *The Life of St Alban in Trinity College, Dublin*. Cf. also Lethaby, *English Primitives*, v (*Burlington Magazine*, 1917, pp. 45 seqq.). The principal manuscripts illustrated by Paris are Corpus Christi College, Cambridge, xxvi (*Chronica Majora*); Brit. Mus. Royal MS. 14 C vii (*Historia Anglorum*); Brit. Mus. Cott. MS. Nero D i (*Lives of the Offas*); Trinity College, Dublin, MS. E i 40 (*Life of St Alban*); Cambridge University Library MS. Ee 3, 59 (*Life of St Edward*). For the work of an imitator (or perhaps, as some critics think, for another work of Paris himself) v. the Apocalypse now in Paris, Bibl. Nat. MS. fr. 403, from which Dr Millar gives a plate (I, Pl. 91).

of colour and composition. Even his more ambitious tinted drawing, so often reproduced, of the Virgin and Child,[1] though not without grace and feeling, cannot compare in beauty and refinement with the superficially similar Chichester roundel. Paris had many pupils, and it is sometimes difficult to distinguish his work from theirs, for in almost all the illustrations known to have been executed at St Albans there is a graphic, secularist tone not noticed elsewhere; the imitators of Paris, however, generally lack his firmness of line or verge upon the grotesque.

From the end of the twelfth century onwards it had been fashionable throughout north-western Europe to decorate elaborately manuscripts of the Apocalypse in accordance with certain conventional schemes or sequences of illustrations.[2] Though by no means a purely English province, one or two families of these Apocalypses may have originated in English monasteries. It is at least certain that the school of St Albans originated a new type of illustration for the Apocalypses painted in the abbey. This was based on the line drawings and pale tints of the school, and was copied extensively elsewhere in England.[3] In a very different manner, the so-called Douce Apocalypse, with its sumptuous and restful scenes, faultlessly executed, reached a higher level of excellence; this also may be a monastic work, and Westminster has been suggested as its place of origin, on account of its manifest affinity to the retable.[4]

Side by side with this monastic work lay, or at least non-monastic, artists of genius were beginning to execute commissions on a commercial basis. Some of them may possibly have learnt their art, and begun their work, in the scriptorium alongside the monks, but very soon they were working in studios of their own. Several of the most notable surviving examples of their art are psalters of the large size then still common, and many appear to have been executed on commission from, or intended as presents for, religious men and women. One of these artists has in our own day been rescued from the iniquity of oblivion by connoisseurs; he was a

1 Brit. Mus. Royal MS. 4 C VII, f. 6. It is reproduced by Millar (1, Pl. 87), Borenius and Tristram (Pl. 18; an extremely good reproduction, which may be compared with the Chichester roundel, Pl. 17), and O. E. Saunders, *English Medieval Art*, fig. 41. It is familiar to many as a Museum Christmas card.

2 For the families of Apocalypses, v. the introduction by M. R. James to his edition of *The Trinity College Apocalypse*, and his introduction to the reproduction by C. H. St John Hornby of *The Douce Apocalypse* (Roxburghe Club, 1910 and 1922); he there summarizes and draws out the conclusions of the pioneer in this field, the great Léopold Delisle, and Paul Meyer. Cf. also Millar, 1, 55, Pls. 85–6, and pp. 62–3, Pls. 93–4. James suggested Canterbury as the source of the Douce book and Canterbury or St Albans for the Dublin Apocalypse. His final conclusions were given in his Schweich Lecture on 'The Apocalypse in Art', delivered in 1927 to the British Academy and published in 1931.

3 Cf. in particular the Apocalypse mentioned on p. 300, n. 4. It is indeed possible that Matthew Paris was the first to exploit the possibilities of the Apocalypse for elaborate illustration.

4 Oxford Bodl. MS. Douce 180, edited by M. R. James and reproduced by C. H. St John Hornby for the Roxburghe Club in 1922. Millar, 1, Pls. 93–4, gives reproductions, and (p. 63) tentatively suggests a Westminster provenance, noting a resemblance to the Westminster retable. James (Introd. p. 11), as has been said, suggests Canterbury.

clerk, and lived and worked at Oxford.[1] Unfortunately, the name of no monastic artist later than Matthew Paris has been preserved, and consequently it is often impossible to know anything of either the artist or the provenance of a manuscript. Thus a work of the first order, dating from the end of the thirteenth century and almost certainly English, may or may not be monastic. This, the psalter whose daintily perched windmill so attracted William Morris, is inspired by contemporary French work and displays delicate skeins of gossamer tendrils together with initials standing in the direct line of descent from older English work; it has been suggested that it was painted at Canterbury.[2]

Equally anonymous are the masterpieces of the East Anglian school of the last years of the thirteenth century and the first decades of the next century, which form a group unsurpassed by those of any single district in any country of the period.[3] It is generally acknowledged that they are not the work of monastic illuminators, though some of them were executed for monks and by artists whose fancies, though anything but spiritual, show an intimate and almost professional familiarity with things ecclesiastical. Whoever painted them, they were highly esteemed by the greater monasteries and nunneries, nor is there any reason to suppose that such monastic illuminators as still existed would have worked in a different or more exclusively religious idiom.

In these later manuscripts, the work ranges from the conventional scenes from the gospels and Old Testament to whimsical and humorous vignettes of country life. Most attractive of all, perhaps, are the incidental glimpses of woodland fur and feather. In these, besides indulging a Puckish humour, the artists not infrequently, as in the altogether charming

---

[1] The name of William de Brailes was first noticed in one of his painted initials by Sir G. F. Warner, but the assembling and identifying of his work has been principally the achievement of Sir Sydney Cockerell, who reproduced all that was then known of it in a monograph for the Roxburghe Club in 1930 (*The Work of William de Brailes. An English Illuminator of the Thirteenth Century*). Since then Hanns Swarzenski has discovered twenty-seven miniatures by him in the Walters Library, Baltimore, and Dr Millar has identified in a Paris collection five miniatures belonging to the same series (*Journal of the Walters Art Gallery*, 1938, pp. 55–69; 1939, pp. 106–9); v. also Millar, 1, 49–51 and Pls. 73–5. To judge from his self-portraits, Brailes was a cleric but not a monk; the psalter he illustrates is of the Sarum, not the monastic, use. His eponymous village is in the Feldon of south Warwickshire.

[2] For a reproduction, v. Millar, 1, Pl. 99; *ibid.* p. 65, Sir Sydney Cockerell is cited as suggesting a Canterbury provenance; an English origin, at least, seems certain. For earlier psalters, almost certainly not monastic in origin, Millar may be consulted; the best are the Psalter of All Souls, done for a nun of Amesbury (1, Pls. 81–2), and that in the possession of the Royal College of Physicians, done for a nun of Wilton.

[3] There is a discussion of these East Anglian psalters in Sir Sydney Cockerell's description of *The Gorleston Psalter* (now in the collection of Mr Dyson Perrins), where the close relationship of the surviving examples and the share taken by several hands is illustrated. Cf. also *Two East Anglian Psalters in the Bodleian Library, Oxford* (Roxburghe Club, 1926), where the Ormesby Psalter (MS. Douce 366) is described by Cockerell and the Bromholm Psalter (MS. Ashmole 1523) by James. The Ormesby Psalter was begun for a lay patron, but completed for a monk of Norwich cathedral priory; the Gorleston Psalter, so called from its place of origin, may have originated in the priory of Austin friars there, though this is not likely.

group of the rabbit's catafalque in the Gorleston Psalter,[1] rise into the realm of pure fantasy, and in their sensitive characterization of the wild creatures foreshadow a trait that has come down the centuries from Chaucer to Kipling, to Kenneth Grahame and to Mr A. A. Milne. If the art of design and colour reached at Lindisfarne and Winchester a height which has never been surpassed, it may fairly be claimed that in the late thirteenth century the art of illustration touched levels of vivacity and imaginative beauty which it was never to reach again in England.

In addition to the negative evidence from surviving painted books, positive statements are not wanting that both illumination and calligraphy were declining in the monastic scriptoria. Richard of Bury, the well-known bibliophile who was bishop of Durham towards the middle of the fourteenth century, contrasts the old days when the monks were busy over manuscripts with the present time, when economic cares and coarser pleasures have driven books from their place of honour.[2] The bishop himself, as he goes on to tell us, employed lay and commercial scribes at all his manors.

Like all complainants, Richard of Bury probably expressed himself in more general terms than the facts warranted. He explicitly included canons in his charge of idleness, yet there is evidence that at some houses of the Austin canons it was the practice for the inmates to complete the script of manuscripts even when destined for private or parochial use, and to leave only the painting to professional artists. A notable example is provided by the so-called Tickhill Psalter, written by John Tickhill, prior of the Augustinian house of Worksop in Nottinghamshire, and a critic who has studied with care a number of psalters of that period has arrived at the conclusion that almost all the survivors of a certain group of illuminated manuscripts can be connected with Augustinian priories in south Yorkshire, Lincolnshire and Nottinghamshire, for whom or for whose patrons they were executed. The script was completed in the monastery, and the illuminations were added, either there or outside, by professional artists.[3]

1 There is a reproduction of this scene in Cockerell (Pl. ix) and also in Millar, *English Illuminated Manuscripts of the XIV and XV Centuries* (cited as Millar II, Pl. 18), who illustrates the Ormesby Psalter in Pls. 1–5. Throughout these manuscripts there is an abundance of wild life—snails, butterflies, squirrels, fighting cocks, cats and mice—but the rabbit, already a favourite in French books, takes pride of place, at least in the Gorleston Psalter, where he enters upon the triumphant saga which he has continued in successive avatars as Brer Rabbit, the White Rabbit and Peter Rabbit.

2 *Philobiblon* (ed. Thomas), pp. 39–44: 'Scribebant namque nonnulli...de quorum laboribus hodie in plerisque splendent monasteriis illa sacra gazophylacia...[at nunc] Liber Bacchus respicitur....Liber Codex despicitur...calicibus epotandis non codicibus emendandis indulget hodie studium monachorum.' These are rhetorical commonplaces, but probably true in part.

3 This Psalter, MS. 26 of the Spencer Collection, New York Public Library, has been critically described and sumptuously reproduced by D. D. Egbert, *The Tickhill Psalter and related manuscripts* (1940). On the general point of origin he concludes (p. 3): 'while the Tickhill Psalter itself is a book that is religious in content and was written by a monastic scribe...it was undoubtedly illuminated...by a group of travelling professional artists.' Later (p. 5) he cites the statement from the Psalter attributing the script to John Tickhill, prior of Worksop 1303–14, removed in the latter year for incontinence and dilapidation, *qui istum librum propriis manibus scripsit necnon deauravit*; v. *VCH, Notts.* II, 127, citing Brit. Mus. Harl. MS. 6972, f. 11.

Whatever the shortcomings of the religious, the age of Richard of Bury saw the decline of the native art of book painting in England. Passing from the monasteries to the ateliers of scattered commercial artists, it died out with the disappearance of a gifted individual or his school, possibly owing in many cases to the mischances of seasons of pestilence, and when, towards the end of the century, illumination of a high order of excellence again appears, it is the work of a few artists of genius in the religious orders, or of commercial groups influenced by the contemporary developments of style in continental Europe.

III

Nothing has hitherto been said of artists among the white monks and canons. The Cistercians had in the beginning been forbidden by rule to paint or even to write manuscripts with any elaboration or ornament, and though this rule was soon broken, and Cîteaux itself amassed a store of illuminated books, the life of the white monks in England was not such as to attract artistic talent or favour its expansion. The like may be said of the Premonstratensian canons. As for the friars, artistic work formed no part of their programme, and we have seen that domestic talent was discouraged by earlier visitors, yet it so happens that the Preachers and Minors had each in their body a great English artist, though the one was separated from the other by almost two centuries.

We owe our knowledge of the earlier of the two and of his work to Matthew Paris, who preserved together with some Franciscan materials in his collection a large drawing, far more delicate and spiritual than any of his own, representing the Son of Man of the Apocalypse, and bearing an inscription attributing it to Brother William, a Minor, the companion of St Francis.[1] We are also told that he was the second to join the order, was holy of life, and English by nationality. In another manuscript, that of the *Chronica Majora*, Paris has executed a small drawing of Brother William the Englishman in a friar's habit.[2]

A Brother William the Englishman duly appears in some early Franciscan documents as a companion of the saint, and as finding a grave near that of Francis at Assisi, where both worked miracles until Brother Elias (or according to another version of the story, Brother Leo) commanded the Englishman's spirit to cease out of reverence for the Founder. No reference is made to any artistic gifts, but the identification seems certain,

---

1 Brit. Mus. Cott. MS. Nero D 1, f. 156: 'Hoc opus fecit Fr Willelmus de ordine minorum socius beati Francisci secundus in ordine ipso conversacione sanctus nacione Anglicus.' For a discussion of this, *v.* A. G. Little, *Brother William of England, companion of St Francis, and some Franciscan drawings in the Matthew Paris Manuscripts*, in *Collectanea Franciscana* (*BSFS*), 1 (1914), 1–8 (reprinted in *FP*), where the two drawings are reproduced. There are large plates of the Christ in Borenius and Tristram, Pl. 27 and O. E. Saunders, *English Illumination*, 11, Pl. 27.

2 MS. Corpus Christi College, Cambridge, xvi, f. 67.

whereas there are serious difficulties in the way of finding the artist in William of London, a dumb tailor who happens to have been the second recruit to the Minors in this country,[1] though it is possible that Paris confused the two. How the chronicler became possessed of the drawing is beyond conjecture; no doubt it was executed before William left for Italy; but had there been a local connection with St Albans this would scarcely have escaped mention. The work is in the traditional English style of outline drawing, with a few touches of colour, and the artist was clearly gifted beyond the ordinary.[2] The casual survival of this single example of his genius should remind us of the danger of any general judgement as to the number and talents of the artists working in England at that time.

III. MUSIC AND THE CHANT

If the part taken by monks of the thirteenth century in the development of manuscript illumination is not easily defined, it is still more difficult to assess their share in contemporary musical achievement.[3] Music, like architecture, was developing very swiftly; at the same time the focus of composition, like that of artistic execution, was shifting from the abbey to the city; but in sacred music, unlike the other two arts, there was for monks and ecclesiastics a fixed continent in an otherwise fluid universe: the traditional Gregorian chant accompanying the liturgy. That could never be wholly changed, and was very slow to decay.

In this field the Worcester *Antiphoner and Gradual*, which, though dating in its present form from *c.* 1230, preserves an antique musical text of remarkable purity,[4] is striking evidence that in the thirteenth century the formulae and melodies of the liturgical chant as performed in the greater churches were identical in almost all respects with those used two or even four centuries earlier. It is even probable that the chant was rendered with greater simplicity than in the days of Ethelwold in the monasteries, for the disappearance of the children of the cloister, and the absence as yet of the

---

1 *Eccleston*, ed. Little, p. 19.

2 W. R. Lethaby, *English Primitives*, v, 51, writes enthusiastically: 'the design of a master who must have been one of the foremost artists of his time.'

3 English medieval music, till recently *terra incognita*, has in common with other fields of medieval thought and culture been the object of intensive research and criticism within the past few years. As in the realm of scholastic thought, much of the best work has been done by continental scholars, among whom Jacques Handschin and Manfred Bukofzer deserve special mention, but more recently valuable research and publication has been undertaken for the Plainsong and Medieval Music Society by Dom Anselm Hughes and others. By far the best general account, which covers all the countries of Europe and supersedes the chapters in the *Oxford History of Music*, is that by Gustav Reese, *Music in the Middle Ages*, a critical and richly documented work with elaborate bibliographies. For the general reader the book suffers somewhat from density of arrangement and from an intermingling of historical with technical and controversial musical matter, but as a work of reference it is indispensable.

4 For this *v. MO*, 553-4.

boys of the almonry or hired singing men would restrict the monastic choir to unison singing of a single register. Moreover, the technical advances that had been made in elaborate solmization, and by the invention of the staff and standardization of the neums and rhythmic signs made it possible to stereotype and transmit chant, thus doing away with the necessity of acquiring and preserving a repertory by a combination of personal tradition and extensive memory work. The history of Gregorian chant itself is, however, very dark between the date of the Worcester *Antiphoner* and the clear evidence of decadence in the fifteenth century.

In all other forms of music it is a different story. There, rapid and observable changes were taking place. In the most accomplished circles descant and polyphony of every kind were being studied and elaborated; the *organum* was being superseded by the *conductus*, and that in its turn by the more flexible *motet*,[1] while the folk-music of England, above all as expressed in the canon or round (*rota*), sprang from below into more sophisticated levels, as appears to be the case with the best known and most exquisite round *Sumer is icumen in* of c. 1240.[2] While the round developed naturally outside the purview of the theorists and professional technicians, and was only accepted when it had reached a pitch of excellence that could not be ignored, the more formal polyphony, at least till far on in the thirteenth century, was almost entirely the preserve of the monastic or cathedral choir. Gradually the break came, and the monasteries surrendered pride of place to the cathedrals, and they in turn to the individual composer. Nevertheless, a few religious houses continued to be centres of musical life; such, it seems, were Bury St Edmunds and above all Worcester, where a very notable school of composers was at work, presumably in the cathedral priory, in the last decades of the thirteenth and the first years of the fourteenth centuries.[3] In addition, there are melodies for hymns and chants for lectionaries of Worcester and York provenance which are of extreme beauty, showing considerable variation from similar compositions from the

---

1 The *organum* in its simplest form consisted of a tenor melody in plain chant accompanied in parallel motion by a *vox organalis* a fifth or a fourth below; to these were added other voices an octave above or below the tenor. The *conductus*, originally a processional piece, came to be the technical name for a composition in which 'the tenor... was an original theme, or in some cases a popular melody [i.e. not a liturgical one] to which one or more parts were added by way of descant' (Grove's *Dictionary*). The *motet*, as a technical term in medieval music, was 'an embroidering of a given (not composed) theme of words-and-music [often a liturgical theme such as *Salve sancta parens*] by two or three other [specially composed] sets of words-and-music' (Grove).

2 *V*. Reese, *Music in the Middle Ages*, 396–7, with references there given.

3 Scattered leaves of this music, sometimes used in later bindings, from the Chapter Library at Worcester, Oxford and elsewhere, were assembled and edited for the Plainsong and Medieval Music Society as *Worcester Medieval Harmony* by Dom Anselm Hughes. He remarks in his introduction (p. 25): 'from the few evidences before us it seems highly probable that Worcester was an important, if not the principal, centre of English musical culture in the fourteenth century, for Bury St Edmund's is the only other locality which can as yet show any traces of a school of composition'. For a criticism of this edition on some points of historical and musical interpretation *v*. the long and important review by J. Handschin in *Zeitschrift für Musikwissenschaft*, XIV (1931), 54–61.

continent;[1] their date is uncertain, but they may represent a tradition of monodic composition existing alongside, or developing gradually into, the later polyphony or such unharmonized melodies as the familiar and beautiful *Angelus ad Virginem*.

During all this period music, as a quasi-mathematical science and as a technical discipline, continued to be the subject of theoretical treatises, and it has not escaped remark that the most celebrated English author of the period, Walter of Oddington, was a monk of Evesham who lived only fifteen miles from Worcester.[2] His treatise *De speculatione musices* is a clearly-written and remarkable work, showing at once a practical interest in the forms and execution of contemporary music and a scientific, mathematical knowledge of harmonics. He is said to have written works on astronomy, and to have migrated to Oxford in 1316, and it was at Oxford that the next great English theorist, Simon Tunsted,[3] flourished a few decades later. Music, at least theoretical music, like all other learning, like all other arts, was passing from the monasteries to the universities, but we shall do well to remember that the Gregorian chant remained, at least in the thirteenth and fourteenth centuries, in all its beauty and solemnity, as a background to the life of the monks year in, year out, and that at some of the greater houses polyphony, ever growing more elaborate and flexible, formed part of the repertory of the choir for extra-liturgical occasions, and occupied the attention of individuals as composers or theorists.

1 A number of these hymn melodies, mainly from Worcester and York MSS., were collected in a *Hymnale* for use by the English Benedictine Congregation; some of the tones for lessons, etc., are in use at Stanbrook Abbey and elsewhere.

2 For Walter of Oddington (probably Oddington in Gloucestershire) *v. DNB*; the text of his work is in C. E. H. Coussemaker, *Scriptorum de musica medii aevi nova series*, I, 182–250.

3 For Tunsted *v. DNB*, and Coussemaker, IV.

CHAPTER XXVI

MONASTIC ENGLAND, 1216–1340

I

In an earlier volume the reader was taken for a kind of circular tour of the black monk monasteries of England.[1] The time was early in the twelfth century, when the old orders were still lords of the ascendant; monastic houses, though numerous, were yet not innumerable; and a well-informed cicerone was at hand in the person of William of Malmesbury. By 1300 much has altered. The new orders of monks, canons and friars far out-number the original followers of the Benedictine rule, and small houses of every kind have so multiplied, that a comprehensive tour, even if possible with our fragmentary records, would be tedious beyond words; moreover, we have no Malmesbury, alert and humane, to accompany us. Nevertheless, after considering at such length the changes within the monastic order, and the organization of institutes that were rival to it, it may not be out of place to glance for a moment at the history of some of the greater houses as it might have appeared to an elderly monk at the turn of the century.[2]

In a survey of this kind it is natural to begin with Canterbury.[3] The cathedral monastery of Christ Church has already occupied space enough

1 *MO*, 176–90.

2 The output of literature on the religious houses of England has been very great, but its bulk is deceptive. With very few exceptions, the monographs or articles are by local historians or antiquarians who at the best give no more than a skeleton chronicle, and at the worst are quite unreliable; where several works exist on the same house, the more recent often do little more than reproduce the material originally collected by a county historian of the eighteenth century or by Dugdale and his associates. Very few attempts have been made to relate the history of a house to the general religious or economic circumstances of the times. Of the exceptions to this judgement several have already been noted, and others are mentioned in subsequent notes.

In particular, a great opportunity was all but lost when the *Victoria County Histories* were first in preparation. The articles on religious houses appeared, with a few exceptions, in the first volume (usually vol. ii) to be published, some forty years ago, and are almost uniformly disappointing, being the work of antiquaries (of whom the late Dr J. C. Cox was the chief) or of young research students who lacked the knowledge and experience needed for the interpretation of their materials. A few articles, however, such as those by F. M. Powicke and James Tait (Lancs.), Miss R. Graham (Glos. and Lincs.), Dr Salter (Oxon.) and Dr Little (friars in general) are of another calibre; and of contributors with less familiar names Miss M. Reddan (Herts.) and Sister Elspeth (Lincs.) did excellent work. Unfortunately, the existence of the *Monasticon*, which it would be difficult either to revise or to supersede, and of the *Victoria Histories* will probably long stand in the way of a fresh detailed survey on more satisfactory lines; all that can be hoped for is the production of monographs on a number of the large houses.

3 Christ Church, moreover, has been fortunate in its historians. In addition to the volumes edited by J. B. Sheppard in the Rolls and Camden Series, and the invaluable lists of monks drawn up by W. G. Searle (*v.* Bibliography), R. Willis in his *History of the Conventual Buildings*, and E. E. Woodruff and W. Danks, *Memorials of Canterbury Cathedral* have surveyed to perfection the fabric with its decorations and associations, while R. A. L. Smith's *Canterbury Cathedral Priory* is perhaps the best example of the type of monograph required.

in these pages. As the strong rule of old Eastry drew to a close, it was in many ways the type of a prosperous, well-organized, extroverted corporation. The great lawsuits, the internecine strife were now old history, and though as recently as the days of Ringmer, and even under Eastry himself, there had been discord and bitterness, the general picture is not an unhappy one: that of a great community with many interests, the centre both of an extensive domestic administration and of the ecclesiastical life of England, guardian of a shrine still second to none in the land as a magnet to pilgrims, strong enough to assert with some success its right to stand outside the orbit of the provincial chapter, and to uphold, not altogether in vain, its claim to elect the primate and to administer the vacant dioceses of England when the primatial see was itself vacant.

Yet even the prestige that clothed the archbishop's monastery did not entirely eclipse the fame of the ancient abbey whose bells mingled their tones with those of the cathedral.[1] Proud in its exemption from the jurisdiction of the metropolitan, and rich in the cornlands of Thanet, St Augustine's maintained beyond the thirteenth century its position of rivalry to Christ Church. Still a home of letters and art, it had recently, in the person of its distinguished Abbot Nicholas Thorne (1273–83), taken the lead in the capitular legislation and domestic reorganization that had marked the last quarter of the century, and now stood, perhaps in natural reaction to the policy of its neighbour, at the head of the movement towards uniformity and centralized direction that was strongest during the reign of Edward I. The customary of the house, dating from this epoch, and the pages of its chronicler give what is perhaps the most pleasing contemporary picture of a dignified and spiritual monastic observance, while the position of the abbey in the social life of the age is seen in the accounts of the numerous visits paid to it by Edward I at the end of the century.

From Canterbury the traveller to London would pass through Rochester, where a small community was long in shaking off the tutelage of Canterbury. At Westminster, he would have found already in existence many of the more admirable parts of the fabric which we admire to-day, together with a dazzling wealth of colour and design that has given place to other modes.[2] A royal *eigenkloster*, endowed by monarchs and the peculiar care of the reigning house since its rehabilitation by the Confessor, Westminster throughout its history was linked closely with public life as

1 St Augustine's had in W. Thorne (fl. 1397) and T. Elmham († 1440) diligent chroniclers, while for our period the Customary of Abbot Nicholas, ed. E. M. Thompson, is precious, but the abbey still awaits its historian.

2 Much excellent work has been done on Westminster in the present century, largely owing to the enterprise of its dignitaries: J. A. Robinson edited Flete's *History of Westminster* (Flete, fl. 1421–65) and H. Pearce compiled a list of Westminster monks, besides throwing much light on the domestic life of the house in his studies of Abbots Walter of Wenlock and William of Colchester; there is also the Customary of Abbot Ware to show the observance in this age. In addition, W. R. Lethaby gave a life's study to the fabric of the Abbey, and H. F. Westlake, in his sumptuously produced *Westminster Abbey* (2 vols.) illustrated every period of the life of the convent; his book, however, does little to interpret the many facts he records.

was no other house. The scene of coronations, weddings and funerals, it was also, owing to its close proximity to the palace, a meeting-place of councils and parliaments, while its strong-room, the chapel of the Pyx, became the receptacle of many of the treasures of the royal wardrobe. The abbot of Westminster by virtue of his office was a person of note, with easy access to the king, and when his personal qualities were above the average it was easy for him to rise to a position of weight and influence. For this very reason it is remarkable that so few abbots of Westminster should have risen to real eminence, and still more remarkable, at least to modern eyes, that so few Westminster monks of any period should have attained to distinction. Nevertheless, the favour of Henry III and the abilities of Abbots Richard of Crokesley, Richard of Ware, and Walter of Wenlock (1246–1307) made of the second half of the thirteenth century a period of celebrity for the abbey. It had been the peculiar delight of Henry III during his long reign to augment and adorn Westminster, and by 1300 its church was probably the most lavishly appointed and gorgeously decorated in England. Towards the end of the century, however, the community became involved in a series of wrangles with its abbot, and these were followed by several *causes célèbres*, which brought notoriety rather than lustre to the house: the dark affair of the burglary, which landed so many of the brethren in gaol,[1] and the quarrel between Wenlock and his prior. It is natural to suppose that such scandals, and the close connection with public life to which they were in part due, were not without influence in lowering and secularizing the tone of the monastery. Contrary to what might be our expectation, the unique position of Westminster did not attract recruits either from noble families or from the leading circles in the city of London. Indeed, many of the monks seem to have come, as in the smaller provincial houses, from the outlying estates of the abbey.

Twenty miles north of London, commanding the first town on the great North Road after the broad belt of heath and woodland had been passed, stood the red tower and walls of St Albans. The position of the abbey, the artistic and literary achievements of its sons, the long succession of eminent abbots, and the abundant and vivid records of its life make of St Albans a monastic microcosm, as they have also made it a type-monastery to writers of every age.[2] Typical St Albans may be, if we

---

1 The Westminster burglary, like the later case of Richard Hunne, has been retailed to satiety without ceasing to remain a historical 'mystery'. T. F. Tout, after dealing with it in passing in his *Chapters*, wrote a more popular account, *A Medieval Burglary* in the *BJRL* (1915), 348–69, in which he passed severe judgement on the community. This Dean Pearce did his best to reverse in *Walter de Wenlok*, ch. ix. The scene of the crime was identified with the Pyx chapel by J. A. Robinson; the crypt beneath the Chapter House, by Tout; the Prior's chamber, by Pearce, *op. cit.* 156–8.

2 References to the vast chronicle literature of St Albans have recurred throughout these pages. The monograph by J. Rushbrook Williams, though perhaps not as full as the subject deserves, is one of the few adequate works of its kind; it is to be regretted that Professor V. H. Galbraith, whose knowledge of the literature is unrivalled, has hitherto not supplemented his earliest essay *The Abbey of St Albans from* 1300 *to the Dissolution of the Monasteries.*

understand by the term the quality of exhibiting clearly defined a number of characteristics and pursuits but dimly seen elsewhere, but it would seem certain that, at least during the earlier centuries, there was in the air of the place a rarity not found elsewhere; there was a circulation of ideas, a stimulating sense of leadership, that in different spheres of life and ages of mankind has made a monastery, a college or a school a focus of the thought and character of its day. In the thirteenth century St Albans had this genial power. The abbey, as a resort of the king and the great barons, and as a kind of hotel for distinguished foreign visitors, was hardly second to Westminster; as the home of artists, and in its possession of Matthew Paris and his disciples, it was unique. All this apart, the abbey was the centre of a private ecclesiastical jurisdiction, of an extensive liberty, and of a group of satellite priories without exact parallel save perhaps at Durham; and being, as Durham was not, exempt and wholly autonomous, its abbot and chapter could feel themselves to bear almost imperial responsibilities. Durham alone has an equivalent of the private legislation of St Albans, of the visitatorial powers of its abbot and of the assemblies of priors which formed a kind of domestic general chapter. When in addition to this the abbots were men of distinction and presidents of the provincial chapter, as happened throughout the greater part of the fourteenth century, it is not surprising that St Albans felt herself to be what her voluminous records have with some justice persuaded posterity that she was, the premier abbey of England.[1]

From St Albans it was not far to the old East Anglian shrine of St Edmundsbury, and though to-day the little town stands apart from the main currents of traffic it continued to be a place of importance in the medieval world, and was the meeting-place of more than one parliament.[2] Bury was rich, and the saint, with his liberties and his hundreds, was a social and economic force. The great Samson had been succeeded by a man of charm and ability, Hugh of Northwold, soon to be bishop of Ely, but those who followed him during the century were not outstanding men. The community, somewhat unmanageable even in the days of Samson, and sharply divided in the election of his successor, was to pass through several crises in the fourteenth century, but in the thirteenth the church was decorated, chronicles kept, and the estates developed in a way that did credit to the farming, rather than to the forensic, abilities of the officials concerned.[3]

Of Norwich comparatively little can be said; abundant records remain, but few have been published or even examined. The cathedral priory had

1 MPChM, III, 337.

2 No adequate account of Bury exists, though it has been the subject of a number of articles and studies. The Memorials of St Edmund's (RS), rich as they are, by no means exhaust the materials with which the historian of the house would have to deal. Prof. V. H. Galbraith, alone of modern scholars, could do justice to the subject.

3 Cf. 'Richard de Horningesheth, c. 1260...vir tantum agriculturae...deditus.' MSE (RS), II, 294.

some administrative features peculiar to itself,[1] and the frequent tenure of the see by monks, either of the priory or from Ely, would make of the relations between bishop and community an interesting study. The house was not noted for learning in the thirteenth century, but its history in the fourteenth century, when it produced a number of eminent Oxford theologians, and the presence within its walls of the Ormesby psalter, suggests that research might show earlier evidences of intellectual life.

Westwards, the coronal of old English monasteries set on islands and river banks round the edge of the Fens continued to draw their large revenues from the rich soil. St Etheldreda, though she still felt the loss of the large fraction of her revenues that had gone to the bishop, still had the liberty of the Isle and six and a half hundreds in the fenland and in Suffolk, where she marched with St Edmund.[2] In the priory itself was a degree of corporate, quasi-democratic government to which a parallel can only be found in a few of the other cathedral monasteries. The monks, as the capitular body of the see, were as persistent as were their brethren of Canterbury in electing members of their own habit, and were more successful. Ely's second age of gold was to come in the middle of the fourteenth century. Less than twenty miles away Ramsey 'the rich' maintained its revenues, and the chronicle and library catalogue show that it long maintained the traditions of Byrthferth, but the house was later to fall into eclipse. Further north, Croyland[3] and Thorney were chiefly notable for their agriculture and sheep farming; the paradisaical fertility of the fenland, with its lofty timber and blossoming fruit trees, and the sacred isolation of the monasteries, so admired by Malmesbury and Ordericus Vitalis, find now no more mention than does the artistic and musical culture which had so impressed visitors two hundred years earlier. Peterborough, however, distinguished as it was for progressive high farming, long retained the traditions of Erwin and his school, and would seem to have been one of the last houses to produce illuminations of high excellence. It also gave birth to a succession of domestic chroniclers.

Beyond the Trent there were, if we except the almost constantly unfortunate Selby, only three black monk monasteries of the first rank. Of these, St Mary's, York, has probably suffered in repute through the destruction of northern records in the Civil War. A short chronicle survives, as do some liturgical and musical texts which suggest that the house was distinguished for its chant. Of Whitby, standing in the path

---

1 H. W. Saunders, in his *Introduction to the Rolls of Norwich Cathedral Priory*, indicates some of the peculiar features of Norwich administration.

2 A monograph on Ely is greatly to be desired. The Sacrist Rolls have been edited, with valuable appendices, by F. R. Chapman, and the history of the conventual buildings is excellently given by T. D. Atkinson in his magnificently produced *Architectural History* (*v.* Bibliography). He has since returned to the subject in his article in *VCH, Cambridge*, vol. II. The interior economy of the priory is well illustrated by *Ely Chapter Ordinances*, ed. Archdeacon S. A. Evans, who will, it is hoped, go on to further studies.

3 The article on Croyland in *VCH, Lincs.* is by Miss R. Graham.

of all the winds, little is known till troubles came later. The third, Durham, has an individuality as striking as that of St Albans.[1] Though rarely a peaceful house in this period, and though struggles with bishop and metropolitan were followed by losses from border forays and organized invasion, Durham never wholly lost her old traditions of intellectual pride, and during the fourteenth century reconquered her old eminent position in monastic England. How proud this was may be judged from her establishment at Oxford, where she disdained to join the southern province and maintained, like Canterbury, a house of her own in which a series of notable masters ruled before returning to Durham to hold high office. Wealthy and enjoying an almost complete independence of the bishop, the monks of St Cuthbert were by situation and tradition alike more severed than others from contact with the circumambient society. Their liturgical life was rich, their social life dignified; history and later theology were in honour, and in their cells on the bleak coast and islands of Northumberland traces lingered of the hermit life of Cuthbert, Godric and Bartholomew.

Of all districts in England the Severn basin was still the richest in great monasteries. At Worcester[2] the cathedral priory of St Mary was fortunate to contain the shrine of St Wulfstan, whither King John came to rest in death, and Edward I more than once to pray for success against the Welsh. The position of the city, where the main road from the midlands to the Shropshire wool markets and to Wales crossed the navigable waterway from Bristol, kept the priory in touch with great events and commerce alike. Nurtured since the days of Wulfstan in diocesan administration the prior and chapter who, like their brethren elsewhere, claimed rights of administering the see during vacancies, claimed also among those rights that of visiting the many other houses of the diocese during vacancies. Worcester, by some persistent trick of fortune, suffered throughout the period from frequent vacancies, and the *Sede vacante* register shows that the priors were almost morbidly active in setting out upon their rounds at the earliest possible moment. Naturally, they encountered difficulties and rebuffs, but on the whole they were remarkably successful in pressing their claims, as they were also in acquiring the use of *pontificalia* in the fourteenth century. Besides these interests, the monks of Worcester owned a large library, and traditions of letters and chant that went back far beyond the Conquest; it is not surprising, therefore, that they should have shown an enthusiasm for theology, and from the foundation of Gloucester College onwards the monks of St Mary's held at Oxford a place second to none in the southern province.

1 The Durham records, including the mass of material in print which has never been analysed or co-ordinated, offer a richer field for research than those of any other house.

2 The Worcester documents have been edited in some profusion: the episcopal registers by J. Willis Bund and Bishop Pearce, the *Registrum Prioratus Wigorniensis* by W. H. Hale, the *Liber Albus* and *Early Compotus Rolls* by J. M. Wilson; in addition, Bishop Pearce's *Thomas de Cobham* is an interesting study. There is, however, no history to supersede Noake.

Almost within sight from the tower of the cathedral, and only a few miles apart from each other across the willows and fruit trees of the rich and beautiful vale dominated by the far-seen eminence of Bredon, lay Tewkesbury and the two ancient houses of Pershore and Evesham. For Tewkesbury, whose Norman tower had even then long been part of the Severn landscape, the thirteenth century was a time of sober prosperity, part of it under the energetic rule of the saintly Abbot Robert.[1] Pershore had long since lost much of its best land to Westminster, which actually owned part of the little town, but what remained was fertile, and Pershore had sheep in plenty at Broadway.[2] Evesham, after the conquest of her exemption, flourished under a succession of able administrators.[3] First among these was Thomas of Marlberge, the protagonist in the Norreys case, who as dean of the Vale, sacrist, prior and abbot helped during more than thirty years to rebuild the abbey's prosperity and augment its beauty. He was followed for more than a century by abbots of ability, of whom Richard le Gras was eminent in public life, while Abbot John (1282–1316) in a long rule that covered the peak period of farming reorganized and equipped the estates and embarked on extensive building schemes. In another sphere Evesham deserves notice as the home of the musician Walter of Oddington (fl. 1240). Compared with Evesham, the career of Winchcombe,[4] a dozen miles away at the foot of the Cotswolds, shows something of a decline; the house never regained the position it had held at its first foundation, and again in the late old English period. It was often in debt, but was settled into fair prosperity by Walter of Wickwane (1282–1314), one more of that large family of high farmers, contemporaries of Henry of Eastry and John of Rutherwick, who gave a peculiar character to the monastic history of their epoch.

Further down the Severn, but still visible from Malvern, St Peter's of Gloucester, though not one of the wealthiest houses, had never wholly deviated from the prospect of distinction that had been opened by its great Abbots Serlo and Gilbert Foliot, and throughout the middle ages occasional royal visits and parliaments gave it public importance.[5] Throughout the thirteenth century, indeed, the growth of Gloucester in fabric and wealth was steady, even though periods of stringency occurred; in the last decades the abbey had the distinction of housing a monk of reputed sanctity, Adam of Emly, and of supplying a local habitation for the black monk settlement at Oxford where, appropriately enough, a Gloucester monk, William of Brock, was the first to incept in theology. The reigning abbot

1 *Ann. Theok. s.a.* 1254: 'Robertus pro quo piissimus Jesus multa pandit miracula.'

2 A valuable monograph on Pershore, a degree thesis of R. A. L. Smith, is in the Library of London University.

3 The *Evesham Chronicle* is one of the few to continue in some fullness throughout the fourteenth and fifteenth centuries, but there is no modern work on the abbey.

4 Winchcombe is well, if briefly, treated by Miss R. Graham in *VCH, Glos.*

5 There is an article in *VCH, Glos.* by Miss Graham, and the Gloucester *Historia* is useful until the end of the fourteenth century, but a critical history of the abbey and its architecture is greatly needed.

at the time, John de Gamages, was the first of a line who made of Gloucester in the fourteenth century one of the leading houses of the kingdom. Noted by that good judge, Edward I, as surpassing all other men in mature dignity of presence, he was also of the brotherhood of the golden hoof; under his rule the flocks of Gloucester on Cotswold were ten thousand strong, and the abbey was wealthy in proportion.

Across the hills from Gloucester the ancient abbey of Malmesbury, though secure in its exemption, had had no distinguished history. William of Malmesbury had no successors in the scriptorium, and the only abbot of note would seem to have been William of Badminton (1296–1324) who was, for a number of years, one of the abbots president, and who may have been yet one more of the farmers of the time. Abingdon, another ancient house with a proud history, was chiefly occupied with domestic activities; more than once the scene of a chapter-meeting in the important epoch of reform, its abbot, Nicholas of Coleham (1289–1306) was president for several years at the turn of the century. At Bath the small community, though successful in asserting its claims as against the bishop and the chapter of Wells, made little mark at this time.

It was otherwise with Glastonbury,[1] always possessed of enormous potential wealth, and now free, after almost a century of tutelage, to be mistress of her own destiny. As might have been expected, elements of discord and disorder remained from the years of strife, and it was not till the election of Michael of Ambresbury, long a strenuous defender of his house's liberties, that Glastonbury, in 1234, found herself as an independent abbey. With his rule began what may be considered the golden age of Glastonbury's prosperity, which reached something of a climax under Abbot John of Taunton, who held office as president during the legislating chapters of the 1270's, and who in 1277 entertained in his abbey for Easter the king, the queen, and Archbishop Kilwardby. The record of his library, and the evidence of chronicles and students at the beginning of the next century, show that Glastonbury had intellectual, as well as economic interests, but it was never the rival here, or in the field of artistic achievement, of St Albans and other houses.

The two small monasteries of the Somerset marshland, Athelney and Muchelney, though escaping the fate, that once had seemed to menace them, of losing their individuality under the control of Glastonbury, never found themselves with the resources sufficient for wide development. Similar reasons prevented the other old houses of Wessex from attaining note. Cerne, Milton and Abbotsbury, though they were able to build churches of moderate size, had no external history, and Sherborne, despite its position on one of the main roads to the west, and Tavistock, the

---

1 There is a good article in *VCH, Somerset* by Chancellor Scott Holmes, but the modern literature on medieval Glastonbury is remarkably scanty. Records exist in abundance at Wells, Longleat and elsewhere; Dom Aelred Watkin is at work upon them.

extreme outpost of monasticism on the borders of Cornwall, remained provincial and unknown.

There remain the two large communities of the old and new minsters at Winchester, once the principal source of a whole world of artistic and religious activity. St Swithun's, the cathedral monastery,[1] though rich and still populous, suffered a grievous dissipation of energy in the vexatious series of struggles—with the bishop for self-government, with the king and bishop over an election to the see, and with bishop and prior over a contested domestic election—that occupied so much of the century. It was not till the fourteenth century that Winchester, having elected an ex-prior Henry Woodlock to the bishopric, entered upon a period of peace and domestic prosperity, but the monastery never, in the later middle ages, gave proof of learning and of keen capitular life such as was shown, in different ways, by Canterbury, Durham and Worcester. Compared with St Swithun's, Hyde had a tranquil life, but the abbey, which lacked the peculiar advantages of St Augustine's, Canterbury, never regained the position it had once held, and was overshadowed, even after a change of site, by the cathedral priory.

II

If it is difficult enough to frame a connected history of most of the black monk houses, it is wholly impossible to do so with the other orders. Of the Cistercian abbeys, only a very few in the thirteenth century show distinguishing characteristics. Thus Beaulieu in Hampshire, by reason of its recent plantation from abroad under royal patronage, and Hayles, chiefly on account of the relic which made it one of the most frequented shrines of England, had a certain celebrity, and the Cistercians in general retained something of their reputation for austerity until the middle of the century, as is shown by the occasional recruits they still drew off from the black monks and canons, but in general their abbeys had sunk into the countryside and lost for ever that compelling charm which had once made them seem like outposts of Jerusalem, the vision of peace. Even the great Yorkshire abbeys, Fountains and Rievaulx, were now distinguished by little save their larger flocks and the superior magnificence of their fabric. Nevertheless, a few notices remain to show that many of them, especially in the north, still stood high in general esteem.[2]

Still less would it be possible to survey the multitudinous foundations of the Austin canons, to which additions were still being made. A few of them, such as Merton, Dunstable and Cirencester, stood out in reputation

---

1 Winchester Cathedral priory is another neglected house. Dean Kitchin's well-known edition of the *Obedientiary Rolls*, Canon Goodman's *Chartulary of Winchester*, and the published episcopal registers show how rich a store has survived; the account rolls of the period immediately before the Dissolution are particularly numerous.

2 The fortunes of two houses may be followed in the *Chronicles* of Meaux and Louth Park.

from the others, and in their economic and cultural life were almost indistinguishable from the black monks; and a small house here and there, such as Barnwell near Cambridge and Bridlington in Yorkshire, may show evidence of individuality, but the records in general are too scanty and too impersonal for this, and it is perhaps unfortunate that it is precisely where all information on the higher level is wanting that the more equivocal evidence of the visitation decrees survives in comparative abundance.

III

It is natural, perhaps, at the end of a survey such as this, to seek to decide what changes life in the old monasteries had undergone between the age of Lanfranc and that of Thomas de la Mare. In what ways had the conditions of daily life been modified, the pursuits of the monks changed? Were their hopes, their aspirations, their convictions the same as of old?

The material developments are easily put out. The monastic buildings had without question become larger, more commodious, more adequately furnished—in a word, more habitable. Throughout every period, indeed, building operations and extensive repairs were going forward, with all the physical inconveniences of exposure to wind and weather that slow execution and a primitive technique of temporary screens must have involved. But no subsequent age can have matched the first fifty or sixty years after the Conquest during which, throughout the land, the small, irregular old English buildings were giving place to the vast Norman churches, cloisters and dormitories, and in which the gaunt new buildings, often incomplete and with many unglazed windows stuffed with straw, afforded more protection against sunlight than against shower and wind, while towers and turrets, lacking firm mortar and foundations, were only too ready to ignite from lightning stroke or plumber's candle, or collapse at shock of tempest or from 'the unimaginable touch of time'. This was past history in 1300-50, and the larger monasteries were beginning to contain some recognizable features of modern domestic architecture. Glazed windows, comfortable desks, well-fitting doors and wainscot, sheltered walks and gardens, met the growing desire for ease and privacy, while in the church the new canopied stalls, weathertight windows, and more efficient lighting made the winter more tolerable for the monks of the cloister, while for abbot, prior and major officials the common life of cloister and hall was being replaced by the private life of a house, with its galleries, chairs and fireplaces. Nor can it be doubted that in every department furnishings and fittings had multiplied.

A change as great, if insensibly wrought, had taken place in the pursuits of the community. In the early twelfth century the majority were normally occupied within the precincts, if not within the walls of the cloister, and the day was passed in liturgical service, private reading and the various processes of book production and ornamentation. This form of work had not been superseded by 1300; there is plenty of evidence that calligraphy and bookbinding survived as the basic or residuary occupation of the monks; but careers for talent had developed to right and to left: on the one hand the discipline of the schools made of study, as it was then understood, and of a teaching post at Gloucester College or at home, the goal of the more studious, while administration, either in the precincts or around the farms, culminating in appointment to one of the major obediences, drew off those with a more practical bent of character. For all, travel, whether to Oxford, to the estates, to villegiatura, or to the homes of relatives, became at once less of a rarity and less of a labour.

The changes of spirit and zeal that come with the lapse of years are so subtle, and so obscured or anticipated by the temporary decline or development of individual houses, that historians have always found it easier to use some sweeping generalization, which in fact holds good only after a long period, than to assess small and gradual, but nevertheless real, changes. Certainly it is the opinion of the present writer, after many years of deliberation, that the greater abbeys, though far from being the abodes of ascetics and solitaries, were c. 1300 still offering a framework within which a devout and worthy life could be lived. The legislation of the chapters, the praise of chroniclers, and the instances, still to be found, of notable holiness in individuals and even in superiors, are strong evidence, and those wholly unfamiliar with the monastic life are perhaps slow to allow for the moulding influence, upon minds and characters attuned to them, of the liturgical texts with their accompaniment of chant and ceremony, which brought to the thirteenth century, as they bring to those fortunate enough to know them at the present day, something of the purity, the austerity, the exquisite employment of type, of symbol and of allusion, and the mingling of all that is best in the Hebrew and Roman genius, which was the supreme achievement of the age before the barbarians conquered Rome. Beauty of word and melody, beauty of architecture and ornament cannot create, and may even hinder, the purest spirituality, but pure spirituality is a rare treasure, and for men of more ordinary mould the liturgy in all its fullness may be a tonic nourishment, as well as an ennobling discipline.

To many, then, during the period 1300–50, the traditional life at one of the larger houses may well have been satisfying enough. Yet it must be admitted that much had changed since the days of Anselm. Then, the monasteries could feel that they were the salt of the earth. Their way of life was the acknowledged way of salvation, and to their intercession all that was best in the world looked. Theirs was the widest learning, theirs the finest art of the age; their abbots were among the trusted counsellors of kings. By 1300 this unique position had been lost. The black monks were still, indeed, an integral and influential part of society, but they were no longer its soul, and society itself was less simple in its composition and less direct in its religious outlook. The monks themselves had in part lost faith in their tradition, and were seeking to adapt themselves to a changing world in the schools. The tide of monastic fervour, after flowing far up the shores, had now receded towards the horizon. The age of Bernard and Ailred was past, the friars had come, and now they too had ceased to be a marvel. The heavy weight of the social and economic fabric of the world was pinning the monks to earth. A despondent religious might well have heard with foreboding the words of the Apostle, when he told how impossible it was that those who had once been enlightened, and had tasted the heavenly gift, and who had fallen, should ever again be renewed to penance.

Yet it must be acknowledged that these are the reflections of a modern: they rest on no contemporary evidence. It was not an age of self-revelation, and no monk of that time has unlocked his heart for us. The impression given by events and chronicles is rather that of a society untroubled by regrets and undisturbed by reforms, a society not so much in decay as in a state of equilibrium, in which monks and canons and friars alike filled a place which their contemporaries were willing enough to allow them, as a tree no longer white as a bride with April blossom, yet not unduly cumbering the ground.

APPENDICES

I. REGULAR BISHOPS 1216-1340

(i) BLACK MONKS

Ralph of Wareham	pr. Norwich	CHICHESTER	1218–1222
Robert Stichill	m. Durham; pr. Finchale	DURHAM	1261–1274
Robert of Holy Island	m. Durham; pr. Finchale	DURHAM	1274–1283
Richard Kellaw	subpr. Durham	DURHAM	1311–1316
Hugh of Northwold	abb. Bury	ELY	1229–1254
Hugh of Balsham	subpr. Ely	ELY	1257–1286
Robert Orford	pr. Ely	ELY	1302–1310
John Keeton	almoner Ely	ELY	1310–1316
William of Goldcliff	pr. Goldcliff	LLANDAFF	1219–1229
Roger Skerning	pr. Norwich	NORWICH	1266–1278
John Salmon	pr. Ely	NORWICH	1299–1325
John Bradfield	m. Rochester	ROCHESTER	1278–1283
Thomas of Wouldham	pr. Rochester	ROCHESTER	1292–1317
Hamo of Hethe	pr. Rochester	ROCHESTER	1319–1352
Henry Woodlock	pr. Winchester	WINCHESTER	1305–1316
Silvester of Evesham	m. Evesham; pr. Worc.	WORCESTER	1216–1218

(ii) WHITE MONKS

Martin or Cadwgan	m. Whitland	BANGOR	1215–1235
Hugh of Beaulieu	abb. Beaulieu	CARLISLE	1219–1223
John of Fountains	abb. Fountains	ELY	1220–1225
John de Ware		LLANDAFF	1254–1256

(iii) BLACK CANONS

Ralph Ireton	c. Gisburne	CARLISLE	1280–1292
John of Halton	pr. Carlisle	CARLISLE	1292–1324

(iv) FRIARS PREACHERS

Robert Kilwardby	provincial England	CANTERBURY	1273–1278
John of Eaglescliff	b. Glasgow 1318; Connor 1322	LLANDAFF	1323–1346
Hugh		ST ASAPH	1235–1240
Anian of Nannau		ST ASAPH	1268–1293

(v) FRIARS MINOR

John Pecham	provincial England	CANTERBURY	1279–1292
Anselm le Gras		ST DAVID'S	1231–1247
Walter Gainsborough	provincial England	WORCESTER	1302–1307

The number of bishops chosen from the regulars in the thirteenth and early fourteenth centuries fluctuated between narrow limits throughout the period, bearing a notable resemblance, alike in its smallness and in its constancy, to the earlier period (v. MO, Appendix XII, pp. 709–10). Standing at zero in 1214, it rose to six in 1220, fell to zero again for a year or so in 1256–7, reached six again in 1280 and stood at two in 1340. A few general observations suggest themselves:

(1) With two unimportant exceptions, all the black monks and Austin canons who became diocesan bishops in this period were elected (usually *e gremio ecclesiae*) by the regular chapter of a cathedral priory. In other words, secular chapters, king and pope, were not favourable to bishops from the older orders—a strong contrast to the decades immediately following the Hildebrandine reform and the Norman Conquest. The disfavour, indeed, was not negative only; it has been shown (Gibbs and Lang, *Bishops and Reform*, 80–2) that during the reign of Edward I alone, at least nine elections of monks by a monastic chapter were rejected by either King or Pope, often without a judgement on the real merits of the candidate. Without such rejections, indeed, the majority of the monastic cathedrals would have had throughout a monastic bishop; the chapters, at least till the end of the fourteenth century, continued to elect a member of the house on almost every occasion, save at Canterbury, which was throughout the period a storm-centre where opposing winds met. While we may think that the monastic bishops as a class have been unduly depreciated (Gibbs and Lang, *op. cit.* 5–10)—for a number of them were excellent men and meritorious administrators—it is comprehensible that those with a wide care for the Church in England should be unwilling that monks should have a monopoly of nine bishoprics, including several of the most important.

(2) The relative absence from the lists of Cistercians and friars is also remarkable, when contrasted with the numbers of white monks and friars serving in the Church elsewhere during the thirteenth century. Taken as a whole, the English Cistercians were a most undistinguished body after the first few decades, and the tendency to elect or appoint university-trained *magistri* told against them. The friars, on the other hand, had plenty of talent, yet the only two appointed to English sees were the two archbishops of Canterbury, both papal appointments. From the end of the thirteenth century onwards, it became common for both pope and king to reward friars (especially of the Order of Preachers), who had done good service in the Curia or in diplomatic missions, with bishoprics in Ireland; such men might be later promoted (like John of Eaglescliff) to Welsh or English sees.

II. THE WORKS AND EXPENSES OF HENRY OF EASTRY (*v.* chap. v)

The British Museum MS. Cotton Galba E IV contains an interesting summary of the works and expenses of Henry of Eastry during his priorate of thirty-seven years; it is printed in full below, save for the omission of the expenses of seven individual manors, which show the same pattern as those of Monkton which are printed in full. The document is an impressive one, both on account of the large sums concerned and of the evidence of lavish 'ploughing-in' of the revenues from the estates. The heavy list of expenses helps to answer the question that often arises in the mind of the monastic historian: that is, where did the vast income go? What follows is not, of course, the complete balance-sheet of the administration; the household and maintenance expenses do not appear at all. We have here, however, the most important, at least, of what may be called the involuntary expenses (subsidies, etc., to pope and king) and of the voluntary and quasi-voluntary commitments (lawsuits, new buildings, large-scale renovations and purchases and improvements of every kind). Of these expenses, excluding the repayment of old debts, about one-third is accounted for by what may be called taxation (royal and papal), one-third is money put back into the estates, one-quarter is represented by litigation and only one-eighth goes to the adornment and improvement of church and monastery. In other words, out of some £18,000, about

£10,500 goes in taxes and lawsuits, £5500 goes back to the land, and £2200 is spent on the church and monastery.

In printing these pages, Arabic numerals have been substituted throughout for the mixture of words and Roman numerals which are used quite unsystematically by the writer, as the purpose of printing the document here is to give the reader a clear view of the various sums in relation to the different years of Eastry's priorate.

(f. 101 r.):

NOVA OPERA IN ECCLESIA
ET IN CURIA TEMPORE HENRICI PRIORIS

Pro vestimentis et aliis ornamentis ecclesiasticis in ecclesia et domibus edificandis et reparandis infra ambitum ecclesia et curie per xxxvii annos tempore Henrici Prioris

	£	s.	d.
1285–90 Camera magna Prioris cum pictura. Camera minor cum capella et novo camino. Camera longa cum novo camino. Camera ad scaccarium cum diversoriis ibidem. Camera nova in veteri plumbario cum capella et camino. Magna grangia ad fenum. Cisterna in piscina. Cisterna juxta scolam noviciorum. Studium Prioris. Reparacio magne Aule juxta portam curie.	230	16	0
1291 Nova camera Prioris plumbata cum garderoba, camino, celatura, pictura, et pavimento aliarum camerarum	36	18	6
1292 Novum orologium magnum in ecclesia	30	0	0
Nova thurris ultra thesaurarium	10	0	0
1294 Novum gablum ecclesiae ultra altare Sancti Gregorii	13	12	0
Nova paneteria et nova coquina plumbata in camera Prioris	13	18	0
1295 Pavimentum claustri et nova Gaola	42	0	2
1298 Decem nove schoppe lapidee in Burgate	40	0	6
1301 Novum stablum thesaurarii cum solario et parvo granario	7	8	0
1303 Novum granarium in Bracina	8	5	10

(f. 101 v.):

	£	s.	d.
1304–5 Reparacio totius chori cum tribus novis ostiis et novo pulpito et reparacio capituli cum duobus novis gabulis	839	7	8
1314 Pro corona Sancti Thome auro et argento et lapidibus preciosis ornanda	115	12	0
Item pro nova cresta aurea feretri Sancti Thome facienda	7	10	0

1316
Quinque campane quarum i que vocatur Thomas in magno clocario que ponderat 8000 libre

Tres alie in novo clocario longo versus North' quarum i ponderat 2400 libre, alia 2200 libre et tercia 2000 libre

Item i campana ad sonitum capituli que ponderat 700½ libre
Precium v campanarum £236. 14s. 6d. sine carpenteria et ferramento

£   s.   d.

1317
Novum clocarium longum versus North'   61   5   3
Item pro plumbo et plumbario   90 12   2
Item tres campane nove in clocario sub angulo quarum prima pon-
    derat 1460 libre secunda ponderat 1210 libre et tercia ponderat
    1124 libre sine carpenteria et ferramento precio   65   0   0
Item tres campane nove minores in eodem clocario que ponderant
    2750 libre precio   10 18   0

1317-18
Pro novis studiis faciendis   32   9   7
Et pro nova bracina cum novo granario et caminis et aliis domibus
    infra curiam per duos annos predictos   144 16   0
In diversis annis:
Pro novis vestimentis et aliis ornamentis ecclesiasticis cum nova
    tabula magni altaris   147 14   0
SUMMA totalis pro vestimentis et aliis ornamentis ecclesiasticis in
    ecclesia et domibus edificandis et reparandis infra ambitum ecclesie
    et curie per 37 annos tempore Henrici Prioris   2184 18   8

Actually the sum is £2184. 18s. 11d.

(f. 102 v.):

NOVA OPERA IN MANERIIS TEMPORE HENRICI PRIORIS

Pro domibus et molendinis edificandis et reparandis in diversis maneriis per 37 annos
tempore Henrici Prioris

MONKETON   £   s.   d.
1287   Nova garderoba   1   12 11
       Nova porta   4   17   6
1289   Nova grangia de Brokesh[end]   8   6   9
1291   Nova bercaria apud Brokesh[end]   1   15   3½
1293   Novum columbarium   1   13   0
1294   Novum granarium   3   13   0
1299   Novum stablum   3   9   1
1303   Nova bercaria de Brokeshend   3   0   6
1305   Nova aula cum solario et aliis pertinentibus   71   7   0
1308   Nova coquina   15   5   0
1311   Pro nova porta, columbario et porcheria   18   8 10
1313   Nova camera lapidea cum camino, capella et garderoba   48   14   6
1317   Nova bovaria apud Brokeshend et nova salina de Monketon   4   5   0
                                                       Total 186   8   4½

*The list is continued for the manors of Eastry, Lyden, Adesham, Ickham, Chartham,
Godmersham and Brooke, and at the end, on f. 108 r. the total for all is given as £3739. 4s. 6d.*

(f. 108 r.):

TERRE REDDITUS PRATA BOSCA & MOLENDINIS
PERQUISITA TEMPORE HENRICI PRIORIS

Pro 286 acris terre arabilis, 51 acris prati, 63½ acris bosci, 8½ molendinis & £57. 2s. 8d.
annui redditus: £1343. 6s. 8d.; que valent annuatim £202. 1s. 11d., ut patet in folio
sequenti
    Certa debita que debebat conventus anno domini 1285, 4 Idus Aprilis, viz. die
electionis Henrici Prioris

	£	s.	d.
Domino Regi Anglie pro diversis debitis	2619	5	0
Item, privatis amicis	438	10	0
Item, obedientiariis et prepositis de ultimo compoto suo precedente	390	10	0
Item, mercatoribus de Florentia	290	11	4
Item, mercatoribus de Pistorio	1085	15	0
SUMMA utriusque debitorum mercatorum	1376	6	4
SUMMA totalis debiti que debebat conventui die electionis predicti Henrici prioris	4924	18	4

Actually the total of the above sums is £4824. 11s. 4d.

(f. 109 r.):

EXPENSUS forinseci et extraordinarii per 37 annos tempre Henrici Prioris

	£	s.	d.
Pro veteribus debitis conventus acquietandis	4924	18	4
Item pro subsidio terre Sancte et ecclesie Rome cum procurationibus cardinalium	1342	13	4
Item pro subsidiis, donis, exheniis et exactionibus solutis domino Regi et Regine et eorum liberis	4611	8	0
Item pro diversis causis, litibus et placitis in curia Romana, in Anglia et Hybernia	4624	0	0
Item pro Warda maris et armis emptis tempore guerre contra Gallicos	274	18	0
Item pro vestimentis et aliis ornamentis ecclesiasticis in ecclesia, et domibus edificandis et reparandis infra ambitum ecclesie et curie cum reparacione chori et capituli	2214	18	8
Item pro domibus et molendinis edificandis et reparandis in diversis maneriis	3739	4	6
Item pro terris marlandis in diversis maneriis	111	5	0
Item pro terris, redditibus, pratus, boscis et molendinis emptis et perquisitis	1343	6	8
Item pro terris intrandis et salvandis contra mare in diversis locis	360	7	0
SUMMA totalis expensarum forinsecarum et extraordinariarum in 10 articulis predictis per 37 annos tempore Henrici Prioris	22,446	19	6

Actually the total of the above sums is £23,546. 19s. 6d. but it will be noticed that the sum for vestments, etc., is less than that given above by £29. 19s. 9d. If this is added, and the total of debts corrected, the total will be £23,479. 6s. 3d.

The items that follow have no introductory rubric. They give in detail the annual income from the lands, etc., listed above (p. 324).

	£	s.	d.
Manerium de Caldecote quod valet per annum	10	0	0
Item 286 acre terre arabilis que valet per annum	21	9	0
Item 51 acre prati que valet per annum	12	15	0
Item 63½ acre bosci que valent per annum	4	15	3
Item 8½ molendini de novo facti et perquisiti, per annum	20	0	0
Item redditus empti in diversis locis cum domibus Judeorum et quinque messuagiis et uno tofto emptis et aliis novis domibus de novo factis in Cantuaria, Suthwerk, Waleworde et alibi, que valent per annum	57	2	8
Item fructus ecclesiarum de Westcliue, Aysshe (Ash) et Westerham perquisiti tempore predicto que valent per annum	76	0	0
SUMMA totalis valoris omnium premissorum annuatim ut supra	202	1	11

BIBLIOGRAPHY

The lists which follow are not a bibliography of the medieval religious orders, still less of the medieval scholastics or Franciscan origins. The aim has been to include in them all, and only, those books and articles which have been used or quoted in the text and notes of this book. The omission of any work, therefore, does not necessarily imply that it has not been consulted, or that it is of slight value, but simply that it has not been used by the writer in this particular connection. In a few cases, when it seemed desirable to give references in the notes to books not so used, they have not been included in these lists.

I. CONTEMPORARY SOURCES

(a) BISHOPS' REGISTERS

Bath and Wells
  Reg. John de Drokensford, ed. Bishop Hobhouse (*SRS* I), 1887.

Canterbury
  Reg. Robert Winchelsey, ed. R. Graham (10 parts, *C & YS*, 1917–42).

Carlisle
  Reg. John de Halton, ed. W. N. Thompson (3 parts, *C & YS*, 1906–13).

Exeter
  Reg. Walter de Stapeldon, ed. F. C. Hingeston-Randolph (Exeter, 1902).
  Reg. John de Grandisson, ed. F. C. Hingeston-Randolph (Exeter, vol. I, 1894; vol. II, 1897).

Hereford
  Reg. Thomae de Cantilupo, ed. R. G. Griffiths (2 parts, *C & YS*, 1905–7).
  Reg. Ricardi de Swinfield, ed. W. W. Capes (2 parts, *C & YS*, 1909).
  Reg. Ade de Orleton, ed. A. T. Banister (2 parts, *C & YS*, 1907–8).

Winchester
  Reg. Joannis de Pontissara, ed. C. Deedes (10 parts, *C & YS*, 1913–24).
  Reg. Henrici Woodlock, ed. A. W. Goodman (6 parts, *C & YS*, 1934–40).

Worcester
  Reg. Godfrey Giffard, ed. J. W. Willis Bund (2 vols. Worcs. Historical Society).
  Reg. of Thomas de Cobham, ed. E. H. Pearce (Worcs. Historical Society, 1930).
  Reg. Sede Vacante, ed. J. W. Willis Bund (Worcs. Historical Society, 1897).

York
  Reg. of Walter Giffard, ed. W. Brown (*SS*, CIX, 1904).
  Reg. of Rolls of Walter Gray, ed. J. Raine (*SS*, LVI, 1872).
  Reg. of William Wickwane, ed. W. Brown (*SS*, CXIV, 1907).
  Reg. of John le Romeyn, ed. W. Brown (*SS*, CXXIII, CXXVIII, 1913, 6).
  Reg. of Thomas of Corbridge, ed. W. Brown (*SS*, CXXXVIII, CXLI, 1925, 8).
  Reg. of William Greenfield, ed. A. Hamilton Thompson (*SS*, CXLV, CXLIX, CLI, CLII, 1931, 4, 6, 7).

(b) Other Printed Sources

Abingdon, Chronicon Monasterii de, ed. J. Stevenson (*RS*, 2, 2 vols. 1858).

Acta Sanctorum Bollandiana (Brussels and elsewhere, 1643 onwards).

Albani, S., Chronica Monasterii, ed. H. T. Riles (*RS*, 28, 12 vols. 1863–76); vols. IV and V contain the *Gesta Abbatum S. Albani* covering this period.

Amundesham, Annales Johannis de, ed. H. T. Riley; in *Chronica S. Albani* above.

Analecta Carmelitarum Discalceatorum (Rome, 1926–).

Analecta Franciscana (Quaracchi, 1885–).

Analecta S. Ordinis Fratrum Praedicatorum (Rome, 1893–).

Annales Monastici, ed. H. R. Luard (*RS*, 36, 5 vols. 1864–9), containing: vol. I, de Margam, Theokesberia et Burton; vol. II, de Wintonia et Waverleia; vol. III, de Dunstaplia et Bermundesia; vol. IV, de Oseneia et Wigornia.

Archivum Franciscanum Historicum (Florence, 1908–).

Bacon, Rogeri, *Compendium Studii Theologiae*, ed. H. Rashdall (*BSFS*, III, 1911).

——— *Opera hactenus inedita*, ed. R. Steele and others (Oxford, 1909—in progress).

——— *Opera inedita*, ed. J. Brewer (*RS*, 15, 1859); this includes the *Opus Tertium* and the *Opus Minus*.

——— *Opus Majus*, ed. J. H. Bridges (3 vols. Oxford, 1897–1900).

Bath Priory, Two Chartularies of, ed. W. Hunt (*SRS*, 1893).

Benedicti, S., Regula Monasteriorum, ed. C. Butler (Freiburg-im-Breisgau, 1912; 2 ed. 1927).

Benet Holme, St, Register of, ed. J. R. West (Norfolk Record Society, 1932).

Bermondsey Annals, *v.s. Annales Monastici*.

Bilsington Cartulary, The, ed. N. Neilson (*PBA*, 1928).

Bonaventurae, S., Opera Omnia, ed. Quaracchi (1882 onwards).

Bullarium Carmelitanum, vols. I and II, ed. Monsignanus (Rome, 1715, 8); vols. III and IV, ed. Ximenes (Rome, 1768).

Bullarium Franciscanum, 8 vols. and 2 supplementary vols. ed. I. H. Sbaralea, continued by de Latera and Eubel (Rome and Quaracchi, 1759–1908).

Burgensis, Historia Coenobii, v.i. Swapham, R.

Burton Annals, *v.s. Annales Monastici*.

Bury, Memorials of the Abbey of St Edmund at, ed. T. Arnold (*RS*, 96, 3 vols. 1890–6).

Bury, Richard of, *Philobiblon*, ed. E. C. Thomas (London, 1888).

Canterbury, Customary of St Augustine's, ed. E. M. Thompson (*HBS*, XXIII, 1902).

Cantuarienses, Epistolae, ed. W. Stubbs (*RS*, 38, 1865).

Cantuarienses, Literae, ed. J. B. Sheppard (*RS*, 86, 3 vols. 1887–9).

Celano, Thomas de, *v.i. Francisci Assisiensis, S.*

Chapters of the Augustinian Canons, ed. H. E. Salter (*OHS*, LXXIV, 1920, and *C & YS*, 70, 1921–2).

Chapters of the English Black Monks, ed. W. A. Pantin (*CS*, 3 ser., 3 vols. XLV, XLVII, LIV, 1931–7).

Chronica XXIV Generalium, in *Analecta Franciscana*, III (1897).

Cisterciensis, Statuta Capitulorum Generalium Ordinis, ed. J. M. Canivez, t. I, 1116–1220; t. II, 1221–61 (Louvain, 1933, 5).

Colecestria, Cartularium Monasterii S. Johannis Baptistae de, ed. S. A. Moore (Roxburghe Club, 1897).

Cronica Ordinis Fratrum Praedicatorum, in *MOPH*.

Croylandiae Historiae Continuatio, ed. W. Fulman in *Rerum Anglicarum scriptorum veterum*, t. I (London, 1684).

Domerham, Adam de, *Historia de rebus gestis Glastoniensibus*, ed. T. Hearne (2 vols. Oxford, 1727).

Dominici, Monumenta S.P.N., ed. M. H. Laurent, O.P., fasc. i, *Historia diplomatica S. Dominici*, in *MOPH*, XV (Paris, 1937).

Dominici, S., Vita, auctore Jordano de Saxonia, in *Acta SS.,* August, I, 545–9.
Dunelmensia, Gesta, ed. R. K. Richardson, in *Camden Miscellany,* XIII (*CS,* 3 ser. XXXIV, 1924).
Dunelmensis, Feodarium Prioratus, ed. W. Greenwell (*SS,* LVIII, 1872).
Dunelmensis, Historiae Scriptores Tres, ed. J. Raine (*SS,* IX, 1839).
Dunstable Annals, *v.s. Annales Monastici.*
Durham Account Rolls, ed. J. T. Fowler (*SS,* 3 vols.: XCIX, 1898; C, 1899; CIII, 1903).
Durham Household Book, ed. J. Raine (*SS,* XVIII, 1844).
Durham Obituary Rolls, ed. J. Raine (*SS,* XIII, 1841), and again by A. H. Thompson (*SS,* CXXXVI, 1923).
Durham, The Rites of, ed. J. Raine (*SS,* XV, 1842), and again by J. T. Fowler (*SS,* CVII, 1903).
Eccleston, Tractatus Fr Thomae vulgo dicti de, De Adventu Fratrum Minorum in Angliam, ed. A. G. Little, in *Collection d'études...du Moyen Âge* (Paris, 1909).
Edmund's, St, Memorials of, *v.s.* Bury.
Ely Chapter Ordinances, ed. S. J. A. Evans (*CS,* Miscellany, XVII, 1940).
Evesham, Chronicon Monasterii de, ed. W. D. Macray (*RS,* 29, 1863).
Francesco, La Leggenda di S., scritta da tre Suoi Compagni, ed. M. da Civezza e Teofilo Domenichelli (Rome, 1899).
Francheto, Fr Gerardi de, *Vitae Fratrum Ordinis Praedicatorum,* ed. B. M. Reichert, in *MOPH,* I.
Franciscana, Documenta Antiqua, ed. L. Lemmens, O.F.M. (Quaracchi, 1901).
Franciscana, Monumenta, ed. J. S. Brewer (*RS,* 4, 2 vols. 1858).
Francisci Assisiensis, S., Vitae et Miracula, auctore Thoma de Celano, ed. Ed. d'Alençon, O.F.M.C. (Rome, 1906).
Francisci, S., Opuscula, v.s. Böhmer, H.
Gervase of Canterbury, Continuation of the *Gesta Regum* of, ed. W. Stubbs (*RS,* 73, 1880).
Gesta Abbatum S. Albani, v.s. Albani, S., Chronica.
Giraldi Cambrensis, Itinerarium Cambriae, ed. J. F. Dimock (*RS,* 21, VI, 1868).
Glastonie, Rentalia et Custumaria abbatiae de, ed. C. I. Elton (*SRS,* V, 1891).
Glastoniensis, Chronicon Joannis, ed. T. Hearne (Oxford, 1726).
Glocestrensis, Historia et Cartularium Monasterii S. Petri, ed. W. H. Hart (*RS,* 31, 3 vols. 1863–7).
Grégoire IX, *Régistres, v.i.* Auvray, L.
Grosseteste, Roberti, Epistolae, ed. H. R. Luard (*RS,* 25, 1861).
Guisborough Chartulary, The, ed. W. Brown (*SS,* LXXXVI, LXXXIX, 1889–91).
Humberti de Romanis Opera, de Vita Regulari, ed. J. J. Berthier (Rome, 1889).
Huntingdon, Henry of, *Historia Anglorum,* ed. T. Arnold (*RS,* 74, 1879).
Jordani, Chronica Fratris, ed. H. Böhmer, in *Collection d'études...du Moyen Âge,* VI (Paris, 1908).
Jordans von Sachsen, Die Brief, ed. B. Altaner (Leipzig, 1925).
Juris Canonici Corpus, ed. E. Friedberg: vol. I, Decretum; vol. II, Decretales (Leipzig, 1881).
Kingswood, Documents relating to the Cistercian Monastery of St Mary, in *Transactions of the Bristol and Gloucestershire Archaeological Society,* XX (1899).
Lanercost, Chronicon de, ed. J. Stevenson (Bannatyne Club, 1839).
Letters relating to the Suppression of the Monasteries, ed. T. Wright (*CS,* XXVI, 1843).
Louth Park, Chronicle of, ed. E. Venables (Lincs Record Society, I, 1891).
Malmesburiense, Registrum, ed. J. S. Brewer (*RS,* 72, 2 vols. 1879–90).
Marsh, Epistolae Adami de, ed. J. S. Brewer, in *Monumenta Franciscana, q.v.*
Melsa (Meaux), *Chronicon monasterii de,* ed. E. A. Bond (*RS,* 43, 3 vols. 1866–8).
Monasticon Anglicanum, by Sir W. Dugdale; new enlarged edition by J. Caley, H. Ellis and B. Bandinel, 6 vols. in 8 (London, 1817–30).

Monumenta Franciscana, v.s. Franciscana.

Monumenta Germaniae Historica, ed. G. H. Pertz and others: Scriptores, vols. I–XXXII (Hanover, 1826–1913).

Monumenta Historica Carmelitana, vol. I (Lérins, 1907; no more published).

Monumenta Ordinis Praedicatorum Historica (Rome, 1897–).

Monumenta S.P.N. Dominici, v.s. Dominici.

Ockham, William of, *Opera Politica,* ed. J. G. Sikes (Manchester, 1940).

Oseney, Annals of, *v.s. Annales Monastici.*

Paris, Matthew, *Chronica Majora,* ed. H. R. Luard (*RS,* 57, 7 vols. 1872–84).

—— *Flores Historiarum,* ed. H. R. Luard (*RS,* 95, 3 vols. 1890).

—— *Gesta Abbatum, v.s. Albani, S., Chronica.*

—— *Historia Anglorum,* ed. F. Madden (*RS,* 44, 3 vols. 1886–9).

Peckham (Pecham), Joannis, *Registrum Epistolarum,* ed. C. T. Martin (*RS,* 77, 3 vols. 1882–6).

—— Fratris, *Tractatus Tres de Paupertate,* ed. C. L. Kingsford, A. G. Little and F. Tocco (*BSFS,* II, 1910).

Petriburgense Chronicon, ed. Th. Stapleton (*CS,* XLVII, 1849).

Praedicatorum, Acta Capituli Generalis FF., in *MOPH,* III *seqq.*

Rameseia, Cartularium Monasterii de, ed. W. H. Hart and A. P. Lyon (*RS,* 79, 3 vols. 1884–94).

Rameseiense, Chronicon, ed. W. D. Macray (*RS,* 83, 1886).

Rolls, Close, *Rotuli Litterarum Clausarum,* ed. Sir T. D. Hardy (London, 1833–).

Rolls, Hundred (2 vols., London, 1812–18).

Rolls, Liberate, Calendar of the Liberate Rolls (London, 1916–).

Rolls, Parliament, *Rotuli Parliamentorum* (6 vols., London, 1767–77).

Salimbene de Adam, Chronica Fratris, ed. O. Holder-Egger, in *MGH, SS,* XXXII.

Soliaco, Henrici de, Liber, ed. J. E. Jackson (Roxburghe Club, 1887).

Speculum Perfectionis, ed. P. Sabatier (*BSFS,* XIII, 2 vols. 1928, 1931).

Swapham, Roberti, *Continuatio Historiae Coenobii Burgensis,* in *Historiae Anglicanae Scriptores,* ed. J. Sparke (London, 1723).

Tewkesbury, Annals of, *v.s. Annales Monastici.*

Thomae Aquinatis, S., *Summa Theologica,* ed. stereotypica.

Thorne, Willelmi, *Chronica S. Augustini Cantuariensis,* ed. R. Twysden, in *Scriptores X* (London, 1652).

Trivet, Nicolai, *Annales,* ed. T. Hog (English Historical Society, 1845).

Waverley, Annals of, *v.s. Annales Monastici.*

Wendover, Roger of, *Chronica,* ed. H. G. Hewlett (*RS,* 84, 3 vols. 1886–9).

Whetehamstede, Registrum Joannis, ed. H. R. Riley (*RS,* 28, 1872–3).

Whiteby, Cartularium Abbathiae de, ed. J. C. Atkinson (*SS,* LXIX, 1879).

Whittlesey, Historia Walteri de, in *Historiae Anglicanae Scriptores,* ed. J. Sparke (London, 1723).

Wigorniensis, Registrum Prioratus B.M. de, ed. W. H. Hale (*CS,* XCI, 1865).

Winchelcumba (Winchcombe) *Landbok de,* ed. D. Royce (2 vols. 1892–1901).

Winchester Annals, *v.s. Annales Monastici.*

Winchester Cathedral Chartulary, ed. A. W. Goodman (Winchester, 1928).

Winchester, Obedientiary Rolls of St Swithun's, ed. Dean Kitchin (Hants Record Society, 1892).

Worcester Annals, *v.s. Annales Monastici.*

II. MODERN WORKS

Albans, St, History of the Abbey of, *v.i.* Williams, L. F. R.

Archiv für Litteratur- und Kirchengeschichte des Mittelalters, ed. H. Denifle, O.P., and F. Ehrle, S. J. (6 vols. Berlin and Freiburg-im-Breisgau, 1885–92; vol. VII, which appeared in 1900, is not referred to). For individual contributions, *v.i.* Denifle, H., and Ehrle, F.

Auvray, L., Les Régistres de Grégoire IX (Paris, 1896).

Bacon, Roger, Commemoration Essays, *v.i.* Little, A. G.

Balič, C., O.F.M., Ratio criticae editionis operum I. D. Scoti. (2 vols. Rome, 1939, 1941).

Barker, Sir E., The Dominican Order and Convocation (Oxford, 1913).

Bateson, M., Archbishop Warham's Visitations of Monasteries, 1511, in *EHR*, VI (1891), 18–35.

Batiffol, P., Histoire du Bréviaire romain (Paris, 1893)

Baudry, L., *Guillaume d'Occam*, vol. i (Paris, 1950).

Baur, L., Der Einfluss der Robert Grosseteste auf die wissenschaftliche Richtung des Roger Bacon, *v.s.* Roger Bacon; Commemoration Essays.

Bennett, H. S., The Reeve and the Manor in the Fourteenth Century, in *EHR*, XLI (1926), 358–65.

Bennett, R. F., The Early Dominicans (Cambridge, 1937).

Bentham, J., The History and Antiquities of the Church of Ely (Cambridge, 1771).

Berlière, Dom U., Honorius III et les monastères bénédictins, in *Revue Belge de Philologie et d'Histoire* (Brussels, 1923), 237–65; 461–84.

—— Innocent III et la réorganisation des monastères bénédictins, in *RB*, XXXII (1926), 22–42; 146–59.

Bierbaum, H., Bettelorden und Weltgeistlichheit an der Universität Paris (Munster-i-Westf., 1920).

Birkenmajer, A., Der Brief Robert Kilwardbys an Peter von Conflans, in *Vermischte Untersuchungen ʒur Geschichte der mittelaltliche Philosophie* (Munster, 1922), 36–69.

Bishop, E., The Methods and Degrees of Fasting and Abstinence of the Black Monks in England before the Reformation, in *DR*, XLVI (1925), 184–237.

Bishop, T. A. M., Assarting and the Growth of the Open Fields, in *EcHR*, VI (1935), 13–29.

—— Monastic Granges in Yorkshire, in *EHR*, LI (1936), 193–214.

Böhmer, H., Analekten zur Geschichte des Franciscus von Assisi (2 ed. Tübingen, 1930).

—— *v.s. Jordani, Chronica.*

Borenius, T., and Tristram, E. W., English Medieval Painting (Paris, 1927).

Brakspear, Sir H., The Abbot's House at Battle, in *Archaeologia*, LXXXIII (83), 139 seqq.

Britton, C. E., A Meteorological Chronicle to A.D. 1450 (Meteorolog. Office, Geophysical Mem. 70, 1937).

Callus, D., O.P., The Introduction of Aristotelian Learning to Oxford, in *PBA*, XXIX (1944).

—— The Oxford Career of Robert Grosseteste, in *Oxoniensia* X and XI (1945–6).

—— Two Early Oxford Masters... Adam of Buckfield and Richard Rufus of Cornwall, in *RNP*, XLII (1939), 411–45.

Cambridge Economic History, vol. I, ed. J. H. Clapham and E. Power (Cambridge, 1941).

Cambridge History of English Literature, vol. I (Cambridge, 1907).

Cambridge Medieval History (Cambridge, 1911–36).

Carton, R., L'expérience physique chez Roger Bacon. Contribution à l'étude de a méthode et de la science expérimentale au XIIIe siècle.

—— L'expérience mystique de l'illumination intérieure chez Roger Bacon.

—— La synthèse doctrinale de Roger Bacon, being t. II, t. III and t. V of *Études de philosophie médiévale*, dirigées par E. Gilson (Paris, 1924).

Cheney, C. R., Episcopal Visitation of Monasteries in the Thirteenth Century (Manchester, 1931).
—— Ipswich, St Peter's Priory, A Visitation of, in *EHR* XLVII (1932), 268–72.
—— Norwich Cathedral Priory in the Fourteenth Century, in *BJRL*, 20 (Jan. 1936), 93–120.
—— The Papal Legate (John of Ferentino) and English Monasteries, in *EHR*, XLVI (1931), 443–52.
Chenu, M. D., O.P., La première diffusion du Thomisme à Oxford; Knapwell et ses 'Notes' sur les Sentences, in *Archives d'Histoire doctrinale et littéraire du Moyen Âge*, III (1928).
—— Les Réponses de S. Thomas et de Kilwardby à la consultation de Jean de Verceil, in *Mélanges Mandonnet* (Bulletin Thomiste, XIII (1930), 191–222).
Chettle, H. F., The Friars of the Holy Cross in England, in *DR*, LXIII (Sept. 1945).
—— The Trinitarian Friars and Easton Royal, in *Wilts Archaeological Magazine*, LI (1946), 365–75.
Chew, H. M., The English Ecclesiastical Tenants in Chief and Knight Service (Oxford, 1932).
Chrysogone du S. Sacrament, P., O.C.D., Maître Jean Baconthorpe, in *RNP*, XXV (1932), 341–65.
Churchill, I. J., Canterbury Administration (2 vols. London, 1933).
Clarke, R. D., Some secular activities of the English Dominicans during the reigns of Edward I, Edward II, and Edward III (London University M.A. thesis, 1930).
Cockerell, Sir S. C., A Book of Old Testament Illustrations (Roxburghe Club, 1927).
—— Two East Anglian Psalters in the Bodleian Library, Oxford (with M. R. James; Roxburghe Club, 1926).
—— The Gorleston Psalter (London, 1907).
—— The Work of William de Brailes. An English Illuminator of the Thirteenth Century (Roxburghe Club, 1933).
Colvin, H. M., *The White Canons in England* (Oxford, 1951).
Copeland, J. L., The Relations between the secular clergy and the Mendicant Friars in England during the century after the issue of the bull *Super Cathedram* (London University M.A. thesis, 1938).
Cotton, C., The Grey Friars of Canterbury (*BSFS*, 1924).
Coulton, G. G., Five Centuries of Religion (Cambridge, vols. I–III, 1923, 1927, 1938).
—— The Interpretation of Visitation Documents, in *EHR*, XXXIX (1914), 16–40.
Coussemaker, C. E. H., Scriptorum de musica medii aevi nova series (4 vols. Paris, 1864–).
Crombie, A. C., *Robert Grosseteste and the origins of experimental science* (Oxford, 1953).
Crowley, T., O.F.M., *Roger Bacon* (Louvain & Dublin, 1950).
Cunningham, W., The Growth of English Industry and Commerce, vol. I (6 ed., Cambridge, 1915).
Cuthbert, Fr, O.S.F.C., St Francis of Assisi (2 ed. London, 1912).
—— The Romanticism of St Francis (2 ed. London, 1924).
Danks, W., *v.i.* Woodruff, C. E.
Davis, H. W. C., An early life of Edmund Rich, in *EHR*, XXII (1907), 84–92.
Dean, R. J., On N. Trivet, in *Medievalia et Humanistica*, II (1945), 86–98.
Delorme, F., O.F.M., Fr Richardi de Mediavilla Quaestio Disputata (Quarrachi, 1925).
Denholm-Young, N., Seignorial Administration in England (Oxford, 1937).
Denifle, H., O.P., Die Constitutionen des Prediger-Ordens vom J. 1228, in *ALKG*, I, 165–227.
—— Die Constitutionen des Predigerordens in der Redaction Raimunds von Peñafort, in *ALKG*, V, 530–64.

Denifle, H., O.P., Quellen zur Gelehrtengeschichte des Carmelitenordens im 13 und 14 Jahrhundret, in *ALKG*, v, 365–84.
—— Quellen zur Gelehrtengeschichte der Predigerordens im 13 und 14 Jahrhundert, in *ALKG*, ii, 165–248.
Denzinger-Bannwärt, *Enchiridion Symbolorum* (15 ed., Freiburg-im-Breisgau, 1922).
Destrez, J., Robert Kilwardby, O.P., 'magnus magister in theologia', in *Bulletin Thomiste*, iii (1933), 191–3.
Dibben, L. B., The Chancellor and Keeper of the Seal under Henry III, in *EHR*, xxvii (1912), 42–3.
Dictionary of National Biography, ed. L. Stephen and S. Lee (London, 1885–).
Dictionnaire d'Histoire et de Géographie ecclésiastiques, ed. A. Baudrillart, Ch. de Meyer and E. Van Cauwenbergh (Paris, 1909–).
Dictionnaire de Spiritualité, ed. M. Viller (Paris, 1932–).
Dictionnaire de Théologie catholique, ed. A. Vacant, E. Mangenot and E. Amann (Paris, 1903–).
Douglas, D. C., The Social Structure of Medieval East Anglia, in *Oxford Studies in Social and Legal History*, ix, 1927.
Douie, D. L., The Nature and Effects of the heresy of the Fraticelli (Manchester, 1932).
—— Three Treatises on Evangelical Poverty, in *AFH*, xxiv–v (1931–2).
Duckett, Sir G. F., Visitations and Chapters of the Order of Cluny (Lewes, 1893).
Dugdale, Sir W., A perfect copy of all summons... to Parliaments, etc. (London, 1685).
—— *v.s. Monasticon Anglicanum.*
Easterling, R., Anian de Nanneu, in *Flints Historical Society Journal*, i (1914–15).
Egbert, D. D., The Tickhill Psalter and related manuscripts (New York, 1940).
Ehrle, Card. F., S. J., L'Agostinismo e l'Aristotelismo nella Scolastica del secolo xiii, in *Xenia Tomistica*, iii (1925), 527–88.
—— Der Augustinismus und der Aristotelismus in der Scholastik gegen Ende des 13 Jahrhunderts, in *ALKG*, v, 603–35.
—— Der Kampf um die Lehre des h. Thomas von Aquin in der erstem fünfzig Jahren nach seinen Tod, in *ZfkT*, xxxvii (1913), 266–318.
—— Franziskanerordens, Die ältesten Redactionen der Generalconstitutionen der, in *ALKG*, vi, 1–138.
—— Peters von Candia, Der Sentenzenkommentar (Munster-i-Westf., 1925).
—— Spiritualen, Die, ihr Verhaltniss zum Franciscanerorden und zu den Fraticellen, in *ALKG*, ii, 108–64; iii, 553–623; iv, 1–190.
—— Sutton, Thomas de, sein Leben, seine Quodlibet und seine Quaestiones disputatae, in *Festschrift Georg von Hertling* (Kempten-Munchen, 1913), 426–50.
—— Trivet, Nikolaus, sein Leben, seine Quolibet und Quaestiones ordinariae, in *Festgabe um 70 Geburtstag Clemens Baeumker* (Munster-i-Westf., 1923), 1–63.
Elisée de la Nativité, Fr, O. C. D., Jean Baconthorpe, in *Études Carmélitaines*, ii (April, 1935), 93–157.
Emery, R. W., The Friars of the Sack, in *Speculum*, xviii, 3 (July, 1943), 323–34.
Études Carmélitaines (Paris, 1920—in progress).
Finberg, H. P. R., The Tragi-comedy of Abbot Bonus, in *Devon and Cornwall Notes and Queries* xxii (1946), 341–7.
Flete, History of Westminster, *v.s.* Robinson, J. R.
Fliche, A., and Jarry, E. (editors), *Histoire de l'Eglise*, vol. 13 (Paris, 1951).
Franceschini, E., Roberto Grossatesta, vescovo di Lincoln, e le sue traduzioni latine (Venice, 1933).
Francis, St (Francesco, Franciscus), *v.* titles in Part i of Bibliography.
Galbraith, G. R., The Constitution of the Dominican Order, 1216–1360 (Manchester, (1925).
Galbraith, V. H., The Abbey of St Albans from 1300 to the Dissolution of the Monasteries (Oxford, 1911).

Galbraith, V. H., New Documents about Gloucester College, in Snappe's Formulary (*OHS*, LXXX, 1924), 336–86.
—— Roger Wendover and Matthew Paris (Glasgow, 1944).
—— The St Albans Chronicle, 1406–1420 (Oxford, 1937).
Gibbs, M., and Lang, J., Bishops and Reform, 1215–1272 (Oxford, 1934).
Gilson, E., *History of Christian Philosophy in the Middle Ages* (London, 1954).
—— *Jean Duns Scot* (Paris, 1952).
—— La philosophie au moyen âge (2 ed., Paris, 1944).
Glorieux, P., Comment les thèses thomistes furent proscrites à Oxford (1284–6), in *Revue Thomiste*, XXXIII (1927), 259–91.
—— La littérature des Correctoires, in *Revue Thomiste*, XXXIV (1928), 69–96.
—— Les polémiques 'Contra Geraldinos', in *Recherches de théologie ancienne et médiévale*, VI (1934), 5–41; and VII (1935), 129–55.
—— Prélats français contre religieux mendicants, in *Revue d'Histoire de l'Église de France*, XI, no. 52 (1925).
—— Répertoire des maîtres en théologie de Paris au XIIIᵉ siècle (Paris, 1933–4).
Grabmann, Mgr M., Die Metaphysik des Thomas von York, in Festgabe um 60 Geburtstag Clemens Baeumker (Munster-i-Westf., 1913).
Graham, R., Cardinal Ottoboni and the Monastery of Stratford Langthorne, in *EHR*, XXXIII (April, 1918), 213–25.
—— English Ecclesiastical Studies (London, 1929).
—— A Metropolitical Visitation of the diocese of Worcester, in *TRHS* 4 ser., vol. XI (1919); reprinted English Ecclesiastical Studies, 330–59.
—— A Papal Visitation of Bury St Edmund's and Westminster in 1234, in *EHR*, XXVII (October, 1912), 728–39.
Gras, N.S.B., The Evolution of the English Corn Market (2 ed., Cambridge, Mass., 1926).
Gratien, P., O.S.F.C., Histoire de la Fondation et de l'Évolution de l'ordre des Frères Mineurs au XIIIᵉ siècle (Paris, 1928).
Gregory IX, *Registers*, *v.s.* Auvray, L.
Gross, C., The Gild Merchant (2 vols. Oxford, 1890).
Grosseteste, Robert, Essays in commemoration of the seventh centenary of his death, ed. D. A. Callus, O.P. (Oxford, 1955).
Grundmann, H., Religiöse Bewegungen im Mittelalter (Berlin, 1935).
Guelluy, R., *Philosophie et théologie chez Guillaume d'Ockham* (Louvain, 1947).
Guignard, Ph., Monuments primitifs de la Règle cistercienne (Dijon, 1878).
Gumbley, W., O.P., The Cambridge Dominicans (a pamphlet, 1938).
—— S.R.E. Cardinales ex Ordine Praedicatorum, in *Analecta S.O.FF.Praedicatorum* (1925), 187–207.
—— St Asaph, Dominican Bishops of, in *Flints Historical Scoiety Journal*, I (1914–15).
—— *v.i.* Jarrett, B.
Gwynn, A., S.J., The English Austin Friars in the Time of Wyclif (Oxford, 1940).
Harris, C. R. S., Duns Scotus (2 vols. Oxford, 1927).
Heimbucher, M., Die Orden und Kongregationen der katholischen Kirche (3 ed. Paderborn, 1933–4).
Hersher, I., O.F.M., Bibliography of Alexander of Hales, in *Franciscan Studies*, vol. 26 (Dec. 1945), no. 4. The number is devoted entirely to Alexander of Hales.
Hinnebusch, W. A., O.P., *The Early English Friars Preachers* (Rome, 1952).
Histoire Littéraire de la France, vols. XXXIV and XXXVII.
Holdsworth, Sir W. S., History of English Law (3 ed. London, 1922–).
Holtzmann, W., Papsturkunden in England (Berlin, I, i–ii, 1932; II, i–ii, 1936).
Hornby, C. H. St J., The Douce Apocalypse (Roxburghe Club, 1922).
Hudson, W., The Camera Roll of the Prior of Norwich in 1283, in *Norfolk Archaeology*, XIX, 268–313.

Hughes, Dom A., Worcester Medieval Harmony, in *Plainsong and Medieval Musical Society Publications* (Burnham, Bucks, 1928).

James, M. R., Aedward le Roi, La Estoire de Seint (Oxford, 1920).

—— Alban in Trinity College, Dublin, Illustrations to the Life of St (Oxford, 1924).

—— Apocalypse, The Douce (introduction to) (Roxburghe Club, 1922).

—— Apocalypse, The Trinity College (Roxburghe Club, 1909).

—— Old Testament, Illustrations of the, an introduction to A Book of Old Testament Illustrations, ed. Sir S. C. Cockerell, *q.v.*

—— Paris, The Drawings of Matthew, in Walpole Society, vol. xiv (1926).

—— Peterborough Psalter and Bestiary of the fourteenth century, A. (Roxburghe Club, 1921).

—— with Sir S. C. Cockerell, Two East Anglian Psalters in the Bodleian Library, Oxford (Roxburghe Club, 1926).

Jarrett, B., O.P., The English Dominicans (London, 1921; 2 ed. revised by W. Gumbley, O.P., 1937).

Jenkins, C., The Monastic Chronicler and the Early School of St Albans (London 1922).

Jenkinson, H., William Cade, in *EHR*, xxviii (1913), 209–27.

Joliffe, J. E. A., Northumbrian Institutions, in *EHR*, xli (1926), 1–42.

Käppeli, Th., O.P., Le Procès contre Th. Waleys, O.P. (Instit. Hist. FF. Praedictorum Dissertationes Historicae fasc. vi. Rome, 1936).

Kingsford, C. L., The Grey Friars of London (*BSFS*, vi, 1915).

—— *v.s.* Peckham, J. and *infra* Little, A. G.

Knowles, Dom M. D., The Monastic Order in England (Cambridge, 1940).

—— Pecham, Archbishop, Some aspects of the career of, in *EHR*, lvii (1942), 1–18; 178–201.

—— The Religious Houses of Medieval England (London, 1940).

Knowles, D., and Hadcock, R. N., *Medieval Religious Houses* (London, 1953).

Koch, J., Durandus de S. Porciano, O.P.; Forschungen zum Streit um Thomas von Aquin zu Beginn des 14 Jahrhunderts, t. 1, in *BGPM*, Texte und Untersuchungen, t. xxvi (Munster, 1927).

Kosminsky, E. A., Services and Money Rents in the Thirteenth Century, in *EcHR*, v (1935), 24–45.

Kralik, R. von, Geschichte des Trinitärienordens (Vienna, 1919).

Lagarde, G. de, La naissance de l'esprit laïque au declin du moyen-âge (6 vols. Paris, 1934–46; especially vol. iv, Ockham et son temps; vol. v, Ockham; bases de départ; and vol. vi, Ockham; la morale et le droit).

Lamond, E., Walter of Henley's Husbandry, including *Reules S. Roberd* (London, 1890).

Lang, J., *v.s.* Gibbs, M.

Laurent, M. H., O.P., *v.s. Dominici, Monumenta S.P.N.*

Lemmens, L., O.F.M., *v.s. Franciscana, Documenta Antiqua.*

Lethaby, W. R., The English Primitives, in *The Burlington Magazine*, xxix (1916) and subsequent volumes.

Levett, E., The Courts and Court Rolls of St.Albans Abbey, in *TRHS*, 4 ser. vii (1924).

—— Studies in Manorial History (Oxford, 1938).

Lindblom, A., La Peinture Gothique en Suède et en Norvège (Stockholm, 1916).

Little, A. G., Bacon, Roger, in *PBA*, xiv (1928). Reprinted, FP, 72–97.

—— Bacon, Roger; Commemoration Essays (Oxford, 1914).

—— Chronicles of the Mendicant Friars, in *BSFS*, Franciscan Essays, ii. Reprinted, *FP*, 25–41.

—— Docking, Thomas, and his relations to Roger Bacon, in Essays presented to R. L. Poole (Oxford, 1927). Reprinted, *FP*, 98–121.

Little, A. G., Educational organization of the Mendicant Friars in England, in *TRHS*, new ser. VIII (1894), 49–70.

―― The Friars and the Foundation of the Faculty of Theology in the University of Cambridge, in *Mélanges Mandonnet* (Bibliothèque Thomiste, XIV), 389–401. Reprinted, *FP*, 122–43.

―― Franciscan Papers, Lists and Documents (Manchester, 1943).

―― Franciscan School at Oxford, The, originally in *AFH*, XIX (1926), and in Essays in Commemoration of St Francis of Assisi; revised version in *FP*, 55–71.

―― Franciscan Studies, Guide to (London, 1920).

―― Friars *v.* the University of Cambridge, The, in *EHR*, L (1935), 686–96.

―― Friars in Oxford, The Grey (*OHS*, XX, 1892).

―― Oxford Theology and Theologians, with F. Pelster, S. J. (*OHS*, XCVI, 1934).

―― Romney, The Franciscan Friary at, in *Archaeologia Cantiana*, L (1938), 151–2.

―― Scotus, Chronological Notes on the Life of Duns, in *EHR*, XLVII (1932), 568–82.

―― Studies in English Franciscan History (Manchester, 1917).

―― William of England, Brother, in *Collectanea Franciscana* (*BSFS*, v). Reprinted, *FP*, 16–24.

―― *v.s.* Eccleston and Pecham, Fr Joannis.

Lobel, M. D., The Borough of Bury St Edmund's (Oxford, 1934).

Longpré, E., O.F.M., Frère Thomas d'York, O.F.M., in *AFH*, XIX (1926).

Lottin, Dom O., O.S.B., La pluralité des formes substantielles avant S. Thomas d'Aquin, in *RNP*, XXXIV (1932), 449–75.

―― Psychologie et Morale à la faculté des arts de Paris aux approches de 1250, in *RNP*, XLII (1939), 182–212.

Lunt, W. E., Financial relations of the Papacy with England to 1327 (Cambridge, Mass., 1939).

―― Papal Revenues in the Middle Ages (New York, 1934).

Maitland, F. W., with Pollock, Sir F., History of English Law (2 ed. Cambridge 1923).

Major, K., An Unknown House of Crutched Friars at Whaplode, in *Associated Architectural and Archaeological Soc. Reports*, LXI (1933), 149–54.

Mandonnet, P., O.P., S. Dominique; l'idée, l'homme et l'œuvre (ed. M. H. Vicaire,O.P.; Paris, 1938).

―― Premiers travaux de polémique Thomiste, in *Revue des sciences philosophiques et théologiques*, XII (1913).

―― Siger de Brabant et l'Averrhoïsme latin (Fribourg, 1898; 2 ed., 1911).

Martin, A. R., Franciscan Architecture in England (*BSFS*, XVIII, 1937).

Millar, E., English Illuminated Manuscripts from the Tenth to the Thirteenth Century (Paris and Brussels, 1926).

―― English Illuminated Manuscripts of the Fourteenth and Fifteenth Centuries (Paris and Brussels, 1928).

Minges, P., Joannis Duns Scoti doctrina (2 vols., Berlin, 1930).

Moorman, J. R. H., Church Life in England in the thirteenth century (Cambridge, 1945).

―― Sources for the Life of St Francis (Manchester, 1940).

―― *The Grey Friars in Cambridge* (Cambridge, 1952).

Nichols, J. F., Custodia Essexae (London University Ph.D. thesis, 1930).

Oakeshott, M., Introduction to the Leviathan of Thomas Hobbes (Oxford, 1946).

Page, F. M., 'Bidentes Hoylandiae', in *Economic Journal* (Economic History), I (1929).

―― The Estates of Crowland Abbey (Cambridge, 1934).

Page, W., The St Albans School of Painting, in *Archaeologia*, LVIII (1902), 275–92.

Palmer, C. F. R., O.P., articles in *The Reliquary* and elsewhere; cf. note 4 on p. 167 *supra*.

Pantin, W. A., Chapters of the Black Monks(*CS*,3ser.,3 vols. XLV, XLVII, LIV,1931,3,7).

―― General and Provincial Chapters of the English Black Monks, The, in *TRHS*, ser. 4, X (1927), 193–263.

Pearce, E. H., Thomas de Cobham (London, 1923).

Pearce, E. H., Walter de Wenlock (London, 1920).
—— William de Colchester (London, 1915).
Pedrick, Gale, Monastic Seals of the Thirteenth Century (London, 1902).
Pelster, F., S.J., Das Leben und die Schriften des Oxforder Dominikanerlehrers Richard Fishacre, in ZfkT, 54 (1930), 518–53.
—— Thomas von Sutton, O.P., als Verfasser zweier Schriften über des Wesenforms, in Scholastik, III (1928), 411–3.
—— Thomas von Sutton, ein Oxforder Vertheidiger der thomistischen Lehre, in ZfkT, 46 (1922), 223 seqq.
—— with A. G. Little, Oxford Theology and Theologians.
Picavet, F., Roger Bacon, La Formation Intellectuelle, in Revue des Deux Mondes, 1 June 1914, 643–75.
Pollock, Sir F., v.s. Maitland, F. W.
Postan, M. M., The Chronology of Labour Services, in TRHS, 4 ser., xx (1937), 169–93.
Power, E., The English Medieval Wool Trade (Oxford, 1941).
Powicke, Sir F. M., Handbook of British Chronology (London, 1939).
—— v.i. Rashdall, H.
Rashdall, H., The Friars Preachers v. the University, in OHS, Collectanea, 2 ser. (1890), 193–273.
—— The Universities of Europe in the Middle Ages (2 ed., F. M. Powicke and A. B. Emden, Oxford, 1936).
Reese, G., Music in the Middle Ages (U.S.A., privately printed, 1941).
Réville, A., Le Soulèvement des Travailleurs d'Angleterre en 1381 (Paris, 1898).
Robinson, J. Armitage, Flete's History of Westminster (Cambridge, 1909).
Rokewood, J. G., Vetusta Monumenta, ed. Societas Antiquariorum London., 1789–1847.
Roth, F., O.E.S.A., 'Cardinal Richard Annibaldi, first Protector of the Augustinian Order', in Augustiniana (Rome, II 1–60, 108–49, 230–47; III 21–34.
Russell, J. C., The Writers of Thirteenth Century England (London, 1936).
Sabatier, P., Examen de la Vie de Frère Elie, in Opuscules de critique historique (Paris, 1904).
—— v.s. Speculum Perfectionis.
Salter, H. E., Chronicle Rolls of the Abbots of Abingdon, in EHR, xxvi (1911), 727–38.
—— v.s. Chapters of the Augustinian Canons.
Saunders, H. W., Introduction to the obedientiary and manor rolls of Norwich Cathedral Priory (Norwich, 1930).
Saunders, O. E., English Art in the Middle Ages (Oxford, 1932).
—— English Illumination (2 vols. Florence and London, 1928).
Schaube, A., Die Wollausfuhr Englands in Jahre 1273, in Vierteljahrschrift für sozial- und Wirtschaftsgeschichte, VI (1908).
Schmaus, M., Der 'Liber Propugnatorius' des Thomas Anglicus und die Lehrunter- schiede zwischen Thomas von Aquin und Duns Scot, in BGPM, xxix.
Schmitz, Dom Ph., articles in DHG.
Seton, W., editor of St Francis. Essays in Commemoration, 1226–1926.
Sharp, D. E., Franciscan Philosophy at Oxford in the xiiith century (Oxford, 1930).
—— Thomas of Sutton, O.P., in RNP, xli (1934), 332–54.
Sikes, J. G., Jean de Pouilli and Peter de la Palu, in EHR, xlix (1934), 219–40.
—— v.s. Ockham, William of.
Smalley, B., The Study of the Bible in the Middle Ages (Oxford, 1941).
—— The Study of the Bible in the Middle Ages (2 ed., revised and augmented (Oxford, 1951).
Smith, A. L., Church and State in the Middle Ages (Oxford, 1913).
Smith, R. A. L., Canterbury Cathedral Priory (Cambridge, 1943).
—— Collected Papers (London, 1947).

Smith, R. A. L., The History of Pershore Abbey and its estates. (London University M.A. thesis, 1938).
—— The Regimen Scaccarii in the English Monasteries, in *TRHS*, 4 ser., XXIV (1942), 73–94.
Sommer-Seckendorff, E. M. F. Studies in the Life of Robert Kilwardby, O.P (Rome, 1937).
Steenberghen, F. van, *Aristote en Occident* (Louvain, 1946; English trans., London, 1955).
—— 'Le XIII° siècle', in *Histoire de l'Eglise* (*v.s.*).
—— *The philosophical movement in the thirteenth century* (Edinburgh, 1954).
Stenton, F. M., Types of Manorial Structure in the Northern Danelaw (Oxford Studies in Social and Legal History, II. Oxford, 1910).
Stewart, Easton, *Roger Bacon* (Oxford, 1952).
Swarzenski, H., on William de Brailes, in *Journal of the Walters Art Gallery* (1938), 55–69; (1939), 106–9.
Tanquerey, F. J., The conspiracy of Thomas Dunheved, 1327, in *EHR*, XXXI (1916), 119–24.
Théry, G., O.P., L'Augustinisme mediéval et le problème de l'unité de la forme substantielle, in *Acta Hebdom. august.-thomisticae* (Rome, 1931, 140–200).
Thompson, A. H., English Monasteries (2 ed. Cambridge, 1923).
—— Visitations of Religious Houses in the Diocese of Lincoln (Lincs Record Soc., vols. 1915, 1919).
—— *v.s.* Episcopal Registers, York.
Thomson, S. H., The Writings of Robert Grosseteste (Cambridge, 1940).
Thorndike, L., The True Roger Bacon, in *American Historical Review*, XXI (1916), 237–57; 468–80.
Tocco, F., *v.s.* Peckham, Fr Joannis.
Toms, E., Chertsey Abbey and its Manors under Abbot John de Rutherwyk (University of London, Ph.D. thesis, 1935).
Tout, T. F., Chapters in the Administrative History of Medieval England (6 vols. Manchester, 1920–33).
—— A Medieval Burglary, in *BJRL* (1915), 348–69.
Trenholme, N. M., The English Monastic Boroughs (University of Missouri Historical Studies; Columbia, Mo., 1927).
—— The Risings in the English Monastic Towns in 1327, in *American Historical Review*, VI (1901), 650–70.
Tristram, E. W., *v.s.* Borenius, T.
Ueberweg, F., Grundriss der Geschichte der Philosophie (11 ed., ed. B. Geyer; Berlin, vol. II, 1928; vol. III, 1924).
Van Moé, E. A., Recherches sur les Ermites de Saint-Augustin, in *Revue des Questions Historiques*, CXVI, 275–316.
Van Ortroy, F., Traité des Miracles de S. François d'Assise, in *Analecta Bollandiana*, XVIII (1899), 81–176.
Van Steenberghen, F., Siger de Brabant d'après ses œuvres inédites, in *Les Philosophes Belges*, XII–XIII (1931–4).
—— Siger de Brabant, Les œuvres et la doctrine de (Brussels, 1938).
Vicaire, M. H., O.P., *Histoire de S. Dominique* (2 vols. Paris, 1957).
—— *v.s.* Mandonnet, P.
Victoria County Histories, The (London, 1900—in progress; the account of the religious houses, which is usually contained in vol. II, has in most cases appeared).
Vignaux, P., *Nominalisme au xiv° siècle* (Montreal, 1948).
Vinogradoff, Sir P., English Society in the Eleventh Century (Oxford, 1908).
—— The Growth of the Manor (3 ed. London, 1920).
Wadding, Luke, O.F.M., *Annales Minorum* (Rome, ed. 1731–45).
Wallace, Dom W., Life of St Edmund of Canterbury (London, 1893).

Warham, Archbishop, Visitations of, *v.s.* Bateson, M.

West, J. R., *v.s.* Benet Holme, St.

Westlake, H. R., Westminster Abbey (2 vols. London, 1923).

Whitwell, R. J., The English Monasteries and the Wool Trade, in *Vierteljahrschrift für sozial- und Wirtschaftsgeschichte*, II, i (1904), 1–34.

Williams, L. F. R., History of the Abbey of St Albans, A (London, 1917).

Willis, R., The architectural history of the conventual buildings of Christ Church, Canterbury (London, 1869).

Wilson, J. M., Early Compotus Rolls of the Priory of Worcester (Worcs Historical Society, 1908).

—— The Liber Albus of the Priory of Worcester (Worcs Historical Society, 1919).

—— The Worcester Liber Albus (London, 1920).

Wood, S., *English monasteries and their patrons in the xiii century*, (Oxford, 1955).

Woodruff, C. E., Notes on the Inner Life and Domestic Economy of the Priory of Christ Church, Canterbury, in *Archaeologia Cantiana*, LIII, 1–16.

—— with Danks, W., Memorials of Canterbury Cathedral (London, 1912).

Wormald, F., More Matthew Paris Drawings, in Walpole Society, XXXI, 109–11.

Wroot, H. E., Yorkshire Abbeys and the Wool Trade, in *Thoresby Society Miscellany*, 1935, 1–21.

Wulf, M. de, Histoire de la Philosophie médiévale (new ed., Paris, 1934, 6; English translation of 6 ed. by E. C. Messenger, London, 1935).

—— Le traité 'de unitate formae' de Gilles de Lessines, in Les Philosophes Belges, I, 16–32 (Louvain, 1901).

Zimmermann, B. M., O.C.D., Les Carmes aux Univerités, in *Études Carmélitaines*, April, 1932, 82–112.

—— De Sacro Scapulari Carmelitano, in *Analecta Carmelitarum Discalceatorum*, II (1927), 70–99.

INDEX

As the custom of using surnames was almost universal in the thirteenth century, persons are so entered in this index; a very few exceptions have been made for saints (e.g. St Francis, St Albert the Great) and others who are currently known by their Christian name alone. Reference to modern scholars whose works are mentioned in the footnotes is given only when an appraisal or discussion of particular points occurs.

The following abbreviations are used: abb. = abbey; Aug. = Augustinian canons; b. = bishop; Ben. = black monk; Cist. = Cistercian; Clun. = Cluniac; m. = monk; OC. = Carmelite; OFM. = Franciscan; OP. = Dominican; OSA. = Austin friar; Prem. = Premonstratensian; pr. = priory.

Abbeville, Gerard of, 221
abbot, position of, 270–9
Abbotsbury, Ben. abb., 315
Abergavenny, Ben. pr., 101
Abingdon, Ben. abb., 192 n., 267, 315. For abbot of see under Coleham, Nicholas of
Ad conditorem canonum, 246, 247
Ad fructus uberes, 186, 189
Agnellus, Agnello. *See under* Pisa
Ailred of Rievaulx, St, 122, 123, 131
Alan the painter, m. of St Albans, 298
Alard, Br., OP, 165
Albans, St, Ben. abb., 266, 270, 271–2, 275, 277, 278, 279, 281, 284, 287, 288, 289, 291–301, 310–11. For abbots of, *see under* Amundesham, John; Hatfield, John of; Hugh; Mare, Thomas de la; Maryns, Thomas; Roger; Trumpington, William of; Wallingford, Richard of. *For* monks of, *see under* Alan; Colchester; Paris, Matthew; Wendover, Roger of
artistic work at, 296–301
literary activity, 291–6
Albert the Great, St, 226
Albigenses, the, 148
Alexander IV, Pope, 20, 185, 190, 200
Alnwick, William of, OFM, 247
Amesbury, Michael of, 37, 45, 315
Amour, William of St, 183, 185, 188, 221
Amundesham, John, 284
Angers, Henry of, 220
Anian of Nannau. *See under* Nannau
annals, monastic, 295 n.
Annibaldi, Cardinal Richard, 200
Anselm, OFM, b. St David's, 193 n.
Apocalypses, illuminated, 301
Aquinas, St Thomas, 161, 166, 188–9, 200, 219, 220, 221, 223, 226, 229, 230, 231, 235 n.

and the essence of perfection, 246
and the soul of man, 227–8
Summa Theologica of, 45, 230 n. *See also* Thomism, Thomist
Aristotle, his influence in the schools, 224–7
and the soul of man, 227, 236–7
arts and crafts, monastic, 296–9
Arundel, Ben. pr., 108
Arundel, Thomas, archb. Canterbury, 256, 261
Asaph, St, bishop of. *See under* Anian of Nannau
Ashby, William of, OFM, 131, 132, 137, 140
Ashridge, pr. Bonshommes, 202
Athelney, Ben. abb., 94 n., 315
Atkinson, T. D., 312 n.
audit, the monastic, 61–2
Augustine, Rule of St, 148, 199, 200, 203, 224
Augustinian canons, chapters of, 28–31. *For* Austin friars (or Hermits), *see under* Friars
'Augustinian' system of theology, 225, 236–7
Averroistic thought, 225–6
Aylesford, OC at, 196, 198

Bacon, Robert, OP, 165, 193 n., 214, 218, 225
Bacon, Roger, OFM, 213–16, 243
on his contemporaries, 210, 211
Baconthorpe, John, OC, 241–2
Badminton, William of, 315
bailiff, the monastic, 35, 36 n., 43–4
Baker, Dom A., 15 n.
Baldock, Ralph, b. London, 104
Bale, John, the antiquary, 128
Balsham, Hugh of, b. Ely, 105
Bardney, Ben. abb., 39 n., 107
Barker, E., 150 n., 155 n.

Barnstaple, Ben. pr., 102, 268
Barnwell, Aug. pr., 317
Barton, Martin of, OFM, 142
Bateman, William, b. Norwich, 105, 278
Bath, Ben. cathedral pr., 102, 255, 259, 315
Bath and Wells. For bishops of, see under
    Burnell, Robert; Button (II), Walter;
    Jocelin
Battle, Ben. abb., 86 n.
    and provincial chapter, 17
Bayham, Prem. abb., 80
Beatific Vision, controversy on, 245, 248–52
Beaulieu, Cist. abb., 5, 73, 77, 316
Beauvais, Laurence of, OFM, 130, 131
Bec, Ben. abb., 26
Becket, St Thomas, shrine of, 297
Bedford, Aug. pr., 28, 58 n.
Bee's, St, Ben. pr., 95
Bek, Antony, b. Durham, 260
Belassise, Stephen of, OFM, 188
Bello, Robert de, 300 n.
Belvoir, Ben. pr., 291
Benedict, St, 158
    Rule of, 18–21, 272
Benedict XI, Pope, 130, 186
Benedict XII, Pope, 30, 282
    Constitutions of, 61
Benet Holm, St, Ben. abb. (Norway), 294
Benet's of Holm, St, Ben. abb., 285
Bennett, H. S., 35 n.
Bergen, 295
Berkeley Castle, 170
Berksted, Stephen, b. Chichester, 4 n.
Bernard of Clairvaux, St, 122, 123
Berthold, St, OC, 196
Berwick, OFM at, 132
Bethlehemites, 204 n.
Bishop, E., 18 n.
bishops and friars, 182–8
    monastic, 257 and Appendix I
Black Death, 103
Blackmore, Aust. pr., 105
Blakeney, OC at, 241
Blois, William de, b. Worcester, 255
Blund, John, 227 n.
Blyth, Ben. pr., 91–2
Bocking, Ralph, OP, 210
Bodmin, Aust. pr., 102, 103
Boethius of Dacia. See under Dacia
Bologna, 149, 160
    Michael of, OC, 242
Bolton, Aust. pr., 86 n., 88, 92, 94 n.
Bonaventure, St, 143, 171, 178, 188–9, 220,
    221, 225, 231, 235
    and Aristotle, 225
    and Franciscan ideals, 178–9
    and Thomism, 228
Boniface VIII, Pope, 52, 158, 183, 186, 189
Boniface of Savoy, archb. Canterbury, 81,
    106, 255, 262 n.

Bonites, the, 199 n., 200
Bonshommes, the, 202
Bonus, abb. Tavistock, 102
boroughs, monastic, 263–9
Boston, OP at, 170
Bovill, Sewal de, archb. York, 4 n.
Bovill, Simon de, OP, 165
Boxgrove, Ben. pr., 107, 109, 282
Boxley, Cist. abb., 80
Brabant, Siger of, 225–6, 228 n.
Bradwardine, Thomas, archb. Canterbury,
    241
Brailes, William de, 302
Brakelond, Jocelin of, 275, 276
breviary, OFM, 174
Brewer, J. S., 134 n.
Bridlington, Aug. pr., 71, 88, 90–1, 94 n.,
    317
Bristol, Aug. abb., 100
    Ben. pr., 192 n.
    OFM at, 132
Brock, William of, m. Gloucester, 314
Bromwich, Richard of, pr. Worcester, 101
Bugton, Hugh of, OFM, 137, 140
Burkitt, F. C., 116 n.
Burnell, Robert, b. Bath and Wells, 98
Burnham Norton, OC at, 196
Burton-on-Trent, Ben. abb., chronicle of,
    295 n.
Bury St Edmund's, Ben. abb., 20, 192 n.,
    193, 264–9, 275, 278, 284–5, 290, 306–7,
    311. For abbots of, see under North-
    wold, Hugh of; Simon
Bury, Richard de, b. Durham, 166, 303
Button (II), Walter, b. Bath and Wells, 4 n.

Cade, William, 68
Caen, Holy Trinity, Ben. nuns, 66
    St Stephen, Ben. abb., 41
Callus, D. A., 210 n., 211 n., 233 n.
Cambridge, OC at, 198, 199, 241
    OFM at, 132, 140, 141, 211
    OP at, 166, 170
    university and friars, 191
camera, the Cistercian, 76–7
Canterbury. For archbishops of, see under
    Arundel, Thomas; Bradwardine, Tho-
    mas; Kilwardby, Robert; Langton,
    Stephen; Pecham, John; Reynolds,
    Walter; Boniface of Savoy; Rich,
    Edmund; Walter, Hubert; Winchel-
    sey, Robert. For abbots of, see under
    Bello, Robert de; Thorne, Nicholas.
    For priors of, see under Eastry, Henry
    of; Ringmer, Thomas
    Christ Church, Ben. cathedral pr., 38–9,
    41, 42, 48 n., 59–60, 70, 108, 131, 132,
    192, 255, 258, 259, 261–2, 271, 282,
    284, 297, 308–9; estates, 37; finances,
    56–7; and provincial chapter, 17

Canterbury. OFM at, 132
St Augustine's, Ben. abb., 20, 39 n., 40, 58, 277, 279, 282, 284, 287, 300, 309
Cantilupe, Thomas de, St, b. Hereford, 99, 165
Cantilupe, Walter, b. Worcester, 4 n., 6
Capes, W. W., 99 n.
Carlisle, Aug. cathedral pr., 112 n. For bishop of, see under Mauclerc, Walter
Carmel, Mount, 196
Carmelites. See under Friars
carrells, 289
Cartmel, Aug. pr., 88
Casale, Ubertino da, 247
Cassian's Conferences, 148
Cathanii, Peter, 129
Ceccano, Cardinal Annibaldo Gaetani de, 249, 250 n.
Celano, Thomas of, OFM, 177 n.
Cerfroy, Trinitarians at, 202
Cerne, Ben. abb., 315
Cesena, Michael de, OFM, 246, 248
chaplains, of abbots, 274
chapters, black monk, provincial, 10-27; attendance at, 16-17
black monk, domestic, 275-6
Cistercian, general, 69
OFM, general, 172-4
OP, general, 156-7, 166
OP, provincial, 156-7, 166
Chatton, Walter of, OFM, 247, 251
chequer, the monastic, 43-4
Cher, Hugh of St, OP, 167, 198
Chertsey, Ben. abb., 104, 299. For abbot of, see under Rutherwyk, John de
chess, 108
Chester, OFM at, 181
Chesterton, OC at, 196, 198
Chichester. For bishops of, see under Berksted, Stephen; Wyche, Richard
roundel, 301
Chirbury, Aug. pr., 99, 100
Chrysogone du S. Sacrament, 241 n.
Churchill, I. J., 107 n.
Cirencester, Aug. abb., 268, 316
Cistercians, 193, 304
abbots at black monk chapter, 10
agrarian economy, 64-75
Carta Caritatis, 153
financial system, 76-7
at Oxford, 25
Clare of Assisi, St, 118
Clarendon, OP at, 182
Clarke, R. D., 168
Clement IV, Pope, 214, 221
Clement V, Pope, 187
clocks, monastic, 289
clothes-money, 105, 106, 288-9
Cluny, Cluniacs, 57, 105-6
Cobham, Thomas de, b. Worcester, 98, 101

Cockerell, S. C., 302 n.
Colchester, Ben. abb., 105, 276
Crutched Friars at, 203
Richard, Simon and Walter of, 297
Colebruge, Ralph de, OFM, 210
Coleham, Nicholas of, 315
collecta (wool), 68
Colonna, Giles, OSA, 201
Colville, William de, OFM, 142
common law and monks, 271
commune in monastic boroughs, 266
comperta in visitations, 82-3
Concordantiae Anglicanae, 167
confessors, royal, from OC and OP, 167
Conflans, Pierre de, OP, 229
conservatores privilegiorum, OFM, 183
constitutions of Narbonne, 143, 171, 175
contemplative life, the, 150 n.
conversi, black monk, 286-7
Cistercian, 69, 71, 73-4, 77, 286
OFM, 174
Conyngton, Richard of, OFM, 247
Copeland, J. L., 184 n., 187 n., 189 n.
Corbridge, Thomas, archb. York, 89, 90, 91, 92
Cornhill, London, OFM at, 132, 134
Cornwall, Richard of, OFM, 211
Cornwall, Richard, earl of, 5, 196
Coulton, G. G., 81 n.
council, the abbot's, 271-2
of seniors, the monastic, 43, 50
Courtenay, John, 102
Coventry, Ben. cathedral pr., 259, 266, 268
Coxford, Aug. pr., 108
Crescenzio (Crescenzius) of Jesi, OFM, 144, 177
Crittall, E., 40 n., 42 n.
Crokesley, Richard of, 277, 310
Cross, friars of. See under Friars
Crowland (Croyland), Ben. abb., 38 n., 41, 42, 70, 276, 290, 312
abbot Geoffrey of, 46, 300
abbot, Thomas of, 290
Crutched friars. See under Friars
Cum a nobis petitur, 185
Cum inter nonnullos, 121 n., 240, 247
Cuthbert, Father, 114 n., 174 n., 175 n., 178 n.
Cwmhir, Cist. abb., 75

Dacia, Boethius of, 225
Dalderby, John, b. Lincoln, 188 n.
Dante, 7, 8, 54
Darlington, John of, OP, 167
David's, St, bishop of. See under Welshman, Thomas the
debts, monastic, 68-9, 73, 99
demesne, leasing of, 35
resumption of, 36-7
Denholm-Young, N., 32 n.

Denifle, H., 148 n., 150 n., 152 n.
Despenser, Henry, b. Norwich, 268, 269
detecta in visitation, 81
Devizes, Richard of, 292, 293
Devon, Richard of, OFM, 130, 132
diffinitores, Austin canons, 30
   black monk, 15
   OFM, 174
   OP, 157
diseases of sheep and cattle, 48 n.
Docking, Thomas, OFM, 212, 223
Domerham, Adam of, 296
Dominic, St, 146–62, 164
Dominicans. *See under* Friars
Douglas, D. C., 33 n.
Douie, D. L., 220 n., 246 n.
Drax, Aug. pr., 29, 88
Drokensford, John, b. Bath and Wells, 101, 102
Dumfries, OFM at, 235
Dunhead, Thomas, OP, 169, 170
Dunstable, Aug. pr., 28 n., 30 n., 67, 192 n., 193, 268, 316
   chronicle of, 295
Dunstan, St, 254
Durham, Ben. cathedral pr., 255, 256, 258, 259 n., 282, 284, 287, 288, 313. *For* bishops of, *see under* Bek, Antony; Bury, Richard de; Hatfield, Thomas; Marsh, Richard
   College, Oxford, 262, 313
   OFM at, 132
Dyes, Thomas, OP, 167 n.

Ea quae (decretal of Honorius III), 79
East Anglian school of illumination, 302–3
Eastry, Henry of, 16 n., 42, 43–4, 49–50, 104 n., 262, 309. *See also* Appendix II
Eccleston, Thomas of, OFM, 127, 136, 137, 139, 140, 141, 144, 177, 203
Edington, Bonshommes pr., 202
Edmund's, St, Walter of, 46
Edward I, 309, 313, 315
Edward II, 266
   abdication, 52
   and OP, 169
Egbert, D. D., 303 n.
Ehrle, Cardinal F., 170 n., 171 n., 174 n., 175 n., 176 n., 177 n., 184 n., 216 n., 224 n., 225 n., 233 n.
Eleanor of Castile, Queen to Edward I, 46
   of Provence, Queen to Henry III, 6, 181–2, 291 n.
election of prior in cathedral monasteries, 154, 255–7
Elias, a novice OFM, 137, 140
Elias of Cortona, OFM, 129, 138, 144, 171, 173, 177, 181, 304
Ely, Ben. cathedral pr., 38 n., 41, 63, 105 255, 258, 273, 288, 312. *For* bishops

of, *see under* Balsham, Hugh of; Orford, Robert of; Walpole, Ralph of
Emly, Adam of, 290, 314
Erwin, abb. Peterborough, 299, 312
Etsi animarum, 185
Euse, Cardinal Gaucelin d', 300
Eustace, m. Christ Church, 261 n.
Evans, S. A., 312 n.
Evesham, Ben. abb., 57, 279, 287, 289, 290, 314. *For* abbots of, *see under* Brock-hampton, John of; Gras, Richard le; Marleberge, Thomas of. *For* monk of, *see under* Oddington, Walter of
   Cardinal Hugh of, 98
   chronicle of, 296
exemption, of abbeys, 12, 80, 98–100, 277–9
   of monastic churches, 258
Exeter. *For* bishops of, *see under* Grandisson, John; Stapledon, Walter
   St James, Ben. pr., 102
Exiit qui seminat, 143, 246
Eynsham, Ben. abb., 27, 47, 62

Faaberg (Norway), 298
Faringdon, Cist. pr., 73, 77
Faversham, Ben. abb., 107, 110 n.
   and provincial chapter, 17
   Haymo of, OFM, 135, 137, 138, 142, 143, 144, 153, 173–5, 205
   Simon of, 233 n.
Felley, Aug. pr., 90, 92, 96 n.
Ferentino, John of, papal legate, 57
finances of canons, 95–6, 103–4
   of monks, 95–6, 108, 109
Fishacre, Richard, OP, 165, 193 n., 218, 235
flesh-meat, eating of, by monks, 11, 17, 107, 281–3
Flete, W., OSA, 242
Flores Historiarum, 291
Foliot, Hugh, b. Hereford, 99
food-farms, 34, 37
Ford, Roger, 37, 45
Fordwich, 36
form, the unity of, in man, 226–32
Fortibus, Isabella de, 72
Fountains, Cist. abb., 68, 69, 71, 316
Francis of Assisi, St, 114–26
   aims and ideals, 114–26, 136, 154, 178, 180, 224, 304
   in East, 128–9
   and England, 130
   and Rules, 129–30
   and St Dominic, 149. *See also under* Friars
Freshbourne, Ralph, OC, 196, 198
Freshbourne, Simon, OC, 196
Fresney, Gilbert of, OP, 163
Fresney, William of, OP, 163 n.
Friars, Austin (Hermits of St Augustine), 182, 183, 195–201, 203; theological school, 242

Friars, Carmelite, 167, 182, 195–9
of Cross (or Crutched), 202
de ordine Martyrum, 204
Minors, constitutions, 172; general chapter, 172; and monks, 131; and poverty, 139, 140, 141, 142–3, 169, 221–4, 246–8; and Preachers, 149
Pied, 204 n.
Preachers, *capitulum generalissimum*, 156–7
Preachers, constitutions, 154–8
Preachers, influence on OC, 198; OFM, 174; OSA, 201
Preachers and poverty, 149–50, 221–4, 247
of the Sack, 202–3

Gaetani, Benedetto. *See under* Boniface VIII
Gainsborough, William of, OFM, 168
Galbraith, G. R., 150 n., 155 n., 156 n.
Galbraith, V. H., 26 n., 292 n., 310 n., 311 n.
Gamages, John de, 290, 315
Gaunt, John of, 167
Gaveston, Piers, 169
Gerald of Wales. *See under* Wales
Germans, St, Aust. pr., 102
Gesta Abbatum (St Albans), 294, 296 n.
Ghent, Henry of, 189, 233 n.
Giano, Jordan of, OFM, 127–8, 139
Gibbs, M., 4 n.
Giffard, Godfrey, b. Worcester, 23, 97, 98, 186
Giffard, Sir John, of Brimpsfield, 26 n., 27
Giffard, Walter, archb. York, 87, 88, 91, 92
Gilbertines, 66, 71
Giles, John of St, OP, 164, 165
Gilson, E., 237 n.
Gisburn, Aug. pr., 29
Glastonbury, Ben. abb., 37, 38, 41, 42, 44–6, 69, 102, 254, 277, 289, 315. *For* abbots of, *see under* Amesbury, Michael of; Ford, Roger; Taunton, John of
John of, chronicler, 296
Gloucester, Ben. abb., 26, 108, 109, 282, 287, 290, 314–15. *For* abbot of, *see under* Gamages, John de. *For* monks of, *see under* Brock, William of; Emly, Adam of
St Oswald's, Aug. pr., 87
OFM at, 132, 141
Godefroid, Raymund, OFM, 78 n.
Gonsalvo, minister-general OFM, 235
Graham, R., 108 n.
grain, export of, 38
Grandisson, John, b. Exeter, 102, 103
grange, the Cistercian, 64–5, 73–4, 75
Gras, N. S. B., 36 n.
Gras, Richard le, 277, 314

Gratien, P., 171 n., 175 n., 178 n., 246 n.
Gray, Walter, archb. York, 87
Greenfield, William, archb. York, 91, 92, 94, 95, 203
Gregory IX, Pope, 19, 58, 85 n., 118 n., 172, 173, 181, 183, 255, 256, 278
and Carmelites, 197
monastic decrees of, 11–12, 78, 80, 270
and OFM, 142, 143
Gregory X, Pope, 200, 220
Grey, Lord, 196
Grosseteste, Robert, b. Lincoln, 4 n., 6, 71, 81, 86, 210, 293 n.
and black canons, 31
and black monks, 19
and Crutched Friars, 203
and OFM, 136–7, 138, 180–1, 207–9
and OP, 165
as reformer, 276
as thinker, 207–8, 211, 214
writings, 207–9
Guant, Simon de, 233 n.
guardians, in OFM, 172, 173 n.
Guildford, friars de ordine Martyrum at, 204
guilds (gilds) merchant, 264, 265
and OP, 160
Gumbley, W., 163 n.
Gynewell, John, b. Lincoln, 203

Haakon IV, King of Norway, 292 n., 294
Hales, Alexander of, OFM, 135, 205, 231
Handschin, J., 305 n., 306 n.
Harding, St Stephen, 163
Harris, C. S., 236 n., 240 n.
Hartland, Aug. abb., 102 n.
Hartlepool, OFM at, 132
Hatfield, John of, 277
Hatfield, Thomas, b. Durham, 262
Hayles, Cist. abb., 6, 81, 316
Helaugh Park, Aug. pr., 88
statutes of, 29–30
Henley, Walter of, 36 n.
Henry III, King, 6, 220, 292 n., 294
and OFM, 181
as patron of art, 294, 297–8
Henry of Blois, b. Winchester, 57
Hereford. *For* bishops of, *see under* Cantilupe, Thomas of; Foliot, Hugh; Maidstone, Ralph of; Orleton, Adam of; Swinfield, Richard
OFM at, 132
Hexham, Aug. pr., 99 n.
Hinton, Simon of, OP, 219
Hobbes, Thomas, 244 n.
Hobhouse, Bishop, 102 n.
Holdsworth, W. S., 271 n.
holidays, monastic, 284–5
Honorius III, Pope, and OFM, 130, 143
and monks, 79
and OP, 149

horarium, the monastic, 280–1
Hothum, William of, OP, 168, 169, 230 n., 231, 232, 233
household of abbot and prior, 273–4
Hugh, abbot of St Albans, 266 n.
Hughes, A., 305 n., 306 n.
Hulme, OC at, 196
Humbert. *See under* Romans
Huntingdon, Henry of, 66
Huy, friars of Cross at, 203
Hyde (or New Minster), Ben. abb., 279, 315

Illumination of manuscripts by monks, 299–304; by friars, 304–5
Immaculate Conception of the Blessed Virgin, 53 n., 239
Ingworth, Richard of, OFM, 130, 131, 132
Innocent III, Pope, 28, 57, 254
  and monks, 270
  and OFM, 128, 143
  and OP, 148
Innocent IV, Pope, and monks, 12, 20, 78, 81, 270, 295
  and OC, 198
  and OFM, 142, 183, 184–6
  and OSA, 200
Inter cunctas, 186
interposita persona, 222
Isabel, Queen, 268

Jacques, St, OP at, 164, 168
James, M. R., 300 n., 301 n.
Jarrett, B., 163 n.
Jervaulx, Cist. abb., 71
Jews and friars, 193
  and monks, 90
Jocelin, b. Bath and Wells, 277
John, King, 313
John XXI, Pope, 228
John XXII, Pope, 101, 166, 234, 245–51
John of St Albans, 164
Joliffe, J. E. A., 33 n.
Jordan of Saxony. *See under* Saxony
Jorz, Cardinal Thomas, OP, 169, 188 n., 191, 233
Joyce fitzJoyce, OFM. *See under* Salomon
justices, abbots as, 276

Käppeli, Y., OP, 249 n.
Kethene, John de, OFM, 142
Keynsham, Aug. abb., 100
Kidwelly, Ben. pr., 107
Kildale, Crutched friars at, 203
Kilwardby, Robert, OP, archb. Canterbury 58, 81, 106–7, 168, 218–20, 223, 282, 315
  and OP, 165, 166
  and Thomism, 228–30
Kimmer, Cist. abb., 75
King's Lynn, 265
  OFM at, 132

Kingswood, Cist. abb., 67 n., 74, 75
Knapwell, Richard, OP, 230, 232, 233

Lacy, Henry, earl of Lincoln, 70
Lancaster, Thomas of, 70
Lanfranc, 254
Lang, J., 4 n.
Langley, King's, OP at, 169
Langton, Simon, 262
Langton, Stephen, archb. Canterbury, 163
Laon, canons of, 66
Lateran, Fourth Council of the, 3, 9, 78, 80, 148
Launceston, Aug. pr., 103
Laurence, Brother, OP, 163
lay brethren. *See under conversi*
Ledbury, William de, 98
Leeds, Aug. pr., 109
Leibniz, 244 n.
Leicester, Aug. abb., 28
  OFM at, 132
  Earl and Countess of. *See under* Montfort
Leighs, Aug. pr., 105
Lenton, Clun. pr., 106
Leo, Brother, OFM, 119 n., 304
Leominster (Lemster), Ben. pr., 99–100
Lesnes, Aug. abb., 108
Lessines, Giles de, OP, 228 n., 229
Lethaby, W. R., 309 n.
Lexington, Stephen of, 6
Lichfield and Coventry. *For* bishops of, *see under* Stavensby, Alexander; Wesham, Roger
Lincoln. *For* bishops of, *see under* Dalderby, John; Grosseteste, Robert; Gynewell, John; Welles, Hugh de
  OFM at, 132
  St Catherine's, Gilbertine pr., 71
Lindeblom, A., 298 n.
Lindsey, Robert of, 18, 46, 299
Little, A. G., 127 n., 206 n., 207 n.
Lobel, M. D., 263 n., 264 n.
Locke, John, 244 n.
London. *For* bishops of, *see under* Baldock, Ralph; Niger, Roger
  council of (1237), 19
  Crutched friars at, 203
  OFM at (Cornhill), 141
  OP at (Holborn), 164
  petition of curates of, 189
London, William of, OFM, 305
Longpré, E., OFM, 211 n.
Losenham, OC at, 196
Louis, St, of France, 294 n.
Louth Park, Cist. abb., 68
Loyola, St Ignatius of, 159
Ludham, Godfrey, archbishop York, 87, 90, 91
Ludlow, OSA at, 201

Luffield, Ben. pr., 107
Lutterell, John, 251 n.
Lyons, Council of (1274), 183, 186, 187, 199, 200, 202

Macclesfield, William of, OP, 169, 230
Maidstone, Ralph of, b. Hereford, 135
Maitland, F. W., 271 n.
Malmesbury, Ben. abb., 27, 278, 315. For abbot of, *see under* Badminton,William of
William of, 293, 312
Malvern, Little, Ben. pr., 99, 107
Great, Ben. pr., 98
John of, OFM, 141, 143
Manchester, Hugh of, OP, 168
Mandonnet, P., OP, 149 n., 155 n., 216 n., 224 n., 226 n.
Mara or Mare, William de, OFM, 229, 230, 233
Mare, Thomas de la, 268, 284
Marsh, Adam, OFM, 134, 136, 138, 143, 144, 173, 181, 205, 211, 212, 214, 220
life and teaching, 209–10
Marsh, Richard, b. Durham, 209
Martin IV, Pope, 186, 189
Marton, Aug. pr., 88, 94 n.
Martyrum, friars de Ordine. *See under* Friars
Mary, Princess (dau. Edward I) 234
Maryns, John de, 278
Matha, St John of, 202
Maturin, St, Trinitarian pr. at Paris, 202
Mauclerc, Walter, b. Carlisle, OP, 166
Maxton, 235
Meaux, Cist. abb., 72, 74
Melioratus, Brother, OFM, 130
Melton, William of, archb. York, 89, 91, 95
Mepeham, Simon, archb. Canterbury, 52
Merk, Eustace de, OFM, 138
Merton, Aug. pr., 104, 109, 316
Michael's Mount, St, Ben. pr., 103
Middleton, Richard of, 234–5
military orders, influence on OP, 153 n.,160
Millar, E., 300 n., 301 n., 302 n.
Millaud, Pierre de, OC, 199
Milton, Ben. abb., 315
Monk Bretton, Ben. pr., 93
Montfort, Simon de, 160, 181–2, 210, 265
Montpellier, OFM chapter at, 143
Moorman, J. R. H., 4 n., 116 n.
More, St Thomas, 297
Mortmain, Statute of, 7, 23
Muchelney, Ben. abb., 315
music and chant, 305–7

Nannau, 168 n.
Anian of, OP, b. St Asaph, 168
Narbonne, constitutions of, 175, 178–9
Neilson, N., 33 n.
Neot's, St, Ben. pr., 26
Netley, Cist. abb., 5

Newark, Aug. pr., 103
Newark, Henry of, archb. York, 89
Newburgh, Aug. pr., 88, 89, 93
Newcastle-on-Tyne, OFM at, 137
Newcastle, Hugh of, OFM, 247
Newenham, Aug. pr., 30 n.
Newstead, Aug. pr., 87, 89–90, 93, 110 n.
Nicholas III, Pope, 193, 231, 232, 246
Nicholas, master-general, OC, 198–9
Niger, Roger, b. London, 4 n., 138, 181, 182
Nimis iniqua, 183, 184
Nominalism, 237–9, 242–5
Normanville, Eustace de, OFM, 210
Northampton, Aug. pr., 30
OFM at, 132, 135
Northwold, Hugh of, 311
Norwich, Ben. cathedral pr., 105, 255, 256, 258, 274, 282, 290, 311–12. For bishops of, *see under* Despenser, Henry; Bateman, William
Nostell, Aug. pr., 91
Nottingham, OFM at, 132
Nottingham, William (I) of, OFM, 137, 138, 141, 142, 143, 144, 211, 212–13
Nottingham, William (II) of, OFM, 247
novices, black monk, reception of, 256; regulations for, 15; training of, 15, 285–6
nunneries, 108

Ockham, William of, OFM, 237, 238–9, 242–5, 248
Oddington, Walter of, 307, 314
Old Malton, Gilbertine pr., 71
Omnis utriusque sexus, 189
Orford, Henry of, OP, 233 n.
Orford, Robert of, b. Ely, 105
Orleton, Adam of, b. Hereford, 100–1
Orsini, Cardinal Matthew, OP, 249
Oswald's, St. *See under* Gloucester
Osyth's, St, Aug. abb., 105
Otho, cardinal and papal legate, 11, 19, 80
Ottoboni, papal legate, 13–14, 80
Ouen, St, at Rouen, Ben. abb., 41
Oxford, Crutched Friars at, 203
OC at, 26, 27, 198
OFM at, 132, 134, 135–7, 140, 141, 142, 222–4; school at, 207–12, 213–16, 236
OP at, 164, 166, 222–3, 240–1; *studium generale* at, 218–19
OSA at, 201
Sack, friars of the, at, 203
university and friars, 190–1

Padua, St Antony of, 144 n.
Page, F. M., 38 n., 42
Palmer, C. F. R., OP, 163 n., 167 n.
Palu, Pierre de la, OP, 189
Pantin, W. A., 10 n., 16 n.
Parenti, John, OFM, 144, 171, 172

Paris, Matthew, 6, 8 n., 165, 192, 202, 292–8
  artistic work, 297–8
  historical work, 292–5
  and friars, 192, 193
  judgements, 210, 218 n.
  references in 277 n., 290
Paris, university of, and friars, 184; and Gallicanism, 189; and John XXII, 248
parliament, monks in, 259, 276
Parma, John of, OFM, 138, 144, 177
Patrington, Stephen, OC, 167
Pearce, E. H., 39 n., 99 n., 309 n.
Peasants' Revolt and monks, 268–9
Pecham, John, OFM, archb. Canterbury, 69, 81, 86 n., 106, 107–8, 220, 223, 235
  and financial reorganization, 58–60
  and monks, 14, 23–4, 26, 39, 52, 98–9, 110, 283
  and OP, 168, 186, 221
  and Thomism, 226–32
peculium, the monastic, 287–9
Pembroke, Ben. pr., 107
Pershore, Ben. abb., 42, 314
Peter, b. Aberdeen, 209
Peterborough, Ben. abb., 19, 39 n., 40, 41, 42, 46, 58, 66, 70, 94 n., 269, 274 n., 276, 281 n., 289, 299, 300, 312. For abbots of, see under Crowland, Geoffrey of; Crowland, Thomas of; Edmund's (St), Walter of; Erwin; Lindsey, Robert of. For monks of, see under Swápham, Robert of; Whittlesey, Walter of
Petit-Dutaillis, Ch., 268 n.
Philip IV of France, 235
Philip VI of France, 251
Picavet, R., 216 n.
Pied Friars. See under Friars
Pisa, Agnellus of, OFM, 130, 131, 132, 138, 141, 182
  Albert of, OFM, 138, 141, 144
  Bartholomew of, OFM, 135 n., 140 n.
plainchant, monastic, 305–7
Platonic theory of man's soul, 227
Plymouth, Aug. pr., 268
Pollock, F., 271 n.
pontificalia, grants of, 259, 313
Pontoise, John of, b. Winchester, 103
Postan, M. M., 37 n., 65 n.
Pouilli, Jean de, 189
poverty. See under Friars, OFM and OP
  of Christ, controversy, 245, 249
Prato, Cardinal Albert di, OP, 234
Premonstratensians, 66, 71, 148, 153
presidents, abbots, of black monks, 17
prison, the monastic, 94
procurators of the OFM, 142
psalmody, shortening of, 22
Psalter, the Bromholm, 302 n.
  the Gorleston, 302 n., 303

the Ormesby, 302 n., 312
the Tickhill, 303
punishments in visitation, 93–4
purgation, canonical, 93

Quarr, Cist. abb., 6
Quasi lignum vitae, 185, 190
Quo elongati, 139, 143, 172, 232
Quum ad monasterium, 19–20, 57, 281–2

Ralph, Brother, OP, 165
Ramsey, Ben. abb., 38, 57, 276, 312
Randolph, F. C. Hingeston, 87 n., 102 n.
Raymund of Ostia, Cardinal, 144
Reading, Ben. abb., 99–100, 107, 109, 192, 265, 269
  John of, OFM, 134, 192 n.
recreation, monastic, 283–5
Redburn, Ben. pr., 284
Reese, G., 305 n.
reeve, the monastic, 35 n., 43–4
registers, episcopal, 86–7 n.
Regula Bullata, 142, 143
Reresby, Henry of, OFM, 137 n.
Réville, A., 268 n.
Rewley, Cist. abb., 6, 26 and n.
Reyner, Clement, 15 n.
Reynolds, Walter, archb. Canterbury, 52, 101
Rhuddlan, OP at, 163
Rich, St Edmund, archb. Canterbury, 106, 166 n., 261–2, 277
Richard, abbot of Meaux, 73
Richard of Chichester, St. See under Wyche
Rievaulx, Cist. abb., 316
  William of, 163
Rigauld, archb. Rouen, OFM, 211
Rimini, Gregory of, OSA, 242
Ringmer, Thomas, 60, 108, 309
Robert, abb. Meaux, 73
Robert, abb. Tewkesbury, 290, 314
Roches, Peter des, b. Winchester, 163
Rochester, Ben. cathedral pr., 39 n., 107, 108, 309. For bishops of, see under Wendeve, Richard
Roger, abb. St Albans, 13
Romana ecclesia (decretal), 81
Romans, Humbert of the, OP, 157, 158 n., 219
Rome, Giles of, OSA, 233 n., 242
Romeyn, John le, archb. York, 89, 90, 93
Romney, OFM at, 131
Rouen, St Katherine's, Ben. abb., 91–2
Roxburgh, OFM at, 132
Royston, Aug. pr., 105
Rufus, Richard. See under Cornwall, Richard of
Rules of St Francis, 128–9
Rutherwyk, John de, 17, 47, 104

Sabatier, P., 114 n., 123 n., 140, 144 n., 173
Sack, Friars of the. *See under* Friars
Salimbene, Fra, OFM, 127–8, 139, 199 n., 202, 203, 210
Salisbury. *For* bishops of, *see under* Scammell, Walter; York, William of OFM at, 132
Salomon fitzJoyce, OFM, 134, 138, 140, 141
sanctity, monastic examples of, 290
Saxony, Jordan of, OP, 148 n., 161 n., 164–5, 205 n.
Scammell, Walter, b. Salisbury, 109
Scarborough, OFM at, 132
scholasticism, historians of, 206 n., 224 n.
Scotism, influence of, 244
Scotus, Duns, OFM, 233, 235–8, 243–4
Selby, Ben. abb., 92, 94–5
Sempringham, Gilbertine pr., 80 n.
Seneca, Trivet's commentary on, 234
senescallus terrarum, 38
Servites, the, 204
Shaftesbury, Ben. nunnery, 71
Shamele, OSA at, 201
Sharp, D. E., 206 n., 216 n., 220 n., 240 n.
sheep-farming, by Austin canons, 67 n., 71
    by black monks, 41–2
    by Cistercians, 65–7
    by Gilbertines, 67, 71
    by Premonstratensians, 17, 71
Sheppard, J. B., 52 n.
Sherborne, Ben. abb., 315
Shrewsbury, OFM at, 141, 143
Shuttington, OSA at, 201
Simon, abb. Bury, 278
Smith, A. L., 292 n.
Smith, R. A. L., 36 n., 39 n., 43 n., 49 n., 56 n., 314 n.
Solomon, Brother, OP, 222–3
Sommer-Seckendorff, E. M. F., 218 n.
Southampton, OFM at, 141
Southampton, William of, OP, 168
Southwick, Aug. pr., 104, 107
Spalding, Ben. abb., and provincial chapter, 17
'spiritual friend', the OFM, 142
Spirituals, OFM, 177–9, 245–6
Stamford, OFM at, 132
Stapeldon, Walter de, b. Exeter, 102
Stavensby, Alexander, b. Lichfield, 138, 165, 181
Stenton, F. M., 33 n.
Stock, St Simon, OC, 196–7
Stoke-by-Clare, Ben. pr., 26
    OSA at, 201
Stubbs, W., 261 n.
studies, organization of, by OFM, 212–13; by OP, 152, 166
Studley, Aug. pr., 99
Subiaco, Ben. abb., 19, 57
Suffield, Walter, b. Norwich, 4 n.

Summi Magistri, 282, 288
Super cathedram, 183, 186, 187, 191
Sutton, Thomas of, OP, 230 n., 233–4
Swapham, Robert of, 296
Swarzenski, H., 302 n.
Swinfield, Richard of, b. Hereford, 99–100
Syreford, Henry of, OP, 181

Tandridge, Aug. pr., 104
Taunton, John of, 13–14, 22, 45
Tavistock, Ben. abb., 290, 314. *For* abbots of, *see under* Bonus; Courtenay, John
Tempier, Étienne, b. Paris, 228
Testament of St Francis, 143
Tewkesbury, Ben. abb., 290, 314
    Peter of, OFM, 136, 143, 181
Thetford, Clun. pr., 106
Thomism, official system of OP, 233
    reactions to, of Baconthorpe, 241; of John XXII, 248; of Ockham, 238; of Scotus, 237; of Sutton, 233; of Trivet, 234
Thomist theses proscribed at London, 232; at Oxford, 229, 231; at Paris, 228
Thompson, A. H., 81 n.
Thompson, E. M., 15
Thorne, Nicholas, 309
Thorney, Ben. abb., 312
Thornham, Robert of, OFM, 138
Thurgarton, Aug. pr., 88, 89, 91, 92, 94 n., 96 n.
Tickhill, John of, 303
Tout, T. F., 49 n., 310 n.
treasurers, monastic, 56, 58, 59–60
    Austin canons, 58, 96
Trenholme, N. M., 263 n., 264 n., 265 n., 267 n.
Trinitarians, the, 201–2
Trivet, Nicholas, OP, 168, 210, 234, 247
Trondhjem (Norway), 294
Trumpington, William of, 10, 18, 22, 277, 281
Tunsted, Simon, 307
Tyler, Wat, 268–9
Tywardreath, Ben. pr., 103

Ugolino, Cardinal, 118 n. *See also* Gregory IX
universities, black monks and, 21, 25–7, 312, 313
    Cistercians and, 25

Valéry, St, Ben. abb., 41
Valois, St Felix of, 202
Valois, N., 249 n.
Vanderwalle, B., 214 n.
Vercelli, St Albert of, Patriarch of Jerusalem, 196
Vercelli, John of, OP, 219
Vescy, Lord de, 196
Vicaire, M. H., OP, 150 n.

Vinogradoff, P., 33 n.
visitation, monastic, capitular, Austin canons, 85 n., 90; black monks, 110; Cistercians, 85, 110; Cluniacs, 105–6; Premonstratensians, 85
monastic, episcopal, 78–112; legatine, 80, 85 n.; metropolitan, 81, 106–10

Walden, Thomas Netter of, OC, 242
Wales, Gerald of, 62, 64, 293
Wales, John of, OFM, 211
Waleys, Thomas, OP, 247, 249–52
Wallace, W., 261 n.
Wallingford, Ralph of, 266
Wallingford, Richard of, 284, 289
Walpole, Ralph of, b. Ely, 105
Walsingham, Thomas of, 288, 295
Walter, Hubert, archb. Canterbury, 57
Waltham, Aug. abb., 57, 107
wardens of manors, monastic, 36 n., 39, 43, 50, 74
Ware, Richard of, 13, 277
Waverley, Cist. abb., 70
Welbeck, abbot of, 29
Welles, Hugh de, b. Lincoln, 86
Wells. For bishops of, see under Burnell, Robert; Drokensford, John; Jocelin
Welshman, Thomas the, b. St David's, 209
Wendeve, Richard, b. Rochester, 4 n.
Wendover, Roger of, 193, 291, 292 n.
Wenlock, Much, Clun. pr., 273
Wenlock (Wenlok), Walter de, 16 n., 26 n., 40; customary of, 13
Wesham, Roger, b. Lichfield, 209
Westlake, H. F., 309 n.
Westminster, Ben. abb., 39 n., 40, 69, 80 n. 98, 277, 290, 297, 301, 309–10. For abbots of, see under Crokesley, Richard of; Wallingford, Richard of; Wenlock, Walter of
Whaplode, Crutched friars at, 203
Whitby, Ben. abb., 93, 94, 95, 282, 312
Whitland, Cist. abb., 69
Whittleseamere, OSA at, 201
Whittlesey, Walter of, 296
Wickwane, Walter of, 314
Wickwane, William of, archb. York, 88, 90, 91, 92, 94 n.
Wigmore, Aug. abb., 100–1
William of England, OFM, 163, 192 (? another), 304
William the painter, 298–9
Williams, J. R., 310 n.

Wilton, Ben. nunnery, 71
Winchcombe, Ben. abb., 287, 314. For abbot of, see under Wickwane, Walter of
Winchelsey, Robert, archb. Canterbury, 52, 83 n., 233, 256, 288 n.; and monks, 108–10; questionnaire of, 83 n.
Winchester, Ben. cathedral pr., 41, 57, 70, 255, 256, 258, 259, 282, 315. For bishops of, see under Pontoise, John of; Roches, Peter des; Woodlock, Henry. For New Minster, Ben. abb., see under Hyde
Winterbourne, William of, Cardinal OP, 169
Woodhouse, OSA at, 201
Woodlock, Henry, b. Winchester, 104, 109, 255, 256, 316
Woodstock, Edmund of, 170
wool trade, the, 67–71
Wootton Wawen, Ben. pr., 97–8
Worcester, Ben. cathedral pr., 101, 255, 256, 258, 282, 306–7, 313; antiphoner of, 303. For monk of, see under Bromwich, Richard of. For bishops of, see under Blois, William de; Cobham, Thomas de; Cantilupe, Walter; Giffard, Godfrey
College, Oxford, 26–7
OFM at, 132, 134, 209
Worcester, Vincent of, OFM, 141
Worksop, Aug. pr., 92–3, 303
Wormesley, Aug. pr., 99, 107
Wulfstan, St, 313
Wyche, St Richard of, b. Chichester, 165
Wyclif, John, 193

Xiberta, B. M., OC, 241 n.

York. For archbishops of, see under Bovill, Sewal de; Corbridge, Thomas; Greenfield, William; Giffard, Walter; Gray, Walter; Ludham, Godfrey; Melton, William of; Newark, Henry of; Romeyn, John le; Wickwane, William of
St Mary's, Ben. abb., 58, 71, 94, 306–7, 312
OFM at, 132
Thomas of, OFM, 211, 214
William of, b. Salisbury, 181

Zealots, ζηλαντι, 144, 145, 177, 245
Zimmermann, B., OC, 195 n.